M000240459

Nymphs for Streams and Stillwaters

DAVE HUGHES

STACKPOLE
BOOKS

Published by
STACKPOLE BOOKS
5067 Ritter Road
Mechanicsburg, PA 17055
www.stackpolebooks.com

Printed in China

First edition

10 9 8 7 6 5 4 3 2 1

Library of Congress Cataloging-in-Publication Data

Hughes, Dave, 1945–
Nymphs for streams and stillwaters / Dave Hughes.
p. cm.
Includes bibliographical references.
ISBN-13: 978-0-8117-0472-4 (hardcover)
ISBN-10: 0-8117-0472-6 (hardcover)
1. Fly tying. 2. Flies, Artificial. 3. Nymphs (Insects) I. Title.
SH451.H7834 2008
688.7'9124—dc22
2008017302

Dedicated to Justin David Hughes,
September 6, 2005–November 19, 2006

Contents

Acknowledgments vi
Introduction vii

PART 1
The Way Nymphing Shapes Itself 1
Chapter 1 A New Nymph Box 2
Chapter 2 Searching Nymphs for Moving Water 7
Chapter 3 Imitative Nymphs for Moving Water 10
Chapter 4 Nymphs for Stillwaters 15
Chapter 5 At the Tying Bench 19
Chapter 6 Hooks, Threads, and Materials 28
Chapter 7 On the Road 36
Chapter 8 Basic Maneuvers 41
Chapter 9 The Rock 62
Chapter 10 Beads and Flash 66

PART 2
Searching Nymphs for Moving Water 71
Chapter 11 Fur Nymphs 72
Chapter 12 Herl Nymphs 107
Chapter 13 Twisted-Strand Nymphs 120
Chapter 14 Wire- and Tinsel-Bodied Nymphs 125
Chapter 15 Rubber-Legged Nymphs 141
Chapter 16 Czech Nymphs 145
Chapter 17 A Searching-Nymph Box 149

PART 3
Imitative Nymphs for Moving Water 151
Chapter 18 Mayflies 152
Chapter 19 Stoneflies 194
Chapter 20 Caddisflies 208
Chapter 21 Moving Water Midges 236
Chapter 22 Craneflies 245
Chapter 23 Sow Bugs and Scuds 251
Chapter 24 Hellgrammites and Fishfly Larvae 265
Chapter 25 Aquatic Worms 274
Chapter 26 An Imitative-Nymph Box 279

PART 4
Nymphs for Stillwaters 281
Chapter 27 How to Murder a Woolly Bugger 282
Chapter 28 Stillwater Mayflies 288
Chapter 29 Stillwater Midges 296
Chapter 30 Damselflies 304
Chapter 31 Dragonflies 315
Chapter 32 Stillwater Caddisflies 327
Chapter 33 Water Boatmen and Back Swimmers 340
Chapter 34 Stillwater Scuds 348
Chapter 35 Leeches 355
Chapter 36 A Stillwater-Nymph Box 362

Conclusion 364
Bibliography 365
Index 367

Acknowledgments

I would like to thank all of the authors and originators whose work is gratefully referred to in the pages of this book.

I always owe Richard Bunse, Jim Schollmeyer, Rick Hafele, and Ted Leeson for time on streams, photo help, and perpetual instruction in the meaning of life, though I still have a long way to go before I get it.

I appreciate the help of Marcos Vergara at Hareline Dubbin' and Bruce Olsen at Umpqua Feather Merchants, and all others who have invented materials or new ways to use old ones. Special thanks to Kimio Yonenoi of C&F Designs for the brilliant mind that comes up with all those useful tools with which to tie flies and fly boxes into which to insert them.

I am indebted to Judith Schnell and Ruth Cohen for enabling the construction of the backyard studio in which I was finally able to settle down, write, and photograph this book.

And as always, thanks to my wife and daughter, who unfortunately had to learn to avoid the untamed bear in its backyard cage.

Introduction

I remember three trout, all of them early, each of them delivering with its capture some sort of minor nymphing epiphany. The first came on a gray September day on the lower Big Hole River near Melrose, Montana. I'd recently been released by the Army, had driven several miles of gravel and dirt road to a cottonwood copse alongside the river, found it a peaceful haven, set up camp there, and fished for three weeks. The weather was autumn in the Rockies: freezing at night, cold in the morning, mildly warm by early afternoon, cooling again at evening. An occasional gust of wind came up, snatched fallen cottonwood leaves off the ground, flung them around that copse of trees like startled flocks of songbirds.

I'd wake every morning when sunshine struck the windows of the camper. After breakfast I'd get out the portable tying kit and replace the half dozen or so size 12 and 14 Royal Wulff dry flies I'd lost to trout the day before. I'd string my ancient floating fly line out between trees to stretch and straighten while I tied on the tailgate. When finished tying I'd run Mucilin over the line a few times before reeling it onto the spool, wadering up, hiking upstream or down to a favored riffle. I'd begin fishing about the time that the world had warmed sufficiently so

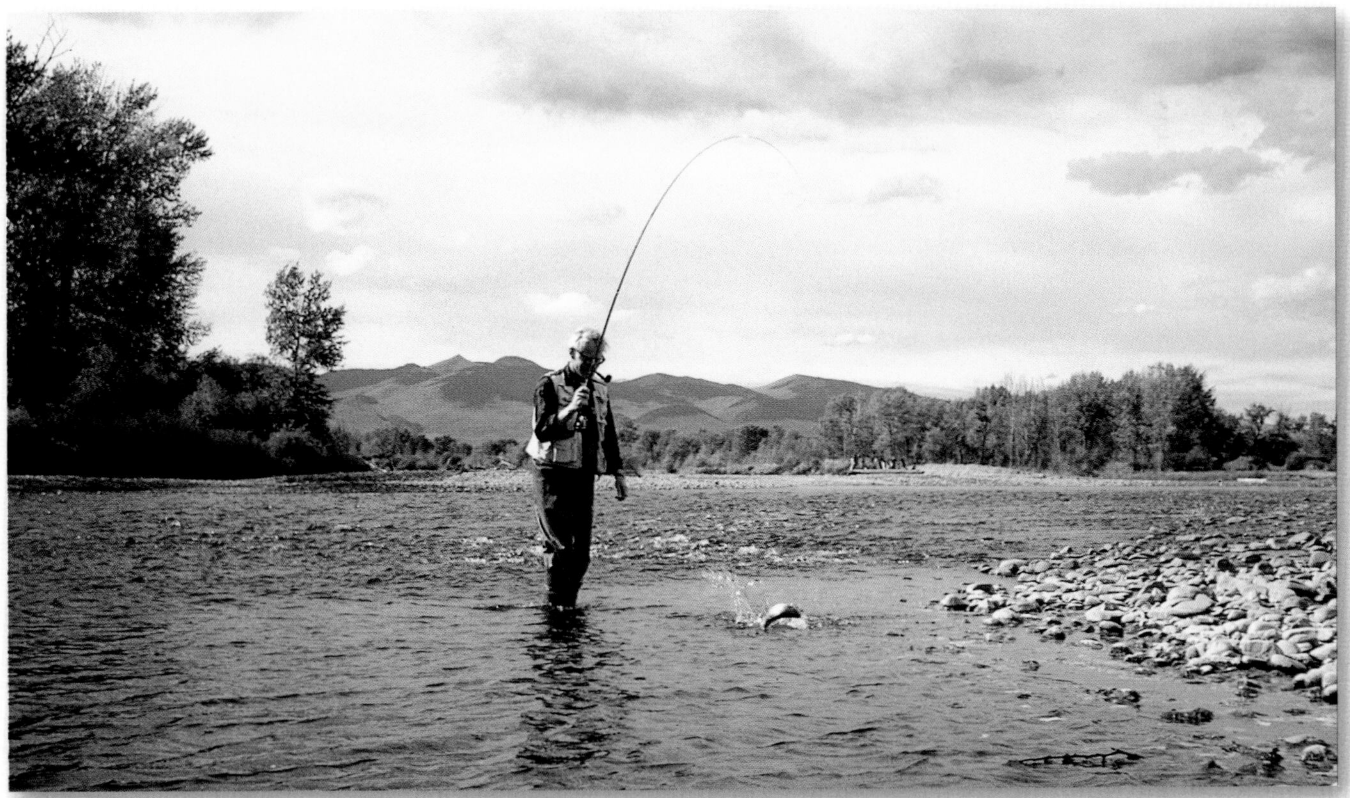

My friend Ernest W. "Tex" Baxter playing a Big Hole River trout hooked on a generic searching nymph fished with a simple down-and-around swing.

trout would begin moving to those drys, which they did daily in enough numbers to keep me happy.

Then a weather front moved in. The sky turned blackish gray, the air turned cold. Trout abruptly turned off. I decided it was time to try a new approach to nymphing I'd been reading about in the breathless *Field & Stream* and *Sports Afield* articles of the day. The prescription was to fish a weighted nymph upstream on a long leader and floating line, in shallow chattery water, watching the line tip for the slight dart that would indicate a trout had intercepted the nymph. I tied on an ugly size 12 Gray Nymph and tried it for an hour or so, but noticed none of those darts. In distant retrospect, there might have been many and I failed to notice them all, but I doubt it. The part of that big and boisterous river that I fished was not suited to the method then, and still isn't.

GRAY NYMPH

Hook:	Standard nymph, size 10–16
Weight:	8–12 turns nonlead wire
Thread:	Black 6/0 or 8/0
Tail:	Badger or woodchuck guard hairs
Body:	Muskrat fur
Hackle:	Grizzly hen

I assumed the building weather was at fault, gave up on the nymph and the method, turned around and flicked the fly across the same broad riffle I'd been fishing upstream, began to wade out and reel up at the same time, in order to head back to camp. The nymph got whacked on its aimless amble down and around below me.

That first epiphanic trout was a brown, about eighteen inches long, plump and pretty. The message it delivered was that nymph fishing might be made easy, and it also might bring a few trout to my hand when dry-fly fishing would not. I spent the rest of the day, and many that followed it, proving to myself that a nymph fished on the simple and ancient wet-fly swing could be very effective. I was amazed by the number of trout I caught then, and still do, fishing nymphs on that simple swing, in violation of almost all that I'd ever read about nymphing.

The second memorable trout came quite a few years later, when the indicator-and-shot method was just beginning to be chronicled in similar breathless articles, but this time in the new fly-fishing magazines of the day. I'd been fishing nymphs with enough success to be pleased during all those years. I was camped on the Deschutes River in central Oregon, which was just then becoming my home river, fishing with Jim Schollmeyer, who was in the earliest instars of becoming the fishing photographer and writer we know today. The season was on the border between late spring and early summer, just after the giant salmon fly and golden stonefly hatches had ended.

An updated edition of Polly Rosborough's *Tying and Fishing the Fuzzy Nymphs* had recently been published, and I was reading it, tying from it, working his theories into my muddled thinking and his nymphs into my tangled fly boxes. At the same time I was kicking around with mesh screen nets, taking bottom samples of aquatic insects, beginning to parse out and identify the things that trout make a living eating. It quickly became clear, from the abundance of tiny larvae and nymphs, pupae and crustaceans that came up wiggling, crawling, and swimming in those early kick-net samples, that trout get chances at a lot more small bites down along the bottom than they do big ones.

Very few big naturals were left down there that day on the Deschutes, because all of the mature salmon flies and golden stones had emerged, laid the eggs of the next generation, and died. Polly called for tying his Muskrat Nymph in sizes 6 to 16. That smallest size was about average for the size food forms I'd been collecting in my thrashing around, even on the big and brawling Deschutes. I set up a portable tying kit in camp and tied a dozen of them on 2XL, size 18 fine-wire dry-fly hooks, because Polly called for long-shank hooks on all of his nymphs, and those were the only elongated hooks I had with me on the trip. I added a layer of fine lead wire beneath each noodled body, in violation of Polly's rule against weighting any of his nymphs.

I hiked downstream from camp and arrived at a riffle that was a big one even on the Deschutes. Shallow water bounded down a long, cobbled, and steeply tilted stretch of bottom that was far too fast to hold any trout. But that kind of water is enormously productive for aquatic insect life. Trout gather up in the nearest soft water downstream from such a delivery system, on any creek, stream, or river, waiting to intercept helpless nymphs and larvae dislodged by the brisker currents upstream. Often these trout are the largest that water offers.

Even trout in such heavy water as this boisterous Deschutes River riffle corner feed on more small insects than large ones. Contrary to what seems like logic, trout can see such tiny bits of food in the drift. If they couldn't, they would never get fat.

MUSKRAT *Polly Rosborough*

Hook: 2XL or 3XL, size 6–18
Weight: 10–20 turns nonlead wire, optional
Thread: Black 6/0 or 8/0
Body: Muskrat fur, noodled
Legs: Speckled guinea fibers
Head: Black ostrich

I stepped into the riffle corner, rigged with a small fluorescent orange steelhead Corky for an indicator, tied one of the size 18 Muskrats to a 5X tippet, and pinched a couple of small split shot about ten inches above the fly. I followed the rough rule of rigging with the indicator about twice the depth of the water above the nymph. I began fishing out along the shelf between the riffle and its runout downstream, where the bottom gradient suddenly leveled out, where the steep riffle ceased and the slower holding water began. I'd make each cast right to the transition line between fast water and slow, give the line a couple of mends to buy time for those split shot to tug the tiny nymph to the bottom, then hoist the rod and high-stick the nymph through a drift ten to twenty feet long.

The water was three to four feet deep, and because of irrigation return, it lacked the clarity you might find in a pristine mountain stream. Visibility, in my mind, was doubtful, and fishing that small fly was, again in my mind, an experiment. I wasn't sure trout would be able to notice such a small fly surrounded by such a vast river. A couple of tiddlers, rare on the Deschutes, took the fly and began to ease my doubts. Then a few fair-sized redside rainbows, fourteen to sixteen inches long, found the fly and did some dancing around with it. By the time I released those, I was beginning to suspect they were not bumping into that small fly by accident.

Then I worked my way into the sweet spot in the vortex of the riffle corner, the angle where the shelf gave way to the run, forming the single holding lie where the most food gets delivered from the riffle above to the softest water below. On the first cast into that water, the indicator settled into its drift, then dipped under. I set the hook and was fairly certain I'd hooked a leftover summer steelhead, a happening that is far from rare on the Deschutes River. But such steelhead, by midsummer, lack vigor. This fish bulled down the riffle, poked itself into the air way down there, shook its head, turned its tail to the current, and ran downstream some more.

I was forced by that small and fragile dry-fly hook to follow the trout until it entered an eddy downstream. I let the fish exhaust itself against the reversed current of the eddy, playing it unfairly from a position upstream while it fought the current and the rod at the same time. When it surrendered I wished Jim was around with his cameras. It was and remains the heaviest trout I've taken on the Deschutes. Though it was not much more than twenty inches long, and I've caught trout longer there, it was portly out of proportion to its length, and I'd guess it at well over four pounds, though probably short of five.

I got the message that day that trout, even large ones, make a high proportion of their living eating very small bites. If they weren't able to see them in the vigorous drift, down near the bottom, they'd quickly starve. It's wise to fish small nymphs more often than it is to fish big ones. It might be wisest of all to fish two nymphs at the same time, at least one of which is a small one.

The third minor but still instructive trout came during a float of the Rio Rivadevia with guide John Roberts out of Esquel, Argentina. The main river was high from rain and not as productive as we'd have liked. Midway through the float we stopped for lunch where a small spring creek emerged out of the forested hills, meandered across a cattle-cropped pastoral flat, and entered the main river in a long, straight glide about fifteen feet wide and four or five feet deep. This glide had eroded its course deeply into the soft soil. The water was about head-height below steep, grassed banks on both sides.

After lunch John headed up the spring creek with another client. I picked up my light rod and started to trot after them, but put on my brakes when I spotted a single nice trout holding on the bottom in a part of the glide they'd already hiked past. The first smart thing I did was nothing, which I do far too seldom. I tend to cast first, ask questions later. This time I froze. My rod wasn't rigged, which made inactivity easier. Since I was still downstream from the fish, though not by much, it had not yet spotted me. I bellied onto the grass on that high bank above it and watched it for a while. Its lie looked bulletproof. The high, exposed banks, the impossibility of getting into the water downstream from the trout without sending wading waves upstream and over the trout, the water clear as air and deep enough to make it difficult to get a nymph to the bottom: all defended that trout.

The streambed was soft clay, with patches of rooted vegetation trailing in the mild current. The trout lay in a narrow slot between two such beds, sunk almost to the bottom, but obviously willing to feed when something was delivered to it. Often it turned aside a bit, or lifted up a few inches eagerly, clear signs of feeding. Sometimes I'd see the white wink of its mouth as it opened to take something, closed to ingest it. I'd sampled enough weed beds in my life, in enough spring creeks, in enough widespread places, to suspect tiny mayfly nymphs or scuds.

At first I enjoyed just watching the trout at its work, at its life. I didn't have any sense that I might catch it if I tried. We'd been hammering the banks of the bigger river with 8-weights, depth-charge lines, big streamers. The line wasn't even strung on my light rod. I didn't want to rig for what I suspected would be a single fruitless cast to that bulletproof trout. But I also didn't want to leave it. So I simply lay in that meadow grass, my back warmed by the Argentine sun, and watched the trout feed on bits of the drift so small I never did see any of them.

You can watch a trout for only so long before you begin to plot against it. I decided that if I were hypothetically going to try for that trout, I'd do it by tying a tiny yarn indicator to the tip of the 9-foot 5X leader already nail-knotted to the line spooled on my reel. Then I'd hinge six feet of 6X tippet from the yarn and tie a single beadhead nymph to that. I wouldn't use weight on the leader, because that would introduce the likelihood that I'd calculate the sink rate wrong and end up anchored in the weeds upstream from the trout. I knew that getting a hung fly unhooked and back into the drift would almost certainly be fatal. I also knew that if I added a shot or putty weight, the trout might see it first and mistake it for something good to eat and take it. That happens.

BEADHEAD SQUIRREL NYMPH

Hook:	Standard nymph or curved scud, size 12–20
Head:	Gold bead
Thread:	Brown 6/0 or 8/0
Tail:	Pine squirrel fur, with guard hairs
Body:	Half tan Antron, half red fox squirrel fur
Thorax:	Pine squirrel fur, with guard hairs

You can devise a plan against a trout and keep it hypothetical for only so long before you've got to put it into play, see if it works or does not. I strung the rod, straightened that 9-foot leader, slip-knotted a half-inch wisp of yellow yarn to its 5X tip, fanned the yarn out, dressed it with dry-fly floatant. I clinch-knotted the long 6X tippet to the leader and jammed the knot down against the indicator, forming the 90-degree angle in the leader critical to the hinge. I selected a size 20 Squirrel Beadhead tied with just a few turns of lead wire under its thorax and fixed it to the tippet with a Duncan loop knot, to give it some freedom of movement in its drift.

I belly-crawled forward a few feet, spooled about ten feet of line off the reel, flicked a single backcast, angled the delivery stroke across the surface, and placed the indicator, not the nymph, as close as I could into the feeding lane of the trout. The nymph pipped into the water the length of that long leader upstream from the trout. I expected the trout to bolt when the leader and strike indicator settled softly to the smooth water, but it did not.

It's always a dilemma whether to watch the indicator, the fly, or the trout. I watched the trout, and out of the metaphorical corner of my eye watched the water just upstream from it. I saw an occasional tiny copper spark of reflected light, which let me know my nymph was riding above the groove between those two weed beds, and sinking slowly toward the trout. When it got about three feet deep, still riding at least a foot higher than the trout, I lost sight of it and shifted my peripheral focus to the indicator while still watching the trout.

When the indicator had slipped past the position of the trout, I thought the nymph had drifted over its head, that the nymph had gone by unnoticed. Just as my meager hopes for that precious first cast began to fade, I saw the trout lift a few inches, then tip back down to the bottom, apparently without ever opening its mouth. My brain registered it as a refusal, but my rod hand, accustomed to such mistakes, made an inspection of the situation by gently elevating the rod tip. The trout exploded upstream.

A three-pound rainbow trout with a bright red stripe down its side might be pretty, but it isn't much of a trout in Argentina. Still, I enjoyed unpinning the little beadhead nymph from the corner of that trout's jaw, hefting the fish momentarily before letting it go back to its station in that glide. It quickly disappeared into the weeds.

I got the message from that single trout that fishing a nymph over a sighted fish can be more challenging than any other sort of nymphing, and that it's best to hold fire until the situation is as figured out as you can get it. I also learned that a wink of light reflecting off a bead can be beneficial, making it easier to follow a nymph in its drift.

Always keep your nymph tying in a tight relationship to your nymph fishing. It's fine, and it's probably even necessary, to wander into experimentation that arises from an excess of fancy materials scattered on the tying bench, but your best experimental ties will be rooted in reasons that you discover in your own fishing on streams and stillwaters.

PART 1

The Way Nymphing Shapes Itself

CHAPTER 1

A New Nymph Box

I've fished with Rick Hafele for more years than either of us would care to count, starting long before he became author of his essential book *Nymph-Fishing Rivers and Streams.* We began by thrashing around, gathering insects, photographs, and anecdotes for a workshop we taught under the unwieldy title "Entomology and the Artificial Fly." It was modestly popular. An outline and then notebook we wrote for the workshop became greatly expanded into the book *Western Hatches.* Work on that book required several more years fishing together, which we called *research.*

We continued our work, planning to expand that first book into a series, each much more detailed, which except for the mayfly portion hasn't happened. We still thrash around streams and stillwaters together. I'll give you an example. Not long enough ago we took a four-

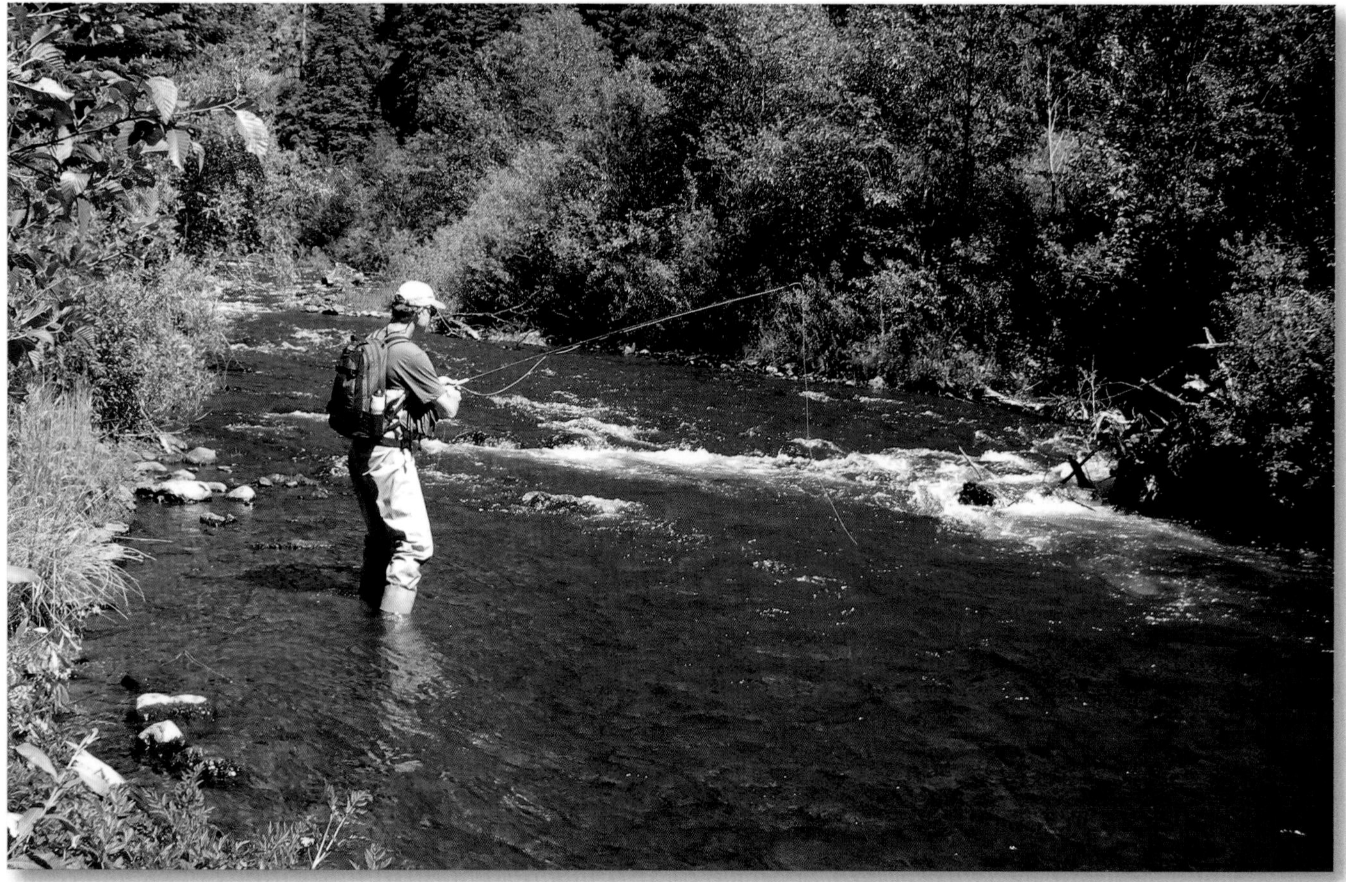

Rick Hafele, author of Nymph-Fishing Rivers and Streams, *nymphing a slick where western green drake duns were hatching sporadically, but trout were ignoring them for the nymphs.*

day trip to a small stream, in the mountains of northeast Oregon, that I'd fished briefly once and long ago, and Rick had not fished at all. I remembered it as tiny, discounted that we'd be going in early July, and took only one pair of wading brogues, those experimental types with sticky rubber soles rather than felt, thinking I'd be doing more rock hopping than wading anyway, so it was a good place to try them. They'd been sent to me years earlier; I'd neglected to get them wet and was feeling guilty about it.

Rick wore his normal sturdy felt-soled brogues. He's a professional aquatic entomologist, spends a lot of time kicking around in streambed stones for his work, so he wears the best.

The stream was just dropping down from runoff. It was clear enough, and quite fishable. But it was boisterous, and filled its channel from bank to bank. There were few exposed gravel bars, and no dry rocks to hop. It was a clean mountain stream, but it also had the normal complement of vegetative growth where the sun struck its bottom rocks. This is algae, what scientists call *periphyton,* and what most anglers call *moss.* Aquatic insects make a living eating it, so we shouldn't always curse it as we do when we skid on it.

PEACOCK HERL NYMPH ***Rick Hafele***

Hook:	Standard nymph, size 8–18
Weight:	6–8 turns of nonlead wire
Thread:	Black 6/0 or 8/0
Tails:	4–6 wood-duck flank fibers, or brown hackle fibers
Rib:	Fine gold or silver tinsel, or gold wire
Body:	2–4 peacock herls
Wing case:	Black Krystal Flash
Thorax:	Pine squirrel fur, with guard hairs

It was slick. My rubber-soled wading shoes found little agreement with it. I had a wading staff, so I stayed upright in the swift current, but I didn't travel much, didn't cover much water. Rick was wading fine until the felts on both of his brogues, the glue overtaxed by years of kicking up insect samples, suddenly let go. One felt washed away in the current and was gone. The other began flapping, and Rick had to tear it the rest of the way off to keep from tripping over it. Then we were both stumbling around.

When one insect, such as this western green drake nymph (Drunella doddsi), *is this abundant in your collecting, you can assume trout want to see a nymph that looks at least a little like it.*

We found ourselves taking root around noon in a long, sunstruck pool. It entered from a riffle upstream, glided along a cliff face on its deep far side, shallowed up toward a submerged gravel bar on our side. It flowed levelly, in a rumpled run that smoothed out at its lower end, for two hundred feet or so before gathering speed and tipping over into a riffle downstream.

A scattering of very large green drake duns boated those currents. They were coming off in what we call a *sporadic* hatch, but enough were present that we could see one or two on the water at any one time. No trout were rising to take the duns, but in their presence I did not feel it was a mistake to try an imitation, a size 12 Green Paradrake, which I happened to have with me. I suspected trout would start rising soon, or that I'd at least be able to coax a few fish to the surface by repeating drifts down the same current lines. It all seemed reasonable; those insects were big, and they were having trouble getting launched off the water.

I began fishing my dry up from the tailout. Rick inserted himself into the pool about midway up, and as usual in the absence of an overwhelming reason that he should do anything else, which reason would have been rising trout, he rigged with a pair of nymphs, a couple of split shot, a strike indicator, and began fishing upstream. One of his flies was his generic Peacock Herl Nymph.

Rick ties it with a pine squirrel thorax and black Krystal Flash wing case. If you were a trout submerged in deep, fast water and in the sort of hurry that brisk mountain currents inspire, you could easily mistake that Herl Nymph for the nymphal stage of a green drake mayfly.

So there we were, in our very common combination: Rick fishing the bottom, and me fishing the top. The results were unfortunately common, as well: Rick began catching trout and I did not. No trout rose to floating duns, either the naturals or my imitation. Because I was idled by the trout, and also my position was just downstream from Rick, I was forced to be a spectator to all the action.

A. P. BLACK *André Puyans*

Hook:	Standard nymph, size 12–16
Weight:	8–12 turns of nonlead wire
Thread:	Black 6/0 or 8/0
Tail:	Dark moose body hair
Abdomen:	Black fur dubbing
Wing case:	Dark moose body hair
Thorax:	Black fur mixed with black Antron
Legs:	Butts of wing-case fibers

I didn't watch long. Rick had only danced half a dozen trout before I decided that the trout, if they had any plans to take on top later, had missed their chance to get caught on my dry fly. My small-stream fly box, the only one I had with me, contains no imitations of green drake nymphs, but it always has a short row of André Puyans's A. P. Blacks in sizes 12 and 14 stuck in its foam, because I catch a lot of trout from small streams by suspending that fly beneath a yellow yarn indicator. I dangled one under a hard indicator for the deeper and brisker water where those big duns were emerging, and pinched a hefty split shot to the leader above the weighted nymph.

Not many casts later, I'd caught a trout and had a throat pump sample to study. It included clear evidence that, while trout refused to swim to the top to take green drake duns, they were not neglecting green drake nymphs as they drifted downstream. Examining the sample made me think that only a small tithe of these nymphs ever succeeded in making it to the top.

I don't want you to conclude that Rick Hafele outfishes me every time, or even very often. But I have arrived at the following conclusion myself: If one of us is going to outfish the other, it's going to be Rick outfishing me, and it's going to be because he begins fishing with nymphs on or near the bottom unless he sees a clear indication that he should do something else, while in my own past I have always started with dry flies or something near the surface unless I see indications that they don't have a hope to work.

In September of that same year, I was on the Bighorn River with Jim Schollmeyer, who has since written and photographed his excellent book *Nymph Fly-Tying Techniques.* We launched Jim's drift boat below the afterbay dam at midmorning, and floated idly downstream, hoping to position ourselves between the surge of guides who had hit the water early, and the second surge of those who would finish their first float and relaunch themselves to make the same float again in early afternoon. It worked to an extent; we didn't have the river to ourselves, but we were able to fish one or two of the productive riffles that we like while we waited for the black caddis *(Brachycentrus americanus)* hatch that we expected to start sometime around the lunch hour. That's the fishing we were there for, but it rarely feels bad to catch a few fat trout on nymphs while you wait for dry-fly activity to start.

Jim parked the boat and I hoisted my vest. On a trip to the varied waters of Montana it is so heavy with fly boxes that I would instantly be dragged under and drowned if I fell in while wearing it. I stepped into a broad, gentle riffle, unzipped the biggest pocket of the vest, and wrestled out my bulky main nymph box, the one into which I had long ago decided to condense almost all of the nymphs that I owned, so I'd always be able to find the nymph that I needed. What I desired to tie on, to explore the bottom of that wide, unfeatured expanse of bumpy water on the Bighorn River, was a pair of nymphs, one small and drab, the other tiny and with some flash. I looked for a size 16 Squirrel Beadhead, a size 20 Flashback Pheasant Tail, perhaps a size 18 Copper John. I knew just what I wanted, or what I thought the trout out there would want. But when I peered into the one box that contained almost all of the nymphs that I owned, I found it empty of any of them. I didn't find a fly that spoke to me, one that I really wanted to tie to my tippet, one that I would fish with the sort of confidence that translates into trout caught.

Fly boxes, at least mine, go through a progression, and at one final point they need to be reworked, or replaced.

Jim Schollmeyer fishing the Bighorn River in Montana on the day I discovered I didn't have any nymphs in my boxes that I desired to tie to my tippet.

At best, all of the flies need to be removed, sorted out, put back in the box in something that resembles order, and some new flies added for refreshment. At worst, fly boxes need to simply be replaced, along with all of their contents. Here's how it happens, at least to me. I buy a new fly box and fill it with nymphs rather haphazardly. Some are patterns that have worked for me for years. Others I've discovered on recent trips; they've solved specific situations. Many are experiments, tied around theories about what I think should work, or tied with materials I've just acquired, or with methods I've just learned, and would like to try against trout.

It's my failing, one I'm warning you about, that I rarely settle on an effective dressing, then tie it by the dozens so they're lined up in rows in my nymph boxes, according to size and according to color if the pattern has variations. The result of my lack of method is that I start each season with a few nymphs in my box that I know will work, a larger scattering of flies that I hope will work. The largest muddle in the box is those nymphs that have failed ever to work at all, and therefore accumulate because they never get tied to tippets and lost.

What happens as each season goes along, and as one season follows another, is that the few essential patterns that catch trout get lost, while the nymphs that don't catch trout never go away. Instead, new experiments are tried, found to fail, and remain in the box. After a time, sometimes a single season and other times several seasons, nymphs that don't work expand to take over the entire box. There would be no room for nymphs that do catch trout even if I got time during the season to tie them. The world might become perfect if only that single formula could be reversed. In your own nymph boxes, patterns that work should expand, and those that fail should contract. With luck or courage, all nymphs that fail might even be made to disappear. Give them to friends, if you have any left.

AQUATIC SOW BUG

Hook:	Curved scud, 2X heavy, size 14–20
Thread:	Black 6/0 or 8/0
Rib:	Heavy copper wire
Body:	Muskrat fur

I found a couple of flies in my unruly nymph box that in combination worked to take a few trout from that Bighorn River riffle, that day with Jim Schollmeyer. One was a size 14 beadhead of some sort; I don't remember its pedigree because none of the trout came to it. The other was a size 20 Aquatic Sow Bug that I tied by ribbing muskrat fur with heavy copper wire. The Bighorn is full of aquatic sow bugs (Isopoda); an imitation for them does not need to be complicated.

The success of that nymph, extracted from my nymph box full of failures, is probably an indication that an old, out-of-control fly box should not neccessarily be discarded. But I felt an overwhelming moment of disgust while I searched through that box for something I thought might work. There were simply no flies in it that I desired to tie to my tippet, and that included the fly that I tied to my tippet and that worked.

The day I got home from the trip to the Bighorn, I drove to my local fly shop and bought a new nymph box, of what I will call medium size. I disciplined myself to spend a large part of my winter tying time filling that box with nymphs that I know catch trout, the kind that I'm glad to see when I open the box, the few dressings that I truly desire to tie to my tippet. I tied them by the dozen, not by ones and twos. I got that box filled by the next spring. I still own and sometimes carry the old and tangled one. But you know which nymph box I reach for when I've got my waders wet in a riffle that I suspect is full of fat trout.

I recommend you begin reading this book with at least one new nymph box, empty, open, and receptive on your fly-tying bench. Better yet would be three—one for searching nymphs, another for imitative nymphs, and the third for lake and pond nymphs.

CHAPTER 2

Searching Nymphs for Moving Water

Everybody knows that a small, black beadhead nymph fished with a dead-drift presentation on or near the bottom, will take an outsized number of trout from creeks, streams, and rivers. Everybody also knows that it's fun to invent flies, go out and catch a bunch of trout on them, name them after yourself, get famous for it. I plotted a minor experiment along those lines last year: I created a simple nymph with a gold bead, peacock herl, black dubbing, and copper wire ribbing, tied up a dozen in size 16, and went out to try it against the trout. Actually I tied up half a dozen of two dressings, and went out to try *them* against the trout, because I assembled those meager materials on the hook in a couple of different ways.

DARING DARK 1

Hook: Standard wet-fly hook, size 14–18
Head: Gold bead
Thread: Black 8/0
Rib: Copper wire
Abdomen: 2 parts black rabbit, 1 part charcoal, and 1 part rust Sparkle Yarn (my standard mix for a salmon-fly nymph)
Thorax: Peacock herl

DARING DARK 2

Hook: Standard wet-fly hook, size 14–18
Head: Gold bead
Thread: Black 8/0
Rib: Copper wire
Abdomen: Peacock herl
Thorax: 2 parts black rabbit, 1 part charcoal, and 1 part rust Sparkle Yarn

The first was by dubbing a black fur body, ribbing it, finishing the fly off with a few turns of herl behind the bead for a thorax. That looked nice; on a size 16 hook the body was slender, the peacock herl, taken from the base of the eye feather, was wider, and therefore the fly had a proper tapered appearance, gaining thickness from back to front in an insectlike shape. The second tie reversed the order of the materials: a ribbed peacock herl body finished off with a black fur thorax. It looked nice as well. By using thinner herls in the eye of the peacock feather, and then dubbing the fur thorax loosely, it was easy to achieve the same tapered shape.

I forgot to name the fly after myself, or at all; we'll call it the Daring Dark, presupposing the need for a Daring Light, a Daring Olive, a Daring . . . on and on. It's

You can make a kick-screen net from two ¾-inch wooden dowels, three feet of fine-mesh window screen, and a staple gun. Do not use the net to collect from fragile environments.

actually quite likely that such a fly has already been tied, tried, named, and is out there in hundreds of fly boxes. That's not the point. The point was to see if one fished better than the other. One did.

I rigged the reversed flies about a foot apart on a 5X tippet, with a bit of putty weight between them, a strike indicator four feet up the leader from them. I fished them in a bright riffle in a favorite stream that is not full of trout, but is also very far from lacking them. I worked slowly upstream, casting short, high-sticking that tandem along the bottom, setting the hook whenever the indicator hesitated or took a dip under. I caught lots of fish. I kept loose time, switched the position of the two flies about every half hour. I also kept a loose count, to see which fooled the most fish.

The results were quite clear: whichever fly was on the point came in a close second to the fly riding above the putty weight. For all I know, the weight itself drew an equal number of strikes, but I didn't catch a single trout on it. I suspect the upper fly took more trout because takes to it were slightly more likely to be reported to the indicator than were takes to the fly dangling on the other side of the slight weight. These takes would have to remove the bit of slack and move the bit of weight before the indicator would react to what happened and I might be made aware of the take. I didn't give much weight to any of my findings. I rated the dressings as equals, and don't know to this day which is the proper Daring Dark.

Either way it's tied, it makes an excellent searching nymph. So would the Daring Light, which I would tie with a gold bead, gold wire rib, hare's mask fur for the abdomen, and hare's mask fur with the guard hairs left in for the thorax. I'd be reinventing the Beadhead Hare's Ear, which would get me in well-deserved trouble the instant I named it anything else.

The point is not that the upper fly worked better than the point fly. It's that neither fly imitated any specific insect in the water I was fishing, but both flies were readily mistaken by the trout for something that ought to be eaten. They became what I call *searching nymphs,* for use in situations when no single insect is dominant, and when trout are not feeding selectively, but opportunistically.

Remember my admonition, in the introduction, to keep your nymph tying rooted in your nymph fishing. If you collect insects from the bottom of trout streams, whether you do it with a kick-screen net you've made yourself, or simply by hoisting rocks and looking at what's clinging to them, you'll find a great number of small, dark ones. These insects get eaten on a fairly consistent basis by trout. Unless a single one of them is dominant in whatever sort of sampling you're doing, they'll be eaten whenever a trout gets a chance at one, which in most creeks, streams, and rivers will be very often. Trout will not often turn down a chance at a small, dark natural nymph or larva.

Sometimes even when a trout is nibbling at a single set of groceries that does not look at all like such a small, dark nymph, it will still move to sample a similar natural drifting helplessly past. That is why the same trout will not often pass up a chance to take a small, dark nymph, whether it's the Daring Dark, Polly Rosborough's Muskrat, Rick Hafele's Peacock Herl Nymph, or André Puyans's A. P. Black. I've taken many throat pump samples from trout that I thought were feeding selectively, only to find them full of a larger potpourri of natural insects than I ever suspected were present in the currents.

I highly recommend you take a bit of time, trot to your local hardware store, spend the very few dollars it requires to construct your own kick-screen net, and carry it with you the next time you go trout fishing. This first step toward collecting insects is not designed to propel you out to your favorite streams, or even stillwaters, to gather what is there, to return to the vise with it in order to tie exact imitations. I suspect, instead, that your initial kicking around in riffles, which are the most productive part of any stream, will inform you of the wide variety of aquatic insects and other beasts that trout see escorted to them on the drift each day. This will be more true on freestone streams than on spring creeks and meadow streams, most true in the rockiest, shallowest parts of those rougher waters. If you collect from a freestone riffle and the sample lacks variety, it's a sign that the stream is unhealthy.

It will be far from rare that a particular insect or crustacean will stand out from all that variety that you collect. It might be surrounded by a lot of different things, but a sample that includes twenty different types of critters will often include half a dozen or more of one of them. In that case you should choose a nymph pattern that looks at least somewhat like the most abundant food form. You don't necessarily need to imitate it, but if you at least approximate it with a nymph that is similar in size, shape, and color, then you'll know you're tumbling something in front of the trout that they've seen, and most likely eaten, recently.

Searching nymphs for moving water are tied to be fished when trout are not feeding selectively. But the best of them are based on some sort of trout food form. You won't, in truth, do badly very often if you carry nothing but exact imitations of the widest variety of aquatic insects, scuds, sow bugs, and aquatic worms. But each of those groups varies considerably in size, shape, and color, as you move from stream to stream, whether they're separated by a continent, a state, or a single ridgeline. It would be quite an assignment to assemble a set of exact imitations for all of the food forms in a single river system of some size and in good health, therefore containing the normal wide variety of things that trout eat beneath the surface.

When one insect is more abundant than others in a collection sample that includes a potpourri of them, a searching dressing that looks at least a little like the dominant insect will take trout. In this case, you would want to use something similar to the golden stone nymph (Hesperoperla pacifica), *though a nymph resembling a salmon-fly nymph* (Pteronarcys californica) *would be a good second choice.*

That's why it's a fine idea to come up with a list of searching nymph patterns that average them out, and to tie those into a fly box that you carry with you everywhere you go. The most beneficial thing about such a set of searching nymphs is that they will catch trout anywhere you might take them, whether it's on your home stream, in your home state, around your home continent, or anywhere else in the world that trout abound.

CHAPTER 3

Imitative Nymphs for Moving Water

I spent a late-winter week at a cabin on the Deschutes River some time ago, alternately working on the last stages of a manuscript and working over a pod of trout that rose for hours every midday, on a flat where that boisterous river paused reflectively for a bit, spread out peacefully over a gravel bottom. I'd get up early every morning, do my editing for an hour or so, then pace out to the deck overlooking the river, look for rises, go back to work. Around the eleven o'clock break I'd begin to see a few sporadic rises, but I'd usually be able to resist them and work for another hour.

When I quit to eat lunch I'd be forced to bolt it, because those trout would be rising steadily by then, and I'd need to be down there, waist-deep in the chilled water, trying to pester them. The first day or two, they bothered me a lot more than I bothered them. I couldn't figure out what they were taking. There were no insects on the surface, at least that I could see. It became fairly

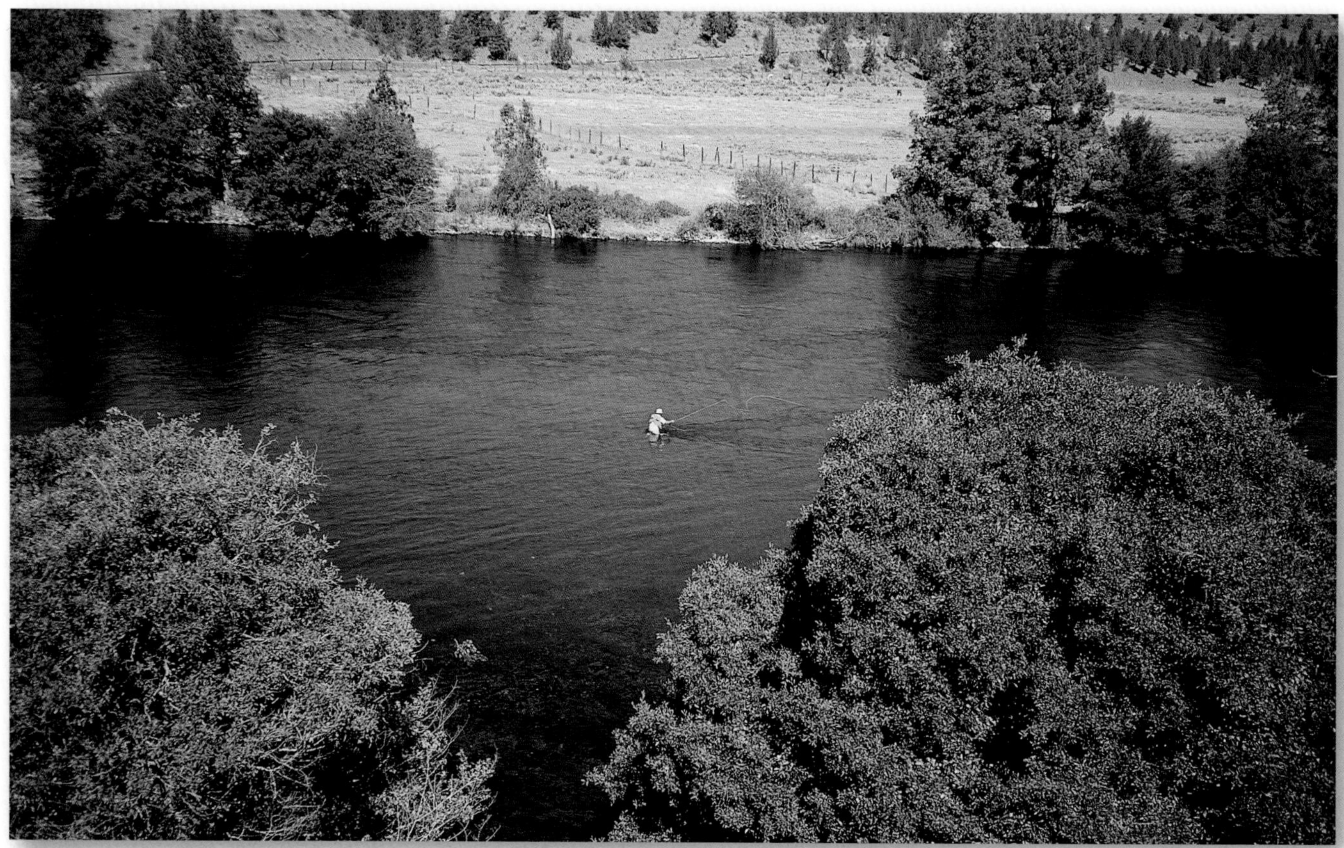

The Deschutes River doesn't have many placid flats, but the few it has can sponsor feeding to tiny midges that require almost exact imitation.

evident that the trout, though they sent rise rings to the top, were actually feeding on something just beneath it. No noses, dorsal fins, or tails broke the surface. No bubbles were left in any rises.

I suspended a kick net in the water once, held it against the current with its top out, the screen vertical to capture whatever mystery might be adrift in the upper foot of the water column where those trout were so busy feeding. When I brought the net up to examine it, I saw nothing of any significance. There were a couple of tiny, dark midge pupae, in my defense so small that if there were many others in the current, most had gone right through the mesh of the net. Nothing else had caught in the net except a few twigs and leaves. I washed the net of this detritus and set it back on the bank, went back to my frustrated fishing.

I didn't discount the idea that the trout might be taking those scant midges. But I didn't give much credit to the idea that they were big enough bites, or in large enough numbers, to cause the type of constant feeding those trout were enjoying.

I did, however, respond to what I saw, but only after another hour of continued failure, during which time I tried out a few extra theories based first on early *Baetis* mayflies, and then on tiny winter black stoneflies, thinking perhaps the trout were feeding on those in some stage that had managed to elude the net. Finally I tied on a size 18 Parachute Adams and suspended the smallest nymph I had on me at that moment, a size 20 Pheasant Tail, beneath the dry fly on twenty inches of 6X tippet. One trout, perhaps what my late friend Col. Tony Robnett called the *duty trout,* intercepted that nymph and caused the sudden disappearance of the indicator dry. The trout was about twelve inches long, but I played it gently out of all proportion to its potential to break me. When I eased it into my hand, and unpinned that Pheasant Tail from its lip, I noticed the fish had a peppering of some sort of tiny, black insect inside its mouth. They were, of course, those midge pupae, most of which had slipped through the meshes of my collecting net.

Having caught one trout on the nymph, I thought I had the problem solved. But you know I did not. That was the only stupid trout in the pod, or it was the only one with the assignment to distract me into thinking I'd worked the problem to its solution. I didn't catch another trout in the hour it took for the feeding activity to taper off, for the chill of the late-winter water to work though my waders and into my bones, for the manuscript spread up there on the table in the cabin to recall me to my work.

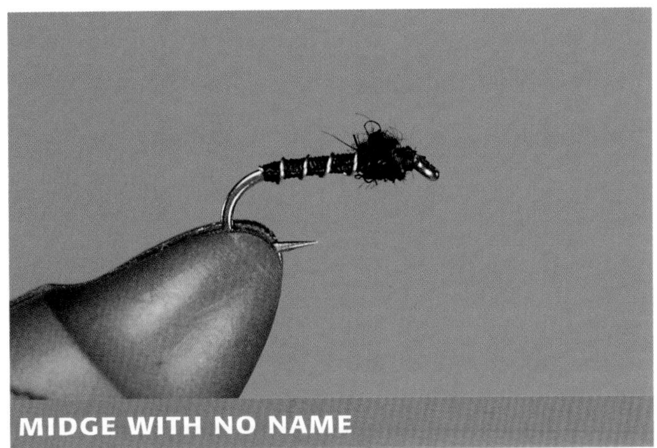

MIDGE WITH NO NAME

Hook:	Standard dry fly, size 22
Thread:	Black 8/0
Rib:	Fine silver wire
Abdomen:	Working thread
Thorax:	Black rabbit fur

That evening I rummaged around the cabin's tying bench, found that the smallest hooks there were size 22 and for dry flies. I wound a few with bodies of black tying thread, fine silver wire ribs, and a small knot of black rabbit fur for the clumped head and thorax of the hunchbacked midge pupae. That was it. They'd have been more imitative on hooks a size or two smaller. I didn't bother to name the fly; something similar to it has surely been invented numberless times.

My world didn't exactly open out the next day on account of that minor fly. But I found close to ten stupid trout during the two hours the rise lasted. I took a throat pump sample from one. It contained more than a hundred of those tiny midge pupae, many of them still kicking

Tiny midge pupae appear in many throat pump samples when trout are feeding just subsurface on invisibles.

feebly for a few moments in the vial of alcohol in which I pickled them. They were not much more than half the size of the size 22 fly which I'd used to imitate them.

Situations in which you'll need to fish imitative nymphs, on moving water, are not as common as a lot of recent fly-fishing literature might make them seem. Almost every article is about a difficult fishing problem solved by a different exact imitation. There are good reasons for such articles. First, they make good literature; it's far more interesting to read about a problem and its solution than it is to read a piece in which the author steps into the stream, ties on any old nymph, and confidently whacks a bunch of trout . . . though the latter is a lot easier, far more fun, and might reflect careful selection of a set of searching nymphs. Second, a mystery makes better reading than the exposition of the obvious, so it's better to write a story, if not to read one, in which the author is forced to trudge back up to the cabin and create something that he comes back down and fishes and it works. Third, and most important, trout fishing does involve many situations in which trout are selective to nymphs, and if nobody solved them and wrote articles about them, fly tying and fly fishing would fail to evolve, and fly fishers would bump into lots of days full of the sort of never-ending frustration I suffered on that Deschutes River flat, until I accidentally figured out what the trout were eating.

Progress does not necessarily entail complexity. Some of the most elegant solutions in nymph imitations are very simple. An example is the Black Beauty and its variations, tied by Colorado guide Pat Dorsey and recorded in Ed Engle's fine book *Tying Small Flies.* The basic Black Beauty has a black thread body, copper wire rib, black synthetic dubbing for the thorax. Variations include the addition of a stub of white Z-lon for a wing, making it an emerger, and either a black microbead or a silver glass bead for the head, the metal one giving it a bit of sink, the glass one a bit of flash. All are simple to tie; each solves a bit different midge pupa situation.

Trout commonly take midge pupae hanging from the surface film, or just an inch or two beneath it.

Some imitative nymphs might be elegant, but also quite complex. Several things propel these dressings into fly-pattern catalogs and fly-shop bins. The first is the desire among tiers to imitate all the complexity of parts insects have acquired to adapt to the aquatic environment: fringed cerci; tergites and sternites; gill filaments; pro-, meso-, and metathoracic segments; legs, which can be broken into their many segments; heads, with eyes and antennae, vermiculations and dots. Some ties, called *realistic,* imitate all of these parts, in the sincere belief that the closer you come to the natural, the more trout you'll catch. That is probably far from true. It is certain that the more complex your tie, the more time you'll spend tying it, and the less time you'll spend fishing it.

Fly tying, in some important circles, has evolved into a separate sport—actually a craft or art—from fly fishing. This book won't go there, because I never go there. My own fly tying is always rooted in my own fly fishing. The flies that I use are rarely complex and never realistic, because I don't believe that complex dressings catch more trout, and I do know that tying them would keep me at the bench when I'd rather be out fishing.

A second and more valid reason for complex ties, at least to me, is that it's simply fun to experiment with materials, old and new, and with ways to attach materials to a hook, again both old and new. Sometimes what gets added adds trout to the catch. An example might be rubber legs on a salmon-fly nymph imitation, though in truth my own book is still open on that. I haven't fished a salmon fly with legs against the same one without them, so I can't say that the legs increase the catch from my own experience. But I can say that I've shown my fly box to an occasional guide, to ask which fly to tie on, and they've always said that they'd prefer I'd tie on the one with rubber legs. I can't say if that's because they think the one with legs is more effective, or prettier to them—it's usually uglier to me—but I do know that the younger and less experienced the guide, the more likely he, she, or it will insist that nymphs with rubber legs are better.

The truth is that the legs will add trout to your catch if they add to the confidence with which you fish the imitation. You'll fish it more diligently, present it more carefully, mind its drift better, expect takes to it more often, and therefore be more likely to detect takes to this fly to which you've begun to ascribe some minor or major magic. You will not be wrong.

I encountered another concrete reason for complexity that you might want to consider when you're tying or buying flies. I talked to the inspector of prospective new flies for a production fly company; his job was to decide

Black Beauty (left), Black Beauty Emerger (center left), Beadhead Black Beauty (center right and right)

BLACK BEAUTY *Pat Dorsey*

Hook:	Curved scud, size 18–24
Thread:	Black 8/0
Rib:	Fine copper wire, reverse-wrapped
Body:	Working thread
Thorax:	Black synthetic dubbing

BLACK BEAUTY EMERGER *Pat Dorsey*

Hook:	Curved scud, size 18–24
Thread:	Black 8/0
Rib:	Fine copper wire, reverse-wrapped
Body:	Working thread
Wing:	White Z-lon
Thorax:	Black synthetic dubbing

BEADHEAD BLACK BEAUTY *Pat Dorsey*

Hook:	Curved scud, size 18–24
Head:	Black Micro-Bead or Hi-Lite silver glass bead
Thread:	Black 8/0
Rib:	Fine copper wire, reverse-wrapped
Body:	Working thread
Thorax:	Black synthetic dubbing

which flies went into the catalog and which did not. We discussed imitations for caddis pupae. I mentioned that a certain simple tie was effective for me. He compared it to a recent invention that had all the core parts and what seemed to me quite a few unnecessary peripheral ones. "But this one," he said, holding up a sample of the more complicated tie, "will sell better. People want to buy something that *looks* like it will fool smart fish."

It is not news that flies are tied to catch fishermen as well as fish. If you enjoy tying a complex tie, and you fish such a fly with more confidence, it's going to be more effective for you. But never neglect the simple ones; they can be just as imitative as their opposite. And you'll fill a fly box with them a lot more quickly.

My experience with those midges on the Deschutes River is an example of the many days when you'll be glad to have imitative nymphs among your possessions. You'll need midge nymphs more often if you fish spring creeks in winter, or tailwaters at any time of year, than you will if your fishing is limited to freestone streams during the central part of the fishing season. But you might run into situations that call for them at any time of year, on any moving water where trout become selective.

Small nymphs of the blue-winged olive mayfly group *(Baetis)* and the slightly larger pale morning duns (*Ephemerella inermis* and *infrequens*) are examples of aquatic insects that are often dominant in the vegetated waters of spring creeks and tailwaters. These stabilized flows allow aquatic vegetation to take root. The rooted plants create a myriad of microniches to which BWO and PMD nymphs are perfectly suited. Their populations explode, while those of other insects less suited to the narrow habitat are either diminished or extinguished. It's a case of limited variety, but an almost overabundance of the few forms that are left. Trout naturally see those most often in the drift, focus on them, and fairly often become selective to them. If your nymph boxes lack imitations of them, you might find yourself fishless at times when those naturals are most active and available to trout.

On a few big western rivers, including my home Deschutes, Montana's Madison and Big Hole, and parts of Idaho's Henry's Fork of the Snake, among many others less famous, giant salmon-fly nymphs make mass migrations to shore each spring and early summer for emergence. When they do, trout become exceedingly well fed, and are willing to take little else. An imitation is necessary. A lot of widespread western streams enjoy the same activity. A salmon-fly nymph is necessary wherever this happens.

Many riffles and rocky runs, especially in tailwaters, have almost overwhelming populations of net-spinning caddis larvae. Many of these are tan, but the most common are green, giving rise to the *green rock worm* moniker. These are filter feeders. They construct tiny nets in the current, which seine bits of decaying leaves and other minute detritus from the water. Their populations explode in top-release tailwaters because plankton grows in the stillwater of the reservoir upstream—plankton does not grow in moving water—and gets delivered over the spillway, gets trapped in their nets, feeds them out of all proportion to the way they were fed before the dam got built. These net spinners can also be abundant on streams with lots of irrigation return, again because the water delivers an unnatural amount of small detrital material.

Dense populations of net-spinning caddis larvae are not always signs of a healthy stream or river. Often they're signs of just the opposite. But great numbers of green rock worms adrift in the currents, along with a sizable number of trout waiting to feed upon them, does little damage to your fishing if you have an adequate dressing in your imitative nymph box.

Those are a few specific species that can dominate the population in a stream or river, and become exclusive in the eyes of the trout, and therefore be taken selectively. But any species of aquatic insect, whether it's a mayfly, midge, caddisfly, or stonefly, can suddenly become the most available insect just before and also during its emergence. Many mayfly nymphs of a single species gather along the bottom, release from it for the hazardous trip to the surface, all during a period of an hour or two. This is a defense against predation: if they all go at once, condensing their emergence into a short period of hours for a minimal number of days, rather than trickling off a few at a time for weeks or months, then trout in the water and swallows in the air cannot eat fast enough to get them all. They cannot wipe out the species in that bit of water. When such a brief but dense emergence happens, that insect is the most important insect around, and you will need to imitate it to do much business with trout. If trout feed on adults, on the surface, you'll want to use dry flies. If trout focus on nymphs making their way to the top, you'll need to use an imitative nymph.

Whenever one insect is so abundant that you suspect trout see little else, no matter its size and kind, you should use a pattern that imitates it as closely as you can. This happens once a year on streams with migrations of the giant salmon-fly nymph (Pteronarcys californica).

The same can be true for caddis. An abundance of pupae of a single species tweezer their way out of pupal cocoons hidden among bottom rocks, drift for some distance along the bottom, make the perilous trip to the surface, where they either drift along subsurface for some time or pop through and emerge quickly. Again, trout become selective to that pupa when it is the most abundant thing around, and you need a nymph that imitates it to fool the fish.

Stoneflies, without any known exceptions in moving water, migrate to shore as nymphs, crawl out on stones or shoreline vegetation for emergence. At times a single species of stonefly nymphs will be so abundant right along the edges, queuing up for emergence, that trout gather there and pick them like berries. Again, these trout are at least somewhat selective whenever they see such a dominance of one insect, and you need to match the natural to catch many trout.

When one insect, whether for reasons of abundance or sudden availability, becomes dominant in the trout diet, you'll catch far more trout if you fish a nymph that at least roughly resembles what they're taking. When any insect is prevalent in your sampling, even if trout are not feeding selectively on it, you still might be wise to imitate it. This reflects the notes in the previous chapter: quite often the best searching nymph is one that imitates the most abundant insect in the water you're fishing.

I've recommended that you buy a specific box and dedicate it to your searching nymphs. Here I'll advise that you buy a box at least as large, and set it aside to be filled, though perhaps more slowly, with nymphs imitative of the insects you find important in your fishing on trout streams and rivers. You'll fill this box over the seasons and the years as you encounter important insects and crustaceans in your own collecting, or find trout feeding on something selectively, and tie, buy, or even invent nymphs to imitate them.

CHAPTER 4

Nymphs for Stillwaters

I set out to prove to myself, one early year in what I'll call my fly-fishing career, that I could fish lakes and ponds effectively out of my stream-fly boxes for a full season, without ever missing the flies that I usually tie exclusively for lakes. For the first day of my experiment, at the leading edge of spring, I left my boat bag and float tube in the rig and hiked a mile through timber, on elk trails, to a very small, forested pond. I'd fished it a few times before. It was shallow, sunstruck, heavily vegetated. Past winter storms had toppled a few big trees from shore and into the pond; they'd been limbed and bleached by time. I hiked out on these and used them as casting platforms, to cast and cover water with nymphs and streamers when nothing specific was happening, or to reach rises with dry flies when trout were actively feeding.

Trout were feeding when I emerged out of the forest and stepped onto a bleached floating log that day, but very sporadically, taking something with strong subsurface swirls in the open water between those fallen logs. I tied on a Hare's Ear wet fly in size 12, because it had often worked on that pond, and on other lakes and ponds as well, whether trout were feeding or not. It was a go-to fly that I used more on streams and rivers than I did on lakes and ponds. But I had enough history with it on stillwaters that I often cast it long across open stretches of water, or to the occasional rises that I could cover, with quite a bit of confidence.

I tried the wet fly with a stripping retrieve of medium speed. Nothing moved to it. I switched to a patient hand-twist retrieve. The wet fly continued to fail. A trout rose in range. I quickly hoisted the fly and cast it beyond the rise, retrieved it back at a gallop. That usually prods a trout into a swift follow and strike. This trout ignored it.

I saw a trout turn to the wet once, as I brought it back to the log on which I stood, in preparation to lifting it for the next fruitless cast. The trout saw the fly, rushed after it. I continued the retrieve without interruption, as you're instructed to do when you see a trout following: don't stop; don't speed up; don't panic and jerk it out of there. The trout surged at the winged Hare's Ear, looked as if it were about to take it, but suddenly put on its brakes, turned and swam disdainfully away.

I sat down on the log, rummaged through the stream-fly boxes to which I'd decided to dedicate myself, tried a bunch of other flies that I found in them. The trout didn't approve any of them. Before I was finished with them, I didn't approve any of them either.

GREEN DAMSEL *Polly Rosborough*

Hook:	3XL, size 10–14
Thread:	Olive 6/0 or 8/0
Tail:	Light green marabou
Body:	Olive fur dubbing
Legs:	Speckled guinea fibers
Wing case:	Dark green marabou

My experiment to fish a season on stillwaters out of my stream-fly boxes didn't last half an afternoon, but it did get me some extra exercise that first day. I thrashed

The natural damselfly nymph is long and slender, with willow-leaf gills in place of tails. No fly in my stream-nymph boxes looks anything like it.

back through the forest to my rig, fetched the fly box I needed, long ago labeled "Lakes," and returned to the pond. I tied on a size 12 Polly Rosborough Green Damsel nymph, one of the earliest and still one of the most effective dressings for those migratory aquatic insects. I cast it out, intending to fish it back with alternate twitches and strips and pauses to simply sit and slowly sink, according to the late Polly's prescription, but I didn't get a chance to put his whole plan into action.

A trout took the nymph almost the instant it landed on the first cast.

That remote pond was underfished and oversubscribed with trout, to the point that some winnowing would increase the groceries for those remaining, and thereby their size, to the improvement of the fishing. So I killed that first trout for the campfire frying pan, opened it with a sharp little pocketknife, squeezed the surprisingly sparse contents of its stomach into a pickle jar lid filled with pond water. It held only half a dozen mature damselfly nymphs, all of them fairly bright green. But it was empty of anything else, which is why, even in that lightly fished pond, the trout refused all flies that failed to look like green damselfly nymphs.

I carry no flies in my stream boxes that look even remotely like green damselfly nymphs.

When trout are not feeding visibly in streams and rivers, you are most likely to do well with a searching nymph, or better yet, two of them in tandem that average out the types of food forms that are most common in moving waters, rather than a fly or two that imitate any specific naturals exactly. You'll never make a mistake by

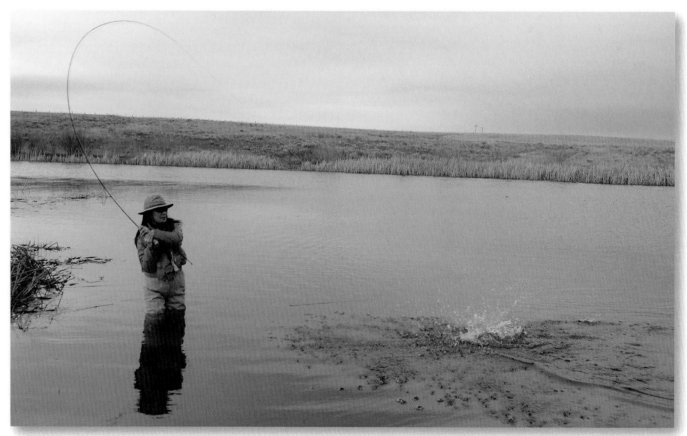

The stillwater environment could be considered analogous to the slowest water in a spring creek or tailwater. You'll find greater abundance of a restricted number of insect species than you ever would in brisk freestone flows.

collecting for a few minutes to see what might be most abundant in any new stream or river, and even on each new day spent on an old stream or river. If you find one insect dominant, or even present in numbers that slightly outweigh all the other insects in the net, choose at least one of your searching nymphs to look at least a little like that particular insect. But you'll do better with searching nymphs than you will with exact imitations.

When trout are not feeding visibly in lakes, it's a bit more difficult to collect from their environment, on account of depth, and you're more often forced to puzzle out what trout might be taking without getting a close look at exactly what insects are out there. But it's not as difficult as you might think.

Stillwaters are more limited environments than moving water. Think of a lake or pond as a creek, stream, or river with its riffles deleted, its runs absent, its pocket water gone. There are no gravel and boulder structures that we have come to call *freestone,* because such features are shaped by currents. Stillwaters, while possessing mild wind currents, have none that would clean gravel of silt, or shift and deposit rocks and boulders, with the possible exception of wave-washed shorelines, which in some big and wind-swept lakes approach riverine environments.

What you have left when you delete the current and stabilize the water level of a stream might make a stillwater correspond most closely to a gentle spring creek flat, defined by the productivity but also by the narrow types of niches in its rooted vegetation. Recall from the last chapter that a spring creek is the most likely type of moving water to have a limited number of insect and crustacean species, but each of them is present in great abundance, and this is the type of moving water in which you'll most likely need to fish imitative nymphs. Slow those gentle flows down a bit further, limit the variety of the niches a bit more, and you approach the shape of a stillwater.

Lakes and ponds tend to offer trout just two to at most four types of mayflies, specifically and by far most widespread the *Callibaetis,* possibly a few scattered *Siphlonurus,* in a few very scattered locations the big *Hexagenia,* and rarely the tiny *Caenis,* these last so tiny and adapted to such marginal lake habitat that it's not clear they're important to trout even where they're very abundant. A wider variety of caddis types live in stillwaters, but all are cased. You'll find none of the free-living and net-spinning caddis larvae that we call green rock worms, and that are so common in the drift and in trout stomach samples in almost all moving waters.

Stoneflies are so rarely found in lakes that even entomologists get excited about it when they discover a species in any numbers. Stillwater stoneflies are almost always associated with shorelines that are rocky and constantly pounded by waves, therefore perpetually aerated. I have yet to collect stonefly nymphs from a lake, or to find trout feeding on them in a lake. Though I know that it happens on occasion, I have no personal experiences to report, and prefer to limit my reports to things I know something about.

Lakes do contain terrific numbers of scuds, leeches, damselflies, dragonflies, midges, and water boatmen. Though there is some overlap between stillwater and stream types among leeches and midges, the rest are almost exclusively stillwater trout food forms, and all are much more important in lakes and ponds than they are in streams and rivers. Where they are important in moving water, it's often in a situation such as a tailwater where the pools are at times of low flow ponded almost to stillness.

When trout feed in a stillwater, even opportunistically, they often see most of just one type of food, because that one is most abundant, or most active, in the specific water the trout are cruising. Sometimes they'll see more than one food type, but they will almost never see, and feed upon, the wide variety that currents trot past the average stream trout almost every day, during almost any season. If trout in a stillwater do not become selective to a single food form on their average travels throughout a day, they are necessarily aware of what is most abundant in their waters, what it looks like, how it moves, where it's most likely to be encountered, and what to do about it when they do see one.

If your nymph looks a lot like the most common food form in the water where you're fishing, and you fish it the way that natural might move, in and around the

The bright pale moon-winged back swimmer is a rare exception to the need for camouflage among aquatic insects and other trout food forms living in lakes and ponds. It depends on speed for protection from predators such as trout.

habitat where that natural might live, then trout are going to know what to do when they see your nymph, too.

Your best searching patterns for streams and rivers usually average out the size, shape, and color of the wide variety of things that trout see and feed upon, rather than imitating precisely any one of them. The most effective searching nymphs for trout in stillwaters tend to be the imitative nymphs you tie for specific insects, crustaceans, and leeches. You will do most of your stillwater searching fishing, looking for trout that haven't told you where they are or what they're doing, with imitative nymphs.

Almost all insects and other food forms depend on camouflage for protection from predators in the aquatic environment. They have no other defense. None can fight back against a trout. Few can flee fast enough to escape a pursuing trout. The bold and brisk back swimmer is a rare exception. Not surprisingly, it is often bright, because it can stroke away with its strong legs, escape from trout . . . sometimes. I've seen back swimmers hunting bravely through clear stillwater shallows. I've also seen a trout dash twenty feet to kill one with a slashing take. Back swimmers are found only in lakes and ponds.

The lake and pond environment tends to be tan to brown on the bottom, green wherever vegetation grows. Most insects and other things that trout eat live in vegetation, and make their living either feeding on plant growth or, if they're predaceous, feeding on the things that feed on the plant growth. It's no accident that most trout foods in stillwaters tend toward tan or brown, and the greater abundance of things that trout eat in stillwaters are some shade of green.

Because the stillwater environment is less expansive than that of moving water, in terms of varied habitat types and therefore trout food types, you'll be even better served by a bit of collecting in a lake or pond than you are in a stream or river. Because stillwater trout are more likely to be narrow-minded even when they're feeding opportunistically, and because they're more likely to be seeing an abundance of one food form, you're less likely to catch many trout if you don't know what they're eating, what it looks like, how it moves, and imitate it, or at least approximate it.

The kick-screen net you made for collecting in moving water will not serve you very well in a stillwater. The broad, open, flat screen depends on current to deliver what you've kicked up, downstream into the waiting meshes. It also needs the current to pin insects there, hold them until you can lift the net out, wade to shore with it, spread it out, see what you've captured. You can roll such a net up to a minimal opening size, say a foot or two, and swish it through aquatic vegetation along the shoreline of a lake or pond, and sometimes come up with a reasonable sample of what is most abundant there. But to do more effective sampling, and at a bit more depth, you need a net that allows you to move it more swiftly through the water.

You can make a stillwater collecting net by taping a kitchen strainer to a wooden dowel or bamboo pole.

A kitchen strainer attached to a dowel will get you started. If your desires take you deeper, attach the same strainer to a bamboo pole, available at any garden-supply store.

Now that you have begun to collect and closely observe the things that trout eat in lakes, you'll want to buy a separate nymph box and slowly fill it with imitations of those specific creatures. I recommend that it be a large one. Most of the time on lakes and ponds you'll keep the box in a boat bag, not have to carry it in a vest pocket, though you should never buy a fly box too large to fit in the biggest pocket of your vest, just in case you need to hike in to some remote bit of water, as I did on that early pond, when I decided I didn't need my lake-fly box, left it in the rig, and had to thrash back through the woods to get it before I could catch any trout.

CHAPTER 5

At the Tying Bench

I made a mistake when I failed to take a photo of Polly Rosborough's fly-tying bench. The author of *Tying and Fishing the Fuzzy Nymphs* was a professional tier for most of his long life. He lived in a double-wide trailer within a long fly cast of southern Oregon's Williamson River, famed for its big lake-run rainbow trout. His tying area was in a back bedroom near windows with a view out over the river. The entire room was given over to materials storage. The closets were stacked with shoe boxes, each containing the materials to tie a particular fly that he tied commercially.

The famous man tied at a big rolltop desk. Bookshelves on the wall above the rolltop were piled with shoe boxes for the flies on which he was working at the time. Some were too full, their lids bulging open, materials hanging out. The top shelf of the rolltop desk had a bunch more overstuffed shoe boxes and some loose piles of yarn skeins, furs on hides, a mixture of debris dominated by all of the etceteras that I can no longer remember.

The desk surface itself seemed a literal pile of tools, materials, yarns of various colors snaking around, hook boxes and shoe boxes piled together, all of it contained by the side walls and back wall of the rolltop. A small arc around Polly's vise, in front of his swivel chair, had been winnowed clean, and was flooded with light. When the great man sat to tie a fly for me, the full shelf above the rolltop, the stack of items on its lid, and the stuff piled up all around him gave me the impression that he was sitting in the ocean surf, with a breaker wave about to topple over onto him.

It took Polly many years to organize his tying area just the way it worked best for him. If anything had ever been moved even slightly by somebody else, Polly would likely have panicked trying to find it.

SAITO-SAN SPECIAL

Hook:	Standard dry fly, size 12
Thread:	Brown 8/0
Wingpost:	White lamb's wool
Tail:	Dark blue dun hackle fibers
Body:	Rusty fine synthetic dubbing
Hackle:	Dark blue dun, parachute

My wife and I spent several days visiting and fishing with bamboo rod maker Megaku Saito, at his home in Furukawa, Japan. We were fishing small streams, most of them hemmed in by trees, and mostly with dry flies, not nymphs. Saito-san had one favorite fly, which I now use often and with great success on small streams in the States, and call the Saito-san Special. It's a simple parachute pattern tied in size 14, with blue dun tails, rusty body, and blue dun hackle wound around a white lamb's-wool wing post. That wool, with all its lanolin, floats like a bobber. It's an excellent searching dry fly, and also a fine imitation of the ubiquitous rusty mayfly spinner. The three of us lost so many of this particular fly in our first two days' fishing that it was necessary to tie more.

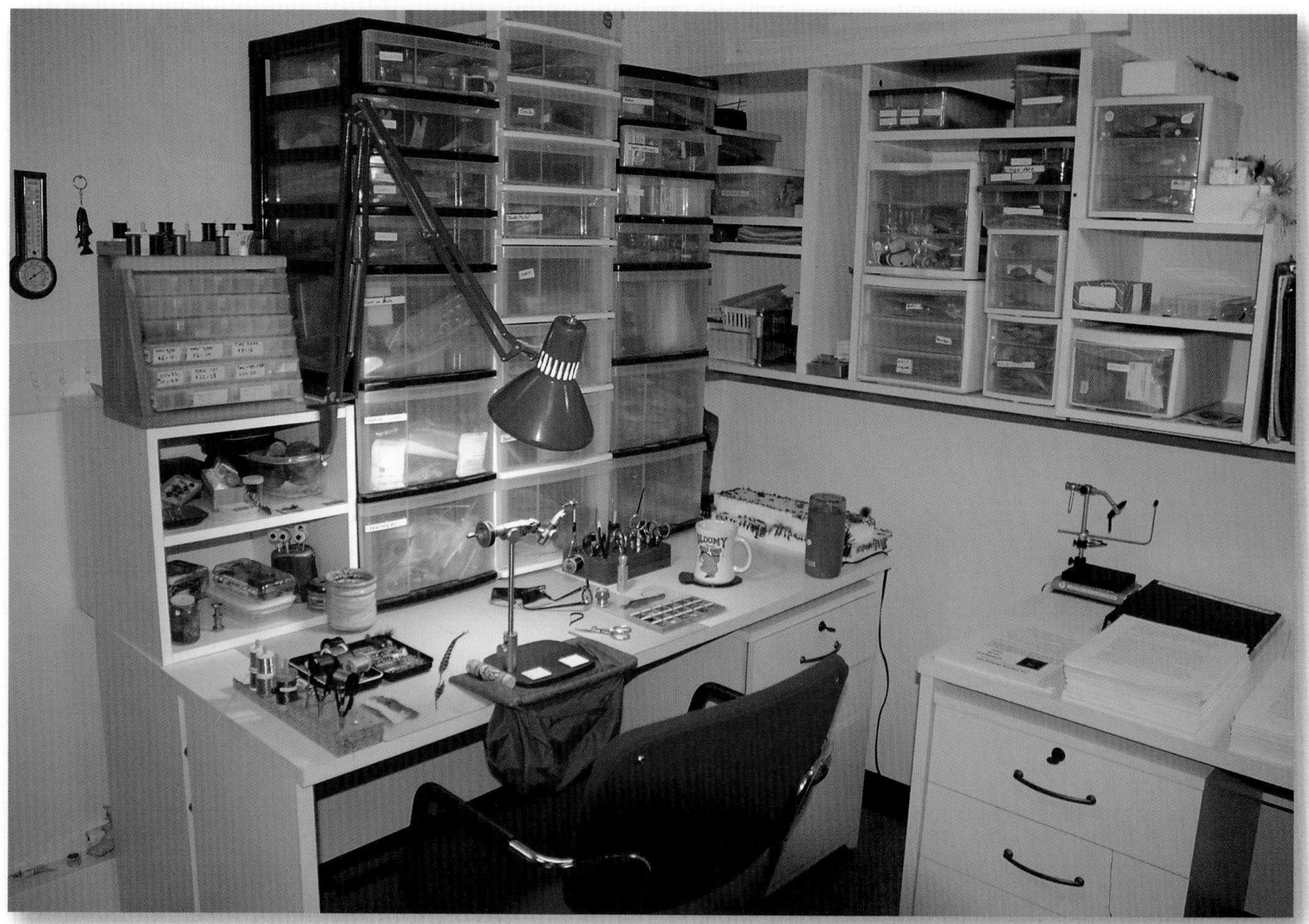

My tying bench in rare pristine condition. It's more often a tangle of tools, hooks, and materials.

Saito-san brought out his tying kit. It was a sewing basket, just big enough to contain his vise, a basic set of tools, and hooks and materials to tie a few favorite flies. He set it on a low table, sat cross-legged, and tied that one pattern briskly while we chatted about the fishing we'd been having on beautiful mountain streams. By the time we were called to dinner he'd finished enough to supply us for two more days of tangling with trees and trout. He parsed out the flies, put the few tying things back in the sewing basket, dropped the lid on it, returned it to whatever small space in which he stored it. That was the simplest home tying bench I've ever seen. If you keep your pattern list reduced to a very few essential flies, there's no reason such a small kit wouldn't contain all you would ever need to tie them.

My own tying bench is not what it should be, and I finally realize it probably never will be. In the last few years it has moved from a bedroom office at home to an office downtown, back into a dimly lit space in the garage, and now into a new writing studio I've had built in our backyard. I haven't had time to get my tying area settled yet, and still consider it temporary. When I reflect over the years, with minor periods that have been wonderful exceptions, my fly-tying bench has almost always been something I consider temporary. I suspect it has reached a permanent state of temporariness, and that I'd better get used to it.

My tying bench is no more than a white desk with a set of drawers under one side, in which I store hooks and tools. The desk is otherwise open underneath. Across the back are two tall, rolling, plastic drawer sets, the kind you can buy at office-supply or big-box stores. To one side are stacks of plastic drawers and Tupperware boxes full of materials: my equivalent to Polly's shoe boxes.

When I'm tying, I try to have just the tools and materials at hand for the pattern on which I'm working. When I'm that disciplined, my bench is quite tidy. But then I begin experimenting, dragging out this material and that, or I finish one fly and start tying another without putting away the materials from the last. My tying bench is more often a disaster than it's not. In truth, your personality will dictate whether your tying area is tame or a tangle. I'm not going to try to explain your personality to you. At the least, I recommend that you clean your bench up once in a while, during which process you're likely to find some things that you've been missing.

You get to define *a while.*

The top of your bench, which becomes the background for every fly that you tie, should be neither bright nor dark. If it's bright, it will reflect the light from your tying lamp. Light-colored materials will blend in with it, be hard to see. The brash reflected light will wear out your eyes. If the top of your bench is dark, anything you tie against it that is moderately drab will disappear. The best background color is a pale gray, green, or blue that is not reflective. I buy a sheet of mat board from an art-supply store, and lay it on top of that white desk. You could as easily paint the top of your own bench, but I find it nice to be able to toss out a stained mat board now and then, start my tying life afresh by buying a new one.

In the past I've used a ceramic mug for a wastebasket, and I'll admit it was because there was something aesthetic about having a classy ceramic mug on my desk into which I deposited the detritus of fly tying. However, it was necessary to reach out and find it each time I nipped off some excess bit of material, which created three to six extra steps for each fly I tied. For some years that was okay with me. If we weren't at least a little bit into aesthetics, we'd be fishing worms rather than tying flies.

One day I was drinking coffee and tying a spun deer-hair fly at the same time. I clipped off a near fistful of deer-hair butts, and without looking, deposited them into what I thought was the ceramic waste mug. The next sip of coffee I took made me sneeze, which blew a damp cloud of hair all over my tying bench. I had to buy a new mat board. After that, I suddenly liked the idea of a Waste Troll that sits under the vise. Not only does it save the steps involved in depositing each thing clipped into a mug, but it also keeps me from spoiling my morning coffee.

I still keep that ceramic mug on my bench, more or less as decoration.

Professional tiers tie flies by the dozen, always of a size and kind. When they have an order they tie them by the hundreds of dozens. Such repetitiveness not only hones their skills on a particular pattern, but also teaches them to tie all flies effortlessly and without any wasted motion. No pro would have a ceramic waste cup in the way on his tying bench. I could not be a professional fly tier. I could not tie size 12 Gold-Ribbed Hare's Ear nymphs by the hundreds of dozens. I have to lash myself to the chair to force myself to tie my old reliables by the dozen. That reflects personalities, too.

Let me establish a rule, one that you'll be able to break without fear of going to jail: If you don't want to tie by the dozen, then tie your nymphs by the half dozen of a single size. This will arm you with enough to give them a fair trial. If you'd like to see if Lightning Bugs are going to find a permanent spot in your fly box, then tie six each in sizes 12, 14, and 16. By the time you're finished, perhaps in a single evening, you'll not only know how to tie Lightning Bugs, but you'll also have enough to take fishing, and if they work wonders for you, you won't run out, and you'll be able to loan one or two to friends.

Another minor rule might help you keep your desk clear of the sprinklings of miscellaneous flies that accumulate over time on almost all tying benches: Try always to tie directly into a fly box. That way all the beautiful experiments that you tie will wind up getting toted to water and have their chance against trout, rather than being swept into the dustbin, the Waste Troll, or the ceramic mug. Maybe I should advise running to the fly shop and buying a fourth fly box, to add to your moving-water searching box, your moving-water imitative box, and your lake-nymph box: an experimental nymph box. If you get your largest fly-tying pleasure from designing and fishing your own flies, which many tiers do, then you should do this. This box might soon outgrow all the other boxes, and become the one that you tie into and fish out of most of the time.

Experimental ties, and tying directly into a fly box, give you good excuses to break the rule of tying by the half dozen. If you're working variations on a theme, then tying just a few is fine, but never tie just one of a fly pattern, experimental or not. If you do, you're going to fish it, it's going to hammer the trout, you're going to lose it, and you're never going to remember what materials and manner of construction caused that magic.

When you tie to replace flies that have been lost out of an old familiar fly box, then you need only replace those that you've lost, in order to fill the gaps in that box. That, to me, is the most pleasurable tying of all.

Vise. Your tying vise can be rotary or fixed, or fixed with a rotating capability. A true rotary holds the hook in line with the handle axis. When you turn the handle, if the hook is properly positioned in the jaws of the vise, the hook shank will rotate in one position rather than describing a circle. This is beneficial if you prefer to tie with the rotary function. If you do, you should clearly buy a rotary vise. I use a rotary vise most often, but don't use its rotary function often enough.

A fixed vise does not allow movement of the hook once it is clamped into the vise. If you don't desire the benefits of rotary, a fixed vise is less expensive and very satisfactory. The shaft angle can be elevated, giving you a larger scope to work with your fingers around the fly. It's not a bad idea to start with an inexpensive fixed vise, and later buy a rotary when you've decided you have use for one. That is the normal progression in a fly-tying life.

A fixed vise with a rotating capability allows the hook to be turned at any angle. This allows you to see

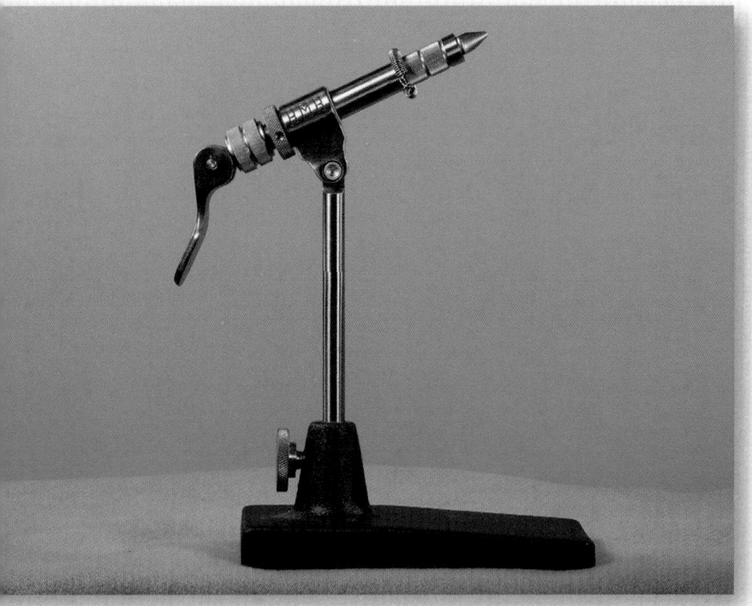

A standard pedestal vise that is partial rotary, a good choice for almost all trout-fly tying.

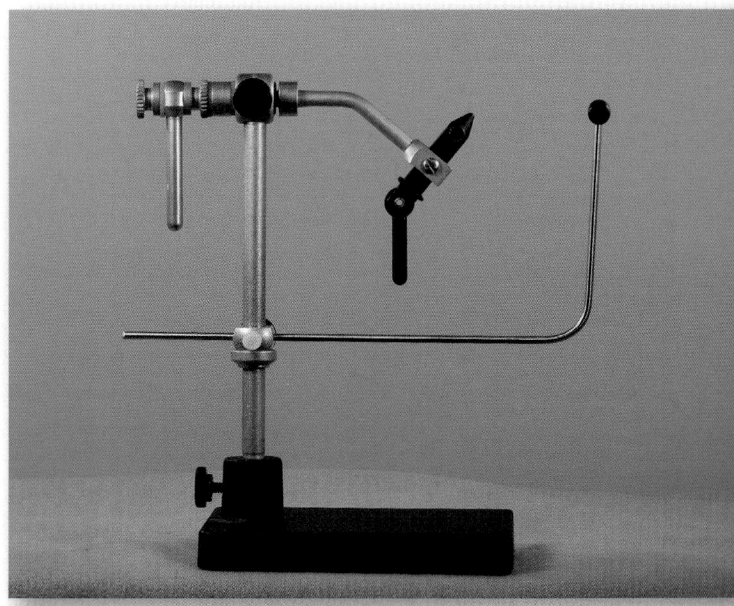

A rotary vise keeps the hook in the same line no matter which way it is turned. This is beneficial when tying many types of nymphs.

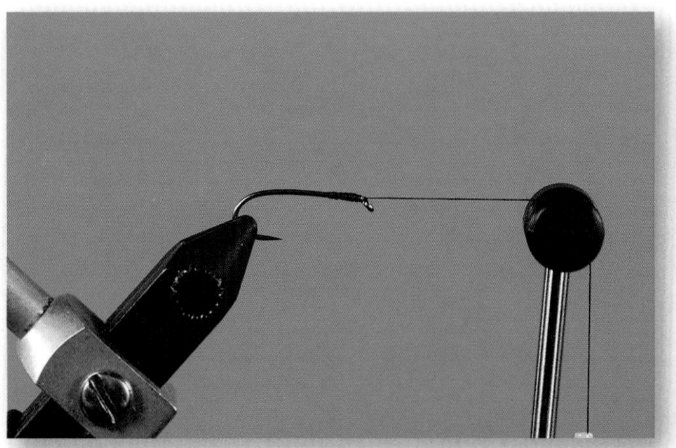

The shank of a hook in a rotary vise that is adjusted properly will maintain its position as you rotate it. You will need to use the bobbin holder to keep your thread out of the way.

how you're doing on the back side of the fly. It also allows you to turn the hook upside down, so you can tie in legs or other parts of the fly that can be cranky when you try to tie them in with the hook in the normal position. Such a vise is usually set at a higher angle than a rotary vise, giving you more room to work around small flies. If you lower the angle to align the vise jaws with the axis of the handle, you will have close to true rotary, but your hook will describe a small circle as you rotate it. If you don't need true rotary, and your budget is not fixed to a fixed vise, then I recommend you buy a vise that you can at least rotate when you desire to. On some types of nymphs, it's easier to tie when you can tilt the hook just a bit to get a different angle of sight at what you're doing.

Any type of vise can be purchased as a pedestal model or in a design to be C-clamped to your bench. If all of your tying will be done at home, the clamp model will be a bit more solid, and will also enable you to adjust the height of the jaws over a wider range. Some pedestal model vises have somewhat short stems. If you're tall or long-necked, consider a clamp model for home and later a pedestal model if you put together a portable fly-tying kit.

The jaws of your vise, for nymph tying, should be capable of holding hooks in a range from size 4 at maximum down to size 24 at minimum. Many vises are adjustable, and will accommodate this range without changing jaws. Other vises have interchangeable medium, midge, and magnum jaws. Either adjustable or interchangeable is fine. If I'm tying tiny, I like to do it on

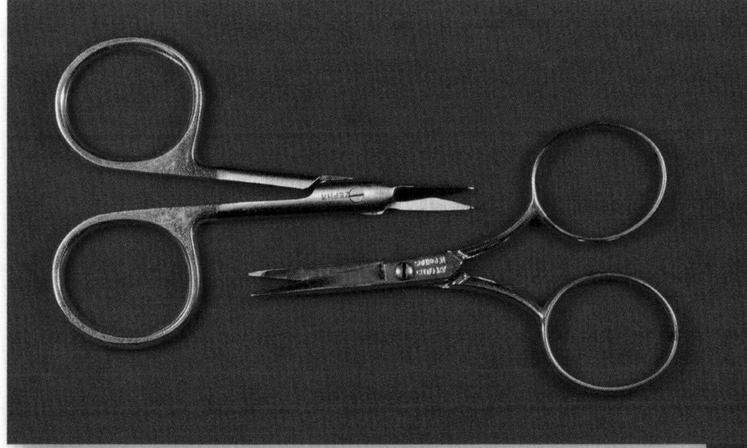

It helps to have two pairs of tying scissors, one for fine work (top) and one for rough (bottom). The finger holes of both should be big enough to allow you to carry them in your hand while you tie.

Use needlenose pliers for debarbing hooks and occasionally for flattening weighting wire wraps.

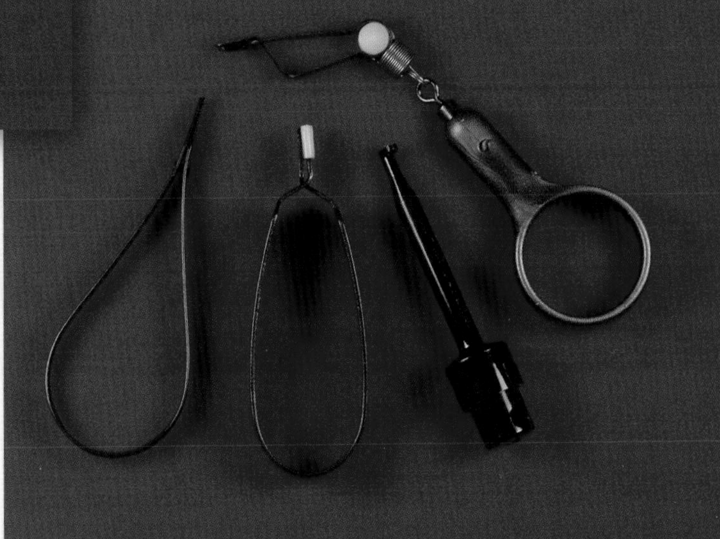

Various types of hackle pliers include fine-tipped and standard pliers, electrical clips, and a spring-loaded type that is easy on fragile hackle feathers.

midge jaws, because they're tapered to a finer point, and therefore expose more of the hook, making it easier to work small magic. So I like to have an interchangeable vise available even if I don't tie all of my flies on it.

Scissors. A good pair of tying scissors should have fine but stiff points, so they cut small things but don't open up when you ask them to cut rough stuff. They should be sharp. You should strive to keep them sharp by cutting only soft materials such as threads, furs, yarns, and feathers with the points. When you need to cut tinsels or wires, work these into the back part of the scissors, to protect the points.

I use two pairs of scissors, one with delicate points, the other with rough points. I use the rough ones for cutting hard materials, the fine ones for delicate materials. Because most of the nymphs I tie have one hard material—weighting or ribbing wire, for example—I use my stout scissors most often, because I do not like to set one pair down and pick up the other to suit what I'm scissoring at the moment.

Your scissors should have fingerholes big enough to slip over the largest knuckle on your tying-hand ring finger. As you gain experience tying, you will almost never set your scissors down. Instead, you'll slip them up your finger and continue tying with them cradled in your hand. When you need to nip something, they're right there and ready to go. It saves an enormous amount of time in your tying.

Many modern fly-tying scissors are sold with sharp spines running down the ridge backs opposite their fine cutting edges. If you use a whip-finish tool, these will cause you no problems. Many tiers, and I am one, whip-finish their flies by hand. The whip knot is finished by placing the tip of the scissors into the loop of the knot, which you then allow to slip off the scissors and onto the head of the fly as you draw the knot tight. If the scissors have that sharp spine, your thread slipping the length of it will be sliced every time. Take fine 320-grade sandpaper to it. I have to do it with almost every pair of specialty fly-tying scissors I buy.

Pliers. You'll need needlenose pliers to debarb your hooks. Any with points fine enough to fit into the hook gap of the smallest-size flies you tie will be fine.

Hackle pliers. Hackle pliers have a myriad of uses beyond their dedication to the winding of hackles. You'll use them to catch the end of dubbing loops, to wind

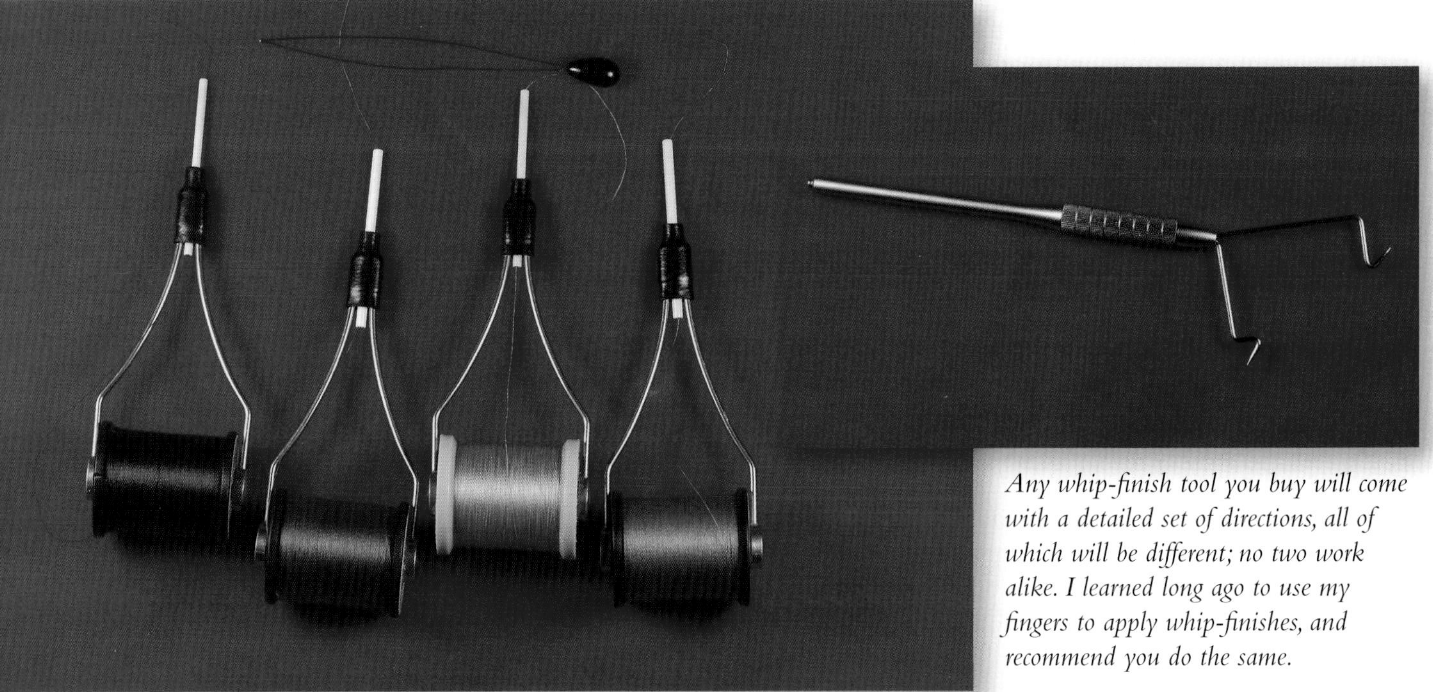

Any whip-finish tool you buy will come with a detailed set of directions, all of which will be different; no two work alike. I learned long ago to use my fingers to apply whip-finishes, and recommend you do the same.

It's helpful to keep a bobbin threaded with each color you use most often.

wire bodies and all kinds of ribbing, to hold the loose end of your thread every time you snap the thread while tying and have to rethread the bobbin to rescue yourself. I use an extra pair of hackle pliers to hold loose strands of Krystal Flash, leftover herl ropes that are long enough to tie a second fly, all the etceteras that often need to be policed up on your tying bench. Hackle pliers are never more than a handsbreadth from my vise, even if I'm tying a nymph with no hackles.

Many tiers prefer electrical wire clips for hackle pliers, and they work fine. I prefer pliers I can slip a finger through, so the conventional hackle pliers are better for me. Whatever you use, take the time to adjust the pliers, bending the frame and the angle of the jaws, so that they hold materials without letting them slip. If your pliers have metal-on-metal jaws, you'll quite commonly need to take the same 320-grade sandpaper to them that you used on your scissor spines. Many metal pliers are sold with such sharp-edged jaws that they cut the hackle you're trying to wind.

Thread Bobbins and Threader. I recommend ceramic bobbins with short barrels, about one inch. Longer barrels are fine for large flies, but you'll be tying a wide range of sizes, and the shorter barrel is better. Metal barrels are cheaper, and fine for a time, but eventually your thread will wear a groove in the barrel, then the bobbin will begin to fray and cut your thread. Anything from dental floss threaders to specific bobbin threaders will allow you to change threads quickly, and to rescue yourself when you break your thread in the midst of tying a fly.

I switch thread colors so much in my own tying that I keep four bobbins threaded at all times. Mine hold 8/0 in black, brown, tan, and olive. That is the size thread and four colors I use most often, in all of my tying, not just for nymphs. If I want to use 3/0, 6/0, or 10/0 thread in a specific color, then I'll switch one of the bobbins. If you're just getting into tying, you might want to use the same four colors in 6/0, since it is a bit stronger, less prone to breaking. One bobbin will do, but you'll need to switch thread spools each time you want a different color.

Whip-Finisher. I learned to tie flies by finishing the heads with half hitches coated with head cement. They frequently came unraveled. Later I learned to use a whip-finish tool. The heads made with it rarely came unwound, and I discovered that head cement was pretty, but not necessary. Finally I learned to whip-finish with my fingers, and no longer needed to set down my scissors, pick up a whip-finisher, wrap a five-turn whip-finish, set down the whip-finisher, pick up the scissors, and nip the thread. Using a whip-finish tool is not nearly as long and slow a process as I've intentionally made it sound. But my fingers are nearly always attached to my hands, and I can whip-finish just as well and a bit more quickly with them, and never have to set down my scissors to pick up my fingers. In my own life, if I can dispense with a tool, I do so.

If you're just beginning to tie flies, I recommend a quality whip-finish tool. The directions that come with it will explain how to use it. I will not, because each type has its own separate set of directions.

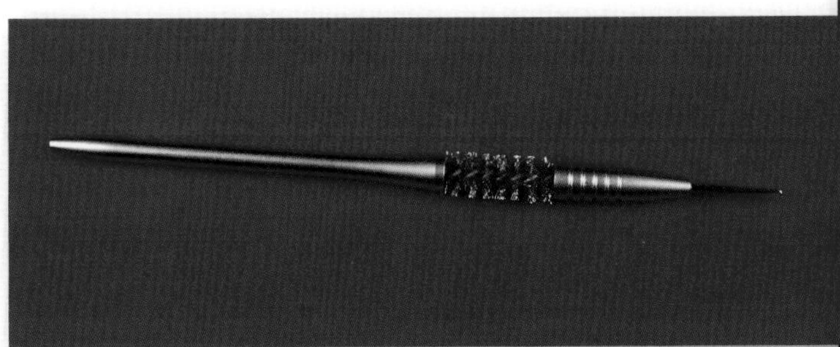

A half-hitch tool at one end, with a dubbing picker at the other end and a dubbing rougher in the middle, becomes a very handy nymph-tying tool.

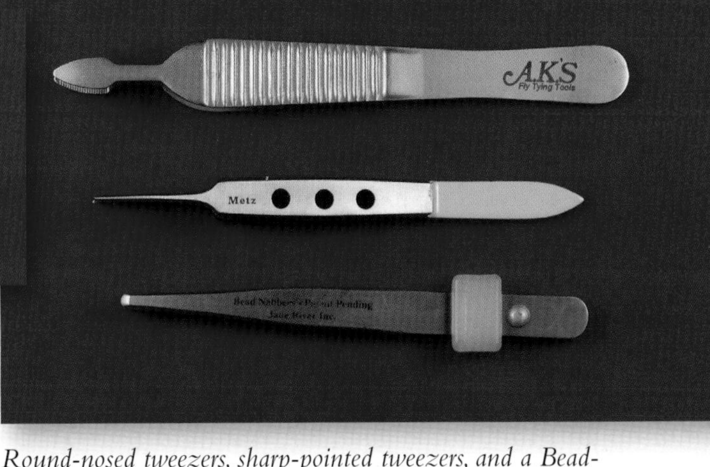

Round-nosed tweezers, sharp-pointed tweezers, and a Bead-Nabber all have a place on your tying bench.

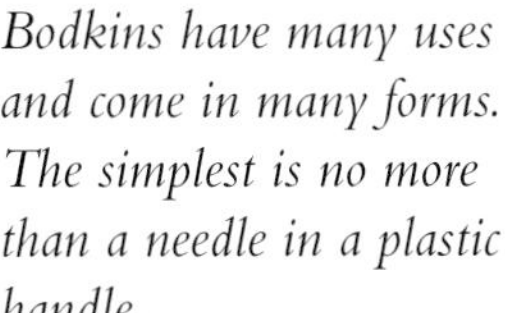

Bodkins have many uses and come in many forms. The simplest is no more than a needle in a plastic handle.

Dubbing twisters can range from one as simple as a hooked wire with a weight that you can twirl, to a collapsible one with arms that make it easy to form a dubbing loop or a fur hackle. Your fingers will serve, but the tools do make the job a bit easier and neater.

Half-Hitch Tool. Though I no longer finish flies with half hitches, I do find common use for a half-hitch tool. When tying rotary, it's necessary to secure the thread with a half hitch before twirling the hook; otherwise the thread will come unwound. On large hooks, I'll use the tip of my tying-hand forefinger to slip a half hitch behind the head of the fly, or behind a bead if the fly has one. But on a small hook, a half-hitch tool allows more precise placement of the knot.

You'll also find use for a half-hitch tool when you break your thread. If enough of the broken end is left, you can make a quick half hitch with it, then clip the excess and restart your thread.

You can make a half-hitch tool by removing the ink cartridge from a ballpoint pen. The half-hitch tool I use has a dubbing picker at its opposite end and a dubbing rougher in the middle, making it a far more useful tool. I use the other parts more often than I use the half-hitch end. But when I need a half-hitch tool, it's often in an emergency, and I'm glad I always have it close to hand.

Tweezers and Bead-Nabbers. When you're tying tiny, a pair of tweezers with slightly rounded ends is invaluable for removing a hook from the box or bin in which it is tangled with its friends. If you're tying for perfection, you can use the same tweezers to pluck out stray fibers from a finished fly.

I also use tweezers for picking up beads and threading them onto hooks. A Bead-Nabber tool is more suited to this use. You need one or the other, or both, or you're going to be down on the floor a lot, looking for runaway beads.

Bodkin. You'll need a bodkin for applying drops of head cement. It can also be used for mixing and applying five-minute epoxy to nymph backs. Additionally, it's useful to pick out or rough up your dubbing, for example when you want your thorax fur to also represent the legs of a natural nymph.

Dubbing Twister. When you make a dubbing or herl rope, you'll start with a thread loop, and capture the material between the threads. Then you'll need to twist it. I

Pill dispenser boxes store beads in a useful range of sizes and colors. In this case, one is for standard gold and one is for tungsten.

Magnetized hook boxes, with eighteen compartments, allow you to keep the three styles of hooks you use most often—in my case, dry fly, curved scud, and standard nymph—in a range of sizes, for use both on the bench and in a portable tying kit. A six-compartment fly box, with foam in the lid to prevent migration of small sizes, carries a full range of a single hook style.

almost always twist the rope with my fingertips, then capture the twirled end in my hackle pliers. Many amateur and professional tiers prefer to use a dubbing twister, because it's easier to twist the metal stem than it is to twist some slippery materials, notably peacock herl. I will recommend that you try a dubbing twister, but will continue to use those attached fingers that I always have handy.

Head Cement, Epoxy, and Zap-A-Gap. I've never been sure that these glues don't add some slight scent to flies. That would be fine on drys. It would not be so good on sunk flies, such as nymphs. Trout feed primarily by sight, but they do have accurate senses of smell. I don't like to think that the sudden sniff of something wrong might turn a trout away from a nymph that it has already decided to take. So I use little to no glue on my own nymphs, and apply it only in cases where the originator of a fly calls for it, such as on the famous and productive Copper John. I'll confess here, and never again, that I often violate the rules and omit the glue and head cement on sunk flies even where it's an elemental part of a dressing.

Dubbing Wax. A tacky wax is helpful when you want to make a dubbing rope or a fur hackle. I use these methods so constantly in my own tying that I keep my wax dispenser tucked behind my vise at all times. When I use a clamp vise, with its convenient long stem, I sometimes tape the lid of the wax dispenser to the stem, so that I can whip out the wax, run it along the thread, and replace the wax, all with one hand. It's one reason I still tie at times on an old C-clamp vise that is far out-of-date.

Tool Caddies. You can buy a wide array of prebuilt tool holders that will help you tame the mess on your bench. I recommend them without hesitation, but I hesitate to use one, because most of them stand in the line of sight behind the vise. I don't want anything behind the vise but the light-colored mat board that lets everything I do to the hook stand out starkly.

I did make up a bit of a tool holder with a couple of boards, some screws, 3/8- and 1/4-inch drill bits, a 1/4-inch dowel, and some paper clamps. When I'm tying, it is to the left of my vise. The materials for the fly I'm tying, and the few tools I need to tie it, are to the right of the vise.

Bead and Hook Storage. I use a bead and hook tower to store the bulk of my brass beads, tungsten beads, glass beads, and hooks. It has pleased me about beads and hooks. The front end of each compartment is curved rather than straight, so it's easy to lift out a small bead or hook.

Tinsels, weighting wires, and body and ribbing wires, separated by diameter, can be tamed by stringing them on 1/4-inch dowels and blocking the ends of the dowel with wine-bottle corks.

I presently store the hooks I use constantly in smaller, flatter holders that I can use on the bench or slip into a portable kit to take on a fishing trip. They organize my most commonly used hook styles in the sizes I use most often: standard dry fly, curved scud, and standard nymph hooks in sizes 12 through 22 in one holder, 3XL nymph and 3XL hopper hooks in sizes 6 to 16 in another.

I keep standard wet-fly hooks, sizes 8 to 18, on which I tie many nymphs, in a small six-compartment fly box. To keep the smaller-size hooks from migrating over the tops of the dividers and into the wrong compartments, in such a box, it is necessary to glue packing foam into the lid. This is a trick you need to know even for some plastic boxes that are designed to hold hooks.

I also use two pillboxes, each with six compartments, each compartment with a separate lid, to hold the beads that I use most often. One holds gold beads in a range of sizes from 1.5 millimeters to 5/32 inch; the other holds tungsten beads in gold and black, each in sizes 3/32, 1/8, and 5/32 inch. When traveling I place these two containers face-to-face, with their lids together, and fasten them securely with a couple of hair bands that my wife and daughter use to restrain their ponytails. The lids are not the best; without banding them, I've had them come open on trips, which is an event that calls for a lot more restraint than a ponytail needs.

Tinsel and Wire Holders. Flat Mylar and oval tinsels, body and ribbing wires, and either lead or lead-free weighting wires are all bought on sewing thread spools, and all tend to loosen up on their spools, unwind, get unruly. When I walk into my studio at night, flick on the lights, I expect to catch a bunch of these spools on the bench top, prancing around on little legs and waving tiny arms, causing mischief, weaving terrible tangles—dancing in the moonlight, so to speak.

You can tame them. Buy a 1/4-inch dowel, and cut it into four one-foot sections. String your spools on them, each according to its kind and your own desires. Drink four bottles of wine—not all tonight—or otherwise acquire four wine corks. Drill a 1/4-inch hole the length of each cork. Cut each in half. Cap the ends of the dowels with the wine corks. Do not use rubber bands to control the wire. They deteriorate and become the cause of the problem, not its cure. Hairbands with a diameter smaller than a thread spool will work. Commercial Spool-Hands are perfect for the purpose; your fly shop should have them or can order them. Place the restraining band around the spool, thread the wire or tinsel through it, and if all of your problems are not solved, at least this one will be.

Coffee Grinder. I often tie nymphs with blends of natural or dyed furs mixed with chopped Sparkle Yarn. The soft fur makes the blend easy to dub. The Sparkle Yarn not only adds flash, but also fluffs the dubbing out, makes it work a bit better when I want to catch it in a dubbing loop and create a loose abdomen or thorax, or even dubbed hackle, that is more active in the water.

These blends are already on the market in a full range of colors, so you don't need to grind your own. But I sometimes want a color that I don't own at the moment, and don't want to rush out and buy. With a coffee grinder on the tying bench, it takes only a few minutes to scissor Sparkle Yarn into quarter-inch lengths, add fur, twirl it up, adjust it by adding different colors, until you've got just what you want.

CHAPTER 6

Hooks, Threads, and Materials

To tie a basic set of nymphs, you'll need a minimal set of hooks, threads, and tying materials. To pursue every direction in which nymph tying might take you, you would need approximately the stock of a small fly shop. It's probable that you'll end up somewhere between the two, likely much nearer the basic load than an investment that would allow you to go into business. But the basics are an almost mandatory place to start, especially if you're just getting into tying. Though it's not likely that you'll stop at the basics, it is necessary to begin there, because you'll need those foundation materials to tie even the most complex flies.

HOOKS

You will choose the brand of hook you prefer by a formula for price and quality that will vary with each tier. If you plan to fish barbless, and would like to avoid the extra step of debarbing each hook before you tie on it, then you will want to buy barbless hooks. I do, in any style for which barbless are offered. Many basic hook styles can be purchased either barbed or barbless for the same price. If you're going to debarb them anyway, you can save that step.

Hooks in trout sizes are numbered in inverse order: the larger the number, the smaller the hook. Thus a size 4 hook would be for a giant salmon-fly nymph, a size 14 for a normal mayfly nymph or caddis larva, and a size 24 for a very tiny midge pupa pattern. Nymphs are typically tied on heavy wire hooks. A hook listed as 2X heavy would be forged from the same wire used for a standard-weight hook two sizes larger. It would be stronger, and would also sink faster, than the same size hook tied with standard or fine wire.

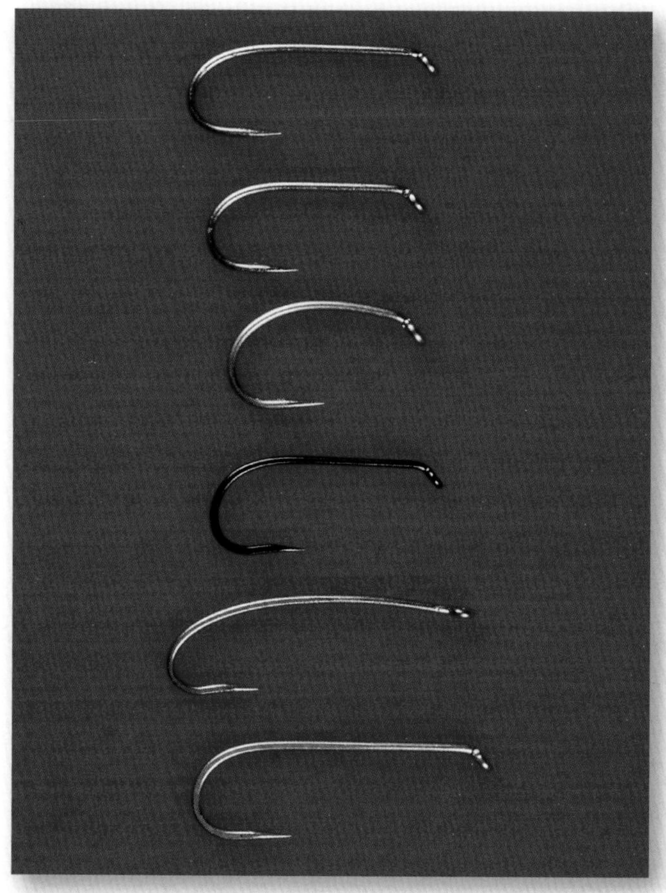

Basic nymph hook styles. All are shown in size 12. From top:

Standard nymph: 1XL, 2X heavy.
Standard wet: standard length, 2X heavy.
Curved scud: 2X short, 2X wide gap, 2X heavy, curved shank.
Standard dry fly: standard length, 1X fine.
Long-shank curved nymph hook: 3XL, 2X heavy, curved shank.
Long-shank nymph hook: 3XL, 2X heavy, straight shank.

Nymphs are also tied on long or short hooks, depending on the shape of the fly you desire to tie. A hook listed as 3XL would have a shank the length of a standard hook three sizes larger. A hook listed as 2X short would have the shank length of a standard hook two sizes smaller. You might tie a long and slender stonefly nymph on the long-shank hook, a short and fat scud imitation on the shorter-shank hook.

Standard nymph hook, 1XL, 2X heavy. When a dressing calls for a standard nymph hook, that hook normally has a bit of extra shank length, and is forged on heavy wire. If you're going to limit your original purchases to one hook style for nymphs, it should be this one in sizes 12, 14, and 16. That would take you a long way toward tying an effective assortment of nymphs that would catch trout in a wide variety of stream and stillwater situations. A full range of standard nymph hooks that I find useful runs from size 10 to 20.

Standard wet-fly hook, standard shank length, 2X heavy. Many traditional nymph dressings, and some newer ones as well, look better when tied on slightly shorter hooks than the standard nymph. If you tie a lot of wet flies, and also want the full range of nymph hooks, then this is one that you will use on occasion. But you'll not be hurt by substituting the above standard nymph hook in a dressing that calls for this one. I find standard wet-fly hooks most useful in my own nymph tying toward the small end of the spectrum, sizes 14, 16, and 18. A full range of them would be from size 8 to 18.

Curved scud hook, 2X heavy, 2X wide, 2X short. This hook is excellent for tying caddis larvae and pupae, scuds, midge larvae and pupae, and mayfly emerger nymphs. It is second in importance to the standard nymph hook. The same hook style is available with 1XF wire for dry flies such as the Klinkhamer Special. If your budget is pinched, and you tie as many dry flies as you do nymphs, which most of us do, then you can save money by substituting the fine-wire hook. It does not serve to do the reverse: tie floating flies on the heavy nymph hook. Your dry flies will fail to float.

The heavy-wire version of the curved hook is better for nymphs, and necessary for the heavily weighted Czech Nymphs, which are working their way toward becoming standard dressings on the North American continent. A narrow range of curved nymph hooks, for standard insect imitations, would call for sizes 12, 14, and 16. For the full range, they're useful in sizes 8 to 18. Heavy-wire nymph hooks are not made smaller than that. If you desire to tie tiny nymph patterns on curved scud hooks, the fine-wire version of the same hook style is made down to size 24.

Long-shank nymph hook, 3XL, 2X heavy. This hook is excellent for stonefly nymphs, and is called for in many dressings that imitate those insects. They're also good for streamers such as Woolly Buggers, which some books list as nymphs. Long-shank nymph hooks are most useful in a narrow range, sizes 6, 8, and 10. A full range of 3XL nymph hooks, from size 6 to 16, would be beneficial for damselfly dressings, and some standard nymphs call for the extra length even in their smaller sizes.

Standard dry-fly hook, 1X fine, standard shank. Some emerger nymphs that are designed to fish just beneath the surface film call for light-wire hooks. It is my assumption that you will not limit your tying to nymphs, and that a range of dry-fly hooks is already among your possessions, or on your list of things to purchase. If it isn't, you'll find them most useful for nymphs in sizes 14, 16, and 18. A full range would extend from size 10 to 22.

Long-shank curved nymph hook, 3XL, 2X heavy, semicurved shank. This is similar to the dry-fly grasshopper hook, which can be substituted for it, though the shank will be standard weight rather than 2X heavy. You can cure that with weighting wire. Some slender nymphs look rakish when tied on the curved-shank hook. While few dressings call for it, you should experiment with it, and see if you like it. I'll be surprised if you don't. Sometimes that little bit of extra appreciation for the appearance of your nymph will cause you to fish it with more confidence. It looks as though it's going to go hunting down there in the water, chase after the trout. I like them in sizes 6 to 16 for a range of stonefly nymphs, caddis larvae and pupae, and a few mayfly and midge nymphs. Damselfly nymphs look good on them as well.

THREADS

The larger the *ought* number, the finer the thread. You could use a full range, 3/0 for big nymphs, 6/0 for medium nymphs, 8/0 for small nymphs, and 10/0 for tiny nymphs. Then you would need each in a narrow set of colors: black, tan, olive, brown, and possibly gray. As the thread gets finer, it is naturally easier to break: 10/0 is fragile; 8/0 takes some getting used to; 6/0 is a good, stout standard, and will not bulk up the heads of any but tiny nymphs if you're somewhat careful about the number of thread turns you take; 3/0 is good for large flies, but is too thick for the standard and smaller nymphs that will constitute the largest number that you tie into your fly boxes.

I tie almost all of my flies—nymphs, wets, dry flies, and streamers—with 8/0, because I tie small more often than I tie large, and 8/0 threads are kept spooled on my bobbins. I have the other threads available. If I'm going to be tying a dozen or more of a fly that will clearly benefit from a different-size thread, I'll respool a bobbin. Most of the time, I'll make 8/0 do the job.

If I were just setting out in nymph tying, I would buy four spools of 6/0 prewaxed thread in black, tan, olive, and brown. If my budget had extra money in it, I would buy four ceramic bobbins at the same time, and keep all of those colors spooled at all times. If it didn't, one bobbin would be fine, since I'd have to buy a bobbin threader anyway, for use whenever I break my thread, and could use it to switch spools.

To get a feel for just how much force any thread will stand, start it on a big hook fixed firmly in the vise, then tug on the thread until you break it. You'll discover that if you don't nick it or otherwise weaken it, even 8/0 is stronger than you think. You'll also get a feel for just how tight you should make each thread winding as you tie any fly, in order to tie the most durable nymphs possible.

MATERIALS

Never neglect the enjoyment of trying new materials that come onto the market, or that you might find in craft shops and other peripheral fly-tying sources. The incorporation of new and *found* materials, tied with new methods, leads toward new and often more effective flies of all kinds. It's not just a theory that trout eventually begin to turn away from old patterns, at least in heavily fished waters where they might get stung by a hook more than once. Not all of your experiments will be successful. On occasions that are not entirely rare, however, experimental patterns will catch more trout than the old standards, and because of that sudden success, will become standards themselves.

Beads. The best metal beads are made of brass, coated for color, and taper-drilled. The hole is small at one end, wider at the other. This allows a bead of proper size to be slipped around the hook bend. If your beads have a straight hole, a single diameter from end to end, the size bead that will go around the bend of a hook will look outsized on most finished nymphs that you tie.

You'll find most use for metal beads in gold, for the little wink of reflected light they give when the nymph is drifting through the water. You will also find patterns that call for black, silver, and brass beads. I recommend that you stock both gold and black. Observant anglers on such heavily fished rivers as the Missouri, Bighorn, and Delaware have noticed that trout are beginning to back away from bright-beaded nymphs, but they are being shown very few nymphs with black beads, and are still eager to take them.

Tungsten beads are heavier than brass. They'll sink a nymph deeper. Perhaps more important, a nymph tied with a tungsten beadhead will penetrate the surface film more quickly, and sink a few inches deep in a fairly brisk current, without any added weight on the leader. A small nymph tied with a tungsten bead and no other weight is excellent for fishing beneath a yarn indicator or as a dropper from a dry fly, because it will attain its depth quickly. A heavily weighted nymph tied with a tungsten bead will be heavier than one tied without a bead, or with a brass bead, and will sink faster and deeper. Tungsten beads are more expensive than standard brass beads. Stock them in gold and black. Use them only when you're trying for quick surface film penetration or maximum depth.

Glass beads are used most often for flash and translucence. They don't add much weight to a nymph, and do nothing to propel it either through the surface film or down to the depths. But a silver glass bead adds a tiny spark of life to a nymph, and a colored glass bead, or sequence of them lined up on the hook shank, will add color and a transparency that can make a nymph look alive. I use glass beads most often for stillwater nymphs or on tiny midge nymphs for slow-flowing water that has many of the characteristics of a stillwater. Glass beads are sized by the number of them that it takes to make a line an inch long. They are drilled with straight holes, so the size bead you use will be dictated by the size you can get around the bend of the hook. See the chart for approximate sizes, but let your eye make the final determination.

The sizes of all bead types that you need will reflect the size hooks on which you tie most often. The chart

Metal Bead Diameter	Hook Size	Glass Bead Size	Hook Size
1.5 mm	20–22	15/0	18–20
5/64 inch	16–18	11/0	14–16
3/32 inch	14–16	8/0	8–12
7/64 inch	12–14	6/0	2–6
1/8 inch	10–12		
5/32 inch	8–10		
3/16 inch	6–8		

You'll need nonlead weighting wire (top row) in .015 and .025 inch. You'll be served well by Ultra Wire in size Brassie (middle row), in black, silver, red, copper, and green. You'll also want to have Mylar tinsel, gold on one side and silver on the other (bottom row, left). Medium-size vinyl ribbing or lace, in amber, black, and green, will be a short start on the stretch tubing you will find useful (bottom row, right).

Krystal Flash in green, red, pearl, and black, plus Holographic Flash in pearl, will serve many purposes.

shows approximate hook sizes for counterdrilled beads. Because beads do not look the same on all hooks, use your eye and vary the bead size to suit your sense of proportions.

Wires. The original use for wire was in fine silver and gold as ribbing for small to medium-sized flies. Wire is now just as commonly used in copper, red, and green for bodies on such nymphs as the Copper John and Brassie. Medium size (.014 inch) is the most useful for sizes 12 and 14, Brassie size (.010 inch) for 16 and 18, and extra small (.008 inch) for tiny nymph bodies. All can be used as ribbing wire.

Weighting wire comes in lead or nonlead. I prefer nonlead. It comes in only three diameters, .015, .025, and .035 inch. Though I wish it came in the full range of diameters, as does lead, the latter is now banned in many places and will be restricted more, not less, as times continue to change. Nonlead wire is better for the environment, so it is wise to use it in all of your tying.

I once weighed equal lengths of lead and nonlead wire. Nonlead is approximately 20 percent lighter. That translates to five wraps of nonlead wire for every four wraps of lead wire, in case you ever need to interpret.

Ribbing and body lace. Vinyl tubing or lacing is available under a variety of brand names, and in two shapes: round, or flat on one side and rounded on the other. It can be wound alone, making tidy and compact segmented bodies. In medium sizes, it makes excellent caddis larva bodies. In small or midge sizes, it is good for midge larva and pupa bodies. Its more common use is as ribs on nymphs with fur or yarn bodies, usually in medium to large sizes and black and amber colors. The most useful colors for bodies are black, olive, and red.

Tinsel. The most common Mylar tinsel is gold on one side, silver on the other. You'll come across patterns calling for oval gold or silver tinsel, and it will be best if you use it. But you can always substitute Mylar, tying it to the hook so the appropriate side shows when it is wound, and get by for all of your tying with a single spool of it in medium size. Oval tinsels fill out the fly a bit, and might add a bit to the sink rate because of their bulk. I recommend you use them where they are called for, if for no other reason than that your nymphs will then have the traditional look their originators intended for them.

Some flashy nymphs such as the popular Lightning Bug call for Mylar bodies and wider Mylar shellbacks. If you desire to tie them in tiny through large, then you might find use for Mylar in the full range of four sizes.

Flash. Many nymphs call for flashy bodies, ribs, shellbacks, or unfettered strands of flash material dangling as stubbed wings or simply loose strands, all for the purpose

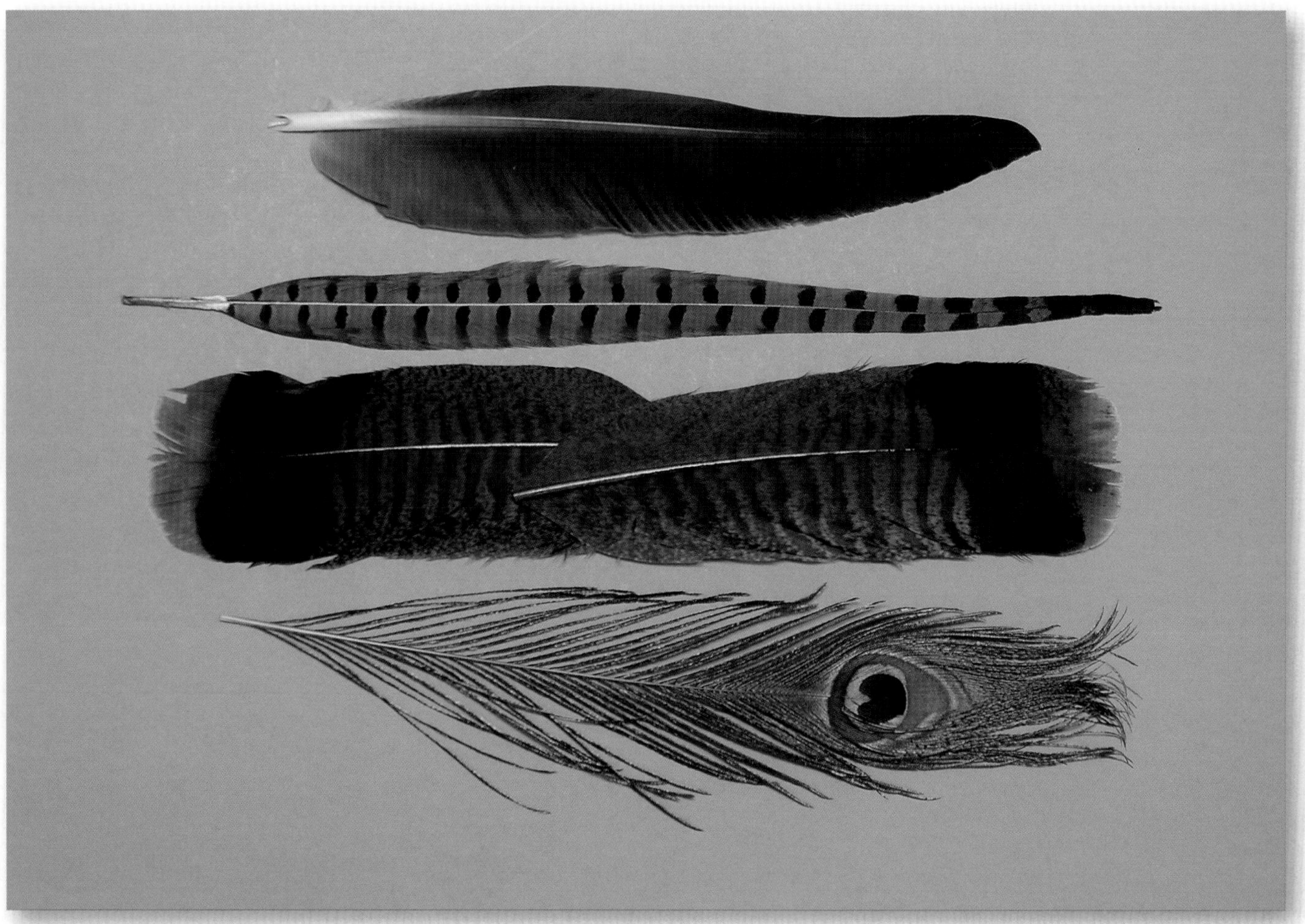

Goose and turkey feather sections from wing cases and shellbacks on many nymphs. Pheasant center tail and peacock eye feathers are the two most useful feathers for herl.

of attracting trout to the fly. The addition of a tiny bit of brightness, such as the shellback on a Flashback Pheasant Tail, can make quite a bit of difference in the effectiveness of a nymph. Red, green, or black Krystal Flash, an imprinted and colored Mylar, can make an effective caddis or midge body when twisted and wound. Pearl Flashabou, Krystal Flash, or other brand of brightness should be available on your bench, along with specific colors that you'd like to use in your own tying.

Rubber and silicone legs. Round black or white rubber legs have been used on nymphs for many years, and are suspected to add to the effectiveness of many nymphs, most likely because of the addition of lifelike movement. The newer silicone legs, with their distinct barring, are available in a variety of colors, and cry out for experimentation.

Wing cases and shellbacks. Many standard patterns call for black goose or mottled turkey feathers for wing cases or shellbacks drawn over the thorax. Moose body hair is used for both the tail and wing case on the A. P. Black, which is one of the most effective nymphs you can tie. Soft synthetic shellbacks such as Scud Back and Body Stretch add realism to many dressings. Thin Skin in clear and black is called for specifically by the originators of some patterns, and you should follow their materials lists, as I will do throughout this book.

Herl. Pheasant, peacock, ostrich, and marabou herl is made by winding the long fibers from a tail feather around a hook. The tiny individual barbules stick out, forming a sort of natural chenille. The result varies from slender in the case of pheasant tail to fairly thick in the case of ostrich or marabou. Peacock herl is the most common and useful. I have heard it called "trout cocaine." Clearly trout are attracted to its combination of color and reflectiveness. Almost any nymph tied with peacock herl will take what seems to be more than its share of fish. Ostrich herl is most often used for the head or gills of a nymph. Marabou finds some use for gills, and is also used as herl on some damselfly dressings.

Herl is fragile, and should be wound with the thread in a herl rope, or counterwound with fine ribbing wire, to secure it against the teeth of trout. Otherwise the nymph you have so carefully tied with it will come unwound after one or two fish.

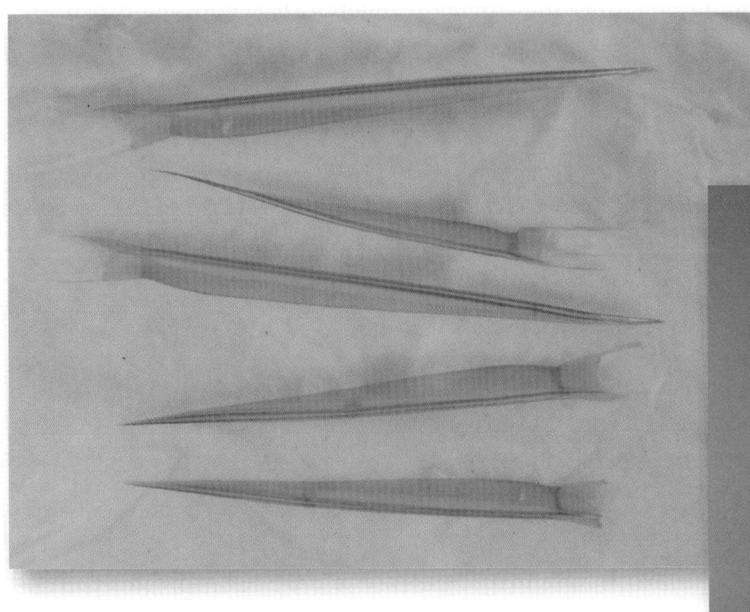

Biots should be peeled, not cut, from the stem, and presoaked in a moistened paper towel to keep them pliable.

A dispenser of nonblended fur, and another blended with Sparkle Yarn, each in a range of the most useful trout colors, will serve for most of your nymphs. They can also form the basis for blends with each other, or with different colors of Sparkle Yarn.

Biot. The leading edge of a goose or turkey wing feather has short, hard, spearlike barbs called biots. These are used for tails on such nymphs as the Copper John, and as segmented bodies on many small imitative nymphs, though the latter use is more common on dry flies, less common on those fished sunk. Before tying with biot, it needs to be soaked at least briefly in water. I usually strip the biots I need for the number of flies I'm tying, and fold a damp paper towel around them, letting them soak up moisture until I'm ready to use them.

Hen hackle. Hen hackle is softer, and absorbs more water, and therefore is more useful than rooster hackle on nymphs. Hen necks are inexpensive, and you might want to keep at least one in brown and another in grizzly on your tying bench. If you use them for no other fly, those two colors are both used on Charles Brooks's necessary Montana Stone nymph.

Partridge, wood-duck flank, and speckled guinea. Many nymph dressings call for speckled brown or gray partridge fibers for legs. You can buy small packages of the separate colors, or get a whole Hungarian partridge skin. I recommend that you buy a skin if you tie soft-hackled wet flies to any extent, which I do to a great extent. They're not nymphs, but they do fool lots of trout. Then you'll have plenty of feathers available for the many nymphs that call for them.

Wood-duck flank fibers are used as tails and legs in many traditional nymph patterns. In more modern patterns, they are often used as antennae. They are expensive, but a few feathers go a long way, and you should have them available on your tying bench.

Just a few traditional patterns, most from the great Polly Rosborough, call for speckled guinea. You can stock it, or hold off on it until you encounter a need for it, or substitute partridge for it. Trout won't scold you.

Dubbing. Every manufacturer of fly-tying supplies has its own line of natural fur and synthetic dubbing colors and blends. You can buy them specific to patterns. I prefer to buy a dispenser that covers the most common color spectrum, which makes it easier to organize them and more tidy to tie with them on the bench, and covers me when I otherwise would not have a certain color that I do not use often, but suddenly need very badly. I can also place the dispensers into my portable kit, and my mind is at ease about the colors I might have forgotten.

For nymph tying, I find two types of dubbing most useful, and stock dispensers with both types in the common color ranges. One is a fine synthetic, for tightly dubbed bodies and more loosely dubbed thoracic segments, especially on small nymphs, size 16 and under. It is not an accident that the same dubbing is used on most of my dry flies. The other is a blend of either rabbit or

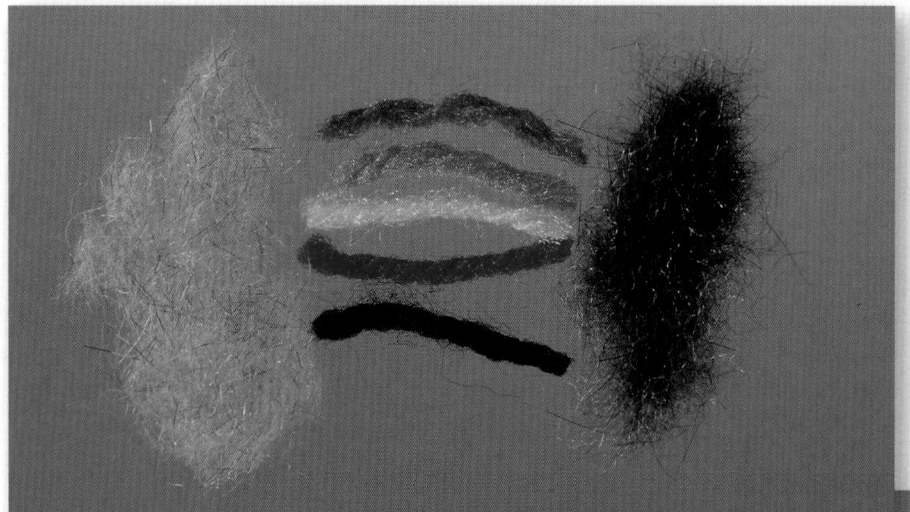

A coffee-grinder blend of natural or dyed fur with Sparkle Yarn that has been cut into short pieces will be a mottled mix of shades, and will have some fibers that reflect light, making a nymph tied with the blend look more alive. Light and dark blends are shown at left and right. Some good yarn colors to keep on hand for blending include green, orange, yellow, brown, and black.

Some furs that are useful by themselves, or when mixed with Sparkle Yarn in blends, are (left to right) Australian opossum, red fox squirrel, gray fox squirrel, pine squirrel, and muskrat.

squirrel fur with chopped Antron, a Sparkle Yarn, added. This makes a rougher dubbing, and also relects bits of light. Some of these I buy, others I blend myself. I use this rougher-style dubbing most often when I'm tying nymphs, especially those in size 14 up to the largest I tie.

This combination of one fine and one rough dubbing will cover almost all of your nymph-tying needs. A narrow color list would include black, brown, tan, olive, gray, and pale yellow. A longer list would extend into the reds and whites, and would cover shades and blends of all the more basic colors. I confess to having one dispenser, though not just for tying nymphs, that has ten different shades of green. I don't use them all.

Yarns. I rarely use wool yarns, but find many uses for reflective Antron Sparkle Yarns, and always have them available in at least the basic set of colors: black, brown, tan, amber, olive, pale yellow, and gray. The yarn can be separated and used for the corona and trailing shuck on Gary LaFontaine's famous Sparkle Pupa patterns. It can be chopped short and blended with natural fur for a loose dubbing blend. It can be used whole as yarn for bodies on large flies, or separated into two strands or a single strand, and wound for bodies on small nymphs. By twisting it tight, then winding it forward, it makes a firm and segmented body for flies such as those in the Serendipity style.

Chenille. Standard chenille is the basic ingredient for the Woolly Worm, a fly so far past its prime that you'll probably make the mistake of never tying and trying it. You'll use chenille far more often for the famous Woolly Bugger streamer, in black and olive, so you'll have it on hand for any nymphs you decide to tie with it.

Vernille, Velvet Chenille, and Ultra Chenille are brand names for a stiff and fine-textured chenille used most commonly in the San Juan Worm. You should stock it in red and natural "flesh" worm color. It is also good in tan for the Poopah pattern.

Furs. I do a substantial amount of tying with furs on the hide. Most of it is with pine and fox squirrel, incorporating the underfur and guard hairs for a spiky dubbing mix. Squirrel fur can also be sheared and mixed with Sparkle Yarn for Dave Whitlock's great Fox Squirrel

Nymph, and variations on that theme in different colors, or it can be captured in a thread loop and turned into a very useful fur hackle.

Rabbit and squirrel hides can be cut into strips and wound for very realistic Rabbit Leeches and Squirrel Leeches. You can buy the strips precut, or buy the hides and tailor the width of the strips to your own tying. I buy rabbit strips precut, but always keep pine, fox, and gray squirrel skins in Ziploc bags somewhere near the bench.

Muskrat fur is also useful, though more often in traditional nymphs than in more recent patterns. It's nice to have a full skin, if you can find one, for the range of grays it gives you from light on the belly to dark on the back. But a small patch of muskrat back fur, with the guard hairs, will cover a wide range of your needs for that animal.

Hare's mask fur is useful in many patterns, not least of which is the famous Gold-Ribbed Hare's Ear. I'm allergic to the dander in unwashed masks, so am forced to buy the necessary blends prepackaged, which are so popular that they're readily available. If you are not allergic to it, you can buy a mask, shear its different parts, and blend them into one light and one dark mixture in your coffee grinder. Then you'll have the real thing, which will catch more trout for you, because you've taken all that time to create it.

Ziploc bags. Ziploc bags are your friends. Moth larvae will do devastation to your fly-tying materials. I bought some fur from a fly shop once, took it home, and placed it in a drawer with my other furs. A few weeks later I visited the same shop for something else, for some reason was invited into the back room to look for it, noticed a few moths flying around in there, closed that door abruptly. As soon as I got home . . . it was too late. I don't like to use mothballs around any materials that I'll use on sunk flies, because they stink, trout can smell, and I suspect trout are not as easily attracted to nymphs that have any stinkum on them. The best way to keep materials away from moths is to keep them tightly sealed in Ziploc bags, and beyond that to keep the bags tightly sealed in Tupperware containers.

If you ever acquire a moth infestation from somebody else, or get ahold of a bit of material that gives you the slightest doubt, put it in a Ziploc bag and stick it in the freezer for at least a full twenty-four-hour day. That will kill all the stages of the insect: adults, larvae, pupae, and eggs. If you discover your materials are already infested, the same procedure will work: bag them, then freeze them.

CHAPTER 7

On the Road

I spent a few days camped in the tent trailer alongside a high-desert lake one recent spring. The water was on the verge of warming up after a long, frigid winter. Midges hatched every morning and evening in the reed-lined shallows. Trout attended them, and though I didn't exactly whack them, I did manage to hook about a dozen during each hatch cycle. The fish had grown so fat on the midges, and whatever else was out there in the depths of the lake, that it took only eight of them to make a dozen.

Most of the trout came to tiny CDC drys during the center of the hatch. I was fairly well satisfied by the luck I was having just after dawn and just before dusk, so I didn't press the fishing during the middle of the day. Instead, I'd make a leisurely brunch, take a walk in the sagebrush hills to startle deer and antelope and jackrabbits, head back to the tent trailer to read a novel, take a nap, eat an early dinner so I could fish until dark without a terrible hunger driving me from those productive shallows while the fishing was still good.

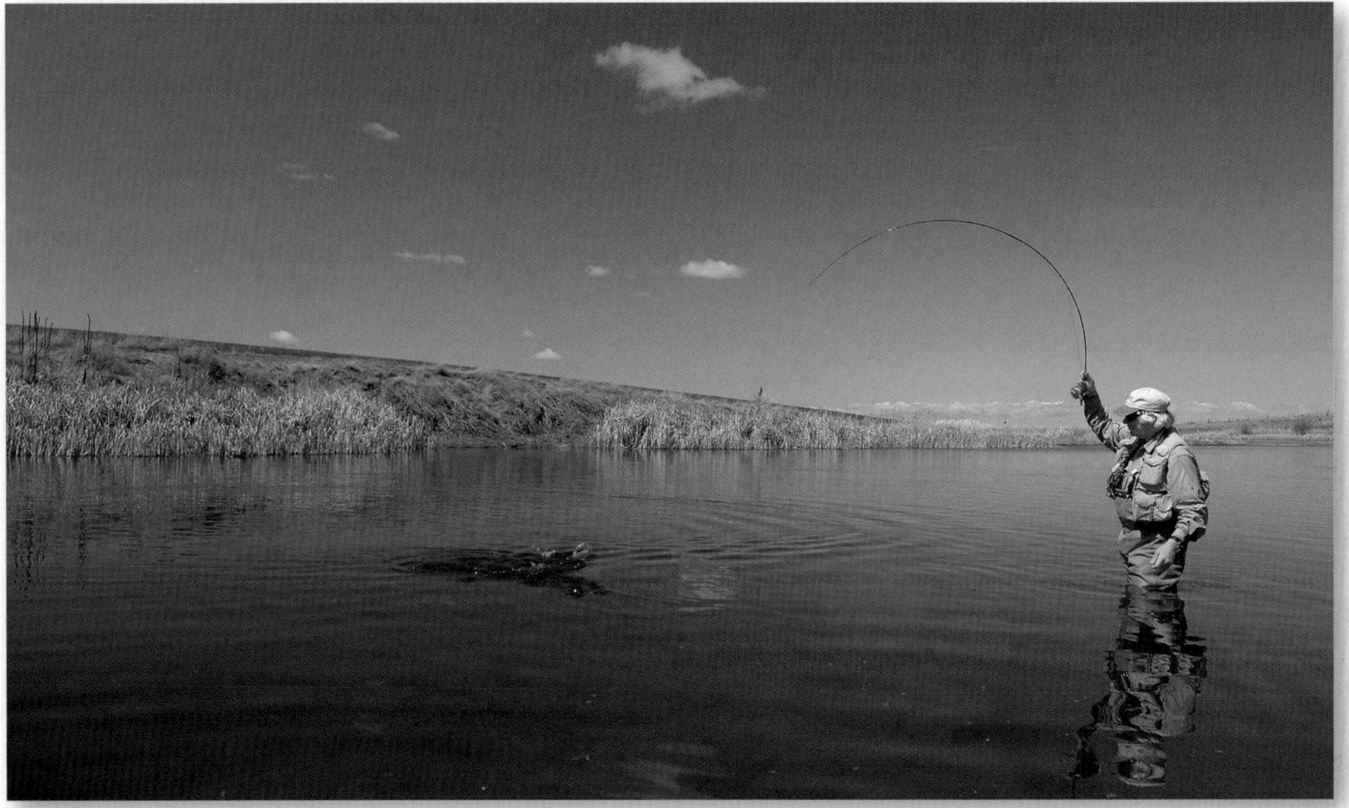

When you see a specific food form in demand by the trout, and have no fly near it, your fishing can improve enormously if you have a portable tying kit along on the trip.

About the third day it occurred to me that I was not really catching the full share of trout that I clearly deserved by fishing just mornings and evenings, and that I might do well enough if I could figure out what the trout were busy doing in the midday hours when they weren't feeding on midges at the surface. Rather than take a long walk after brunch, I pulled on my waders and took a long wade, rod in hand. It was frustrating. It also became educational.

It was frustrating because the sun struck down through the water, and revealed an occasional gliding, turning, flashing form that was obviously a trout feeding on something. But I couldn't tell what. The normal prescription at such times is to try nymphs or even streamers that are based on the most abundant food forms either in the lake you're fishing or in all lakes—they're usually not all that different from lake to lake. That's what I did. I tried midge pupa patterns first. They made the most sense, since trout were making most of their living in that lake feasting on midges, at least when I was there. But they ignored all the normal midge nymphs that I tossed at them, whether I fished them on the sit, retrieved them slowly, galloped them back out of desperation, or suspended them beneath yarn indicators at the very depth where I noticed those occasional ghostlike forms feeding.

After the midges I tried damselfly nymphs, dragonfly nymphs, water boatmen and back swimmers, scuds, and leeches. Nothing worked. I finally ceased casting, reeled up, and did what you would have done in the first place: stood still and watched down into the water. That's when it became educational.

The water was a stew of tiny lives, all suspended and all drifting slowly through the water column on the slightest of wind currents. The sun struck through it and ignited tiny animated bits of life that appeared to be zooplankton in its typical broad variety of forms. I had to get my nose down close to the water to notice a few bright red water mites stroking along among the smaller animals, and a few minute crustaceans. Then a midge larva entered my cone of vision from the left, and thrashed along aimlessly, sightlessly, all the way across my bow and out of sight to the right. It took a long time. It twisted its body and flipped it constantly, which seemed to have no effect on the speed or direction of its travel. Its movement seemed fruitless to me, but I suppose just making progress through the water is fruit to a tiny midge larva.

It was bright green. It was size 22. It stood out among the smaller bits of aquatic life in that stew as a pink elephant might show among a herd of gazelles on a flat African plain . . . that's a bad metaphor, but that tiny midge larva looked big and bright down there, surrounded by all the minute life forms wiggling and squirming around it.

Tiny green midge larvae were adrift that day on the pond, struggling through a cloud of zooplankton that must have made the midges look large to cruising trout.

I watched awhile. A few more green midge larvae drifted by, all in constant motion, all lit by the sun, all obvious at a range of six to ten feet through that clear water. It seemed obvious that cruising trout would have no trouble seeing them. It also seemed obvious that trout would recognize the midge larvae as the biggest bites available at the moment. I needed a throat pump sample to provide proof.

My lake-fly box at that time did not contain anything to match such a small and bright midge larva. But I had a portable tying kit in the tent trailer.

It took half an hour to break out the kit, set it up on a table, and construct a half dozen of what I suspected would be an acceptable imitation. I did no more than wrap the shank of a curved size 22 scud hook with bright green wire. The flies were finished in such a short time that I took the time to wrap a half dozen more shanks with bright red wire. These had no counterpart in nature out there in the lake, at least that I had seen. But most stillwaters have bloodworm midges, and red is pretty, so I decided to try it.

WIRE MIDGE LARVA

Hook: Curved scud, size 18–24
Thread: Olive or red 8/0
Body: Green or red wire

I tried them by suspending a pair of them, one green, the other red, from a yarn strike indicator on five feet of straight 6X tippet. Because they were so tiny and, consisting only of wire, would not have enough weight to achieve their depth very quickly, I pinched a tiny split shot to the leader halfway between them. That was it. I waded as deep as I dared, cast the rig upstream in the barely perceptible wind current, gave it all the time in the world to sink, then settled in to watch that indicator suspend my two tiny flies through that stew of little living things.

It took quite some time for a trout to find the flies. By the time it did, my attention had wandered to the shoreline reeds, where a flock of yellow-headed blackbirds fought over territories, argued over hens, screamed obscenities at each other. When I glanced back at my indicator once, it wasn't there. I raised my rod inquisitively, to find out where my indicator might have gone, and felt weight. Not long later I held that weight thrashing in my hands, subdued it by holding it upside down, unpinned the tiny, green midge pattern from its upper lip, took that throat sample.

When I released the trout and squeezed the bulb to shoot the sample into a white pickle jar lid, it writhed with green midge larvae. I broke off more trout than I landed the rest of the afternoon. More of them took the green midge than took the red one, but enough took the red one to make me wonder why they did it. I didn't catch a big bunch of trout, but I spent a lot more time engaged with them than I would have had I gone for another long walk.

You can approach a portable fly-tying kit—I'll not restrict it to a nymph-tying kit, because that would be illogical if you're at least a somewhat rounded fly fisher—from three different directions. The first is not to even own one. That makes sense if you take just short trips. If you're going fishing for a day, or a weekend, you're not likely to have time to tie even if you discover the need for it. Quite often a short trip is to familiar water. You might know what flies you need anyway.

A trip taken by air, by the simple rules of logistics, might eliminate the possibility of taking a fly-tying kit. Your luggage is limited. Your time, on such a trip, is often tight. The right flies, determined beforehand, are a lot easier to carry than a kit constructed to tie them. They also have the advantage of being tied, and therefore ready to fish. Most of the trips I take by airplane, especially overseas, leave little time in an average day for fly tying. The lodge or a fly shop or friend at your destination can probably supply you with a list of the flies you'll need before you go. It's best to tie them at home, before the trip, and have them with you when you arrive.

Many experienced folks do not have a portable kit assembled and would never consider putting one together. It's a matter of personality. Again, I'm not going to try to explain your own personality to you.

I don't get as much tying time at home as I'd like. I spend more time fishing new places than I do old and familiar waters. I prefer to go to a river, lake, stream, or even pond for the first time without all the foreknowledge that would be available if I did the thorough research I recommend you always do. I enjoy getting surprised by a hatch, collecting it, figuring out which stage of it the trout might be taking, finding or tying or even inventing a fly to match it, succeeding or failing with it.

If I'm going on a trip of more than one or two days to water where I'm not sure what I might encounter, I like to have a portable tying kit along. I don't always have it. If I do have it, I'll use it less than half the time. If I don't have it, I won't miss it half the time. But when I don't have it and do want it, I'm going to regret it. I'm going to solve fewer situations when I don't take a tying kit, and I'm probably going to catch fewer trout.

The second approach to a portable fly-tying kit is to construct one and keep it packed and ready to travel at all times. This necessitates the purchase of a second set of tools, in addition to those you'll use at home at the tying bench. It also requires the assembly of a selection of hooks, beads, hackles, wires and tinsels, furs and feathers, dubbing mixes and herls, and all of the etceteras. That can cost a bunch. It has the advantage of always being ready to grab and go, with the secure sense that you won't be forgetting anything. It does demand that you have the discipline to leave everything in it, not tie out of it at home, or if you do, that you pack back what you've used, or it will be missing and be precisely the thing you need when you open the kit to tie at your destination.

A portable kit, always kept packed, was my own solution for many years. About five years ago mine was stolen. I haven't had the heart to reconstruct it, which leads to the third way to address the need for a portable fly-tying kit.

The least expensive and perhaps most efficient way to have a portable fly-tying kit is first to select the transportation for it—a daypack or old briefcase or bag made exactly for a portable fly-tying kit—and then make a list of all that you'd like to remove from your bench and place into the kit when you take a trip. That's what I do now. And that's why I store a lot of things for my home bench in the sorts of containers that will fit in a portable fly-tying kit. I keep the range of hooks and beads that I use most often in small, compartmented boxes that can be banded together and slipped into a kit. I have a Tupperware sandwich box that will hold a basic set of tools,

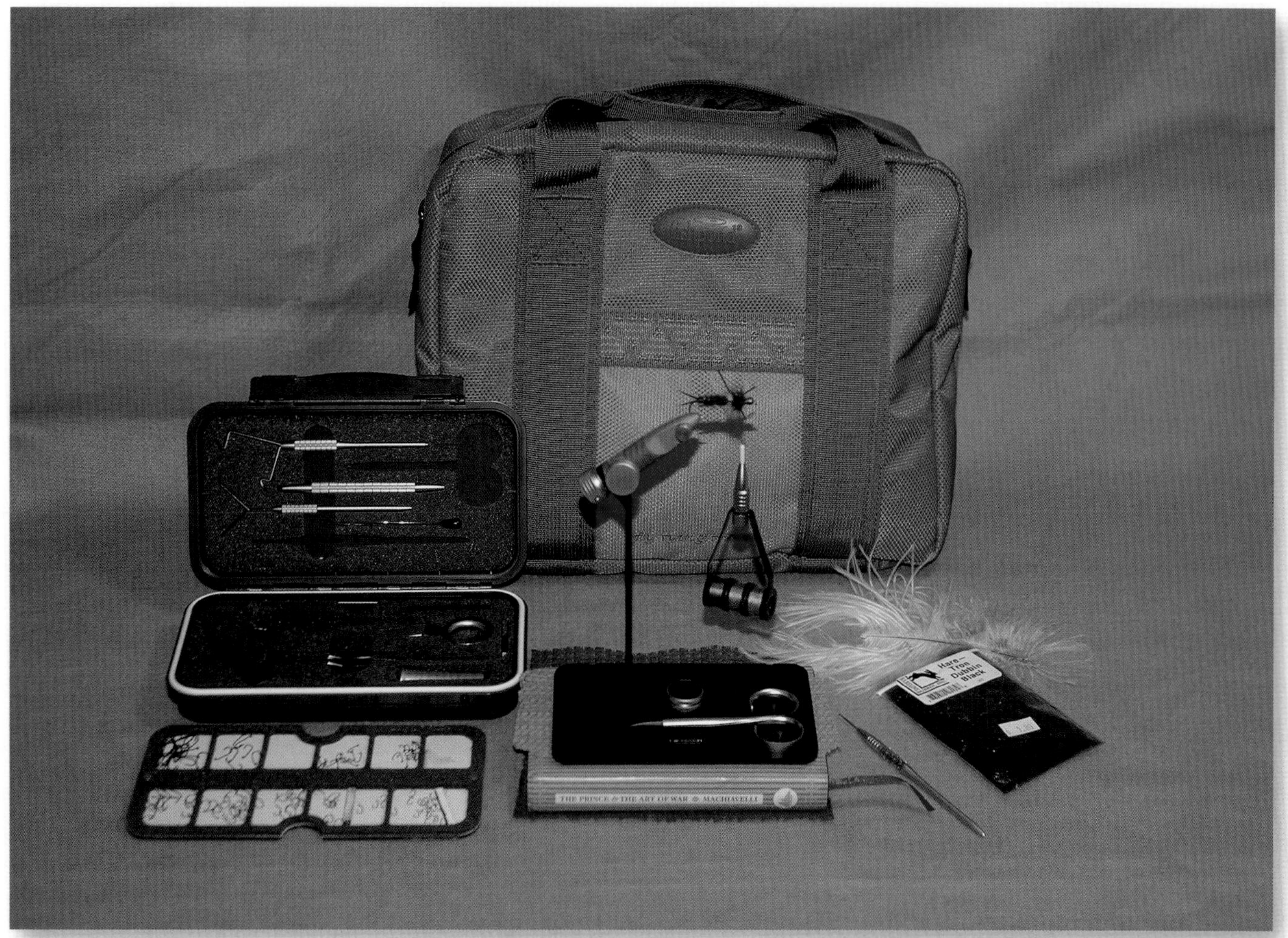

A portable tying kit can be set up at streamside or lakeside, in camp or in a motel room, to supply just the right nymph for the moment.

though I also have a C&F Designs Marco Polo portable tool set that is complete and beautifully engineered. I keep my basic dubbings stored in dispensers that let me grab one with the fine colors, another with the rougher blends, and I've got all I need.

Beyond those basics, I have a checklist of all the things I need on a normal trip. If I'm about to depart on a trip on which I'll want a tying kit, I go quickly through my list, gather everything into the bag I keep for the kit, check things off as I go, and end up with all that I might need. This approach also lets me tailor the kit to the trip.

The list I've supplied for my own portable kit is extensive, though it's probably missing some things that should be on it. I would be unlikely to take everything on the list on every trip. The list does not reflect the minimal kit I recommend you consider constructing. Instead, it contains everything I'd like to at least consider taking on a trip. Many of the things I'll glance at and decide I don't need. But it's better to have them listed, to consider them and reject them, than it is to neglect them and forget what might be the one item that solves a certain situation during a hatch out on trout water.

I'm unable to explain why the list ends with Machiavelli's *The Prince* and *The Art of War.* That must be what I was reading when I assembled the kit for a trip sometime in the past, and I added it to the list whimsically and have left it there. But it's a fine book, actually a compilation of his two fine books, gathered into a pocket-sized hardbound that has been able to withstand the rigors of many travels without adding much bulk or weight to the portable kit. It's full of enough blood, conflict, and consternation to be very entertaining. I pulled it out of the kit on a trip to Canada once and a friend said, "That's an appropriate book. You can apply its principles against the trout."

That's not why I read it, but it's good to have a book of your own choosing in your own portable fly-tying kit. If nothing else, it might be the right size to put under the vise, lift it up to the right tying height, if the pedestal stem is too short for you.

PORTABLE FLY-TYING KIT

- [ ] Marco Polo tool kit
- [ ] Tying light/extension cord
- [ ] Cheater glasses
- [ ] Lt. green napkin/tying background
- [ ] Vise w/ large & small collets
- [ ] Scissors: fine and coarse
- [ ] Bobbins: black/olive/tan/gray/brown, 8/0
- [ ] Pearsall's gossamer silk: primrose/orange/green/crimson
- [ ] Bobbin threader
- [ ] Pliers
- [ ] Bodkin
- [ ] Stacker: large & small
- [ ] Hackle pliers
- [ ] Parachute hackle pliers
- [ ] Dubbing spinner
- [ ] Half-hitch tool/dubbing rougher
- [ ] CDC clamp
- [ ] Bead-Nabbers
- [ ] Tweezers
- [ ] Steel comb
- [ ] Dubbing wax
- [ ] Head cement
- [ ] Water Shed
- [ ] Razor blade
- [ ] Std. dry-fly hooks, 12–22
- [ ] Curved scud hooks, 12–22
- [ ] Std. nymph hooks, 10–20
- [ ] 3XL hooks, 4–16
- [ ] Hopper hooks, 6–16
- [ ] Gold beads: 1.5 mm, 5/64, 3/32, 7/64, 1/8 inch
- [ ] Tungsten beads, gold: 3/32, 1/8, 5/32 inch
- [ ] Tungsten beads, black: 3/32, 1/8, 5/32 inch
- [ ] Weighting wire: .015-, .025-, .035-inch nonlead
- [ ] Wire: fine/med. copper/olive/red
- [ ] Tinsel: oval silver/gold, small/med./large
- [ ] Mylar: fine/med./large
- [ ] Scud back: dark olive
- [ ] Pearl flash
- [ ] Rubber legs: black/white/barred
- [ ] Chenille: black/olive
- [ ] Z-lon: olive/amber/gray/clear
- [ ] Mayfly tails: dun/PMD/tan
- [ ] Parachute post: white/gray/yellow
- [ ] White lamb's wool
- [ ] Foam: black/olive/yellow/orange/tan
- [ ] Rooster necks: black/brown/ginger/dun/grizzly
- [ ] Hen necks: brown/ginger/dun/grizzly
- [ ] Chickabou: olive
- [ ] Biots: black, brown, red, olive, PMD
- [ ] Hackle stems: selection
- [ ] Peacock eye
- [ ] Partridge skin
- [ ] Starling skin
- [ ] CDC selection
- [ ] Oak turkey: treated w/ Flexament
- [ ] Pheasant tail
- [ ] Turkey flats: gray/white
- [ ] Marabou: black/olive/white/brown
- [ ] Squirrel: pine/fox/gray
- [ ] Muskrat back
- [ ] Superfine, color selection
- [ ] Nymph fur/Sparkle Yarn mix, color selection
- [ ] Touch dubbing, color selection
- [ ] Sparkle Yarn, color selection
- [ ] Snowshoe feet: black/cream/gray
- [ ] Rabbit strips: black/olive/brown/white
- [ ] Comparadun/X-Caddis hair: lt/med./dk.
- [ ] Yearling elk hair: natural/olive/gray
- [ ] Calf body hair, white/dun
- [ ] Moose body hair
- [ ] Machiavelli: *The Prince* and *The Art of War*

CHAPTER 8

Basic Maneuvers

A limited number of basic tying procedures are used on nearly every fly you tie, whether it's a nymph or not, and it's best to get them down correctly before you begin to tie completed flies. For example, you'll be very wise to practice mounting the hook securely in the vise, starting your thread, and then breaking it a few times. You'll quickly learn if your vise needs to be adjusted to hold the hook the way it should. You'll also begin to get a feel for just how much pressure you can put on your thread before it snaps and causes an emergency.

If you buy a whip-finish tool, follow the directions that come with it, and learn to use it on a bare hook shank, not a finished fly. If you prefer to whip-finish by hand, again it's easier to master on a bare shank, where the finishing of a nymph does not depend on your getting the final whip-finish just right.

Some steps, such as weighting a shank or placing weighting wire wraps behind a bead, will be done so repetitively in nymph tying that it's best to practice them until they become almost instinctive. But you needn't do all of your drills on a bunch of bare hooks, then undo what you've done or toss them away. Instead, choose a simple dressing that incorporates the method you're learning, and tie a dozen in a single size. Not only will you know by the end of that practice exactly how to weight a shank or a beadhead nymph, but you'll also have a dozen finished flies that will give you some tugs by trout.

This will all be *preview* if you've never tied flies before. If you're more experienced, it might be worthwhile as an exercise in *review.*

MOUNTING THE HOOK IN THE VISE

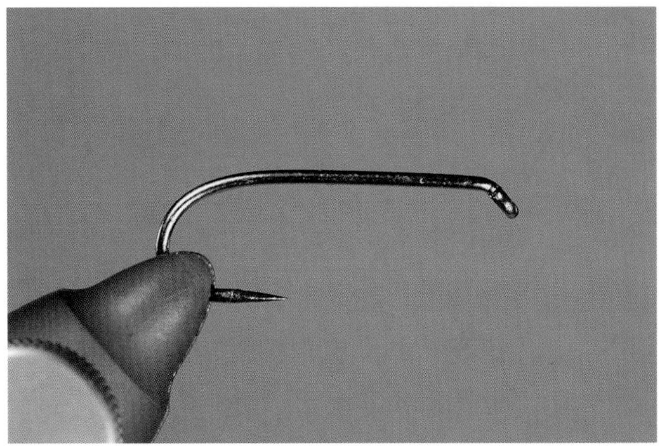

When a hook is correctly mounted, the lower half of the hook bend will be captured by the vise jaws, spreading their force evenly over the widest portion of the wire, and over none of the tapered point.

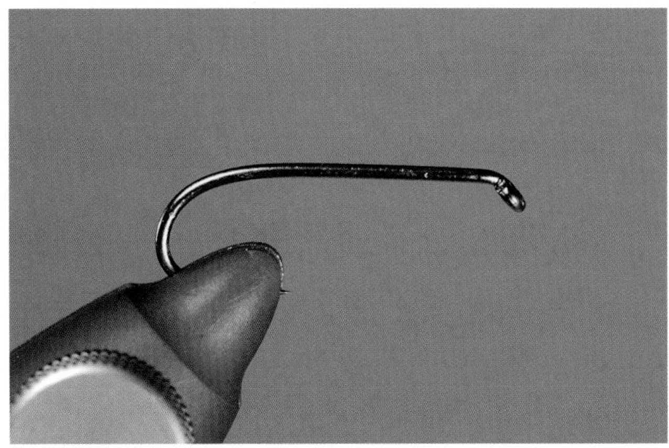

If you capture the point of the hook beneath the vise jaws, they'll clamp over the tapered part of the shank; the upper side of the jaws will pinch the hook and weaken it.

Place the hook in the vise jaws so that when clamped they cover the lower half of the bend of the hook, but do not cover any of the taper toward the point. The jaws should trap the hook wire where it has an even diameter, thereby spreading the force of the jaws. If you include the tapered wire toward the point, the jaws will pinch the upper end of the bend, and the hook will be weakened. It's not likely to break as you're tying, but it is likely to break later, on a big trout. You'll be left forever wondering just why it broke, and blame it on the hook manufacturer.

STARTING THE THREAD

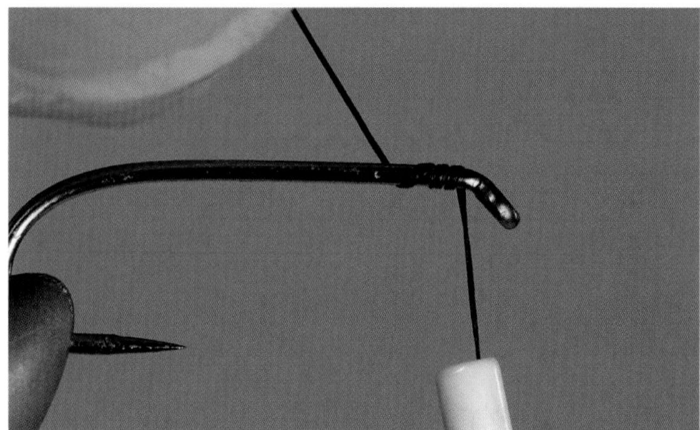

Start the thread by taking three or four wraps forward just behind the hook eye.

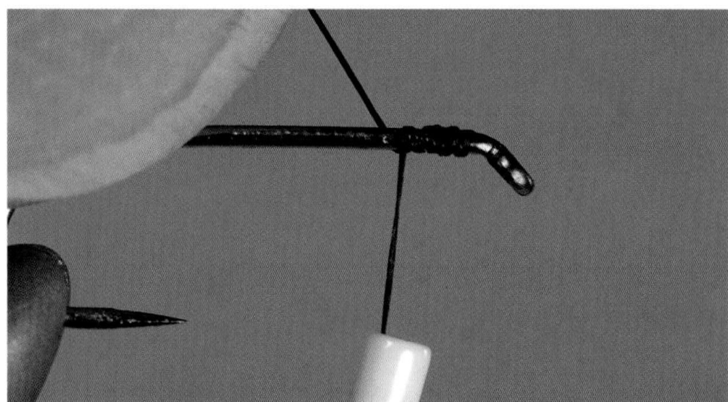

Take three or four wraps back over the previous wraps, and your thread will be securely attached to the hook.

Hold the thread bobbin loosely in your tying hand—we'll not talk about right and left hands here—and with one or two inches of thread beyond the end of the bobbin barrel, grip the thread end between the forefinger and thumb of your off hand. Hold the thread tip below the hook shank, on the near side. Cross the thread over the shank just behind the hook eye.

Take three to four abutting thread wraps toward the hook. Reverse direction and take three to four wraps over the top of the first layer. You can clip the tag end at this point, or wait until you've made a base layer that covers the hook shank, then clip the excess at that point.

BASE THREAD LAYER

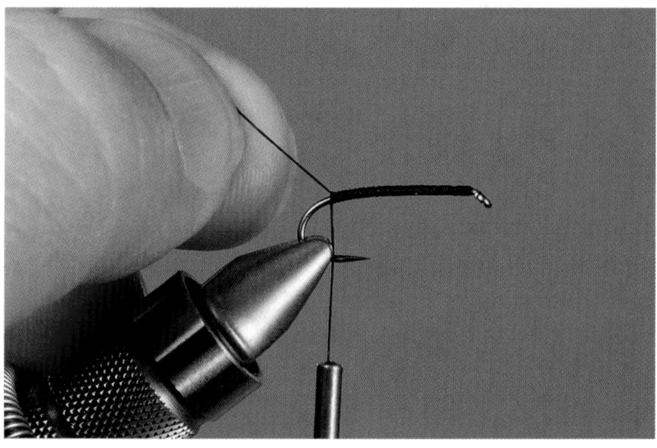

Hold the tag end of the thread above the shank while making your base layer, and the thread wraps will slide down and abut tightly against each other.

The hook shank is slippery, and it's always wise to cover it with a layer of thread before you begin to tie materials to it. This is most easily done if you begin tying in materials at the tail end of the hook, which is the common case. Simply start the thread behind the eye, wrap it to the back, and cut or break off the tag. The exception to layering the hook with thread first, also common in nymph tying, is a weighted shank. The weighting wire wraps should be placed before you start the thread.

To make the base thread layer on an unweighted hook, simply start the thread and continue winding it toward the bend of the hook. Be sure that the wraps are tightly abutted. If it helps, hold the tag end of the thread elevated above the shank, and each wrap will slide down it and nestle against the previous wrap. Stop at the beginning of the hook bend, and clip the excess thread tag.

BREAKING AND RESCUING THREAD

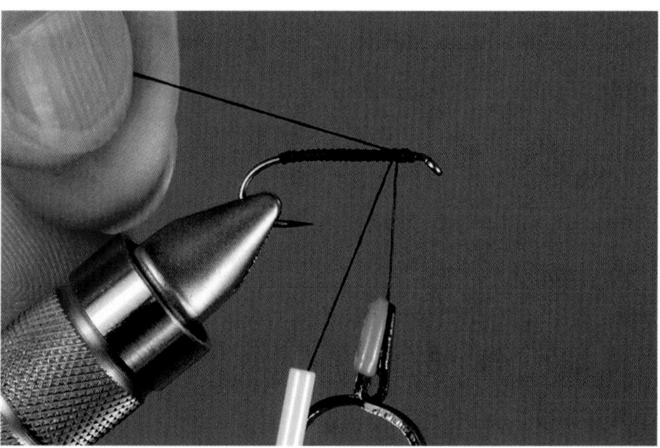

To rescue broken thread, attach your hackle pliers to the broken thread end, let them dangle, and restart the thread with three wraps forward and three wraps back, over the last thread windings you made before the thread broke.

If your thread breaks in the middle of tying a nymph, it's not the emergency it might seem, unless you've just finished winding a springy ribbing material, and the break causes it to unwind. Even in that case, you can easily restart the thread and rewind the rib.

The moment your thread breaks, pinch the broken end with your off-hand fingertips. Find those handy hackle pliers, and clip them to the loose end. The weight of the pliers will keep your previous thread windings secure.

Rethread your bobbin if necessary. Then repeat the procedure you used to start the thread, but do it over the last windings where the thread just broke. Take three wraps forward, and three wraps back. Don't use excess turns and bulk up the break point. Gather the broken tag of thread along with the tag of the thread you've just started, and nip them both together.

HALF HITCH

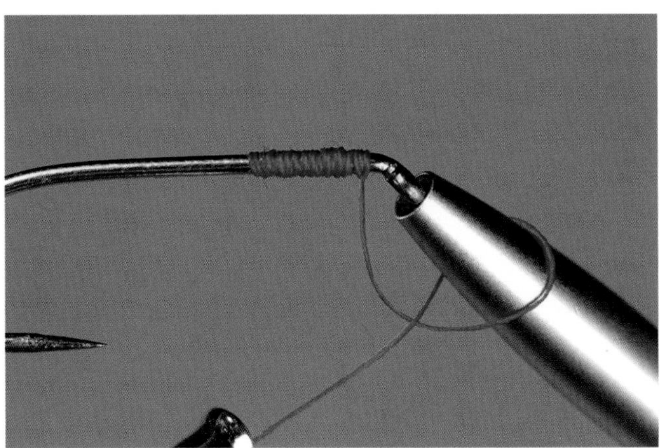

To use a half-hitch tool, throw a loop around the barrel, brace the barrel against the hook eye, and slide the loop down the barrel and over the eye, seating the half hitch where you want it.

You'll use an occasional half-hitch knot to rescue your thread, in the rare event that a long-enough tag is left after the break to make one. If you're tying rotary, you'll use a half hitch to secure your thread every time you employ the rotary function, to keep the thread from unwinding as you twirl the vise and thereby rotate the hook.

To use a half-hitch tool, roll the thread once around the end of the barrel, then brace the open end of the tool against the hook eye, or over the hook eye if the opening is so large that the hook eye fits into it. To finish the half hitch, simply slide the thread off the end of the barrel and over the eye of the hook. Seat it where you want it, then draw it tight.

WHIP-FINISH

It takes considerable practice to learn the hand whip-finish, but it will cut out a tool and eliminate the need to pick it up and set it down to finish each fly for the rest of time. I recommend you try it; better yet, get a friend to teach you, or best of all, take a fly-tying class. A whip-finish tool will ease the pain of learning, and will finish heads that are just as tidy and every bit as secure. If you buy a whip-finisher, follow the directions that come with it. The following instructions are for the hand whip-finish.

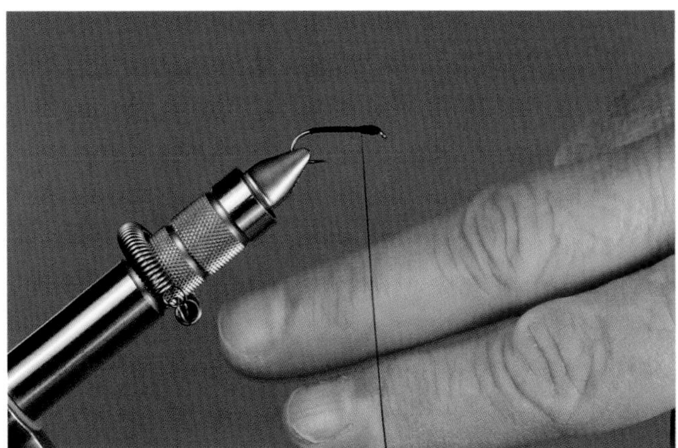

Step 1. Spool five to seven inches of thread off the bobbin, and hold the bobbin in your off hand, below the vise. Extend the forefinger and middle finger of your tying hand, with their backs to you, and place them behind the thread at about the first knuckle. The forefinger should be down, the middle finger up. Your tying scissors should be riding high on the ring finger of your tying hand, though in the beginning you might decide to practice a few whips without the minor bother of the scissors.

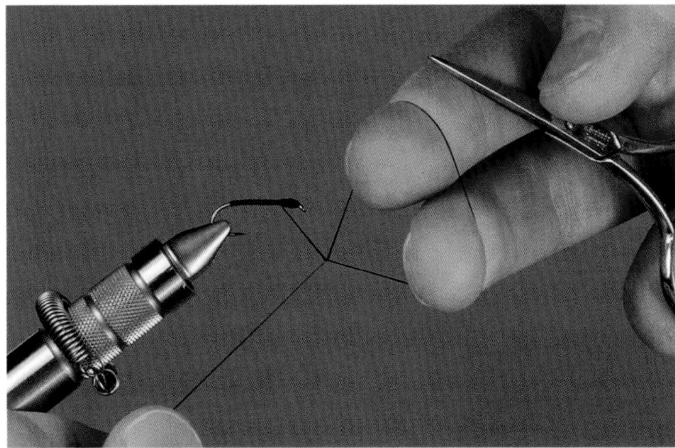

Step 2. Bring your two fingers up and rotate your wrist down so that your fingers make a 180-degree turn, and capture a loop of thread around them. End with your palm facing you, your forefinger up, your middle finger down, and your tying hand near the hook eye with a loop of thread around it. The bobbin will be pointed in the direction of the hook bend. The thread will form a distinct X in the air between your fingers and the hook eye.

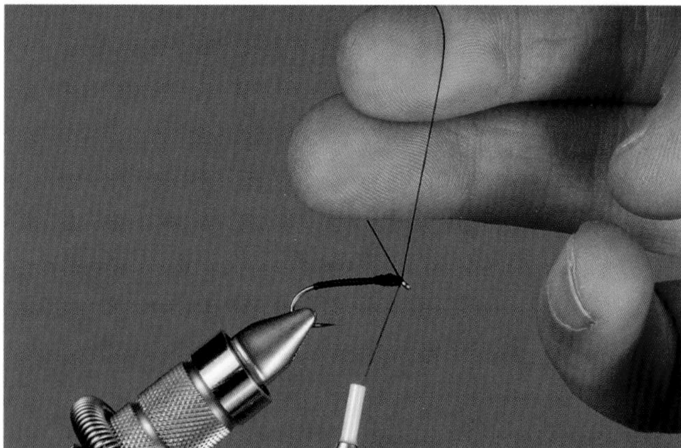

Step 3. Move your forefinger over the top of the hook and behind it, at the same time moving your middle finger under the hook and behind it. This will slide the X in the thread to a position directly behind the hook eye. Rotate your fingers inside the loop, behind the hook, so that they are together, with their palm sides toward you, and point in the direction of the bend of the hook. End with your hand behind the hook shank, your forefinger high, your middle finger low, and the thread secured to the hook shank right behind the eye of the hook. The thread loop will still be around your fingers.

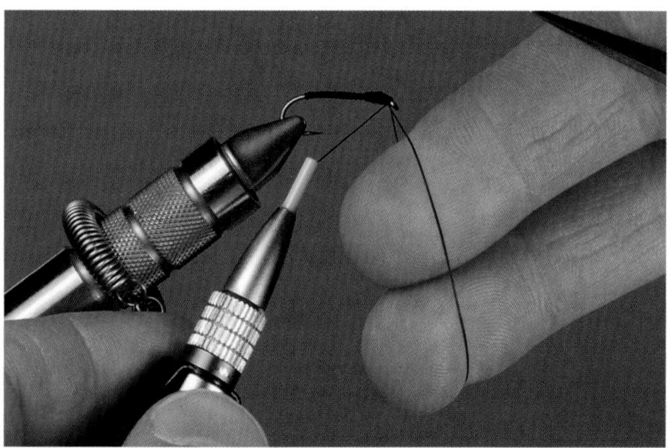

Step 4. Bring your two fingers underneath the hook shank together, delivering the loop of thread that is around them with them. End with your hand between you and the hook shank, your forefinger on top, your middle finger under, and your palm facing you.

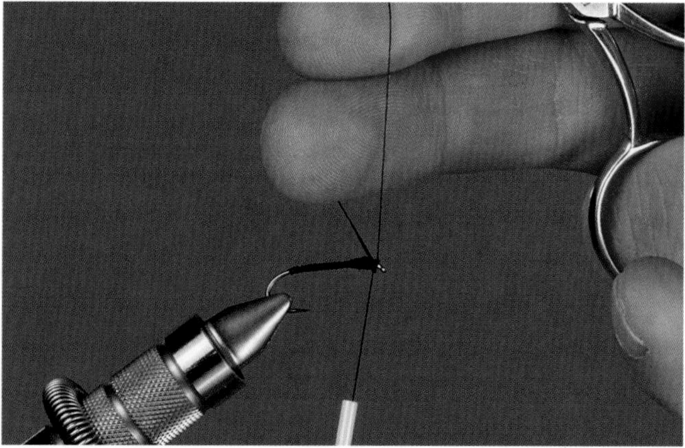

Step 5. Move your forefinger over the top of the hook, and your middle finger under it, just as you did in Step 3. Rotate your fingers inside the loop behind the hook, so that your ending position is exactly as it was in Step 3: your hand behind the hook shank, your forefinger high, your middle finger low, and the thread loop going around your fingers. In Steps 3 and 5 you have essentially taken two turns of the thread over itself. A completed whip-finish will have four or five of these turns before it is drawn tight.

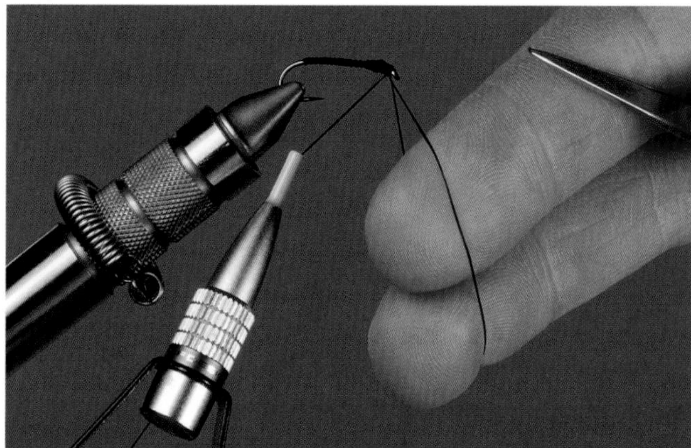

Step 6. Repeat Step 4, bringing your two fingers together underneath the hook shank, delivering the loop of thread with them, ending with your hand between you and the hook shank, your forefinger on top, your middle finger under, and your palm facing you. You have now positioned yourself to repeat Step 5, taking another turn of thread over itself.

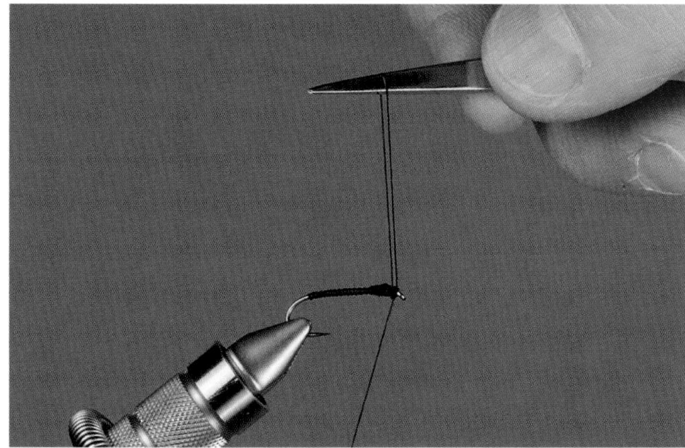

Step 7. Repeat Steps 3 and 4 twice more, splitting the thread loop around the hook shank to make a thread wrap over itself, bringing the thread wrap forward to reposition it for another wrap. End with the thread loop behind the hook. Draw your middle finger out of the loop, replace it with the scissor points, and remove your forefinger from the loop, shifting the loop from your forefinger to the scissors. Be sure to keep the loop tight.

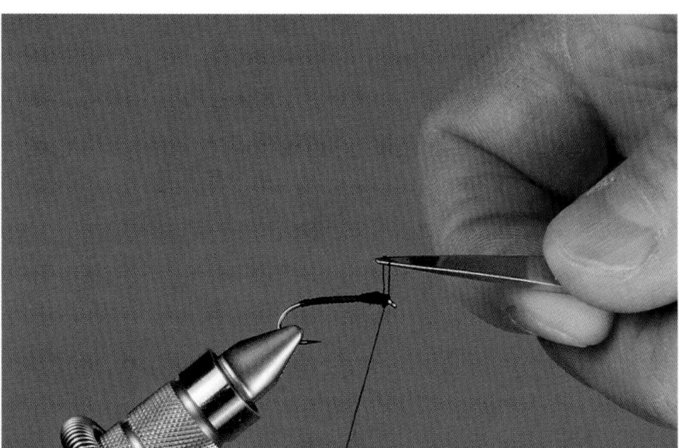

Step 8. Pull the thread bobbin down and away from the hook, drawing the loop down just behind the eye. Let the loop slip over the scissors, using the points to direct the final and precise placement of the finished whip. Clip the thread and you're finished.

PINCH WRAP

If you lay a bit of material, say fibers for a tail, on top of the hook shank, then take thread wraps around the material, the thread wraps will drive the material off the top of the shank, and you'll end up with your tail coming off the far side of the hook shank at best, or scattered around the far side and bottom at worst. To place any material on the shank precisely where you want it, use the *pinch wrap,* which in many books is also called the *soft loop.* The pinch wrap allows you to apply the force of the first turn of thread directly down onto the material, capturing it against the hook shank in the exact position where you want it.

The pinch wrap is essentially a loop of thread lofted loosely over the material you're tying in, and pinched between the forefinger tip and thumb tip of your off hand. The thread bobbin is then held beneath the hook shank, or even on your side. As the thread is drawn tight, the loop slips between your forefinger and thumb, and draws straight down on top of the material. A single pinch wrap locks the material where you want it. Subsequent thread wraps, made in the normal manner, will not drive the material off the top of the shank, so long as you make those wraps forward of the pinch wrap. If you make them behind it, you'll once again drive the material around the shank of the hook. So you make that first pinch wrap at the back of the tie-in point.

You will employ the pinch wrap on nearly every fly, nymph or not, that you tie. It should become so routine that you don't even notice you're using it.

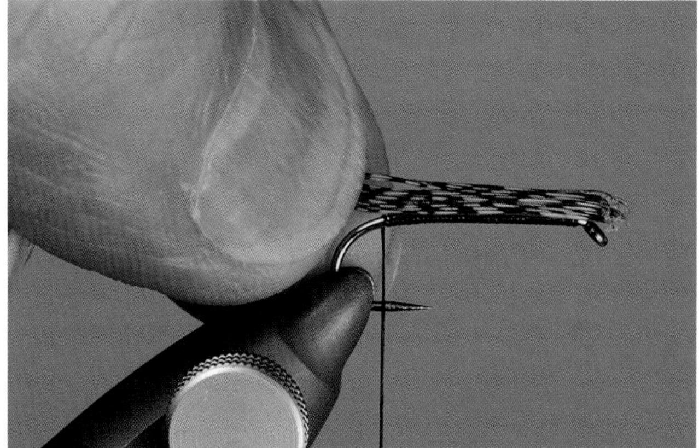

Step 1. Make the base layer of thread over the hook shank before tying in parts such as tails. Select the fibers you want for the tail, prepare them by evening their tips and removing any fuzz from their butts, if they're the type of material that has underfur, and measure them to the correct length. Pinch them between the forefinger tip and thumb tip of your off hand, and hold them on top of the hook at the tie-in point, usually the beginning of the bend of the hook.

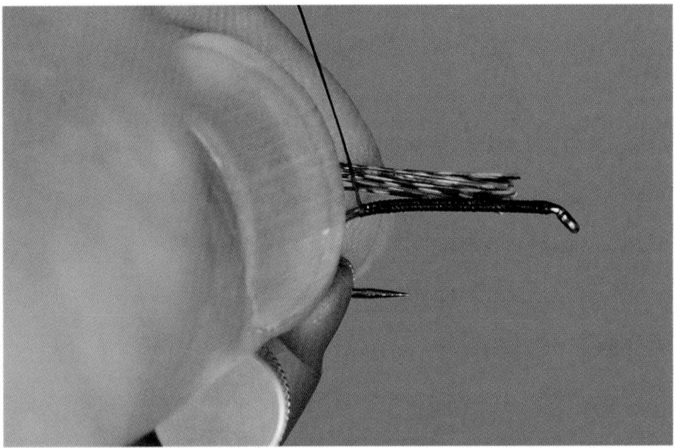

Step 2. Run your thread up between the forefinger and thumb tips that are holding the material in place. Pinch the thread along with the material. (*Note:* In order to show the thread, the thumb is moved back in the photo, but when executing the pinch wrap, the thumb and forefinger would be even and held firmly together, pinching the thread.)

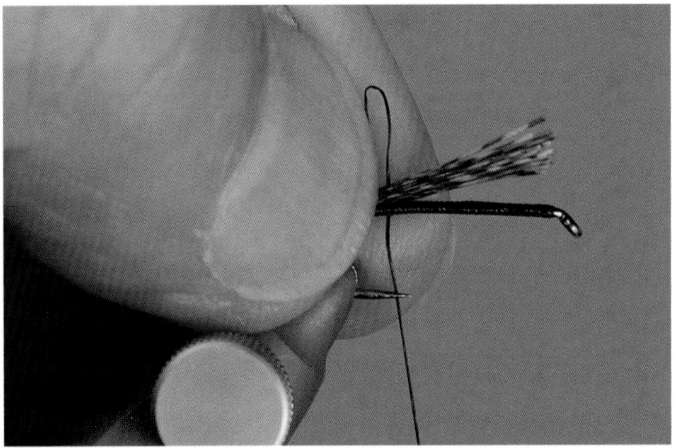

Step 3. Bring the thread back down between the forefinger and thumb tips that are holding the material and first leg of the loop. Pinch the loop, and bring the thread bobbin to a position directly beneath the hook shank, or even around toward your side. (*Note:* The thumb is held back in the photo to reveal the loop above the hook shank, around the tail material. You will hold the thumb tight against the forefinger to pinch the thread loop along with the material it will capture against the hook.)

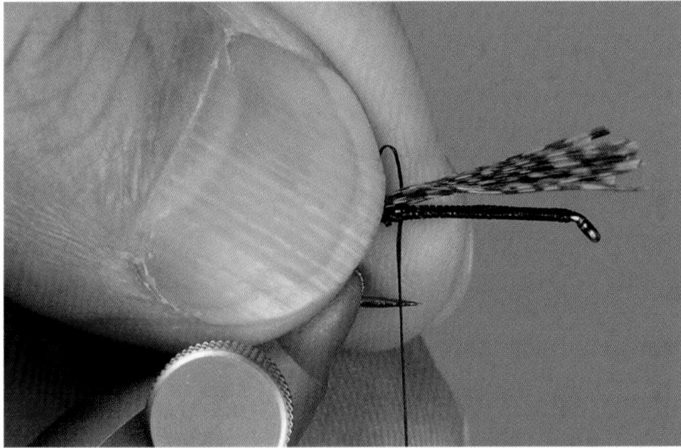

Step 4. Draw the bobbin down or slightly toward you, pulling on the loop. As the loop shrinks in size, let it slide between your forefinger and thumb without releasing the pinch on the thread and tail material. (*Note:* Again the thumb is repositioned back a bit in the photo to reveal the descending loop.)

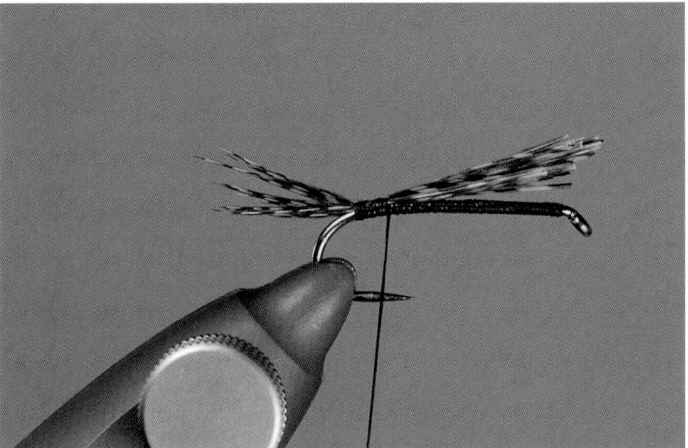

Step 5. After the pinch wrap is drawn tight, take three to six wraps of thread forward to secure the material in position.

SHANK WRAP

When you tie in a material that has substantial thickness, especially a body wire, ribbing tinsel, or yarn, it should be overwrapped with thread the length of the hook shank, rather than tied in just at the bend of the hook. If you tie it in with just a few turns of thread over a small portion of the hook shank, and clip the excess, it will leave a lump, making it difficult to wrap an even or slightly tapered body. This is critical with slender biot and wire-bodied nymphs.

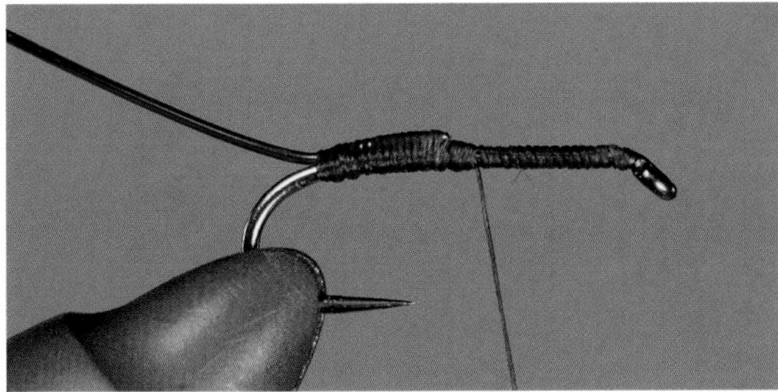

If you tie in a material with substantial thickness, such as this copper wire, and use only a few turns of thread at the back of the hook, then clip the excess, the finished body will have a lump in it.

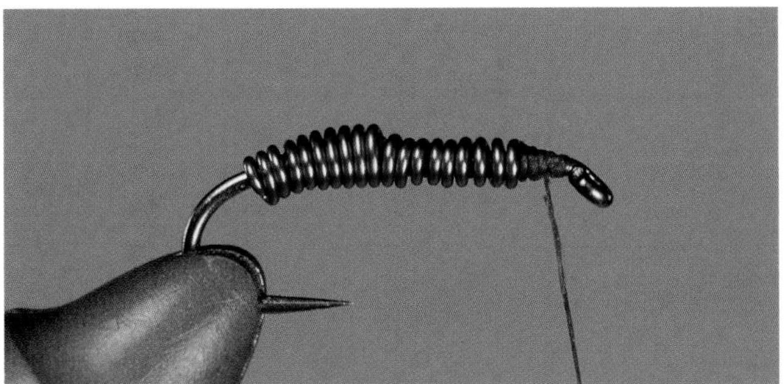

The result of tying a short section of wire to the shank is a body with a lump at the tie-in point.

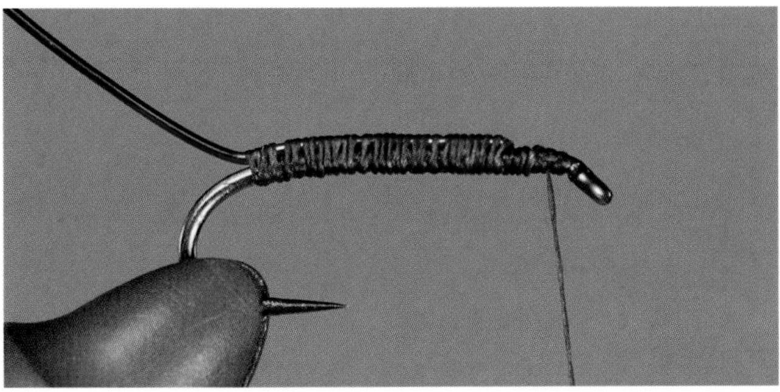

To create an even underbody, overwrap the entire length of the wire with thread. End with the thread at the point where you'd like to tie in the next material, or where you will tie off the wire after it is wound.

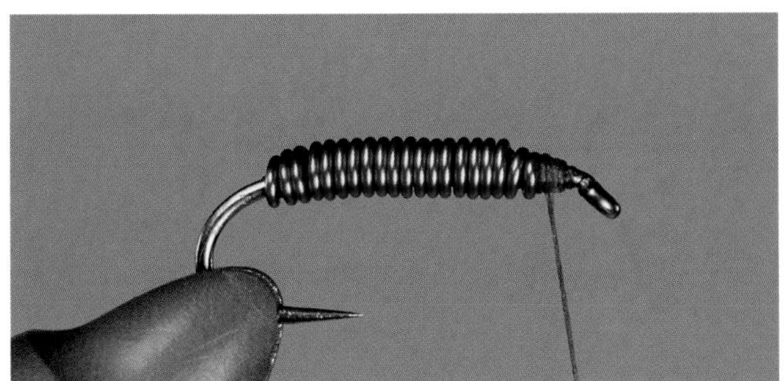

An even wire underbody results in a finished body with no lumps. If you want a tapered body, then create an appropriate tapered underbody with extra thread wraps before wrapping the final body.

WEIGHTING THE SHANK

The standard rule for weighting nymphs is to use lead or nonlead wire about equal in diameter to the hook shank. A hook weighted normally will have ten to fifteen wraps of lead. A heavy nymph will have from fifteen to twenty-five wraps. A few very heavy nymphs call for a layer of weighting wire the length of the hook shank, with a second layer wrapped back over the first for a few turns in the thorax area. I *underweight* many of my own nymphs, using the number of turns specified for the dressing, but with weighting wire one size smaller than the diameter of the hook shank. This gives me the option to fish them shallow. If I want to fish them deep, I add split shot or putty weight to the leader.

Weighting wire should be wrapped onto the hook shank before the thread is started. The thread should then be used to secure the weight, and also to build ramps or shoulders at both ends, so subsequent materials can be wrapped over the weight smoothly.

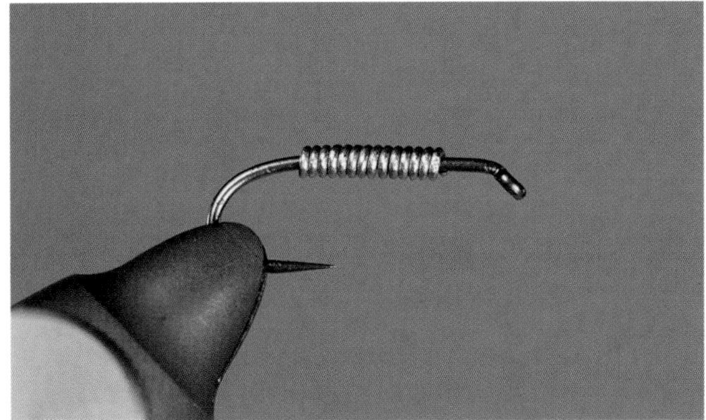

Step 1. Select weighting wire with a diameter approximately equal to the hook wire diameter. Start it by holding the end of the wire close above the hook shank, in front of the bend of the hook, in your off hand. Keep a firm grip on the tag end while taking the number of wraps forward that you want on the hook. Clip the weighting wire close to the hook shank in front, with your rough scissors. You can also tug on the wire until it breaks. It will usually, though not always, break at the shank, right where you want it to. You can either clip the tag end, or wrap it around the shank and flatten it with your thumbnail or fingernail. Position the weighting wire in the center of the shank.

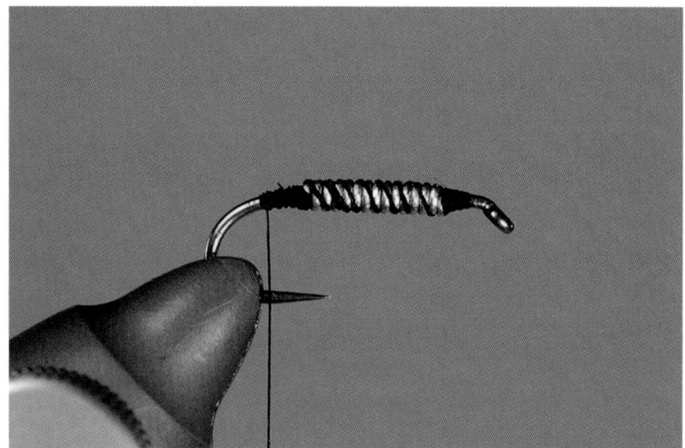

Step 2. Start the thread behind the weighting wire. Wrap it forward, letting a turn of thread slip between each gap in the turns of wire. Layer thread wraps to the hook eye, then return it to the front shoulder of the lead. Use enough thread wraps to create a sloped shoulder in front of the weighting wire, then overwrap the wire and make the same sort of shoulder in back of it. If you're tying with a material that will fill in the shoulder, omit the thread ramps.

WEIGHTING WITH BEADHEADS

The whip-finish on a beadhead fly gets tucked in between the bead and the forward end of the body or whatever other material constitutes the front of the fly. If the bead is not locked in tight, the whip slides into the hollow chamber in the back of the bead, comes undone, and the fly quickly decomposes. After a trout or two, the bead slides back on the shank, and the fly is finished, though in truth if you continue to fish it, you will probably continue to catch fish. But it won't look very good, and won't speak well of your tying.

Since most beadhead nymphs will be tied with weight, the weighting wire can be used to secure the bead. Try to use weighting wire in a diameter that allows it to slip into the back of the bead.

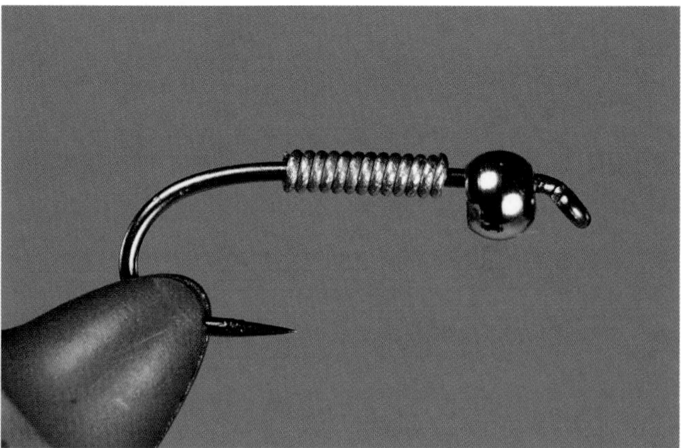

Step 1. Debarb the hook, if it is barbed, and slide a taper-drilled bead around the bend and to the hook eye. Be sure the narrow opening of the bead is braced against the eye, the open end toward the back of the fly. Select the appropriate size weighting wire, and take five to fifteen turns on the shank. Clip the front of the wire, and clip or flatten the tag at the back.

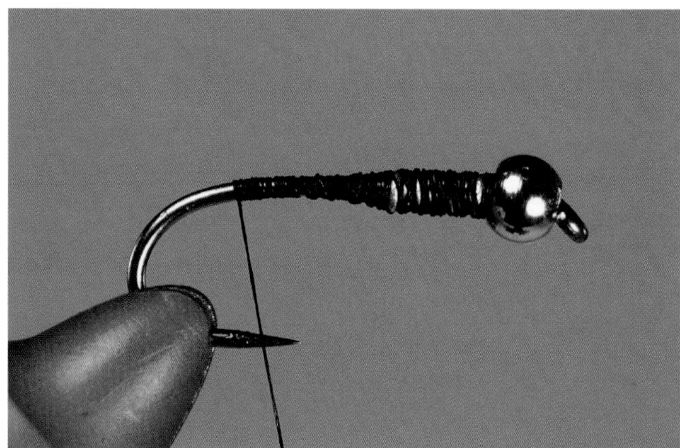

Step 2. Slide the front end of the weighting wire wraps into the back end of the bead. If the weighting wire is too thick to fit into the bead, or if your bead is not tapered, jam the weighting wire tightly against the back of the bead. Start your thread just behind the weighting wire. Make a thread ramp up onto the wire, then wrap thread forward through the wire and back over it to the bend of the hook, layering the shank with thread and locking in the bead.

DIRECT DUBBING

Many natural nymphs are slender, and should be imitated with slender imitations. Dubbing for such bodies should be applied to the tying thread in a thin, compacted skein, so that when it's wound on the hook, the result is not thick. Many naturals also have somewhat long and tapered abdomens that broaden out in front into more portly thoracic segments. You want a thin dubbing for the back, a thicker one in front. Direct dubbing is a method that lets you determine the thickness of the material on the thread. By making it thin at the back and thicker at the front, you can wind a tapered body.

Use the direct-dubbing technique to affix fur or synthetic dubbing material directly to the thread. Your standard tying thread should be prewaxed. If you're using unwaxed thread for a particular fly, you might have difficulty getting your dubbing to stick to it unless you wax it. I always use prewaxed thread, but also keep a stick of beeswax on my bench, though I use it more often for tying wet flies such as soft-hackles and flymphs than I do when tying nymphs. Once in a while, however, it helps to add a bit of beeswax to a thread that is already waxed, to make it stiffer, and also to make it hold dubbing a bit better.

Many of the larger 3/0 threads are not prewaxed, and you'll need to wax them almost every time you use dubbing. Beeswax will work in most cases, but you'll also find a tacky fly-tying wax very handy, though it is used more often in making the following dubbing loop than it is for direct dubbing.

Direct dubbing is easiest with soft furs, such as squirrel or rabbit, and synthetics with soft, long fibers. It is more difficult, though it will work, with coarse dubbings such as mixed blends of fur and Sparkle Yarn. The finer the material, the more slender the body you can wind with it. The coarser the material, the thicker the resulting body will be, no matter what dubbing method you use. In general, use the direct-dubbing method on a nymph when you're imitating a slender natural, such as a midge pupa, and the dubbing-loop method when you want a looser, thicker dubbing.

To achieve a tapered body with direct dubbing, simply apply the dubbing to the thread thin near the hook, thicker as you move away from it, then a short taper down for the tie-in point. Experience, gained quickly when you tie nymphs by the dozen, or at least half dozen, will quickly tell you the correct amount of dubbing for the size hook on which you're tying.

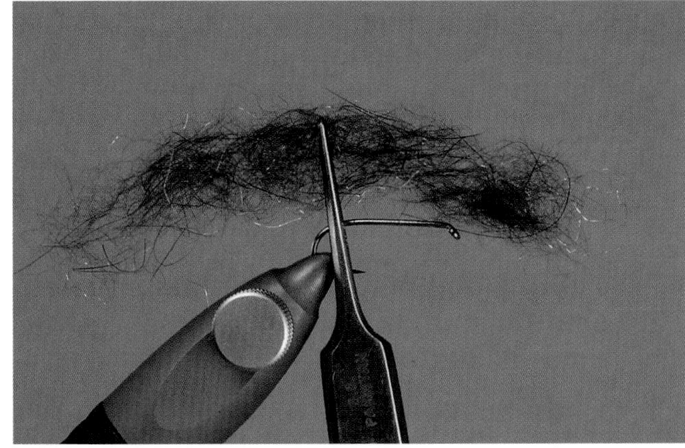

Step 1. Tease the approximate amount of dubbing for the size hook you're using from the package. Shape it into a rough skein in the palm of your hand, and distribute more toward the end you'd like to be tapered more fully.

Step 2. Place the dubbing skein against your waxed thread, and use the thumb and forefinger of your off hand to roll the top end of the dubbing, near the hook shank, tightly to the thread. Do the same at the distal end. This locks the fur skein to the thread.

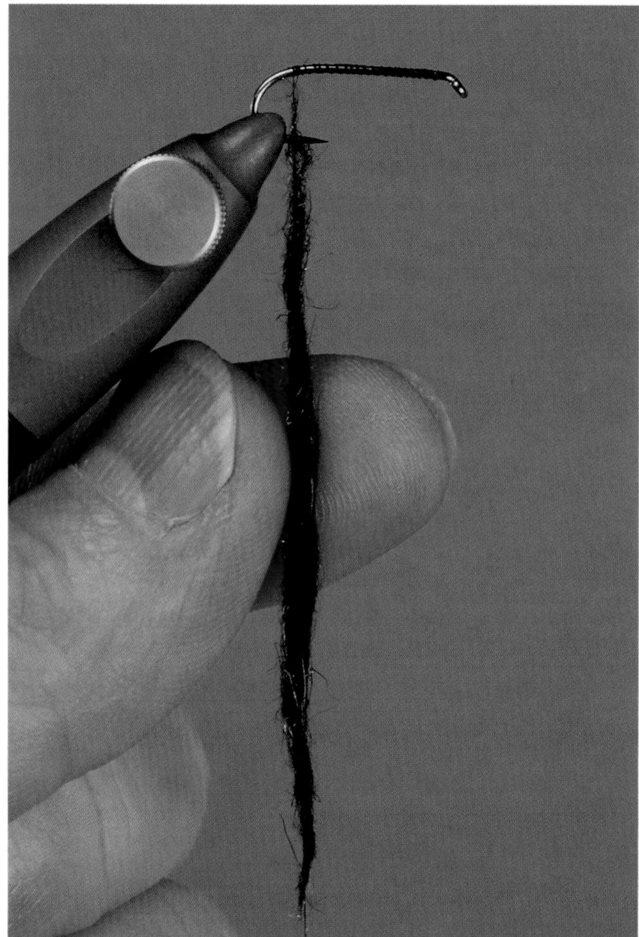

Step 3. Attach the rest of the fur skein onto the thread by rolling the ball of your thumb over the ball of your forefinger. If the material slips, moisten the ball of your thumb, though you'll rarely need to do this. Roll in only one direction, not back and forth. If you roll your thumb back and forth over the ball of your fingertip, with the dubbing captured between them, you will merely tighten and then loosen the dubbing. By rolling in one direction, you continually tighten the dubbing into a more slender skein on the thread. Work your way from the hook shank toward the thicker end, which will become the front end of the dubbed body. You can easily add dubbing to make it thicker, pluck out dubbing to make it thinner, or redistribute dubbing from one part of the skein to the other to achieve the taper you'd like.

Step 4. Wind the dubbing from the beginning of the bend of the hook forward to where your nymph body will end. It should be slightly tapered from thin at the back to thicker at the front. You can vary the proportions, and the taper, by choosing how much dubbing you use in the skein, how tightly you roll it onto the thread, and how you distribute it on the thread, thereby changing the thickness and taper of the resulting body.

You can vary the amount of either a fine or coarse dubbing material to achieve a thicker finished body on a nymph, or part of a nymph. For example, you might dub a slender abdomen on an A. P. Black, with a tight direct dubbing, add a shellback, then dub a thicker, looser thorax with the same material and method, then pull the shellback over the thorax.

DUBBING LOOP

Coarse dubbings, most often those that are a mix of fine fur and Antron Sparkle Yarn, are difficult to dub directly to the thread. If you do, you'll wind up with a ragged body if the material is too loosely attached to the thread, or a body that is too slender and tight if the material is rolled too tightly to the thread. If you're after a tight body, you can achieve it better with finer dubbing. If you're after a rougher body, you can achieve that effect, and a more durable fly, by using a dubbing loop.

The dubbing loop captures the rough dubbing material between two strands of thread, which when twisted lock in almost all of the fibers. The result is a very rough, loose dubbing that has many moving parts when the nymph is wet and in the water. It looks alive. The dubbing is locked in, so it will not be torn away by the teeth of the many trout you'll catch on a single nymph. The more trout you catch on a nymph with a dubbing-loop body, the rougher it gets, and the better it fishes.

The dubbing-loop method is very useful for blends of fur and Sparkle Yarn. It's also important when you desire to use natural furs with a mix of soft underfur and longer guard hairs. The dubbing-loop method captures the guard hairs but leaves them free to stick out in all directions, looking like legs or antennae. The direct-dubbing method either flattens the guard hairs into the rest of the fur, resulting in a thin body with few guard hairs sticking out, or it fails to capture the guard hairs, allowing them to pull out as soon as you begin fishing the fly.

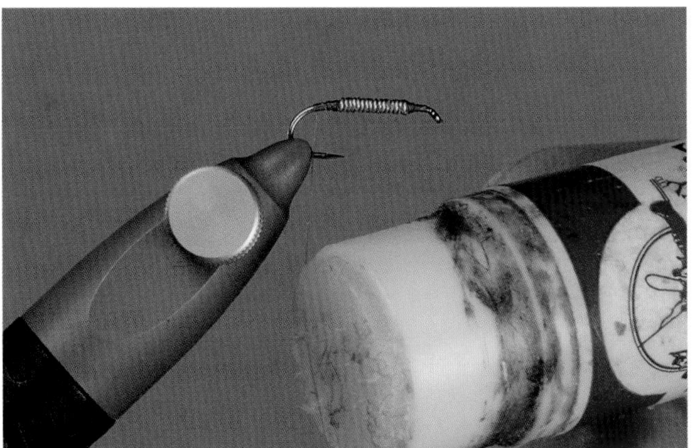

Step 1. Coat one to three inches of your thread with a sticky dubbing wax. The length needed depends on the size fly you're tying.

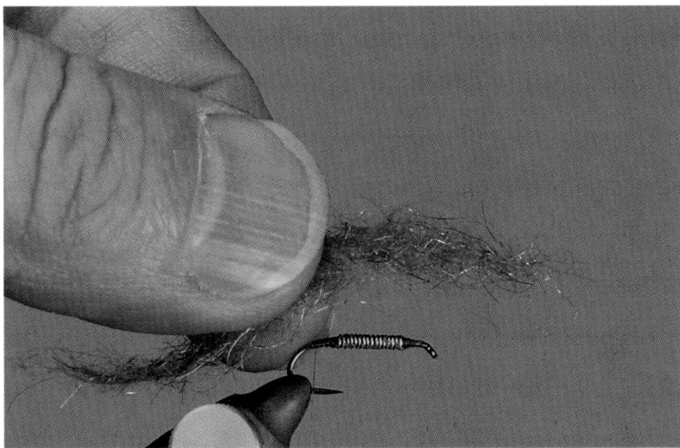

Step 2. Tease a skein of mixed dubbing blend from the package and stretch it into the rough shape you'd like. If you're using fur cut from the hide, with guard hairs, then rough it up in the palm of your hand and tease it into a skein with the proportions you want, usually thin at one end and thicker at the other.

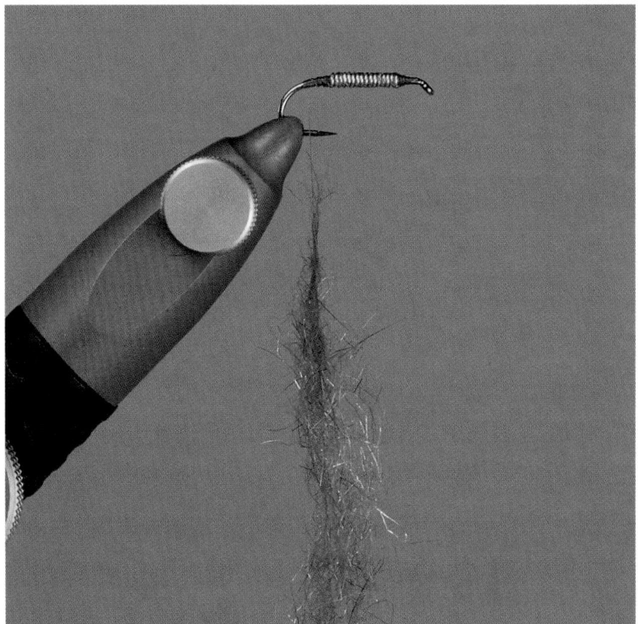

Step 3. Roll the upper and lower tips of the skein slightly to the thread, to tack it in place in case you sneeze before you capture it between two strands of thread. But do not roll it on too tightly, and do not roll any of the rest of the skein onto the thread. You just want to hold it in place for the moment.

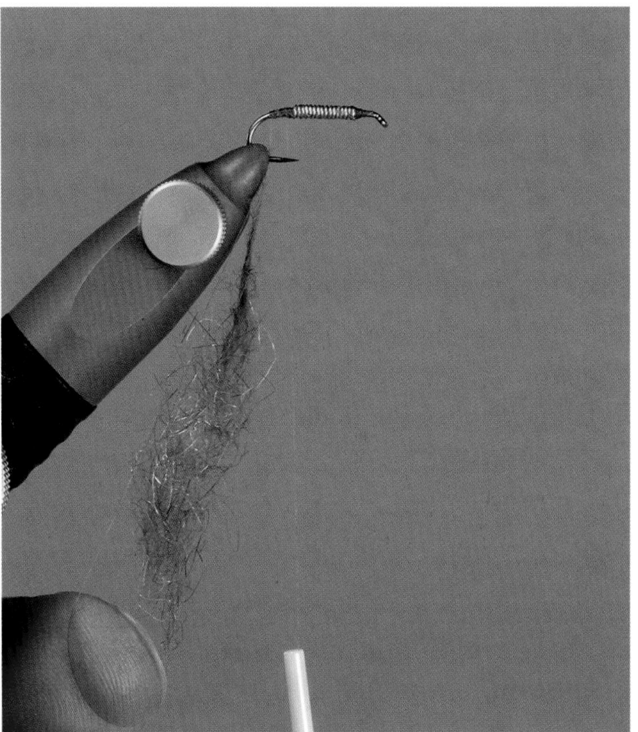

Step 4. Capture the thread over the tip of your off-hand forefinger, just below the skein of dubbing. Roll enough thread off the bobbin to return it to the hook shank. Take three to four turns of thread over the hook shank at or near the same point where the thread departs the shank to hold the dubbing. This forms the dubbing loop.

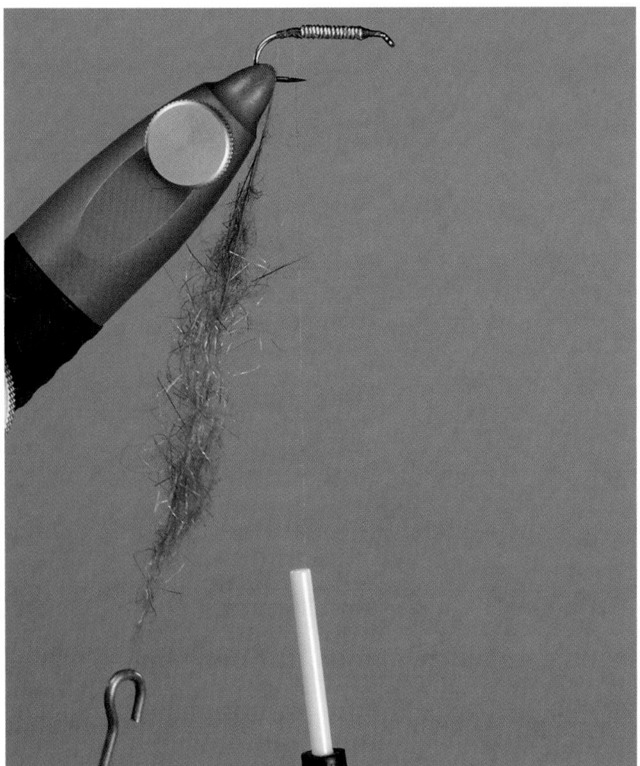

Alternate Step 4. Capture the thread over the end of a dubbing twister tool, and return the thread to the hook shank, being sure to catch the dubbing between the two strands of thread. Take three to four turns of thread around the hook shank to lock in the loop.

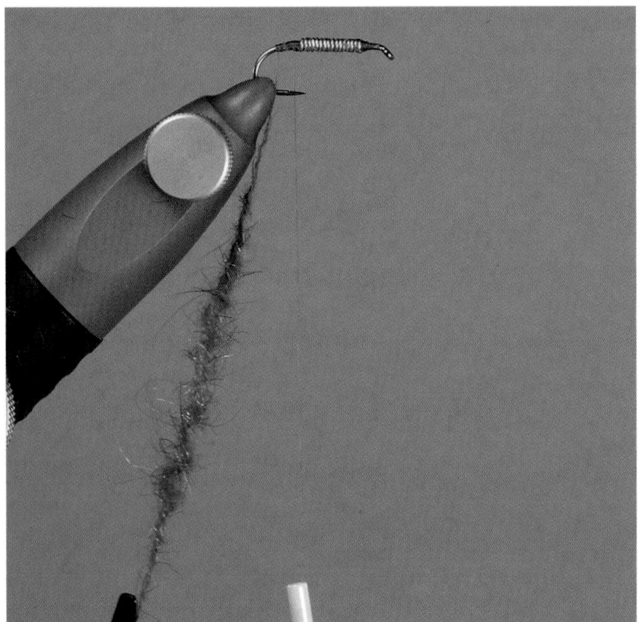

Step 5. Capture the dubbing between the two strands of the loop, and roll the end of the loop between your thumb and forefinger. Adjust the tightness of the finished dubbing loop, and therefore the slenderness or portliness of the finished nymph body, by how tightly you roll the skein of dubbing at this point in the tying. When finished, clip your hackle pliers to the end of the dubbing loop.

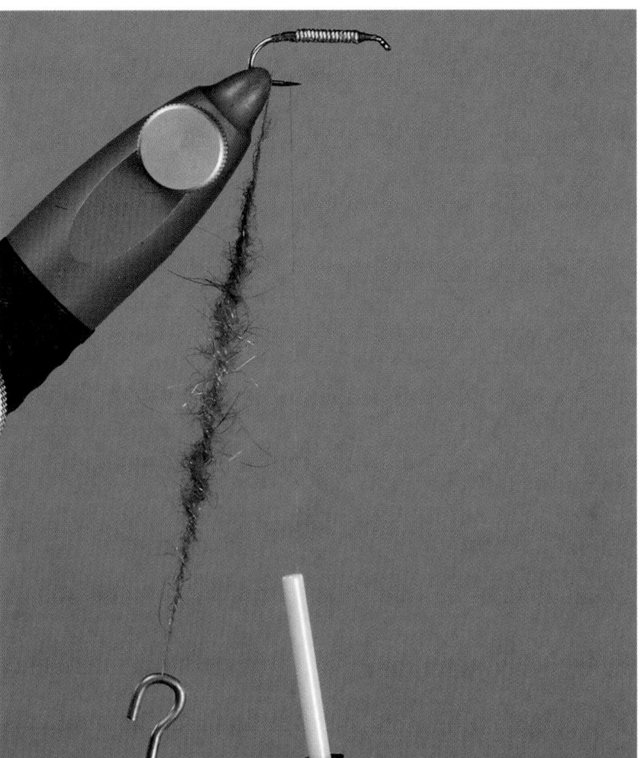

Alternate Step 5. Capture the dubbing between the two thread strands, and use your dubbing twister to tighten the dubbing rope to the slenderness or fatness you want.

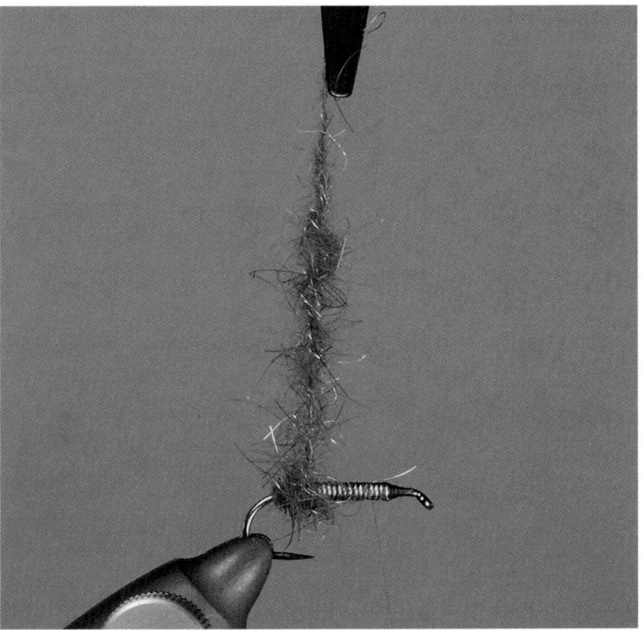

Step 6A. Wind your working thread forward to where you want the dubbing loop tied off. Wind the dubbing loop forward on the hook shank. Because you do not wind the dubbing loop from the thread bobbin as you do with the more simple direct-dubbing method, it is necessary to reposition your off hand on the hackle pliers or the dubbing twister on each wind, because at the end of each wrap around the shank, your off hand is positioned behind the hook shank, and you need to bring it to the near side for the next wrap. To make each wrap, keep the bobbin cradled in your tying hand, with your handy scissors kept there as well, and take your turns around the hook shank with your off-hand forefinger through the hackle pliers, or your off-hand fingers holding the dubbing twister.

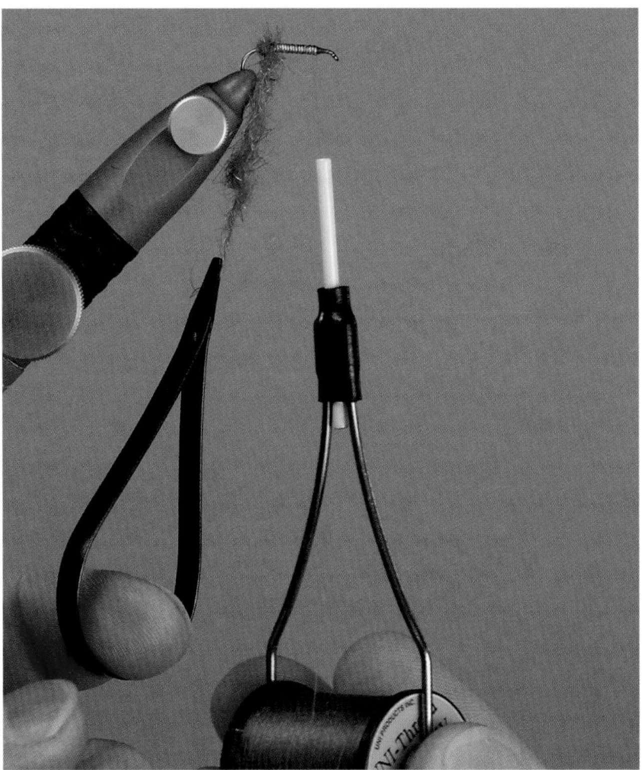

Step 6B. At the bottom of each wind, transfer the hackle pliers or dubbing twister briefly to your tying-hand fingers. Reposition your off hand to the near side of the hook, and either insert your off-hand forefinger through the hackle pliers or regrasp the dubbing twister for the next wrap. This will quickly become so instinctive that you will no longer notice you're doing it.

The finished body, when tied with a dubbing loop, will be anywhere from fairly compact to very loose and fibrous.

FUR NOODLE

You won't find many modern nymphs that call for fur noodles, and I won't dwell on them. They were popularized in Polly Rosborough's *Tying and Fishing the Fuzzy Nymphs.* His noodling method is the source for the dubbing loop. Polly used natural and dyed furs, and he mixed them in proportions that gave him the colors and textures he wanted for his proprietary patterns. Once he had what he wanted, he sheared full skins and made up a big batch, then stored it in one of those shoe boxes that stood on the shelf above his rolltop desk, or in his closet.

A body tied with a fur noodle, such as this Muskrat Nymph, or with a tightly twisted dubbing loop, will have a segmented appearance, much like the average natural nymph.

Polly's prescription for a fur noodle was to twist it so tight, with a thread loop, that when wound on a hook the result is a segmented body. He also called for roughing the body with a hacksaw blade—hence his *fuzzy nymphs*—after finishing the fly. You can accomplish the same thing by using somewhat soft fur, and twisting it into a compact dubbing rope. When it is wound, it will reveal segmentation in the finished body, and have the fibrous effect you want.

When tying a fur noodle, you need to retighten the dubbing rope after every turn or two of the dubbing around the hook shank, because each turn untwists it a bit, loosening it. Do this simply by taking a few turns of the hackle pliers, or the dubbing twister, as you wind the body forward.

FUR HACKLE

A fur hackle is an extension of a very loose dubbing rope, but it is a bit more difficult to achieve. It can be tied with nearly any natural fur that combines underfur with guard hairs. The length of the fur dictates the size fur hackle you can tie with it. Polly Rosborough used muskrat fur hackles on some of his famous flies, but he tied them on size 6 and 8 hooks. I almost always use the fur hackle method with pine squirrel, because the fur is much shorter than muskrat, and I'm able to tie with it through the more normal range of nymphs, sizes 12, 14, and 16. Natural pine squirrel is a good grayish brown color, and can also be bought bleached or dyed olive.

The fur hackle is an old technique, originated in the late 1800s in Great Britain. It still makes a very nice thorax on a nymph, with the underfur representing the muscular core of the natural, and the guard hairs looking much like legs and antennae.

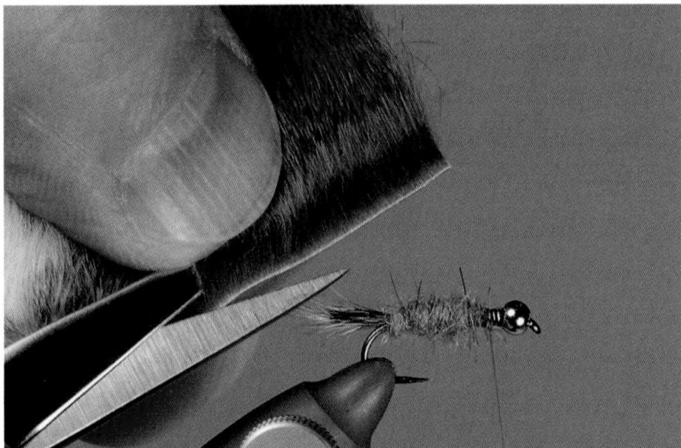

Step 1. Begin with a nymph tied to the point where you're ready for the thorax. In this case I'm tying a favorite searching nymph, a beadhead version of Dave Whitlock's famous Fox Squirrel Nymph. To prepare for tying the fur hackle, wax one to two inches of the thread with a very tacky wax, or apply head cement to the thread with a bodkin. You can cut squirrel fur directly from the whole hide, but using a razor blade to cut out a small square of hide will give you an even *shelf* of fur. Slip your fine-pointed scissors laterally under the fur along this shelf. The resulting snip will give you a thin but wide patch of fur. Hold the tips of the fur under your thumb while you make this snip.

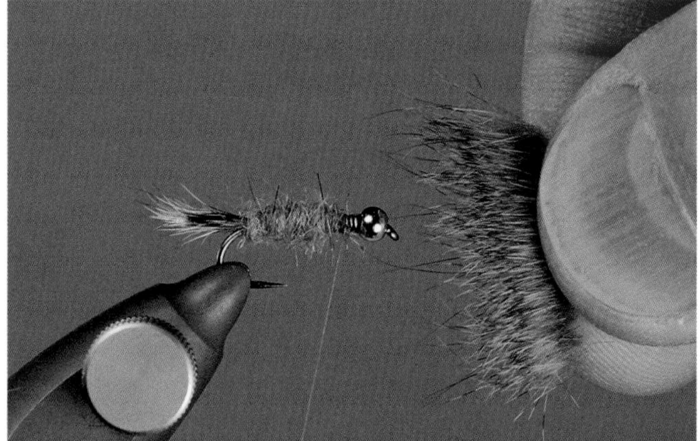

Step 2. Bend the fur piece a bit with your off hand, to lift the fur butts away from the hide. Grip the fur butts between the forefinger and thumb of your tying hand, and lift the fur from the hide. Be sure to keep it spread out and even. If you rough it up at this point, it will not make a successful fur hackle. Any wax on your fingers will be fatal in this stage; if your fingers are not perfectly clean, wipe them on your pant leg before grasping the fur.

Step 3. If the fur is too long for the hook on which you'll tie it, trim the cut ends of the fur to the length you suspect will be about right. Do this by carefully transferring the fur to your off hand, again without roughing it up. Trim the butts, keeping the cut even.

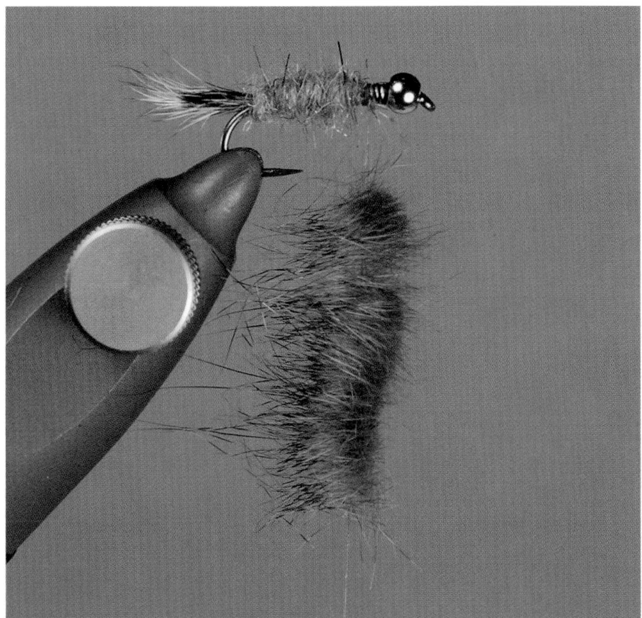

Step 4. Place the fur carefully against the waxed thread. Be sure the thread is at about the middle of the fur, not toward the tips or the butts. If your wax is tacky, the fur will stick to the thread and stay there. But be careful not to thump the thread or *twang* it like a guitar string at this point. If you do, fur will fly.

Step 5. Making every move smoothly, capture the end of the thread over the forefinger tip of your off hand. A dubbing twister does not work for this, though you can buy a special fur hackle tool with springy spread arms that collapse to capture the fur, if you find the need for it. Return the thread to the hook shank, and secure it as you would for a dubbing loop. Take the working thread forward to the whip-finish point, in this case just behind the bead.

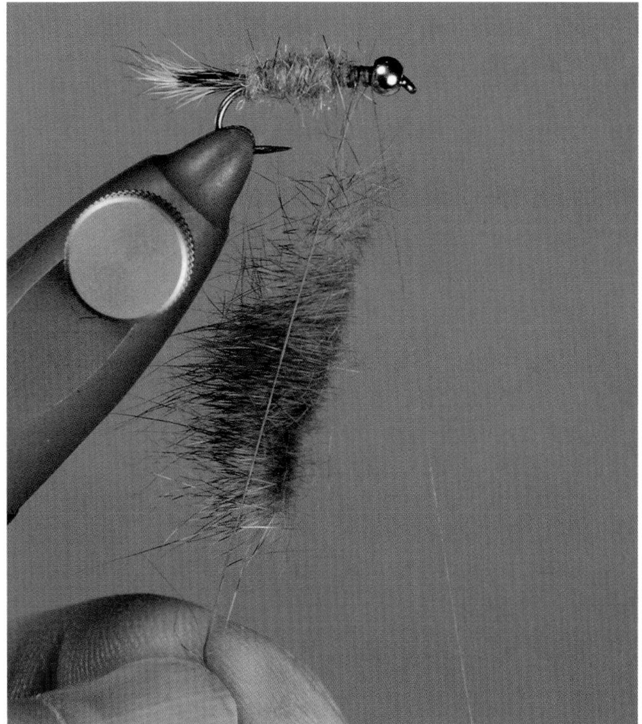

Step 6. Capture the fur between the two strands of thread, and allow the thread loop to collapse onto it. If the fur is not equally distributed at this point, you can spread it slightly within the loop, or tap the butts or tips to move it to the midpoint. But it's best if you leave yourself with no adjustments to make by getting it as right as you can in the first place.

Step 7. Twirl the end of the thread loop in your fingertips. The proper fur hackle will look like a bottle brush at this point, and it is no longer adjustable.

Step 8. Capture the end of the rope in your hackle pliers.

Step 9. Wind one full turn of the fur hackle at the end of the abdomen.

Step 10. Use the forefinger and thumb of your off hand to stroke the first turn of hackle back. If the material is unruly, it will help to wet your fingertips. Take another turn of hackle in front of the first. If enough hackle is left, and some hook space in which to wind it, take a last turn of fur hackle, ending against the back of the bead, or just behind the hook eye if you're tying a nymph without a bead.

Step 11. Stroke the fur hackle out of the way, and place a whip-finish in front of it. Clip the thread. You can tug out stray fibers that don't please you, and prune the fur hackle down to the exact size and shape you desire. The fur and guard hairs are securely locked in, so whatever you leave will not come undone.

TWISTED YARN BODY

Many nymphs call for yarns that are twisted tightly, resulting in segmented bodies. The popular and productive Serendipity series is tied with this method. It's not difficult to master, and one you should be able to execute very quickly. Before beginning, you'll need to adjust the size of your yarn to the hook on which you're tying your nymph. Most yarns are woven of four or more strands. Though the full yarn might be right for a size 10 or 12 fly, if you're going to tie smaller, which most of us do, then you'll need to separate out the yarn strands. Sometimes you'll tie with two or three strands, at other times just one. Since yarns vary in the number and thickness of their strands, you'll have to learn to judge the number of strands you need for the size fly you're tying.

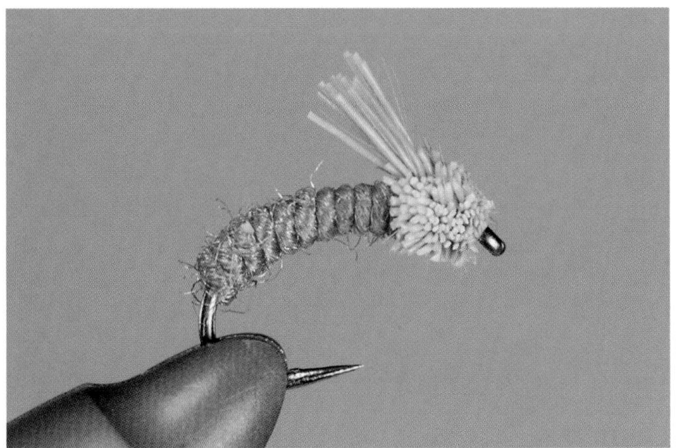

Nymphs such as the popular Serendipity style are tied with twisted-yarn bodies, for the segmented effect desired in the finished fly.

Separating yarn into strands is best done by cutting the length you need, long enough to tie several flies, not just one. Clip a pair of hackle pliers to one end, then separate the strands by pulling them apart at the other end. If you do not attach hackle pliers or otherwise hold the end of the yarn, the strands will tangle, and you'll have to tear them apart.

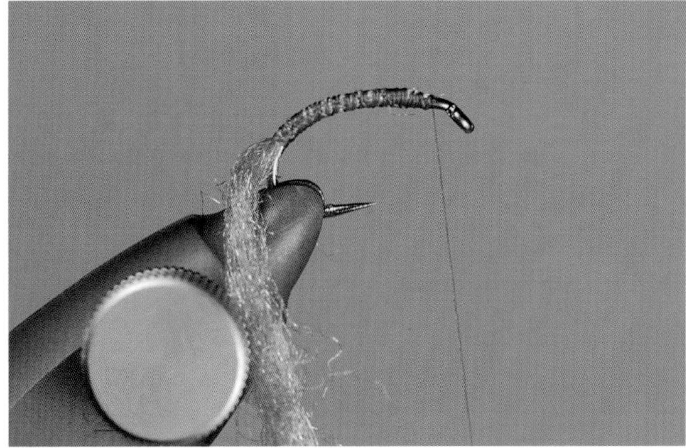

Step 1. Place the hook in the vise and layer it with tying thread. If you're using a curved scud hook, as shown here, layer the thread well down on the bend. Tie the yarn in at the end of the layer of thread, and secure it with thread wraps back to the hook eye, or wherever the body will end. This forms an even underbody for the nymph.

Step 2. Use your fingertips or hackle pliers to twist the yarn tightly, and wrap the body forward. After each wrap, twist the yarn again, or it will loosen up and your body will flatten out. On the last turn, at the tie-off point, let the yarn relax and flatten out, and tie it off on the underside of the shank. This creates a less bulky and more secure tie, without sacrificing any of the segmentation in the body.

KRYSTAL FLASH BODIES

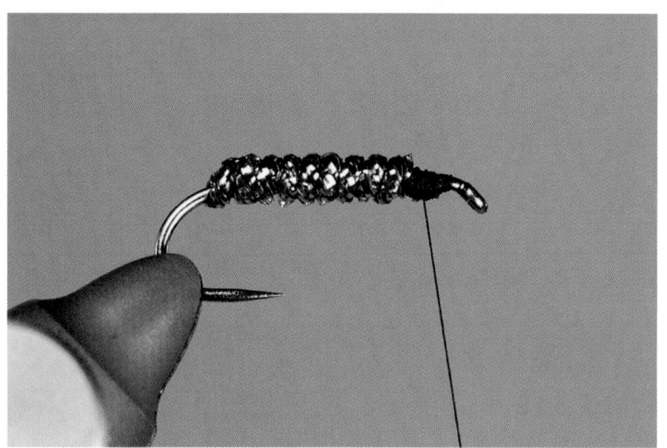

To get a substantial and segmented Krystal Flash body, you need to tie in the strands and twist them.

You can tie a nymph body with Mylar strands, such as Krystal Flash, in the standard fashion, by tying in a few strands at the bend of the hook, wrapping them forward, tying them off. But that body will be slender unless you use an excess of strands, in which case it will be difficult to keep tidy because the strands will splay. Use that method for thin nymphs. For fatter bodies use twisted Krystal Flash. By tying in a substantial number of strands, then twisting them into a body, you get a result that can be thicker or thinner as you choose, depending on how much Krystal Flash you tie in, and how tightly you twist it.

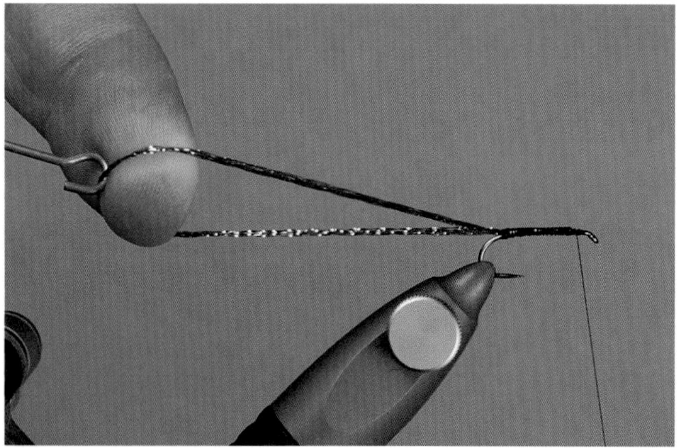

Step 1. Cut from two to ten long strands of Krystal Flash, keeping the ends gathered together. Tie them in at the beginning of the bend of the hook, or wherever you want the body to begin. Use your forefinger tip or a dubbing twister to capture the strands in the center and form a loop (the photo shows both options). Bring the ends of the Krystal Flash back to the tie-in point and lash them forward, along with the butts of the opposite end, to the point where you would like the body to end. Clip the excess at that point.

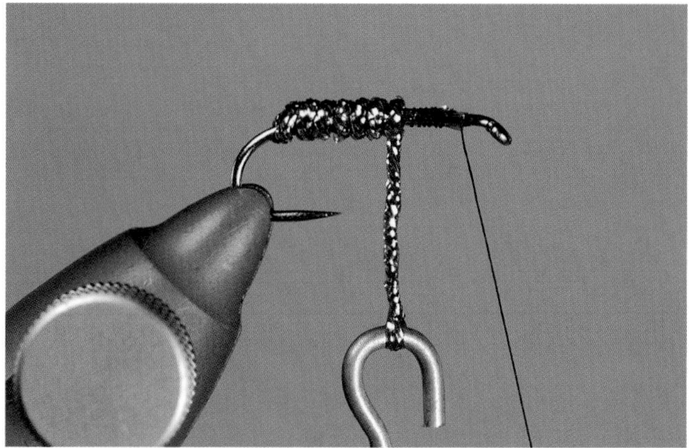

Step 2. Twist the Krystal Flash with your fingers or the dubbing twister, and wind it as the body, continuing to twist it as you take wraps forward. Let the last turn relax before tying it off and clipping the excess.

COUNTERWOUND HERL

FLASHBACK PHEASANT TAIL

Hook: Standard nymph, size 14–22
Thread: Brown 8/0 or 10/0
Tails: 3–4 pheasant tail fibers
Rib: Copper wire, counterwound
Abdomen and legs: 3–4 pheasant tail fibers
Wing case: Pearl Flashabou
Thorax: Peacock herl

When you wind a body of herl, whether pheasant, peacock, ostrich, or marabou, the stems will be fragile, and the body needs to be protected against the teeth of trout. One of the oldest and surest methods to accomplish this is to counterwind wire over the body. The famous Pheasant Tail Nymph, and its derivative Pheasant Tail Flashback, are tied with pheasant tail fibers counterwound with copper wire.

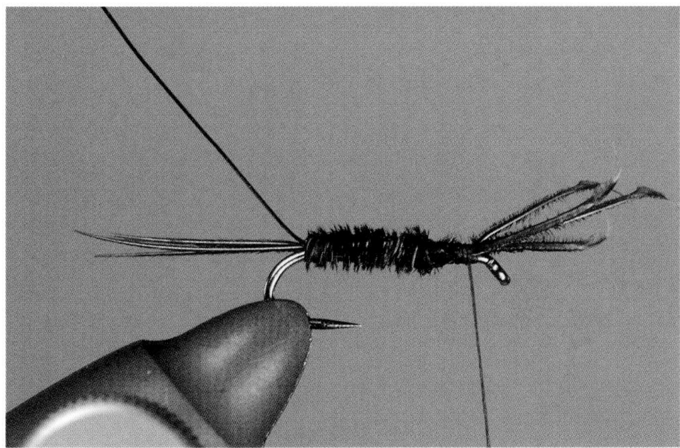

Step 1. Tie in the tail of your nymph, wrapping the butts of the tail material to a point just behind the hook eye, to make an even underbody. Tie in your ribbing wire at that point, and secure it the length of the shank, ending with it on the far side of the hook shank and even with the base of the tail. Tie in the body herls and wrap them forward. Clip the excess, or in the case of some versions of the Pheasant Tail, leave the butts of the body herls to become the thorax or legs of the finished fly.

Step 2. Wind the ribbing wire in evenly spaced turns over the body herl, in the opposite direction from which the herl was wound on the hook shank. This locks it in. If a large trout with sharp teeth through some unfortunate circumstance gets an opportunity to chew on your nymph, it might bite through the herl, but only a short portion will come undone.

HERL ROPE

If a herl dressing does not call for a counterwound rib, then you need to secure the herl by winding it together with the tying thread. You can do this in one of two ways. The first, and seemingly simplest, is to twist the herl with the single strand of the working thread: tie in the herl, twist it together with your thread, wind the body forward. You should try it this way, and might prefer it. I find it more difficult to get the herls twirled around the thread. When you use the length you want for the body, there will be herl left over, still wound around the thread. It's necessary to untangle this remainder from the working thread, which I sometimes find difficult.

The second method to secure herl, seemingly more complicated, is to form the same sort of thread loop you did in making a dubbing loop: tie in the herl, make a loop, twirl the herl with the thread, wind the body forward, clip the excess. I prefer this method because I use so many thread loops for both dubbing and herl that the process is less awkward than twisting the herl with the thread without the loop. Using a loop does not slow me down, and I feel it results in a more secure herl body.

Peacock herl is annoyingly slippery. If you cut two or three herls from the eye, tie them in, catch them together with your thread, and try to twist them with your forefinger and thumb tips, you'll get little traction. The balls of your forefinger and thumb will slide over the herl instead of twisting it. Always peel the herls from the stem, rather than cutting it, leaving tiny curled ends. When you twist the rope, get your grip over those rough ends, not the herl itself.

When you make a peacock herl rope, shown here combined with a few strands of Krystal Flash the same color as the herl, be sure to use herl that has been peeled, not cut, from the eye feather. Note the rough curled ends of the herls in this photo; without these, the slippery herl is very difficult to twist into a rope.

Another alternative, effective for nymph bodies, is to tie in two to four strands of Krystal Flash to make the herl rope: tie in the herl and Krystal Flash together, twirl them, wind them forward, clip the excess. This secures the fragile herl, and also adds a bit of flash to the finished nymph. The following steps show how to tie a standard herl rope.

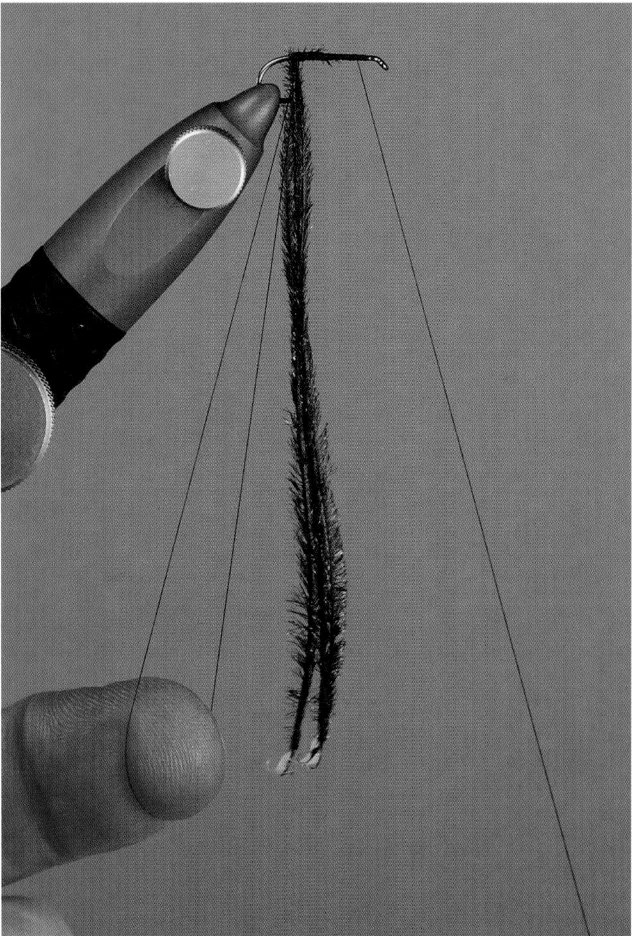

Step 1. Peel two to four peacock herl fibers from the eye feather—do not cut them from it. Break off and discard about an inch of the herl tips; they're too weak, and will break if you use them in a herl rope. Tie the herls in by their tips. Make the last turns of thread at the back soft; turns of normal tightness will often cut through the herl stems, or the weakened herl will break as soon as you twist it to make the rope. Double the thread over your off-hand fingertip, return the thread to the shank, and secure it with three to four turns of thread. Be sure the thread loop is at least as long as the herls.

Step 2. Remove your forefinger tip from the loop and let it collapse—no need here to capture the herls inside the loop. Grasp the herls at the ends, where they have been pulled from the stem, between the ball of your forefinger and thumb. Twist the herls and thread together just until the herl fibers near the shank have made a rope; do not overtwist it or the herls will break at the tie-in point. (If you find the herl too slippery, capture the thread and ends of the herl together, attach your hackle pliers, and twist the herl rope with the pliers.)

Step 3. Clip your hackle pliers to the end of the herl rope. Take your thread forward to the tie-off point. As you wind the herl rope forward, twist it a few turns after each wrap or two around the hook shank, to keep it wound tight and fluffed up.

Step 4. Tie the rope off at the point where you want the body to end, and clip the excess. If enough is left to tie another fly, clamp the herl and thread together in your hackle pliers, and save it.

TYING ORDER

Materials in a dressing are listed in the order they're to be tied on the hook, in this book. It would seem logical to list materials from stern to stem of a fly. That's the way it's often done: the pattern lists the hook style and size, the thread size and color, then begins at the tail and lists things as things go forward—the abdomen, thorax, shellback, legs, and finally head, which might be a bead. If the pattern is described that way, and you wait until you get to the head to put the bead on the hook, you're in for an adventure. If a nymph calls for a bead, you need to put it on the hook before you even put the hook in the vise. If it calls for a thorax with a hackle wound over it to represent the legs of a natural, and a shellback to be drawn over the thorax and legs to represent the wing case of the natural, then the shellback must be tied in first, the hackle second, and the thorax last, not first.

Learn to read patterns carefully, and parse out the order in which materials must be tied to the hook, before you begin tying. Then place all that you need to tie the fly, both tools and materials, within easy reach. If you're tying a half dozen or full dozen of a fly that calls for a wire rib, spool off several inches of the wire, enough to rib the lot, or half of the lot, so that you don't need to clip and discard the excess wire after ribbing each fly, then cut and tie in a new piece of ribbing.

If you're going to tie a dozen nymphs on hooks that need to be debarbed and then beaded, count out the dozen hooks, pinch their barbs, and slip a bead around the shank of each as you're handling it to debarb it. Do the dozen all at once, and set them on the vise pedestal or very near it. Set the furs and feathers and etceteras that are called for in the pattern to your tying-hand side, out of their packages. Take out a wad of dubbing, enough for all the nymphs you'll be tying, and put it in a slide film lid or dish that is deep enough that the dubbing won't blow away if you sneeze, but convenient enough that you don't need to dig into a Ziploc baggie to get what you need for each separate fly.

Certain steps in tying should be left until you've completed the set of flies on which you're working. If you're tying a dozen Copper Johns, then it would waste a fortune of time and glue if you were to mix a drop of five-minute epoxy for the shellback each time you finished tying a nymph. Tie the dozen and line them up in Styrofoam. Mix enough epoxy for the dozen, and dot the shellbacks all at once.

CHAPTER 9

The Rock

Quite a few years ago, in what I thought was going to be an idle experiment, I tied sixteen nymphs and glued them in rows to a flat, white river rock. My bright idea was to tie a fly with every shade of olive I could find, take them to a favorite riffle on my home Deschutes River, dunk them in water, then collect a bunch of naturals, toss them in with the imitations, see what color looked most like the naturals.

I knew that riffle was full of net-spinning caddis larvae, green rock worms in the common tongue, *Cheumatopsyche,* or little sister sedges, for readers of Gary LaFontaine's fine book *Caddisflies.* I also knew that trout in the riffle got most of their calories from precisely those insects. They often get cut loose from their moorings by the brisk current. They also get restless on account of overcrowding, and cut themselves loose, to join the biotic drift that is so

My favorite wife fishing my favorite riffle on my home Deschutes River, where I put the first rock experiment into play. The river bottom under that big water is crawling with free-living and net-spinning caddis larvae: green rock worms.

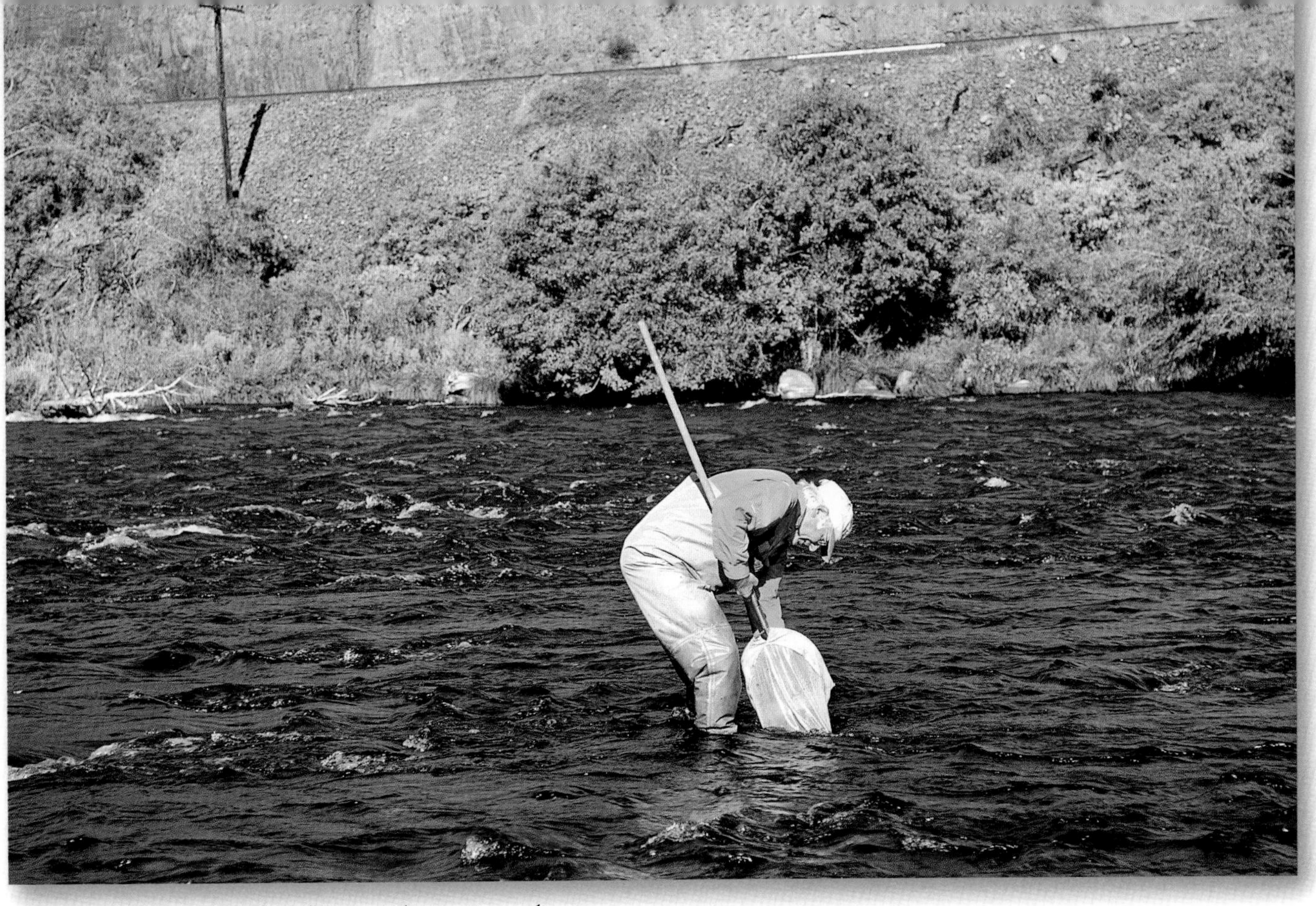

Here I am collecting samples of green rock worms to release on the submerged rock with its sixteen olive nymphs.

favorable to trout. I'd collected in the riffle often; green rock worms were so abundant that a kick-net sample would usually crawl with them.

It turned out I was unable to tie flies with all the olives I could find. That would have taken a boulder so big I'd not be able to hoist it to the riverside. Instead, I tied with a few shades of olive-dyed rabbit fur, some of Krystal Flash, and a few more of Antron, or Sparkle Yarn. Since I was interested in imitations, not pure science, I tied entire flies, complete with beadheads and fur thoracic segments. My next rock will be constructed with pure bodies wound on long-shank hooks of substantial size, so I can get a better look at just the body color. But I got a very good look with the sixteen that I did tie.

I glued the sixteen flies to the rock, lined up in rows, keyed to a template on which I wrote down the type of material and the manufacturer's name for each shade I'd used. Then I drove to the river, placed the rock in a pan, filled the pan with water, and had a gander at the flies before I launched myself into the riffle with my collecting net.

The experiment with the rock was more educational than I'd expected. For the first part, and sadly to me because I've always preferred to tie with natural materials as opposed to synthetics, the furs lost some of their color the instant they got wet. They did not lose it all, and the experiment came far from precluding their use, but I did discover that furs are better for achieving a soft, subtle color than they are for a vibrant, bright one. Synthetics, on the opposite hand, retained their color fairly precisely when they went from being dry to getting wet.

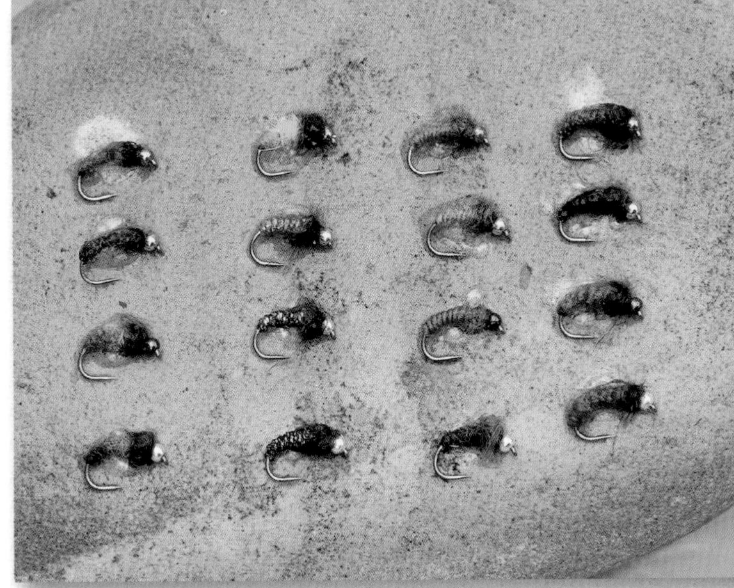

In my original rock experiment, I tied sixteen nymphs with a fairly narrow set of materials—dyed rabbit fur (row 1 and top fly on row 2), Krystal Flash (bottom 3 flies in row 2), and Antron, or Sparkle Yarn (rows 3 and 4). This photo was taken in sunshine, with the bodies damp.

A predaceous Rhyacophila *larva heads toward its imitation, Rick Hafele's Beadhead Green Rock Worm, though probably not with the intention of asking it for a date.*

The riffle, as I expected, was full of olive caddis larvae. I went out to collect, and within minutes I was back on the bank, tweezering green rock worms onto the submerged rock, where they wandered among the imitations that they failed to mistake for friends. Most of what I collected were the little sister sedges. One of what I collected was a free-living caddis larva, a predaceous green rock worm, in the genus *Rhyacophila,* which has dozens of species, including representatives that are dark green to some that are almost fluorescent green. This one was dark.

One of the flies I'd tied and glued to the rock was Rick Hafele's Beadhead Green Rock Worm, an imitation of that precise insect from the Deschutes River. It turned out that Rick's pattern was effective for a set of very good reasons. It was the right color, the right shape, and if a bit small for the one I'd collected, just right for the size of the average of them I collect throughout most of their spring and summer season.

Most of the larvae in the net were the smaller net-spinning little sister sedges, and all were a pale shade of green. I let them crawl among their imitations, and I took a few photos while they did, using natural sunlight rather than the flash on the camera. The colors would likely vary under different kinds of light, and would also vary at different depths. It's my guess that as a set of flies got deeper, where less light strikes through, their colors would tend toward fewer differences, and the beads and Krystal Flashes would be less prone to throwing off reflections. Those speculations might make the basis for some future experiment.

I do suggest that you take my experiment for what it is—speculation—and make up your own rock, go out to your own waters and collect your own insects, come to your own conclusions about what you see. I'll be surprised if it doesn't cause you to make some changes in the materials, or at least the colors of the materials, with which you're tying your favorite nymphs. I had always used a standard green rock worm imitation tied with a medium-olive rabbit fur body. After dunking the rock, I now use one with a Sparkle Yarn body of about the same shade. But it keeps its color, and is the same shade when I fish it as it is when I tie it.

In all honesty, I can't report that my take in that riffle has suddenly jumped up. It's about the same as it has always been, and the number of trout that take the green rock worm imitation, when I fish it as part of a tandem, has remained about the same. If I fish it in size 14 or 16 as a dropper off a much larger salmon-fly nymph, then I catch most of my trout on the smaller fly except during the salmon-fly nymph migration, when trout prefer the bigger bite. When I fish it in size 12 or 14 as the large fly in tandem with a size 16 or 18 generic beadhead, usually the favored Fox Squirrel, then again I often catch more trout on the smaller fly.

Don't think I'm leading you toward a conclusion that size matters but color does not. You'll get into some situations where trout focus on one size and color natural nymph, and while size matters most, color can help you increase your catch. And if the color of your imitation is too far off from the abundant naturals you've collected, the correct size is unlikely to compensate for the mistake, and you're not likely to catch many trout at all.

If making up your own rock, taking it out and dunking it next to your own home water, does nothing more, it will prod you to collect the naturals you're trying to imitate, and encourage you to take a close look at them, in water the way trout see them. You'll notice the way they're shaped, alongside the imitations you've shaped to look like them. And you'll see the way they move, which will inform your presentation when you fish your flies to behave like them. It might seem least that you'll notice their colors, but you'll begin honing the colors of your flies to come closer and closer to them. When all the information you gain from your own rock is added together, it's likely to become very educational, and it's doubtful you're going to catch any fewer fish because you did it.

This experiment with the rock might prompt you to do one more thing, as it has me. I now keep a container filled with water on my tying bench. A shallow dish or glass will do, if all you want to see is the color of a material when it's wet. Simply remove the finished fly from your vise, pitch it into the dish or glass, and you'll see the change at once, know whether that material color works for you, or if you need to go to a drabber or brighter shade of the same material.

A deeper container can tell you more about the finished fly. For example, it's surprising how often I tie a nymph on a heavy-wire hook, with just a few turns of weighting wire, and discover that when I toss it on water it floats rather than sinks. Mostly that means that the nymph has to be wetted before it can be fished subsurface. But you might find that nymphs tied with certain materials either continue to float even when they're wet, or sink much more slowly than you have it in your calculations. If nothing else, keeping a water container that is three to four inches deep on your tying bench will allow you to adjust your thinking about sink rate when you're fishing. Most often, you'll discover the need to adjust the amount of weight you're adding to the hook shank when you tie the nymphs, or the number of split shot you add to the leader when you fish them.

NOTES AND CONCLUSIONS FROM THE FIRST ROCK EXPERIMENT

Naturals are *Cheumatopsyche* sp. and one *Rhyacophila* sp. larva from a Deschutes River riffle. Insects are alive, and light is natural sunlight.

Key:

1	5	9	13
2	6	10	14
3	7	11	15
4	8	12	16

Bead:	Body:	Thorax:
1. Brass.	Light olive rabbit.	Pine squirrel.
2. Gold.	Olive rabbit.	Pine squirrel.
3. Black.	Caddis green rabbit.	Pine squirrel.
4. Silver.	Olive-brown rabbit.	Pine squirrel.
5. Brass.	Hareline Fluor. Lime #05.	Pine squirrel.
6. Gold.	Gold Krystal Flash.	Pine squirrel.
7. Silver.	Pale olive Krystal Flash.	Pine squirrel.
8. Silver.	Dark green Krystal Flash.	Pine squirrel.
9. Brass.	Apple green Sparkle Yarn.	Natural hare's ear.
10. Gold.	Medium green Sparkle Yarn.	Natural hare's ear.
11. Black.	Bright green Sparkle Yarn.	Natural hare's ear.
12. Silver.	Dark green Sparkle Yarn.	Natural hare's ear.
13. Brass.	Antron Sparkle Dub green.	Pine squirrel.
14. Gold.	Antron Sparkle Dub medium olive.	Pine squirrel.
15. Black.	AZ Micro Sheen caddis green.	Pine squirrel.
16. Silver.	AZ Micro Sheen BWO.	Pine squirrel.

Conclusions:

1. Brass bead seems the most natural color. Gold bead gives a sparkle of light.
2. Apple green Sparkle Yarn seems the best match for *Cheumatopsyche* larvae.
3. Dark green Krystal Flash seems the best match for *Rhyacophila*.
4. Pine squirrel back fur has the darkness for the thorax; hare's ear seems to wash out.

CHAPTER 10

Beads and Flash

The use of beadheads and flashy materials such as Krystal Flash and Flashabou, and a dozen others under a wide variety of brand names, is at least mildly controversial. Many experienced anglers believe they have no place on a fly, that they're not *natural* materials, which is true. These are often the same folks who believe that strike indicators should be called bobbers and be restricted to baitfishing. In one sense they're right: beads and flash are not found sprinkled around out in nature. But neither are hooks, and most folks I know who don't like beads and flash don't mind tying their flies on hooks, or even winding them with traditional oval and embossed tinsel ribs, which are also not natural.

The key word is likely *traditional,* and tradition is a very fine criterion on which to base any personal opinion about fly fishing. I taught a fly-tying class at a community college many years ago. A student who worked as a lineman for an electric utility asked me, "Why don't you use electrical clips for hackle pliers? They're cheaper and just as good, maybe better."

I had to think awhile before I answered him. I agreed that they were cheaper and perhaps just as good. Finally I could think of no other reason and said, "Because they're not traditional." That was enough reason for me, and it must still be, because I have electrical clips on my tying bench today, but very rarely reach for them. Clearly the use of beadheads or anything else to add a bit of brightness to a nymph falls into the realm of personal opinion. I have nothing against anybody who is against using these materials. I do have something against anybody who says that I should not use them.

I like having flies with beads and flash in my nymph boxes. I also feel that though beads and flash are not found in nature, they do imitate a few phenomena observed in natural nymphs, and in that sense are, if not natural, imitative of nature and therefore no more pernicious than hooks or those traditional tinsels.

The bit of brightness that beads and flash add does seem to make nymphs tied with them more effective. Rick Hafele's self-published little booklet *Favorite Fly Patterns and How to Fish Them* lists his dozen favorite flies for trout, of which six are nymphs. Rick is the best nymph fisherman with whom I fish. For many years after beads reached our shores from Europe, and began to become popular here, Rick did not get around to using nymphs with beadheads. I don't think he was reluctant to try them out of any sense that they violated tradition. I just think that what he was using was working, and that like most smart fly fishermen, he considered pattern secondary to presentation and wasn't in a hurry to try the new beads. But that was years ago. Out of the six nymphs in his current booklet, five have either beads or some other source of flash. One, his Beadhead Green Rock Worm Nymph, which I wrote about in the last chapter, has both a beadhead *and* a Krystal Flash body.

My own searching-nymph box, the one I bought and began tying into after being humbled so often by Rick, then discovering one day while fishing with Jim Schollmeyer that I didn't see anything in my old nymph boxes that I desired to tie to my tippet, contains nymphs with beads or flash in about the same proportion: four or five out of six have flash of some sort. Many of my favorites, including the Beadhead Fox Squirrel, have small beads. Some, such as the Flashback Pheasant Tail, have subtle single-strand shellbacks. Others, like the popular Copper John, have reflective wire bodies, bright shellbacks, and bright beadheads as well. The Lightning Bug, with its Mylar tinsel body, Mylar shellback, and bright bead, is almost all flash. A row of them in the fly box looks like a beam of light shined across it. Not all of the searching dressings that I use have flash, but when I tie on a tandem of them, to explore the water, it's almost certain that at least one of the two flies will have something bright incorporated into it.

I notice, looking into this searching-nymph box of mine with some embarrassment, that I've tied a tidy row of salmon-fly nymph imitations, the same insect for which Rick and I both use the Montana Stone, and more than half of my own salmon-fly imitations have somehow gotten beads slipped onto them. I'm sure somebody else did that.

The question is not whether flies with beadheads catch more trout, but rather, *why?* I've come across three primary answers to the question in fly-fishing literature, and will add a fourth.

The first reason usually given for the effectiveness of beadhead nymphs is that they sink faster and deeper. Everything else being equal, that would be true: an unweighted nymph with a bead added would sink faster than one without it, and a weighted nymph with a beadhead would sink faster than one lacking the bead. In the latter case, it wouldn't sink much faster. There are other ways, besides adding a bead, to sink a nymph deeper and faster. You can add more weighting wire wraps to the hook shank. You can pinch split shot to the leader near the nymph you're trying to sink at full throttle. You can drop an unweighted or lightly weighted nymph off the hook bend of a depth-charge nymph, and that will get the smaller fly down farther and faster than adding a bead to its head. But given that all else is equal, including the depth at which both nymphs are fished, the nymph with a beadhead will usually outfish the same dressing tied without it.

If a beadhead nymph outfishes the same fly tied without the bead, at the same depth, it's not likely to be because the bead causes it to sink faster and therefore fish deeper.

The second reason commonly given for the effectiveness of beadhead nymphs, which can be applied just as well to those tied with flash added in any other way, is that the wink of reflected light catches the attention of trout busy feeding on the drift. They notice the nymph because of that wink, drive over to inspect it more closely, find it acceptable as food, open their mouths and take it. I find this reasoning very reasonable, and would have no trouble accepting it as the sole reason for the added effectiveness of flies with flash, if I didn't think there was another, perhaps larger, reason. I suspect that this factor—attracting the attention of feeding trout—accounts for a high proportion, though likely not all, of the benefits given by winks of reflected light.

The six nymphs in Rick Hafele's booklet Favorite Fly Patterns and How to Fish Them *are the Peacock Herl Nymph with a Krystal Flash shellback, Beadhead Green Rock Worm Nymph, Krystal Flash Blue-Winged Olive Nymph, Beadhead Pale Morning Dun Nymph, Midge Pupa with a Krystal Flash body, and Charles Brooks's Montana Stone, the only one without a bead or some flash added.*

A third reason, argued by the late Gary LaFontaine, and supported by experiments that he made by skin diving and watching trout as they fed, is that the jigging action given to a nymph by a bead on its head triggers trout to take a beadhead nymph. I have no reason to think this would not be true, and I've done no diving of my own to either confirm it or refute it. I have spent

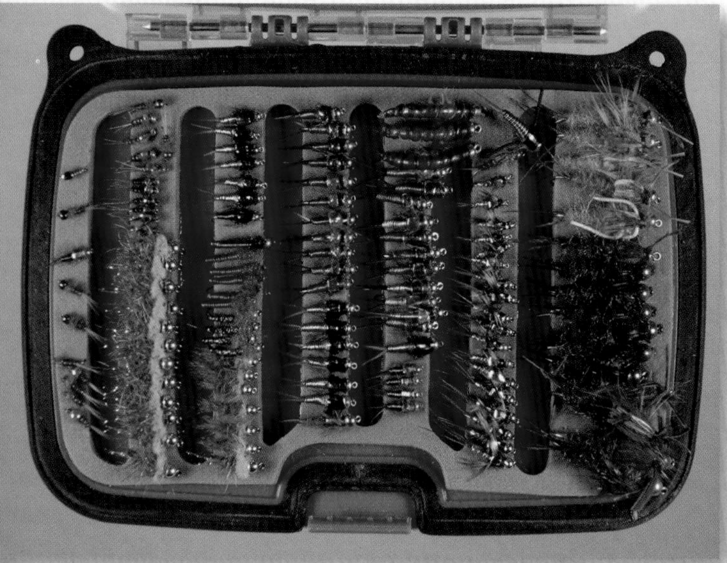

Many of my favorite nymphs incorporate bits of flash in one way or another: the Beadhead Fox Squirrel, Flashback Pheasant Tail, Copper John, and Lightning Bug are examples. The overall brightness of the resulting fly box is a bit embarrassing.

more time than I should watching the movements of aquatic insects, and can think of one or two types that might make jigging motions when they swim. For example, water boatmen swim to the surface, grab a bubble of air, dive back toward the vegetation. They're found in lakes, but only along the still edges and in the very slowest vegetated flows in moving water. Damselflies might be another example. When they see or sense that a trout is after them, they dive.

I've not observed it myself, but it would be easy to guess that when any of the swimmer mayfly nymphs, among them the abundant moving-water *Baetis* and stillwater *Callibaetis,* see a trout on their tails, they might dive toward the nearest shelter. That might be imitated by a jigging action. It would also be a speculation that I'm hesitant to ascribe as a motive to a trout for taking a beadhead nymph. But I'll accept Gary's findings, whether I'm able to confirm them or not.

I do believe that a wink of reflected light is imitative for a lot of subsurface insects that trout feed upon out in unruly nature. I construct my own reasoning for the success of beadhead nymphs around things that I see in natural nymphs. For example, I've noticed that natural nymphs and pupae in my aquariums, getting ready for emergence, sometimes turn a shiny, brassy color. I suspect it is due to gases exuded between the outer skin of the nymph or pupa, which is about to be cast, and the inner skin of the adult, which is about to be exposed. I don't know why the result is a brassy brightness, not related to the color of either the immature or the dawning adult, but I do know that a nymph tied with a bead or a reflective body, especially if it's a brass color, is often a more exact imitation than a nymph tied without that flash.

It is common scientific knowledge that many mayfly nymphs and most caddis pupae exude gases into the space between the exoskeleton that is about to be shed and the skin of the adult inside it. These gases serve two purposes: first, to float the immature from the bottom, where pupation takes place, to the surface, where emergence can take place; and second, to separate the old skin from the new, so the adult can escape from the nymphal or pupal exoskeleton more quickly, without becoming stuck in it. If emergence were to be delayed, trout would have a prolonged period to feed. If more than a few adults got their legs, tails, or wings trapped and were unable to free them, the result would be more frequent fishing over trout feeding on cripples.

This midge pupa is an example of an insect taking on quite a bit of shine when it is just about to emerge.

This fast-water cased caddis larva has bits of bright sand incorporated into its case. It is an excellent model for the Brassie nymph, or any nymph with a beadhead or reflective body.

BRASSIE
Gene Lynch, Ken Chandler, and Tug Davenport

Hook: Standard nymph, size 12–18
Thread: Black 6/0 or 8/0
Body: Copper wire
Thorax: Peacock herl

Many cased caddis larvae make their cases out of bits of sand, or embed sand into their pebble cases. Sometimes these flecks are mica, quartz, perhaps even flakes of gold: all bright colors and many that are reflective. A bead or a bright body makes a more imitative nymph than a drab one. It's no accident that these types of caddis are most prevalent in fast water, and that the Brassie was first tied and fished in bounding Colorado streams where they're abundant.

A common thread runs through these examples: a bit of flash on a nymph, whether a natural or an imitation, equates to something alive and nutritious if you're a trout. It's just a theory, to add to the others, but it leads me to think that beadheads, wire bodies, flashbacks, epoxied wing cases, and other types of brightness are more natural than they are the opposite. Perhaps today's beadheads and Krystal Flash and Pearlescent Flashabou are yesterday's tinsel ribbing, and are added to a fly for the same reason: to add a sparkle of light, a bit of flash, to attract trout.

I'll end this chapter about brightness by repeating one darkening warning: trout on heavily fished waters are beginning to become shy about bright. You will need to do some experimenting of your own, on your home waters, which you know better than anybody else. If your trout are often pestered, you might get well ahead of the curve by being a contrarian: head your flies with black tungsten beads while everybody else is brightening theirs with gold beads, and you might surprise some trout that are beginning to be bashful about brightness.

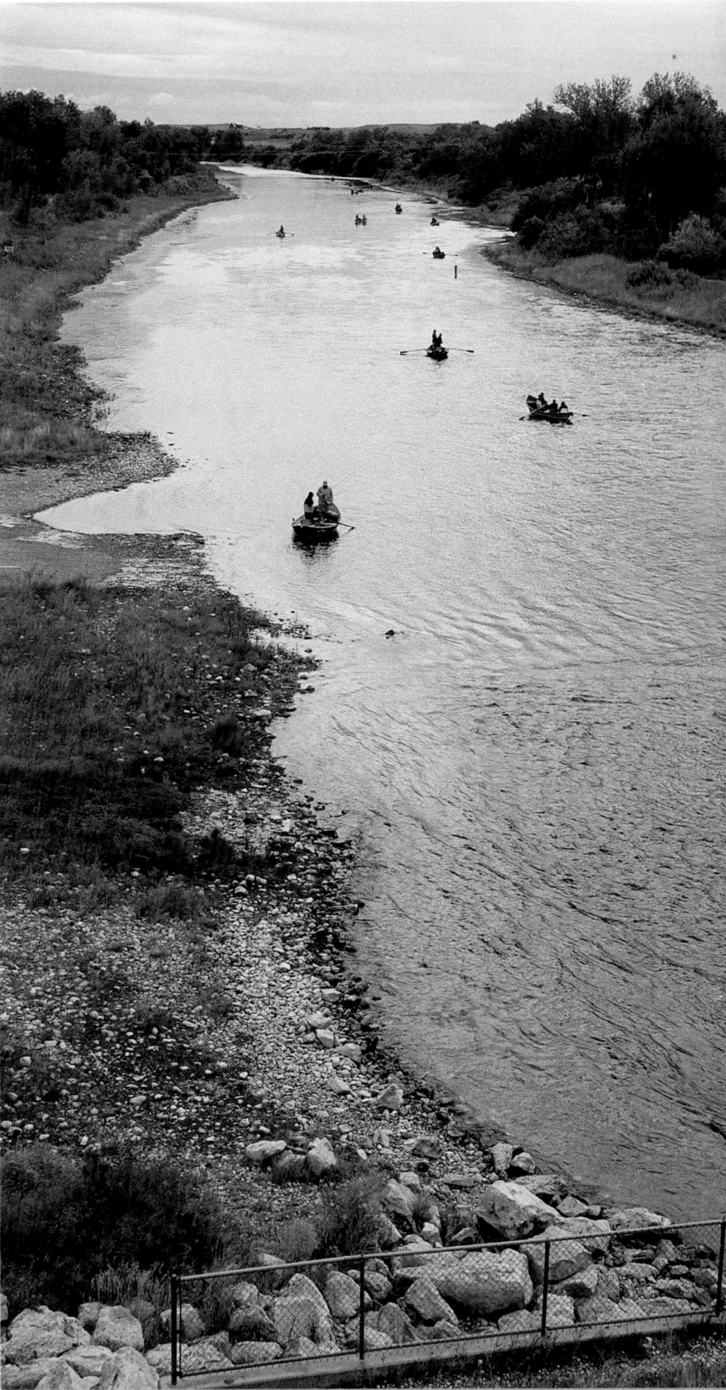

On such heavily fished waters as the Bighorn River in Montana, trout are showing early signs of being bashful about bright nymphs tied with gold beads. If your home waters fall in this category, you might consider tying your nymphs with black tungsten beads.

PART 2

Searching Nymphs for Moving Water

CHAPTER 11

Fur Nymphs

I mentioned in Chapter 2 that most effective searching nymphs are based on the shape of a common trout food form such as a mayfly nymph or caddis larva. When you select a set of searching nymphs to fill a fly box, to prepare yourself to fish for trout in the widest array of possible trout stream situations, it's wise to choose patterns that cover the basic shapes of the things trout eat most often. Your searching nymphs should also cover the most common size range, and a narrow set of colors that are repeated most often in naturals.

When I began fishing nymphs, long before I began studying the aquatic insects on which most of them were at least loosely based, the average fly in my nymph box was a size 10 or 12. When I explored water I'd never fished before, or fished known waters with unknown nymphs for the first time, I wanted to show trout a fly that I knew they'd be able to notice. I had no concept that they might see a nymph and refuse it because it didn't look like anything they'd eaten recently. I assumed that if a trout saw a nymph adrift in the currents, the trout would automatically assume it was something good to eat, and go get it. The key criterion, in my early estimation, was visibility, and that was solved with size.

Collecting insects, and also taking an occasional stomach sample from a mortally wounded trout, or a throat pump sample from one caught and about to be released, quickly educated me about the average-size naturals that trout see and eat. They're about size 16, and my nymph boxes reflect that now, though not precisely, because I live in salmon-fly and golden stone country, and the big imitations for those skew averages. The larger nymphs, and even medium-sized ones, are also very useful as delivery systems in two-nymph tandems to get the more effective small nymphs down to the bottom where they work best.

The most common colors that natural nymphs and larvae assume are those of the background colors against which they live. These are typically dark and drab rock bottoms, hence the weight of effective searching nymphs tied for moving water toward blacks, browns, and grays. But trout also feed opportunistically on many small caddis larvae that redistribute their populations by abandoning their cases and floating naked, if you will, in the biotic drift. Many of these are creamish white, and you will do well to let your searching-fly boxes represent this color with at least an occasional searching nymph.

Many natural aquatic insects take on the color of vegetation for their camouflage, ending up some shade of olive. Most of these live in stillwaters, where green is average for the immature stages of the aquatic insects. But creek, stream, and river forms arrive in the same olive to green shades wherever you find rooted vegetation. Since plant habitats in moving water are found most often in spring creeks and tailwaters, you need olive versions of your searching nymphs if you fish those two types of water with any regularity. Aquatic insects in freestone environments will often be olive or green in their immature stages, and that color becomes quite common as soon as they emerge. It's likely that nature knows the winged stage is headed for the protection of streamside vegetation as soon as it emerges.

A searching nymph with a somewhat slender abdomen and enlarged thorax looks like more than one type of aquatic insect. If you discount their peripheral parts, many mayfly and small stonefly nymphs are very difficult to tell apart. The most common taxonomic error, among anglers and entomologists just beginning to look at the aquatic insects, is the confusion of crawler mayfly nymphs with immature stonefly nymphs. Perhaps we can forgive the trout if they mistake a slender searching nymph for one or the other, and in the end take it for both. Trout don't sit in on many entomology workshops, and are not very adept at looking through microscopes.

Though an entomologist and even practiced amateur can tell at a glance that this is a mayfly nymph, trout, with their lack of ability to distinguish gill structures and count tails, often misidentify naturals, or they would never take our imitations.

In their small and early stages, stonefly nymphs can be difficult for anglers to distinguish from mayfly nymphs. Trout have that same difficulty, and will take the same searching nymph for either one.

Your searching-nymph box should contain dressings that look at least a little like free-living caddis larvae, because the naturals are often so abundant that even in a searching situation, you need to at least approximate them.

Your searching-nymph box will be more effective, even with fewer flies, if it covers the larger distinctions rather than the smaller ones. Caddis larvae, for example, are the most common insects in the drift in many large and brisk riffles, and also in almost any top-release tailwater, where plankton feeds net-spinning caddis larvae and prompts them into growing in great abundance. A few patterns that roughly approximate them will add to your catch, or put more precisely, add to the number of searching situations you can successfully cover, and thereby catch more trout.

MIDGE NYMPHS

I've often caught trout on nymphs as simple as a few twists of the right colored fur dubbing on a hook, usually when I'm fishing over trout that are busy feeding on a tiny aquatic insect or crustacean. All insects and crustaceans begin life tiny and spend a large part of their life that way. It's probable that more than half of those that escape the egg fail to escape the trout, and end their lives while still less than half the size they would attain at maturity.

The last instance I can recall in which I approximated a natural with a simple ball of dubbing on a hook took place on a weedy desert tailwater that was used primarily for irrigation, got shut down in late fall, became good for fishing when its water dropped and cleared. Its long and deep pools almost became ponds. Mats of vegetation took root, with deep channels through the weeds where the minor current threaded its way. Vast numbers of water boatmen thrived in the vegetation, but all were small, around size 20. The same vegetation held a myriad of scuds, again most of them small, size 16 at largest. All depended on camouflage for cover. In that vegetation, all were olive.

Trout cruised in the channels, occasionally nosed into the vegetation, obviously frightening up water boatmen and scuds, chasing them down and eating them whenever they strayed into more open water. I tried a number of both searching and imitative dressings, but none that I owned were olive and small enough. The closest I had on me were peacock-bodied Zug Bugs in size 14. Some trout made the mistake of accepting them, but most turned away from them.

That evening after dinner I lit the lantern, opened a portable fly-tying kit in the tent, and because of the poor light and cold fingers, came up with the simplest solution I thought might work. I wound about five turns of weighting wire on a size 20 hook, and took two or three turns of loose olive fur dubbing over it. That was it. I tied half a dozen before my fingers seized up and I could tie no more.

On weedy tailwaters, when irrigation is over and flows are lowered, trout move into pools and feed on a variety of small scuds and water boatmen, among other insects and crustaceans.

When trout nose into vegetation to frighten out such food forms as these small scuds, a simple searching nymph about the same color as the vegetation will always be a good choice.

I waited the next morning until the sun climbed above that desert canyon, warmed the water a bit, and perhaps more important, struck down through it, lighting the channels in the vegetation. At midmorning I began to notice the occasional flash of a turning flank, indicating that trout were cruising and hunting again. I took a position at the downstream end of a thirty-foot-long channel between banks of vegetation, then rigged with three feet of 6X tippet and one of those rough nymphs I'd tied in the tent. I began working my way upstream, casting the nymph just as if it were a dry fly. It would *plip* through the surface film and begin to tug that fine tippet slowly down behind it. Sometimes I could see the turn of a take, because the fly fished so near the surface, but more often I'd be forced to watch for any twitch taken by the line tip.

The results were far from devastating to the trout population. But the difference in my take was sufficient to ensure that I'm always armed with something at least similar to that simple olive nymph.

The origins of Midge Nymphs are found in Ed Koch's wonderful book *Fishing the Midge.* He originally called them Sim-fectives: simple to tie and effective when fished. He tied them without weight or wire ribs, and fished them most often on spring creeks in the Carlisle, Pennsylvania, area. Koch considered them to have a general resemblance to small mayfly nymphs such as *Baetis* and *Caenis,* and tied them in sizes 16 to 28, in three colors: gray with muskrat fur, brown with weasel fur, and cream with fur from the belly of a red fox. Perhaps most interesting, he wrote of an instance in which he used a size 18 Shenk's Special, originated by Ed Shenk: "This little creation is no more than a body of dubbed weasel fur ribbed with extra-fine gold wire . . . a tailless, wingless, thoraxless little nymphet." Koch's three color variations of the Midge Nymph are all as simple as those I tied by lantern light in the tent, though he didn't call for one in olive.

My own version of the Midge Nymph is closer to Shenk's than to Koch's, on account of the wire rib, but I use thick copper wire, the same diameter as that used for Brassies in sizes 14 and 16, and consider it important more for the added weight than for any added lifelikeness. But it does give off winks of light, and we do use beads and flashbacks to achieve that very thing, so it's possible the copper rib adds some trout to the catch. The most important thing, when you tie so tiny and with fur, is to add enough weight on the body or in a rib to propel the nymph through the surface film.

MIDGE NYMPH, OLIVE

Hook: Curved scud, size 14–24
Weight: 5–6 turns lead-free wire
Thread: Olive 8/0 or 10/0
Rib: Copper wire
Body: Olive-dyed rabbit or squirrel fur

To ensure that my olive retains some of that desired color when the fly is wet, I often use what many materials manufacturers label as Caddis Green, especially when I'm using dyed furs rather than synthetics.

MIDGE NYMPH, GRAY

Hook: Curved scud, size 14–24
Weight: 5–6 turns lead-free wire
Thread: Black 8/0 or 10/0
Rib: Copper wire
Body: Muskrat fur

MIDGE NYMPH, CREAM

Hook: Curved scud, size 14–24
Weight: 5–6 turns lead-free wire
Thread: Tan 8/0 or 10/0
Rib: Copper wire
Body: Cream-dyed rabbit or squirrel fur (You can substitute Light Cahill or use Ed Koch's red fox belly.)

MIDGE NYMPH, TAN

Hook: Curved scud, size 14–24
Weight: 5–6 turns lead-free wire
Thread: Brown 8/0 or 10/0
Rib: Copper wire
Body: Hare's mask fur or blend

MIDGE NYMPH, BLACK

Hook: Curved scud, size 14–24
Weight: 5–6 turns lead-free wire
Thread: Black 8/0 or 10/0
Rib: Copper wire
Body: Black-dyed rabbit fur

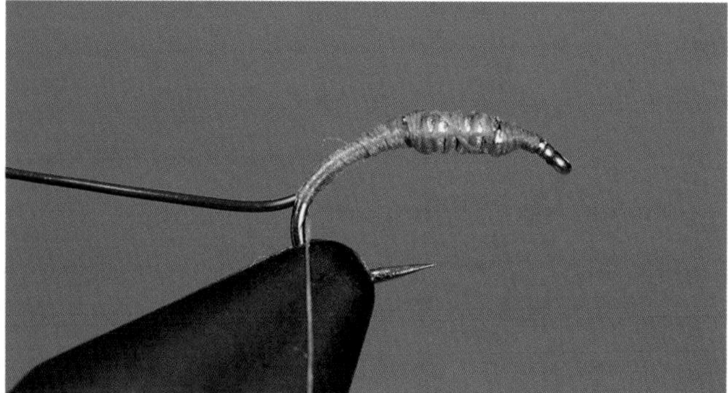

Step 1. Weight the hook with five to six turns of lead-free wire the approximate diameter of the hook-shank wire. It should be slightly forward of the midpoint of the hook, to give the finished fly a stouter thorax. Start the thread and make a thread base, locking in the lead with a thread ramp at the front end, to form an even transition for the fur body. Butt the ribbing wire against the back end of the lead wraps, and secure it to the hook with a layer of thread wraps, continuing down the hook bend to where you want the body to begin.

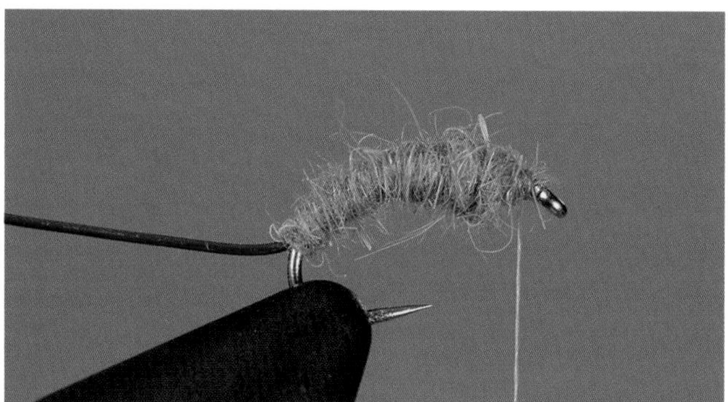

Step 2. Using the direct-dubbing method (see page 49), fix a slender amount of fur dubbing to the thread and wind it forward to the hook eye, to make a fairly tight and compact body.

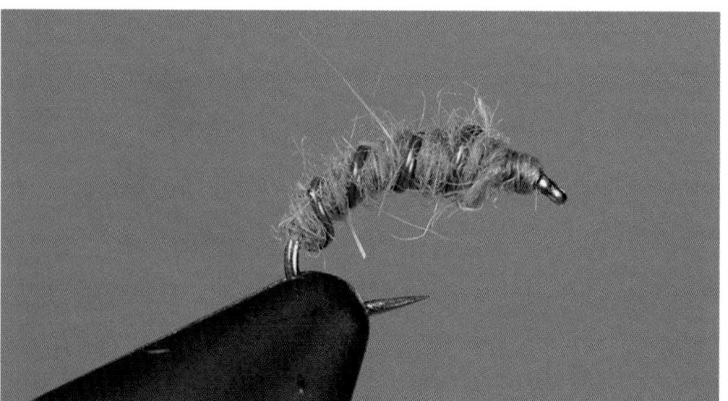

Step 3. Wrap the ribbing wire forward in three to six evenly spaced turns, depending on the size hook on which you're tying. Tie the ribbing wire off and clip the excess. If you don't have scissors for rough work, don't cut the wire with the tips of your fine pair. Instead, bend the wire back and forth until it breaks. Whip-finish and the fly is complete.

A narrow selection of simple Midge Nymphs is an excellent way to arm yourself with searching nymphs that cover the color spectrum of natural nymphs in very small sizes. I recommend you consider carrying at least half a dozen each in size 20. It won't take much time to tie them, and you'll never lack for a tiny fly to tie to your tippet, either alone or as a point fly, in a situation that demands something small.

ALL-FUR NYMPHS

One of the first books I bought in my early curiosity about the history of fly-tying was *All-Fur Flies and How to Dress Them,* by the British author W. H. Lawrie. A large part of the book was devoted to saving money by substituting furs for exotic feathers in fancy Atlantic salmon flies. That part didn't interest me because I live near the Pacific, and I nearly set the book aside, but noticed a section on wet flies, and in it the description of a method for tying fur hackles. (I described that method on page 54).

Lawrie credits the fur-hackle concept to Captain George Marryatt, in the mid-1800s, with interpretations of how to execute it based on turn-of-the-century notes from G. E. M. Skues and Frederick Halford. Both methods called for creating the fur hackle separately from tying the fly, and incorporating it into the fly as the pattern is tied, much as one might pluck a hackle from a neck, tie it in by the stem, and wind it.

Because I lack the sort of focus required to form a hackle one day and tie the fly the next, I create the fur hackle on a thread loop in the process of tying a fly. It is quicker, simpler, allows tailoring the size of the fur hackle to the size hook on which it will be wound, and doesn't test my attention span. An occasional hackle, however, will blow up when you slip while trying to capture the fur in the thread loop.

I originally tied a narrow size and color range of these and called them variously All-Fur Wets and All-Fur Nymphs. I used them most often for swinging, exploring the riffles and runs of medium streams and large rivers when I had no indication that anything specific would work better and I wanted to cover lots of water, find the preferred addresses of trout, so I could later focus on that sort of water, perhaps with other kinds of flies. In that sense, these fur-hackled flies looked more like nymphs but were fished more like wets.

In recent years I've added gold beads to their heads, and that has completed their conversion from wet flies to nymphs. I use a few turns of lead wire to brace the bead. I still fish them on the swing, still use them almost exclusively in searching situations. But I fish them on the bottom as well, with a strike indicator-and-split shot setup, usually as part of a two-fly tandem with either a large nymph opposed to a small All-Fur Nymph, size 16 or 18, or with a tiny nymph trailing a medium-sized All-Fur Nymph, size 12 or 14. They work well in a wide array of searching situations, and again they're a simple way to cover a size and color spectrum that agrees with most of what nature offers trout in moving waters.

Squirrel makes the best fur for All-Fur Nymphs, because it has the right mix of underfur and guard hairs, and also because it is about the right length for the sizes of most nymphs. Fox squirrel and gray squirrel are good for large nymphs, sizes 6 to 12. But I rarely tie these flies in those sizes. I tie many more small, size 14 and under, than I do large, size 12 and up. Pine squirrel fur is just right for the small sizes, but even it often has to be trimmed shorter to accommodate hooks smaller than size 16. You'll have to search for skins with an appropriate balance between underfur and guard hairs. A summer-killed squirrel will have almost no underfur. A winter-killed squirrel might be too plush. Paw through bins of them, if you can, looking for what you want. If you must order them, which you almost surely will, order two or three, rather than one, to be sure you get one that is right.

Pine squirrel is now available in bleached, which is almost blond, and very useful for the cream tie, and also in olive, which is obviously preferred for the olive version of the fly. If you can't get either of these colors, substitute the natural dark grayish pine squirrel, which will give you a nice contrast between the abdomen and thorax, resulting in an effective searching fly.

In small sizes, 18 and 20, I tend to use rabbit fur or even a fine synthetic for the body, because it's easiest to dub. In size 16 and larger, I prefer a blend of rabbit fur and Sparkle Yarn, for the slight sparkles of light it adds to the pattern. In size 16 and smaller, I also tend to escape the difficulty of creating a fur hackle by simply dubbing the squirrel fur. In the tiniest sizes, I'll just direct-dub it, twisting the fur loosely to the thread and taking a couple of turns with it behind the beadhead. More often I'll rough the fur up, mixing the underfur and guard hairs, then wax an inch of my thread, capture the rough mixture in a thread loop, and wind a couple of turns as a dubbing loop rather than a fur hackle. The procedure can vary, but the results you're after should not: you want a fairly robust abdomen behind a loose and fibrous and much thicker thorax or fur hackle. If you find the fur hackle difficult to create even in the larger sizes, dispense with it and use a dubbing loop to form a thorax. It won't look quite the same, but trout will still applaud it.

ALL-FUR NYMPH, OLIVE

Hook: Standard wet fly or standard nymph, size 12–20
Head: Gold bead
Weight: 8–10 turns nonlead wire
Thread: Olive or brown 8/0
Abdomen: Olive fur, synthetic, or fur-Sparkle Yarn blend
Hackle: Olive-dyed pine squirrel (substitute natural pine squirrel)

ALL-FUR NYMPH, GRAY

Hook: Standard wet fly or standard nymph, size 12–20
Head: Gold bead
Weight: 8–10 turns nonlead wire
Thread: Brown 8/0
Abdomen: Muskrat fur, gray synthetic, or fur-Sparkle Yarn blend
Hackle: Natural pine squirrel

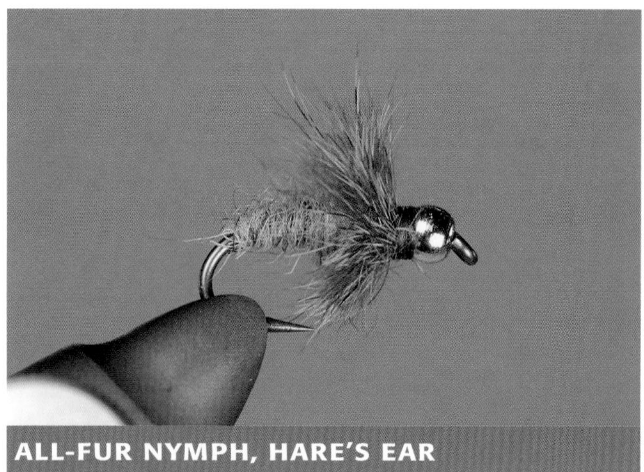

ALL-FUR NYMPH, HARE'S EAR

Hook: Standard wet fly or standard nymph, size 12–20
Head: Gold bead
Weight: 8–10 turns nonlead wire
Thread: Brown 8/0
Abdomen: Hare's mask fur or blend
Hackle: Natural pine squirrel

ALL-FUR NYMPH, CREAM

Hook: Standard wet fly or standard nymph, size 12–20
Head: Gold bead
Weight: 8–10 turns nonlead wire
Thread: Tan 8/0
Abdomen: Cream fur, synthetic, or fur-Sparkle Yarn blend
Hackle: Bleached pine squirrel (substitute natural pine squirrel)

ALL-FUR NYMPH, BLACK

Hook: Standard wet fly or standard nymph, size 12–20
Head: Gold or black bead
Weight: 8–10 turns nonlead wire
Thread: Black 8/0
Abdomen: Black fur, synthetic, or fur-Sparkle Yarn blend
Hackle: Natural pine squirrel

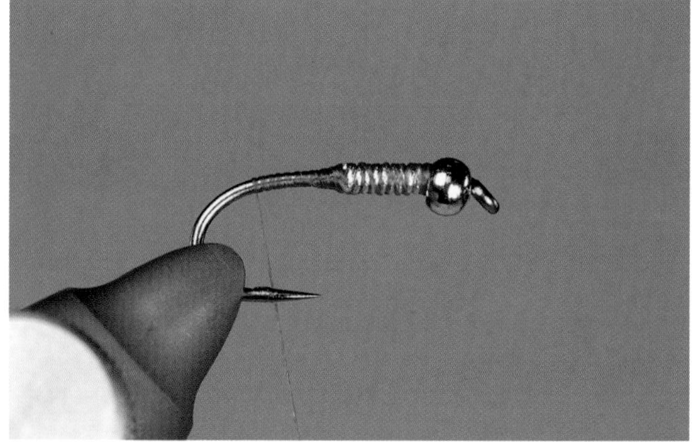

Step 1. If the hook is barbed, debarb it with needlenose pliers. Place a taper-drilled bead on the hook with the small end of the tapered hole toward the hook eye. Fix the hook in the vise. Take eight to ten turns of weighting wire at midshank. If your wire is soft enough, you can often wind it from the spool, then pull it against the hook shank until it breaks. It will usually break against the shank and save you the step of cutting it with scissors or pinching it off with your fingernail. Wrap the butt end of the weighting wire tight to the shank, and press the wire forward, working the front turns inside the back of the bead, or tight against it if they don't fit inside. Brace the weighting wire with a thread ramp, and overwrap the wire to the bead and back. Layer a base of thread to the hook bend.

Step 2. Using the direct-dubbing method, twist a proportionately fat amount of dubbing to the thread, and wind a body that is more stout than slender, and tapered slightly from back to front. Though you should tweezer or clip any obvious wild hairs, don't wind the body tightly, and don't trim it to neatness. Stray fibers kick loose in the water, and make the fly look more alive.

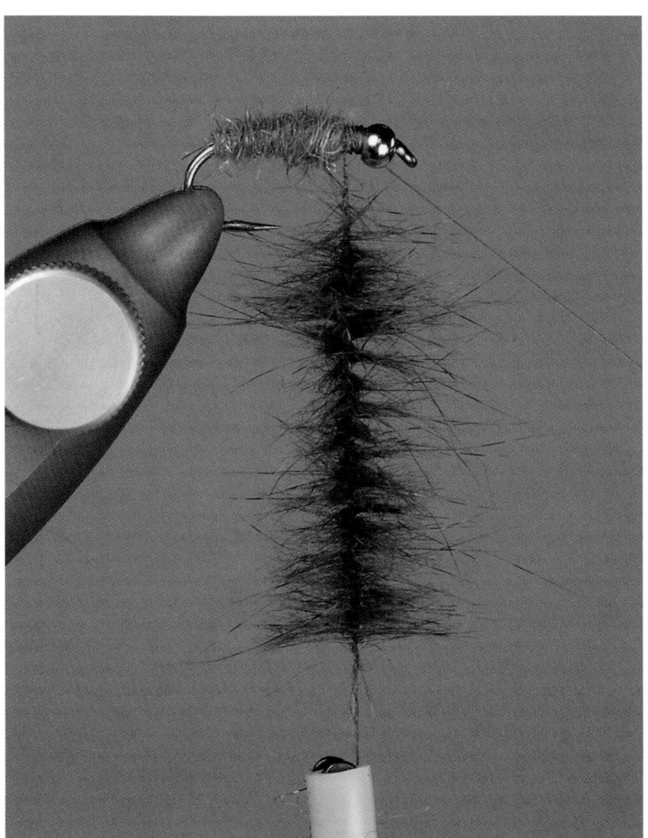

Step 3. Create a fur hackle captured in a thread loop (see page 54). Use a sticky dubbing wax on one to two inches of your tying thread. Be careful to keep the length of the guard hairs in the fur in balance with the size hook on which you're about to wind the hackle. The hackle should be about one and a half hook-gap widths long. Trim the butts of the fur, if necessary, and align the fur so that it is centered when captured in the thread loop. Let the thread loop collapse and twist the end of the loop, then capture it in your hackle pliers. The fur hackle should look just like a bottle brush at this point.

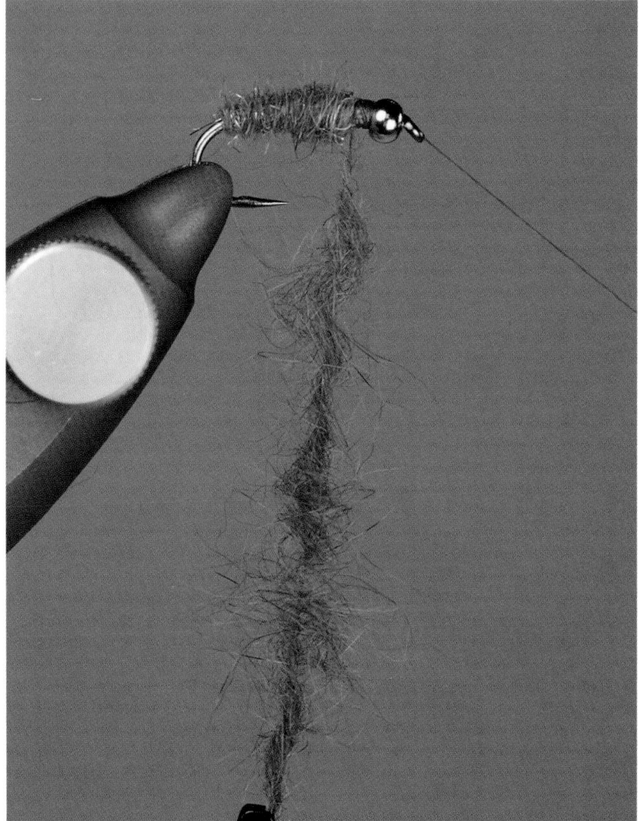

Alternate Step 3. If the above fur hackle seems too difficult, or you're tying on a size 16 or smaller hook, use a dubbing loop in place of the fur hackle (see page 50). Touch one to two inches of your tying thread with sticky wax. Use the forefinger tip of your tying hand to stir the dubbing mix in your off-hand palm, mixing the underfur with the guard hairs. Tack the mixed fur lightly to the waxed thread, make a thread loop, and twirl it to form a very loose dubbing. Capture the end of the loop in your hackle pliers.

Step 4. Wind the fur hackle or dubbing loop forward in one to at most three turns, from the end of the abdomen to the back of the bead. Use the forefinger and thumb of your off hand to stroke the fur back after each turn of hackle or dubbing. The result should be a thick thoracic area, with plenty of guard hairs sticking out to represent legs, antennae, and life in general. Secure the thread loop

with three to four turns of thread, and clip the excess. Stroke any stray fibers back, and take four to six turns of thread tight behind the beadhead, then place a whip-finish over them. Draw it tight and clip the thread. If you feel it necessary, tidy the fly by plucking out any disturbing stray guard hairs. But don't overdo it; those fibers are what make the fly look alive in the water.

Alternate Step 4. Wind the fur loop from Alternate Step 3 forward to the back of the bead. Tie it off there and clip the excess loop. Take three to four turns of thread for a base, and apply your whip-finish. Use your fingers to preen the thorax into shape, plucking out any stray fibers that you feel detract from the appearance of the finished fly. Again, don't pretty it up too much, killing all the action.

I use All-Fur Nymphs most often in sizes 14 and 16, and usually consider them exploratory patterns for pure searching situations, when I don't have any idea what trout might be taking and have only a hazy idea about where they might be holding. I'll use them as often on the swing as I do to probe the depths on dead drifts.

If you see evidence that adult caddis are diving down to lay their eggs on the bottom—or in this case, on your waders—then consider switching to an All-Fur Nymph the approximate size and color of the egg-laying female.

It's well known that many moving-water female caddis adults dive down to the bottom to lay their eggs on submerged logs, stones, and trailing vegetation. If you ever see caddis adults in the air, and you have any doubt that such activity is taking place, examine your waders when you emerge from the water. You might find them covered with egg masses deposited there by caddis mistaking you for bottom structure.

If you get into a situation where you see adult caddis in great abundance in the air, but you can't bring any trout to an imitative dry fly, make a quick switch to an All-Fur Nymph the approximate size and color of the natural. You can either nip off the dry and tie on the nymph, and fish the nymph on the swing, or add twenty inches of tippet to the hook bend of your dry, and trail the nymph off its stern. The failed dry fly then becomes your strike indicator. A note of caution when you do this: use a tippet to the nymph one size finer than that to the dry, so you don't lose them both when you lose the nymph to a big and nasty trout, and use a dry fly at least a size larger than the nymph, so the submerged nymph doesn't tug the dry fly under, which would end its usefulness as an indicator.

If you find that the nymph is the solution, that you're catching all of your trout on it and none on the dry fly, then replace the dry with a yarn indicator. It will be easier to see, will float better, and will be less likely to hook you when you try to release a trout dancing on the dangling nymph.

WHITLOCK RED FOX SQUIRREL NYMPH

As editor of *Flyfishing & Tying Journal,* I get to work with some greats, and I'm also able to acquire some great information when I want it. Having Dave Whitlock as a columnist, with permission to fire at will at any subject he'd like, has been a great honor, and an education as well. I haven't admitted to Dave, and I hope you won't tell him, that I've occasionally asked him to write his column on a subject about which I'd like to become better informed. As an example, I mentioned in chapter 5 that my own tying bench has reached a permanent state of *temporariness.* That may seem like an oxymoron, but there is unfortunately such a state. I've long dreamed what it would be like to have a permanent setup, not one moved from here to there. I suspect I'll never achieve it, so I asked Dave to write about his own fly-tying bench.

His bench is a wonder, an oak rolltop desk inherited from his great-grandfather, augmented by three large wooden cabinets built expressly to hold an overflow of materials. Dave referred to this in his article as an *orderly chaos,* and it was one of the most highly regarded pieces the magazine has ever published.

I also asked Dave to write a piece about his Red Fox Squirrel Nymph, again with my own education in mind, though I didn't think it would do any harm to readers. That fly has been my favorite nymph—as it is the great Dave's—for so long that the way I tie it has wandered so far from the original that I doubt Dave would recognize it as his. I wanted to get back in touch with the way he tied it. I discovered from his subsequent article that he ties it in seven different versions: the original standard nymph, one on a curved hook for larvae and scuds, another with eyes and antennae for caddis pupae, a fourth on a long-shank hook for damselfly nymphs, a fifth with rubber legs and dumbbell eyes for the saltwater flats, a sixth in soft-hackled wet-fly form, and a seventh with a foam carapace to hang the nymph from the surface as an emerger. Add a beadhead version, which is sold commercially, and which I use most often, and you have eight variations on Dave's fine theme.

My Red Fox Squirrel began to lose its red almost at once. The dressing calls for a mix of one-half red fox squirrel back fur with one-half tan Sparkle Yarn. I was on a camping trip the first time I tied the nymph. The only Sparkle Yarn I had available was a strand unraveled from the carpet on the tailgate of my pickup. It was more light beige than tan, but I clipped a few inches into quarter-inch snippets, sheared some fox squirrel, and blended a batch of dubbing by hand. I tied a dozen flies with it. It was easy to see that they were not the reddish color Dave called for, but I took them out and had the misfortune of catching an outsized bunch of trout on them. What was I to do then, call them failures and toss them?

I made a patchwork of my tailgate carpet and blended enough of that dubbing to last several years. The Less-Than-Red Fox Squirrel became the first fly I'd tie on whenever I decided to fish a nymph, but had no hint that I should try any exact imitation, which means most of the time. I became so dependent on the fly that I finally ran out of the dubbing I'd mixed to tie it with. By then I'd sold that ancient pickup, but had bought a supply of tan Antron.

Because I tie the fly most often in sizes 14, 16, and 18, I noticed that pine squirrel fur, with shorter guard hairs, was a more suitable length, if a less appropriate color, than the original red fox squirrel. I tried a few of Dave's nymphs with pine squirrel for the thorax, and trout seemed to approve. I use pine squirrel fur from the hide a lot, for other flies, and nearly always have it at hand. I slipped into tying my Squirrel Nymphs with pine rather than fox squirrel, and they took one more migration away from Dave Whitlock's original.

You begin to see why I asked Dave to write that article: I'd lost my way. I'm glad that he responded with such a thoughtful and thorough treatment. It turns out that you can now buy dubbing blends specifically for the abdomen and thorax of the Red Fox Squirrel Nymph, as Dave recommends them, and that is precisely what I did and advise you to do.

RED FOX SQUIRREL NYMPH *Dave Whitlock*

Hook: 2X or 3XL, 2X heavy, size 2–18
Weight: 10–15 wraps nonlead wire
Thread: Orange or black 6/0 or 8/0
Cement: Dave's Flexament
Tail: Tuft of red fox squirrel back guard hair and underfur
Rib: Oval gold tinsel or orange Flashabou
Abdomen: Red fox squirrel belly hair and Hare's Ear Antron, 50–50 blend, or Dave Whitlock SLF dubbing blend #02, Red Fox Squirrel Nymph-Abdomen
Thorax: Red fox squirrel back hair and RFSN Antron, 50–50 blend, or Dave Whitlock SLF dubbing blend #01, Red Squirrel Nymph-Thorax
Legs: Dark ginger hen hackle on sizes 12 and larger

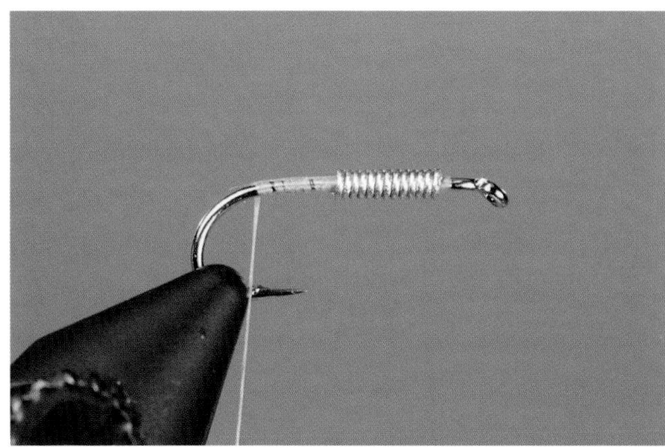

Step 1. Start thread and layer hook shank to the bend. Wrap ten to fifteen turns of weighting wire around the hook shank, with the preponderance of it under what will become the thorax area of the fly.

Step 2. Clip a small tuft of squirrel hair from the hide, including both guard hairs and underfur. Measure it one-third to one-half the hook length, and tie it in at the bend of the hook. Overwrap the tail hair to the back end of the lead wraps, and cut the excess there. This forms an even underbody. Tie in two to three inches of tinsel or Flashabou, beginning at the back end of the lead wraps, and securing it to the base of the tail. Coat the hook shank and wire wraps with Flexament.

Step 3. Using the direct-dubbing method, apply the abdomen blend to the thread, tapering it from slender near the hook shank to a bit thicker at the farther end. It will take some practice, tying by the half dozen or dozen, to work out the right amount of dubbing for each size hook on which you tie. You can always add extra, or pinch off excess. Wind the abdomen forward, with a slight taper from the back up to the front. Cover about two-thirds of the hook shank.

Step 4. Take three to five evenly spaced turns of ribbing forward to the end of the abdomen. Tie it off there and clip the excess.

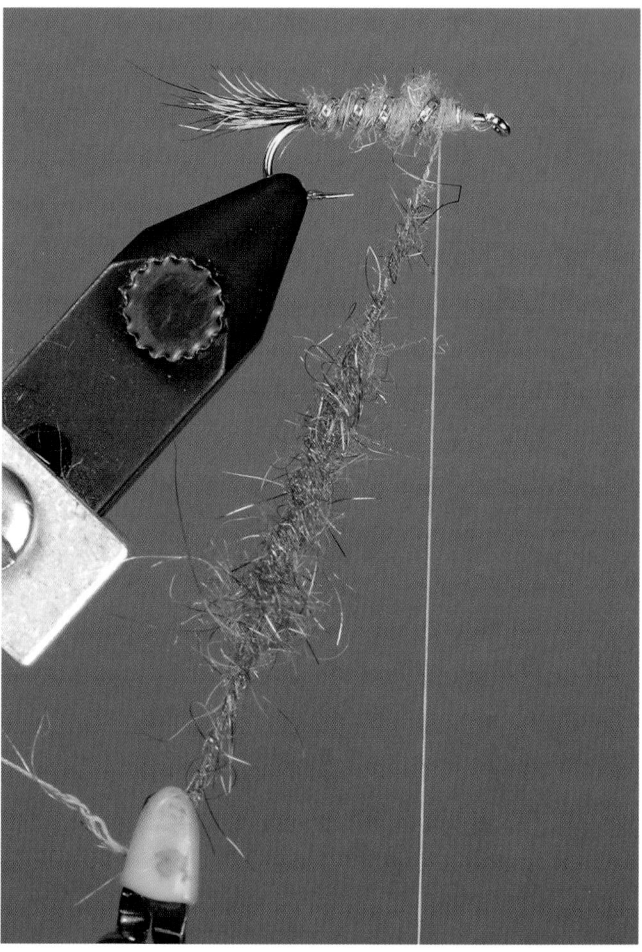

Step 5. Wax your thread with a sticky wax. Tease your thorax dubbing into a wide, loose skein before tacking it to the waxed thread (see page 50). Twist it to the thread at each end, just enough to secure it to the thread. Capture the dubbing in a dubbing loop, and twist it with just a few turns, leaving it loose and fibrous, before catching the end in your hackle pliers.

Step 6. Wrap the thorax dubbing forward from the end of the abdomen to about one hook-eye length behind the hook eye, and clip the excess dubbing loop. If your fly is size 14 or smaller, whip-finish it at this point, and coat the head with Flexament. Use a bodkin or dubbing tool to pick out the thorax dubbing to represent legs and make the fly more lively in the water. If your fly is size 12 or larger, go on to the next step.

Step 7. Select a hen neck or saddle feather with barbs one-half to two hook gaps long, or about the length of the hook shank. Tie it in behind the hook eye with the concave side away from you, so that when wound the hackle will sweep back.

Step 8. Take a single turn of hackle, tie it off, and clip the excess. Form a neat thread head, whip-finish the fly, clip the thread, and coat the head with Flexament.

Some of the most important variations of the Dave Whitlock original Red Fox Squirrel Nymph, for trout fishing, include the Larva/Scud, Caddis Pupa, Damsel, Soft-Hackle, and Beadhead Red Fox Squirrel Nymphs.

I still use my accidental color variation of Dave's dressing as often as I use his original, due to its habit of success. I'd feel in danger and disarmed if I were to go fishing without them. So I continue to tie them when I lose them. Because I don't want to confuse the dressing for my version with the original, I'll list it here as the Pine Squirrel Nymph, though for my own purposes I continue to call it the Dave Whitlock Red Fox Squirrel Nymph.

I fish it most often in sizes 16 and 18. It's rare that I tie it without a gold beadhead, and that's the way I'll describe it. It's also very rare that I tie this workhorse with anything added but the basic tail, abdomen, and thorax. I omit the rib and hackle, in the interest of getting more of them into my fly box in a hurry, so I can get back out and go fishing.

BEADHEAD PINE SQUIRREL NYMPH

Hook:	Standard nymph, size 12–20
Head:	Gold bead
Weight:	8–12 turns nonlead wire
Thread:	Brown 8/0
Tail:	Pine squirrel guard hairs with underfur
Abdomen:	Half pine squirrel back fur, half tan or beige Antron, blended
Thorax:	Pine squirrel fur with guard hairs

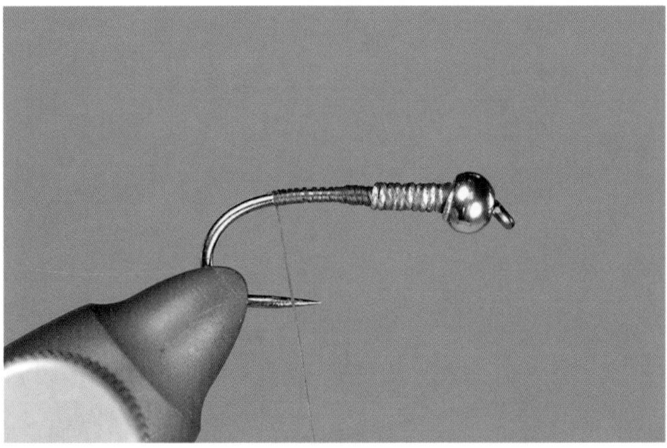

Step 1. Place a bead on the hook, insert the hook in the vise, and wind eight to twelve turns of weighting wire on the hook shank. Slide the front end of the weighting wraps into the back end of the bead. Start your thread behind the weighting wire, build a slight thread ramp at the rear wraps, work the thread through the lead to the bead and back, then layer a base of thread to the hook bend.

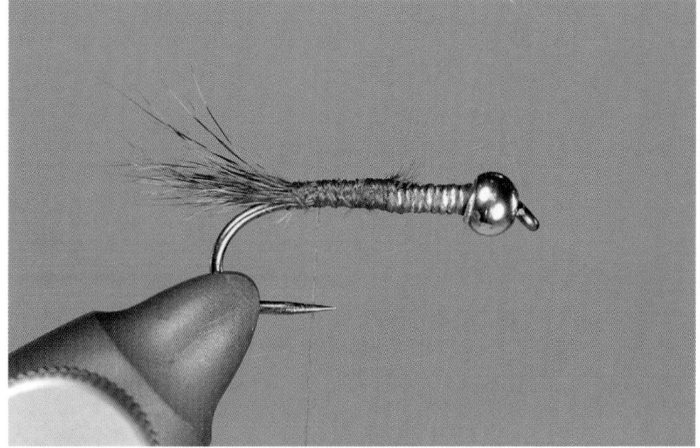

Step 2. Clip a small tuft of pine squirrel hair from the back of the hide. Remove any stray guard hairs that are excessively long. Pluck away any loose underfur, but do not remove the underfur from the guard hairs. Measure the tail one-half the hook length, and tie it in at the bend of the hook. Secure it with thread wraps to the back end of the weighting wire, and clip the excess there.

Step 3. Use the direct-dubbing method to twist a slender amount of dubbing to the thread. Wind this forward just past the midpoint of the hook. It should be at least slightly tapered, slender at the back, more portly at the front. This has not been reported by trout to be a critical factor, but it does make a more attractive and buggy finished fly, one you'll fish with a bit more confidence.

Step 4. Wax an inch or two of thread. Clip a tuft of fur from the back of the same pine squirrel hide from which you clipped the tail. It should be about twice the amount you used for the tail, but this will vary, and you'll begin to calculate the correct amount after tying a few flies. Mix the guard hairs and underfur in the palm of your hand. Place the fur against the waxed thread, and twist it very lightly, not tightly, onto the thread. Capture it in a thread loop. You can dispense with the loop if you like, but the fur with guard hairs tends to be unruly, and the loop helps tame it. Wind two to three turns of fur between the abdomen and bead. Use the thumb and forefinger tips of your off hand to hold the fur back, and take three or four turns of thread between the fur and the bead.

Step 5. Whip-finish the fly, and clip your thread. Use your fingers or tweezers to pluck out any fibers that you consider to be sports, detracting from the appearance of the fly. But don't tidy it up too much. My rule is to leave any fibers that protrude less than the hook-shank length, but that is arbitrary, and you should make your own rule. Trout value liveliness above neatness.

GOLD-RIBBED HARE'S EAR

John Merwin, past editor of *Fly Fisherman* magazine, founding editor of *Fly Rod & Reel,* current fishing editor at *Field & Stream,* is as knowledgeable about flies as anyone else who has ever invited me fishing and then handily outfished me. He recently wrote an article about nine essential trout flies, and listed the Gold-Ribbed Hare's Ear nymph first. John wrote, "It's the one fly to have if you're having only one." I would have trouble being restricted to one nymph, but I would also have trouble disagreeing with John's statement.

The standard Gold-Ribbed Hare's Ear has been around so long that I'm not aware of its origins. It was the first nymph with which I had more than a moderate amount of luck. I was armed with a Gold-Ribbed Hare's Ear the day I had my moment of epiphany in the use of the split-shot-and-strike-indicator method. This was a while ago. I'd been reading early articles about slipping a red steelhead Corkie high on the leader, pinching a couple of split shot above a nymph, fishing the rig on upstream casts so the nymph tumbled right along the bottom. I tried it many times, but for a season or so it remained a theory to me. The trout I caught seemed almost always to be accidents. I'd raise the rod for the next cast and a trout would be there. I would have no idea how or when it got hooked.

One late winter I got desperate to get the coastal rains out of my system. I drove to the dry side of Oregon's Cascade Mountain Range, set my tent on a flat next to the Deschutes River, shivered through a cold night. I parted the tent flaps and looked outside the next morning. The sky was gray; the rain was following me. I got dressed and stepped down to the riverside. The water, reflecting that dull sky, was just as gray. I worked up a campfire, cooked a leisurely breakfast, glassed some mule deer browsing on a sagebrush hillside across the river. It was a bachelor band of about a dozen, all bucks. I layered long johns under latex waders, strung my fiberglass fly rod—I'm giving you a sense of time here, if you've not noticed—and stepped to the bank of the big and brawling river once again, stood looking at it, pondering what to try. The entire world was gray and cold. My chances with a dry fly looked black.

I rigged reluctantly, because of all my past failures, with a red Corkie, a couple of big split shot, a weighted size 12 Gold-Ribbed Hare's Ear. The river where I was about to step into it was shaped perfectly for the method. A long and boisterous riffle upstream bounded into a long central current tongue outboard, one that was far too fast and deep to wade. But it left what I call a *riffle corner* on the inside, where the riffle shallowed up, chattered over a steep gravel bottom, broke over a shelf, leveled out and slowed down at the same time. Where

In any riffle corner, trout hold on the soft water to the inside of the swifter current, where they can maintain a feeding station without fighting heavy currents, but rush out to intercept whatever those currents deliver down to them. Make sure you fish the shallower water before you wade through it.

The standard Gold-Ribbed Hare's Ear looks a lot like the average crawler mayfly nymph, such as this western green drake (Drunella grandis), *as well as a wide variety of mayfly clinger and swimmer nymphs. In the right sizes, it resembles many stonefly nymphs as well. Its resemblance to so many natural trout food forms, while not precisely imitating any of them, is the probable cause for its widespread and long-lived success against trout.*

this shelf edged out against the deeper and stronger current tongue, it formed a wedge of water that was two to four feet deep, had a modest current, and was braced against the much more forceful current that whisked down from the riffle, where would be delivered a steady stream of drifting aquatic insects. I had no difficulty reading the riffle corner, and deciding exactly where trout would be holding, if any trout were in there and feeding at that early time of year.

Trout were in there, and hungry.

My first cast danced a seventeen-inch rainbow that made a bold dash down and out of the corner, flapped into the air, smacked back into the water, and broke off my Gold-Ribbed Hare's Ear.

I tied on another, and made the same cast. The indicator hesitated while the surrounding water by which I was measuring the speed of its drift kept moving. I raised the rod in that eternal query—Is anybody out there?—and got the same dashing and dancing response from a smaller rainbow. I was able to subdue it, estimate that it was plump and about fifteen inches long, release it away from the corner pocket so that it would not disturb any more trout that might be in there.

I quit at seven, counting the first lost trout and another about the same size that also broke off. I was able to hold the largest in my hands, estimated it at about eighteen inches; I never measure trout, because they seem to shrink so badly. But you'll have no trouble estimating my sudden satisfaction with the split-shot-and-indicator method. In that one brief burst of trout, I got a firm sense of how to rig correctly for the water, what a strike looked like when it happened, and how to set the hook when the indicator gave me a hint that a trout had a grip on my Gold-Ribbed Hare's Ear and was about to decide it was not good for groceries.

I did not become an expert at fishing nymphs in that instant. But shot-and-indicator nymphing is at the core of success with nymphs, and ever since that single hour in that single riffle corner, which left me somewhat stunned and instilled a sudden confidence in the flies and the method, I've been progressively catching more and more trout on nymphs. Before that, nymphing seemed a series of mysteries without any solutions. After that, nymphing became a series of mysteries, some of which at least seemed to have solutions.

If you're fairly new to tying and fishing nymphs, and haven't enjoyed that epiphanic moment, be assured it's coming to you. You just need to keep your nymphs in the water. One day you'll feel you're fumbling. Then the moment will arrive. The next day you'll be casting nymphs upon the water with confidence that trout are out there and eager to take them.

You can tie the Gold-Ribbed Hare's Ear with foreknowledge that if you get it in front of a trout that is at all receptive to nymphs, one not feeding selectively on something shaped and sized and colored quite differently, the trout will accept it. It's likely that more trout have been caught on Gold-Ribbed Hare's Ears than have been fooled by any other nymph. In its standard dressing, it looks like a wide variety of mayfly and stonefly nymphs. I tie it down to size 14 with all of its prescribed parts. In size 16 and smaller, I omit the rib and shellback.

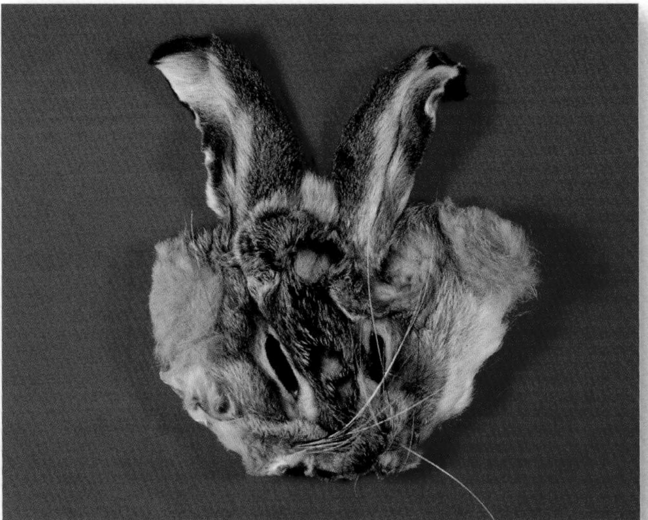

The mask from a proper English hare surrenders its fur for the Gold-Ribbed Hare's Ear nymph from different parts: the poll between the ears for the tail, the cheeks for the abdomen, and the face and ears for the thorax.

Because it is one of the oldest, most successful, and therefore most used and useful nymphs, more variations have been worked on the Gold-Ribbed Hare's Ear than on any other nymph. You'll find one version or another occupying a favored spot in nearly every experienced angler's nymph box. You'll find your own preferred way to tie the fly, but I recommend you begin with the standard, and let experience with trout nudge you toward a variation that suits you.

GOLD-RIBBED HARE'S EAR

Hook:	Standard nymph, size 12–20
Weight:	10–20 turns nonlead wire
Thread:	Black 6/0 or 8/0
Tail:	Hare's mask guard hairs, with underfur
Rib:	Oval gold tinsel
Abdomen:	Natural hare's mask dubbing or commercial blend
Wing case:	Dark turkey tail feather section
Thorax:	Dark hare's mask dubbing, with guard hairs, or commercial blend

For the tail, use hair from the poll, or space between the ears of an English, not an American, hare's mask. The abdomen fur is sheared from the light-colored cheeks of the mask, with most of the guard hairs removed. The thorax fur is sheared from the face, between the eyes, and from the ears, where the fur is dark, and blended with the guard hairs left in. The result is a tan tail and abdomen, contrasted against a darker thorax. Every dubbing manufacturer has blends for the abdomen and thorax, for example Hareline Dubbin' Hare's Ear #4 and Dark Hare's Ear #5. I'm allergic to the dander in hare's mask and don't dare to shear one. I wear a bandanna like an old movie bandit when tying Gold-Ribbed Hare's Ear Nymphs, and cut the tail from the mask, but use commercial blends for the abdomen and thorax.

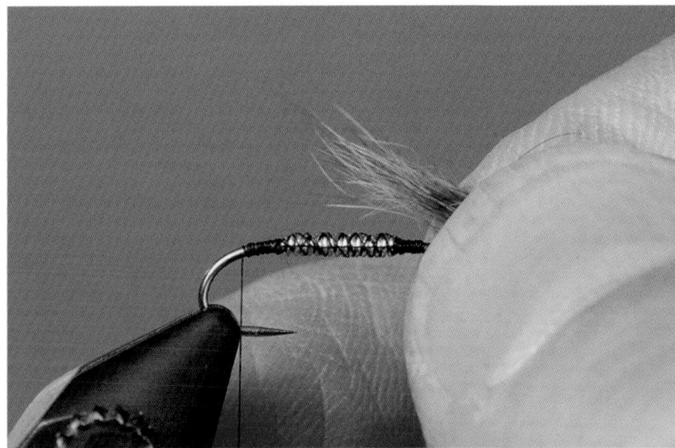

Step 1. Fix the hook in the vise, layer the midshank with weighting wire wraps, and start your thread, securing the weight with slight thread ramps at both ends. Clip a tuft of guard hairs from the poll. Remove any excessively long guard hairs from the tips of the tuft, and winnow the excess underfur from the butts. Measure the hair half the length of the hook shank.

Step 2. Tie the hair in at the bend of the hook, and make thread wraps over it forward to the back shoulder of the weighting wire. Clip the excess there, to form an even underbody. Clip two to three inches of oval gold tinsel from the spool, lay it over or alongside the weighting wraps, extending just beyond them, and tie it in with thread wraps from back to front, then back to the base of the tail. Layering the thick ribbing the length of the shank in this way maintains the even underbody.

Step 3. Clip a small bunch of fur from the hare's cheek, and remove most of the guard hairs, or use an available hare's mask blend. The abdomen should not be as spiky as the thorax, but it should not be a tight and tidy dubbing, either. Use the direct-dubbing method to twist the fur to the thread, being sure it is tapered slightly from thin near the hook shank to a bit more portly away from it. Wrap the abdomen forward to just past the midpoint of the hook shank.

Step 4. Take three to five evenly spaced wraps of ribbing forward over the abdomen. Tie it off and clip the excess.

Step 5. Clip a section of dark turkey tail feather approximately the width of the hook gap. If you prefer, you can precoat a turkey feather with Flexament and allow it to dry ahead of time. Holding the section by the tip, make a cut across the butts to square it. Tie it in just in front of the abdomen, with the butts toward the hook eye and the dark side down. Take thread wraps back over the wing case and abdomen until you are sure the fly will not have a narrow wasp waist when you pull the wing case forward over the thorax.

Step 6. Clip a tuft of hair from the face or ear of a hare's mask, or a small tuft from each, and blend them together. Mix the underfur and guard hairs together in the palm of your hand. Use either the direct-dubbing method or a dubbing loop to form a loose, spiky thorax dubbing. Wind it forward to a point about one hook eye length behind the hook eye. It should be darker, thicker, and more loosely dubbed than the abdomen.

Step 7. Bring the wing case forward over the thorax, holding any forward-leaning guard hairs back out of the way when you do. Tie the wing case off with a few turns of thread behind the hook eye. Clip the excess tip.

Step 8. Use enough thread turns to make a neat thread head. Whip-finish and clip the thread. Use your fingers or tweezers to pluck out any wildly stray fibers. If the thorax is too tightly wound, use your bodkin point to tease out guard hairs and underfur until the fly looks as though it has legs.

To tie the Flashback Gold-Ribbed Hare's Ear, just substitute pearl Krystal Flash or silver Mylar tinsel for the turkey wing case.

A recommended variation that gives the fly a bit of brightness is conversion of the nymph to a Flashback Gold-Ribbed Hare's Ear. I haven't made the minute experiments that would be required to determine whether the Flashback catches more trout than the original. I'll give myself an assignment, and ask you to consider it as well: tie a half dozen each of the standard Gold-Ribbed Hare's Ear, Flashback Hare's Ear, and the following Beadhead Hare's Ear, all in size 14 or 16, and fish them against each other in a searching situation, to see if one outfishes the others. I don't have a guess about which one it might be. I do have a guess that the excercise will prod you toward one of the three, and that one of the variations of the Gold-Ribbed Hare's Ear will become a fixture in your searching-nymph box.

I've arrived at the following version for my own box.

BEADHEAD HARE'S EAR

Hook:	Standard nymph, size 14–20
Head:	Gold bead
Weight:	8–12 turns nonlead wire
Thread:	Brown 8/0
Tail:	Hare's mask guard hairs
Abdomen:	Hare's mask fur or Hareline #4
Thorax:	Dark hare's mask fur or Hareline #5

Step 1. Slide a taper-drilled bead onto the hook with the small end toward the eye. Fix the hook in the vise and wrap eight to twelve turns of weighting wire. Push the forward end of the wire into the back end of the bead. Start the thread behind the wire, create a small thread ramp, and take a set of thread turns forward and back over the wire. Wrap the thread to the bend of the hook. Clip a tuft of hare's mask guard hairs, and remove the excess long fibers from the tips and any excess underfur from the butts. Measure half the shank length and tie it in, overwrapping the butts to the back of the weighting wire before clipping the excess.

Step 2. Clip a tuft of underfur from the cheek area of a hare's mask. Remove most of the guard hairs, though the resulting dubbing won't suffer if it's a little bit rough. Use the direct-dubbing method to twist the fur to the thread, and wrap a few turns forward to just past the midpoint of the hook shank.

Step 3. Clip a tuft of underfur and guard hairs from the hare's face or ear. Mix the fur together, and use either the direct-dubbing method or a dubbing loop to secure it somewhat loosely to the thread. Wrap it forward from the end of the abdomen to the back of the bead. Take just two to four thread turns behind the bead, then tuck a whip-finish over those turns. Clip the thread. Tidy the fly if you feel it necessary.

This Beadhead Hare's Ear, with its omissions of the rib and wing case, is easy to tie, but has a very buggy appearance. I tie it and use it most often in sizes 16, 18, and 20. I often reach for this nymph rather than a more exact imitation when I find nymphs of the pale morning dun *(Ephemerella inermis)* dominant in a kick-net sample. This happens often in late spring and early summer on such waters as the Deschutes, Henry's Fork of the Snake, Madison, and many smaller and less famous moving waters from East to West.

The Beadhead Gold-Ribbed Hare's Ear is a logical extension of the standard pattern, one I would tie more often if I fished Hare's Ear nymphs more often in sizes 12 and 14, less often in smaller sizes 16 and 18, in which sizes it is more practical to tie the fly without the turkey wing case.

Variations on the Hare's Ear theme are almost endless. Perhaps the first and most logical is simply to add a beadhead to the standard Gold-Ribbed Hare's Ear, tied with its ribbing and wing case. I've used it this way often enough to know that it makes a very effective searching dressing. The only reason I haven't settled on it for my own fly boxes is my propensity to use the Hare's Ear in smaller sizes, in which case the truncated Beadhead Hare's Ear is simply faster to tie, so I can get a bunch done in more of a hurry. If I had more time to tie, and didn't mind having less time to fish, I'd be glad to tie the more detailed version.

A. P. NYMPHS

The late André Puyans's All Purpose nymph series makes an excellent way to cover the color spectrum of fur nymphs, with a shape that roughly resembles a myriad of mayfly and stonefly forms. I've already mentioned that the A. P. Black is one of my favorite nymphs on small waters. It is excellent as a generalized black pattern to cover that necessary color in your searching-nymph box.

Puyans tied the series in the full range of colors, listing the A. P. Black, A. P. Beaver, A. P. Hare's Ear, A. P. Muskrat, A. P. Olive, and A. P. Herl. You could easily disregard all other fur searching nymphs, select from the A. P. series to cover the natural color spectrum of black, brown, tan, gray, olive, and green, and you'd kill two problems with a single fly style: most of your searching nymph needs would be covered, and your tying life would be simplified.

I use the A. P. Black, and cover most other natural color phases with other patterns. I suggest, however, that you give serious consideration to the A. P. Muskrat as an excellent way to cover gray, which is at least as necessary as black. For some reason gray is not covered by many choices among searching-nymph styles. You might want to tie and try all of the A. P. Nymph colors. It's almost certain that you'll be fishing one day and all the factors in nymphing—weather, prevalent naturals, eager trout, and so on—will align themselves, and the nymph you have on your tippet at that moment will work sudden wonders. You'll have a new go-to fly based on this all-purpose concept that has been around for many years. I have no idea which A. P. color you'll be using the day that happens, and neither do you. It might not matter. If you catch fish on any searching nymph, you'll develop confidence in it, and you'll fish it into your future with continued, though of course not continual, success. It will find its place in your fly boxes. One or two of the A. P. Nymph series are likely to deserve such a place in yours.

Remember that your purpose is to fill a fly box with searching nymphs that fish in the widest variety of situations with the minimum, not maximum, number of dressings. If the full range of the A. P. Nymph series turns out to be your way to do that, it's far from a bad decision. But you're more likely to want one or two of them to augment other choices you've made. For me, the A. P. Black is a natural choice to go along with Hare's Ear and Fox Squirrel nymphs.

A. P. BLACK *André Puyans*

Hook:	Standard nymph, size 10–16
Weight:	10–20 turns nonlead wire
Thread:	Black 6/0 or 8/0
Tail:	Moose body hair
Rib:	Copper wire
Abdomen:	Black fur or fur-Sparkle Yarn blend
Wing case:	Moose body hair
Thorax:	Black fur or fur-Sparkle Yarn blend
Legs:	Tips of wing-case hair

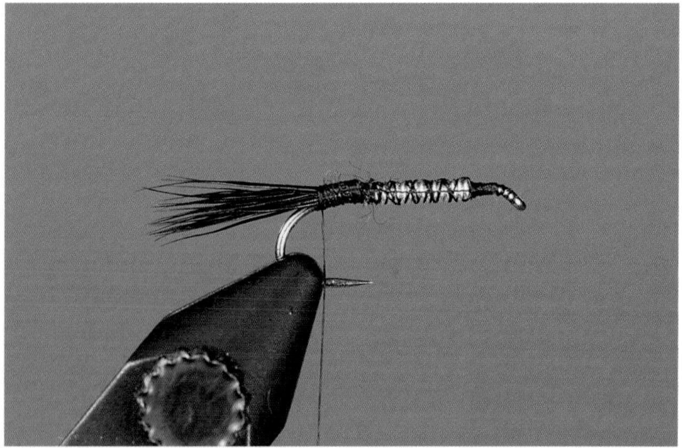

Step 1. Fix the hook in the vise, weight it, start the thread, and secure the weighting wire. Select a small bunch of dark moose hair fibers for the tail. Clip them from the hide, remove fuzzy underfur, and align the tips in your stacker. Measure the tail one-half to two-thirds the hook-shank length, and tie it in at the bend. Overwrap the tail butts to the back shoulder of the weighting wire before clipping the excess.

Step 2. Tie in the ribbing wire alongside the tail and weighting wraps, ending between the hook eye and front shoulder, to maintain the taper of the body. Using the direct-dubbing method, twist enough fur, or fur and Sparkle Yarn blend, to the thread to make a substantial and slightly tapered abdomen. Though there are no rules, I prefer rabbit or squirrel fur, dyed black, for the abdomen, because it can be dubbed tightly, and a fur-Sparkle Yarn blend for the thicker thorax, because it looks better when dubbed loosely or when spun in a dubbing loop.

Step 3. Wind the rib forward in three to five evenly spaced turns over the abdomen, and clip or break off the excess. Select a bunch of moose hairs for the wing case, about twice the amount you used for the tail. Remove underfur from the butts, and make a straight clip across them so they are aligned. Most moose hair is brown close to the hide, blacker as you move toward the tips. Make this alignment cut above the lighter brown part of the hair. Tie it in just in front of the abdomen, and overwrap it back onto the abdomen to be sure there will be no wasp waist when you draw the wing case forward over the thorax.

Step 4. Use a dubbing loop to capture a wide and loose skein of fur and Sparkle Yarn blend. Twist it just enough to capture the fibers, but not enough to form a tight dubbing rope. Wrap it forward to a point two hook-eye lengths behind the eye, leaving room for the wing-case tie-off. I use Hare's Ear Plus, a mix of Sparkle Yarn and rabbit fur with the guard hairs left in, for the thorax. I usually pick out the fur to represent legs, and omit the wing-case tip-fiber legs called for in the original. But we'll tie it according to plan here, and you can choose your own method later.

Step 5. Gather the wing-case hairs between the thumb and forefinger of your tying hand. Give them a slight twist to compact the wing case, then draw it over the hook eye. Use your off hand to take one or two tight wraps of thread over the wing case at the front end of the thorax, to hold the hair in place. Switch the bobbin to your tying hand and take four to eight more thread wraps, drawing each tight. Moose hair is hard, and needs to be tied in tightly. Hold the hair tips up, and take about five thread wraps between the hook eye and the moose hair to hold it upright.

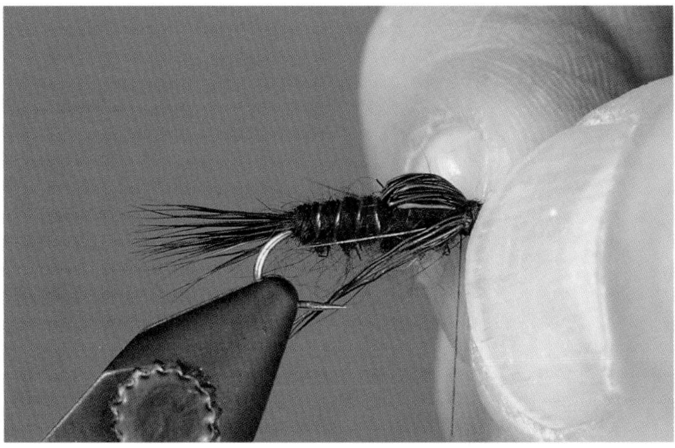

Step 6. Draw three to six wing-case fibers back along the nymph body, on the near side, and capture them under two to three turns of thread. Draw three to six fibers back on the far side, and capture them with the same number of thread wraps. Clip the remaining fibers. If you have crowded the head, which is normal with this fly until you've tied a few, use the thumbnail and forefinger nail of your tying hand to force the moose hair back from the hook eye, leaving enough room to place a thread head and whip-finish.

Step 7. Whip-finish the fly, clip the thread, and apply head cement. Clip the leg fibers just beyond the back edge of the wing case, and the fly is finished.

A. P. BEAVER *André Puyans*

Hook:	Standard nymph, size 10–16
Weight:	10–20 turns nonlead wire
Thread:	Brown 6/0 or 8/0
Tail:	Moose body hair
Rib:	Copper wire
Abdomen:	Beaver back fur
Wing case:	Moose body hair
Thorax:	Beaver back fur
Legs:	Tips of wing-case hair

I mentioned in the A. P. Black that the lower part of the moose fibers, close to the hide, are more brown than black. For the wing case here, use the part closer to the hide.

A. P. HARE'S EAR *André Puyans*

Hook: Standard nymph, size 10–16
Weight: 10–20 turns nonlead wire
Thread: Tan 6/0 or 8/0
Tail: Wood-duck or mallard flank fibers
Rib: Copper wire
Abdomen: Hare's mask fur or Hareline Dubbin' #4
Wing case: Wood-duck or mallard flank fibers
Thorax: Hare's mask fur or Hareline Dubbin' #4
Legs: Tips of wing-case fibers

A. P. OLIVE *André Puyans*

Hook: Standard nymph, size 10–16
Weight: 10–20 turns nonlead wire
Thread: Olive 6/0 or 8/0
Tail: Wood duck or mallard flank
Rib: Copper wire
Abdomen: Olive fur or fur-Sparkle Yarn blend
Wing case: Wood duck or mallard flank
Thorax: Olive fur or fur-Sparkle Yarn blend
Legs: Tips of wing-case fibers

A. P. MUSKRAT *André Puyans*

Hook: Standard nymph, size 10–16
Weight: 10–20 turns nonlead wire
Thread: Black 6/0 or 8/0
Tail: Moose body hair
Rib: Copper wire
Abdomen: Muskrat back fur
Wing case: Moose body hair
Thorax: Muskrat back fur
Legs: Tips of wing-case hair

A. P. HERL *André Puyans*

Hook: Standard nymph, size 10–16
Weight: 10–20 turns nonlead wire
Thread: Brown 6/0 or 8/0
Tail: Pheasant tail
Rib: Copper wire
Abdomen: Peacock herl
Wing case: Pheasant tail
Thorax: Peacock herl
Legs: Tips of wing-case fibers

The A. P. Herl is not a fur nymph, and might be out of place here, but it's part of André Puyans's All Purpose series, and covers a color at one end of the spectrum. It fits as a reminder that you should consider the color range of natural stream and river nymphs carefully when you select a set of searching nymphs to fill a fly box for all the situations you might encounter on moving waters.

The addition of a bead to the head of any fly in the A. P. Nymph series might be a wise idea. Note that when stiff moose hair is used for the wing case, it's best to whip-finish behind the bead before the hair is trimmed. The butts of the hair should be left sticking out a bit, so they cannot pull free and loosen the whip-finish after you've caught a trout or two.

Give serious thought to the option of adding a beadhead to any of the flies in this series. Most beadhead dressings began as standard nymphs, to which beads were later added. If you look through fly-fishing catalogs, you'll see the A. P. Black listed more than any other fly in the series, and it will be offered as a beadhead about half the time. I carry the nonbeaded variety in the box of flies that I set aside specifically for small-stream fishing, which is where I use the A. P. Black most. For other searching situations, I add the bead.

BIRD'S NEST

Cal Bird's famous nymph is excellent when it's rigged to tumble along the bottom. But it also looks racy when fished on the swing, higher in the water column, a method that is overlooked in modern nymphing's emphasis on the shot-and-indicator method. Many natural mayfly swimmer nymphs live in slow edge currents, or migrate to them before emergence. When they're active along the edges, or on tailwater and spring-creek flats, trout get used to chasing them, and can be fooled by a nymph of the proper size, shape, and color fished on the swim.

The Bird's Nest can fill that niche for you. It can be tied in a range of colors from black, through brown, to light cahill and olive. I'll list it here in brown and olive, the two most popular and useful colors. This is one of those rare dressings that looks as though it might go out and swim aggressively after trout, chase them down, and catch them for you. It winds up being the opposite—trout chase it down—but it will indeed catch lots of trout for you.

BIRD'S NEST, BROWN *Cal Bird*

Hook: Standard nymph or 2XL, size 10–16
Weight: 10–15 turns nonlead wire
Thread: Brown 6/0 or 8/0
Tail: Bronze mallard flank
Rib: Copper wire
Abdomen: Australian opossum belly fur
Legs: Bronze mallard flank
Thorax: Australian opossum back fur

Step 1. Fix the hook in the vise, weight the shank, and start the working thread. Build a slight thread ramp at the front end of the weighting wire wraps, and layer thread to the bend of the hook. Clip several bronze mallard flank fibers from the feather, measure them two-thirds the length of the hook shank, and tie them in for the tail, overwrapping the butts to the weighting wire before clipping. Clip two to three inches of ribbing wire from the spool, eight to ten inches if you're tying a dozen Bird's Nests as you should. Overwrap the ribbing wire to the back shoulder of the weighting wire.

Step 2. Clip fur from the belly of an Aussie opossum hide, or use prepackaged light Australian opossum fur. Rough up the fur in your palm and use the direct-dubbing method to twist it to your thread, being sure it is thinner toward the hook, more substantial as you move away from the hook, for a tapered body. Wrap the abdomen forward to a point about one-quarter the shank length behind the hook eye. Make four to six turns of evenly spaced ribbing through the abdomen fur, tie off, and clip or break the excess wire.

Step 3. Clip or strip a section of bronze mallard flank fibers from one side of the feather, about equal to the width of the hook gap. Measure these to the end of the nymph body, and tie them in on the near side of the shank, in front of the abdomen, with the curve, if there is any, inward toward the shank. Clip or strip an equal amount of fibers from the opposite side of the same feather, and tie them in on the opposite side of the hook shank, again with their curved surfaces, if any, toward the hook shank. Clip the butts.

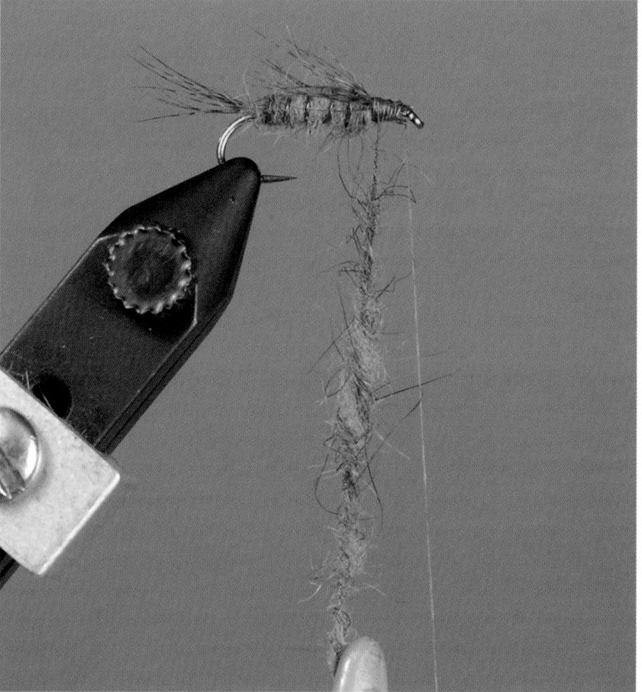

Step 4. Clip a small amount of fur from the back of an Aussie opossum hide, or use prepackaged dark Australian opossum fur. If you're using fur from the hide, leave the guard hairs in, but rough the fur up in the palm of your hand, so that the underfur and guard hairs are mixed. Wax one to two inches of your working thread with tacky wax. Twist the top and bottom tips of the fur to the thread, to hold it in place, then capture the fur in a spiky dubbing loop.

Step 5. Take two to three turns of thorax dubbing, stepping it down to a point one hook-eye length behind the eye. Tie off and clip the excess dubbing loop. Form a neat thread head and whip-finish the fly. Clip your thread. If you desire, you can tidy up the thorax, plucking out or clipping any excessively long guard-hair fibers. Don't trim it too much. This nymph is better left ragged, with lots of fur and fibers to work in the currents, to make it look alive and attractive to trout.

BIRD'S NEST, OLIVE *Cal Bird*

Hook:	Standard nymph or 2XL, size 10–16
Weight:	10–15 turns nonlead wire
Thread:	Olive 6/0 or 8/0
Tail:	Wood-duck flank fibers or mallard-dyed wood duck
Rib:	Copper wire
Abdomen:	Olive-dyed Aussie opossum or squirrel fur
Legs:	Wood-duck flank fibers or mallard-dyed wood duck
Thorax:	Olive-dyed Aussie opossum or squirrel fur

My favorite version of the Bird's Nest is the following unauthorized crossing of the original brown dressing and the olive variant, with an olive body and brown thorax. I tie it most often in sizes 14 and 16, and fish it most often in slow to stillwaters, the kinds of tailwater and spring-creek flats and pond or lake shallows that are loaded with scuds, *Callibaetis* mayfly nymphs, predaceous damselfly nymphs, all of them camouflaged in olive.

BIRD'S NEST, OLIVE-BROWN *Cal Bird*

Hook:	Standard nymph or 2XL, size 14–16
Weight:	8–12 turns nonlead wire
Thread:	Olive 8/0
Tail:	Wood-duck flank fibers
Rib:	Fine copper wire
Abdomen:	Caddis green rabbit fur
Legs:	Wood-duck flank fibers
Thorax:	Light Aussie opossum fur

The abdomen could be any fur or even synthetic dubbing. You will suffer no fatal harm if you substitute hare's mask fur or a prepackaged blend for the thorax.

CHARLES BROOKS'S MONTANA STONE

I don't find giant salmon-fly nymphs *(Pteronarcys californica)* everywhere that I fish for trout, but I find that trout are willing to take Charles Brooks's Montana Stone nymph no matter where I fish it. I've used it on my home river, the Deschutes in Oregon, and on the South Fork of the Snake, Madison, Big Hole, and Yellowstone Rivers in Idaho and Montana, where the naturals are abundant. I've also caught trout on it in Patagonia and New Zealand, where nothing like it exists in nature.

The fly is a good color for a searching nymph—black—and has a general insect shape. When tied the way its originator intended, it's a depth charge. It bangs through the surface film with a wallop and gets on its way toward the bottom in a hurry. If you're hitting bank water from a moving boat, that is excellent. If you're wade-fishing fast riffles, runs, or pocket water with more than two-foot depths, it's necessary. If you're counting a nymph down into the dark depths of a slow run or almost still pool, all that weight is a distinct advantage.

If you're fishing the indicator-and-shot method, and desire a heavily weighted nymph to deliver a smaller, lightly weighted nymph to the bottom, the Montana Stone is your best candidate. You can accomplish the same thing by adding split shot to the leader, but your hooking rate on split shot will be considerably lower than with this portly, attractive nymph.

Charles Brooks's heavily weighted Montana Stone is most useful in the brutal flows of big rivers, where you want your fly to get deep quickly and stay on the bottom throughout the length of its drift.

I once ordered a dozen Montana Stones from a catalog, for a trip at some distance for which I had no time to tie, and was surprised to discover that they were tied with slender bodies and very little weight. They were effective enough on waters where salmon-fly nymphs were abundant. I simply added enough split shot to get them to the bottom. But they were of no use for the kind of fishing to which I normally assign the fly: to scour the bottom in brutal water, or to deliver one or even two smaller nymphs to the bottom in water where I'd rather double my chances by using a heavily weighted nymph rather than shot.

The big and ugly Montana Stone is also useful when you fish for trout in such waters as the Deschutes, where trout are likely to take a small trailer nymph but the occasional summer steelhead is more apt to prefer bigger groceries. I've caught a lot of accidental steelhead in my life. Most of them have taken a Montana Stone employed to get my trout fly to the bottom. Trout will also mistake the big salmon-fly imitation for a natural when the migration is on, or even in the weeks and months before it, when the most common big bite is a *Pteronarcys californica* nymph. But I use it more often as a searching pattern than I do as an imitation. That's why I list it here, though it's also my primary salmon-fly nymph imitation.

I tie and fish the fly in sizes 6 through 12. The late Charles Brooks, in his 1976 book, *The Trout and the Stream,* gave only one hook size: 4XL size 4. That is the

The Montana Stone was orginated as an imitation for the large salmon-fly nymph (Pteronarcys californica), *and it is excellent for that. But it has become one of my favorite searching nymphs, even for waters where none of the naturals live.*

maximum size of a mature natural. They have a three- to four-year life cycle; the second- and perhaps third-year classes are always out there, available to trout. That is one reason I tie it in smaller sizes. I also like it as an exploring nymph, not necessarily related to the natural, and therefore more effective when it's not tied to the maximum size of the most mature specimens during the week or two of the migration. I also use fly rods that are far less stout than Charles Brooks used, and I don't enjoy pelting myself with heavily weighted size 4 nymphs. Even when

I'm using it as an imitation, and the naturals have attained that size, I've found that trout are willing to accept one in size 6 or even 8.

Brooks's directions on lead were quite specific: "Weight the hook with twenty-five turns of .025-inch lead wire." Given the calculation that nonlead wire is 20 percent lighter than lead, that adds up to thirty turns. Even at twenty-five turns, the nymph usually calls for a double-deck of wraps in the thorax area. That is not all bad; it thickens the fly there, where the natural is also most robust. If your weighting wire is in keeping with the standard formula—approximately the same diameter as the hook shank—and you use the same twenty-five to thirty turns, your smaller flies will also be weighted in the proper proportions of the originals, and will serve the purpose of fishing deep or tugging smaller nymphs quickly down behind them.

I've heard that I should weight some Montana Stones heavily, others moderately, and some not at all, each with a different thread color on the head, so that I can tell them apart and fish them in various water types. When I turn to this fly, however, I'm doing so for its weight, not because it's pretty. I don't want to confuse myself by carrying it in different versions. When I pluck a Montana Stone out of my fly box, I want to know that its fuselage has an outsized bunch of weighting wire wrapped around it. If I want a lighter black fly, I'll turn to the A. P. Black.

MONTANA STONE *Charles Brooks*

Hook:	3XL or 4XL, size 4–12
Weight:	25–30 turns nonlead wire
Thread:	Black 3/0 or 6/0
Tails:	Black crow, raven, goose, or turkey biots, forked
Rib:	Copper wire
Abdomen:	Black fur or yarn
Gills:	Gray or white ostrich herl
Legs:	One grizzly and one brown-dyed grizzly hen hackle
Thorax:	Black fur or yarn

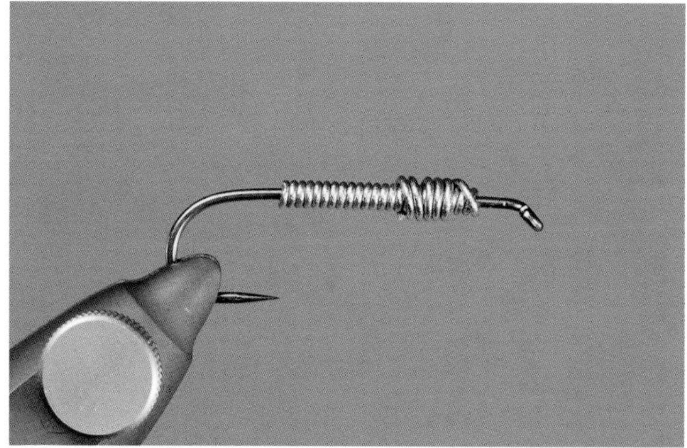

Step 1. Start the weighting wire just in front of the hook bend, and take twenty to twenty-five wraps forward to a point one-fifth to one-sixth of the shank length behind the eye. Double the wire back over itself, and take the remaining five to six wraps as a second deck over the first wraps.

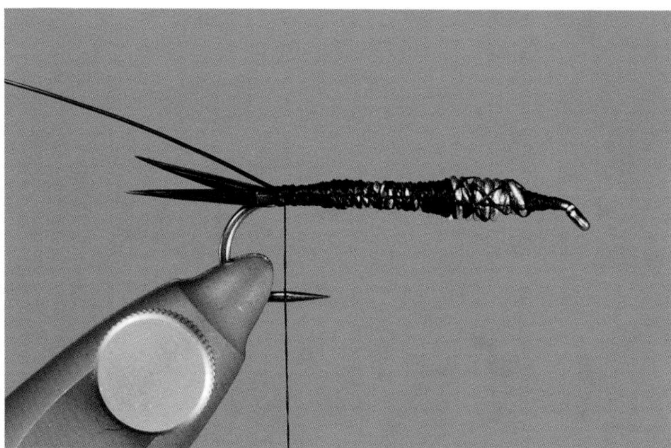

Step 2. Start your thread behind the hook eye. Thicker 3/0 thread is an advantage unless you're tying on a hook in the small size range for this nymph. Build a thread ramp in front of the weighting wire. Take your thread over the wire to the hook bend. Measure a black biot one-quarter to one-third the shank length, and tie it in on the near side of the hook, with the curve outward. Tie in another on the far side of the hook. Clip several inches of ribbing wire from the spool, and tie it in from the back of the second deck of weighting wire to the base of the tails, to form an even underbody. Use your thread to even out bumps in the underbody.

Step 3. Use the direct-dubbing method to twist a somewhat thick amount of black fur to the thread. Charles Brooks called for black yarn in the original dressing, but listed fur as an option. I prefer rabbit fur, or a blend of black-dyed rabbit fur and Sparkle Yarn. The abdomen should be portly, with a small amount of taper. Wind it forward just past the midpoint of the hook, leaving plenty of room for the thorax, gills, and legs. Wind five to seven evenly spaced turns of ribbing forward over the abdomen. Tie off and clip or break the excess ribbing wire.

Step 4. You'll need high-quality hen necks with long feathers to tie this fly. Hen saddle is excellent. You can also use poor-quality rooster. If you don't have a grizzly hen dyed brown, substitute a brown or furnace hackle and the trout won't notice the difference. Select one grizzly and one brown-dyed grizzly feather with fibers equal in length to one and a half to two hook gaps. Strip the fuzz from the base, and tie them in just in front of the abdomen, with the concave side toward the back, so that when wound the fibers will sweep back. Tie in two gray or white ostrich herl fibers, or one gray and one white.

Step 5. Use the direct-dubbing method or a dubbing loop to dub a thick thorax that tapers down to the hook eye, leaving room to finish the head.

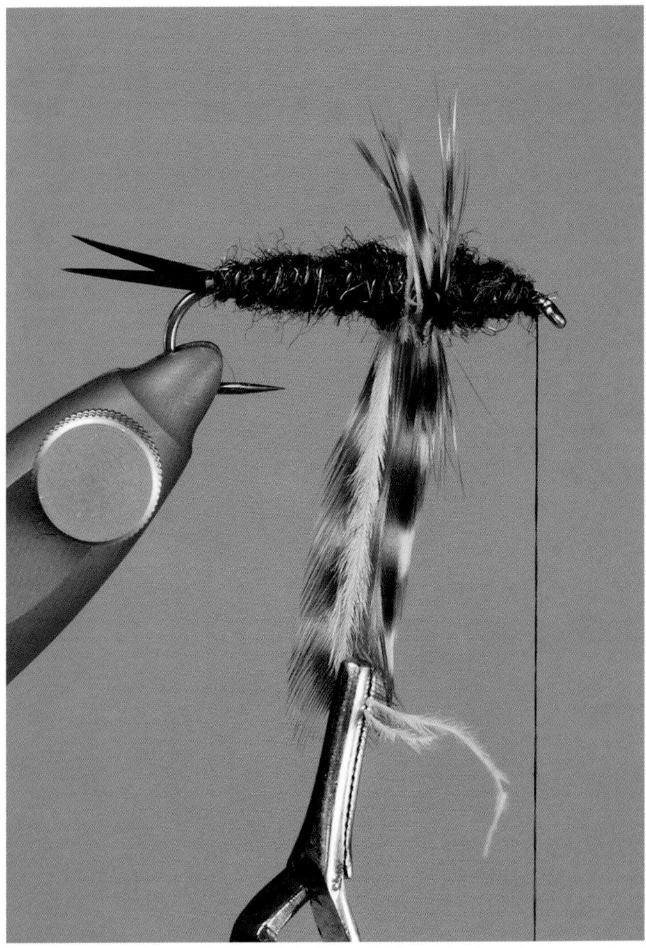

Step 6. Gather the two hackle feathers and the ostrich herls together, and fix your hackle pliers to their tips. Take a single turn of all together, just in front of the abdomen.

Step 7. Take a second turn of hackle and ostrich halfway between the first turn and the hook eye.

Step 8. Bring the hackle and herl forward under the hook eye, and use four or five turns of thread to tie it off. Do not clip the excess until you're sure the unruly affair is captured securely with your thread.

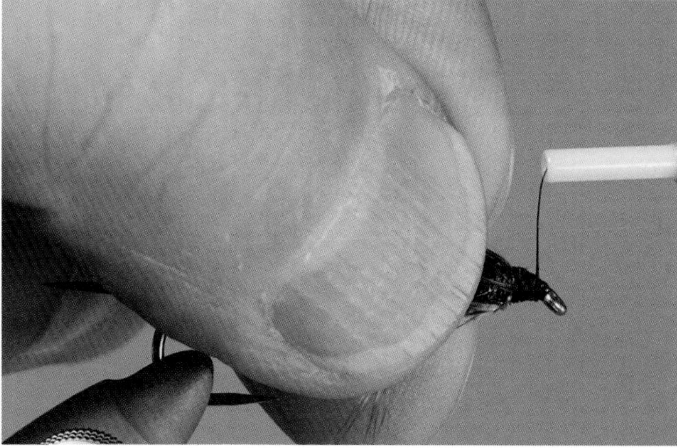

Step 9. Use the thumb and forefinger of your off hand to hold any stray hackle fibers back from the head, and make a layer or two of thread behind the hook eye to tidy up the head.

Step 10. Before whip-finishing, take two or three turns of thread back through the hackle and herl to the abdomen, and bring it forward through the hackle to the hook eye. This forms two or three X-turns of thread over the hackle and the fragile herl, and secures them against the teeth of the many angry trout you are going to catch on this fly. As you work the thread through the hackle and herl, wobble your bobbin back and forth, to seat the thread without matting down any more hackle fibers than necessary. This will make the finished fly less tidy and attractive, but much more durable. I have seen directions for the tie with the rib wound after the hackle and herl are completed, carrying the rib all the way to the hook eye, serving this same purpose: to guard the fragile herl from the teeth of trout.

Step 11. Whip-finish the fly and clip the thread. It is wise at this point to apply head cement to the whip-finish. It is more common among experienced tiers who fish their own flies to add a second quick whip-finish at this point, and omit the head cement.

The Montana Stone is tied in the round, so that a trout sees the same thing no matter how the fly tumbles in the current.

Charles Brooks commented that if this fly looks neat when it exits your tying vise, you've made a mistake, and should drop it on the ground, grind it under your foot to mess it up. He also wrote that he designed his fast-water nymphs to be tied *in the round,* so that no matter the view a trout got of them—top, bottom, or either side—it saw the same thing. Natural salmon flies, in his underwater observations, did not tumble with the currents, flashing now the underside, now the top, but stabilized themselves, and showed trout the same side as they drifted downstream.

There can be little doubt that a Montana Stone tricked out with a tungsten bead and rubber legs would get down deep, scare up some trout. But it might not be any more effective than similar patterns that would be a lot easier to tie. And it would be difficult to fish it without the feeling that the great Charles Brooks might be looking over your shoulder, scolding you for what you've done to his famous nymph.

I have never seen this fly with a bead added, and have never tried it that way myself. I've also not seen it with a flashback, rubber legs, or any other of the many ways that it might be tricked up. I don't know if they would make it better or worse. There is little question they would make it look more like other flies that you can tie to accomplish the same thing, and less like the wonderful original that catches so many trout, in so many places, far removed from the presence of the naturals Charles Brooks tied it to imitate.

ALL-FUR SWIMMER

One fur nymph that I tie and use consistently could be considered a simple elongation of the beadhead Pine Squirrel Nymph that I listed earlier as my modification of Dave Whitlock's Red Fox Squirrel Nymph. The entire fly, except the bead, is tied from the hide of a pine squirrel. It is tied on a 3XL hook, most of the time with a straight shank, but sometimes for a racier look on a curved-shank nymph hook.

I use it mostly on small to medium-sized trout streams with mild gradients. Such streams have a lot of deep water moving slowly along undercut banks, usually with grass drooping over the edges, trailing almost into the water. Trout hang back beneath those protective undercuts. A lot of long and slender mayfly swimmer nymphs, and other types of agile nymphs and even small minnows, live there as well. Trout are accustomed to hiding in ambush, dashing out into the near currents to intercept food dashing past.

ALL-FUR SWIMMER

Hook:	3XL, size 12–16
Bead:	Gold
Weight:	10–20 turns nonlead wire
Thread:	Brown 8/0
Tail:	Pine squirrel guard hairs
Body:	Pine squirrel fur
Hackle:	Pine squirrel fur hackle

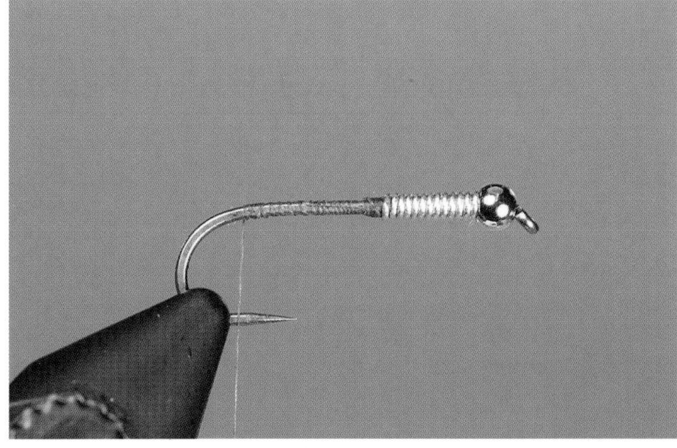

Step 1. Place a bead on the hook, fix the hook in the vise, and weight the hook with ten to twenty turns of nonlead wire. Because I want to keep this fly slender, I tend to use weighting wire that is one size undersized, and take fifteen to twenty turns. Work the front turns of weighting wire into the open back end of the bead. Start the thread behind the weighting wire, create a thread ramp behind the shoulder, then take the thread to the bend of the hook.

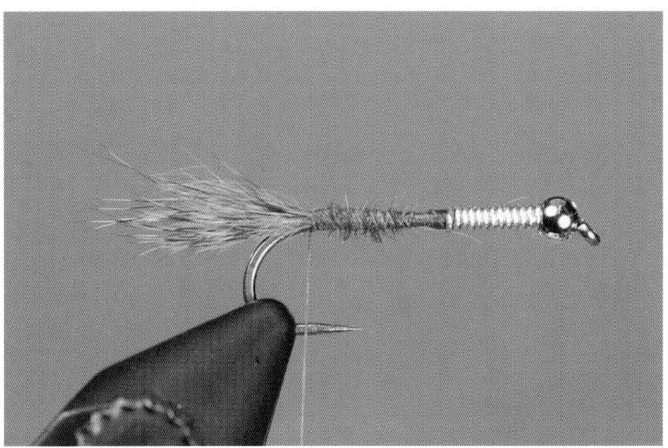

Step 2. Clip a substantial clump of hair from the hide of a pine squirrel. Remove the excess underfur from the base, but not from the guard hairs; this represents an extension of the body as much as a tail, and should be left full. Measure the hair two-thirds the length of the hook shank, and tie it in at the bend of the hook.

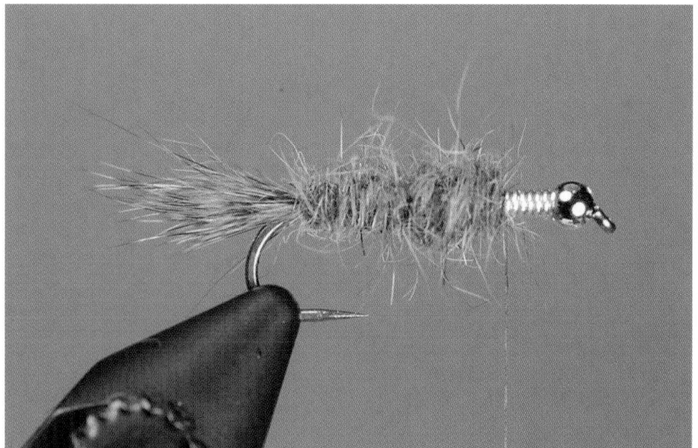

Step 3. Clip a larger portion of fur from the same squirrel hide. Remove the guard hairs, and rough up the underfur in the palm of your hand to mix it. Using the direct-dubbing method, tease the fur out along your thread, twisting it to the thread at the same time. Make a long, slim dubbing skein, and wind it forward over the hook shank and weighting wire wraps to a point about one-quarter the shank length behind the hook eye. It should be somewhat slender, and tapered slightly from the back up to the front.

Step 4. Use the fur hackle technique (see page 54) to finish the fly. Wax one to two inches of thread with sticky wax. Clip a wide and thin patch of fur from the pine squirrel hide, with the guard hairs and underfur left in. If necessary for a small hook, shorten the fur hackle with scissors. Place the fur gently against the waxed thread, and capture it in a thread loop. Twirl the end of the loop to turn the fur into a bottle brush, and catch the end of the loop in your hackle pliers.

Step 5. Wind two to at most four turns of fur hackle forward between the end of the abdomen and the back of the bead. Use the thumb and forefinger tips of your off hand to stroke the fur back after each turn, so that when finished it is swept back, as it might be for a streamer or wet-fly hackle. It's not likely to be tidy at this point.

Step 6. Stroke any stray fibers back, and hold them while you take just a few turns of thread between the end of the fur hackle and the back of the bead. Place a whip-finish behind the bead, and use the thumbnail and forefinger nail of your tying hand to seat it securely before you clip the thread. You can pluck out any wild hairs from the fur hackle, but it should be thick and fibrous, and more unruly than it is pretty.

Most fur searching nymphs are designed to be fished dead drift along the bottom, but this All-Fur Swimmer, like the Bird's Nest, is designed as much for fishing with a teasing swing as it for tumbling deep. I generally cast this streamlined nymph upstream along undercut edges, and fish it back downstream with very short, staccato strips that move it just a bit faster than the current would escort it, swimming right along the length of the undercut.

When the stream is wide enough to take a position upstream and across from an undercut bank, I'll sometimes cast directly to the bank, setting the fly down as close as possible to the edge. After giving it a bit of time to sink, I'll retrieve it out away from the bank, as if it's a natural swimmer nymph escaping out into the open current. Trout often chase it down and thrash it with one of those turning takes that tell of the sort of size that often lurks beneath undercut banks.

OLIVE BEADHEAD

Your searching-nymph box should contain at least one fur dressing that represents the very common free-living or net-spinning caddis larva shape: essentially, the green rock worm. So many of these live in brisk riffles, and so often get kicked loose into the currents, that trout in fast water are always aware of them, and almost always willing to take a searching nymph that looks a little like them. Most of them are some shade of green.

I was distressed a few years ago to discover that no fly shop or catalog offered an olive nymph tied on a curved-shank hook with a beadhead. It seemed such an elemental addition to a trout-fly box that I sat at a picnic table, in the backyard of Andy and Marie Davidson's home in Fennimore, Wisconsin, and invented a bunch in a hurry, because the trout in those tiny limestone spring creeks in the area seemed to cry for them. It turned out not to be as true as I'd hoped. The nymph worked no wonders there, but it did when I began using it in the riffles of larger streams and rivers.

This gap in flies has now been filled: fly-shop bins and catalogs offer a wide variety of beadhead, olive-bodied, curved-shank nymphs. None of them are mine, but mine seems to work as well as any I've tried, and I'll offer it here in case you'd like to try it.

OLIVE BEADHEAD

Hook:	Curved scud hook, size 12–16
Bead:	Gold
Weight:	10–15 turns nonlead wire
Thread:	Brown 8/0
Rib:	Yellow buttonhole twist or doubled Pearsall's Gossamer silk thread
Abdomen:	Caddis green fur or synthetic dubbing
Thorax:	Hare's mask fur or Hareline Dubbin' Dark Hare's Ear Plus #5

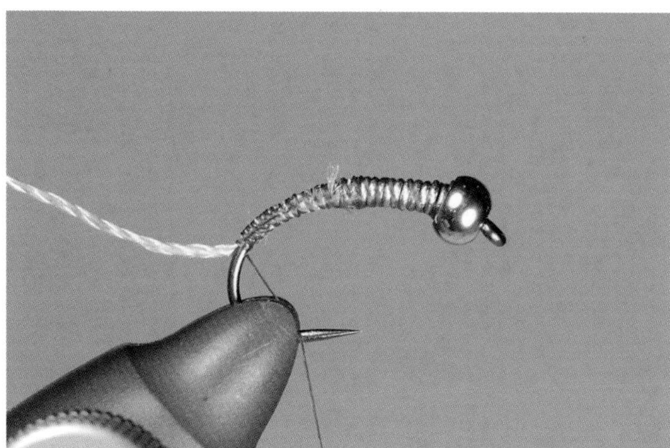

Step 1. Place a bead on the hook, fix the hook in the vise, and take ten to fifteen turns of weighting wire. Work the front of the wire into the back of the bead, start the thread behind the wire, and build up a thread ramp onto the shoulder. Take thread wraps forward and back through the wire to lock it in place, then take the working thread well down on the curve of the hook. Tie in several inches of thick silk thread at this point, or double or quadruple 6/0 or 8/0 yellow tying thread, and use that for the rib.

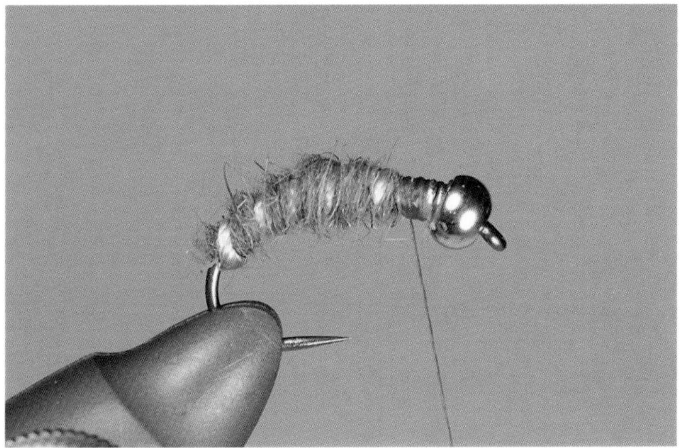

Step 2. Using the direct-dubbing method, twist fur or synthetic dubbing tightly to the thread, and take it forward to a point about one-quarter the length of the shank behind the hook eye. It should be a compact and only slightly tapered body. Rib the body with four to six evenly spaced turns of ribbing, and clip the excess. If you're using doubled thread, twist the strands together before ribbing the body.

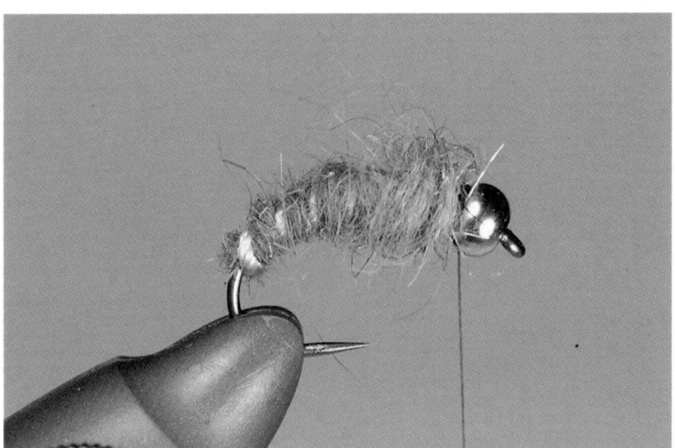

Step 3. Use the direct-dubbing method to twist a small amount of dark hare's mask fur, with the guard hairs left in, loosely to the thread. Wind it forward in just two or three turns from the end of the abdomen to the back of the bead. If a few wild guard hairs stick out, that is good: caddis larvae have legs. If the dubbing is too tidy, I'll usually pick it out with my dubbing needle.

SUMMARY

You could easily fill an entire nymph box, or several of them, with nothing but fur searching nymphs, and you'd be assured of catching a lot of trout on moving water, often even those trout that might be feeding selectively. But you might be better advised to pick just a few, at least to start, especially those that cover the color spectrum of natural insects that live most often in rivers and streams, and tie those in a range of sizes, so that you have covered the averages of the things that trout eat. That is what searching nymphs are all about: lifelike and lively nymphs that average out what the trout eat rather than precisely resemble any one insect or crustacean.

The few fur nymphs that I tie and use most often include Dave Whitlock's Red Fox Squirrel, or my Beadhead Pine Squirrel misinterpretation of it; the A. P. Black for small streams, half the time with a beadhead and half the time without; Charles Brooks's Montana Stone as an exploring fly in brutal water, and for delivering smaller nymphs to the bottom; the All-Fur Swimmer for low-gradient undercuts; and the Olive Beadhead for covering riffles and fast runs in midsized streams and rivers. Those make a good start on a box of searching nymphs for trout.

CHAPTER 12

Herl Nymphs

Trout are attracted to herl, at least in part because of the reflectance of light off the myriads of tiny barbules that line each quill. But herl is fragile. If the quill is simply tied in, and the herl wound around the hook shank so the barbules stand up short but as thick as chenille, the teeth of the first trout you catch will cut the stem, the herl will come unwound, and you will no longer have a fly with which to beguile the trout. Fragile herl must be protected against the sharp teeth of the trout.

You can protect herl in two primary ways. The first is to counterwind it with fine ribbing wire (page 58). The second is to gather it along with your tying thread, and twirl them into a herl rope (see page 59). A third method, little used in modern nymphs, is to twirl the fragile herl together with the ribbing wire. The original Frank Sawyer Pheasant Tail was tied with fine copper wire in place of thread. The pheasant herls for the body were twisted with the wire, and the resulting body was both secure and a bit more substantial. The wire also served to weight the fly, to help it penetrate the surface film and sink a few inches. This served Sawyer's method and the water on which he fished his Pheasant Tail Nymph.

He was riverkeeper on the peaceful Avon River in England. He fished his Pheasant Tail to visible trout that were feeding during olive *(Baetis)* hatches, but subsurface rather than on top. He would cast upstream from the trout, let his little nymph sink to the level of the fish, then animate the fly in front of the eyes of the trout, using his *induced take* method to make the fly suddenly look alive and as if it were escaping toward the surface for emergence. The weight of the copper wire, used in place of tying thread, helped get his nymph to the level of the trout.

The directions for tying, as given by Sawyer in his 1958 book, *Nymphs and the Trout,* call for using copper wire "little thicker than a human hair," and layering it from back to front and front to back before tying in the tail. The best wire I've found for tying the fly is Ultra Wire in size X-small. The best result I've been able to achieve for the fly, tied with wire, is from Darrel Martin's interpretation of the Sawyer method in Darrel's very fine 1987 book, *Fly-Tying Methods.* With Darrel's technique, it is possible to achieve Sawyer's described result. I tie the PT with wire so often that I tried threading a spool of the Ultra Wire on an old bobbin. It didn't work. The wire twisted and broke at inopportune moments.

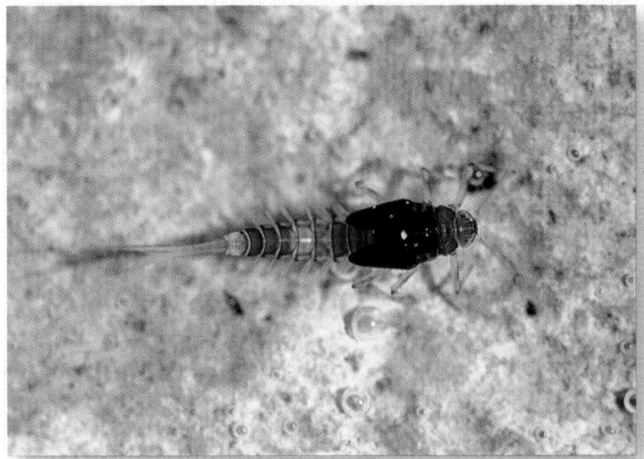

The Sawyer Pheasant Tail was originated as an imitation for the blue-winged olive nymph (Baetis), *which occurs in waters all around the world. This specimen, with its almost black wing cases, is mature and ready to emerge.*

Because it was the foundation method for handling herl, I'll list the original Sawyer Pheasant Tail here, tied with wire. It's interesting to note that some famous British writers pointed out to Sawyer that his copperish nymph did not capture the true colors of the natural *Baetis* nymph, which varies in color from place to place but is more likely to be brownish olive. Sawyer agreed, but noted that the fly as he tied it captured more trout than one tied with more realistic colors. My own experience lends itself toward Sawyer's observation.

I have noticed that many nymphs in the Baetidae family turn a shiny copper color just before emergence, presumably because they exude bubbles of air between the inner skin of the dun about to be born and the outer exoskeleton of the nymph about to be shed. It's possible, even likely, that trout are triggered to take by the copper sheen of the nymph the way Sawyer tied it. Because natural swimmer nymphs tuck their legs against their bodies while swimming, Sawyer tied his nymph without legs.

PHEASANT TAIL *Frank Sawyer*

Hook:	Standard nymph, size 14–20
Wire:	X-small Ultra Wire
Tail:	Pheasant tail fibers
Body:	Pheasant tail fibers
Shellback:	Butts of body fibers

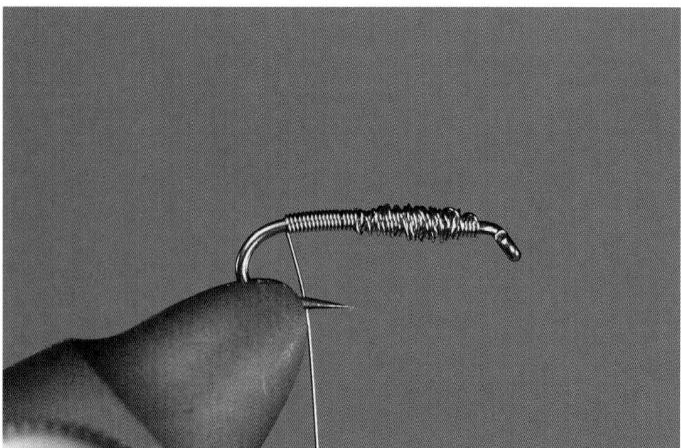

Step 1. Fix the hook in the vise. Start with a size 18; it's most suitable to the length of the pheasant fibers and diameter of the wire, in my experience. Cut a ten- to twelve-inch length of wire from the spool; waste some at the start, and don't short yourself. Start the wire at about the midpoint of the shank. Make a layer forward, stopping well short of the eye. Use the thumbnails and forefinger nails of both hands to compress the wraps and to move the wire to where you want it on the hook. Layer wire back and forth three to four times to build up an oval underthorax. Take the wire in tight turns to the hook bend. Compress the wraps again.

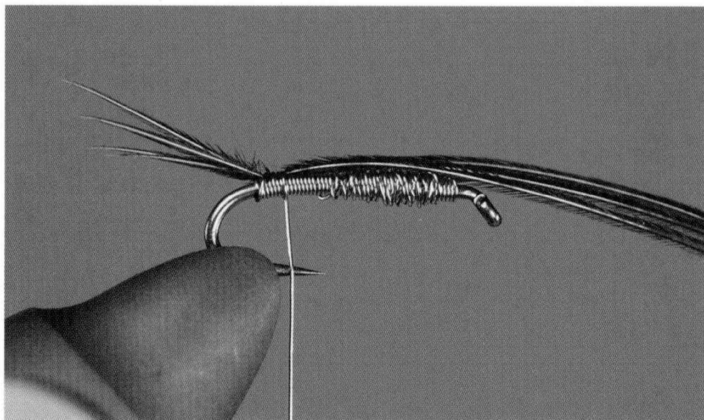

Step 2. Align the tips of four long pheasant tail fibers, and strip or clip them from the feather. Measure the tips one-third to one-half the hook shank, and hold them in a pinch at the bend of the hook. Use a wire pinch wrap (see page 45), just as you would with thread, to attach the tails directly onto the top of the hook. Take two to three wraps of wire forward. If the tails are not centered on top of the hook shank, or are too long or short, you can reposition them at this point.

Step 3. Gather the wire and herls and gently twist them together, but not tight enough to break the herls. If you do, which will be common at first, unwind the wire to remove the tail, select and even four more herl fibers, and tie the tail in again. Wind the herl and wire forward together to the hook eye. Abut the turns but do not overlap them, or you'll run out of herl. Continue to twist the herl and wire together as you go forward. Separate the herls from the wire behind the hook eye, and take two to three turns of wire over the herls to hold them in place. Be careful not to crowd the hook eye.

Step 4. Take a single turn of wire back over the thorax to place it at the back of the thorax lump. Bring the herl butts back, and take one or two turns of wire over them to secure the first layer of the shellback.

Step 5. Take one or two turns of wire over the shellback to return the wire to a point just behind the hook eye. Draw the herl butts forward, and take three to five turns of wire to secure them.

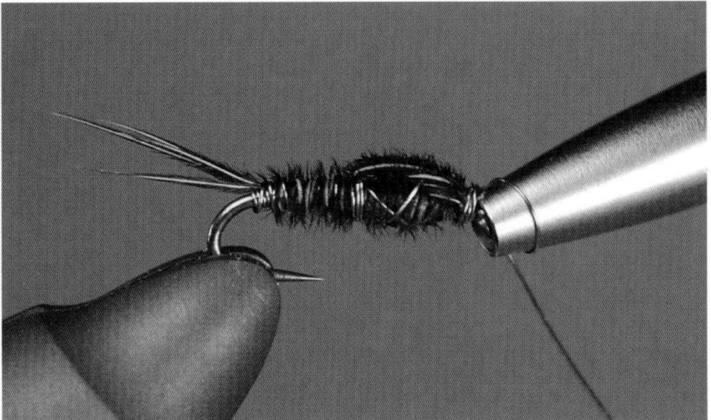

Step 6. Clip the excess herl. Directions for the Sawyer original call for clipping the wire and letting its natural tension hold it in place. I enjoy using a half-hitch tool to place a single half hitch tight behind the eye (see page 43). It thickens the head slightly, but the resulting fly is at least slightly more durable.

It adds little difficulty to draw two herl butts back to the near side, take a turn of wire over them, then do the same on the other side, before finishing the head. Clip the herls to leg length after the fly is finished, and the fly might look a little more rakish and complete to you. But it would also violate the originator's intentions for his Pheasant Tail, which was to tie it without legs.

If you master tying the Pheasant Tail with wire, you'll find it easy to tie it with thread and counterwound ribbing wire, in what has become the standard method for North American waters. Be aware that the nymph is far less heavy without the underlayment of copper wire. It can be weighted with nonlead wire under the thorax area, or weight can be omitted. Because of its compactness, the fly will rarely get hung up in the surface film, and it's often an advantage to be able to fish it on a natural drift just an inch to a few inches deep, when trout are taking emerging naturals just beneath the surface film. So tying the Pheasant Tail without any weight is the standard method.

If you desire to get it deep, you can add split shot to the leader, or use a heavily weighted nymph such as Charles Brooks's Montana Stone to escort it down there. The Pheasant Tail Nymph in sizes 16 through 22 makes an excellent small nymph in a two-fly tandem.

PHEASANT TAIL *Al Troth*

Hook:	Standard nymph, size 14–22
Thread:	Brown 8/0
Weight:	6–10 turns fine nonlead wire, optional
Tail:	3–4 pheasant tail fibers
Rib:	Fine copper wire
Abdomen:	Tail fibers wound as herl
Legs:	Pheasant fiber tips
Thorax:	Peacock herl
Wing case:	Pheasant tail fibers

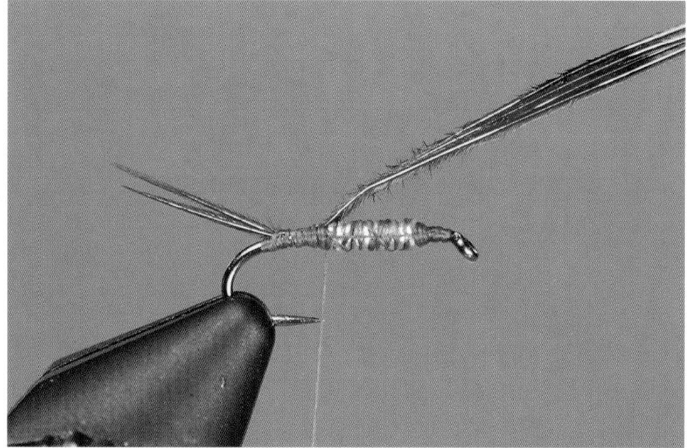

Step 1. Fix the hook in the vise, and layer the thorax area with fine nonlead weighting wire wraps, if desired. Start the thread behind the hook eye, layer it over the weighting wire and back, and build slight thread ramps at the front and back shoulders of the wire. Layer thread to the hook bend and clip the excess. Select four pheasant herl fibers, even the tips, and clip or pull them from the feather. Measure them one-half to two-thirds the shank length, and tie them in at the bend of the hook. Overwrap them to the back of the weighting wire wraps.

Step 2. Lay the ribbing wire alongside the hook shank with its tip abutted against the back shoulder of the weighting wire. Gather it together with the herl stems, and overwrap them with thread to the base of the tails.

Step 3. Wrap the herl forward to a point just past the midpoint of the hook shank. Tie it off there. If you're tying a very small fly, size 20 or under, and the abdomen herl will be sufficient for the wing case, do not clip the herl butts. If you're tying size 18 or larger, clip the butts, as shown here. Counterwind the ribbing wire in four to six evenly spaced turns to the end of the abdomen. Clip the excess wire there.

Step 4. Even the tips of six pheasant tail fibers, and clip or strip them from the feather. Measure the tips two-thirds the length of the hook shank, and tie them in just behind the hook eye, so they stick out over the front of the hook. Overwrap the butts back to the end of the abdomen. Bend the herl butts into a loop, and tie them down. This doubles the amount for the wing case, and also brings the black part of the herls into the right position for the wing case, which should be darker than the abdomen.

Step 5. Select two or three peacock herl fibers from the eye feather, appropriate to the size fly you're tying. If it's size 14, take them from near the eye, where they have longer barbules. If you're tying smaller, take the herl fibers from farther down the stem, where they become slimmer. Tie them in by the tips, and take two to at most four turns forward to the hook eye before tying them off and clipping the excess.

Step 6. Bring the pheasant herl butts forward over the peacock herl, and tie them off behind the hook eye, leaving room for a thread head. Clip the excess butts. Be careful not to clip your leg fiber tips with them.

Step 7. Separate out three fiber tips, and draw them back along the near side. Take two to three turns of thread over them to lock them back and down. Do the same with the remaining fiber tips on the far side of the hook. Take a minimal number of thread turns to tidy the head, and whip-finish the fly.

The Pheasant Tail Nymph has been interpreted in more ways, it seems, than there are folks who tie and fish it. That might be because some of us use it in more than one style. The least commonly used is the original Frank Sawyer version, tied with wire, though learning to tie it the way he did is more than an excellent academic exercise. Such a heavy Pheasant Tail, wound with copper wire, causes the fly to sink quickly even when no weight is added to the leader. If you're working a sighted trout, as Sawyer often did, on smooth currents, as Sawyer's home waters were, and you need the fly to reach the depth of the trout without any other delivery system that would disturb the trout, then the original would serve you well. I use it often, in part out of nostalgia, in another part out of effectiveness.

The Americanized brand of the fly, tied with a peacock herl thorax and usually credited to the famous Montana guide Al Troth, has been the most popular version of the fly on our waters, until the introduction of beads and flashbacks. It's likely that the fly is fished most often in its flashback variation on the Al Troth pattern. Certainly the combination of pheasant herl, peacock herl, and a bit of flash is deadly. The only difference is replacement of pheasant tail fibers with pearl flash for the wing case.

FLASHBACK PHEASANT TAIL

Hook:	Standard nymph, size 14–22
Thread:	Brown 8/0
Weight:	6–10 turns fine nonlead wire, optional
Tail:	3–4 pheasant tail fibers
Rib:	Fine copper wire
Abdomen:	Tail fibers wound as herl
Wing case:	Pearl Flashabou or Krystal Flash
Legs:	Pheasant fiber tips
Thorax:	Peacock herl

I tie and fish the Pheasant Tail most often in this flashback form. The fly was originally tied by Sawyer for trout feeding selectively on emerging *Baetis* nymphs in British chalkstreams. The same nymph, in a wide number of species but a narrow spectrum of colors, hatches all across our own continent. With the added bit of sparkle, the Flashback Pheasant Tail makes an excellent imitation wherever you find *Baetis* hatching, which might be nearly anywhere you fly-fish for trout. It will be most useful as an imitation of these small insects in sizes 18 and 20.

I also use the flashback version of the same fly as an imitation of stillwater *Callibaetis,* which like their sister *Baetis* are common in lakes and ponds from the Atlantic Ocean to the Pacific. Also like the smaller *Baetis,* they often take on a brassy appearance just before emergence. I have tried exact imitations of the naturals I collect during hatches, but have always caught more trout on the Flashback Pheasant Tail in sizes 14 and 16.

This chapter is about searching nymphs, not imitations, but I've made it clear that the best searching nymphs are often based on abundant natural trout foods, such as those ubiquitous *Baetis* and *Callibaetis.* The Flashback Pheasant Tail, in sizes 14 through 20, would be an obvious addition to any searching box of nymphs. But I tie it as listed for imitations, and use a bit simpler and buggier variation in my searching fishing.

I have never considered it necessary to name this variation, which makes the fly a lot easier to tie by substituting pine squirrel fur for both the thorax and legs of the standard flashback version. I'd be surprised to find out I was the first to tie it this way. It is, however, the way I tie and use the Pheasant Tail most often.

PHEASANT TAIL FLASHBACK SQUIRREL

Hook:	Curved scud, size 14–22
Thread:	Brown 8/0
Weight:	6–10 turns fine nonlead wire, optional
Tail:	3–4 pheasant tail fibers
Rib:	Fine copper wire
Abdomen:	Tail fibers wound as herl
Wing case:	Pearl Flashabou or Krystal Flash
Thorax and legs:	Pine squirrel fur, with guard hairs

When tying the Flashback PT with squirrel fur for the thorax and legs, I use a dubbing loop in the larger sizes, 14 and 16, but use the simpler direct-dubbing method on smaller flies. If you wind up with wild hairs sticking out, and find your fly untidy, then pluck them out with tweezers. If you feel the fur is wound too tight, and would like to rough it up, merely take your bodkin, scissor points, or other sharp tool to it to pick it out. I prefer it rough, with some fibers sticking out to work in the water, to make the fly look alive. But Frank Sawyer, who originated the Pheasant Tail Nymph, tied his without legs because the naturals fold theirs in when swimming.

PHEASANT TAIL BEADHEAD

Hook: Curved scud, size 16–20
Bead: Gold
Weight: 5–10 turns fine nonlead wire, optional
Thread: Brown 8/0
Tails: Pheasant tail fibers
Rib: Fine copper wire
Abdomen: Pheasant tail herl
Thorax: Pine squirrel fur

Beads have been added to every nymph ever tied, and the Pheasant Tail is not an exception. I think it's a great idea; it's just not one I've taken up with any enthusiasm. The bead disrupts the slender, tapered, insectlike look of the nymph, and though I consider the addition of some flash beneficial to the nymph, as a searching dressing and as an imitation both, I prefer to achieve it with the pearl flash wing case, which maintains the shape of the slender fly, rather than with a bead.

You'll want one version or another of the Pheasant Tail Nymph in your searching-nymph box, though if you're like me, it will find a surer seat in both your still-water and moving-water imitative boxes, in one size for *Callibaetis* and another for *Baetis.* In my own searching-nymph box, I use the Pheasant Tail tiny, in size 18 and smaller. It's almost always fished as the smaller fly of a two-fly tandem, with a size 16 lead fly and size 20 or even 22 Pheasant Tail point fly. Trout in smooth flows make more of their living than you might suspect on tiny bites. If you decrease the size of the nymphs you use, you might be surprised at the increase in the size of your catch.

Pheasant Tail Nymphs are an excellent way to tie and fish tiny flies.

HERL NYMPH

I've already mentioned Rick Hafele's Peacock Herl Nymph (see page 3). He's an aquatic entomologist; it's a lifelike rendition of an old standard. The original Herl Nymph resembles a caddis larva in its case, more than anything else, and it's well known that trout take cased caddis opportunistically, ingesting case and all, but might not do that when more amenable groceries are present in any abundance. Clearly the Herl Nymph is best tied and fished as a searching dressing, for use in those times when you don't know what trout might be taking.

Herl has that well-known universal appeal. The Herl Nymph is an excellent way to take advantage of the failing trout have for any fly tied with peacock.

HERL NYMPH

Hook: Standard nymph or 2XL, size 10–18
Weight: 10–20 turns nonlead wire
Thread: Black 6/0 or 8/0
Body: Peacock herl
Legs: Black hackle fibers
Head: Black ostrich herl

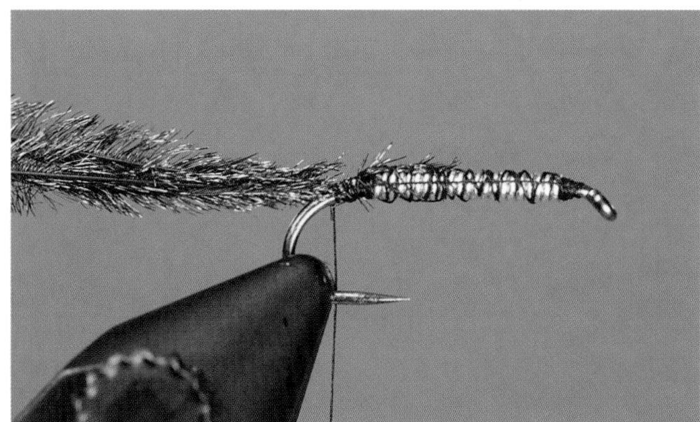

Step 1. Fix the hook in the vise and layer the shank with the desired number of weighting wire turns. You'll rarely want to fish this fly anywhere except on or very near the bottom, so your weighting wire should be about the same diameter as the hook wire, not undersized, and should cover most of the hook shank. Start the thread, and build

ramps at the front and back of the weighting wire wraps. Strip two to four herls from the eye feather, break or cut a half inch to an inch off the very fragile tips, and tie the herl in by the tips at the bend of the hook.

Step 2. Using the herl rope method (see page 59) form a thread loop over the forefinger of your off hand. Be sure it is a bit longer than the herls. Twist the herls together with the thread loop, forming a herl rope. Use your hackle pliers to wrap the herl forward, and stop at a point about one-quarter the shank length behind the hook eye. Tie it off there and clip the excess. Be sure to twist the herl rope after each turn or two around the hook shank.

Step 3. Even the tips of a substantial bundle of black hackle fibers, and clip or peel them from the feather stem. If you're tying rotary, it's easiest at this point to rotate the hook so that it is upside down. If not, this is the point where you learn to execute a pinch wrap on the underside of the hook. Measure the fibers to the hook point, hold them between the thumb and forefinger of your off hand, and place them between the end of the body and the hook eye. Slide your thread between thumb and forefinger, then form a loop of thread by sliding it back between them, around both the hook shank and the hackle fibers. Draw the thread tight while letting the loop slip onto the fibers, locking them against the hook. Take a few more turns of thread, then clip the butts.

Step 4. Clip or peel two black marabou fibers from the feather. Marabou stems are less fragile than peacock or pheasant, and do not need to be secured with wire ribbing or a thread loop, though you can add those things if you desire. The herl can simply be tied in, wound, and tied off. Tie the herls in together in front of the abdomen. Keeping them together, take two to five wraps forward to a point just behind the hook eye. Tie them off and clip the excess; most times I simply snap them back against the thread wraps to break them off, rather than cut them. Make a neat thread head, whip-finish, and apply head cement.

By tying the Herl Nymph on a 2XL or even 3XL hook, and using slightly slimmer peacock herls, you can turn it into a more elegant affair. The shape that pleases you should be the one that seems to you to best please the trout.

The Herl Nymph can be portly or slender, depending on the shank length of the hook on which you tie it and the diameter of the herl you use. Though it is typically tied on a standard 1XL nymph hook, it looks at least as good when tied on a 2XL or even 3XL hook. Your eye should tell you which you prefer, or you should try a few on each hook style.

The Herl Nymph in its various forms bears a striking resemblance to many cased caddis larvae, which trout take case and all, and which might explain some of the success of the pattern as a searching nymph.

Rick Hafele's version of the Herl Nymph (see page 3) moves the shape of the Herl Nymph only slightly away from the shape of a cased caddis larva, and brings it much more in line with the common mayfly crawler and stonefly nymph shape. As such, it might make a more realistic searching nymph on the peacock herl theme.

Though Rick doesn't tie or fish this nymph with a bead, I find that the addition of a small bead, one size smaller than normal for the size fly being tied, doesn't do it any damage and improves my attitude about fishing it. I will list it here with a gold beadhead, and suggest that you tie and try a few both ways, to see which might work best for you. Rick lists it in sizes 8 to 18, but it's likely to be most useful to you in sizes 12, 14, and 16.

PEACOCK HERL NYMPH, BEADHEAD
Rick Hafele

Hook:	Standard nymph, size 8–18
Bead:	Gold
Weight:	10–20 turns nonlead wire
Thread:	Black 6/0 or 8/0
Rib:	Fine gold or silver tinsel or wire
Abdomen:	Peacock herl
Wing case:	Black Krystal Flash
Thorax:	Pine squirrel fur

Step 1. Place the bead over the hook shank, fix the hook in the vise, take the desired number of weighting wire turns, and insert the forward end of the weighting wire wraps into the open end of the bead. Start your thread behind the weighting wire, build a slight thread ramp up onto the wire, and take turns forward to the bead and back to secure the weight. Layer thread to the hook bend. Tie in your ribbing wire and peacock herl, butting them against the back shoulder of the weighting wire, and overwrapping them with thread to the bend of the hook.

Step 2. Using the herl rope method (see page 59) twist the herl together with a thread loop, and wind it forward to a point just past the midpoint of the shank. Tie it off and clip the excess. Wind the ribbing forward in three to six evenly spaced turns through the herl. Tie it off and clip or break off the excess. Tie in several strands of black Krystal Flash for the wing case. Be sure that the Krystal Flash is overwrapped in the thread tight back against the abdomen, to avoid a wasp-waisted appearance when the wing case is brought forward over the thorax.

Step 3. Use the direct-dubbing method or fur loop method to wrap a somewhat loose and spiky thorax of pine squirrel fur. Be sure to leave the guard hairs in the fur, to act as legs on the finished fly. Bring the wing-case fibers forward, and take three to five tight turns of thread to lock them in behind the bead.

Step 4. Clip the excess wing-case fibers at the back of the bead. Do not try to cut them tight against the thread wraps holding them down; this only increases the chance that they'll work loose later. Leave just a fringe at the back of the bead. Tuck a whip-finish tight behind the beadhead, over the wraps securing the wing case. Clip the thread, apply head cement, and the fly is finished.

PRINCE NYMPH

Entire articles have been written speculating why a nymph that looks so little like anything in nature could possibly catch so many trout as the Prince Nymph, with its white wings held tight over its peacock herl body. It almost seems as if the deletion of those unnatural wings would increase the catch, but that turns out to be far from true. Whatever triggers they trip in trout, they definitely make the fly more effective.

The nearest I've been able to speculate is the relationship between the white wing of the fly and the white back of the pale moon-winged back swimmer natural. Back swimmers are predators; they hang in the surface, their butt ends up absorbing atmospheric oxygen through spiracles, their big eyes down, looking for prey on which to pounce. Just about as often as the back swimmers see prey, trout see them, and the chase gets on. Trout win. I once guessed that the wings of the Prince Nymph reflect in the surface film, trout see that reflection, mistake it for a back swimmer waiting for prey, make the mistake of taking the artificial.

Back swimmers live only in lakes and ponds. The Prince Nymph works there, especially in the presence of back swimmers. But I catch far more trout on it in moving water, where no back swimmers live, and so far as I've been able to figure out, no other natural insects look remotely like a Prince Nymph. It works wonders as a searching nymph, and in its beadhead version is one of the most popular and productive flies you can fish. It should have a distinct presence in your own searching-nymph box.

I carry the Prince Nymph tied in two ways: the standard beadhead dressing in sizes 12 and 14, and a truncated version, missing many of its parts, in sizes 16 and 18. I'll list both here.

PRINCE NYMPH, BEADHEAD *Doug Prince*

Hook:	Standard nymph, size 12–18
Bead:	Gold
Weight:	10–20 turns nonlead wire
Thread:	Black 6/0 or 8/0
Wings:	White goose biots
Tails:	Brown goose biot, forked
Rib:	Oval gold tinsel
Body:	Peacock herl
Hackle:	Brown hen, short

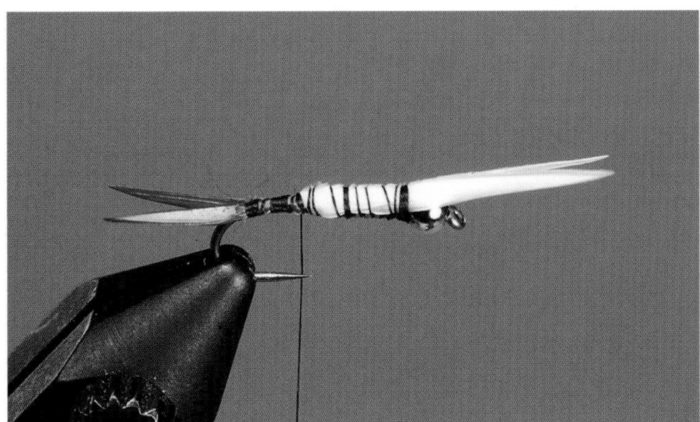

Step 1. Slip a bead onto the hook, fix the hook in the vise, add weighting wire, and start your thread, securing the weighting wire and making a thread ramp at the back shoulder. Select two white goose biots, and clip them from the stem. Measure the first biot the length of the hook shank only, and tie it in tight behind the bead with two to three turns of thread, just off-center on the near side of the hook. The tip should be to the front, the concave side up. Measure the second biot the length of the first, and tie it in overlapping the first, just off-center on the far side of the hook.

Take the thread to the bend of the hook. Clip two brown goose biots from the stem. Measure the first biot half the shank length, and tie it in on the near side of the hook, with the concave side toward you. Measure the second the same length as the first, and tie it in on the far side of the hook, with the concave side away from you. This creates a forked tail. Layer thread over the base of the tail butts and wing butts to form a tapered underbody.

Step 2. Tie in the ribbing material. Select two to four herls from the part of the eyed feather that will make the appropriate thickness body you desire: fat herls from near the eye for large hooks, slender herls from the lower end of the feather for smaller hooks. Tie them in, being sure the last turns of thread toward the back are soft, so they do not cut the fragile herl when you make a herl rope. End with the thread at the base of the tails.

Step 3. Using the herl rope method (see page 59), wind the body forward to a point just behind the bead, leaving a gap the width of a single turn of herl. Tie it off, clip the excess, and wind the ribbing forward in three to six evenly spaced turns. Tie off the tinsel and clip the excess. Select a hen hackle with fibers about the length of one hook gap. Strip fuzz from the base, and tie it in with the concave side to the rear, so that when wound the fibers will sweep back. Clip the stem.

Step 4. Wind a single turn of the hackle, and tie it off. Clip the excess tip. The hackle should be short and sparse. It should never be obtrusive on the Prince Nymph.

Step 5. Double the wing biots back over the body, and take three to five thread turns over them to lock them in place. If necessary, tug them into the proper position on top of the hook shank and take a few more turns of thread to hold them in place. Keep all thread turns at this point minimal, or you'll have an overly thick neck on the fly. Whip-finish tight behind the bead, clip the thread, cement the head, and the nymph is finished. By tying the wing biots in first, rather than last, they will never pull out, as they might if you were to tie them in as the last step in completing the fly.

The truncated version of the Prince Nymph, which I confess to using far more often than I do the standard version shown above, has only a herl body and white biot wings. I tie it in sizes 16 and 18, sometimes 20, and use it as the trail fly in a two-fly tandem with a size 14 or so searching nymph above it. Most trout take the smaller of the two. I've caught uncounted numbers of trout on a small, abbreviated Prince Nymph used as a trailing fly behind a slightly larger nymph.

PRINCE NYMPH, ABBREVIATED

Hook:	Standard nymph, size 16–20
Bead:	Gold
Weight:	5–10 turns nonlead wire
Thread:	Black 8/0
Wings:	White goose biots
Body:	Peacock herl

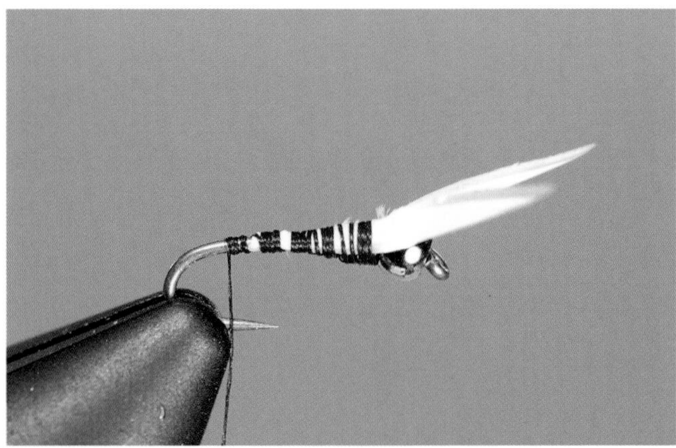

Step 1. Place a bead on the hook, fix the hook in the vise, and secure the bead with just a few turns of weighting wire tucked into the open end. Start your thread behind the weighting wire, build a slight thread ramp at the rear shoulder, and take your thread forward to the bead. Measure one white goose biot the length of the hook shank only, and tie it in behind the bead, with the tip forward and the concave side up, slightly off-center to your side of the hook. Repeat with a second biot on the far side.

Step 2. Tie in two to four slender peacock herl fibers, catch them with a thread loop, and wind the herl rope forward to the back of the bead. Tie it off there with minimal turns of thread to hold it, without building up a thick thread neck, and clip the excess herl rope.

Step 3. Double the goose biots back over the herl body of the nymph. Hold them in place and take five to ten thread turns over them to lock them in place. Tuck a whip-finish behind the bead, over the same wraps that secure the biots. This very simple Prince Nymph seems to be just as effective as the more complicated full tie, and a bunch of them can be tied in a lot less time.

SUMMARY

My searching-nymph box contains just a couple of herl nymphs, the Flashback Pheasant Tail and the Prince Nymph, mostly in its abbreviated form. It's difficult for me to decide whether the Pheasant Tail is a searching nymph or an imitative nymph. I carry it and use it often, and usually first, during both *Baetis* and *Callibaetis* hatches. In that sense it is imitative. But I also use it often as the tiny trailer fly in a two-fly searching tandem, and catch more trout using it that way than I do as an imitation. I use the Pheasant Tail far more often in sizes 18 through 22 than I do in anything larger.

Though I like to have the Prince Nymph in sizes 12 and 14 aboard, I don't use it very often except in the smaller sizes, and without all of the tails and hackles and ribs that are called for in the original version. It's my chosen way to show peacock herl to trout. It's an unlikely combination, the dark and drab herl topped with that bright white wing. For whatever reason, it appeals to fish, and that criterion boils to the top whenever I'm trying to prod trout off the bottom with a searching nymph.

CHAPTER 13

Twisted-Strand Nymphs

Yarns and floss find little play in tying modern nymphs, likely because when they're wound directly onto a hook they form relatively unfeatured bodies, with few loose fibers to wave in the currents, and to make nymphs tied with them resemble anything alive. But when the same materials, and some newer ones such as Z-lon and Krystal Flash, are twisted as tightly as ropes, and wound while the tight twist is maintained, they form nicely segmented bodies, and resemble many of the things that trout make a living eating down along the bottom. Among those things are midge and caddis larvae, both of which are eaten often and opportunistically by trout. A few searching nymphs tied with twisted-strand bodies will go a long way toward rounding out your nymph fly boxes.

The late Ross Marigold was a guide on Montana's Madison River, and became famous for catching large trout on small nymphs. He was best known as the orgina-

Montana's Madison River, often called one long riffle, is where Ross Marigold originated the Serendipities, and also where Craig Mathews worked his beadhead changes on the original.

tor of the Serendipity series of nymphs, and they're as useful today as they were when he fished them in the 1970s and '80s. In their original incarnation, they had heads and stubby wings of spun deer hair. Craig Mathews, co-owner of Blue Ribbon Flies in West Yellowstone, Montana, adapted the beadhead to Marigold's concept. If the result is not more effective, it catches at least as many trout, and is a bit quicker and easier to tie.

The original Serendipity is listed in most catalogs in sizes 14 through tiny 22s. I find them most useful in sizes 16 and 18; when I'm tying tinier than that, I want to tie something less complex than these. Without doubt a workable variation would be to tie the smallest of them without the deer-hair head and wing, but they would no longer be Serendipities if you tied them that way. I almost always fish Serendipities as point flies in combination with a larger nymph of some sort, though two of them in slightly different sizes and dramatically different colors would help sort out quickly which small fly trout might prefer on a given day.

Though it's likely they were first tied with wool yarn, the standard has become Z-lon. Antron yarn works very well; if you have it in a range of colors, and lack Z-lon, don't hesitate to tie your Serendipities with what would be Sparkle Yarn if you didn't wind it so tight. Krystal Flash retains its reflective sparkle when wound tight, but is difficult to confine to a rope that results in much segmentation. In truth it's likely to be the small size, natural appearance, and free drift along the bottom that attracts trout to these productive nymphs, and it will make less difference than you think whether you tie them with Z-lon, Antron, Krystal Flash, wool yarn, or floss. Carry just a few in a narrow range of colors, and use them when you're not sure what trout might desire, but you suspect they'll be more susceptible to something small than anything large.

The three Serendipities shown are tied with Z-lon (olive), Krystal Flash (red), and Antron yarn (black).

SERENDIPITY *Ross Marigold*

Hook: Curved scud, size 14–22
Thread: White 8/0
Body: Red, olive, or black Z-lon, Antron, or Krystal Flash
Head and wing: Trimmed deer hair

These three body colors have proved to be universally effective, but the Serendipity has been tied in almost any color you can imagine, and. it has worked in all of them. Nor should you confine yourself to the listed body materials. Anything that can be twisted into a rope, so that when wound it forms a segmented body, will work well.

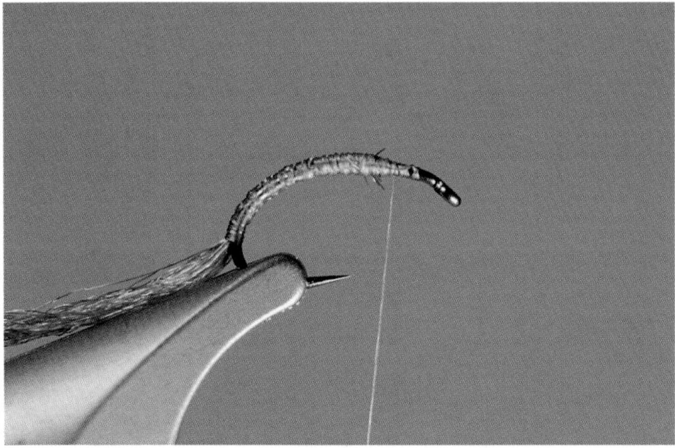

Step 1. Fix the hook in the vise, start your thread behind the eye, and wind a layer halfway down around the bend. Clip a strand of body material from the skein; a bit of practice will inform you about the amount to use. When twisted it should form a rope at least a bit fatter than the diameter of the hook shank. Lay this alongside the hook shank, and lash it forward with thread to a point about one-fifth the shank length behind the eye.

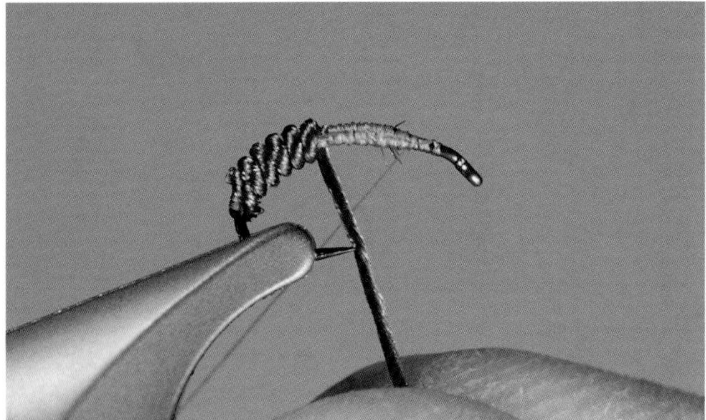

Step 2. Grasp the body material between the thumb and forefinger of your tying hand. Twist it into a tight rope (see page 57). Wind it forward in wraps that are butted together, passing the rope from your tying hand to your off hand on top of the hook, bringing the rope under the hook, and passing it off to the tying hand again there. Before beginning to wrap each new turn of the body, retwist the rope until it is tight.

Alternate Step 2. You might find it easier to attach your hackle pliers to the end of the rope, and take your turns with the pliers, rather than your fingers, retwisting the rope after each turn.

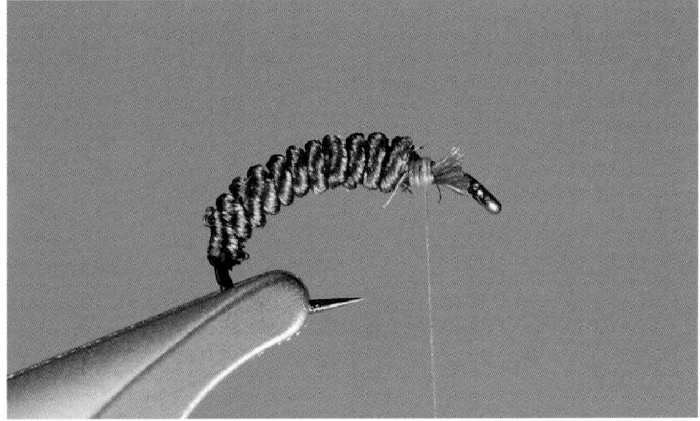

Step 3. Take the body material forward to a point about one-fifth the hook-shank length behind the eye. Let the last turn of the body untwist beneath the hook before using several turns of thread to tie it off. This avoids a lumpy tie-in point, which would make tying in the deer hair awkward.

Step 4. Clip a half-pencil-diameter patch of deer hair from the hide. Clean fuzz from the butts, and trim the hair to an inch or so in length. Lay it on top of the hook shank between the end of the body and the hook eye. Take two loose turns of thread around it while holding the hair in place. Let go of the hair and draw the thread turns firmly around it at the same time. The hair will spin around the shank. If it does not, encourage it to surround the shank with your off-hand fingers. Wrap several more tight turns of thread through the hair to the hook eye. Hold the hair back from the eye with your off-hand thumb and forefinger, take a few turns in front of it, make a whip-finish behind the eye, and clip the thread.

Step 5. Use sharp scissors or a single-edge razor blade to trim the deer hair close on the bottom, sides, top, and front. Leave a few fibers of hair protruding over the back, about half the body length, to serve as a wing. This can be dressed with floatant to fish the fly in the surface film, though that is rare. It can also be cut off, if you're sure you won't ever want to fish the fly as an emerging nymph.

The Beadhead Serendipity adds that universal wink of light to this small-fly concept. It also speeds up tying this useful set of flies by doing away with the deer-hair head and wing. You will, however, no longer be able to dress your Serendipity with dry-fly floatant and fish it in the surface film as an emerger. I have never used them that way, anyway, and prefer mine tied with beads.

BEADHEAD SERENDIPITY *Craig Mathews*

Hook:	Curved scud, sizes 14–18
Head:	Gold or brass bead
Weight:	8–10 turns nonlead wire
Thread:	Brown 6/0 or 8/0
Body:	Olive, red, or black Z-lon, Antron yarn, or Krystal Flash
Thorax:	Australian opossum (substitute hare's mask fur)

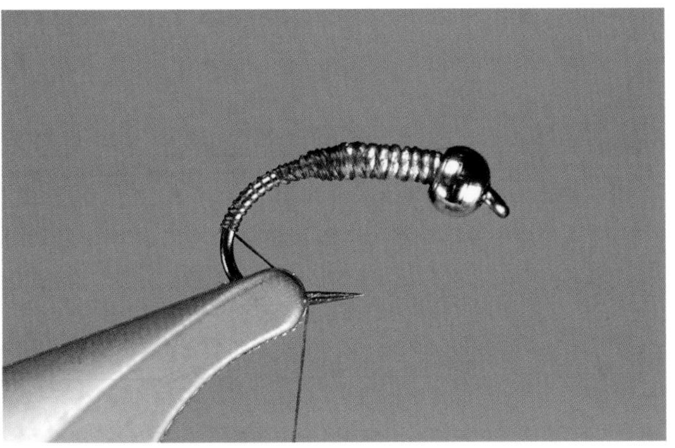

Step 1. Place a taper-drilled bead on the hook with the small hole toward the hook eye, the wider hole toward the back. Wind about eight to ten turns of nonlead wire around the hook shank. Work the front end of the wire into the open end of the bead, or jam the wire tight to the bead if it will not fit into the opening. Start your thread behind the weighting wire wraps, take turns forward to the bead and back to lock the wire in place, then build a ramp of thread from the bare shank up onto the wire wraps. This is critical for a smoothly tapered body.

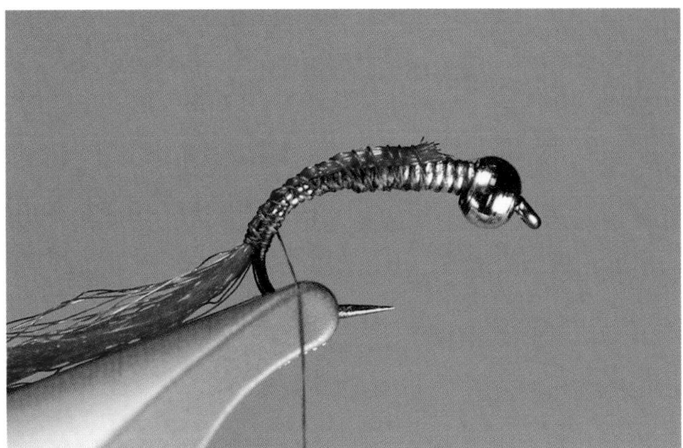

Step 2. Clip a strand of body material that when twisted will form a rope the diameter of the hook shank or a little larger. As you get familiar with tying on a certain size hook, you'll begin to add or delete strands, and sometimes even double the material by folding it, or whatever else it takes to get the segmentation you're after in the finished fly. Secure it with thread wraps from just behind the beadhead to the center of the bend of the hook.

Step 3. Take your thread forward to a point about one to one and a half bead diameters behind the beadhead, leaving room for the fur thorax. Twist the body material tightly into a rope, using your thumb and forefinger tips or attaching hackle pliers, and wind it forward to the same point. Be sure to take an additional twist after each wrap around the hook shank, to keep the body rope from loosening and thereby flattening. Let the rope relax on the back side of the hook after the final turn, before tying it in with several tight wraps of thread. Cut the excess body material.

Step 4. If you have Aussie opossum fur, select a patch, remove most of the guard hairs, and mix the fur in the palm of your hand, to form a rough dubbing. Hare's mask fur or any packaged fur that is somewhat spiky will do almost as well, but won't conform to Craig Mathews's prescription for the fly. Use the direct-dubbing method to attach the fur loosely to the thread. Wind sufficient turns to fill in the gap between the end of the body and the back of the bead. You should have a fibrous thorax greater in thickness than the diameter of the bead.

Step 5. Slip a five-turn whip-finish between the thorax and the bead. Draw it tight, then work it in further with the thumbnail and fingernail of your off hand while tugging on the bobbin, to seat the whip as firmly as possible. Clip the thread. If any guard fibers stick out and make your fly appear unduly unruly, you can pluck them out with tweezers. But refrain from cropping the thorax close; the tidier you make it, the less it will work in the water.

The Olive and Red Beadhead Serendipities are tied with Z-lon, the Black Beadhead Serendipity with Krystal Flash.

Endless color choices in the Serendipity series would without doubt contain some that would fool trout under certain circumstances. But I generally stick to the three main colors listed—olive, red, and black—and try more exact imitations from those patterns listed in part 3 if I feel trout are seeing so many of a particular insect that they've become selective.

SUMMARY

All of the Serendipity series could be listed as caddis larva imitations, but in smaller sizes they're also effective as midge larva or pupa patterns. It would be difficult to choose where to put them in part 3, under caddis or midges, but it's that very application to more than one type of insect that makes them ideal searching patterns. Trout might mistake them for many of the things they've eaten recently, and therefore will take them often, whether they're feeding selectively or opportunistically. That willingness of trout to make mistakes about them makes them perfect additions to a searching-nymph box.

CHAPTER 14

Wire- and Tinsel-Bodied Nymphs

Nymphs tied with bodies of wire or tinsel, whatever the color, have a bit of brightness to them. They reflect any light that reaches them underwater, whether it's brash sunlight or faint light in the dimness of the depths. They always have a bit of a spark, though sometimes it's tiny. I listed several reasons earlier that might be responsible for the effectiveness of beadheads: the quicker sink, the jigging movement, the wink of light that looks like life. In my opinion, that wink of light is what often elevates nymphs with wire or tinsel bodies over drab nymphs, and makes them highly effective as searching nymphs. That spark of light separates them, in the eyes of trout, from detritus in the drift.

Twigs, bits of bark, decaying leaves: none of them shine when in the drift, and none of them are nutritious to trout. Many aquatic insects, though far from all, entrain bubbles of air between their inner and outer exoskeletons to help propel them from the bottom to the top. Since this happens during emergence, it's a time of both concentrated numbers and utter defenselessness. If you're a trout, any spark of light in the drift might signal groceries, and incite the feeding response.

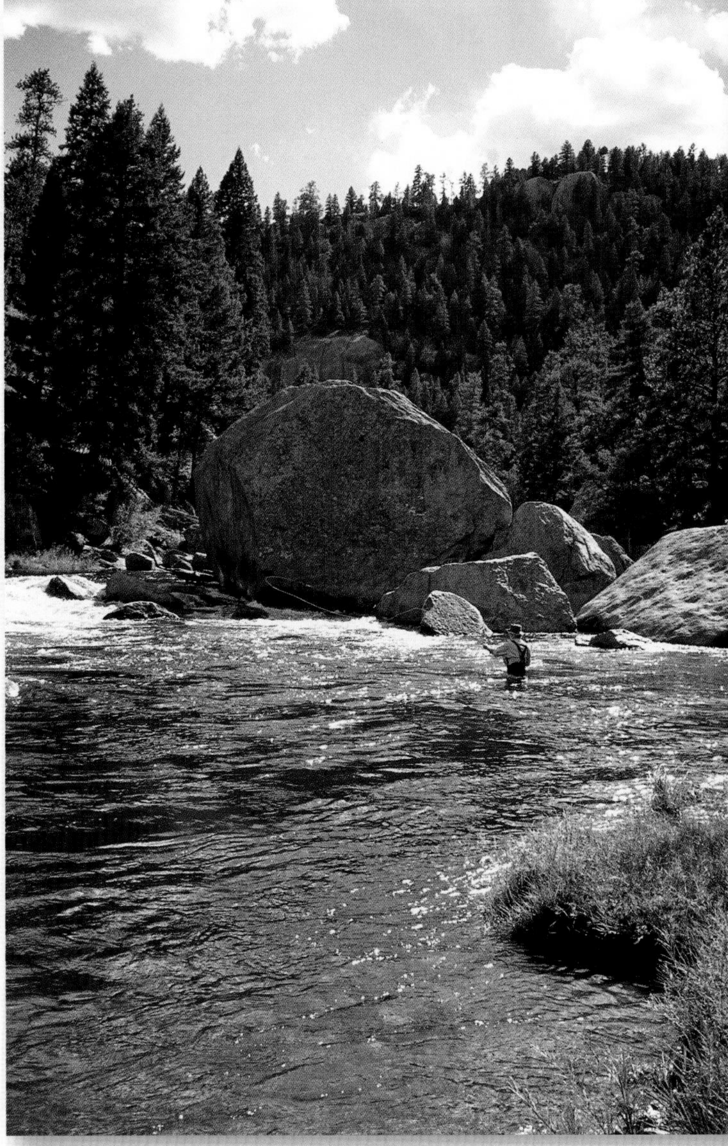

Not all reaches of the South Platte River, where the Brassie was first fished, are as deep and swift as this.

BRASSIE

It's been obvious for many decades that nymphs such as the famous Brassie are attractive to trout. Its orginators, Gene Lynch, Ken Chandler, and Tug Davenport, fished it in Colorado, not on the Roaring Fork, but on the less boisterous South Platte. Clearly its success was not related to any jigging motion and, because it was fished most often in small sizes, not entirely to its quick sink, though that could not have hurt it. Most likely it worked because that wink of light separated it from detrital drift.

Those original Brassies, in the early 1960s, were tied with copper wire from electric motors, or stripped from electrical and telephone wires. That can still be your source for body wire today, though it's wise to recall that the wire will oxidize and tarnish. Your Brassies will darken and lose their spark after a few months in a fly box. Ed Engle, in his *Tying Small Flies,* notes that the originators tied the flies just a few at a time, as need for them arose, rather than tying a season's supply ahead of time. When manufacturers began to market Brassies, they packaged them in gelatin capsules, in which the flies would retain their reflective qualities for years, until removed and exposed to air, and one supposes, to trout.

Copper wire is now available under the brand name Ultra Wire, is coated with polyurathane so its shine lasts forever, and comes in a wider array of colors than I can imagine using when tying flies for trout. It's available in four sizes: extra small, small, brassie, and medium. Since that nomenclature is a bit confusing, medium is good for size 14 and 16 nymphs, Brassie for sizes 18 to 22. Small is useful for size 24 and 26 nymphs. Extra small is best for ribbing wire and size 28 to 32 nymphs if you desire to tie wire-bodied nymphs that small. I recommend you buy at least two sizes, Brassie and medium, in three colors, copper, red, and green. Silver and black in the same sizes will let you experiment with two-tone Brassies.

Brassies can be tied on a 3XL nymph hook (top), curved scud hook (center), or standard nymph hook (bottom).

The original Brassie had a copper body and heat-shrunk black tubing at the head. The accepted version today has a peacock herl head. Though the dressing calls for a standard straight-shank nymph hook, 1XL and 2X heavy, the fly looks very good and fishes very well when tied on either a curved scud hook or a 3XL curved nymph hook.

BRASSIE
Gene Lynch, Ken Chandler, and Tug Davenport

Hook:	Standard nymph, size 12–22
Thread:	Black 8/0
Body:	Copper, red, or green wire
Head:	Peacock herl

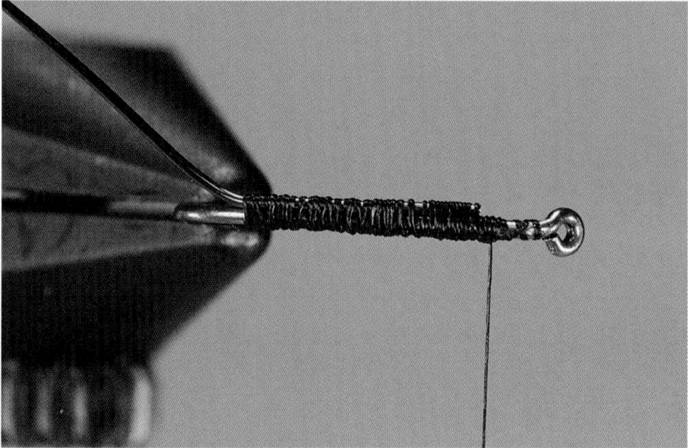

Step 1. Fix the hook in the vise, and make a layer of thread from the eye to the beginning of the bend and back. This double layer of thread forms a firm base for the body. Clip several inches of wire from the spool, of the appropriate size for the nymph you're tying. The standard is wire close to the diameter of the hook shank. If you're tying several nymphs at a time, clip eight to ten inches of wire; this will reduce wasted wire. Lay the wire alongside the shank from a point about one-fifth the shank length behind the hook eye. Layer the wire with thread to the bend and back to the tie-in point. This will provide an even underbody for the wire wraps.

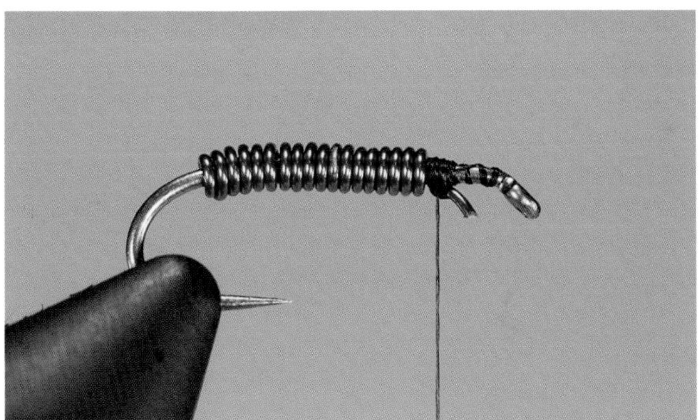

Step 2. Wind the wire forward to the tie-in point in tightly adjacent wraps. Avoid gaps between wire wraps; though they won't turn trout away, they'll make the resulting fly less pretty, and pretty is part of what you're after when you tie flies, though fishability comes ahead of it, at least in my tying. Tie the wire off on the underside of the hook. Leave a slight tag, not long enough to reach the hook eye, when you cut the wire. Flatten this tag to the shank with your fingernails, and overwrap it with thread to secure the wire. (In the photo, the tag is shown before it is flattened and overwrapped.)

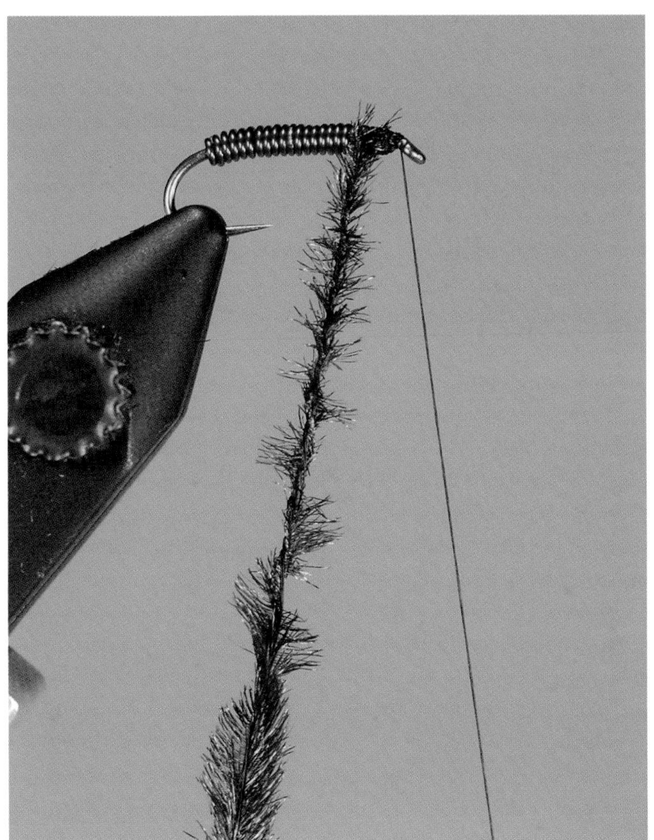

Step 3. Select two or three peacock herl fibers with barbules appropriate to the size fly you're tying. Those near the eye of the feather are generally longer in the barbule than those farther down the stem. Tie the fibers in at the end of the wire body, about an inch from their fragile tips. Break off or cut the excess tips, and discard. Unspool a few inches of tying thread from the bobbin, capture it over the forefinger of your off hand, return the thread to the shank, and take several turns of thread to form a thread loop. Twist the herl and the thread together to make a herl rope (see page 59).

Step 4. Wind the herl rope forward to the hook eye. Use enough turns of herl, overlapping them if necessary, to form a head two to three three times the diameter of the wire body. Secure the herl rope with five to ten turns of thread tight behind the hook eye.

Step 5. Clip the excess herl rope. Use the thumbnail and forefinger nail of your tying hand to clear thread and herl fibers back from the hook eye, and take enough turns of thread to form a smooth and clear base behind the eye for your whip-finish. This clears it so your whip-finish wraps will tuck behind the hook eye, not clog it. When you tie the fly to your leader, the eye will be open. Whip-finish behind the eye, apply head cement, and the Brassie is finished.

The three most popular and useful colors in the Brassie theme are copper, green, and red.

I usually drop the Brassie in size 16 or 18 on a short point tippet below a larger Montana Stone or heavily weighted scud. The combination is best in brisk water: a riffle or run in a medium to large mountain trout stream or river. But Brassies are used more often in tiny sizes 20 and 22 in and around the waters where they originated, on the South Platte and other heavily fished Colorado trout streams. Such small Brassies are excellent either as part of a two-nymph or even three-nymph rig, with strike indicator and split shot, fished down near the bottom, or as part of a dry-fly-and-dropper rig, fished just a foot or so beneath the surface.

You can create all sorts of variations on the original Brassie theme, using different hook styles, wire colors, and head materials. As long as your ideas don't disrupt the clean body outlines, or hinder the quick sink of the original, you're likely to take trout no matter what you do. Some of the prettiest and most useful variations have been worked in two-tone combinations by Rick Murphy, using wires of different colors, again on the South Platte River. When the wire colors contrast sharply, such as black and silver, the result is a nymph with distinct segmentation.

MURPHY'S TWO-WIRE BRASSIE *Rick Murphy*

Hook: Straight-shank or curved scud, size 18–24
Thread: Black 8/0 or 14/0
Abdomen: Contrasting copper wires
Wing: Clear Z-lon or similar flashy material
Thorax: Peacock herl

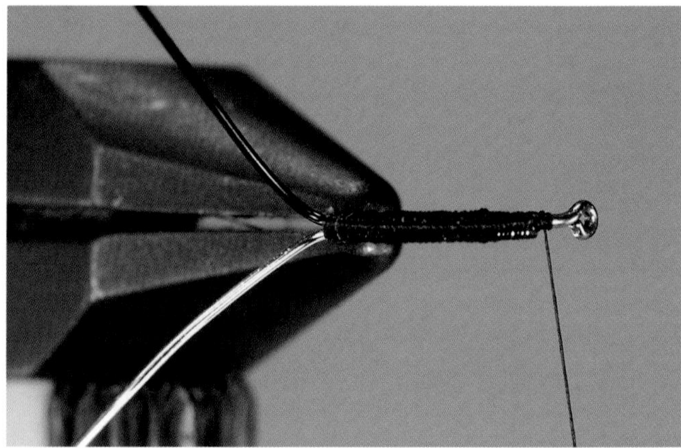

Step 1. Layer thread over the hook shank. Select two contrasting colors of copper wire, in the appropriate diameter for the hook size on which you're tying. Tie them in on top of the shank, side by side, and overwrap them firmly well down the bend of the hook and back to the eye, so they will not slide off the shank when you begin to wind them. Keep the two wires separate so they do not twist as you wind them forward in the next step.

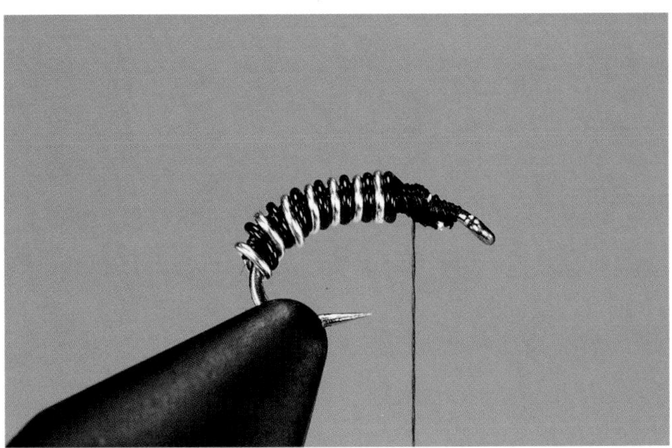

Step 2. Grasp the wire strands in your fingers, and take a careful first wrap around the hook shank, being sure the wires do not cross but lie smoothly on the hook, alongside each other. Continue wraps forward, keeping them tightly adjacent. Stop the wraps about one-quarter the shank length behind the eye, leaving room for the wing and herl thorax.

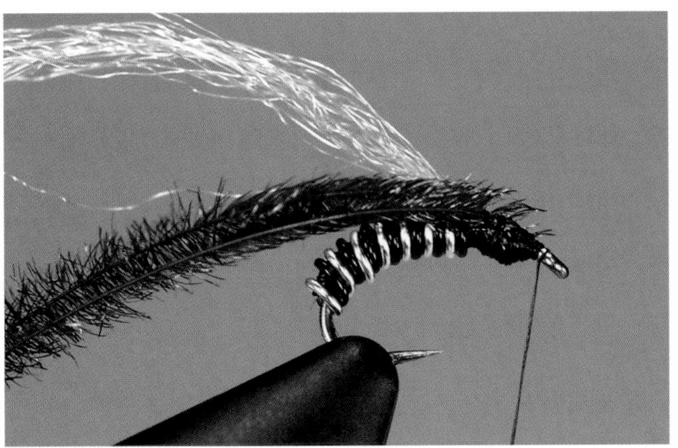

Step 3. Clip a small skein of Z-lon or other wing material. Leave it long; if you're tying by the half dozen or dozen, you'll work a two- to three-inch skein down without any waste. Tie the wing material in front of the body, leaving room for one or two turns of herl behind it. Select one or two peacock herl fibers with barbules the appropriate length for the size fly you're tying. Tie these in front of the wing.

Step 4. Twist the herl together with a single strand of thread, or double the thread and make a herl rope. Wind one or two turns of herl behind the wing, then two or three turns in front, to the hook eye. Tie the herl off there, and clip the excess.

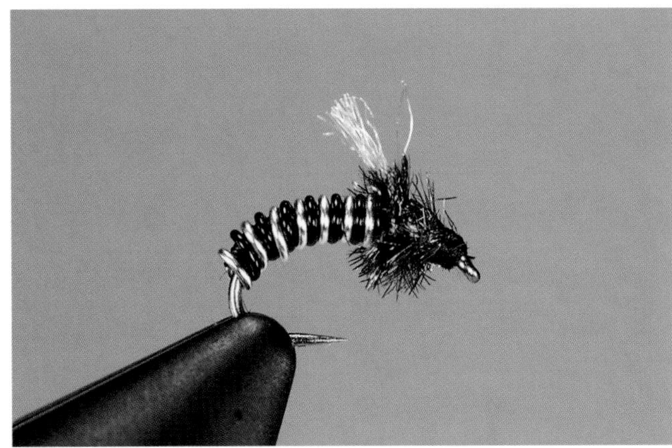

Step 5. Coax any stray herl fibers back from the eye, and use enough turns of thread to secure them. Whip-finish the head and clip the thread. Clip the wing to about half the body length.

Beadhead Brassies are fished as often as standard versions today, but the beadhead seems to me to add a bit of complexity to a tie that is flashy enough already.

You can work endless color variations on this segmented dressing, but the one shown, tied with black and silver wire, is excellent in the types of waters where midges are most abundant: tailwaters and spring creeks. It is effective whether fished near the bottom, or dangled just beneath the surface film.

COPPER JOHN

Originated by John Barr in the early 1990s, the Copper John has become the most popular searching nymph in all of trout fishing, almost everywhere. If it's not the most effective searching nymph as well, it's difficult to imagine what fly might be. In my own fishing, I still affix my tan variation of Dave Whitlock's Beadhead Fox Squirrel Nymph to my tippet more often than I use a Copper John. But that is due to many years of continual success with the great Dave's Squirrel Nymph. Using it first has become a habit that is hard to break. Recently, in nymphing situations where I have no idea what trout might prefer, it's become a secondary habit to knot a size 12 or 14 Copper John to the end of a 4X tippet, then to drop the perpetual size 16 Squirrel Nymph off the Copper John's hook bend, on about ten inches of 5X tippet.

John Barr, of Boulder, Colorado, originally tied the Copper John as an attractor nymph, with the idea that it might draw the attention of trout to a more realistic dropper, which they would then accept. He found that trout accepted the Copper John more often than the fly to which it was designed to draw attention.

The Copper John is extremely effective as a delivery system. It is nearly pure weight, with almost nothing to hinder its sink. It is beaded, and has lead wraps tucked behind the head. That tightly wound copper wire body adds to its plummet. The only peripheral parts, the biot tails, peacock herl thorax, and hen fiber legs, do little to impede the sinking of the nymph. The fly has been corrupted in every manner you can imagine. I am among the corrupters; I've used pine squirrel fur for the thorax on some tiny versions, in most part because it's easier to twirl a bit of spiky dubbing onto the shank than it is to wind herl and add fiber legs. But the fur decreases the sink rate of the fly. I've found that the addition of fur to the fly has necessitated the addition of split shot or putty weight to the leader.

I always find that it's best to stick with an originator's dressing until I discover a need, and therefore initiate a modification, that arises out of my fishing, not out of my laziness at the tying bench. John Barr has detailed the origins, tying steps, and presentation methods for his most famous fly in his 2007 book, *Barr Flies.* It includes his own modifications and variations on the theme.

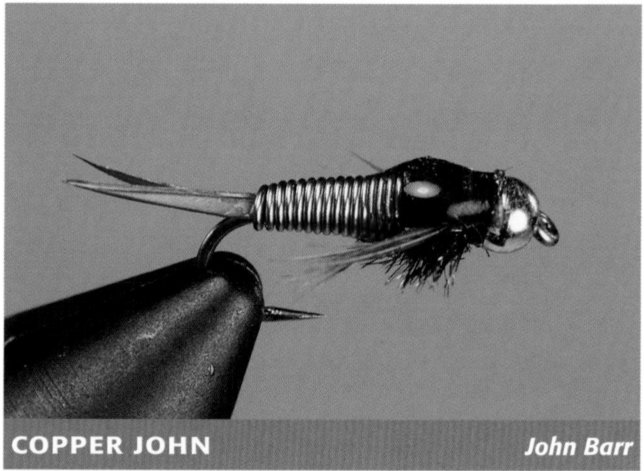

COPPER JOHN ***John Barr***

Hook: 2XL, 2X heavy, size 10–18
Bead: Gold
Weight: 13 turns nonlead wire
Thread: Black 70-denier Ultra Thread
Tails: Brown goose biots
Abdomen: Copper Ultra Wire
Wing case: Pearl Flashabou, black Thin Skin, and 30-minute epoxy
Thorax: Peacock herl
Legs: Mottled brown hen back fibers

In his book about his nymph, John Barr calls for thirteen turns of lead wire. I call for nonlead wire, as it's already a requirement on many waters, and I feel it will be a requirement in more and more places as time goes on. If I find that the designated number of turns throws the weighting wire shoulder too far back on the hook shank, I use fewer turns. The shoulder should be about one-fifth to one-quarter the length of the shank forward of the midpoint of the shank. If the shoulder extends farther back, it will be difficult to create a slender, tapered underbody without a hump in it. When I tie Copper Johns, I substitute 6/0 or 8/0 thread because that's what I keep spooled on bobbins. For gluing the wing case, you can use five-minute epoxy, but it will cause you to work at a scramble before it hardens. Whichever you use, tie up a batch of flies and epoxy them all at the same time.

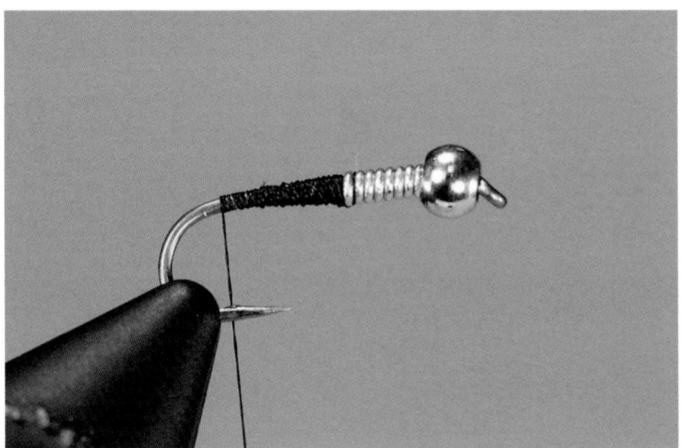

Step 1. Debarb the hook if it's barbed, and slip the appropriate size bead for the size fly you're tying over the bend and up to the eye. Take approximately thirteen turns of nonlead wire around the hook shank. Jam the front of the wraps into the back of the bead. If they do not fit, either use a finer weighting wire or fewer turns, to be sure your shoulder is forward of the midpoint of the hook. Start your thread behind the shoulder, and build a thread ramp from the shank up to the shoulder. Take your thread to the beginning of the hook bend.

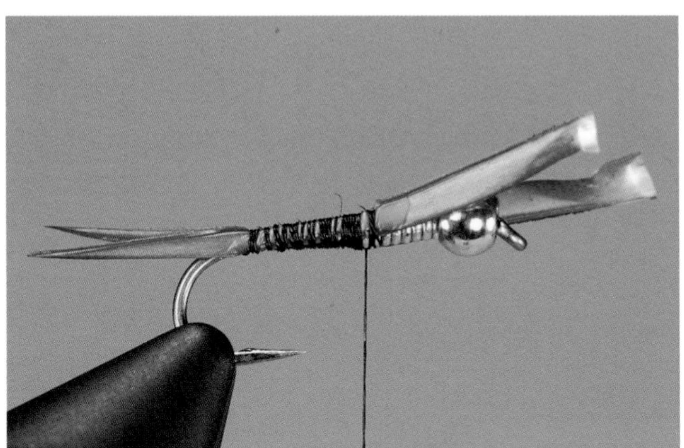

Step 2. Remove two adjacent goose biots from the feather stem, place them back-to-back so the tips flare, and align the tips so they are even. Measure them one-half the hook-shank length. Hold them at the hook bend, split on either side of it and canted slightly toward you. Your first thread wraps will remove this cant and place them perfectly. Use one or two pinch wraps (see page 45) to lock the biots into position. Overwrap the biot butts forward to a point one-quarter the shank length behind the bead. They will form a substantial part of the tapered underbody of the fly.

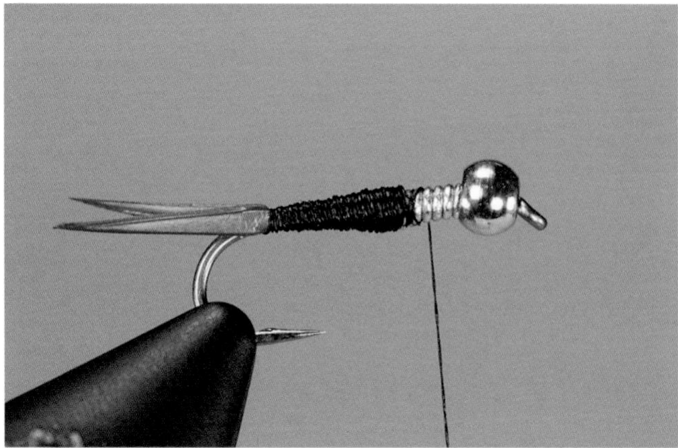

Step 3. Clip the biot butts. Take a layer of thread to the base of the tails, and another back to the front, using any extra turns necessary to form an even and smoothly tapered underbody for the copper wire.

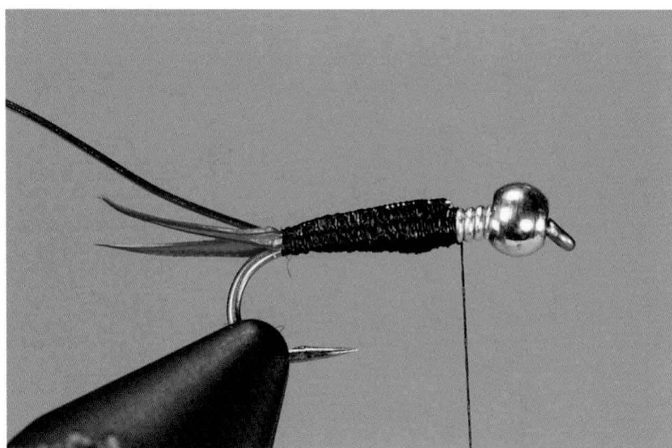

Step 4. Clip a six- to eight-inch length of copper wire approximately the diameter of the hook shank. Until you've tied a few Copper Johns in a particular size, don't worry about a bit of wasted wire. Lay the wire along the top or far side of the hook shank, beginning at the end of the biot butts. Overwrap the wire securely with thread to the base of the tail, where your wraps should be firmest. Take another layer of thread forward to the wire tie-in point, being sure to retain your evenly tapered underbody.

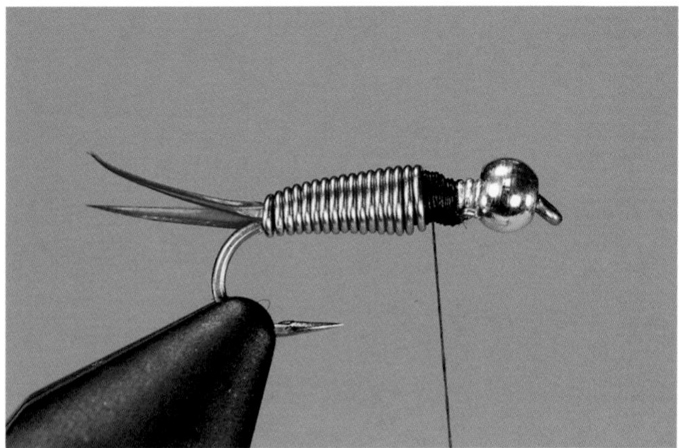

Step 5. Wrap the copper wire forward in tightly abutted turns to the tie-in point. Leave a sufficient gap between the front of the body and the back of the bead for the herl, shellback, and legs of the fly. Tie the wire off and clip the excess.

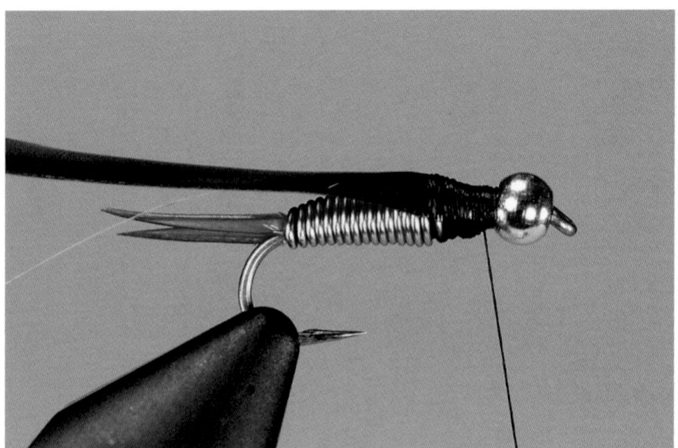

Step 6. Tie in a single strand of Pearl Flashabou at the front of the copper wire. It should be perfectly centered on the shank. Cut a section of black Thin Skin, while it's still on the paper backing, not quite as wide as the hook gap. Remove it from the backing, and tie it in with the shiny side up. Overwrap the Thin Skin and Flashabou back over the front wrap or two of copper wire. Barr calls for wrapping it to the 70 percent point on the hook shank. Take your thread forward to the bead to fill in any gaps between the lead wraps.

Step 7. Tie in three to five peacock herls with barbules the appropriate length for the size fly you're tying. You can form a herl rope, or twist the herls together with your thread, but the wing case is going to keep this herl from coming unwound if a stem is broken by the teeth of a trout. You can simply wind a few turns forward to the bead, tie it off, and clip the excess, if you prefer.

Step 8. Select a hen back feather with fibers of the appropriate length for the size fly you're tying. Remove fuzz and soft, poorly marked fibers from the lower end of the stem. Even the tips of a clump of fibers on one side, and peel them from the stem. Measure the tips to reach the hook point on the far side of the hook, and use a couple turns of thread and a pinch wrap to secure the fibers behind the bead. Peel a clump of similar size from the opposite side of the feather, measure the tips to the hook point, and tie the clump in on the near side of the hook shank.

Step 9. Clip the butts of the leg fibers. Bring the Thin Skin wing case forward and secure it with a couple of turns of thread tight behind the bead. Follow with the Flashabou strip, securing it as well. Use a few extra turns of thread to be sure both are locked in securely.

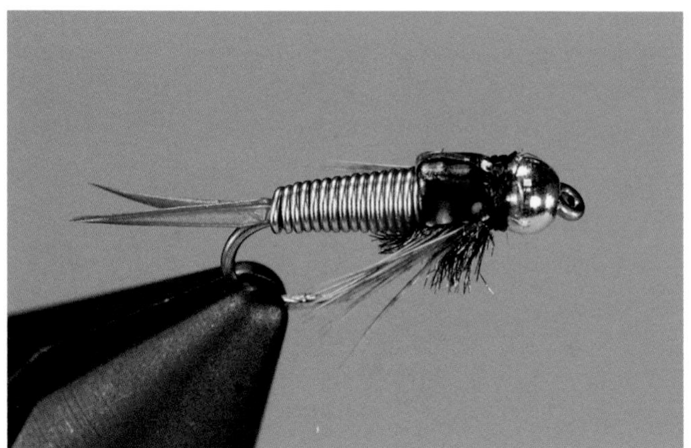

Step 10. Clip the Thin Skin and Flashabou at the back of the bead. Don't worry if some rides up onto the bead; this will give your thread head a better grip and make a more secure fly. Tuck a five-turn whip-finish behind the bead, over the wraps that secure the wing case. Clip your thread.

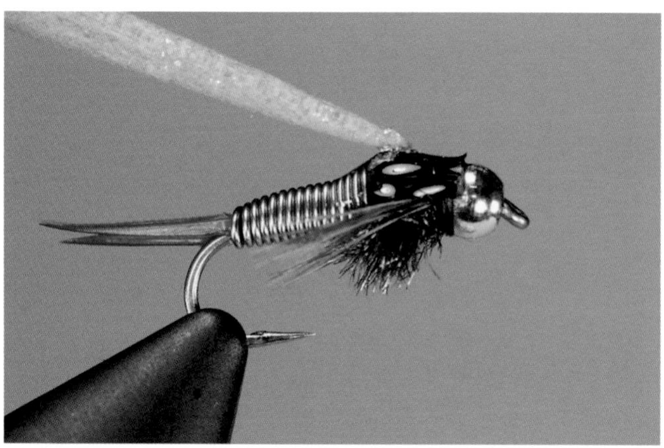

Step 11. Mix a small batch of epoxy. Use a toothpick point to apply a drop to the wing case. Spread the glue from the back side of the bead, over the wing case, and onto the first one or two turns of copper wire behind the wing case. Be sure the epoxy covers the whip-finish and runs up onto the back of the bead.

My corrupted Green Copper John, tied in small sizes, substitutes pine squirrel fur for the thorax and legs, but I haven't discovered it to be an improvement on the original Copper John in its green-bodied variation.

In his valuable book, John Barr details thirty-one steps in tying the Copper John. If you tie it as it was designed, it will never be a quick tie, though you can speed it up by first laying out all the materials for it in handy order, and second developing a routine for tying it that you repeat and refine. In my own past I've condensed out some of the design's peripheral parts, for example replacing the herl thorax and hen fiber legs with fur, and omitting the Flashabou racing stripe. I've even neglected to epoxy the Thin Skin wing case. The results catch trout, though I'm never sure these truncated Copper Johns catch their full share of them. I've gone back to tying the fly as it was intended to be tied, relaxing into a tying session and tying the fly by the half dozen or dozen of a size and color. The results are a lot prettier than my corruptions were, and I fish them with more confidence because of that.

Some favorite Copper Johns (from left): Copper, Green, Red, Chartreuse, and Zebra.

You can tie the Copper John in any color for which you can find suitable wire, which is currently almost any color you can imagine and some you might not, including zebra dressings, which are combinations of two colors, most often black and silver. Barr states, "If I was limited to three sizes and four colors, I would carry sizes 14-18 in natural copper, red, chartreuse, and black." His experience with the style is far more extensive than mine. I haven't tried the chartreuse. I do use a green that is so dark it might look black when wet and appearing before the eyes of a trout. If I were limited to a couple of colors, I would fish the original copper color in sizes 14 and 16, and the dark green version, which I like to think looks a little like a small *Baetis* mayfly swimmer nymph, in sizes 18 and 20.

COPPER JOHN, GREEN — *John Barr*

Hook: 2XL, 2X heavy, size 10–18
Bead: Gold
Weight: 8–15 turns nonlead wire
Thread: Black 70-denier Ultra Thread
Tails: Black goose biots
Abdomen: Green Ultra Wire
Wing case: Pearl Flashabou, black Thin Skin, and 30-minute epoxy
Thorax: Peacock herl
Legs: Black hen back fibers

COPPER JOHN, RED — *John Barr*

Hook: 2XL, 2X heavy, size 10–18
Bead: Gold
Weight: 8–15 turns nonlead wire
Thread: Black 70-denier Ultra Thread
Tails: Brown goose biots
Abdomen: Red Ultra Wire
Wing case: Pearl Flashabou, black Thin Skin, and 30-minute epoxy
Thorax: Peacock herl
Legs: Black hen back fibers

COPPER JOHN, CHARTREUSE — *John Barr*

Hook: 2XL, 2X heavy, size 10–18
Bead: Gold
Weight: 8–15 turns nonlead wire
Thread: Black 70-denier Ultra Thread
Tails: Black goose biots
Abdomen: Chartreuse Ultra Wire
Wing case: Pearl Flashabou, black Thin Skin, and 30-minute epoxy
Thorax: Peacock herl
Legs: Black hen back fibers

COPPER JOHN, ZEBRA — *John Barr*

Hook: 2XL, 2X heavy, size 10–18
Bead: Silver
Weight: 8–15 turns nonlead wire
Thread: Black 70-denier Ultra Thread
Tails: Black goose biots
Abdomen: Black and silver Ultra Wire
Wing case: Pearl Flashabou, black Thin Skin, and 30-minute epoxy
Thorax: Peacock herl
Legs: Black hen back fibers

The Tungsten Bead Copper John can be tied on either curved or standard hooks, but when you get to the smallest sizes, it's wise to consider the wider gap of the scud-type hook. The tungsten bead can be substituted for a brass bead on any of the listed patterns, or used in any experiments you care to carry out on the Copper John theme.

The Copper John tied with a tungsten bead sinks faster than the standard tie. I find it most useful in the smallest sizes, when dropped off a dry fly with substantial flotation. The general formula is to suspend a nymph from a dry that is one size larger. For the standard Copper John, use a fly two sizes larger, and if you tie with tungsten, it should either be three sizes larger or incorporate extra flotation. Barr and his friend Charlie Craven created their bullet-headed and foam-bodied B/C Hopper primarily, it seems, as a suspension system for Copper Johns. It looks a lot like a grasshopper, and is clearly an excellent imitation. It also looks a bit like a battleship at sea, and is unlikely to be pulled under the water by a Copper John tied with a tungsten bead.

The tungsten version can be tied on standard or curved scud hooks. When tied small, the wider gape of the curved hook is beneficial. Barr calls specifically for the Tiemco 2488 hook, for the width of its gape. I generally tie it on heavy-wire curved scud hooks.

The Rubber Leg Copper John is a useful concept in larger sizes, the kind used as attractors in two- or even three-nymph rigs. It can also be fished by itself in situations where trout are feeding on a variety of larger insects such as golden stonefly nymphs or free-living caddis larvae. It's far from an imitation of anything, but the best thing about all good searching nymphs is their ability to incite trout to strike without looking precisely like what the trout might be taking in the way of naturals. The Rubber Leg Copper John has a lot of things about it that make it look alive and good to eat, to a trout.

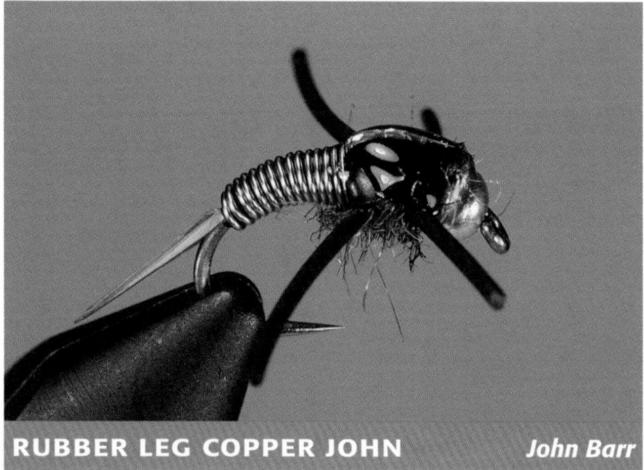

RUBBER LEG COPPER JOHN *John Barr*

Hook: Curved hook, size 8–18
Bead: Gold tungsten
Weight: 8–15 turns nonlead wire
Thread: Black 70-denier
Tail: Brown goose biots
Abodomen: Copper Ultra Wire
Wing case: Silver Holographic Flash, black Thin Skin, and 30-minute epoxy
Thorax: Bronze Arizona peacock dubbing
Legs: Round black rubber legs

Step 1. Affix a bead, weight the hook shank, form an even underbody, place the tails, and wind a wire body just as you would with a standard Copper John. Tie in a single strand of Holographic Flash, and the Thin Skin wing case, just as you normally would. Dub a somewhat portly thorax with the synthetic dubbing, from the front of the abdomen to the back of the bead. Return your thread to the midpoint of the thorax dubbing and take a couple turns of thread there.

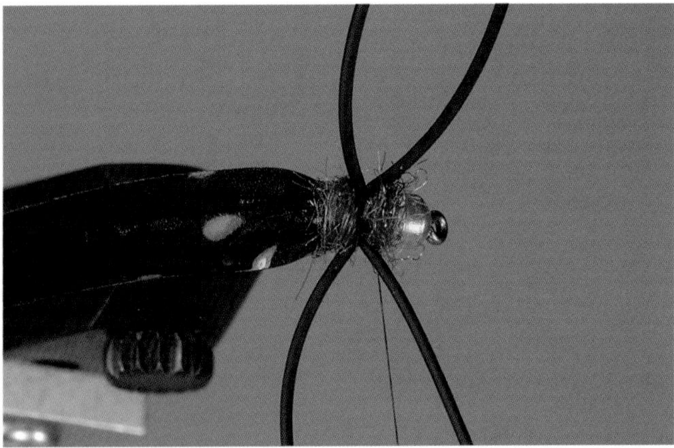

Step 2. Cut two strands of rubber leg material extra long. Tie one strand in on the near side, at the midpoint of the thorax, using just a couple turns of thread. Tie the second leg strand in on the far side of the thorax, again using just a couple turns of thread to lock it in place.

Step 3. Fix a small amount of dubbing to the thread in a slender skein. Take two to three turns of this over the leg tie-in wraps. This secures the legs to the body, covers the tie-in point, and also serves to splay the legs at least slightly. When finished wrapping the dubbing, take your thread forward to the back of the beadhead.

Step 4. Draw the Thin Skin wing case forward, and secure it with a couple turns of thread. Draw the Holographic Flash over the center of the Thin Skin, and secure it. Clip the flash and wing case as close as you can over the back of the bead. Whip-finish behind the bead and clip your thread. Hold the rear legs together as a pair, and snip them a bit longer than the end of the abdomen. Hold the front legs together, and snip them a bit shorter than the rear legs. Apply epoxy to the wing case.

The Rubber Leg Copper John can be tied in an array of combined colors, limited only by the availability of wires.

In his book, Barr calls for single-wire bodied Rubber Leg Copper Johns in copper, chartreuse, black, green, and red. He also lists some exquisite two-wire combinations that result in gorgeous flies: zebra (black and silver), black and olive, red and blue, and copper and copper-brown. That last one sounds perfect for streams in which golden stonefly nymphs, in first-, second-, and third-year classes and therefore a wide array of sizes, are dominant in riffles and runs. I haven't tried it, but one thing is certain: when I do, I'll have no trouble getting the fly to the bottom rocks where golden stone nymphs live and trout scurry around eating them.

One of my favorite days astream contains a perfect example of the kind of situation the Copper John, in its

Neal Mitchell on a perfect North Carolina trout stream pool, where a Copper John suspended beneath a big dry fly on four feet of fine tippet found a few trout.

various forms, was designed to solve. It was a March day in the mountains of North Carolina, just south of the Virginia border. The unnamed stream would have been considered small anywhere else I fish, but the southern Appalachians are so beribboned with gorgeous tiny trout streams that what I define as small is more toward medium for those who are lucky enough to fish them often. I'm not that lucky, but I was in the area to give a slide show at the Nat Greene Trout Unlimited chapter banquet in Greensboro, and members Jack Patterson and Neal Mitchell blindfolded me and took me to their favorite stream the day before the banquet.

The day was intermittently cloudy and splashed with sun. The stream was not low, but it was also far from high and muddy, as we think most trout waters might be in early spring. Instead, water flow was brisk and clear, bounding around boulders and gliding over a clean bedrock bottom. Wherever the stream spread out into small and graceful plunge pools, it was overhung and crowded in by mountain laurel.

I did fine under the tutelage of Jack and Neal. Because I'd departed for the trip completely unarmed for fishing, I was wearing their waders, carrying their rods, fishing their flies. They instructed me to rig a size 14 Copper John on a two-foot dropper tippet tied to the hook bend of a size 10 Royal Wulff. That big, white-winged dry didn't fool any trout, but it dipped under often enough to keep me, if not busy, at least pleased. The trout that came to hand were a mix of brookies, rainbows, and browns from ten to fourteen inches long.

After a couple of pleasant hours spent fishing this combination of flies in small pockets and pools, we arrived at a place where the stream opened out, put on its brakes, deepened up. We hit it first with the rigs we already had tied to our tippets, but maximum sink was the length of the short tippet, about two feet, which in that clear water we could see was about halfway to the bottom. We'd probably have moved on without rerigging, but Jack spotted a small hover of trout, obviously at work feeding along the bottom, right where the main entering current flowed down a slot and pooped out, lost its energy, dropped off into those four-foot depths.

Jack added a couple feet of tippet to his rig, retied his Copper John, cast about ten feet upstream from the trout, watched his dry fly drift downstream several times without dipping under. Then he placed a cast fifteen feet upstream from the trout, far up into the area where the current still had most of its energy. The dry fly settled into its long float, and had already gone past the trout, when it suddenly was no longer there. The first few times you fish a dry fly and dropper, the sudden absence of your dry fly seems a mystery. But Jack was not new to this. He instantly lifted his rod and danced the nicest trout of the day.

After he released it, I rerigged with a small fan of indicator yarn and five feet of 5X tippet to the same size 14 Copper John I'd been using all day. I copied Jack and cast fifteen feet upstream from the bottom-feeding trout, far up into that entering current. A couple of casts later, the indicator darted under, I set the hook, and a trout just a bit smaller than Jack's came up for a brief rest in my hand.

Neal followed suit, and we'd each caught one trout from that small covey of them, all on Copper Johns. After Neal released the last one and Jack stepped up for what we hoped would be a pleasant rotation on the one place in the pool that held trout, we beheld the bottom, and it was empty of them. They'd had enough, but so had we.

When we reentered the stream above that broad pool, and began to fish water that was once again brisk, shallow, and surrounded by mountain laurel, we were forced to nip off those long tippets, revert to our earlier dry-and-short-dropper rigging.

LIGHTNING BUG

The first time I fished the Lightning Bug, three brown trout of two to four pounds jumped it. I dropped it off a dry fly on Oregon's Owyhee River, and it provided one of those rare occasions when I outfished Rick Hafele. I offered to sell him some, but he didn't want to meet any price. As its name implies, it's a flash of light, and as we know, that is sometimes all that is required to con trout. Since many insects capture bubbles of air between their inner and outer exoskeletons, and rise to the surface looking more like reflective bubbles of air than insects, it's possible the Lightning Bug is more imitative than it looks. But I've listed it here as a searching nymph because I have no idea where it would fit as an imitation, and also because it's the sort of nymph that should be tied on when you have no idea what else might work.

The late Larry Graham originated the Lightning Bug in the early 1990s on the Yakima River, in central Washington. Its use has since spread over the entire continent, and it has become what might be called a *guide fly:* one of the few flies that guides reach for when the situation is difficult and they'd like their clients to dangle a nymph and feel the rewarding tug of a trout. It's most often rigged as an attractor fly, with a less showy and usually smaller nymph trailing a few inches behind it.

LIGHTNING BUG *Larry Graham*

Hook: Standard nymph, size 12–16
Bead: Gold brass or tungsten bead
Weight: 8–15 turns of nonlead wire
Thread: Black 8/0
Tail: Pheasant tail fibers
Rib: Fine copper wire
Body: Flat pearlescent or holographic Mylar
Wing case: Flat pearlescent or holographic Mylar
Thorax: Peacock herl
Legs: Hen back fibers

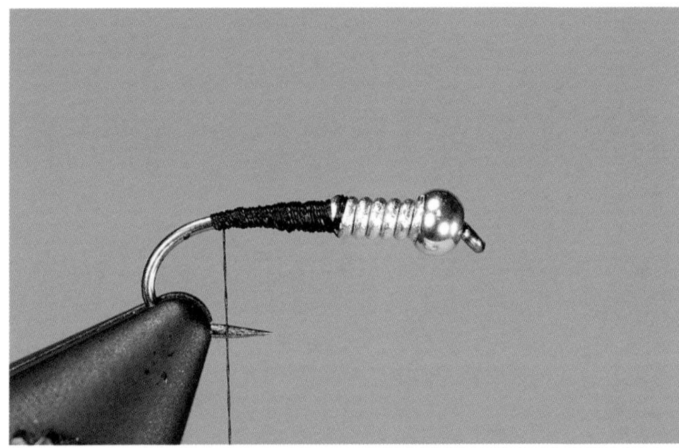

Step 1. Debarb the hook, slip a tapered bead over it with the wider opening toward the back, and take a few turns of nonlead wire about the diameter of the hook shank. Slip the front of the weighting wire into the back of the bead, or jam it against the bead. Be sure the back shoulder of the wire is forward of the midpoint of the hook shank. Start your thread behind the wire, build a thread ramp to the wire shoulder, and layer thread in an even taper from the back of the wire to the bend of the hook.

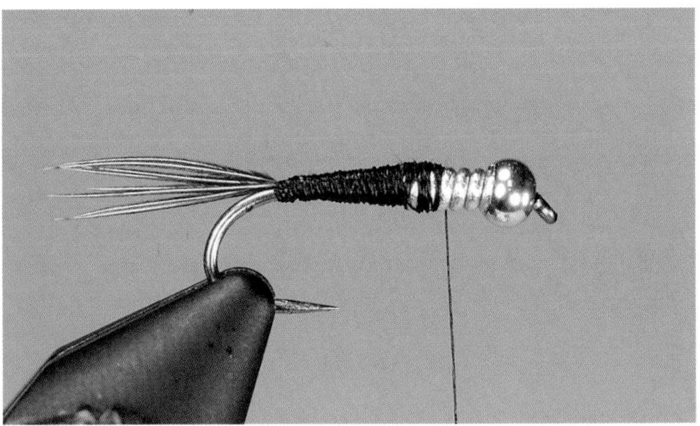

Step 2. Align the tips of several pheasant tail fibers, and either strip or clip them from the feather. Measure them the length of the hook shank or a bit shorter, and tie them in at the bend of the hook. Overwrap the fibers past the weighting wire shoulder, maintaining an even underbody, before clipping the excess.

Step 3. Tie in the ribbing wire at the front of the fly, and overwind it back to the tail tie-in point and then back to the front, to maintain the underbody taper. Tie in several inches of body tinsel over the weighting wire wraps at the front of the fly.

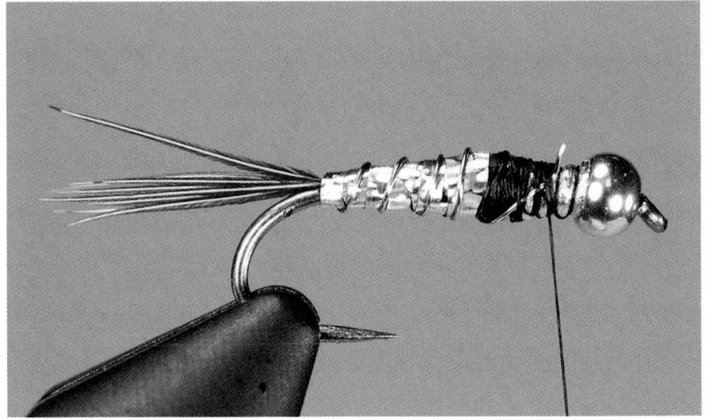

Step 4. Wrap the body tinsel to the base of the tail in adjacent turns. Take a second layer of body tinsel forward over the first layer, returning it to the tie-in point. Clip the excess there. The double layer of tinsel ensures that the thread underbody will be covered. Wind the ribbing wire forward in evenly spaced turns, and tie it off in front of the tinsel tie-off point, to avoid a lump under the thorax.

Step 5. Tie in a short section of the same Mylar tinsel you used for the body. If you'd like to save a step in tying the fly, rather than cut the body tinsel after you've wound it, simply bend it back and overwrap it with thread so that it will emanate from a point a bit back on the body when it is later pulled forward as a wing case. If the wing case is tied in too far forward, when it is pulled forward it will cause a wasp-waisted gap between the body and thorax. Tie in three to five peacock herl fibers, twist them together with the working thread, and take three to four turns of herl forward to the back of the bead. Tie it off there and clip the excess.

Step 6. Select a hen back feather with tip fibers appropriate to the size fly you're tying. Hold the feather by the tip, and reverse the fibers. Select the few you desire to become legs on the fly, and peel the rest of the fibers from both sides of the stem. Clip out the tip, and the feather is prepared. As an alternative, you can strip fibers from the feather and tie them in one side at a time, as you did on the Copper John and do on most flies. The method given here was used by Larry Graham, and does result in a prettier fly. However, it wastes all the fibers on a feather except those few near the tip.

Step 7. Lay the prepared feather over the thorax of the nymph, and use just a couple turns of thread to lock it in. Do not cut the stem yet. Instead, use it to tug the feather forward until you've positioned the legs precisely where you want them. Their swept-back tips should extend approximately to the hook point.

Step 8. Clip the feather stem tight behind the bead. Draw the wing-case tinsel forward over the leg feather, separating the sides neatly. In a perfect world, the wing case will lie directly over the feather stem, covering it and keeping the legs in equal proportion, side to side.

Step 9. Clip the excess wing-case tinsel. Place a five-turn whip-finish tight behind the beadhead. Head cement is beneficial on this fly, though your author usually adds a quick second whip-finish and dispenses with cement. The finished fly will be more attractive, to you and perhaps to the trout as well, if you cement the head as you should.

Because I think tiny winks of light are more effective than bigger ones, I tie this fly more often in size 16 than I do in anything larger. I haven't tried it on smaller hooks, but suspect it might be better the smaller it's tied. I also suspect that as time goes on, as it tends to do, trout in heavily fished water will become educated about this bright fly. I haven't heard of that happening with the Lightning Bug yet, however. Perhaps, if the fly is imitative of emerging insects with bubbles of air captured between their exoskeletons, just the opposite will happen: more realistic dressings that lack the brightness resembling the bubble will become less effective, and the bright Lightning Bug will catch more trout rather than fewer.

If you want the fly to sink fast, tie it with a tungsten bead instead of brass. You can tie the fly with any color Mylar you choose, and with any configuration of Mylar as well. Krystal Flash is an embossed Mylar tinsel, and comes in any color you'd like. But to remain true to the originator's concept, it should be a bright and reflective tinsel, or it will no longer be a flashy Lightning Bug. Graham tied it in silver and his favorite, pearlescent Mylar with a greenish cast.

SUMMARY

You could easily let the Copper John, the most popular nymph in terms of pattern sales, stand by itself as your wire-bodied searching nymph. It would be wiser to carry the standard Copper John in a range of sizes from 12 to 18 than it would be to carry the same fly in a dozen colors, all in a single size.

I recommend you carry the Copper John in original copper in a full range of sizes, and add some in green and red in smaller sizes, 16 and 18, because they can be mistaken by trout for a variety of swimmer mayfly nymphs, small caddis larvae, and midges in both larval and pupal stages. Add the Lightning Bug in a couple of sizes, say 14 and 18, for their flash, and you would have a fine bright section in your searching-nymph box.

CHAPTER 15

Rubber-Legged Nymphs

I was in Chile recently, trying to select a nymph to probe a deep run in a big river, and held my fly box out to my guide, Juan-Ramon Astorga, for his advice. He'd recently led a successful pancora hunt on the Rio Huemules, and we'd captured a couple dozen of that peculiar cross between crayfish and crabs. The ones we'd caught, between dime and silver-dollar size, were dunked in Tupperware containers, taken back to the lodge at Estancia del Zorro to pose for photos. But I might have learned as much from those that escaped as we turned over rocks in the swift shallows, grabbing for them as they bolted away backward.

The fleeting impression the pancora left as they dashed was of a brickish brown body and flailing legs. Because those legs were pale grayish white on the underside, they flashed white. That is what one would expect a trout to see of a pancora it was chasing down to eat: a blur of brown surrounded by an impression of flashing white legs. It came as no surprise, then, when Juan-Ramon looked at my fly box, pointed at a big ugly nymph with rubber legs, and said, "Tie on that one with the white legs." It was an unnamed nymph, portly, wound with a rabbit strip to give it maximum fluff and movement when wet in water. I'd tied several with tungsten beads for

When it's necessary to probe the depths of a big river, such as this side channel of Chile's Rio Yelcho, in hopes of big trout, the addition of rubber legs to your nymphs might make a difference. Your guides will always think so.

A pancora at rest looks a lot like a North American crayfish, but when one is in motion, trout see a brownish red blur dashing through the water, with whitish legs flailing all around it. A rubber-legged nymph makes the best imitation of many such aquatic animals.

extra weight, and had added white legs to just a couple, to see what they might look like.

It was one of the two nymphs with rubber legs that Juan-Ramon picked out. He liked it. The trout liked it. They quickly separated me from the only two I'd tied with legs. They didn't show much desire for the same nymph tied without legs.

I'll address rubber legs as a tying concept here, rather than list a long line of individual dressings, because you can add them to almost any nymph or streamer. As noted in the previous chapter, one very useful variation of the Copper John, in its largest sizes, is the Rubber Leg Copper John. The standard dressing for pancora in Chile is a Brown Girdle Bug, a simple tie constructed of brown chenille, white rubber legs, and nothing more. It's a variation of the Black Girdle Bug, tied with black chenille and white legs. It's long been a standard in the Rocky Mountain West for the salmon-fly nymph, but it is used most commonly as a searching dressing in big water.

I'd recommend you tie the black version for North America and the brown variation for South America. I'll add the hint that your guides will be happiest, almost all over the world, if more than half of the largest searching nymphs in your traveling fly boxes are equipped with rubber legs.

GIRDLE BUG, BLACK

Hook: 3XL or 4XL, size 4–10
Weight: 15–25 turns of nonlead wire
Thread: Black 3/0 or 6/0
Tails and legs: White round rubber legs
Body: Black chenille

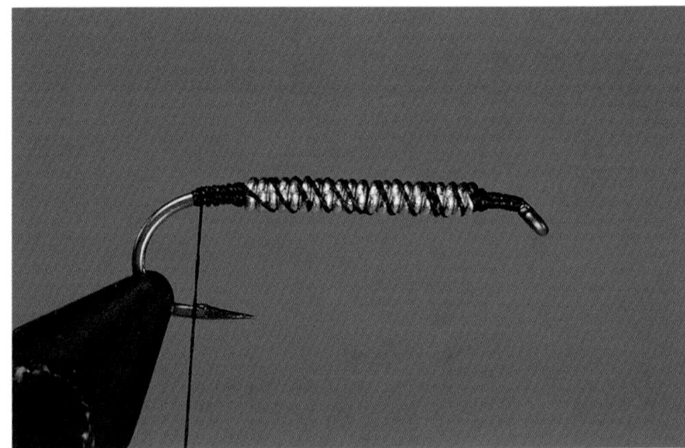

Step 1. Fix the hook in the vise, and weight it with fifteen to twenty-five turns of nonlead wire approximately the diameter of the hook shank. Attach your thread behind the hook eye, and layer it over the shank and weighting wire wraps. You can build thread ramps up to the front and back wire shoulders, if you'd like, but chenille will even out these bumps even if you neglect this step.

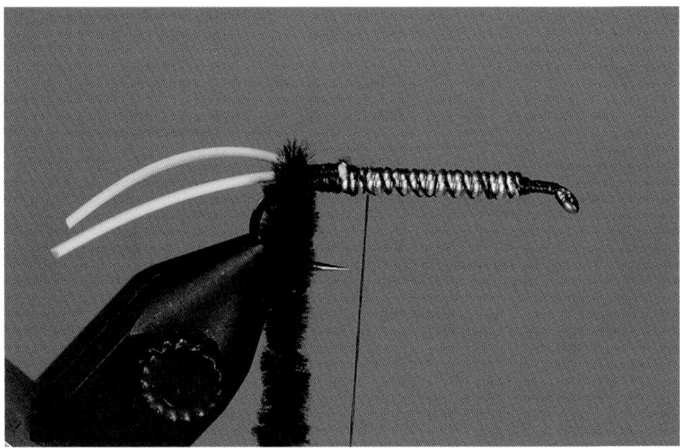

Step 2. Measure four sections of white rubber leg material twice the length of the hook shank, and clip them from the strand. If you're tying a bunch of this fly, measure and clip enough leg sections in advance, so you won't be forced to measure and snip each set of legs and tails as you go. Double one section of leg material so the tips are even. Hold it at the bend of the hook, and tie it in to form tails set in a V-shape. Clip any excess tail butts at the weighting wire shoulder. Clip a three- to five-inch section of chenille, strip one-eighth inch of fuzz from its core threads, and tie this in at the base of the tails.

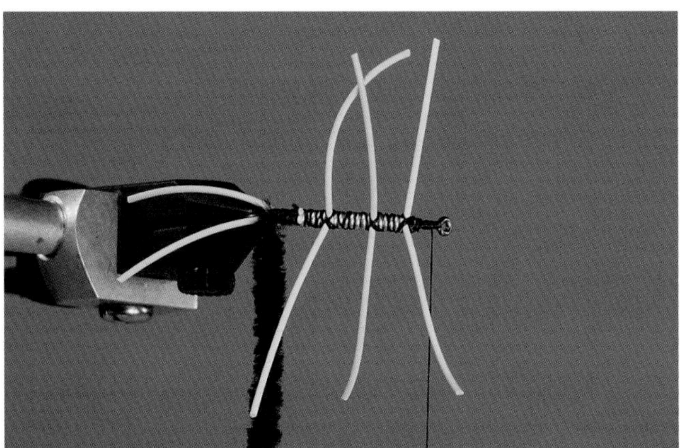

Step 3. Move your thread to approximately the one-third point on the shank. Set a section of rubber leg material across the hook shank, half on one side and half on the other. Tie it in with three to six figure eights of thread. Move the thread to about the midpoint of the shank, and tie in another section in the same way. Tie in a third and final set of legs one-quarter to one-third the shank length behind the eye. You can reduce this to two sets of legs if you'd like; trout are not known to count well. You can also add a final set projecting out over the hook eye, as antennae, if you'd like to complicate the fly a bit.

Step 4. Wrap the chenille forward, using it to hold the legs in proper position as you do. It will be necessary to use your off-hand thumb and forefinger to hold the legs back out of the way as you make winds of chenille between them. Snug the chenille wraps against both the back and front of each leg set, to hold them firmly in place. Take the chenille forward to the hook eye, tie it off, clip the excess, and whip-finish the fly.

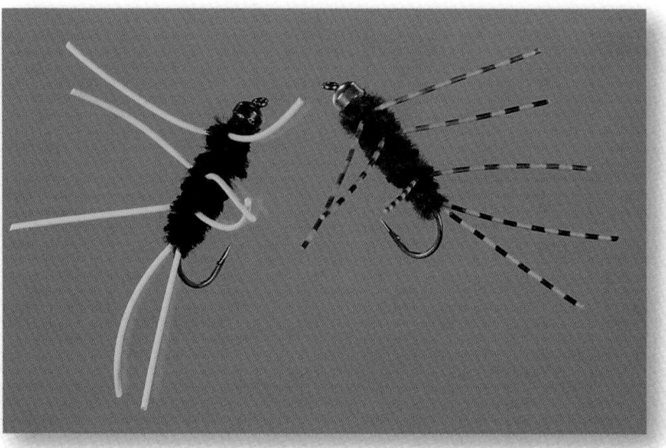

The addition of tungsten beads helps get rubber-legged flies down quickly in fast water. The Black Girdle Bug with black tungsten bead (left) is a standard. The Brown Girdle Bug with gold tungsten bead (right) is excellent for crayfish and pancora. Speckled Tarantu-Legs add a bit of extra life to any rubber-legged nymph.

The addition of tungsten beads to any rubber-legged nymph will help deliver it down quickly. Since I almost always use this style nymph either when bombing banks from a boat, or when trying to probe the depths of a medium to large river, I usually tie my rubber-legged nymphs with either black or gold beads, most often the heaviest I can find.

It's difficult to imagine any effective searching nymph to which a beadhead hasn't been added, sometimes with a change of name, more often without. The same is true for rubber legs: if a nymph catches trout, somebody will add legs and declare it to catch even more. They might be right. Without doubt, rubber legs add movement to any dressing, and it's not a theory that movement, mimicking life, is one of the key triggers to a take by a trout. I suspect you would not have to fish a Black Girdle Bug alongside a Black Woolly Worm for many days before you decided that the nymph with legs was more effective. But I haven't made that experiment, and I haven't fished a Black Woolly Worm in so many years that I'm not sure I even own any.

The Gold-Ribbed Hare's Ear (left) and Dave Whitlock's Fox Squirrel Nymph (right) are two famous searching nymphs to which both beadheads and rubber legs can be added with beneficial effects.

I don't own many rubber-legged nymphs, either, but I keep enough in my searching-nymph box to apply against the banks when I'm fishing big western rivers from a boat. I use them even more often in my sparse foreign travels, and most often then because my guide glances at my fly box and instantly requests that I tie on a big, ugly nymph with rubber legs.

I fished a lake system in central British Columbia recently, and got into a tributary river where Kamloops trout of fair size had run upstream and clustered to pester spawning kokanees, whether to eat kokanee or kokanee eggs it was not quite clear. Whatever they were taking, the trout crouched in darknesses along undercut, overhung banks, and they pounced on big nymphs that were smacked back in there, allowed to sink, retrieved on a slow strip. The most effective flies looked like nothing in nature, but they had rubber legs.

Deke Meyer's Yellow Bead Head Rubber Legs has taken trout for me on more than one continent, but I'm still not sure whether it's a nymph or a streamer.

The best fly I found for these rapacious trout was a Deke Meyer cross between a nymph and a streamer. A dozen were sent to me from Umpqua Feather Merchants, for a trip to Argentina, and I applied them to trout with good results down there. But they were even more effective against smallmouth bass, and I later lost all but one to them. The one I had left on that trip to Canada had a gold bead, yellow rubber legs, a brown chenille body, and olive marabou tail with lots of flash added. It's a takeoff on the Woolly Bugger, and had an olive-dyed and an orange-dyed saddle hackle wound over the chenille.

The Woolly Bugger itself, originated by Russell Blessing, is one of the most effective searching dressings ever tied. It is listed in many catalogs as a nymph, but I've always considered it a streamer. I consider myself stuck with my own definitions on the subject of Woolly Buggers, and won't list them here as searching nymphs, though I'll list them later in the chapter on leeches, because I consider them imitative for those undulating beasts, and imitative dressings are naturally nymphs, not streamers. That, of course, is also by my own narrow set of definitions, and I don't mean to foist them onto you.

SUMMARY

I don't tie and carry many rubber-legged dressings. The few I do, which amount to the Black and Brown Girdle Bugs, have tungsten beadheads. When I toss something so ugly, I want it to sink out of sight quickly, where nobody but the trout are ever able to see it.

CHAPTER 16

Czech Nymphs

Czech nymphing, also referred to as Polish nymphing, is a method in which a very heavy nymph is used to deliver a pair of smaller and less heavy nymphs to or near the bottom in fast water. The rod is long, the cast is short, the angler's position almost on top of the trout to be caught. Only the upstream portion of the drift is fished. The cast of flies is led through the water, the line kept only tight enough to keep in touch with the flies. Once the nymphs have reached the position of the angler, they are lifted and lobbed upstream, and fished through short drifts repeatedly to cover the water.

The leader is about six feet long, the heavy Czech nymph rigged in the center position, the other two nymphs on droppers about eighteen inches above and below it. At most half a rod length of line is extended for the short cast. If you're fishing much farther off than that, then you're no longer Czech nymphing. It's not a method I employ often, or well, because to me fly fishing is defined by the act of fly casting, and it's been said that Czech nymphing must be done with a fly rod but does not necessarily need to be done with a fly line. That short length of line beyond the rod tip could just as well be monofilament.

I've applied the method enough to be surprised, and even pleased, by the trout I've caught using it. Because the line is kept at least somewhat tight to the nymphs while leading them through their drift, a take is felt rather than seen as the dipping of an indicator, and that felt take gives a nice goose of excitement to the game. I can't say that I've gotten good at it, and I'm not sure that I ever will. Those who are experts at it routinely win international fly-fishing competitions, which is how the method came to light. I fish enough swift water to have use for the method. If you fish such water as well, you should at least tie a few of the nymphs, arm yourself with them, try them the next time you're in fast water and not doing well with your normal nymphing techniques.

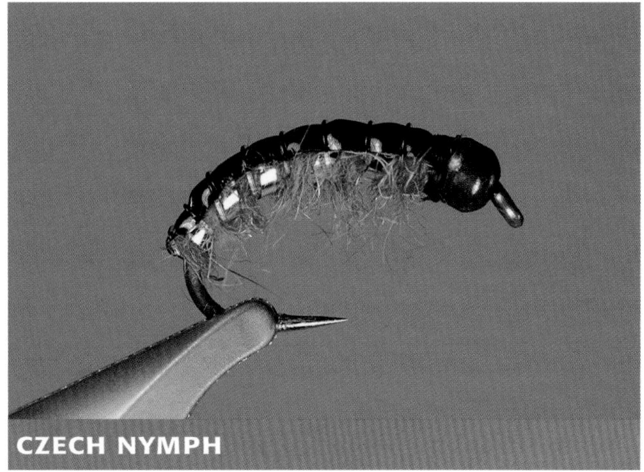
CZECH NYMPH

Hook:	Curved scud, size 8–12
Head:	Black or gold tungsten bead
Weight:	15–25 turns nonlead wire
Thread:	Black or brown 6/0 or 8/0
Overrib:	3X or 4X monofilament
Shellback:	Clear or black Thin Skin or similar material
Body rib:	Flat gold tinsel
Body:	Tan fur-green fur-tan fur

Nothing is set in stone about the materials or colors in tying the Czech Nymph, except the amount of weight. The original was tied as an imitation of a large green rock worm larva, and the shape of the nymph echoes that. But body colors vary from tan with a green midsection to green with an orange midsection. My favorite has a black tungsten bead, black shellback, and the standard tan-green-tan body. That's the one we'll tie here.

Because the Czech nymph itself is largely a delivery tool for a couple of lighter nymphs, the essence of the fly is weight. Because I use nonlead weighting wire, and it is 20 percent lighter than lead wire of the same diameter, I tie my Czech nymphs with tungsten beads, though that is a peripheral option in all of the literature I have read on Czech nymphing. If you don't mind using lead wire, you'll do fine without the tungsten bead. In my experience, using what I'll call the *thump test*—dropping nymphs weighted in different ways into the palm of my hand, and discerning the difference in how heavy they feel when they land—the addition of a tungsten bead makes a considerable difference in the authority of the thump, and therefore the swiftness with which the nymph will plummet toward the bottom. You could perform a more accurate experiment by dropping them into water and watching the rate at which they actually sink. That would be far more scientific.

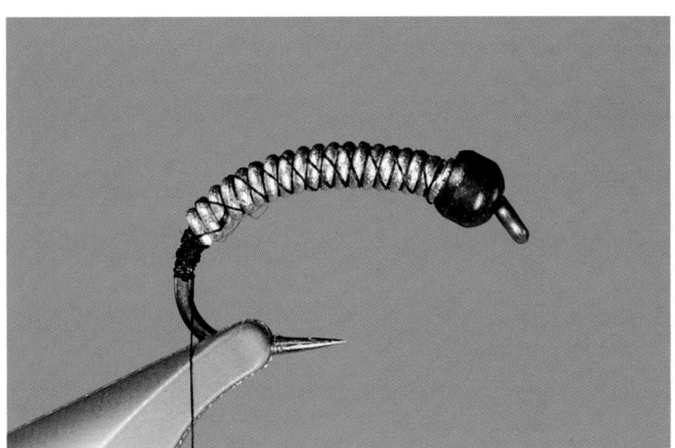

Step 1. Debarb the hook, slip a taper-drilled tungsten bead over it, with the small opening braced against the hook eye. Wrap as many turns of weighting wire as you can get on the shank, beginning well down around the bend and ending at the back end of the bead. Start your thread behind the weighting wire, and use enough turns to secure the wire, and also build at least a slight ramp at the rear shoulder of the wire.

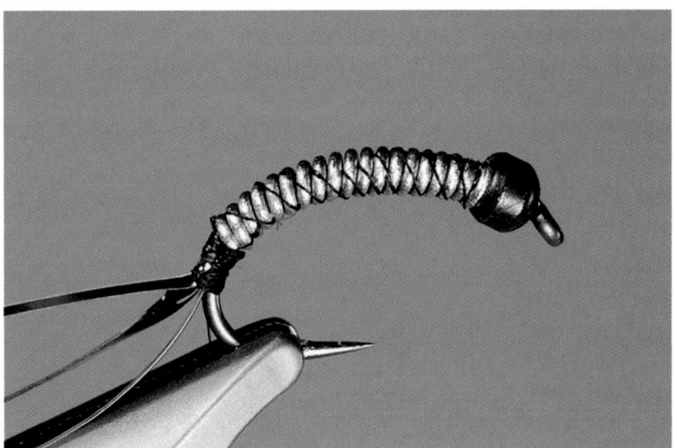

Step 2. Tie in a few inches of 3X or 4X monofilament behind the weighting wraps. I use retired tippet spools for ribbing. Clip a strip of Thin Skin or other shellback material about half the hook gap wide, taper one end with your scissors, and tie it in behind the weighting wire with the shiny side down, so that when you draw it over the body the shiny side will be up. Tie in a few inches of flat gold tinsel behind the weighting wire; if you're using silver and gold Mylar, tie it in with the gold side down, so that when you wind it, it will reverse itself and the gold side will be out.

Step 3. Fix a small amount of tan dubbing to the thread. Keep it slender; it should be just enough to cover the weighting wire. A bulky body will hinder the sinking of the fly, and that firm plummet is the primary goal when you tie this fly. Wind the dubbing to a point just short of the midpoint of the hook. Fix a shorter skein of green dubbing to the thread.

Step 4. Wrap a short section of green dubbing in the middle of the body. Fix a similar amount of the same tan dubbing that you used for the rear section of the body, and wrap it forward to the back of the bead.

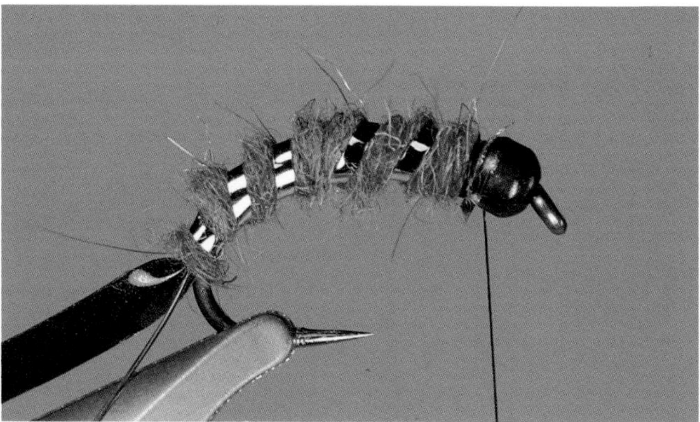

Step 5. Wrap the ribbing tinsel forward in evenly spaced turns to the back of the bead, and secure it with a few turns of thread. Clip the excess. Be sure you do not obscure the green section of the body.

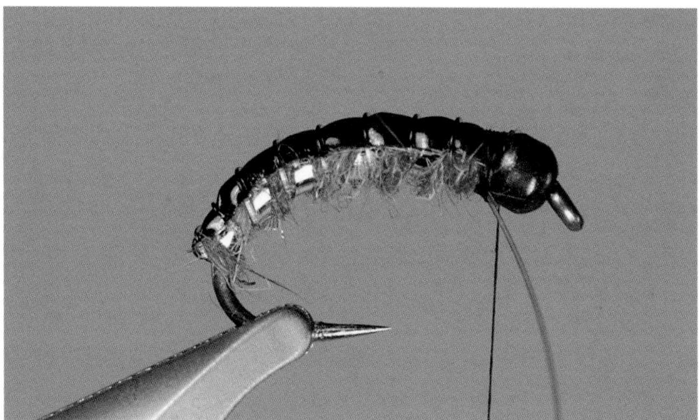

Step 6. Draw the shellback over the body, and tie it off with a few turns of thread tight behind the bead. Clip the excess. Wind the monofilament ribbing forward over the shellback in evenly spaced turns. Tie it off behind the bead with a few turns of thread.

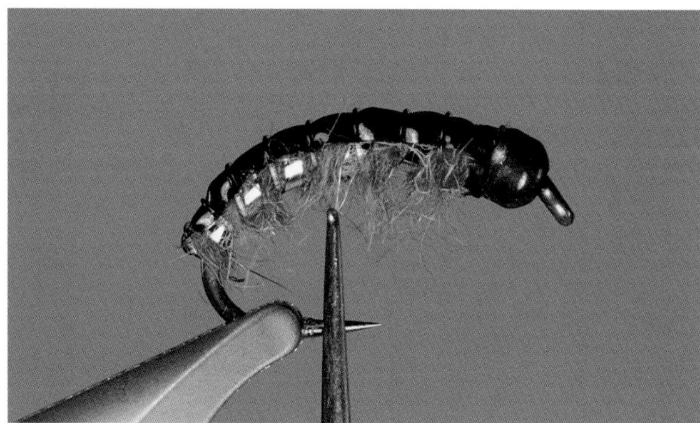

Step 7. Clip the excess monofilament ribbing. Whip-finish the fly behind the bead, and apply a drop of head cement over the whip. Use your bodkin point to tease out a bit of the belly and green accent fur, if you'd like, though this is not necessary.

To be applied correctly, the Czech-nymphing method calls for 10-foot and longer rods, in 3-, 4-, or 5-weight. The prescribed action of the favorable rod could fairly be called a noodle, because that type of slow action is best for lobbing three flies short distances without tangles, and a soft rod also protects tippets when the action is in close and comes upon you suddenly. I suspect this description of the perfect rod is another factor preventing me from perfecting this method: I rarely find myself astream armed with a 10-foot-long noodle. That type of rod would be appropriate only for this type of fishing, although it might also be useful for some short indicator-and-shot nymphing, and could perhaps be used for some very light yarn indicator and tiny nymph fishing. It wouldn't serve very well if trout began rising, and I decided to switch from nymphs to dry flies and emergers.

The best outfit for Czech nymphing would not be suitable for dry-fly fishing on the same type of water where you'd want to use the Czech nymph. It would be far from my first choice for indicator fishing on swift water. It's one of the limitations of the method: when you arm yourself to apply it, you might be giving yourself the best chance to catch trout in the water where you'll use it, but you'll be limited to the one method, and might need to gallop back to your rig for a different rod if you desire to do something different.

You can, however, apply the Czech-nymphing method more than marginally with the equipment you would normally carry on the type of fast water where you would want to apply the method. A 9-foot rod, even if its action is a bit brisk, will work; it just won't be perfect. You'll certainly be able to use tackle you already own for Czech nymphing, at least well enough to decide whether you'd like to outfit yourself precisely for the method in order to apply it more effectively. I've never done that. I've always rigged for Czech nymphing with whatever rod I held in my hand at that moment. I prefer to retain my option to fish any method, and would never want to have anything less than the best rod I could have in my hands if I encountered trout rising to insects on the surface, and I suddenly wanted to present a dry fly to them.

So I'll never be your best source of information on Czech nymphing. But at least you can now tie a few of the flies, and see how they work for you.

SUMMARY

You should at least prepare yourself to experiment with the Czech-nymphing method, to see if it suits you, and if it suits the types of waters where you fish most often. You might discover it's just the thing for your personality, and your home stream. That would not be an accident, just as it's no accident that the method has won many fly-fishing tournaments.

To arm yourself initially, try the standard Czech Nymph as listed, with lots of nonlead wire, a tan fur body with a green fur midsection, and a clear shellback. Tie it on a heavy wire curved hook, in size 8 or 10. If you'd like, tie the same version with a tungsten bead added. It won't take long to tie a half dozen of each, the standard and tungsten variety, and it won't take losing more than that to decide whether the method is suited to both you and your waters. If it is, your take of trout is about to increase dramatically.

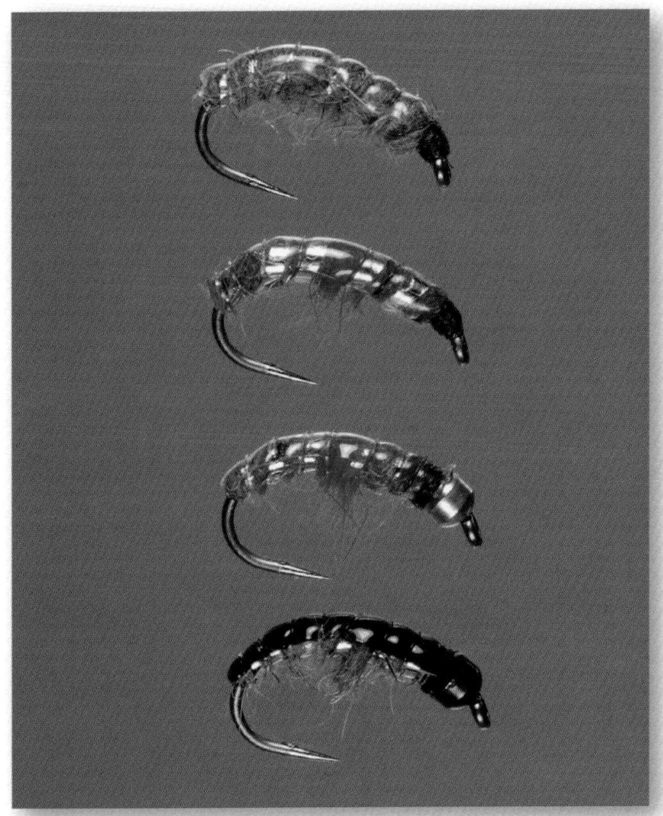

Czech nymphs are defined by their compact bodies and heavy weight. You can tie them with a variety of materials and colors, and with gold or black tungsten beads.

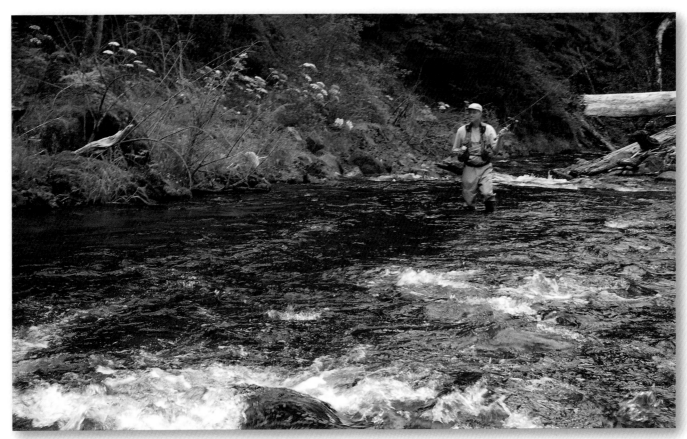

Rick Hafele nymphing the type of water where the Czech Nymph could be nicely applied.

CHAPTER 17

A Searching-Nymph Box

You've already fished long enough to have favorite nymphs, those that have caught trout for you in your past, and therefore those that you naturally tie to your tippet first when you get to a stream or river, gaze around, decide it's a day for nymphing as opposed to dry-fly, wet-fly, or streamer fishing. Nymphs that you already fish with confidence should be the first you tie and place in your new searching-nymph box.

I do recommend that you buy a new fly box. It will accomplish three quick things. First, it will clear out room for a seat of honor for those nymphs you've already established as your favorites. Second, it will give you a clear field for your thinking: what should go into the remainder of those spaces? Third, it will give you room for expansion, unless you buy a very small one, into which you can tie a variety of new searching nymphs that you feel might cover certain situations for you.

Only after you've placed your own current favorites in your box should you open up to consideration of the many nymphs I've listed in the preceding few chapters. Clearly you don't want to tie them all. You need to winnow them down to the few you feel will work best for you. You might want to pick only one or two, add them to a box that is already almost full of your favorites. You might have few favorites, and therefore want to pick half a dozen to a dozen of them, and then tie those by the half dozen or dozen so you can give each a fair test. It's a rule never to tie one of a size and kind of fly; surely you'll catch trout on it and lose it and abruptly forget what it was. Always put yourself in a position to repeat your successes.

One way to tie a trial sample of a specific nymph is to tie a dozen, three in each of four sizes, or four in each of three sizes. It's very rare that you'll land on a specific dressing as an addition to your list of favorites, without at the same time deciding that a specific size is precisely the correct one. The first time I had great success with Dave Whitlock's Red Fox Squirrel Nymph, I was fishing it in my off-color rendition, because I'd failed to get the right colors to follow the great Dave's prescription. The fly I fished had a gold bead, and was tied on a size 16 hook. It was weighted with eight turns of lead wire. I would feel totally disarmed if I were to go astream today without that exact fly, in that same size. I've gone to nonlead wire, so now I tie it with ten turns instead of eight. I suspect you'll think this is all pure superstition, but I think repeating the formula that brought good fortune is never a mistake. It certainly gives me confidence: whenever I dunk that particular nymph, I'm pretty sure I'm going to catch some trout.

One way to ensure a distinct range of sizes for a nymph pattern you'd like to give a fair trial is to skip sizes: tie Dave Whitlock's Beadhead Red Fox Squirrel, as shown here, in sizes 12, 16, and 20. The gaps between will be clear, and you'll have no trouble telling which trout prefer on a given day.

It's also never a mistake to tie a single dressing in a range of sizes. Another way to accomplish that, especially when you begin experimenting with a searching dressing, is to skip hook sizes. Tie the same nymph in sizes 12, 16, and 20. That gives you a clear choice between small, medium, and large, which is not far off from doing the same thing when you choose colors for a style of searching nymph: choose a light color, a medium color, and a dark color.

As an example, you might be making a mistake to tie the A. P. series in Black and Muskrat, because both have a similar dark aspect when wet. You would do better to tie it in Black and Beaver, because that would give you a couple of colors that have some contrast, light and dark, and therefore you'd be able to offer trout a choice, and would be able to make a clearer choice yourself about which one worked best for you.

Your entire searching-nymph box should reflect those types of contrasts. Your selection should run from small size 20s to large size 8s. Some should be light, others dark, some drab, many bright. Some should be long and slender, most should be substantial and tapered neatly, following the shape of most natural insects, but a few should be portly, because if trout ever like a mouthful, it's when they're feeding nonselectively, and are therefore susceptible to your searching nymphs.

When choosing colors for a style of nymph, tie it in ones that contrast rather than ones that are similar in shade, so you're able to choose clearly between a light and a dark. If you fish the two together, you'll quickly get a sense which one trout prefer that day.

Your searching-nymph selection should include patterns that are slender, such as the Flashback Pheasant Tail (left); tapered and toward the center of the natural insect range of shapes, such as the Bird's Nest (center); and portly, such as the Herl Nymph (right).

PART 3

Imitative Nymphs for Moving Water

CHAPTER 18

Mayflies

It's heresy to begin by stating that most mayfly nymph situations can be solved with nymphs selected from your searching box. Most mayfly crawler and clinger nymphs, as broad examples, live along the bottom in water that varies from brisk to brutally fast. Such water delivers a mix of aquatic insects to trout: mayfly and stonefly nymphs, caddisfly and midge larvae. The same water also gives trout little time to examine what the drift delivers to them. In the average type of water where crawler and clinger mayfly nymphs are abundant, trout are forced to make quick decisions. They'll routinely accept any fly that is roughly the size, shape, and shade of something they've been eating lately.

The most successful searching nymphs—the Gold-Ribbed Hare's Ear, Red Fox Squirrel, Herl Nymph, on and on—resemble more than one aquatic food form. Both the Hare's Ear and Squirrel Nymph have the shape and general coloration of the average dislodged fast-water mayfly nymph. If you select one of those patterns in an appropriate size, usually 16 or at most 14, as opposed to 10 or 12, you're very likely to fool a bunch of trout in water that is moving at least moderately.

If you take a kick-net sample in such water, it will almost invariably come up crawling with a wide variety of insect types. If one of them is clearly dominant—in terms of numbers, not necessarily size—you should examine your searching-nymph box for the fly that's nearest to it, and tie it to your tippet. If it's a somewhat large fly, again a size 12 or 14, you'll be smart to drop a size 16 or 18 searching nymph off the hook bend, on an eight- to ten-inch tippet. You'll be surprised to discover, even in the presence of a dominant larger natural, how often the smaller nymph outfishes the larger, in this case more imitative, nymph.

Most mayfly situations can be solved out of your searching-nymph box. The key to imitative nymphs is recognition of a situation in which you need to get imitative. Two things, easy to observe, will inform you that you're in such a situation.

The first is abundance. At times you'll encounter a bit of water that contains one species of insect heavily outweighing all others. The faster water flows, the more silt and pea gravel it washes away, the more its bottom is composed of cobble and rock, and the more varied environments it offers to aquatic insects. That's why a kick-net sample taken in such water comes up awiggle with variety. The slower and more stable the water, the more deposition it permits, and the more aquatic vegetation is able to take root. Plants form a myriad of microniches, all of which are pretty much alike. The telling result: on spring creeks and in tailwaters, you often get a narrowing of the list of species, with each species existing in overwhelming abundance. It's a prescription for selective feeding.

You're most likely to get into a situation where you must match a mayfly nymph on the relatively peaceful waters of a spring creek or tailwater, least likely to run into a similar situation on the brisk flows of a freestone stream or river. However, if your collecting scoops up a netful of a single dominant species, in any kind of water, that spells an abundance that you should match.

The second factor pointing toward the need for imitation in nymph fishing is availability of a particular insect. Sometimes the water, whether fast or slow, is full of a variety of aquatic insect types, but only one of them is engaged in some activity that makes it vulnerable to trout. Among stoneflies, it might be a mass migration toward shore, where emergence will take place. With caddisflies, it might be the staging of pupae in the drift inches from the bottom, preparatory to their fateful swim to the surface for emergence.

In the mayflies under our current examination, availability of nymphs is almost always increased in the hours

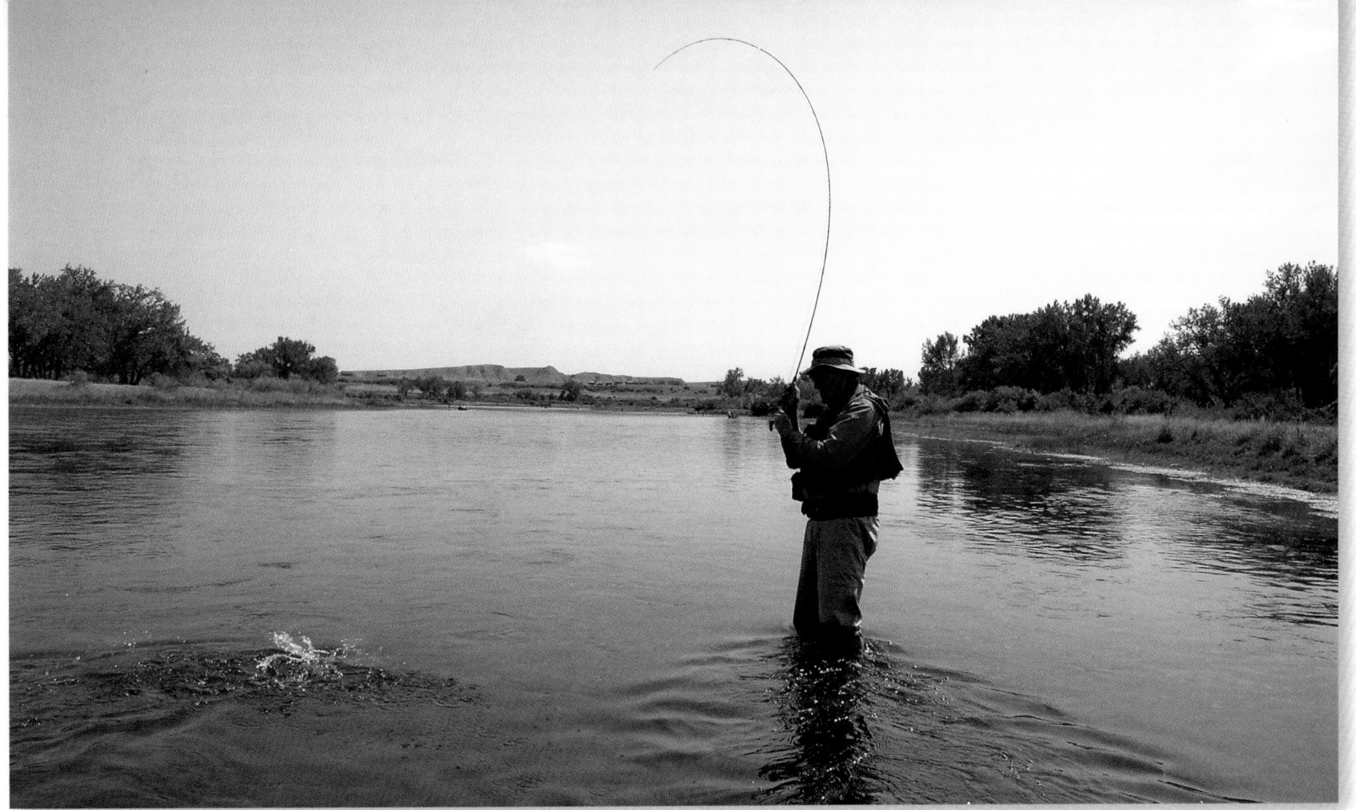

The Bighorn River in Montana is typical of the type of tailwater that has heavy hatches of tiny blue-winged olive mayflies. You won't do well on such water if you're fishing a dry fly when trout are focusing on nymphs.

before emergence. If you see a few duns on the surface, but no trout feedng on them, quite often those duns are an indication that trout are feeding on nymphs just beneath the surface. It becomes critical, during a mayfly hatch, that you observe the rises with which trout take insects. If no floating duns disappear, if no noses break the flow, if no bubbles are left in rise rings, it's more likely that trout are feeding just beneath the surface than they are on top. This reflects both abundance and availability of the nymph that goes before the dun you're able to observe. Those are the two factors that prompt trout to feed selectively on a nymph. You need to be prepared to collect and match whatever nymph is both abundant and available at that moment.

I'll give you an example. In a recent early October, Jim Schollmeyer and I floated the Bighorn River in Montana, hoping to get into daily hatches of black caddis (Brachycentridae), which can be so heavy on the river. But our timing was off; the caddis hatch was over. We didn't get into more than a trickle of them. But we did get into early-afternoon hatches of the tiny mayfly that used to be called *Pseudocloeon,* but has since been shifted to some other taxonomic location in the extensive *Baetis* complex. Call them blue-winged olives; they were tiny. The duns, visible boating the smooth currents among pods of rising trout, were no larger than size 22s; they might have been 24s.

I tried nearly every dun imitation I owned in those small sizes before I ceased my frantic casting, paid close attention to a few rises. Once in a while a trout back

When trout ignore duns and feed just beneath the surface during a hatch, it's logical to conclude that they're taking nymphs of the same species, such as this blue-winged olive (Baetis), *and that you should try an imitation fished inches deep.*

would break the water. More often a tail would break the surface and wag happily in what has appropriately been termed a *satisfaction rise.* Most of the time, only the rise rings would reach the surface, with no bubbles left in them: a sure sign that more than 90 percent of the takes were to something just beneath the surface. I began doing what I should have done in the first place: I got out my compact Nikon binoculars and followed the floats of a few duns. Not one went down in a swirl.

It took scant minutes to rerig with a white yarn indicator about the size of a pea, with a foot of 5X tippet to a size 20 Pheasant Tail, and another foot of 6X to a size

22 Flashback PT. It was my misfortune that most of the trout passed up the big nymph and sipped in the small one. Half the time I'd see my indicator dip from sight. The other half I'd see the rise itself, and set the hook gently to that. I'd made the great mistake of tying my smallest nymphs on light-wire dry-fly hooks. Those Bighorn trout had broad shoulders. Close to a third of them snapped the 6X. More than that straightened the fine-wire hooks. Only a tithe of the trout that I hooked let themselves get coaxed into my hands.

The Bighorn River is a large tailwater. It has rooted vegetation, smooth flows, heavy hatches of blue-winged olives. During those hatches, the two key components of imitative nymphing, abundance and availability, often arrive together. When they do, it's easy to notice it. On many streams you'll encounter less abundance though similar availability, and you'll have more trouble noticing when you should use a nymph as opposed to a floating dun dressing. The easiest, but also most frustrating, way to notice that you need to switch to a shallow nymph is failure of all your attempts with a variety of duns. If you can't catch trout on top, switch to a nymph, or at least trail a nymph.

That last prescription, while easy to write, is not always as easy to execute. The formula goes like this: If you're not catching trout on your floating imitation, just add a couple feet of tippet to the hook bend of the dry fly, and tie a nymph imitation behind it. That sounds fine, but most of the time a nymph big enough to imitate the natural will sink a dry fly small enough to imitate the dun. Mayflies lose about a size in the transition from nymph to dun. If you feel you need to try a nymph, usually it's beneficial to take a bit of time to rerig with a yarn indicator. You can always slip-knot a yarn indicator into the leader four feet or so from the dry fly, then dangle the nymph, and hope the dry floats. If you see any rise near the indicator, set the hook gently. Don't set it hard, or you'll rip everything out of there if the rise was not to your dry fly or submerged nymph. That will scare the trout, put them down.

Mayfly nymphs are traditionally broken into four categories, defined by behavior: swimmers, crawlers, clingers, and burrowers. Since behavior shapes bodies, they also have four fairly distinct shapes.

Mayfly swimmer nymphs live on bottom rocks or in rooted vegetation. They can be found in fair abundance in fast water, but usually in sheltered spaces between bottom stones, or in slower water along the margins. In swift streams and rivers, you'll find the most swimmer nymphs tucked back beneath undercut banks. They reach their greatest numbers in aquatic plant beds in spring creeks and tailwaters, where they find millions of microniches, all of similar shape.

Swimmer mayfly nymphs are long and slender, adapted to flitting from stone to stone in freestone streams, or among the myriads of microniches in spring-creek and tailwater aquatic plant beds.

Members of the small blue-winged olive, or *Baetis,* complex can be dominant on such waters as the Henry's Fork of the Snake and the Bighorn, but are far from limited to the West. They're found all across our continent and all around the world. They are the famous olives of early British writings, which not accidentally were about limestone stream hatches: the exact type of water where swimmers often dominate other aquatic insects. Swimmer nymphs are the most abundant of the four mayfly types in stillwaters, but we'll leave that to a later chapter.

The swimmer nymphs' shape reflects their dashing lifestyle. They're long, slender, and have tails that are usually fringed with hair, to increase their surface area and make them better propellants. If you drop a swimmer mayfly nymph into the palm of your hand and add water, it will react the same as a tiny minnow, flipping its body around, trying to swim.

Mayfly crawler nymphs are typically more blocky and stout than swimmers, reflecting their lifestyle of patiently hiking, rather than swimming, when they want to move from one part of the aquatic environment to another.

Most mayfly crawler nymphs live on the bottom, in moving water that varies between slow and so fast that you wouldn't dare to wade it. They are typically distributed in riffles and runs of freestone streams and rivers, and spend almost all of their time sheltering in the spaces between stones. They feed on the thin layer of vegetation that grows on the surfaces of rocks, the same slippery stuff that causes you to slip and fall while you're wading.

When knocked loose from the safety of their shelters, crawler mayfly nymphs tumble with the currents until they're delivered safely back to the bottom, or into the waiting jaws of bottom-feeding trout. Many try to swim feebly, but few are able to take control of their own fate when they're cast into the currents. Their main way of moving from place to place is by crawling from stone to stone.

A few crawlers do live in rooted vegetation, in spring creeks and tailwaters. Where they have adapted to such microniches, they're found in the same sort of abundance as swimmer nymphs. The pale morning dun hatch on many scattered streams reflects this adaptation. The famous western green drake hatch on the Henry's Fork of the Snake River in Idaho is another example, though this large mayfly crawler nymph is unfortunately not adapted to many other spring creeks.

The shape of the mayfly crawlers reflects their type of movement in the water. They are less slender than swimmers, and have strong legs. The stout body shape is exaggerated in those that live most commonly in fast water, less pronounced in those that have adapted to slower waters and to the margins of swift water. A few crawlers are able to swim fairly well, but if you were to set one on the starting blocks next to a swimmer and fire off a pistol, you would have no trouble telling them apart as they raced away.

Clinger nymphs are flattened in aspect, with heads wider than their bodies, for living in the microscopically thin layer of water slowed by friction on the faces of stones in the fastest currents.

Mayfly clinger nymphs live on the bottom, almost always in moderate to swift water. They expose themselves to the current, flattening against the surfaces of stones, browsing the same thin and slippery layer of algae that crawler nymphs feed upon in more sheltered spaces. You can often see them in shallow riffles, where thin water shears over a rock, right out in sunlight. If your shadow crosses them, or you wave your hand too near them, they'll scuttle quickly to the underside of the rock. But they won't let go and enter the drift. They're adapted to clinging to the surfaces of stones right in the current, not to swimming if for some rare reason they're knocked loose from their perches in that current. They keep their grip tenaciously.

Clingers have adapted over about 250 million mayfly generations to a lifestyle cramped into the very thin layer of current that is slowed by friction as it passes over the face of a bottom rock. As a consequence, their bodies have become flattened. From the top or bottom view, they're as stout as crawlers. From the side view, they're flat as Frisbees.

Burrower nymphs are typically long and have little taper to their bodies. Though they are cryptic, coming out of their burrows to feed or emerge only in the low light of evening or after dark, they're able to swim quite fast when they feel the need.

Mayfly burrower nymphs, as their name implies, create their own shelters in the bottom, either by digging U-shaped tunnels, or by nestling into soft sands and fine gravels. A nymph that digs a burrow creates a tiny current by waving its gills in a synchronized movement that pulses water from one end of the tunnel to the other, thus constantly delivering oxygen. Digging a burrow requires a bottom that is soft enough to dig in, yet firm enough not to collapse once the tunnel has been excavated. Nestling into the bottom requires a consistency that collapses around the buried insect, but does not capture it or deny it oxygenated water. These requirements are very specific.

You'll find populations of burrower nymphs scattered all over the continent, but only where the bottom is firm mud, clay, sand, or very fine gravel. Fast water does not allow the deposition of such material. You'll find burrowers only in slow water with stabilized flows. If silt were to be washed out by winter spates, you'd have a typical freestone bottom, and you wouldn't find burrowers.

The burrowers' shape reflects their digging or sheltering lifestyle. They're long, somewhat slender, with little taper to the body. The most important species to trout fishermen are all large, size 6 down to about 12, probably because it takes some heft to wield burrowing tusks like you would a garden spade. When it comes time for emergence—or, one would presume, for escape from a hungry trout—burrowers are able to swim fairly fast, and that should shape both the nymph patterns you tie to imitate them, and the way you retrieve those patterns.

MAYFLY SWIMMER NYMPHS

Moving-water swimmer nymphs can be roughly divided into two groups, the widespread and small but often very abundant members of the blue-winged olive, or *Baetis,* group, and the less abundant, less widespread, but larger members of the gray drake, or *Siphlonurus* and related genera. The first will be encountered most often, and will be most difficult to match. Because their hatches are so often concentrated, and trout feeding on them are so often selective, you'll need to have imitations, or you're likely to harvest nothing but frustration. The larger insects of the second group will cause you fits far less often, and can usually be solved with one of the searching dressings listed earlier, if the retrieve is right. Most of them live along stream edges, and you'll do your best fishing for them if you use a retrieve that seems more appropriate to a streamer than to a nymph.

The size 16 and smaller blue-winged olive nymph (Baetis) *is typical of small swimmer nymphs that are both abundant and available in great numbers during a hatch on the smooth waters of many spring creeks and tailwaters. They must be matched at least in terms of size and shape, and with a fly that is fairly close in color.*

PHEASANT TAIL NYMPH

The standard imitation for the smaller swimmers is the Pheasant Tail Nymph. The same nymph was listed as a searching dressing in chapter 12, because the constant presence of the naturals, in all types of moving waters, means they're being seen and eaten by trout almost all the time, and trout are therefore almost always susceptible to a fly that looks like a small blue-winged olive nymph. Few people fish the Pheasant Tail in its orginal form, as tied by Frank Sawyer, with copper wire rather than thread. The early American version of the nymph, using pheasant tail fibers for the tail, body, wing case, and legs, is still very effective. It's a toss-up whether the most common tie for the nymph is now the Al Troth variation, with peacock herl for the thorax, or the Flashback Pheasant Tail, with some form of bright material tied in as the shellback.

I prefer the flashback style, not based on any exact science, but out of the belief that I've caught more trout on the Pheasant Tail Nymph with that bit of brightness added. That could simply reflect that I fish the fly most often in the flashback variation, and I'm naturally going to catch more trout on the fly I fish most often.

I suspect you can tie any version of the fly you prefer, and do well with it, so long as you get the size right. At one time I thought a size 16 Pheasant Tail Nymph was a small nymph. In many places, that is still true. But if you begin fishing the sorts of waters where trout see lots of blue-winged olive naturals, and are pestered by an almost constant parade of BWO imitations, then a critical measurement of the size insect you're imitating becomes much more important.

It's easy enough to get the size of your nymph right by simply collecting a dun, setting it into your nymph box, selecting a fly that is at most a size larger. It is, of course, more accurate to acquire a natural nymph, using a kick net or a throat pump, but not all of us carry a net around, and it's not always easy to catch that first trout for a sample until after you've estimated the size of the insects it has been eating.

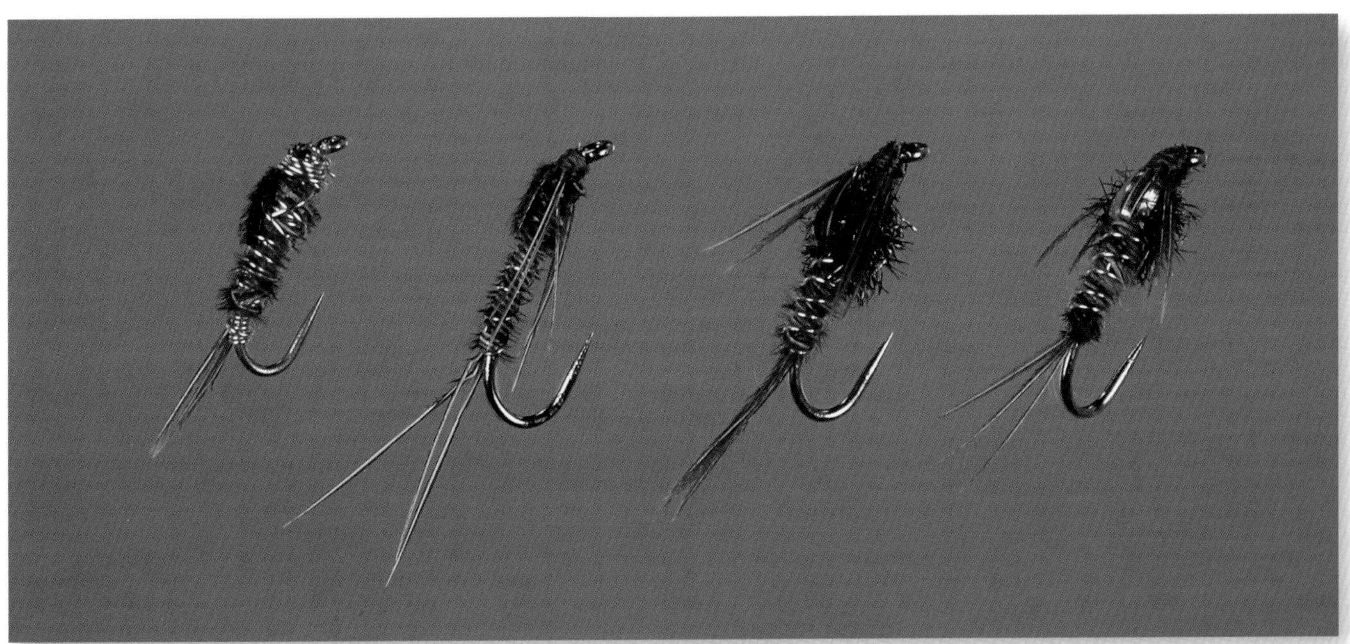

You can use the version of the Pheasant Tail Nymph that suits you best; all will catch trout so long as the size is right. From left: original Frank Sawyer version, standard tie, Al Troth variation with peacock herl thorax, and Flashback Pheasant Tail. See chapter 12, Herl Nymphs, for tying instructions.

When you're trying to match a blue-winged olive nymph, with a Pheasant Tail or any other nymph, size is critical, and a size 16 is large. A size 20 or 22 will take trout more often when they're selective to BWOs.

Most of the time, the Pheasant Tail I tie on during a blue-winged olive emergence is a size 20 or 22. Now I consider a size 18 a big one. Exact imitation of the minute peripheral parts of a tiny insect is mostly an exercise in fly-tying skills. If you get the size right, and approximate the shape of the natural, capturing the essence of its most important parts, you'll likely catch just as many trout. You might catch more, because you'll spend less time tying, more time fishing.

RS-2

Tailwater flows, heavy fishing pressure, and heavy hatches all lead toward selective trout, which in turn prod pattern development. The South Platte River, not far from Denver, Colorado, has become the proving ground for many of the best small flies, both nymphs and drys. Rim Chung's RS-2, developed in the 1970s and detailed in Ed Engle's *Tying Small Flies,* is one of the best, and is fished as an imitation of the blue-winged olive nymph in the beginning stages of emergence.

The RS-2 stands for Rim's Semblance, version two. It is tied with beaver fur and the fluff from the base of a pheasant neck feather. Many variations have been tied on the original theme. The most common calls for muskrat fur and natural dun CDC. Some folks now add a touch of flash, in the form of Krystal Flash strands standing up in front of the wing. I recommend you try it as its originator called for it, and fish the original against variations that you'd like to work on it.

The RS-2 appears to be an emerger, and its shape suggests it should be fished in the surface film. It's possible to fish it that way if you tie the wing stub of CDC. But even then it will usually soak up water and subside after a cast or two. It was designed to be fished just subsurface, and that is the way I have found it most effective. It's also excellent as a tiny dropper behind a "big" size 16 or 18 nymph rigged to be fished along the bottom, with an indicator and microshot attached to the leader.

I find the RS-2 most effective when fished twelve inches to two feet from a tiny yarn indicator, usually in tandem with a slightly larger fly fished a foot from it on the same rig. I rarely use the RS-2 unless blue-winged olives are hatching, and trout are working the hatch but taking more nymphs just before emergence than they are duns just after they've emerged.

RS-2 Rim Chung

Hook:	Ring-eye or standard dry fly, size 16–26
Thread:	Black or gray 8/0 or 10/0
Tail:	2 dark dun Microfibetts, split
Abdomen:	Beaver fur
Wing:	Fluff from pheasant feather
Thorax:	Beaver fur

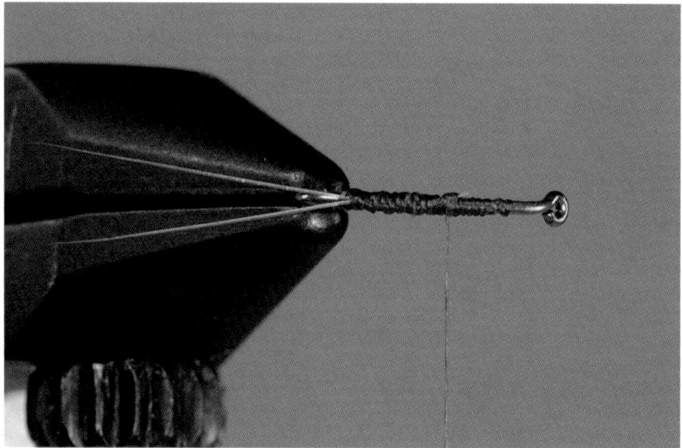

Step 1. Debarb the hook if needed, and fix it in the vise. Layer the shank with thread. Twist your thread to fatten it, by spinning the bobbin clockwise. Use three to five turns of thread at the beginning of the bend of the hook to make a tiny thread bump. Flatten your thread again by twirling the bobbin counterclockwise. Measure a tail fiber one to one and a half times the length of the shank, and tie it in on the opposite side of the hook. Measure another fiber the same length, and tie it in on the near side. Work your thread back against the thread bump to separate the tails. If necessary, take a thread turn between the tails to hold them apart.

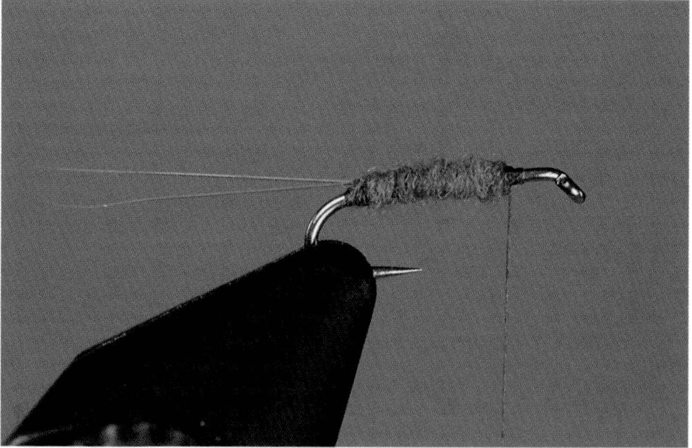

Step 2. Pick the guard hairs from a very small amount of fur dubbing. Use the direct-dubbing method to twist it to the thread tightly; the body should be slender and compact. Wrap the abdomen forward to a point just past the midpoint of the hook shank.

Step 3. Strip or cut the fluffy fibers from one side of the base of a pheasant back feather. Clip across the butt ends to even them. Hold them in front of the abdomen, and use several tight thread turns to lock them in at that point.

Fix a small amount of the same fur to the thread, twisting it tightly as you did with the abdomen. Wrap three to four turns of dubbing forward to a point just behind the hook eye. Whip-finish the head and clip your thread.

Step 4. Grip the wing fibers with the thumb and forefinger of your off hand, and use your scissors to snip the wing to a stub about even with the end of the abdomen, or a bit shorter. Slant the cut downward, so the wing has the shape of the wings of a natural dun just beginning to unfurl from the nymphal shuck.

In his book *Advanced Fly Tying,* A. K. Best offers a carefully explained adaptation of the RS-2, which he developed by wading into the middle of a bunch of trout feeding on blue-winged olives, and observing exactly what the insects looked like on the water, while being fed upon by the trout. He calls his pattern the RS Quill. It is tied to imitate the insect in the earliest stages of emergence, when the wing is just beginning to emerge from the nymphal shuck. It can be fished in any of the ways that Rim Chung's original RS-2 is effective: along the bottom, just subsurface, or dressed with dry-fly floatant and fished in the surface film. A. K. calls for tying it on "any dry fly hook," which would give you that last option, whereas a heavy nymph hook would not.

RS QUILL *A. K. Best*

Hook:	Standard dry fly, 1XF, size 16–22
Thread:	Olive 8/0
Tail:	4–5 wood-duck flank fibers
Body:	Olive-dyed hackle stem
Wing:	Light gray poly yarn
Thorax:	Medium dun fur or synthetic dubbing

You can buy prepared and dyed quill stems, though you can also strip them with a bleach solution and dye them yourself. Whichever you use, be sure to soak the quills in water before trying to wind them as the body of a fly. I fold them into a paper towel and wet the towel, which keeps them flat and dampens them at the same time.

KRYSTAL FLASH *BAETIS* NYMPH

Rick Hafele is an aquatic entomologist, and you would think he would be further into exact imitation than the average angler. But Rick has long recognized that behavior is often more important than precisely copying an

RS-2 variations tied (from left) in the original with beaver fur, with a muskrat fur body, with muskrat fur and a couple strands of pearl Krystal Flash in front of the wing, and with a CDC wing.

insect's peripheral parts. His Krystal Flash *Baetis* Nymph is based on the prescription of a slender, reflective body; a dark wing case that captures the trigger of a nymph about ready for emergence; and a balance between a fly that can be fished shallow and one that will also work well when fished deep, with weight added above it on the leader.

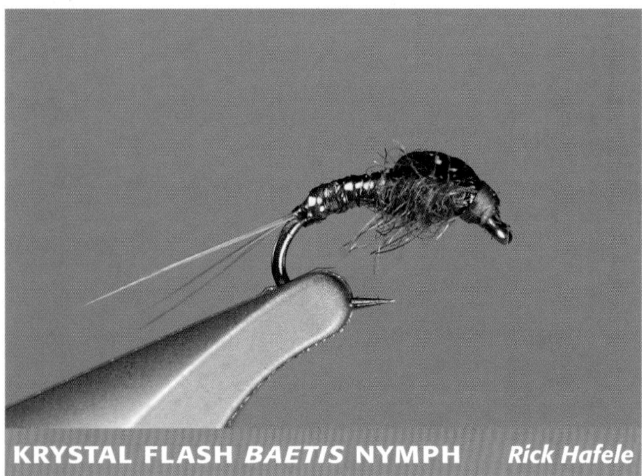

KRYSTAL FLASH *BAETIS* NYMPH ***Rick Hafele***

Hook:	Curved scud, size 16–20
Thread:	Olive 8/0
Tail:	3–6 light dun hackle fibers
Abdomen:	4–6 strands peacock Krystal Flash
Wing case:	Dark turkey or black Krystal Flash
Thorax:	Brown fur dubbing

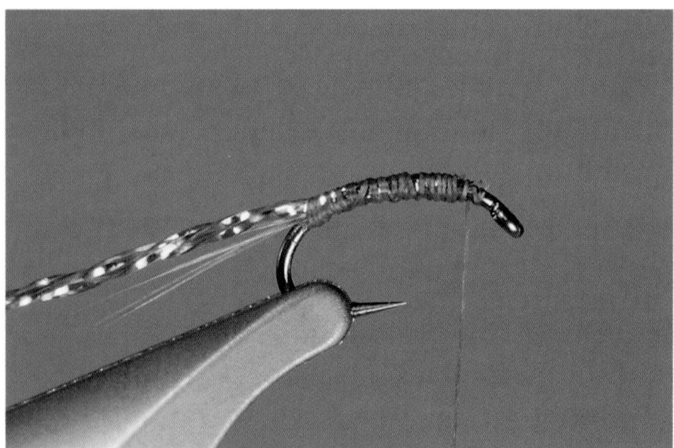

Step 1. Debarb your hook, start the thread behind the hook eye, and layer thread partway down the bend of the curved hook. Select three to six light dun neck fibers, measure them the length of the hook, and tie them in on the hook bend. Even the tips of four to six strands of Krystal Flash, and tie them in firmly at the base of the tail. Overwrap the tails past the midpoint of the hook shank, to form an even underbody for the abdomen.

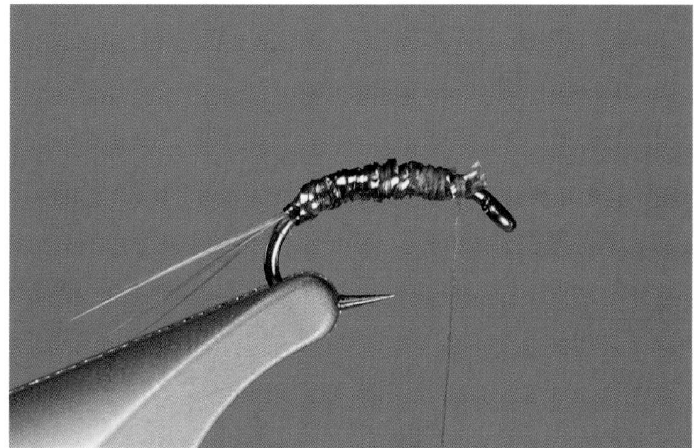

Step 2. Twist the Krystal Flash strands together, enough to keep them from splaying as this material tends to do. Wind this forward to a point just past the midpoint of the hook shank. Be sure to retwist the flash strands after each turn around the hook shank, to keep them from splaying. Tie it off securely and clip the excess.

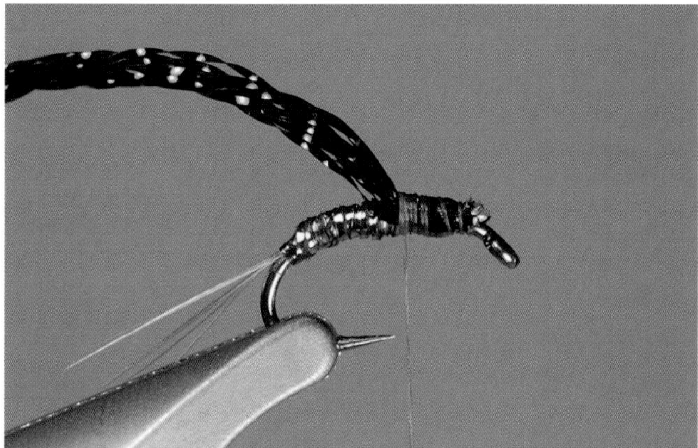

Step 3. Even the tips of ten to twenty strands of black Krystal Flash, depending on the size nymph you're tying. Tie them in at the end of the abdomen, overwrapping them forward to a point about one or two hook-eye lengths behind the eye, leaving room for the head. Clip the excess.

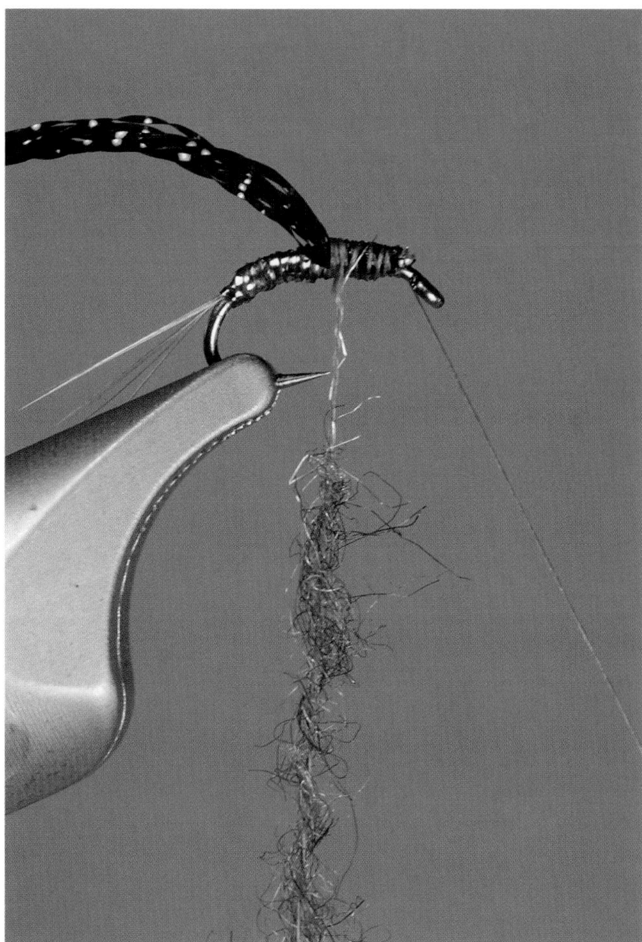

Step 4. Extract a small amount of dubbing from the package, and work it into a loose skein. Attach this lightly to the hook, capture it in a thread loop, and twist it only enough to make sure the fur is captured between the threads. You want a loose dubbing, with many fibers sticking out to represent the legs of the insect.

Step 5. Wrap the dubbing forward in two to four turns to form a loose, spiky thorax. Clip the excess thread forming the fur rope. Refrain from tidying the thorax at this point; leave the maverick strands.

Step 6. Bring the wing-case Krystal Flash forward, and tie it off behind the hook eye. Be sure to leave enough room for a thread head. It helps to twist the Krystal Flash strands just a bit as you draw them forward; this keeps the strands gathered so they form a dense, dark wing case. Clip the excess Krystal Flash, use just enough thread turns to cover the butts, make a neat thread head, and whip-finish tight behind the hook eye. You can now tidy up any maverick strands of thorax dubbing.

The density of the Krystal Flash *Baetis* makes it an excellent upper fly in a two-fly combo to be fished near the surface, just before or even during a blue-winged olive emergence. It is sure to get through the surface film, and to get down a few inches. Use a lighter fly as the trailer, perhaps in a size smaller. A killing combination is a size 18 Krystal Flash *Baetis* on one and a half feet of 5X, suspended from a small yarn indicator, followed by a size 20 or 22 Pheasant Tail or RS-2 on a foot of 6X tippet. It has been interesting to note how often one or the other of the nymphs in such a tandem will take most of the fish, but will suddenly stop working if the other nymph is snipped out of the equation. Two nymphs often fish much better than one, even when trout are taking one and ignoring the other.

BIOT NYMPH

Shane Stalcup is an innovative Colorado tier whose home range contains those difficult Denver-area tailwaters, with heavy fishing pressure and big hatches of tiny blue-winged olive mayflies. His Biot Nymph is about the prettiest you'll be able to tie for the group. His book *Mayflies Top to Bottom* addresses the other stages of the insect as well, but our interest here is limited to nymphs.

I'll make a quick confession: Shane's Biot Nymph is far more graceful and attractive on the hook he uses for it, a 3XL hook with a slight arc, than on a straight-shank. I use that hook in larger sizes, to imitate long and slender naturals, and also tie fair-sized dry flies on it, such as Stimulators in size 12 and up. But it presents a problem in tiny sizes. The long shank makes it difficult to tie a truly small nymph. A size 22 nymph tied on a 3XL hook is by definition about a size 18.

Perhaps all of that is justification for tying a fly that is not nearly as beautiful as Shane would tie it, on a standard nymph hook. He is a very fine tier, and a thoughtful innovator, and his Biot Nymph reflects that.

BIOT NYMPH ***Shane Stalcup***

Hook:	Standard nymph or 3XL, size 16–22
Thread:	Olive 8/0
Tail:	Brown partridge fibers
Body:	Olive-dyed turkey or goose biot
Wing case:	Medallion sheeting or flash material
Thorax:	Brown fur or synthetic dubbing
Legs:	Brown partridge

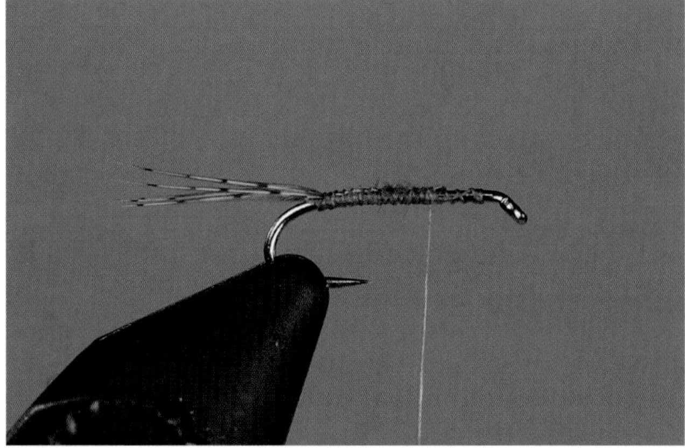

Step 1. Debarb the hook, start the thread behind the hook-eye, and make a single layer to the beginning of the hook bend. Strip or clip three to five partridge fibers from the stem. Measure them about the length of the hook shank, and tie them in at the bend of the hook. Make a single layer of thread over the tail butts to a point about one-quarter to one-third of the shank length behind the eye, and clip the excess there. Be sure this leaves an even underbody for the biot body.

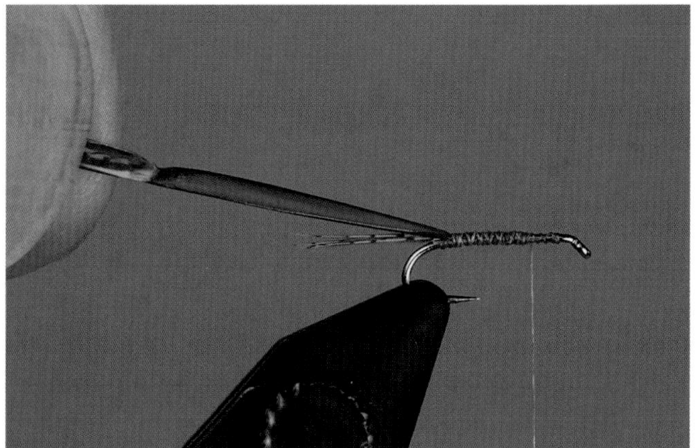

Step 2. Tie in a biot by the tip, beginning at the front and winding back over it to the base of the tail. Bring your thread forward to a point about two-fifths of the shank behind the eye, leaving a perfectly even underbody. Be sure that the slight notch in the base of the biot is up, or you will not get a segmented body. Your biot must be moist before tying it in. I remove the number I need from the feather stem, with a few extra for mistakes, and lay them on a paper towel that has been folded several times. Then I fold the towel once more over them, and pour enough water onto the towel to soak through it.

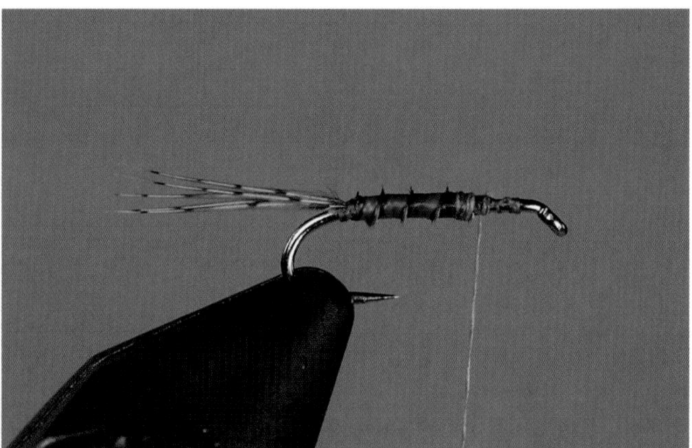

Step 3. Use your hackle pliers to wind the biot forward to the tie-off point, about one-quarter to one-third the shank length behind the eye. Each turn of biot will leave a distinct fuzzy ridge. Be sure to space the turns so they do not overlap and cover these ridges; they represent segmentation of the natural. Tie off and clip the excess biot.

Step 4. Shane Stalcup has encorporated Medallion sheeting into many of his proprietary patterns, and it is available in most fly shops. If you lack it, and substitute turkey quill or another flash material, the fly will not be precisely as its originator intended, but trout might still take it. Cut a strip of Medallion sheeting about half the width of the hook gap, or select a few strands of Krystal Flash or other flash, and tie it in at the end of the biot body. Use the direct-dubbing method to dub a fairly tight thorax forward to just behind the hook eye.

Step 5. Prepare a partridge feather for legs by stripping all but a few fibers from each side of the stem. A natural has no more than three legs per side, though trout can't count and you can have a few extra. Draw three to five fibers out to each side of the feather, and snip the remaining tip. Stroke the fibers back into their original position, and you will have a perfect V of feather to tie in as legs.

Step 6. Use just one or two soft turns of thread to position the leg feather over the thorax. At this point they will usually be much longer than you would like them to be on the final fly. That's all right; at this time, just get them secured lightly and centered.

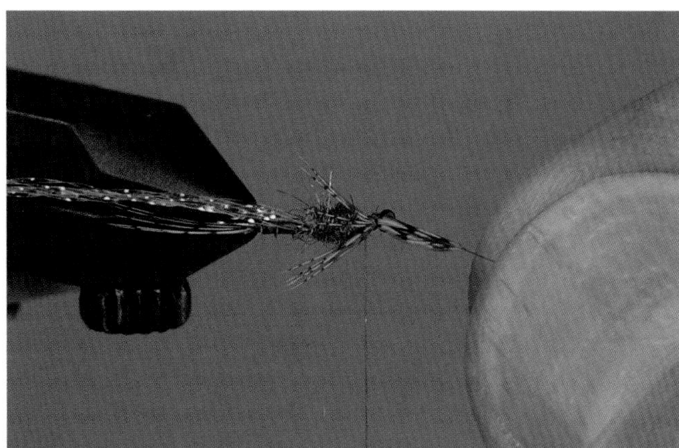

Step 7. Use your tying-hand thumb and forefinger to tug the stem of the feather, carefully pulling it under the loose thread wraps, until you have the legs shortened to about half the hook-shank length. Use the thumb of your off hand to separate the legs equally to each side of the thorax, and hold them in position while you secure the stem firmly with a few more thread turns. Clip the excess feather stem.

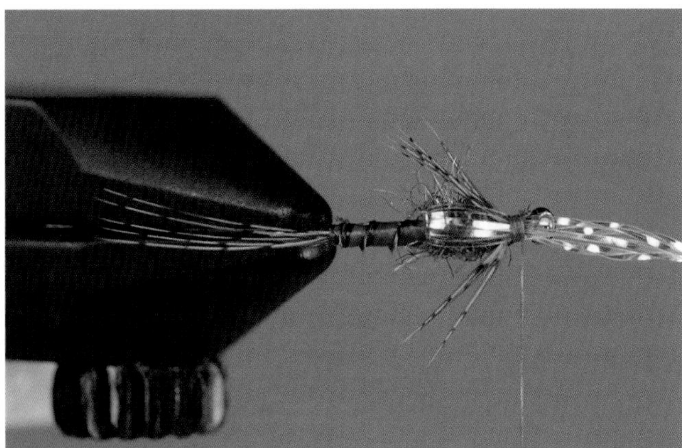

Step 8. Draw the shellback forward over the center of the feather stem, being sure to split the legs so that equal numbers project to each side. Take a couple firm turns of thread to lock the shellback in place. If necessary, at this point, press the legs from the top, working them into a position that is swept back and down.

Step 9. Take a few more turns of thread to secure the shellback material tightly, clip the excess, and whip-finish the fly.

Shane Stalcup's Biot Nymph is prettier on a 3XL, curved-shank hook, but because of that long shank, it's difficult to reduce it to blue-winged olive sizes.

Shane Stalcup recommends tying a few of his Biot Nymphs on heavy-wire curved scud hooks. It's probably the best way to reduce this fine fly to the tiniest sizes that are most useful during blue-winged olive hatches.

The Biot Nymph is useful when fished on the bottom, and makes a fine tiny nymph, size 18 to 22, in combination with a larger scud or searching nymph, size 12 to 16. I use it most often when trout have been drawn toward the top by prehatch or emergence activity of blue-winged olives. Even when trout appear to be feeding on the surface, a significant proportion of them continue to concentrate on nymphs drifting just beneath it. This imitative dressing is excellent suspended behind a tiny yarn indicator.

Shane recommends dressing the fly with floatant and trailing it behind a dry fly that imitates the dun of the same insect. To do this you'll need to tie a few on light-wire hooks.

BLUE-WINGED OLIVE NYMPH

A traditional fur *Baetis* nymph is still nearly as effective as any other dressing, if it is tied slender enough and in the right size, which is usually 18 down to 22. It's simple to construct, so you can get a bunch up in a hurry. It also has the advantage of letting you simply alter the dubbing color to imitate blue-winged olive nymphs in different waters. They vary considerably across their broad range, though size is probably a more important trigger than color. If that were not true, the Pheasant Tail Nymph in its single shade of brown would not work so well from its sources in Britain to waters all over the world. But I've bumped into trout that were more pleased by a blue-winged olive nymph dressing in a pale shade of olive.

If you tie the Blue-Winged Olive Nymph in sizes 20, 22, and even 24, omit the legs and pick out a bit of dubbing. Trout won't notice the difference.

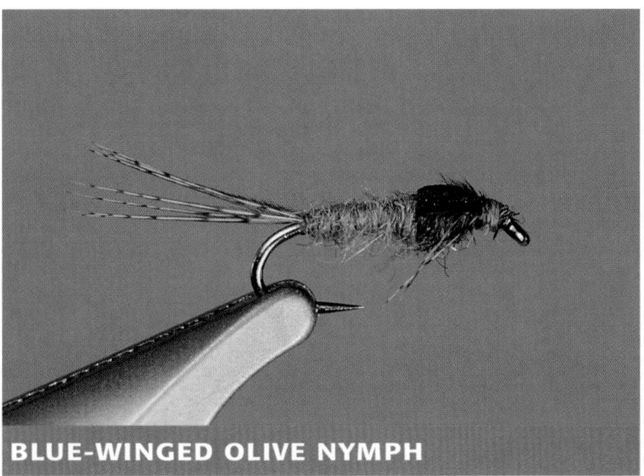

BLUE-WINGED OLIVE NYMPH

Hook: Standard nymph, size 16–24
Thread: Olive 8/0
Tail: Partridge fibers
Body: Olive dubbing
Wing case: Dark turkey or goose feather section
Thorax: Brown-olive dubbing
Legs (optional): Partridge fibers

Step 1. Layer the hook shank with thread. Clip or strip several well-marked partridge fibers from the feather stem, keeping their tips even. Measure them the length of the hook shank, and tie them in at the hook bend. Use the direct-dubbing method to fix a thin amount of fine-textured fur or synthetic to your thread. Roll it tight; you want a slender body. Wrap a slightly tapered body forward to a point about one-third the shank length behind the hook eye.

Step 2. Select a dark section from a turkey or goose feather; the contrast between the body color and wing-case color indicates an insect that is ready to emerge, and is a trigger on this fly. Clip a strip of feather about a hook gap wide. Tie it in at the end of the abdomen, being sure to take thread wraps up onto the front of the abdomen, to avoid a wasp-waist effect when the wing case is pulled forward later. Choose a slightly darker and rougher dubbing for the thorax. Use a small amount, and dub it more loosely on the thread. If you're tying a small fly, this will serve as both thorax and legs.

Step 3 (optional). Strip or clip three to five fibers from a partridge feather, measure them about two-thirds the length of the shank, and tie them in with a single pinch wrap on the near side of the thorax. Take a second pinch wrap to secure them. Repeat the process on the far side of the thorax. Use about three more turns of thread to secure them; thread economy is very important on small flies. Clip the butts.

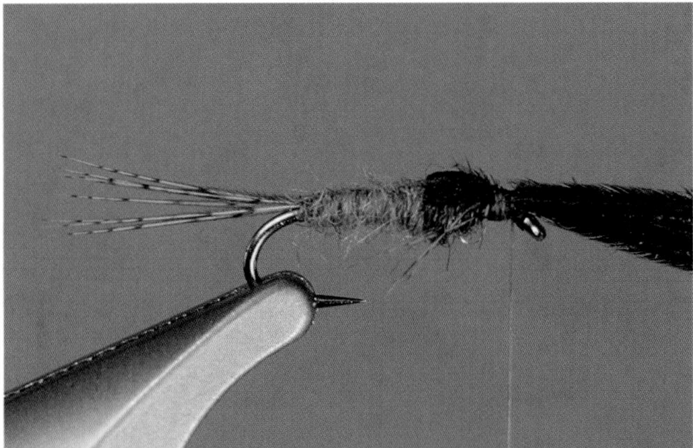

Step 4. Draw the wing case over the thorax, and take three to five tight turns of thread to secure it behind the hook eye. Clip the excess butts, and use just enough turns of thread over them to form a neat head. Whip-finish, clip the thread, and apply head cement.

The Blue-Winged Olive Nymph is a generic nymph for small mayflies. You can tie it in an average color, using olive dubbing for the abdomen, brownish olive dubbing for a bit fatter and darker thorax, and it will fish over most species in the *Baetis* complex, wherever you find them. You can also collect specimens of the same complex that are dominant on the waters you fish most often, record their colors carefully, and compare them with the colors of the materials you select for the abdomen and thorax. Be sure to compare the colors when both the insects and dubbings are wet. When you've worked out the precise right colors for the insect over which you're fishing, you might notice a firm uptick in your take. Your close observations will never harm you if they extend beyond color to the exact size and shape of the natural you're examining.

VINYL RIBBING AND TUBING NYMPHS

Rather than address soft stretch materials, such as D-Rib, Liqui-Lace, Larva Lace, and other tubings, in specific patterns, I'll touch on them here as materials you can incorporate into small mayfly dressings in different ways to achieve varied looks. Most of the mayfly nymph dressings I've seen listed for these materials are fine until you get smaller than about size 16 or 18; then they are too compact and bulky to represent the slender naturals. Since those sizes are where small starts, the materials are of little use for this group of insects unless you can find ways to tie tinier flies with them. That usually requires no more than using the material in the finest sizes you can find, and stretching it as you tie.

The best way to use these stretch materials might be simply to replace the standard dubbing you've been using on a given pattern, see how you like it, and more important, notice how the trout take to it. A couple of variations on simple themes will show you how to go about your own experiments with these materials.

OLIVE NYMPH

Hook: Curved scud, size 16–22
Bead: Gold or brass, optional
Thread: Olive 8/0
Tails: Brown partridge
Abdomen: Fine olive D-Rib, Liqui-Lace, Larva Lace, or similar
Thorax: Brown-olive dubbing mix of Antron and fur

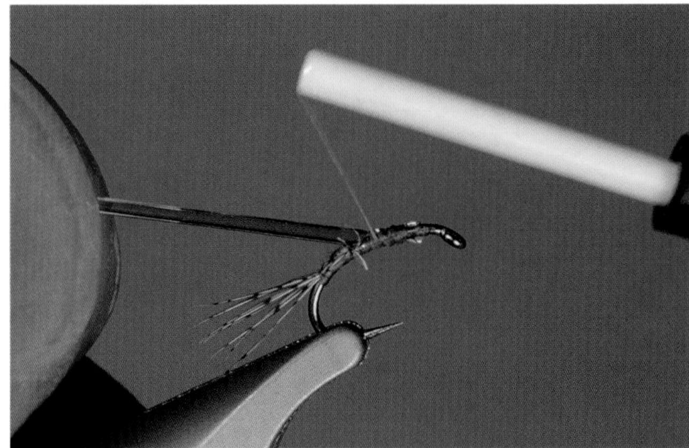

Step 1. Layer the hook shank with thread. Measure the tails about the hook length, and tie them in well down around the bend. Clip three to four inches of stretch material from the strand. Later you can clip enough to tie a few flies, and thereby save the waste of discarding a tag, but for now it's easiest to work with a shorter section of this slightly unruly material. Prestretch the material to make it easier to work with. Place the material alongside the hook shank, and take two or three tight turns of thread over it at about one-third the shank length behind the eye. Stretch the material with your off hand while you overwrap it tightly with thread from the tie-in point to the base of the tail and back to the tie-in point.

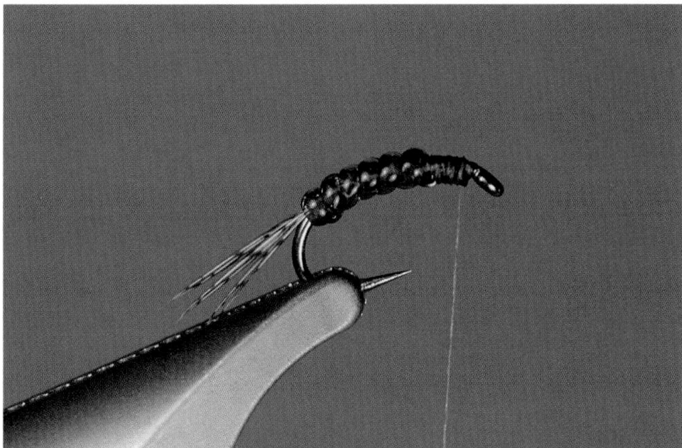

Step 2. Stretch the material and wrap it forward in adjacent turns to the tie-in point. Be sure that you keep it stretched as you go forward, and that the turns touch each other without overlapping or separating, which would interfere with the segmented effect you're after.

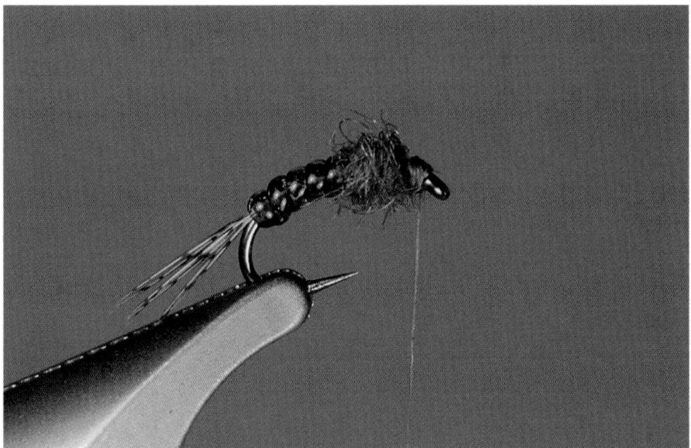

Step 3. Fix a bit of rough dubbing to the thread, without twisting it so tightly that it becomes compact. I prefer a mix of Antron and fur, because it gives a bit of sparkle to the finished fly, and also because the loose fibers of yarn will look like legs on the natural insect. Wind this dubbing forward to the hook eye. Form a neat thread head and whip-finish the nymph.

Such a simple lace or rib dressing will be all you need in the smallest sizes. Be sure the diameter of your material is in keeping with the size hook on which you're tying. If you use medium stretch lace or rib, rather than fine, on a size 18 to 22 curved scud hook, you'll wind up with a portly nymph that looks more like a scud or aquatic worm than a slender swimming mayfly nymph.

For a different look, you can tie the Blue-Winged Olive Nymph on a standard nymph hook, with a stretch body rather than standard fur. You can also substitute Larva Lace, Liqui-Lace, or D-Rib for the body on any swimmer nymph dressing. If you keep it thin, it will look fine, and will fool trout.

BLUE-WINGED OLIVE NYMPH

Hook: Standard nymph, size 16–24
Thread: Olive 8/0
Tail: Partridge fibers
Body: Olive Larva Lace, Liqui-Lace, D-Rib, or similar
Wing case: Dark turkey or goose feather section
Thorax: Brown-olive dubbing
Legs (optional): Partridge fibers

Step 1. Fix the hook in the vise, start the thread, and tie in the tails just as you did for the standard Blue-Winged Olive Nymph above. Clip three to four inches of lace or rib, prestretch it, and tie it in over the rear two-thirds of the shank.

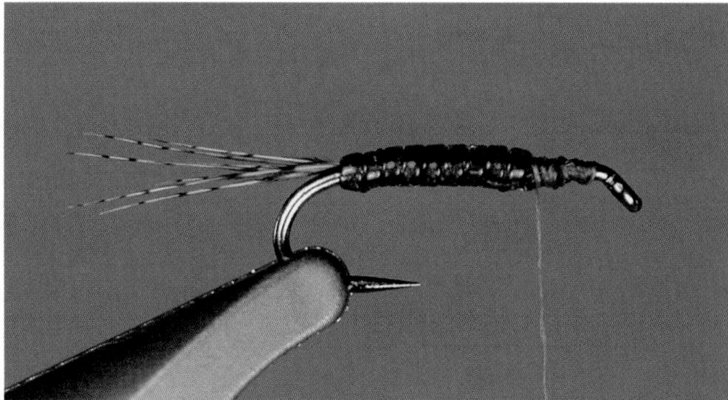

Step 2. Wind the body forward to the tie-in point, stretching the material as you go, abutting the turns to form a slender body. Tie it off and clip the excess.

Step 3. Tie in the wing-case material, being sure to wrap it back tightly over the front of the body, to avoid a wasp-waist effect when you pull the wing case over the thorax. Dub a thorax that is slightly larger in diameter than the lace or rib body. Place the legs behind the hook eye if you want them. Draw the wing case forward, and tie it off behind the hook eye. Clip the excess, form a neat head, and whip-finish the fly.

Nearly every angler who has ever fished over the blue-winged olive hatch has created a series of imitations for the nymph, dun, and spinner, named them after himself, staked a claim to fame on them. So long as they're the right size, tied slender, and have the colors close to correct, they all work. These results are somewhat unfortunate. First, a book could go on and on about nothing but them. Second, many very good nymph patterns get left out of any book about them. The answer, in my estimation, is to study the listed dressings, from the simple and traditional Blue-Winged Olive Nymph and RS-2 through the slightly more complex, but not much more difficult to tie, Biot Nymph. Try them, and see which style suits you and your trout. Alter them until you find a variation that pleases you and your trout even more. Name that one after yourself.

I've done a lot of experimenting, but don't think I'll bore you with it. I've never come up with any evidence that any of my small swimmer nymphs outfish the famous old Flashback Pheasant Tail, so long as I get its size right, which is usually between 18 and 22.

LARGE MAYFLY SWIMMERS

Large mayfly swimmer nymphs are not fed upon selectively as often as the smaller types, though they are clearly bigger bites, and obviously make trout happy whenever they are available. But the most abundant of them, among them the gray drakes *(Siphlonurus),* white-gloved howdies *(Isonychia),* and western leadwing drakes *(Ameletus),* have the unfortunate habit of crawling out of the water as nymphs for emergence into duns. This causes two problems. First, it takes them into marginal edge waters, where trout are not as able to get at them as they are the nymphs of smaller swimmers that emerge out in open water. Second, that dangerous swim to the surface, and staging just beneath it, that puts so many *Baetis*-complex nymphs at risk is traded for a stealthy crawl up the side of a protruding rock or a plant stem.

Capturing a big gray drake swimmer nymph (Siphlonurus) *in an aquarium net is almost like leading a lunker trout into landing net. This one is not yet mature, as its light-colored wing pads indicate, but is already a size 10, 3XL.*

Trout get most of their opportunities at larger swimmer nymphs during the longer period of their growth, and in some concentrated numbers during their migrations toward shore to stage for emergence. They do not get much of a crack at them when they are massed for the hatch, or in the process of performing that magic transformation.

When Rick Hafele and I were doing the research for *Western Hatches,* we got into a blitz of gray drake spinners on southern Oregon's Williamson River. The spinner fall started at dusk and went on far into darkness, but fishing is not allowed on those waters at night, so we went looking for the nymphs as our best hope of enticing some trout to our flies. We got out kick nets and sampled the bottom in open water, where we found a scant few. We swept the nets in closer to shore, along undercut banks, and found more, though hardly enough to cause much enthusiasm among trout that were probably waiting for their daily gorge on the spinners.

It was late June, and some grassy meadows along the stream were flooded by receding high flows. The water

The Wood River, in southern Oregon, with its low gradient, smooth flows, and grassy banks, is an example of prime gray drake (Siphlonurus) *water.*

back there was from an inch or two to about six inches deep. It was no place for a trout interested in avoiding osprey predation. But it must have been the safest habitat around for gray drakes nymphs to gather and emerge. When Rick and I dipped our nets into that water that was marginal to the margins, they came up massed with squirming, wiggling, thrashing *Siphlonurus* nymphs. They were accomplishing their emergence to duns by crawling up grass blades rather than rocks.

In terms of abundance, it was a wondrous hatch.

In terms of availability, it was a bust.

You must carry imitations of the smaller mayfly swimmer nymphs if you fish widespread waters, especially if you spend time on spring creeks and tailwaters. You will have no trouble doing all of your fishing over the larger groups of mayfly swimmer nymphs with searching dressings selected in the right sizes and colors. The standard dressing for the *Isonychia velma* hatch on California streams such as the Pit, McCleod, and Sacramento is the A. P. Black in size 10 or 12. The A. P. Beaver and A. P. Muskrat are both excellent imitations for the heavy *Siphlonurus* hatches. My own All-Fur Swimmer (see page 103) is an imitation of the same gray drake nymph, tied mostly for use on low-gradient small streams, to be fished along undercuts and grassy banks where the naturals gather for emergence when there are no backwaters and flooded meadows nearby.

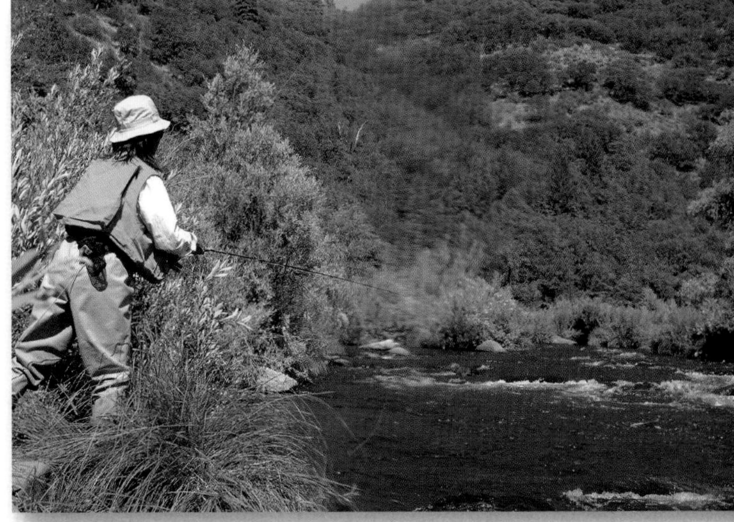

California's Pit River is known for its Isonychia *hatch.*

I have collected *Ameletus* nymphs along the edges of nearly every western trout stream and river I have fished, but have never discovered trout feeding selectively on them, though collecting them is a signal to position yourself next to a good pool at dusk, armed with a size 12 or 14 Rusty Spinner dry fly. When your nymph collecting begins to lead you to such associations, it helps you catch more trout even if you don't catch them on nymphs.

Among my favorite nymphs when the famous gray drake nymph is showing itself to trout is the Beadhead All-Fur Swimmer.

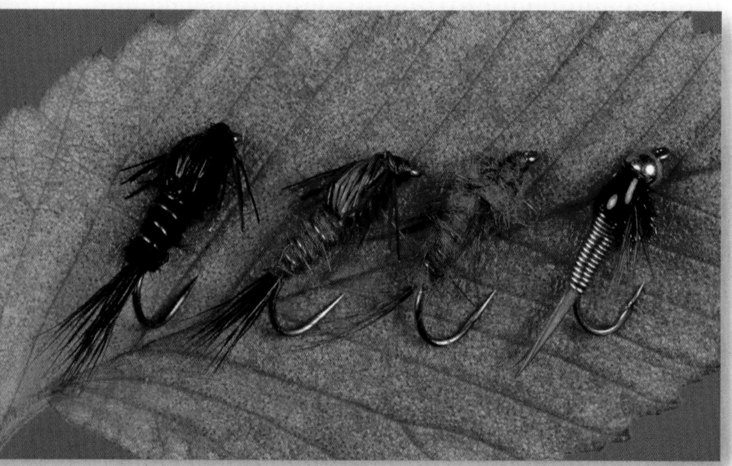

Some searching nymphs that are often effective when trout find large swimmer nymphs available are (from left) the A. P. Black, A. P. Beaver, Bird's Nest, and Copper John.

If you do find good numbers of the dark amber to brown *Ameletus* nymphs, it probably won't hurt to drift a size 12 Copper John along the banks. If the banks are deep enough or undercut sufficiently to hold trout, then there are lots of reasons to let that famous fly idle along there, and these big swimmer nymphs are chief among them.

Because they are large and visible, collected often and at times do prod selective feeding by trout, the larger mayfly swimmer nymphs have been imitated often, and have often been imitated with complicated, exact dressings. It would be a shame to neglect them. You might even find a time when one will save a fishing trip.

POXYBACK SWIMMER

At least one large mayfly swimmer nymph imitation should be built around Mike Mercer's Poxyback concept, described in his 2005 book, *Creative Fly Tying*. Though Mike lists no particular pattern for the larger swimmers, he does urge adapting his procedures to your own needs. I've applied his principles to the gray drake nymph, because it's the one I encounter most often, and suspect you will, too. I do, however, recommend that you read his book, mine it for both the patterns and techniques it offers, and apply all that you can to your own nymph tying and fishing situations.

POXYBACK SWIMMER
interpreted from Mike Mercer

Hook: 3XL, size 10–14
Thread: Brown 8/0
Tail: Partridge center tail fibers
Abdomen shellback: Partridge fibers
Rib: Copper wire
Abdomen: Gray Antron and fur mix
Wing case: Dark turkey tail feather sections
Thorax: Gray Antron and fur mix
Legs: Partridge fibers

Just as the feathers we use most often from a pheasant skin are the long center tails, the Hungarian partridge has useful center tails, though they're rarely put to use. They're well marked with contrasting colors. You must buy a whole skin to get them. If you buy partridge feathers by the package, substitute the longest fibers you can find from the feathers you have. Many dressings call for ostrich herl tips as the tails on swimmer nymphs. These look most like the tails of naturals in the vise, but they usually get nipped off by the first or second trout that takes the fly.

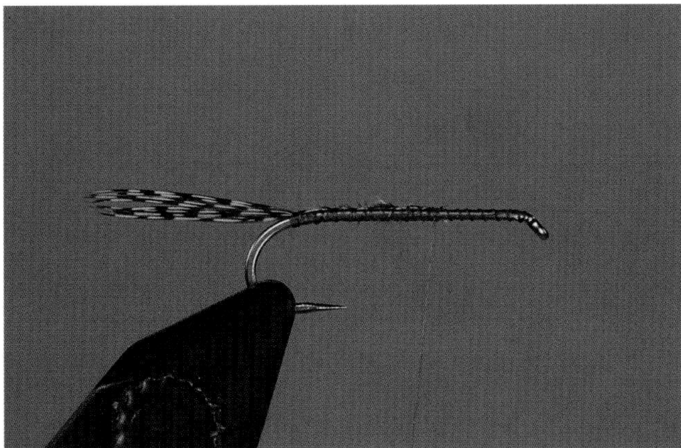

Step 1. Fix the hook in the vise, and layer it with thread to the beginning of the bend. Select a substantial clump of partridge center tail fibers, even their tips, and clip or strip them from the feather stem. Measure them just short of the hook-shank length, and tie them in at the beginning of the bend. Overwrap the butts beyond the midpoint of the hook to about one-third the shank length behind the eye before clipping the excess.

Step 2. Tie in fine copper wire at the point where you clipped the excess tail butts, and overwrap the wire to the base of the tails. Select a larger clump of partridge center tail fibers, even the tips, and strip or clip them from the feather stem. Tie these in at the tip end, but far enough from the tips that the clump will be substantial, not thin. Be sure you leave the shellback clump long enough to draw over the abdomen and reach far enough beyond its end to leave room to tie it off.

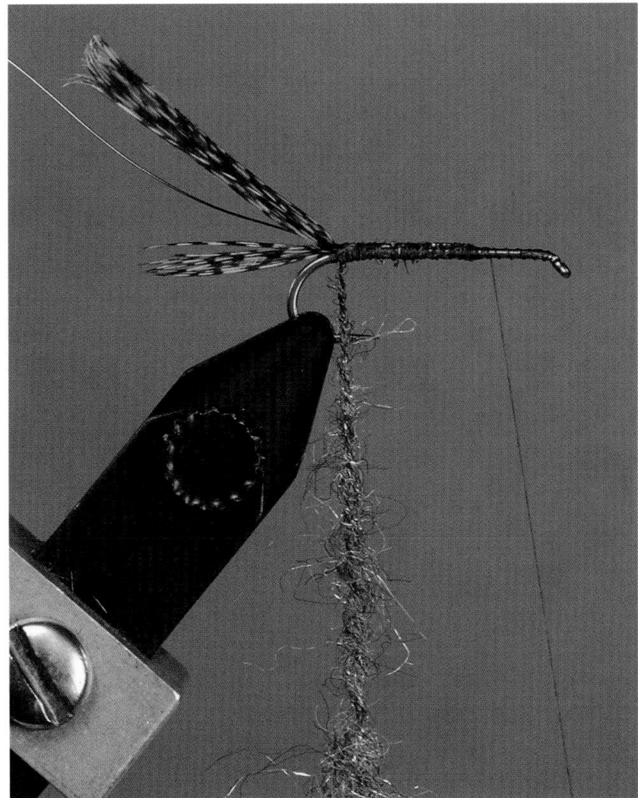

Step 3. Wax your thread with a tacky dubbing wax. Use a rough dubbing mix; tease it into a long and fairly thin skein. Touch both ends of this to the thread, and twist the ends just enough that it will adhere to the thread (see page 50). Loop the thread over the forefinger of your off hand, and bring the bobbin back to the hook. Take sufficient turns of thread around the shank to form a dubbing loop. Twist the loop just tightly enough to capture the dubbing. Don't twist it up tight; the loose dubbing sticking out to the sides will represent the prominent gills of the natural nymph.

Step 4. Wind the dubbing loop forward to a point about one-third the shank length behind the eye. Tie off the doubled threads of the dubbing loop there. If the resulting abdomen is tight, use your bodkin point or a roughing tool to tease it out to the sides.

Step 5. Bring the shellback forward and tie it in at the end of the abdomen. Clip the excess. Rib the abdomen and shellback with evenly-spaced turns of the ribbing wire. Tie off the wire and clip the excess.

Step 6. Measure a section of dark turkey tail a little less than the hook gap in width. Clip it from the feather stem, trim it even across the thicker end, and tie it in at the end of the abdomen. Clip a second section the same size from the stem, and tie it in the same way, at the same point. The doubled wing case ensures that no gaps will result when you pull it forward and the feather sections split, as they will. Be sure to overwrap these wing-case sections back onto the abdomen, to avoid a wasp waist between the abdomen and thorax when you pull the wing case forward.

Step 7. Make a dubbing loop that is somewhat shorter but even looser than that used for the abdomen. Wind it forward in three to four turns to a point at least one hook-eye length behind the eye, to leave room to tie in the legs, wing-case sections, and head of the nymph.

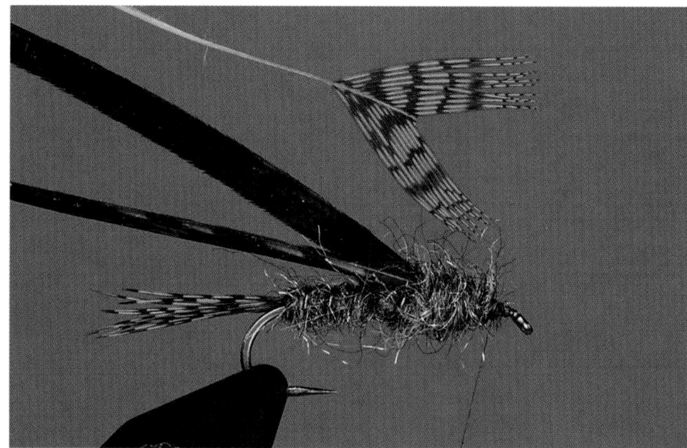

Step 8. Prepare a partridge feather for legs by stripping all but a few fibers from each side, reversing those that are left, and clipping the tip of the feather. Stroke the remaining leg fibers back to their original direction, and you will have a V of fibers.

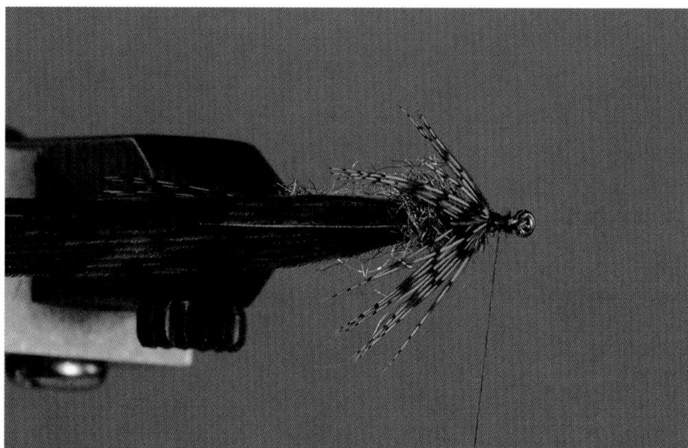

Step 9. Hold the leg feather in place over the thorax, and tie it in by the stem with a couple loose turns of thread. Grasp the stem and tug the feather forward until the

fibers are the right length to reach approximately to the end of the abdomen. Lock the stem in with a few more turns of thread and clip the excess.

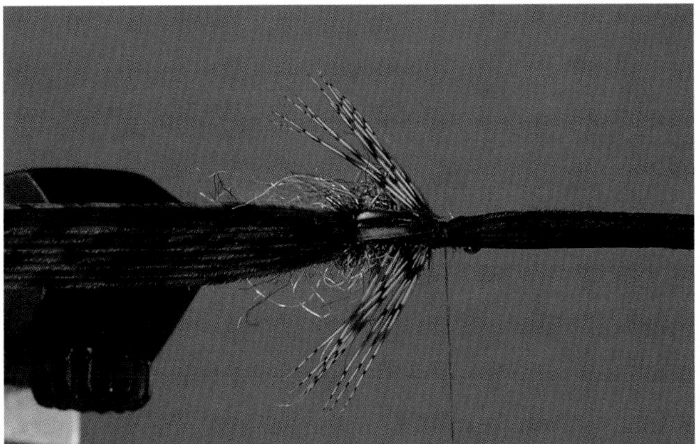

Step 10. Bring one wing-case section forward, splitting the legs so an even number lie on each side. Mike Mercer, in *Creative Fly Tying,* warns against drawing the wing case too tight, as this will split the fibers and allow the epoxy to seep through to the body. Tie the section off behind the hook eye.

Step 11. Draw the second wing-case section over the first, and tie it off in the same place. Clip the excess of both feather sections. Use just enough thread turns over the butts to cover them and form a neat thread head. Whip-finish the fly and clip your thread. Apply a drop of head cement to the whip-finish. I don't recommend using epoxy, in the following step, in place of head cement. Even if you clear the eye carefully, epoxy might flow back into the opening, in which case you'll have the tragedy of an eyeless hook when you go to tie it to your tippet. Hardened epoxy is not easy to clear from the eye of a hook.

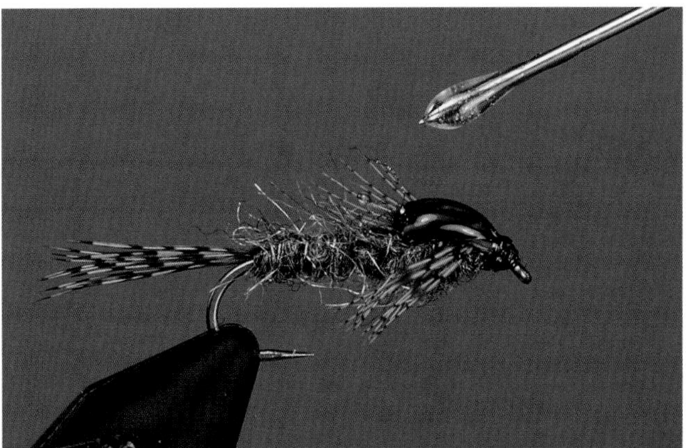

Step 12. Mix a generous drop of five-minute epoxy with a toothpick point or your bodkin. You'll be wise to tie half a dozen to a dozen of any Poxyback dressing, and apply the epoxy to all of them at the same time, just as you do with the Copper John. Spread a thin layer of epoxy over the entire wing case. Before the epoxy has a chance to begin hardening, apply another drop in the center of the wing case. This will self-level and result in a shiny wing case, the essential trigger to this style of nymph.

The colors of the above dressing can be varied from light to dark to suit the various large swimmer nymphs you might encounter. A dark brown version would match many of those that I've encountered, but I've not found it necessary in my fishing, and recommend you hold off tying one until you not only collect naturals on your own streams, but also see signs that trout feed on them with the sort of avidity that would preclude success with a searching nymph. The Poxyback is a fairly complex tie, with an abundance of steps, but none of them are heroic, so you'll find the style slow but pleasant when you're sitting down to construct a bunch in reaction to some need you've found in your fishing.

GILLED NYMPH

Shane Stalcup, in his *Mayflies Top to Bottom,* lists two series of nymphs that he uses to imitate swimmer mayflies, including the largest of them. The first, the Gilled Nymph, uses ostrich herl to represent the bodies and gills of the naturals. The second, his Marabou Nymph, is tied the same but uses marabou wound as herl to accomplish the same effect. They're essentially one style, tied with two different body materials. Shane uses them most often in sizes 14 and 16, but for the larger mayfly swimmers that have become our current subject, you would need to tie them in sizes 10 and 12 as well.

It's important to note that for larger sizes, in which the insect imitated is more meaty, Shane calls for an underbody beneath the ostrich or marabou. That is important when you're tying his nymph for swimmers size 14 and larger. Simply choose a dubbing that is approximately the same as the gill color, and lay a slightly tapered underbody before winding the ostrich or marabou.

By varying the ostrich or marabou colors, and the dubbing color used for the thorax, you can imitate any of the large mayfly swimmer types with these Gilled Nymphs.

GILLED NYMPH *Shane Stalcup*

Hook: 3XL, curved-shank nymph hook, size 10–16
Thread: 6/0 or 8/0 to match thorax color
Tails: Tips of three gray, brown, or black ostrich or marabou fibers
Rib: Fine copper wire
Underbody: Match abdomen color
Abdomen: Remainder of tail fibers wound as herl
Wing case: Medallion sheeting to match thorax color
Thorax: Rough dubbing or marabou fibers to match abdomen
Legs: Partridge fibers

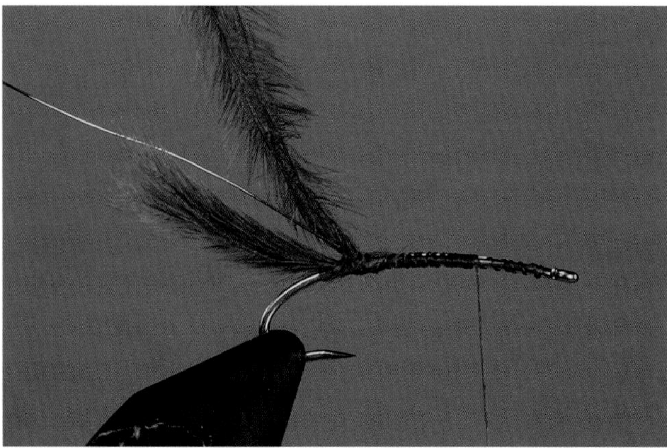

Step 1. Start the thread behind the hook eye, and layer it to a point straight above the hook barb, or where the barb would end if you weren't using a debarbed hook. Select three ostrich or marabou herl fibers, measure the tips two-thirds to the full length of the hook shank, and tie them in above the barb. Tie in your ribbing wire at the same point. Stroke the abdomen fibers back out of the way, and take your working thread forward to a point one-third the shank length behind the eye, tying down the ribbing wire as you go.

Step 2. Use the direct-dubbing method to create an underbody. Taper it from slender at the back to a bit fatter at the midpoint of the shank, tapering off in a sloped shoulder at the front. The underbody can be made of fine dubbing, leaving the gill fibers to do their enticing work. It can also be of slightly rough dubbing, perhaps a mixture of Antron fibers with natural fur, for a fatter body with some sparkle added.

Step 3. Twist the three herl strands together, and wind them forward to a point one-third the shank length behind the hook eye. Tie them off there, at the end of the underbody. If you're using ostrich herl and a dubbed thorax, as shown in the fly being tied, clip the excess herl. If you're using marabou, and will use the same herl for the thorax, do not clip it at this point. Just tie it off. Wind the ribbing forward in evenly spaced turns through the herl, being careful not to mat down any more fibers than necessary.

Step 4. Cut a strip of Medallion sheeting a bit thinner than the width of the hook gap. Tie it in at the end of the abdomen, being sure to take thread wraps up onto the abdomen to prevent the wasp-waist effect. Dub a slightly rough thorax, tapering it down to the hook eye, leaving at least a hook-eye length behind the eye for the legs and head of the nymph. If you're using marabou, twist the herls together again and wind them forward to the same point, tie them off, and clip the excess.

Step 5. Prepare a partridge feather as legs by stripping all but a few fibers from each side, stroking the leg fibers back, nipping out the tip of the feather, and stroking the remaining fibers into their original orientation. Lay this on top of the thorax, and tie it in with a couple loose turns of thread over the feather stem. Tug the stem to position the leg fibers so they reach the end of the abdomen or just short of it. Secure the feather with a few more tight turns, and clip the excess.

Step 6. Bring the Medallion sheeting forward over the leg fibers, splitting them so that equal numbers lie on each side of the wing case. Tie the sheeting in behind the hook eye. Clip the excess, make a neat thread head, and whip-finish the fly. Clip your thread, cement the head, and the Gilled Nymph is ready to fish.

It's most likely you'll find use for the Gray Drake Gilled Nymph (left) in size 12, because of the abundance and widespread distribution of the nymph it imitates. The Brown Gilled Nymph (center) will serve you well in sizes 12 and 14 if you find an abundance of dark swimmer nymphs tucked up beneath undercut banks. You might find rare cause to tie and fish the Black Gilled Nymph (right), likely in size 10 or 12.

This is neither a difficult nor time-consuming style of fly to tie. You can get a bunch done in a hurry, if you want, and still have a nymph that is quite stylish and also very effective. You can vary the colors of the abdomen and thorax to match any large swimmer mayfly you find important on your own waters.

Both the Poxyback and Gilled Nymph, when tied to imitate large swimmers, should be left unweighted if you're fishing them shallow, which will be common, because you'll use them most often when trout are gathered to feed on the naturals in or near marginal shallows. But you might desire to tie a few with the heresy of a beadhead and a few nonlead weighting wire turns behind the bead to lock it in. You could also underweight them, using the standard ten to twenty wire turns, but with nonlead wire one size undersized for the size hook shank on which you're winding it. That is my normal preference for any nymph that I might want to fish shallow, but also might want to give a few seconds to sink deeper before I begin my retrieve.

In any case, I recommend you wait until your own fishing predicts a need for these slightly intricate imitations of the large swimmer mayfly nymphs. Then the situation will dictate the exact color you need, and the amount of weight that will serve you best. Meantime, most of the situations you encounter in which trout are feeding on swimmers larger than those of the *Baetis* complex can be successfully solved with one of the searching nymphs you should already have handy.

As their name implies, the naturals are bold in their movements along the bottom, and in aquatic vegetation. Whether you fish them out in open water or tight along the banks, retrieve them like little streamers, which is essentially what they are. One of the most effective presentations is upstream, from a position on the bank or just out from it, with the line landing nearly parallel to the bank. Let the fly sink a bit, then retrieve it downstream in tiny darts, just a bit faster than the current would deliver it. This works especially well when you're making your way up a small to medium-sized stream, the size water that lets you position yourself a few feet out from the bank, so you can cast up along it without lining trout that are tucked under it.

Another effective method is to take your initial position at the head of a stretch of current that sweeps along an undercut bank, or any bank water that drops off fairly steeply into two to four feet of water. The long curve of an outside bend pool is perfect for this. Make your cast at an angle down and across the current, and tight to the bank. Let the fly sink a few seconds, then retrieve it out with staccato pulses of your rod tip, making it swim in short bursts. You're less likely to line trout this way, as opposed to fishing directly upstream, and more likely to coax out big ones that are moderately to heavily pestered by other fishermen.

If these seem a bit like streamer tactics, that's because the naturals swim like little minnows, and your imitations should be presented like little streamers.

MAYFLY CRAWLER NYMPHS

Mayfly crawler nymphs can be looked at from a couple of directions that seem to conflict. From one angle, they seem so unimportant that very few specific imitations of them have ever been devised, tied, and fished. You'll find a few dressings tied for them, but not very many, and many of those you do find will be what I call *paper patterns,* written up in books but rarely tied and taken to waters. Some of those are so intricate that you could nearly key them out, and you're permitted to wonder if these were designed to be fished or to be mounted on wine-cork pedestals and admired.

Large crawler nymphs, such as this size 10 Drunella grandis, *are the likely models for many of the most effective searching nymphs, and searching nymphs are about all you'll ever need to imitate them.*

From a second, and perhaps more realistic, angle, crawler nymphs have been the inspiration for a very high proportion of the most successful searching nymphs. In that sense, when you're fishing a Gold-Ribbed Hare's Ear, you're not just fishing a searching pattern, you're fishing a mayfly crawler nymph imitation. It doesn't work only because it looks a little like a lot of things out there in nature, tumbling along the stream bottom. It works because it looks a lot like a crawler nymph, and it's likely that the originator of the pattern was looking at a big crawler nymph when he first tied it.

I subscribe to the latter view. So many very fine searching nymphs are tied with the blocky crawler shape, and in the predominantly dark crawler colors, that there is no drastic need to tie specific imitations for at least the largest of them. This abundance of effective searching patterns combines with the habits and habitat of the naturals to reduce the need for exact imitations. They gener-

On waters such as the Henry's Fork of the Snake, in Idaho, less robust crawler nymphs, the pale morning duns (Ephemerella inermis) *are abundant in rooted vegetation.*

When large crawler nymphs are present in kick-net samples, or found clinging to the sides of rocks hoisted from the stream, I usually turn to such searching nymphs as beadhead versions of the Hare's Ear, Red Fox Squirrel, or A. P. Black.

Crawlers such as the pale morning dun nymph are slender, and are often found in great numbers in spring-creek and tailwater vegetation beds. Often a slender searching nymph such as a Flashback Pheasant Tail will imitate them closely enough to catch trout.

ally live in the boisterous parts of freestone streams, and they rarely live in such concentrated numbers that trout are likely to become selective to them. When trout see them, it's most often as big and gratifying bites, but in ones and twos, adrift on the currents, down near the bottom stones. And they're usually taken by trout along with whatever else is adrift down there.

A few small crawler nymphs are less robust, and are also found in great abundance in the vegetated areas of spring creeks and tailwaters. The pale morning dun *(Ephemerella inermis)* is the most common example. The nymphs are present in many freestone environments, but will rarely be found there in such concentrated numbers that you would need more than a size 16 Beadhead Fox Squirrel or Hare's Ear to imitate them. But their numbers get concentrated in some famous trout-fishing meccas, such as the Henry's Fork of the Snake River in Idaho and parts of the Bighorn River in Montana. Because those rivers draw fishermen in almost equally concentrated numbers, it might be beneficial to imitate them, especially in the early stages of an emergence.

A size 16 or 18 Pheasant Tail, either in the standard version or tied with a flashback, will be all you need most of the time, even on the most heavily fished waters. As with the smallest swimmer nymphs, getting the size right will outweigh all other factors. The second most important factor will be your presentation, which should usually be a dead drift beneath a small yarn indicator, especially since you'll almost always be using the pattern as a specific imitation for PMD nymphs on the smooth currents of a spring creek or tailwater. It will never hurt to get the shape and finally the color precisely right when you're fishing over such selective trout, but you'll be surprised how often getting the size and presentation worked out correctly solves the problem of catching selective trout, and therefore how seldom you actually need an exact imitation of any nymph, especially these crawlers.

BEADHEAD PMD NYMPH

Rick Hafele, in his *Nymph-Fishing Rivers and Streams,* calls for a Flashback Hare's Ear in sizes 14 through 18 to imitate the PMD nymph. He also lists his own Beadhead PMD Nymph, which is worth learning how to tie. You can use it as a specific small crawler dressing, when they're abundant in your collecting samples. You can also use it when the naturals are either about to hatch, or already emerging, and a certain number of feeding trout focus on drifting nymphs subsurface.

BEADHEAD PMD NYMPH ***Rick Hafele***

Hook:	Curved scud, size 14–18
Bead:	Gold
Weight:	5–10 turns nonlead wire
Thread:	Brown 8/0
Tails:	Partridge fibers
Rib:	Copper wire
Abdomen:	Light hare's mask fur
Thorax:	Darker hare's mask fur

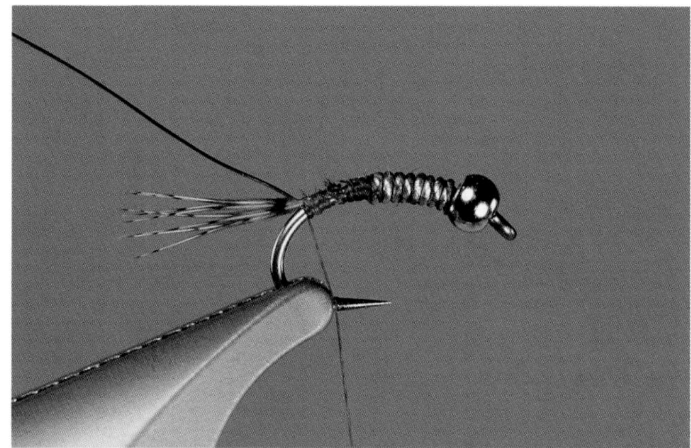

Step 1. Debarb the hook, fix a bead to it, and place the hook in the vise. Take five to ten turns of nonlead wire behind the bead, and jam the front wraps into the back of the bead. Start your thread behind the weighting wire wraps. Remove a few partridge fibers from the feather, measure them the length of the hook shank, and tie them in partway around the bend. Tie in the ribbing wire, and overwrap it with thread to the back weighting wire shoulder, along with the tail butts. Clip the excess ribbing and tails, and use a few turns of thread to form an even taper from the tail base to the back of the weighting wire.

Step 2. Dub a slender and tight abdomen over two-thirds to three-quarters of the hook shank. Rib it with four to five evenly spaced turns of copper wire. Tie off the wire and clip the excess.

Step 3. Use a bit rougher dubbing to make a slightly darker thorax. Don't twist it tightly to the thread. You might want to form a dubbing loop, and twist it to capture the dubbing in a fibrous rope, but that is not usually necessary on such a small fly. Just dub a rough thorax, whip-finish the fly, and tidy up any wild hairs that you feel would detract from the appearance of the fly in the water. But don't preen it to perfection; you want some fibers sticking out to look like the legs of a natural.

Rick Hafele designed this dressing for the PMD hatch on Oregon's Deschutes River, which is not the gentlest bit of water around. Hatches of these small crawlers do tend to come off at the edges of riffles, and even on some edge flats near, but not in, rough water. The Beadhead PMD Nymph can be fished on the bottom, more or less as a searching nymph, whenever an abundance of the naturals are found in collecting net samples. It can also be suspended on a couple feet of fine tippet beneath a yarn or small hard strike indicator, or even a dry fly, when a few duns are boating the currents but trout are not yet working them sufficiently to make the switch to a dry fly profitable. It's not a mistake to continue fishing the nymph all the way through the hatch, even after trout have shown a willingness to take dry dun dressings. The largest trout might just prefer to work under the hatch, and be vulnerable to a nymph, but without interest in the most imitative drys.

PMD TRIGGER NYMPH

When trout work a PMD hatch on smooth water, such as the Henry's Fork of the Snake River in Idaho and many other waters of that gentle kind, they often take emerging nymphs near the surface. Many PMD naturals begin the process of emergence just subsurface. The nymphal exoskeleton splits along the back of the thorax, and the wings begin to escape the darkened wing cases, just before the insect reaches the top. Mike Mercer, in *Creative Fly Tying,* calls these "wing buds," and ties his PMD Trigger Nymph to match them.

PMD TRIGGER NYMPH *Mike Mercer*

Hook: Standard nymph, or 2XL, 2X heavy, size 14–18
Bead: Gold
Thread: Camel brown 8/0
Tail: Three pheasant center tail fibers
Abdomen: Rusty brown turkey biot
Legs: Partridge fibers
Thorax: Brown Buggy Nymph dubbing, or similar
Wing buds: Pale yellow Ice Dub or similar

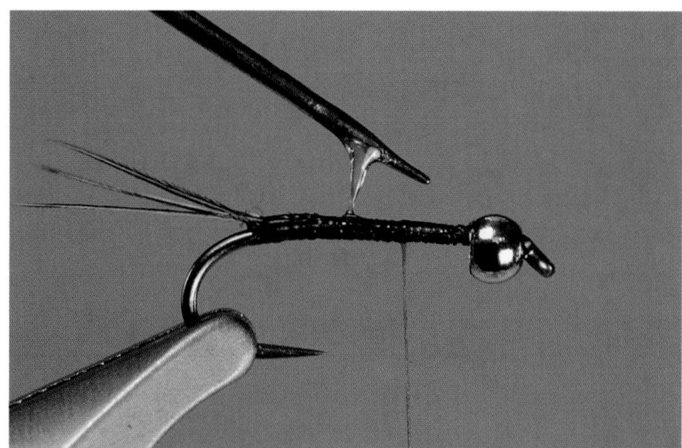

Step 1. Slide a bead onto the hook and place the hook in the vise. Cover the shank behind the bead with thread. Select three pheasant tail fibers, measure them about two-thirds the length of the shank, and tie them in at the bend of the hook. Cock them upward as you take thread turns back over them. If they do not retain this upward

tilt, push them up with the ball of your thumb and take a turn of thread behind them. Take your thread to the front portion of the hook, being sure to leave an even underbody for the biot body. Apply a thin layer of Flexament or head cement to the shank.

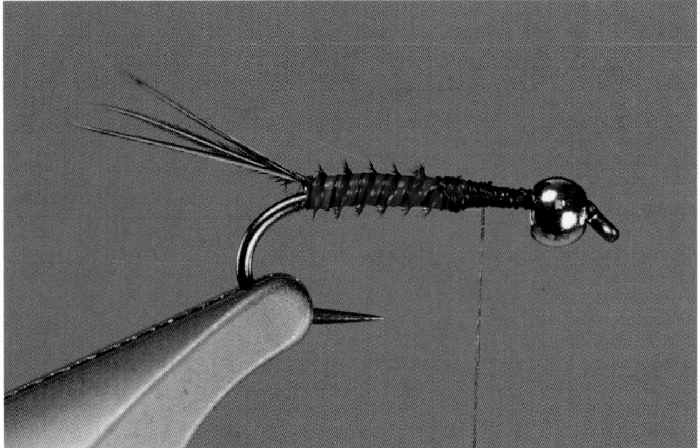

Step 2. Tie in a predampened turkey biot with the notch up, for a segmented body. Mercer describes the biot in terms of a straw sliced in half lengthwise; tie it in on your side of the hook with the curved side of the straw/biot against the shank. Wind it forward to a point just past the midpoint of the shank, being careful not to overlap the turns and mat down the rib. Tie it off and clip the excess.

Step 3. Dub a slight ball of thorax material at the front end of the abdomen. This forms a seat for the leg fibers, to flare them. Even the tips of four to six partridge fibers, and strip or clip them from the feather stem. Measure them to the end of the abdomen, and tie them in on the far side of the hook with a couple loose turns of thread. Repeat on the near side. If they are not positioned correctly, tug them into position by their butts. Secure them with a few turns of thread, and clip the excess butts.

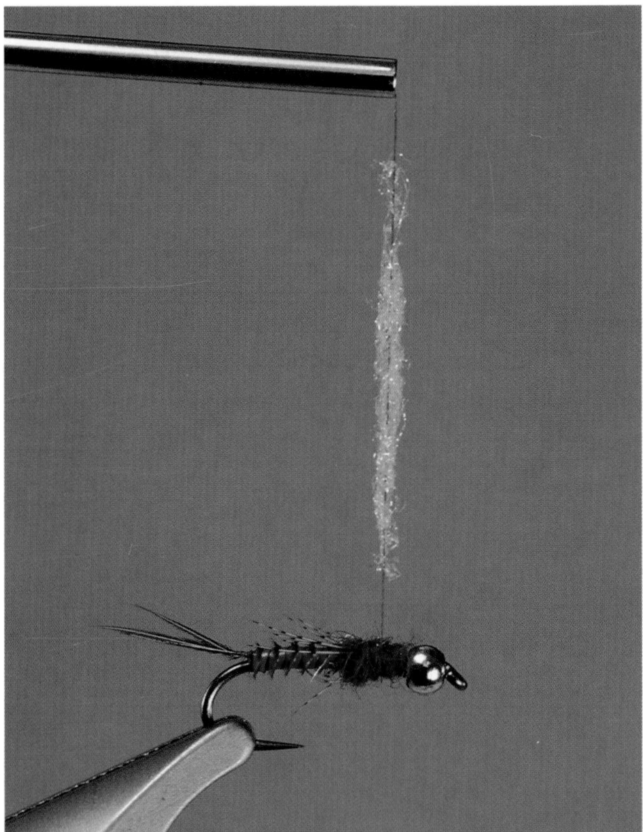

Step 4. Fix a bit more thorax dubbing to the thread, keeping it slender, and wind it forward to a point just behind the bead. Use the last turn of dubbing to return the thread to the midpoint of the thorax. Fix a short and slender skein of pale yellow Ice Dub to the thread. Raise the thread with the dubbing straight above the hook shank.

Step 5. Use the forefinger and thumb of your off hand to slide the dubbing down the thread to the top of the hook shank. Hold it there and take a loose turn of thread around the thorax. Take a second turn of thread around the thorax, and the wing bud will be secure.

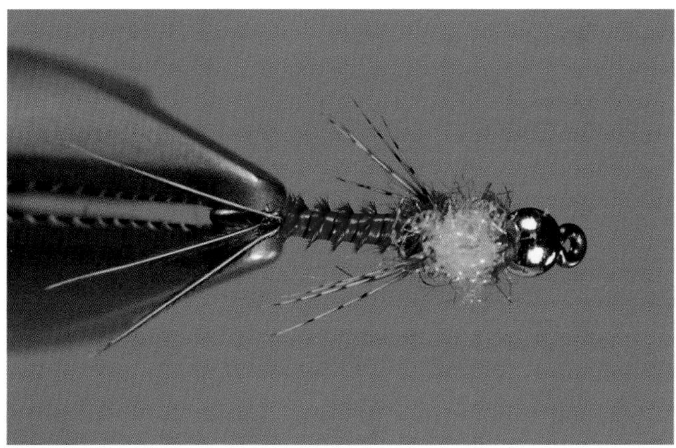

Step 6. Fix a small amount of thorax dubbing to the thread. Take one turn behind the wing buds, another in front, and use the rest to fill in the gap behind the bead. Place a whip-finish there, work it well into the gap behind the bead, and clip your thread.

The PMD Trigger Nymph is a dressing style as much as a single pattern. It can be varied to match almost any mayfly nymph in the stage immediately preceding the dun, when the wings have begun to extract from their cases. It should always be fished just beneath the surface. If you would like to experiment, you could omit the bead, dress the thorax and wing buds with floatant, and you would have a floating nymph. It would be worth trying, but Mike Mercer's intent is to fish it a few inches beneath the surface, to trout feeding on nymphs that are about to pop through into the aerial stage of the mayfly life cycle.

I've been brief about mayfly crawler patterns, not because I think they're unimportant, but because they've been so important over so many years of nymph pattern development that a lot of searching nymphs have their roots in the group. A second part of that is their favored habitat, almost always on the bottom in water that is at least brisk, often nearly violent. An exact imitation of a crawler nymph would clearly catch trout, were you to tumble it along down there. But trout feeding in such circumstances are nearly always opportunistic: they take what the current delivers, and it's rare that a fast current trots a constant supply of a single insect past the noses of bottom-feeding trout.

Trout in fast water are forced to make fast decisions. If your nymph roughly resembles a natural crawler mayfly nymph, it's got as much chance of acceptance as any exact imitation, maybe more, because it will be more likely to look alive than a fly tied with imitative but immobile peripheral parts.

The key to fishing crawler nymphs is always presentation. You need to get them to the bottom, and tumble them along as the feeble-swimming naturals might move. In most water types where the naturals are dominant, that calls for rigging with one or two nymphs, usually a size 12 or 14 followed by a size 16 or 18. It's no accident that the larger of the two falls into the size range of the larger crawler nymphs, while the smaller of the two is the size of the smaller crawlers. If the water calls for it, add split shot or putty weight to the leader between the two nymphs. Place a hard or yarn indicator up the leader about twice the depth of the water.

Make your casts short and upstream, mend and tend the line to get the nymphs to the bottom, follow their drift, watching the indicator for any hesitation or movement in conflict with the current. Be sure to turn and fish the drift out downstream from your position. It took a while to get those nymphs down to where trout might get a chance at them; don't lift them out of that strike zone any sooner than necessary.

Green drake and pale morning dun crawler nymphs are found in concentrations in some spring creek and tailwater plant beds, such as those on the Henry's Fork. During an emergence, you'll usually do well fishing an emerger or dun pattern in or on the surface, but some trout will continue to focus on ascending nymphs throughout the hatch, and you might need to match the nymph to catch them. At such times it's best to rig with a yarn indicator just large enough to suspend the size nymph you're using. You'll be fishing over fairly smooth flows; take your casting position off to the side, rather than directly downstream from the trout, to avoid lining trout you're trying to catch. On such heavily fished waters, trout might not even cease feeding if they see your line fly through the air over their heads, but if they know you're there, your chances of hooking them, even with nymphs, will plummet.

MAYFLY CLINGER NYMPHS

If you search the literature, you can find patterns tied specifically for flattened mayfly clingers. They usually entail strips of lead wire lashed to the sides of the hook shank. Called *outriggers,* these widen the profile of the finished fly, and at the same time help get it down to where natural clinger nymphs spend all of their time: clinging to bottom stones in modest to swift currents. The same dressings usually call for a loose dubbing that is then clipped close on the top and bottom, again broadening the resulting fly while flattening its profile. These things are all beneficial, and it's wise to know how to execute them. We'll tie one here for exercise, but I doubt you'll ever need it.

Clinger mayfly nymphs live in the very thin layer of slow water caused by friction as fast water rushes over the face of a rock or boulder. If you've ever hoisted such a stone from the bottom and tried to pry a clinger nymph away from it for closer inspection, you'll know why they're rarely knocked loose by the currents and delivered to waiting trout. If one does get dislodged, it tumbles with the current, and there is little reason to imitate that flattened profile, because what the trout sees is rolling over and over, showing its broad belly and back as often as its thin sides.

Trout are not selective in the types of water where mayfly clingers are the dominant insect form. If they took time to examine the shape of everything the current delivered past them, they'd never get enough to eat.

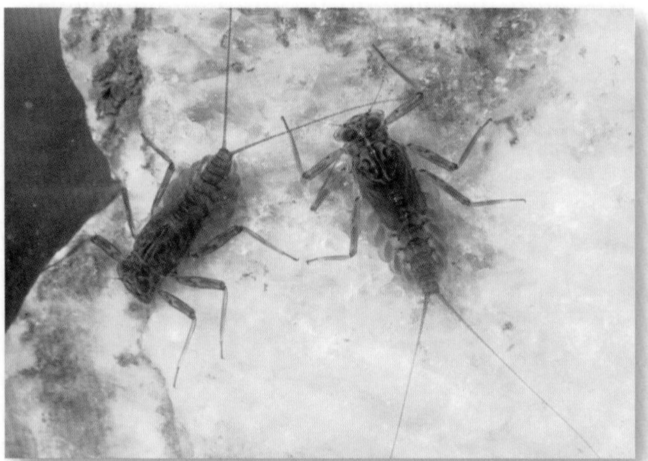

Mayfly clinger nymphs such as these Epeorus *have adapted to living in the very thin layer of water that is slowed by friction as swift water passes over the face of a rock. They are rarely dislodged by the current, and are not the most promising models for imitative nymphs.*

MAYFLY CLINGER NYMPH

The following clinger dressing is fashioned together with ideas from Ernest Schwiebert's *Nymphs,* in which he discusses the outrigger technique, and Poul Jorgensen's *Modern Fly Dressings for the Practical Angler,* in which he outlines the technique for making a thick dubbed body, which is then trimmed to the broad but flat clinger shape. You would do well to collect specimens of clinger nymphs that you feel are important on your own waters, and add your own interpretations to these ideas.

MAYFLY CLINGER NYMPH

Hook: Standard nymph, size 12–16
Thread: Brown 6/0 or 8/0
Tails: Three pheasant center tail fibers
Weight: Two sections nonlead wire, lashed to sides
Body: Brown dubbing, trimmed top and bottom
Wing case: Black Thin Skin, Scud Back, or similar
Legs: Partridge fibers

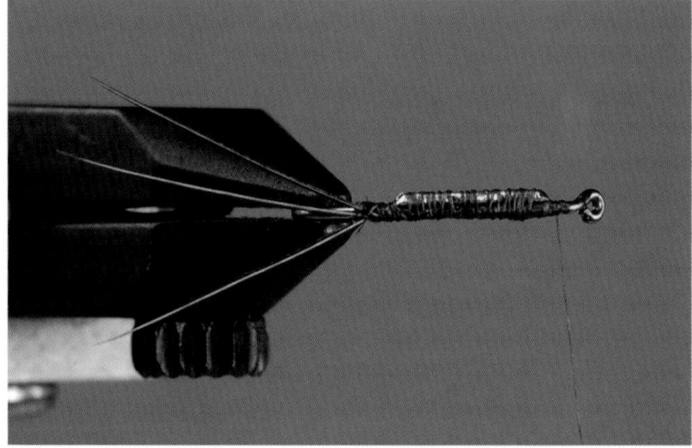

Step 1. Layer the hook shank with thread. Make a thread or fur bump at the bend. Measure three pheasant tail fibers the length of the hook shank, and tie them in so they are splayed widely. Use figure-eight turns of thread

to lock them into position. Clip a section of nonlead wire about the diameter of the hook shank, no more than two-thirds the shank length. Lay it alongside the far side of the hook, and lash it to the shank with two layers of thread. Be sure to leave about two hook-eye lengths behind the eye, or you'll not have room to tie off the fly and finish the head.

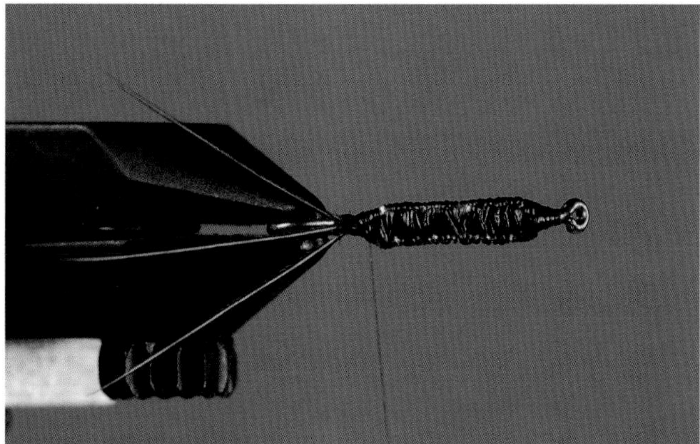

Step 2. Measure a second section of nonlead wire the same length as the first. Lash it in on the near side of the hook shank, with three to four layers of thread that cover both outriggers and form a bit of taper from the tails to the back shoulder of the outriggers, and from the hook eye up to the front shoulder of the outriggers. Use your thumb and fingernail to level the outriggers if necessary, so they lie in the same plane on both sides of the hook shank. Coat the outriggers and base of the tails with head cement, Flexament, or Zap-A-Gap glue.

Step 3. Layer a few inches of your tying thread with a sticky dubbing wax. Use the dubbing loop method to create a very loose abdomen. Wind this just past the midpoint of the hook shank. I like a spiky, fibrous material for this fly, such as Hareline Dubbin's Hare-Tron or Hare's Ear Plus, or René Harrop's Caddis/Emerger/Nymph mix in an appropriate color. Use your scissors to clip it tight to the hook shank and outriggers on the top and bottom.

Step 4. Trim the abdomen in a taper on each side, from wide at the front to narrow at the back. Be careful not to clip off the tails. The result should be an abdomen that is very thin when looked at from either side, but a wedge when seen from the top or bottom.

Step 5. Clip a section of wing-case material almost a hook gap wide. Resist the temptation to make it narrow; the natural clinger nymph is wider at the thorax and head than it is in the abdomen. Though you can't keep the head of the imitation as wide as the head of the natural, do keep the fly broad as far to the front as you can. Tie in the wing-case material in front of the abdomen, being sure to take thread wraps over it back onto the abdomen, to avoid a wasp waist when you pull it forward later.

Step 6. Dub a loose thorax, and wind it forward to just behind the hook eye, leaving room for legs, the wing-case tie-off, and the fly head. Don't crowd it. If you desire, you can trim the thorax on the bottom, but don't tidy it up too much. The finished thorax should be wider than the front end of the abdomen.

Step 7. Strip or clip a few partridge fibers from the feather stem, measure them about two-thirds the hook-shank length, and tie them in on the near side of the thorax. Repeat on the far side with a few more fibers. You can prepare the feather for legs by stripping all but a few fibers from the end, clipping out the end fibers, and tying in the feather over the top of the thorax, as shown for previous swimmer nymphs. This might be easier for you, and will ensure the same number of legs on each side.

Step 8. Draw the wing case forward over the thorax, and tie it off behind the hook eye. Clip the excess as tight as you can over the eye. Use enough thread turns to secure the wing case and to form a neat thread head. Whip-finish the head, clip the thread, and apply head cement.

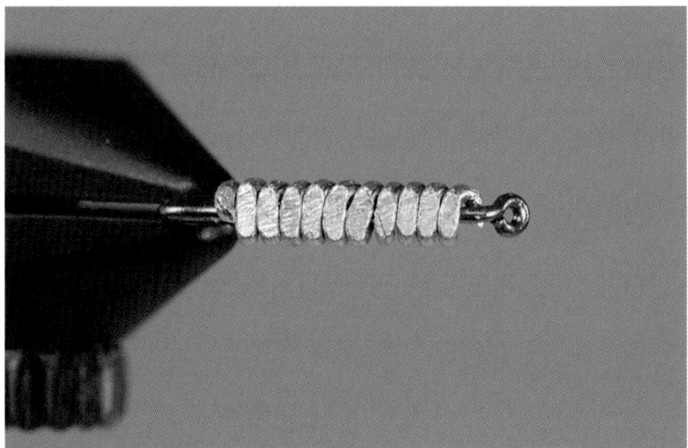

A simpler, though less elegant, way to lay a flat base for the nymph is to wind weighting wire over the body in the normal fashion, then flatten it with pliers.

Though a bit darker, the finished Clinger Mayfly Nymph is a lot like the excellent Gold-Ribbed Hare's Ear. It's likely both would make fair imitations of clinger nymphs, and both do make fine searching nymphs.

When you have finished tying your Mayfly Clinger Nymph, you will find that it is remarkably similar to a traditional Gold-Ribbed Hare's Ear. Perhaps it will be more pleasing to your eye, and it's clearly more imitative of the broadened clinger natural. Trout might never notice the difference.

It is a concept that can be varied to match any clinger you encounter. Most will be dark, for camouflage on the bottom stones on which they live. But you might find yours living on a light-colored substrate, in which case they might be pale to better blend with the lighter stone. The most important clinger naturals will be covered by size 14 and 16 nymphs, but you might encounter clingers on your own waters as large as size 12 and small as size 18. Since they will be most available to trout, and therefore most likely to be important in your fishing, when they are mature and ready for emergence, the darkened wing case is an important feature, and might well be the trigger that prompts trout to take the nymph.

Obviously, you will want to rig the Mayfly Clinger Nymph in a way that lets you fish it along the bottom in at least moderately fast water. Most of the time, you'll need to get it deep in riffles and boisterous runs. The shot-and-indicator rig will almost always be your best bet.

MAYFLY BURROWER NYMPHS

My own experience with burrower nymphs is more theoretical than concrete. Andy Davidson, of Fennimore, Wisconsin, took me out one warm summer dusk to position me over a favorite pool, to await the great *Hexagenia limbata* on one of his favorite local streams. Somebody else was already perched on the water Andy wanted me to fish. We had a short conversation, then backed out of there, went to wait for darkness and the Hex hatch on less favorable water.

Half an hour later, darkness had almost descended when we heard somebody hurrying along the same path we'd taken earlier, toward that favored pool. Andy said to whoever was thrashing past, "That pool's already taken."

"I know," the fellow called back, so we assumed he was a friend of the fisherman who had staked out the pool earlier, and was rushing to meet him before the good fishing started. A few minutes later, we heard a burst of less-than-friendly shouting from the pool we'd wanted to fish, and then somebody tramping back up the trail. It was the fisherman who had been there first. Andy realized what had happened and said something in sympathy.

"The *[fill in the blank]* moved right in on me," he answered. "There's only room for one down there. The dirty . . ." He grumbled on toward his car. It started and we heard him drive away angrily. I can't say that I learned any new words that night, but I did learn a new reason to apply them. Nothing happened on the water Andy and I had retreated to, and I believe the same took place on the ill-gotten water the interloper fished. It's probably as well that the hatch didn't happen; we didn't have time to scout out the new water in daylight, and might have gotten into trouble trying to fish it in the dark.

I've collected Hex nymphs from the tidal flats of the lower Columbia River near my old home in Astoria, Oregon, but it's brackish water; no trout live there. I've also collected them from the Williamson River in southern Oregon, famous as home to both the Hex hatch and the late Polly Rosborough, who researched and wrote his *Tying and Fishing the Fuzzy Nymphs* on that water. I've seen them on Fall River in California, some lakes sprinkled on both sides of the Cascade Range, and of course in the Midwest, where I had only that one missed chance to fish over them.

The Ephemera guttulata *numph is typical of burrowers, with its feathery tails and gills, dark wing cases, and burrowing tusks.* THOMAS AMES

Other important burrowers include *Ephemera simulans,* the widespread brown drake, and *E. guttulata,* known variously as the eastern green drake, the coffin fly, and as entomologist W. Patrick McCafferty points out in his wonderful book *Aquatic Entomology,* "at least six different fishermen's names." *E. varia,* commonly the cream variant or yellow drake, is also an eastern burrower.

These nymphs vary somewhat in body color, but all are large, long, and somewhat slender, have burrowing tusks and plumose gills. All can be imitated with varia-

Fall River in California has placid waters with a bottom of the right consistency to hold heavy populations of the burrowing Hexagenia limbata *nymph.*

A Tan or Brown Woolly Bugger will normally be all you need to imitate most burrower nymphs. You want to imitate movement, and the marabou does it as well as anything.

tions on a limited number of themes. I've fished nymph imitations in waters where the naturals were common, and have found that these nymphs became effective searching dressings in those places. But I've never been able to hit a hatch, so will offer the following patterns with the advice that you should do your own research, and come to your own conclusions, based on the pattern styles listed here.

It's important to know that a Woolly Bugger in an appropriate color is likely all you'll ever need to imitate any burrower nymph. The shape is right. The naturals, when ready to emerge, leave their burrows on the bottom and swim at a surprising clip toward the top, with an up-and-down undulating motion of that long body, and those feathery gills along the back. The marabou tail and palmered hackle of a Woolly Bugger capture that movement about as well as anything you can find. A Tan Woolly Bugger imitates the Hex nymph quite well, and a darker Brown Woolly Bugger is close enough for most of the other species.

CLARK'S HEX EMERGER

This dressing appeared in an article by Lee Clark in the summer 2005 issue of *Flyfishing & Tying Journal.* The listed dressing is imitative of the Hex; color variations would make it a fine dressing for any burrower mayfly nymph. As Clark points out in his article, color and size variations make it a very fine generic searching pattern.

CLARK'S HEX EMERGER *Lee Clark*

Hook:	3XL, size 6–12
Bead:	Gold
Weight:	10–20 turns nonlead wire
Thread:	Tan or brown 6/0 or 8/0
Tail:	Tan to brown marabou
Body:	Tan to brown fur and Antron dubbing mix
Hackle:	Partridge

A proper Woolly Bugger-type tail calls for using the center of the marabou feather. But I prefer the fluffier fibers from the sides of a marabou feather, and usually strip or clip most of the fibers from one side, tear off the less substantial ends of the fibers, then measure and tie in the remaining marabou.

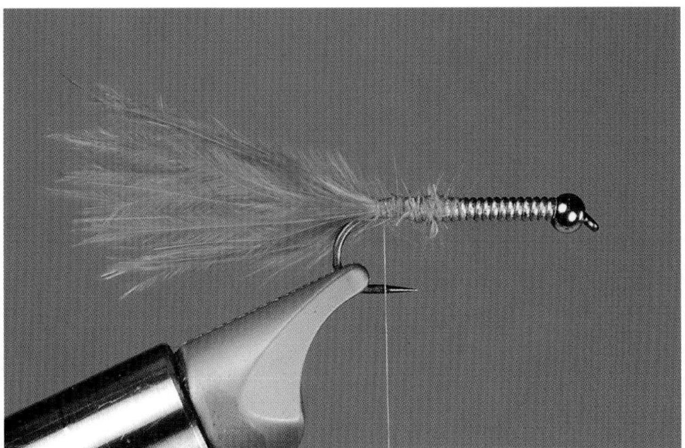

Step 1. Slip an appropriate-sized bead onto the hook, and wrap ten to twenty turns of nonlead wire behind it. Jam the front lead wraps into the bead. Start your thread behind the weighting wire, and layer it to the bend of the hook. Select a substantial clump of marabou fibers, strip or clip them from the feather stem, and measure them the length of the hook shank. Tie them in, overwrapping the butts with thread to the back shoulder of the weighting wire. Clip the excess butts there.

Step 2. Use the direct-dubbing method, or a dubbing loop, to dub a stout and very loose body forward to the back of the bead. The originator calls for combed tan polypro yarn, mixed with copper Lite Brite, for the body on his Hex pattern, and this is the perfect combination. But a blend containing reflective Antron fibers will also work if you don't have the precise right materials and a coffee grinder to combine them. Use a dubbing roughing tool to tease fibers out to both sides of the body.

Step 3. Prepare a partridge feather for tie-in by stripping all of the fuzzy fibers from the lower end of the base of its stem, and stroking the remaining fibers until they stand out straight from the stem. Tie the feather in by its tip, being sure the concave side is toward the hook, so that when wound the fibers will sweep back. Clip the excess tip.

Step 4. Take one turn of partridge hackle behind the bead, then a second turn behind the first. Catch the stem with your thread, and take two to three tight turns to secure it. Clip the excess stem, and work your thread forward in two to three more turns through the hackle, securing it against the teeth of trout. Hold the hackle in the swept-back position, and place a whip finish between the front of the hackle and the back of the bead. Work the whip into this space with your forefingernail and thumbnail before clipping the thread. Apply a generous drop of head cement on the whip finish windings.

HEXAGENIA NYMPH

In his classic 1976 book, *Modern Fly Dressings for the Practical Angler*, the late Poul Jorgensen listed a *Hexagenia* Nymph and variations for all the burrowers. His ideas were ahead of his time, and therefore quite current for ours. With the addition of monofilament eyes, the dressing looks very much like the real thing. I've interpreted it to accommodate the more *modern* list of materials you're more likely to find on your desk three decades after the arrival of Jorgensen's book. Though he called for a straight-shank hook, I find the fly looks racy when tied on a 3XL curved-shank nymph hook. The natural has a three- to four-year life cycle, so first- and second-year-class nymphs are always available to trout, even in the aftermath of the hatch. You might want to tie this fly in sizes 10 and 12, and use it at any time of year on waters where burrowing mayfly populations are heavy.

***HEXAGENIA* NYMPH** *Poul Jorgensen*

Hook: 3XL, size 4–12
Thread: Brown 6/0 or 8/0
Eyes: Black Monofilament Eyes, small or extra small
Tail: Three tannish gray ostrich fibers
Weight: 10–20 turns nonlead wire
Abdomen: Harrop Pro-Dub, Caddis/Emerger/Nymph, golden brown, or similar dubbing
Center stripe: Brown waterproof marker
Wing case: Black Thin Skin or similar
Thorax: Hare's Ear Plus, gold, or similar fur and Antron mix

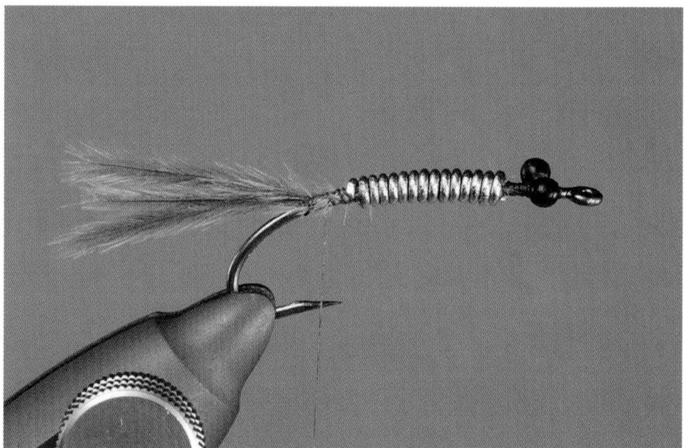

Step 1. Fix the hook in the vise, and start your thread behind the eye, layering the front one-quarter of the shank. Hold a set of Monofilament Eyes in place about a hook-eye length or two behind the eye, and tie it in with figure eights of thread. Layer thread to the bend of the hook. Even the tips of three ostrich fibers, measure them two-thirds the length of the shank, and tie them in. Layer thread over the butts to the eyes and back before clipping the excess. Wrap ten to twenty turns of nonlead wire over the shank.

Step 2. Dub a very loose and somewhat thick abdomen to a point about one-third the shank length behind the eyes. Use a dubbing roughing tool, or your bodkin point, to tease the dubbing out to both sides of the hook shank. With a brown waterproof marker, draw a line down the back of the body.

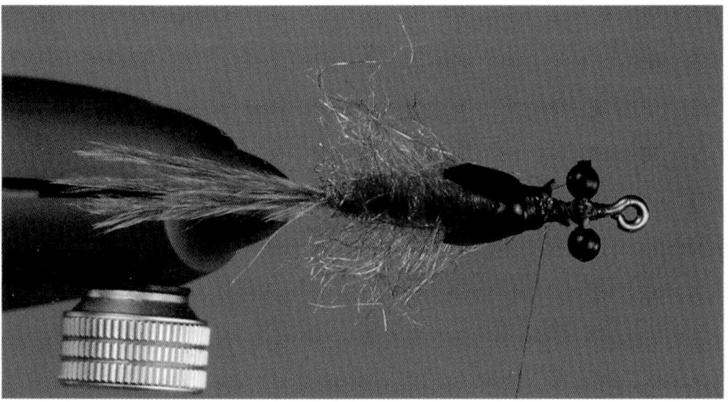

Step 3. Cut a strip of Thin Skin or similar material about two-thirds the width of the hook gap. Round the square corners, and cut a notch out of the center, forming a wing-case shape at one end of the strip. Tie it in at the front of the abdomen, so it extends about to the midpoint of the hook. Clip the excess wing-case material. Leave a gap between the wing-case tie-in pont and the eyes sufficient for at least one full turn of thorax dubbing.

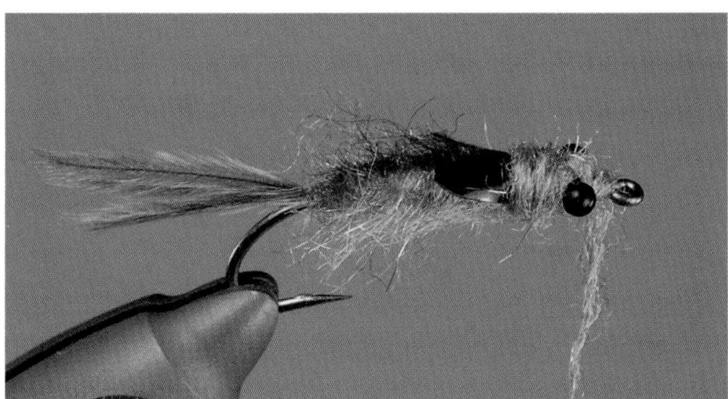

Step 4. Apply thorax dubbing to your thread, and take a turn or two between the wing case and eyes. Take a turn forward between the eyes from back to front, then a second turn between them from front to back. Bring your dubbing forward and take a single turn in front of the eyes. Form a neat thread head, whip-finish, and clip your thread.

HEXAGENIA

Andy Burk's *Hexagenia* is a more complex pattern, but uses a pheasant aftershaft feather to capture perfectly the feathery gills of the natural nymph. This feather is tucked in behind the outer feathers on a ringneck rooster's back; if you don't have a full skin, you can buy aftershaft prepackaged. You can also substitute larger emu aftershafts, or use those from a partridge skin, though they'll be smaller, just long enough to cover the back of a size 6 nymph, and with a less feathery result. Pheasant aftershaft is just the right length and texture.

The pattern also calls for gray marabou for the tail. Just the right color can be found on the same pheasant cape from which you get your aftershaft. A full rooster skin is surprisingly cheap when you consider all the useful feathers you'll find on one.

HEXAGENIA *Andy Burk*

Hook:	3XL curved nymph hook, size 6–12
Weight:	10–20 turns nonlead wire
Thread:	Yellow 6/0
Tail:	Natural gray marabou
Rib:	Copper wire
Shellback:	Dark turkey feather section
Gills:	Pheasant aftershaft (or philoplume)
Abdomen:	Pale yellow nymph dubbing
Wing case:	Dark turkey feather section, continued from shellback
Thorax:	Pale yellow nymph dubbing
Legs:	Mottled brown hen back

Step 1. Fix the hook in the vise, and take ten to twenty turns of nonlead wire midshank. Start the thread behind the hook eye, make a slight ramp to the front weighting wire shoulder, overwrap the wire, and make another slight ramp to the back shoulder. Take the thread to a point just above the hook barb. Select a substantial clump of gray marabou, clip or strip it from the feather stem, and measure it about half the hook-shank length. Tie it in and overwrap the butts to the back shoulder of the weighting wire before clipping the excess.

Step 2. Tie in a length of ribbing wire. Cut a section of turkey tail about two-thirds the width of the hook gap. It helps if this has been sprayed with artist's fixative or given a light coat of Flexament, and allowed to dry. Tie it in by the thinner end, with the darker side down. Tie an aftershaft feather in at the base of the tails, by its tip, with the concave side down, so it will reverse when you pull it over the back, and the posture of the gills will be upward rather than down over the ribbing and shellback.

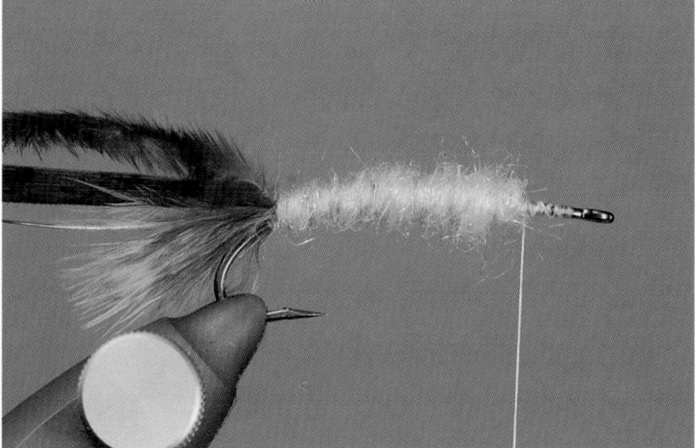

Step 3. Dub a substantial and fibrous abdomen forward over two-thirds of the hook-shank length. It should have a slight taper, but the taper should not be dramatic. The naturals have little taper in the body.

Step 4. Pull the aftershaft feather forward and tie it off at the front of the abdomen. Work your thread turns carefully through the plumes so you don't mat them down. Clip the excess.

Step 5. Pull the shellback forward and tie it off at the end of the abdomen. Do not clip the excess. Work your ribbing wire forward in five to eight evenly spaced turns. Work it back and forth as you wind it through the plumes, to avoid matting them down. You might find it necessary to separate the plumes with your fingers to open a channel through them for the ribbing. Tie off the ribbing and clip the excess.

Step 6. Hold the wing case back and overwrap it with thread up onto the front of the abdomen, approximately at the end of the gills.

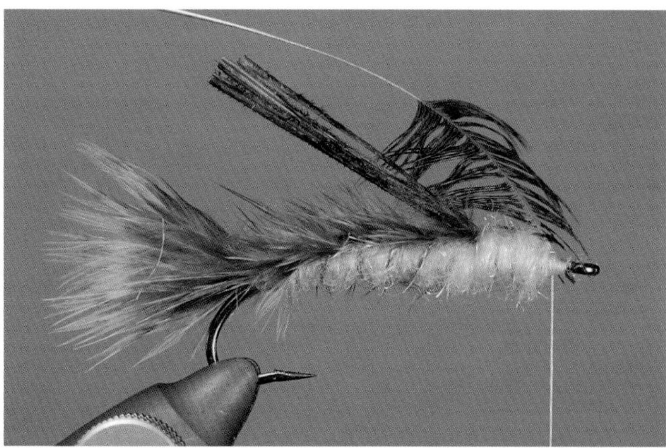

Step 7. Strip fuzz from the lower stem of a hen back feather, stroke the remaining fibers back, and tie the feather in by its tip, just behind the hook eye, leaving room to bring the wing case forward and tie it off. Clip the excess feather tip.

Step 8. Wind one or two turns of hackle behind the hook eye. Tie it off and clip the hackle stem.

Step 9. Bring the wing case forward over the hackle, splitting it evenly on each side. Tie it off behind the hook eye, and clip the excess. Use enough turns of thread to form a neat head, whip-finish, and cement the head.

This is a fairly technical pattern, but it imitates a big insect, one at which trout get a good look if there's enough light to see when they decide to take a whack at one. It's probable that Andy Burk designed the fly to fish the *Hexagenia limbata* hatch on Fall River, in his home area in California. It's a big spring creek, with clear water and constant flows. The river is well attended by anglers, and you can assume that trout there will be as snotty about fly patterns as they are anywhere in the world. Because the naturals hatch at dusk and after dark, except on rare cloudy late afternoons, their habits mitigate against the need for such imitative patterns. But if you ever do need one, Burk's *Hexagenia* will fool the fish.

The colors of this dressing can obviously be altered to suit any other burrower nymphs that you find important on your own waters.

All of the listed dressings for the burrowers are tied on weighted hooks. If you find a need to fish them shallow, for example high in the water column during a hatch, then you'll do better with unweighted versions. But the naturals leave their burrows on the bottom and make a dash to the top. If your fly is weighted, you'll be able to let it sink, then retrieve it upward, which will be the direction taken by the naturals seen by trout during an emergence.

Because burrower nymphs swim at a fair clip, a stripped retrieve will be most effective. They're the size of streamers, and should be fished with streamer retrieves.

SUMMARY

Any mayfly nymph that you find in such concentrated numbers that it dominates all other food forms will at that moment be the most important insect in your world. You should be armed with a fly pattern to match it. That happens more predictably with some insects than it does with others. Among the mayflies, it happens often with the small swimmer nymphs, rarely with the larger swimmers, infrequently with the crawlers, almost never with the clingers, and again rarely with the burrowers. Obviously, you should go prepared with imitations of the small blue-winged olive, or *Baetis* complex, already tied and in your fly boxes. For most of the other mayfly nymphs, you can get by with searching nymphs, if you're well stocked with a wide variety of them.

It's necessary to crank your own fishing preferences into these equations. If you fish tailwaters and spring creeks more often than freestone streams, you will likely encounter the need for a specific imitation of slender crawlers such as the pale morning dun nymph. If your home waters have heavy populations of certain large swimmer nymphs along their edges, then you want to carry at least one dressing that represents them quite closely. If you fish the rare water that throws up a big burrower hatch at evening, then you'll be almost certain to go fishless if you don't have something on you to approximate the nymph.

Your fly boxes should reflect these preferences. I enjoy fishing hatches. My own fishing travels are shaped by my desire to study the aquatic insects. As a consequence, I often get onto the sorts of waters where a particular insect is abundant, and trout are feeding on it selectively. I fish a bit more often on freestone streams than I do on spring creeks and tailwaters, but I find myself challenged by difficult trout more often on those latter waters than I do the rougher types. I tend to lean heavily on my searching-nymph box when I'm on freestone waters. I usually take a portable fly-tying kit on trips to spring creeks and tailwaters. But I fish out of my imitative-nymph box on those waters more often than I do the searching box.

I prefer to depend less than I ever recommend on foreknowledge of what hatches I might find; I like to get surprised, and I don't mind being forced to put that tying kit into play, so long as the trip is for more than a couple of days. On a short trip, it's difficult to work out what trout might want. I do my observing, fishing, and collecting during the day. I tie in the tent trailer or motel room in the evening or morning. I suppose I should start carrying the tying kit in the boat, while floating rivers, but I'm too tuned to the enjoyment of being out there, trying to figure out how to catch trout with the flies I've got on me, to take time to tie on the stream. I know that's a mistake, but I also know it's one I'll probably keep making for the rest of my life.

Getting to specifics, I would feel unarmed if my fly box lacked Flashback Pheasant Tails in sizes 16 through 22. Those will almost always catch trout when small swimmer nymphs are abundant, which in my life happens with fair frequency. Quite often I create some offshoot of the Pheasant Tail, or something else simple, when I'm on a trip and find I need to match a small *Baetis* nymph.

For the larger swimmers, I rely on my All-Fur Swimmer, always present in my searching boxes, until a selective situation presents itself, in which case I'll try to solve it with my portable tying kit. I don't carry a specific dressing for the large swimmers unless I'm on stillwaters, where I'd feel unarmed without a *Callibaetis* imitation . . . but that is the subject of a later chapter.

I've never had trouble solving any large crawler presence with nymphs out of my searching box. A size 12 or 14 Beadhead Hare's Ear or Fox Squirrel looks remarkably like many of them. If they're darker, then the A. P. Black is always there, though I use it more often on small streams than I do on medium streams to large rivers. I have an excessive amount of success with Dave Whitlock's Fox Squirrel nymph, tied with a beadhead and in a little bit of a bastardized color, almost always on a size 16 hook. I don't think it's an accident that this fly is not far off in size, shape, and color from the abundant small crawlers in the PMD group that I find so often in trout streams. I call it a searching nymph, but I could just as well declare it an imitation when I tie it to my tippet.

I don't carry any nymphs specific for clingers. I find them almost everywhere I collect in freestone streams, and in many spring creeks. But I don't recall ever finding a trout taking them selectively. I don't think a trout taking clinger naturals, in the sort of fast water where those flattened nymphs are most common, would turn away from a searching nymph in a similar size and color, rigged with a shot-and-indicator setup to fish right along the bottom.

If you get into a rare concentration of burrower nymphs, especially when they're active just before their evening emergence, then you'll find trout able to ignore everything else. With the widespread *Hexagenia,* it will happen as often on lakes as on streams. If you have Woolly Buggers in the right colors, they will almost certainly solve the problem. I don't know about you, but I carry Woolly Buggers in black and olive, but not in tan, the needed color. It's possible that one of your searching nymphs, in its lightest colors and largest sizes, will solve the problem. Most likely you'll not do well without an imitation. It's my recommendation that you tie and carry at least a half dozen of a specific dressing for these large nymphs, against the chance that you land on water where they're emerging, because not much else is likely to work, and also because these big insects cause the largest trout in any body of water to show up hungry, willing to feed.

CHAPTER 19

Stoneflies

No group is treated with more complexity, yet lends itself more to simplicity, than stonefly nymphs. Half of what I call the *walk-aways*—nymphs tied with so many precise parts that they can nearly be keyed to species—are constructed for stoneflies. These flies are works of art. They deserve to be displayed under glass cases. But you wouldn't want to take them out to a typical stonefly stream and dunk them in water. You'd likely lose a bunch of them on bottom rocks. And then you'd have something to cry about. I wouldn't blame you. I also wouldn't join you. The stonefly nymphs I use are heavily weighted toward the simple end of the spectrum.

Stonefly imitations range in size from 4 to 18, always on 2XL or 3XL hooks. The naturals vary in color from pale yellow to black. Unlike mayfly nymphs, which come in four shapes, swimmers, crawlers, clingers, and burrowers, stonefly nymphs are all elongated, proportionately slender, and with rare exceptions have tails and antennae that are paired, somewhat short, and fairly stout. That is a single shape, and the source of their simplicity. You can choose a single pattern style, vary its size and color, and easily match every stonefly nymph you'll ever encounter.

Stonefly nymph colors can be reduced to a few repeated themes, a bit simpler even than the adults, which

If you settle on a single pattern style, and tie it in a narrow range of sizes and colors, you will be able to cover all of the stonefly nymphs you ever encounter.

themselves are far from complicated. In the winged stage, there are little browns, little greens, and little yellows, medium browns, golden stones, and the giant dark salmon flies. In the nymphal stage, the naturals rely on camouflage in their aquatic environment, and the color schemes get condensed. The little browns are small and dark brown. The little greens and little yellows both tend toward pale olive-tans as nymphs. The medium browns and golden stones tend to mottled golden-browns. The giant salmon-fly nymph ranges from dark brown to almost black.

Little brown stone nymph (Zapada).

Little yellow stone nymph (Sweltsa).

Medium brown stonefly nymphs (Skwala).

Stonefly nymphs come in just one essential shape and four primary color schemes. It's our further good fortune that each color is somewhat retricted to a narrow range of sizes. The little browns are sizes 16 and 18. The little greens and little yellows are size 14 to 18. The medium browns and golden stones are size 6 to 10. The giant salmon fly is size 12 when in its youth, but size 4 or 6 when it's mature and ready to emerge.

Golden stonefly nymph (Calineuria).

Giant salmon-fly nymph (Pteronarcys).

Rare stonefly nymph caught in the brief vulnerable period after a molt (Hesperoperla).

Again, you can condense the stonefly nymphs into a single pattern style, tie a few colors, each in a narrow range of two to three sizes, and you'll have all of them covered in a scant few evenings of tying. They won't take up much room in a fly box, if you tie just a few of each for emergencies. If you encounter one or the other of them frequently, however, you'll need a substantial number of them because the waters in which you'll fish, and the ways you'll need to rig them, cause a lot of them to be lost.

The naturals, as their name implies, live on the bottom in stone-filled waters. Because few stonefly nymphs have external gills, and they depend on transpiration of oxygen directly through the exoskeleton for respiration, they typically live in fast riffles and runs, where the water is rough and oxygen content is highest. If you fish stonefly nymph imitations where the naturals are most abundant, you're going to lose a few.

Though I do all of my stonefly tying and fishing from a stance of simplicity, you might prefer the opposite, and I'll offer some complexity to you, though none of the walk-away kind. I'm a rough tier, usually in a hurry, and couldn't tie one of those if I desired to, and I don't have that desire. I don't get enough fishing time, and don't want to expend any potential stream time at the vise, creating something I'd hate to take a chance on losing, and that I don't think would fish as well as a simple dressing, anyway.

You can fish over most stonefly nymphs with variations on a few searching nymphs. The A. P. Black tied slender, on a long-shank hook, would suffice for the little brown nymphs. A Gold-Ribbed Hare's Ear, again elongated and tied slender, would work for almost all of the little greens, little yellows, medium browns, and golden stones, if tied in a range of sizes from 6 to 16. I listed Charlie Brooks's Montana Stone, his salmon-fly imitation, in chapter 11 as a searching dressing because I use it in such a wide variety of situations, many of them in an entire absence of salmon-fly nymphs. It should be fairly obvious that the same fly is my choice when salmon-fly nymphs are actually present and abundant.

That has been true for a lot of years, though I experiment with other patterns whenever I get into a bunch of salmon flies. They all seem to work. My theory has been reduced to this: If a nymph is big, ugly, black, and fished along the bottom, it will work when trout are feeding on salmon-fly nymphs.

BOX CANYON STONE

The starting point for stonefly simplicity is based on a Mims Barker dressing called the Box Canyon Stone. The original was tied in black, for the salmon-fly nymph. It had forked black goose biot tails, a black yarn body, a mottled turkey feather section wing case, and a dark furnace hackle wrapped through the yarn thorax to represent legs. It is still an excellent imitation; I put it to use against some Deschutes River redsides during the salmon-fly nymph migration early last spring, just to see if they still approved it. They did.

You can vary the size and color of the Box Canyon Stone concept to cover all stonefly nymphs, from size 18 and brown to size 4 and black. Antennae could easily be added to any of the flies, simply by peeling away the outer wing-case butt fibers on each side before clipping out the excess fibers in the middle. But A. K. Best, in his brilliant *A. K.'s Fly Box,* notes that most stonefly nymphs tuck their antennae along their sides when they're attempting to swim and wishing they weren't, and also that every time he tries to tie a stonefly dressing with antennae sticking out, he catches one in his tippet knot and has to cut it off. I'll leave it to you. I tie mine without antennae.

Though they are more precisely imitative without beads, I suspect that the addition of a beadhead will make any of the following stonefly nymph dressings based on the Box Canyon Stone more effective. I'll list them with beads here, because even if I didn't, you'd probably wind up adding them anyway. I do that myself.

LITTLE BROWN STONEFLY NYMPH

Hook: 3XL, size 16–18
Bead: Gold or black
Weight: 10–15 turns nonlead wire
Thread: Brown 8/0
Tails: Dark brown biots, forked
Rib: Fine copper wire
Abdomen: Dark brown Antron and fur dubbing mix
Wing case: Dark brown turkey tail feather section
Thorax: Dark brown Antron and fur dubbing, picked out for legs

LITTLE YELLOW STONEFLY NYMPH

Hook: 3XL, size 14–18
Bead: Gold
Weight: 10–15 turns nonlead wire
Thread: Tan 8/0
Tails: Tan biots, forked
Rib: Fine copper wire
Abdomen: Tannish olive Antron and fur dubbing mix
Wing case: Brown turkey tail feather section
Thorax: Tannish olive Antron and fur dubbing, picked out for legs

GOLDEN STONEFLY NYMPH

Hook: 3XL, size 6–12
Bead: Gold brass or tungsten
Weight: 10–20 turns nonlead wire
Thread: Brown 6/0
Tails: Rust biots, forked
Rib: Medium copper wire
Abdomen: Golden brown Antron and fur dubbing mix
Wing case: Brown turkey tail feather section
Thorax: Golden brown Antron and fur dubbing, picked out for legs

GIANT SALMON FLY NYMPH

Hook: 3XL, size 4–12
Bead: Gold or black tungsten
Weight: 15–25 turns nonlead wire
Thread: Black 6/0
Tails: Black biots, forked
Rib: Heavy copper wire
Abdomen: Black Antron and fur dubbing mix
Wing case: Dark brown turkey or black goose feather section
Thorax: Black Antron and fur dubbing, picked out for legs

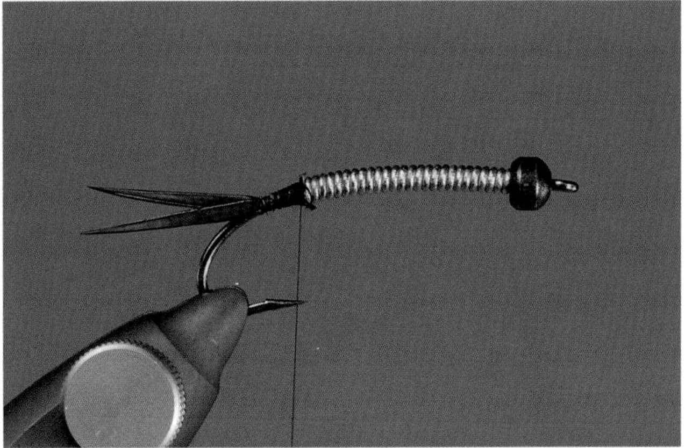

Step 1. Slip an appropriate taper-drilled bead onto the hook. Wrap ten to twenty-five turns of nonlead wire, and jam the front wraps into the back end of the bead, or tight against the back of the bead if the weighting wire is too thick to fit into the bead. Start your thread behind the wire, and form a slight thread ramp to the back shoulder of the wire. Measure one biot half the shank length, and tie it in on the far side of the hook bend. Measure another even with the first, and tie it in on the near side. Overwrap the biot butts to the shoulder of the weighting wire, and clip the excess there.

Step 2. Tie in a few inches of copper wire for the rib. Use the direct-dubbing method or a dubbing loop to wind a slightly tapered body forward from the base of the tails to just beyond the midpoint of the hook shank.

Step 3. Wind the rib forward in four to six evenly spaced turns through the abdomen. Tie it off and clip the excess. Select a wing-case segment about the width of the hook gap, and clip it from the feather stem. It helps keep it together if your feather has been sprayed with artist's fixative or lightly coated with Flexament. Tie the feather section in by the thicker end, with the lighter side up, so that when it is brought forward, the darker side will be up. Wrap thread turns onto the wing case well up onto the abdomen, to prevent a wasp waist when you bring it forward.

Step 4. Dub a substantial thorax forward to the back of the bead. It should be thicker than the thorax at the back, tapering slightly down to the bead. Lay your bodkin point across the wing-case feather section, just behind its tie-in point. Hold it there and fold the section forward over it. Tie the wing case in tight behind the bead.

Step 5. Take a few more turns of thread to secure the wing case. Whip-finish over these wraps, and clip your thread. Clip the wing-case butts close behind the bead. Don't worry about a short section sticking up behind the bead; these ensure that the wing case is fixed in tight, and won't pull out after you've caught a few trout on the fly. Use your bodkin or a dubbing teasing tool to work out some thorax dubbing to both sides, representing legs of the natural insect.

BIRD'S STONE

Matching all of the stoneflies with variations on a single theme is not a new idea. In their book *Stoneflies,* Carl Richards, Doug Swisher, and Fred Arbona Jr. list a series of what they call *prototypical patterns* for both nymphs and adults. They name the Bird's Stone as a pattern style you might want to tie for your "type species" and vary as your encounters with stonefly nymphs up and down the size and color scales demand it.

BIRD'S STONE *Cal Bird*

Hook:	3XL, size 6–12
Weight:	15–20 turns nonlead wire
Thread:	Orange 6/0 or 8/0
Tail:	Brown goose biots
Rib:	Orange floss
Abdomen:	Brown Antron and fur mix
Wing case:	Dark mottled turkey tail
Legs:	Furnace hen or saddle
Thorax:	Peacock herl

Step 1. Debarb the hook and fix it in the vise. Layer the shank with fifteen to twenty turns of nonlead weighting wire. Start your thread behind the wire, and layer it to the bend of the hook. Measure a biot about two-thirds the shank length, and tie it in on the far side of the hook, with the tip splayed away from the hook. Repeat the process on the near side, to form a forked biot tail. Overwrap the biot butts to the rear shoulder of the weighting wire, and clip the excess. Tie in a few inches of orange floss, overwrapping it from the shoulder of the wire to the base of the tail. Dub a fairly stout and slightly tapered abdomen just past the midpoint of the hook shank.

Step 2. Rib the abdomen with four to six evenly spaced turns of floss. Tie off and clip the floss. Measure a section of turkey tail about the width of the hook gap, and clip it from the feather. Tie this in by the softer tip end, with the darker side down. Select a hackle feather with fibers about one and a half hook gaps long. Strip the fuzz from the lower end of the stem, and tie it in so that when wound the fibers will sweep back.

Step 3. Select four to five peacock herls with bushy rather than slender barbs. Strip them from the stem, clip about one-half inch off the tips, and tie them in at the end of the abdomen. Catch the thread over the forefinger of your off hand to form a thread loop, and twist the herls into a herl rope (see page 59). Wind this forward to a point one or two hook-eye lengths behind the eye. Tie it off and clip the excess. Wind the hackle forward in two or three widely spaced turns through the thorax. Tie off the tip and clip the excess.

Step 4. Bring the wing case forward, and tie it off at the end of the thorax. Clip the excess there, and take enough thread turns over the tie-in point to form a neat thread head. Whip-finish and cement the head.

Step 5 (optional). Many experienced tiers remove the hook from the vise and use their fingers and thumbs to crimp about a thirty-degree bend in the shank. This gives the fly a bit of a curved look, which can also be accomplished by tying it on a curved-shank hook in the first place. The original is tied with a straight shank, but you should tie it and fish it the way it looks best to you. The trout probably won't notice the difference.

The Bird's Stone can be varied in size and color to match the four primary stonefly groups: little brown, little yellow, golden, and salmon fly.

It is easy to vary the colors and sizes of the Bird's Stone to represent all of the stonefly nymphs, from small to large. The smallest, for the little brown stones, should be tied on size 16 and 18 hooks in chocolate brown. The next size up, for the little yellow stones, should be tied in sizes 14 and 16 with tannish olive bodies. The midrange of sizes, for the *Skwala* and golden stones, should be tied on size 6 to 12 hooks with golden brown bodies. It's misleading to say that the largest, for the salmon flies, should be tied on size 4 and 6 hooks with black bodies. That's because those large naturals have three- and four-year life cycles. The immature year classes are always out there, year-round, getting eaten by trout. Rick Hafele and I don't agree on everything, but we fish together a lot, and he wrote in *Nymph-Fishing Rivers and Streams* that he uses his salmon-fly imitations more often in the smaller sizes 10 and 12 than he does in the normal sizes 4, 6, and 8. I agree with that.

Stonefly nymphs do not emerge into the adult stage out in open water, as most of the mayflies do. Instead, they migrate to shore, sometimes en masse, where they crawl up the sides of protruding boulders, sticks, or the bank itself, and emerge where trout can't get at them. It's a defense against predation. Another defense, this one against birds, is to make this dangerous transition late in the evening or at night. As a result of this behavior, you don't fish a stonefly hatch in the same sense that you fish a mayfly hatch, especially when the consideration is nymph imitations. Instead, you fish stonefly nymph patterns in one of three situations.

First, you need an appropriate size and color nymph when your kick-net sampling, or simple hoisting of bottom stones, reveals that a particular stonefly species is the most abundant trout food in the bit of water you're about to fish. Second, you try to become aware of a migration whenever one is in progress, because trout will never neglect it. With the larger golden stones and salmon flies, and the smaller stoneflies to a lesser extent, the presence of a few adults in streamside vegetation is your signal that the hatch is about to begin and the migration is likely already in progress.

The third situation in which you'll want a specific imitation for a certain stonefly nymph is that gathering of them right at the shoreline, after completion of their migration, while they wait for the arrival of the right moment to emerge. It's easy to see when this condition exists: step into the shallow edge waters and hoist a few flat stones off the bottom. Sometimes their undersides will reveal half a dozen to a dozen or more stonefly nymphs of a single species, always specimens that are mature, with wing cases ready to pop. When those insects are size 4 and 6 salmon-fly nymphs, you'll have no trouble figuring out why trout have followed the migration in toward shore, and have posted themselves in favorable lies right at the edges.

One bit of trout behavior that you need to know about is their preference for stonefly nymphs over adults. Perhaps the crunchy wings on an adult are distasteful, or the ease of nibbling a nymph as opposed to the difficulty of capturing an adult makes them seem better. Whatever the reason, when stonefly nymphs are gathered along shore in fair numbers, trout will continue to focus on them to the neglect of adults, even after the emergence is well under way and adults in streamside vegetation often fall to the water.

When you arrive at a bit of water, and see lots of a single stonefly species crawling around in the grass and willows, it's easy to get excited and tie on a floating imitation. Before you do, take a few moments to examine a few streambed stones close to the shoreline. If they conceal more than a very few nymphs of the same type of stonefly you see as adults in the nearby vegetation, you're going to catch a lot more trout on a nymph than you will a dry. If nothing else, dangle a nymph imitation off the stern of your dry, and give trout a choice.

In the fairly rare circumstance that you find trout feeding with single-minded selectivity on one of the smaller stonefly nymph groups, it will almost always be at the edges of the stream, at the end of a migration, in the early stages of an emergence. You might see a few little brown, little green, or little yellow stonefly adults in streamside brush or even in the air. It's your clue that trout might be lined up along the edges, in favorable lies, nibbling at natural nymphs.

Knowing their location and behavior, you might solve these trout with a slender searching nymph in the right size and color. The Pheasant Tail in size 14 or 16 is about as close as you can get to an imitation of the little brown stones. Slim Gold-Ribbed Hare's Ears or Whitlock Fox Squirrels might be such effective searching dressings because of their minor resemblance to nymphs of the little yellow stones and smaller golden stones. The Copper John might not be the perfect imitation for any of these naturals, but trout seem to accept it even when it misses by a feature or two, perhaps because it has that slender and slightly tapered shape and general buggy look. It's not a bad idea to follow John Barr's prescription for the fly, in his book *Barr Flies,* to fish it in combination with one or even two nymphs that might be closer imitations.

BEADHEAD BIOT STONEFLY NYMPH

If you want to get imitative of these smaller stonefly nymphs, you'll want to do it with a biot dressing, to capture the slenderness and segmentation of the naturals. The following Beadhead Biot Stonefly Nymph is an interpretation of the Gold Bead Biot Epoxy Golden Stone Nymph, which John Barr recommends be tied small and in different colors for the little stonefly groups.

BEADHEAD BIOT LITTLE BROWN STONEFLY NYMPH

Hook:	3XL, size 14–18
Bead:	Brass or tungsten, gold
Weight:	5–8 turns nonlead wire
Thread:	Brown 8/0
Tails:	Rust or brown turkey biots
Rib:	Fine copper wire
Abdomen:	Rust or brown turkey biot
Thorax:	Rust or brown dubbing
Wing case:	Black Thin Skin or similar
Legs:	Brown partridge fibers

A goose biot will give the same type of body as the turkey biot, but is usually too short to use on long-shank hooks.

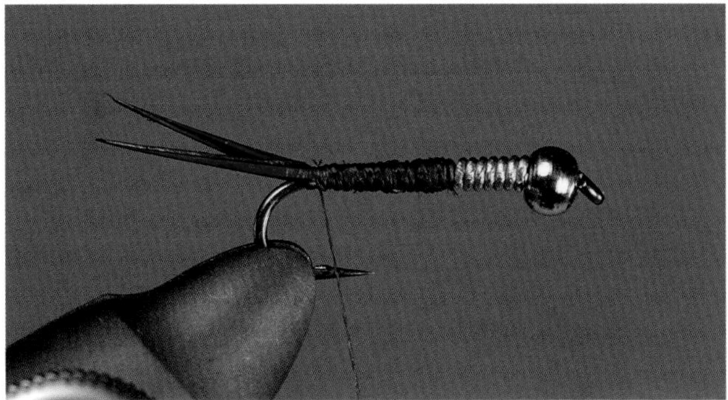

Step 1. Slip a bead over the hook, and fix the hook in your vise. Take just a few turns of nonlead wire behind the bead; it should stop short of the midpoint of the shank. Start your thread behind the wire, and use thread turns to create a slight tapered ramp to the shoulder. Lay an even base of thread to the hook bend. Measure a biot

one-half to two-thirds the shank length, and tie it in on the far side of the hook. Repeat on the near side, to form a forked tail. Use thread wraps to form an even underbody tapering up to the back shoulder of the weighting wire wraps.

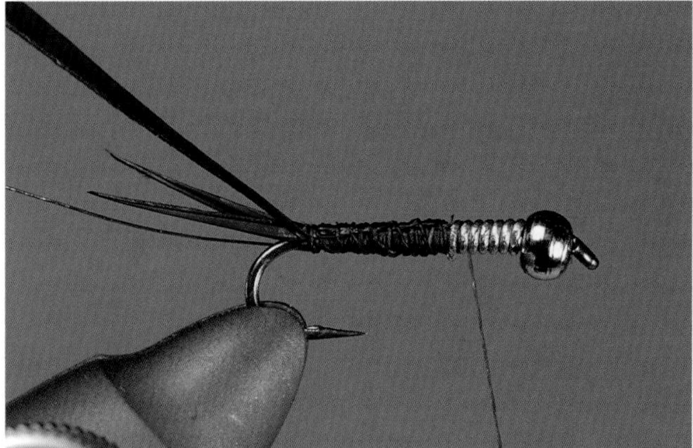

Step 2. Tie in a few inches of fine copper ribbing wire, with an even layer of thread wraps to the back of the weighting wire. Tie a predampened turkey biot, the concave side of the feather toward the hook shank, with an even layer of thread to the base of the tail. Use any necessary thread wraps forward to lay an even underbody for the fly.

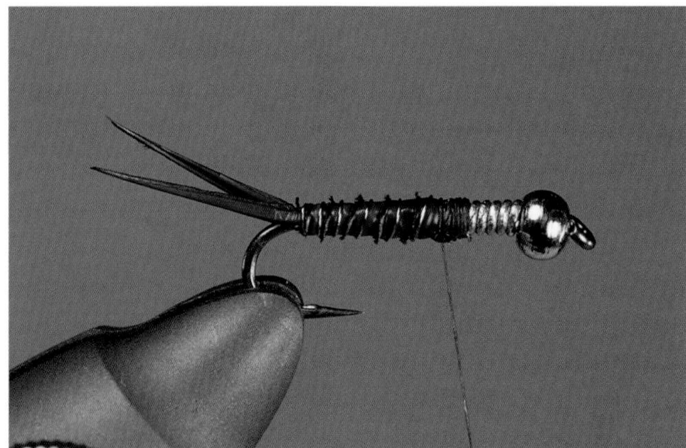

Step 3. Wind the biot forward in slightly wider turns just past the midpoint of the shank. Tie off and clip the excess there. You should have nicely spaced segments with slight ridges on the back side of each. If your body is smooth rather than ridged, tie your biot with the opposite side facing the hook, and the result should be ridged segments. Wind the ribbing wire forward, placing each turn over a segment of the biot body. Tie off the wire and clip the excess.

Step 4. Twist a small amount of dubbing onto the thread, and dub it forward from the front of the biot body to about one hook-eye length behind the bead. Leave a bit of room to tie in the wing case and legs.

Step 5. Even the tips of a few partridge fibers, and clip or strip them from the feather. Measure them so they reach approximately to the hook point, and tie them in on the far side of the hook, in front of the thorax. Repeat on the near side. Clip the excess butts.

Step 6. Clip a section of Thin Skin about the width of the hook gap. Be sure one end is cut square across, then round the corners and cut a small notch in the tip, to shape it as a wing case.

Step 7. Hold the wing case in position so it reaches just beyond the end of the thorax. Use four to six firm thread turns to secure it in place behind the bead. It should cup slightly around the thorax and drive the legs into a downward and swept-back posture.

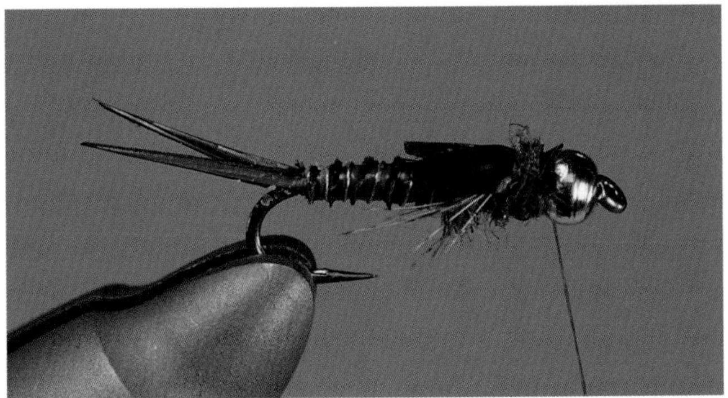

Step 8. Clip the wing-case butts as close as you can behind the bead. Apply a very small amount of dubbing to your thread, and take just a turn of it to cover your thread wraps. This is optional; you might feel you've already done enough, on this small hook, to please the trout. Whip-finish behind the bead, and be sure to nestle the knot securely into the gap between the wing case and the bead before clipping the thread.

Though the biot concept can be applied to the larger stoneflies, it takes careful construction of proper underbodies, sometimes with wire outriggers lashed to the hook shank as demonstrated for the clinger mayfly nymphs (see page 182). I feel that it's difficult to get biots long enough to work on the bigger hooks, and also that I don't want to tie in the detail required, since the way I fish golden stone and salmon-fly nymph imitations puts them into constant peril of being lost on the bottom. I don't enjoy rerigging constantly, and avoid it if I can and still catch trout. But I have a distaste for tying a complex dressing and then losing it on the bottom, especially in situations where I know a simpler fly would work as well.

The biot-bodied nymph is, however, effective for the little yellow stones, with their tannish olive bodies. If you feel the need for exact imitations, the following fly will work well.

BEADHEAD BIOT LITTLE YELLOW STONEFLY NYMPH

Hook: 3XL, size 12–16
Bead: Brass or tungsten, gold
Weight: 5–10 turns nonlead wire
Thread: Tan 6/0 or 8/0
Tails: Tan or rust turkey biots
Rib: Fine copper wire
Abdomen: Tan or rust biot
Thorax: Tan or rust dubbing
Wing case: Black Thin Skin or similar
Legs: Brown partridge fibers

GENERAL STONEFLY NYMPH

The Montana Stone, listed in chapter 11 as a searching nymph, remains my go-to salmon-fly nymph imitation as well.

It would seem necessary to imitate the larger stonefly nymphs, the golden stones and salmon flies, more accurately. I've never found that true, though I've also never been willing to tie and fish entomologically correct walk-aways, and therefore might be failing to catch a lot of trout that I don't know are passing up my less imitative nymphs. It's easy to keep track of the trout you catch; it's more difficult to make a list of the trout that refuse your fly, especially when you're fishing on the bottom. But I seem to be satisfied with the luck my simple

Golden Stonefly Nymph and Brooks Montana Stone provide when the larger stoneflies are present.

I don't know of any angler who has gone out to a river, fished a heavy presence of one of the big stoneflies, collected a few specimens, and failed to trot back to the tying bench and invent an imitation of his own. It's an instinct. Usually we name it after ourselves. I did it myself once.

The first year I fished the Deschutes River salmon-fly hatch extensively, I created my own nymph dressing. I arrived before the hatch was well under way, and found a few adults prowling in streamside grasses. I tied on an Improved Sofa Pillow with the certainty that I had the hatch solved. I was almost shocked when the trout ignored it. I began frantically hoisting bankside stones, and discovered dozens of salmon-fly nymphs, which quickly added up to hundreds, and must have multiplied into thousands and perhaps even millions under all the stones that I left unturned up and down the river. It was easy to see why trout kept their attention turned down.

I pickled a few of the monstrous specimens in alcohol, trotted back to my tent, set them next to a portable tying vise, and whipped up something that was mostly lead and black fur with very minimal appendages. It worked wonders. I wrote an article about it. I called it the Leaded Stone. It still works today, though I would have trouble picking it out of a police lineup of the dozens of similar generic salmon-fly nymph imitations. The truth is, a Black Woolly Worm still works when giant salmon-fly nymphs are on the move. That does not stop me from recommending that you take time to collect a few naturals the next time you're on the water, at the same time they're in the water. Invent an imitation of your own. Name it after yourself. Fish it with confidence. If it's big, black, and preferably ugly rather than pretty, and you tumble it along the bottom, you're going to catch trout on it.

The basic parts from which you assemble the nymph should include a long-shank hook, lots of weighting wire, and black fur or synthetic dubbing, or yarn, or tubing, or stretch lace, or . . . on and on. The peripheral parts to consider are a black or gold bead, regular or tungsten for added weight; biots for tails; rubber legs for legs; and anything black for the wing case. Add something for flash, or some combination of wizardry and magic powder, to personalize it. It's not fair in this complicated age to just throw the basic ingredients onto the hook and place your name on it. Once you've constructed something that looks a little like a salmon-fly nymph, and as little as you can like the myriads of patterns that have already been created for it, you'll have what you're after. It would be a shock if you applied it to water and the trout didn't go after it as well, so long as some naturals were around, tickling trout memories.

The following dressing is from Jim Schollmeyer's book *Nymph Fly-Tying Techniques.* Jim is a rarity among us: he didn't name it after himself.

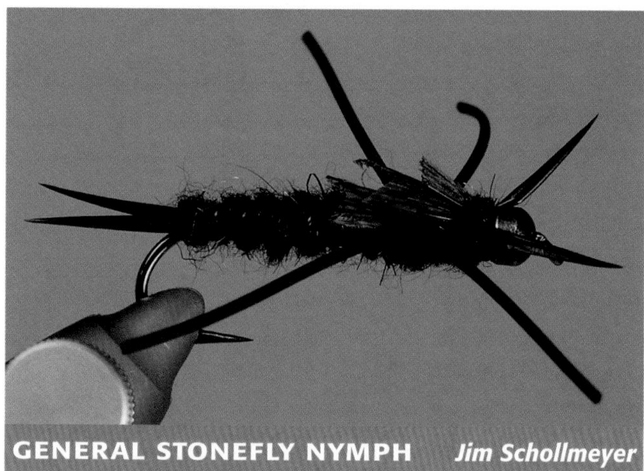

GENERAL STONEFLY NYMPH ***Jim Schollmeyer***

Hook:	3XL, size 4–14
Head:	Black or tungsten bead
Weight:	20–25 turns nonlead wire
Thread:	Black or brown 3/0 or 6/0
Tail:	Black or brown goose biots, forked
Rib:	Black or amber vinyl ribbing
Antennae:	Black or brown goose biots
Body:	Black or golden brown dubbing
Wing case:	Turkey tail feather sections
Legs:	Black or speckled rubber legs

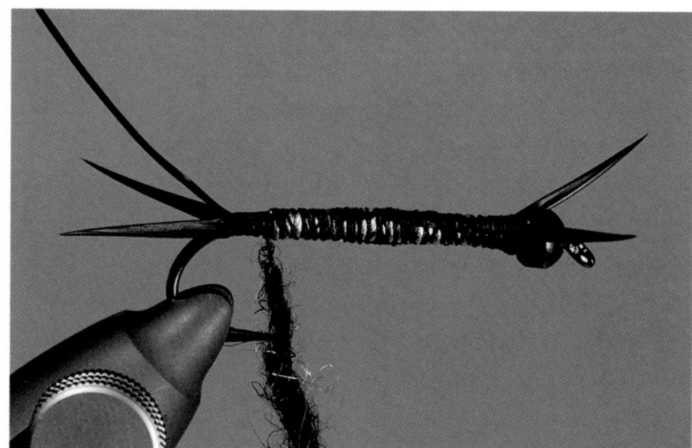

Step 1. Debarb the hook, slip a bead to the eye, and fix the hook in the vise. Wrap twenty to twenty-five turns of weighting wire around the shank, start the thread behind the wire wraps, and layer it to the hook bend. Measure a biot one-half to two-thirds the shank length, and tie it in on the far side. Repeat on the near side. Overwrap the butts to the back shoulder of the weighting wire, and clip the excess there. Tie in a few inches of vinyl tubing for the rib. Take the thread forward to the back of the bead, and use a few wraps there to form a base for the antennae. Measure a biot half the shank

length or a bit shorter. Tie it in on the far side, against the back of the bead. Repeat on the near side. Overwrap the butts of the antennae and the weighting wire to the back shoulder of the wire. Wax your thread and twist a substantial amount of body dubbing to the thread.

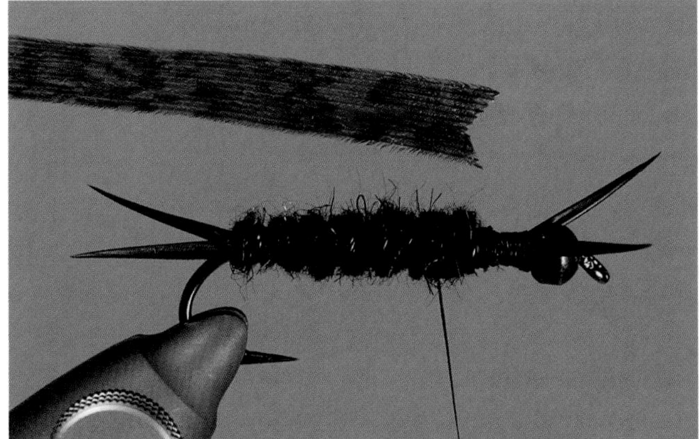

Step 2. Wrap a stout and slightly tapered body forward to a point well past the midpoint of the hook. Wind the ribbing forward in evenly spaced wraps to the end of the body. Tie it off there and clip the excess. Return the thread onto the body at a point about two-fifths the shank length behind the bead. From a turkey tail that has been treated with head cement or Flexament, clip a section a bit wider than the thorax. Fold it in half, and clip the folded corner at an angle, so that when it is unfolded it will have a V notch.

Step 3. Tie the wing case in so that the points are at or just past the midpoint of the hook. Clip the excess butts. Measure two sections of rubber legs about one and a half to two shank lengths. Tie one in on the far side of the hook, over the wing-case tie-in point. Repeat on the near side. Fix a substantial amount of dubbing to the thread. Use enough turns to cover the rubber-legs tie-in point. Hold the front legs back out of the way, and take dubbing turns tapered down to a point just behind the bead.

Step 4. Cut a second turkey feather section for a wing case as you did the first. If desired, you can use the remainder of the first section to form the second, and thereby form the entire wing-case portion of a nymph from a single feather section. Measure this so that it covers the tie-in point for the legs, and extends about halfway over the first wing-case segment. Tie it in and use enough thread wraps to fill in behind the bead. Do not cut the excess wing-case butts.

Step 5. Apply a little dubbing to the thread and wind it forward. Fold the butt of the wing case back over the first and second wing cases. Use just a few thread turns to hold it in position. Fill in between the bead and the wing case with a bit more dubbing. Tuck a whip-finish tight behind the bead, and clip the thread.

Step 6. Clip the wing case butt straight across so that it forms a third section of wing case. In a literal sense, the natural has only two wing-cases, but this third section represents the broad pronotum shield—the hardened plate over the top of the first thoracic segment behind the head, which is represented by the bead and bit of dubbing behind it. This third wing case, and the antennae as well, could easily be omitted without the trout, which have poor inventory methods, ever noticing. But the idea is to offer an imitative dressing, and the extra detail does make it a more exact imitation.

I often put a crimp in my finished salmon-fly nymph imitations, but I always wonder if it pleases the trout as much as it does me.

I've often held natural salmon-fly nymphs in my palm, in which case they curl up. When released into the currents, they keep this same posture until they make contact with the bottom, at which moment they uncurl and scramble for a grip on whatever it is they've touched down upon. As a consequence, I've joined the multitudes and put a crimp in my finished salmon-fly nymphs. The great A. K. Best, in his book *A. K.'s Fly Box,* lists his own salmon-fly dressing, which he calls the Black Ugly Nymph, though it's a beautifully functional imitation of the natural. He calls it foolish to suppose that because a salmon-fly nymph is curled in your hand, it is also curled in nature. He puts a slight bend in the opposite direction.

I've also often held golden stone nymphs in my hand. They do not curl up. When released into the currents, they splay their legs like sky divers, and wiggle in an attempt to swim to the bottom. It's a fair guess that salmon-fly nymphs have the same posture when they're knocked loose from their grip on the bottom stones by natural means. It's also a fair guess that A. K. is right about anything to do with insects and fly fishing far more often than he's wrong.

You'll have to make your own observations, and decide whether to bend your hooks up, down, or leave them straight. Since it's an operation that can be performed on the stream, when you tie the fly to your stout tippet, you can tie a bunch now, leave them straight, and do what you will at streamside, after you've turned over a few stones, dislodged a few salmon-fly nymphs, seen which posture they take in your own opinion. I haven't made that experiment myself; I've always held them in hand, thereby corrupting the results of my own science.

Salmon flies are western, their importance greatest on, though not restricted to, a handful of waters that are famous for their trout fishing, though in part they might be famous because they have the salmon-fly hatch. It would be rare water that was suitable to great numbers of these large insects without being suitable at the same time to great numbers of large trout. I don't know the reason, but salmon flies are most abundant in medium to large trout streams and rivers, more scattered though commonly present in smaller waters. They are important to trout wherever they are found, but they will cause selective feeding only where they dominate other insects.

Salmon-fly nymphs tend to dominate other trout food forms during their mass migration to shore for emergence. That happens in spring, either just before or during snowmelt and heavy runoff. It is often speculated that nature has calculated that this important event should be concealed by turgid flows. Without doubt water that is off-color serves to protect these big, clumsy insects from trout.

On waters with stabilized flows, such as the Deschutes, which is now a tailwater but before dams were built got most of its water from a giant aquifer, the water is clear at all times. Trout respond predictably to the gathering of such big bites: they line up along shore and wait to whack them. On streams such as the Yellowstone River, which turns opaque during the average salmon-fly migration, trout might respond, but it's difficult to know it's happening.

Whenever you have evidence that trout are feeding selectively on salmon-fly nymphs, you should match them. If you don't see such evidence, but do find the big nymphs in your collecting, then a big, black nymph might be your best choice for part of any two- or three-fly nymph rig. For that majority of each year when mature salmon-fly nymphs are not present, but the first- and second-year classes are getting eaten by opportunistic trout, you'll rarely go wrong fishing a smaller imitation, say in size 10 or 12, again as the larger nymph in a two-fly tandem.

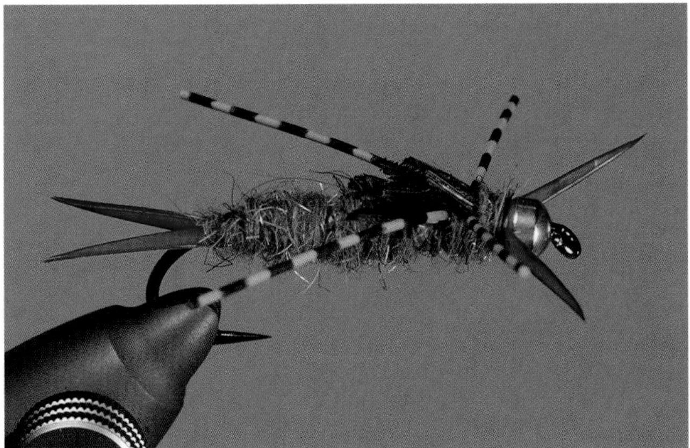

The General Stonefly Nymph in its golden stone colors.

The golden stone nymph is now known as mostly western, but that is misleading. The greater populations are in western streams and rivers, but the most widespread distribution is in the East. More species are adapted to eastern than western waters. It's very likely that historical numbers of golden stones were higher in the East, but a longer period of habitat destruction has caused them to dwindle. Still, they are present in nearly every water that approaches pristine condition, and you'll not be far from wrong fishing an imitation in more places than you might suspect. I would advise, however, that you recall the presence of first- and second-year classes, which always outnumber, if not outweigh, the mature third-year class. Keep your golden stonefly nymph imitations on the small side, sizes 10 and 12, and you'll do better than you will with imitations of mature size 4 and 6 specimens.

SUMMARY

It's a rare water on which you'll find yourself in need of an exact imitation of one of the smaller stonefly nymphs, the little brown, yellow, or green stones. The naturals might be present in abundance, but they'll not often dominate other nymphs and larvae to such an extent that trout will feed on them to the exclusion of everything else. It's fairly important to understand that you only need an exact imitation of any insect when trout include only that insect in their diet. If they're feeding opportunistically, you can catch them with an exact imitation of some small part of that diet, but you can also catch them with searching patterns that roughly resemble other items in the diet.

You should keep your eyes sharpened for situations in which trout feed selectively on one of the smaller stonefly nymphs, and be prepared to tie imitations if you encounter such a situation. I'll declare it unlikely. I've never felt unarmed with a few Pheasant Tail Nymphs, Copper Johns, Beadhead Hare's Ears, and Fox Squirrels, when I'm on waters that contain lots of the smaller stones. That doesn't preclude the likelihood that they're important on scattered waters, and that one of those waters might be your home stream. If you collect and find them dominant, be prepared with imitations whenever you go astream.

If you fish any of the famous western waters that have heavy populations of golden stoneflies or salmon flies, your nymph boxes should contain at least a few imitations for their nymphs. You are almost certain to use them successfully, especially in their smaller sizes, several times each season. You are also quite likely to get into a circumstance where fishing will be a bit slow and dull if you don't have at least an approximation of the large stonefly that is in the midst of its annual migration for emergence.

CHAPTER 20

Caddisflies

Nymphs tied to imitate caddisflies must be categorized differently than those for mayflies, which were broken into swimmers, crawlers, clingers, and burrowers, and for stoneflies, which adhered to a single shape, but could be separated by size and color into little brown, little yellow, golden stone, and salmon-fly nymphs. Both of those orders of aquatic insects undergo *incomplete metamorphosis,* in which the nymph evolves directly into the winged adult. Caddis undergo *complete metamorphosis.* Like butterflies, they progress from larva through the intermediate pupa stage before emerging into the reproductive adult. Your nymph patterns should be tied to reflect both larval and pupal stages.

Caddis larvae live their lives and present themselves to trout in two separate ways. Most are *cased,* concealing themselves inside compact houses that they creep around inside. Many others are *uncased.* These either are free-living, without any type of shelter, or construct crude retreats of leaves, twigs, and pebbles, into which they can retire. Uncased caddis larvae are more exposed to trout predation than cased larvae when they lose their grip on the bottom and are tumbled by the currents. Your patterns should reflect these two larval types.

Slow-water cased caddis (Leptoceridae) choose vegetative matter for their cases, because they have little need for ballast to hold them on the bottom, but they have a great need for camouflage.

Fast-water cased caddis (Dicosmoecus) *make their cases of sand grains and tiny pebbles, to hold them to the bottom if they lose their grip on the streambed.*

Cased caddis choose their materials based on the speed of the currents in which they live. Those living in modest flows have little need for ballast, and usually make their cases from vegetable matter, such as bits of leaves, conifer needles, and twigs, sometimes with grains of sand or small pebbles included. Many cased caddis types live in the quiet edge flows of fairly fast streams. These will also have light cases. Though we're still on the subject of moving waters, lakes and ponds are an extreme example of nil flows: stillwater caddis larvae need no ballast, and always construct their cases out of the local vegetation.

Cased caddis larvae that live in the swifter currents of riffles and runs would fare poorly if every tendril of current that came along could easily pry them from their perches on stones. They build their cases of sand grains, fine bits of stone, and in some cases even larger pebbles, depending on the velocity of the water in which they live.

Trout will ingest any of the cased caddis, at times, but they're more likely to feed frequently on those with soft cases of soft vegetation, and less likely to feed on those with hard cases of sand and pebbles. I've caught trout in small mountain streams with so many pebbles in their stomachs, of such size, that they felt knobby when cradled in the hand for release. These environments were poor, but had good populations of large fall caddis larvae (*Dicosmoecus* sp.). These swift-water larvae had incorporated pebbles into their cases as ballast against the brisk currents. It's easy enough for a trout's strong stomach acids to digest the nutritious larva out of its case. It's less easy for a trout to pass the remainders through the digestive tract.

Cases made of vegetation are not difficult to digest, and it's common to find trout feeding almost exclusively on cased caddis, case and all, but most often in stillwaters, not streams. On occasion, I've found trout feeding on cased caddis in slower edge waters, or in streams and rivers with stabilized flows and extensive rooted vegetation. It happens just often enough that you'll be wise to carry one or two patterns to solve such a situation if you get into one. A cased caddis imitation can also be a good choice for the large fly if you decide to rig with an indicator and split shot, and fish the bottom with a two-nymph setup, in any water that has a heavy and obvious population of cased caddis crawling around on bottom stones.

Free-living caddis larvae (Rhyacophila) *are fleshy and wormlike predators. They live most often in brisk water, and are unable to swim if knocked loose by the currents.*

Uncased caddis larvae either are free-living or construct retreats. Free-living types (Rhyacophilidae) are predaceous. They prowl around in the spaces between bottom stones in the fastest riffles and runs, capturing and devouring anything that doesn't capture and devour them. They are fleshy and wormlike, and are almost

Net-spinning caddis larvae (Hydropsyche) *often live in less boisterous currents than their free-living relatives, but they are also fleshy, wormlike, and unable to swim. This one is shown next to its retreat and partially collapsed net.*

invariably some shade of green, which has given rise to the common name *green rock worms.*

Net-spinning caddis larvae (primarily Hydropsychidae) build a crude retreat of pebbles, twigs, and leaves in crevices, or on the faces of stones, always exposed to the current. They often live in large colonies. Each spins a fine-mesh net of silk across the opening of its shelter, and eats whatever gets delivered into the meshes by the current. In some cases they eat the net along with the trapped material, then spin a new net to capture their next meal. When separated from their retreats, which happens often, these are fleshy and wormlike, very similar in appearance and often in color. They are difficult to distinguish from their green rock worm relatives until you start parsing out their parts with the aid of a microscope. Though fly tiers often distinguish between net spinners and free-living caddis larval types, it's an affectation: trout don't own microscopes.

Caddis pupae, in contrast to cased and uncased larvae, revert to a single shape, though with wide variations in size and color. Pupation takes place over a period of three to five weeks, in the safety of the larval case or the sanctuary of a sealed retreat. They are not available to trout during this slow change from larva to what we anglers still call the pupa, but entomologists call the *pharate adult:* the fully formed adult caddis enclosed by the exoskeleton of the transformational pupa.

When ready to emerge, caddis pupae cut their way out of their cases or retreats. Sometimes they drift for some way along the bottom, then rise to the top, and again they sometimes stage just subsurface, then break through, and the adult escapes the pupal exoskeleton. At other times, the pupa cuts free of the pupal chamber, makes a dash for the top, pops through the surface, and flies off immediately. The ascent, whether it's immediate

Fast-water cased caddis make their cases of sand grains and tiny pebbles, to hold them to the bottom if they lose their grip on the streambed.

Caddis pupae vary in size and color, but all have the approximate same shape: curved bulbous body, wing cases, legs, and antennae all folded down alongside the body, and somewhat large, beady eyes.

or after staging, is usually aided by gases trapped between the inner adult cuticle and the outer pupal exoskeleton. These gases often reflect sparks of light.

Caddis emergence can take place at any time of day, but often happens in the evening, or even after dark. You will encounter many important daytime caddis hatches, but not quite as many as you will dense midday mayfly hatches. Some caddis species have the same defense against predation that is so universal in mayflies: mass emergence. Others trickle off over wider spans of time. Both types are seen by trout, mostly in the ascending pupal stage, often enough that they cause interest at the least, and often prompt selective feeding.

When trout are selective to caddis, you need to have an imitation. Very often, what you are able to observe, from your view above the water, is a few to a lot of caddis adults boating the surface for scant seconds before flying away. What that informs you is that trout are very likely feeding subsurface on pupae, either those ascending toward the top, or those staging just beneath the surface. If you learn to interpret the presence of caddis adults into the need for an appropriate caddis pupa imitation, then you'll begin to solve these situations far more often than you have in the past, sticking to dry flies.

If you do nothing else, when you see adult caddis in the air but trout ignore your floating imitations, select a pupa pattern the same size and color as the adult you see on the surface, and suspend it on a couple feet of tippet from the hook bend of the dry fly you're already using to match the adult caddis. Continue fishing the dry fly just as if the nymph were not there. But don't forget to set the hook if your dry fly suddenly disappears.

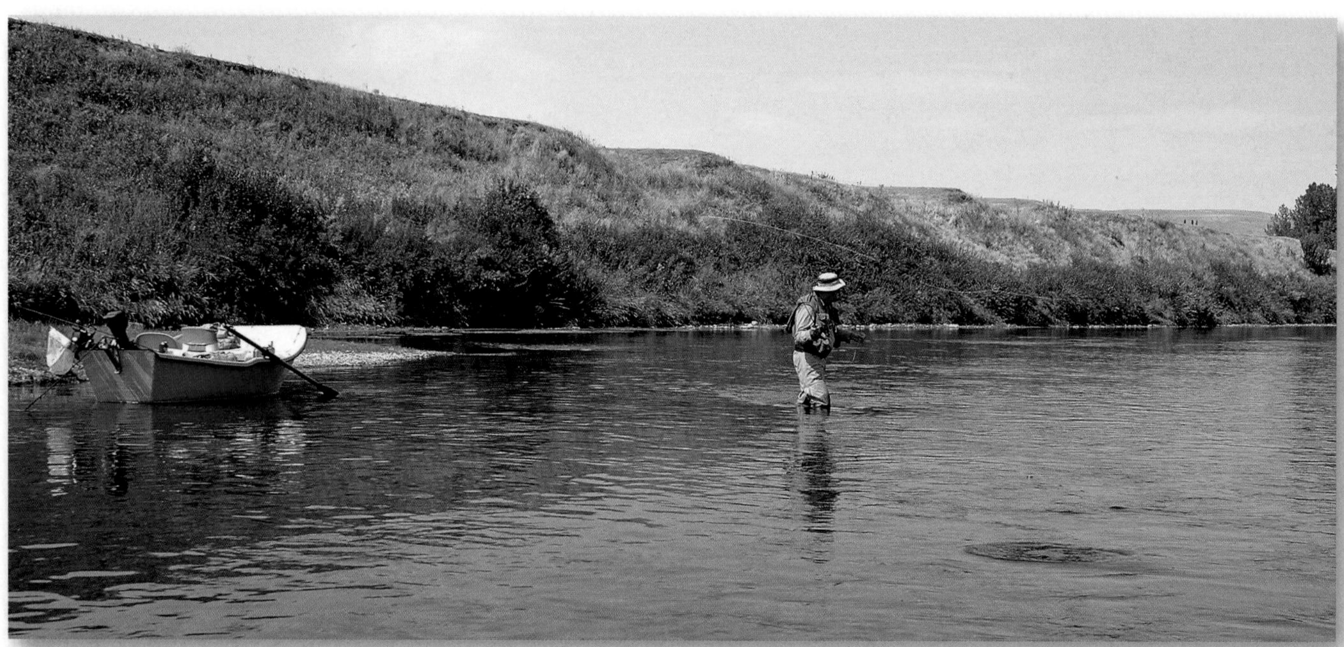

When trout appear to be rising during a caddis hatch, but are taking subsurface rather than on top, you won't do well until you switch to a pupa pattern and fish it a few inches deep.

CASED CADDIS LARVAE

Before you tie a bunch of exact imitations for cased caddis, consider that some of your searching nymphs strike a certain likeness to the same naturals. To a trout, the Gold-Ribbed Hare's Ear might look enough like a caddis that has constructed its case of tan to brown vegetation. The Herl Nymph, with its cylindrical body of dark green peacock herl and its black legs and head, looks like the head and legs of a caddis larva protruding from the front end of a case constructed of dark needles and leaves. The Hare's Ear is not often mentioned in realationship to cased caddis, but its effectiveness as a searching pattern might be enhanced by a resemblance to them, as it is to so many other natural insects. The Herl Nymph is often listed as a cased caddis imitation.

The Brassie, with its bright copper body, has the shape and reflective qualities of many caddis larvae that construct their cases of sand and bits of mica. These are common in the Colorado mountain streams where that wire nymph originated. They are also common wherever the water is swift, erosion is violent, and bits of eroded rock make up a good proportion of the stream bottom. It's hard to imagine any foothill or mountain stream where that is not true, and where a Brassie will not be effective. It's possible that trout take the Copper John for the same reasons, when it's tumbled along the bottom in fast water. But that is speculation. It is not speculation, however, that the Copper John is an excellent nymph to try when you're on mountain water.

PEEKING CADDIS

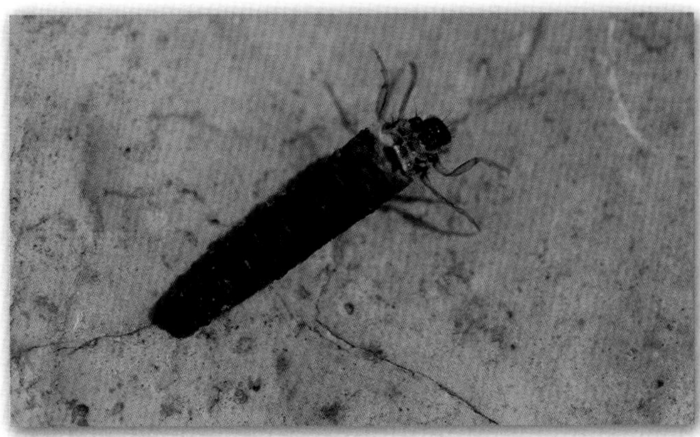

George Anderson's Peeking Caddis is an excellent imitation of the many cased caddis forms that panic when they lose their grip on the bottom, and stretch out their heads, legs, and some of the abdomen in their attempt to regain a hold (Brachycentrus). *The contrast between the case and head color is captured by his dressing, and is probably the trigger that causes trout to take it.*

George Anderson, owner of the Yellowstone Angler Fly Shop in Livingston, Montana, originated the Peeking Caddis, and has proved its effectiveness by winning one-fly contests with it. The nymph imitates a cased caddis larva with its head, legs, and "neck" all stretched out and straining to regain a grip on the bottom. The neck region

The Brassie or Copper John (from left) might do a fine job of representing sand-and-pebble-cased caddis. The Gold-Ribbed Hare's Ear or Herl Nymph resemble quite a few vegetation-cased caddis.

of the fly represents the forward part of the body. Inside the protection of the case, caddis larvae are portly, pale, and grublike. Perhaps the Peeking Caddis is so successful because it captures many triggers that might cause a trout to strike. That stretched neck is the most obvious of them.

PEEKING CADDIS, CREAM *George Anderson*

Hook:	2XL, 2X heavy, size 12–16
Weight:	10–15 turns nonlead wire
Thread:	Black 6/0 or 8/0
Rib:	Oval gold tinsel
Body:	Hare's mask fur
Neck:	Cream dubbing
Legs:	Brown partridge fibers
Head:	Black ostrich herl

PEEKING CADDIS, OLIVE *George Anderson*

Hook:	2XL, 2X heavy, size 12–16
Weight:	10–15 turns nonlead wire
Thread:	Black 6/0 or 8/0
Rib:	Oval gold tinsel
Body:	Dark hare's mask fur
Neck:	Pale olive dubbing
Legs:	Brown partridge fibers
Head:	Black ostrich herl

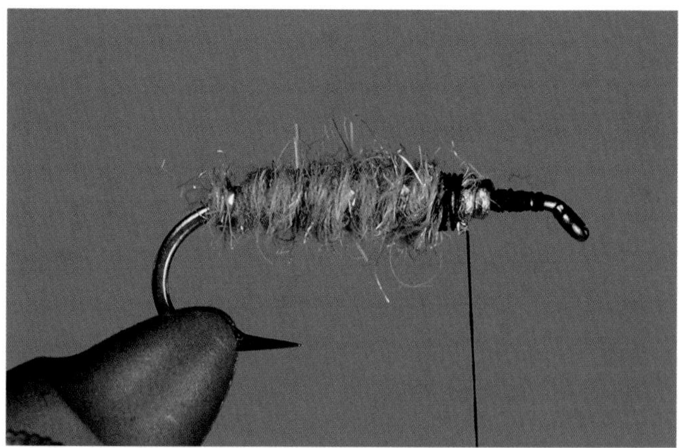

Step 1. Fix the hook in the vise, and weight it with ten to fifteen turns of nonlead wire. Start your thread behind the eye, and take enough turns to form a slight thread ramp to the front shoulder of the weighting wire. Run the thread to the back of the wire and repeat the process there. Tie in oval tinsel between the back shoulder of the wire and the bend of the hook. Use the direct-dubbing method to form a somewhat stout and slightly tapered body forward, stopping about two-fifths the shank length behind the eye. Wind the ribbing forward in four to six evenly spaced turns, tie it off, and clip the excess.

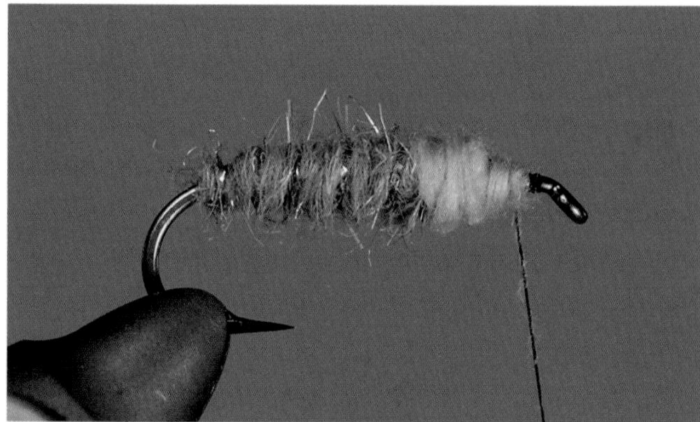

Step 2. Dub a neck of lighter fur or synthetic forward over half the remaining shank, between the body and hook eye. In order to appear as a trigger to trout, this neck must be in strong contrast to the body color. It represents the almost white or pale green body of the natural larva straining out the front of the case.

Step 3. Even the tips of five to ten partridge fibers, and clip or strip them from the feather. Measure them to a point just short of the hook point. Tie them in on the far side of the hook, at the end of the neck. Their tips should angle more down than out to the side. Repeat on the near side with five to ten more fibers. Clip the butts.

Step 4. Tie in two or three black ostrich herls behind the hook eye. Wind three to five turns of the herl from the end of the neck to the hook eye. Tie it off and clip the excess. Form a small thread head, and whip-finish the fly. Clip the thread. Use the forefinger and thumb of your off hand to stroke the ostrich herls back. The contrast between the body, pale neck, and black head should be distinct.

Cased caddis larvae cannot swim. Any imitation for them should be fished on the bottom, with a dead-drift presentation. The way you rig to fish the Peeking Caddis will depend on the type of water in which you're fishing it. If the water is deep, or fast, or deep and fast, then use the traditional shot-and-indicator rig to get the fly down to the bottom and keep it there. If the water is shallow, or slow, or shallow and slow, then rig it with an indicator but without added weight on the leader. You can also try it as a dropper off a dry fly that is at least one size larger—better yet, two or three sizes bigger to be sure it floats over the weighted nymph. If you fish the Peeking Caddis often in gentle currents, you might want to weight it lightly, or not at all.

PEEPING CADDIS

Carl Richards and Bob Braendle list an interesting Peeping Caddis in their book *Caddis Super Hatches.* It is tied backward, with the head and legs of the imitation protruding out of the case and over the bend of the hook. I'll confess to not having fished it myself, but will list it here because it offers concepts to which you should give serious thought if you collect a cased caddis on which trout are feeding selectively. Though the orginators list it with both a fur case and a hard sand and pebble case, I'll describe only the fur-cased variation. To convert it to a hard-body, coat the fur body with epoxy, and bury it in sand and pebbles. When the glue is dry, brush off the material that fails to stick, and the remains will look remarkably like a natural cased caddis larva.

Because I feel that trout feed most often and most happily on vegetation-cased larvae, I recommend trying that version before coating it with glue and rolling it in sand. Save that for occasions that clearly call for it. However, don't eliminate those moments from streamside possibilities, or you'll fail to notice them when they happen.

PEEPING CADDIS ***Carl Richards and Bob Braendle***

Hook:	2XL, 2X heavy, size 12–16
Weight:	10–15 turns of nonlead wire
Thread:	Brown 6/0 or 8/0
Head:	Olive or yellow Antron yarn, singed
Legs:	Partridge hackle
Case:	Spun squirrel or hare's mask fur, with guard hairs, clipped

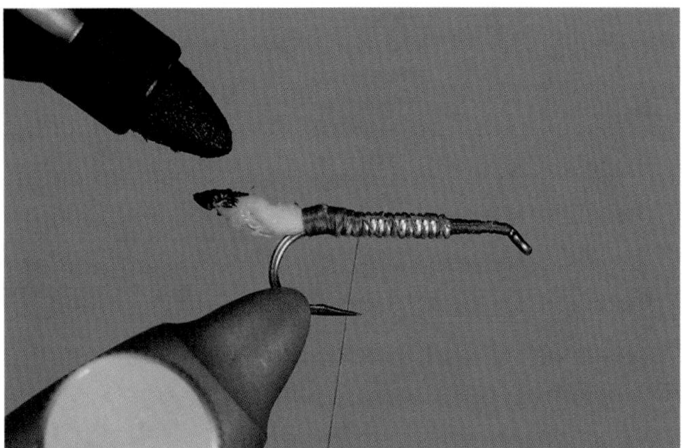

Step 1. Debarb the hook and fix it in the vise. Take ten to fifteen turns of nonlead weighting wire over the shank, positioned so that the balance of the weight is behind the midpoint of the hook. Start your thread and build slight ramps to the front and back shoulders of the wire. Tie in one-quarter to one-third inch of Antron yarn, extending over the bend of the hook. Use a cigarette lighter to singe it to the desired length, a bit short of the hook-gap width. If the lighter does not blacken the tip, use a waterproof black marker to darken it.

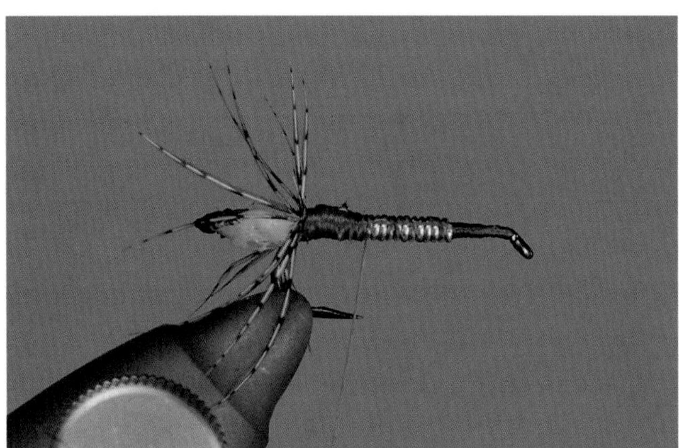

Step 2. Select a brown partridge feather with short fibers, remove fuzzy fibers from the lower stem, and tie it in behind the head. Take a turn or two of the hackle and tie it off, clipping the excess. Hold the fibers forward, and use thread turns to both secure the fragile stem and lock them in that position.

Step 3. Using the dubbing loop method (see page 50), capture a substantial portion of hare's mask or squirrel fur between waxed strands of thread. Twist them into a loose loop, what would be a fur hackle if we weren't using it to make a fur body.

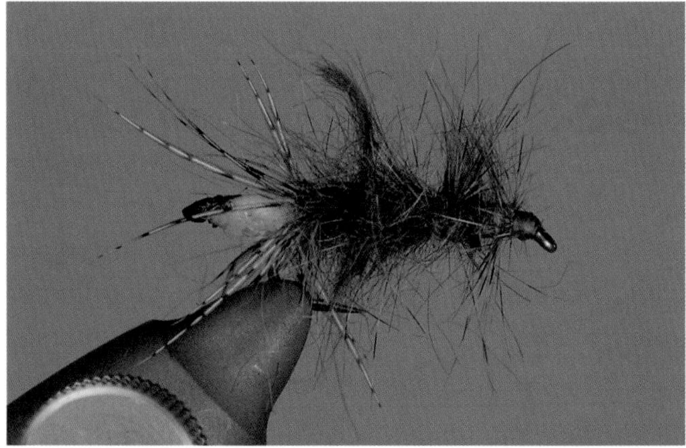

Step 4. Wind the dubbing loop to the eye of the hook. Tie it off there and clip the excess loop. Use a few turns of thread to make a head. Whip-finish the fly and clip the thread. At this point, the body of the fly should be a shaggy mess.

Step 5. Use your scissors, laid parallel to the hook shank, to clip the unruly fur into a tapered body, representing the case of the natural caddis. This procedure will be much easier in a rotary vise.

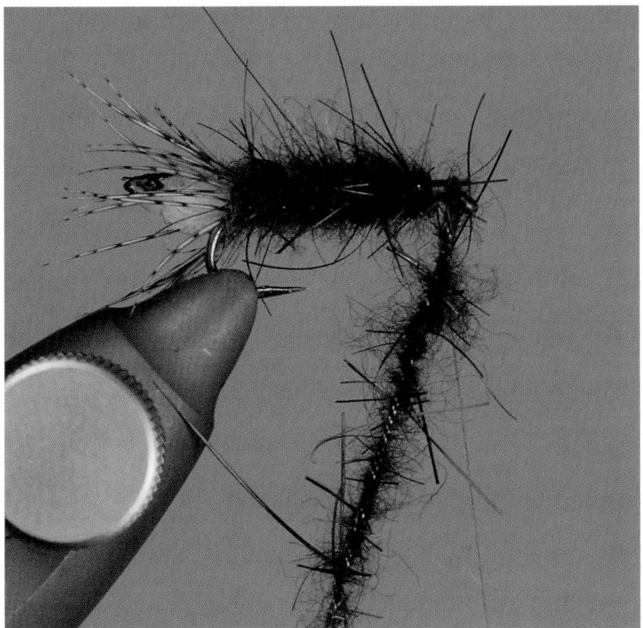

Alternate Body Step 1. Many commercial dubbing brushes, available at fly shops or through mail-order catalogs, can be purchased premade. They're wound on fine wire, so they hold their shape and are very easy to work with. If you try one, it's unlikely you'll go back to making your own dubbing loops for this particular fly type.

Alternate Body Step 2. If you use a premade dubbing brush, you'll often find that it's not necessary to give the fly a final haircut. Pluck out a few wildly stray fibers, if you desire, but don't forget that many cased caddis larvae incorporate conifer needles into their cases, and those stray fibers might make your fly look better rather than worse to a trout.

You can change the initial yarn color to reflect any color "neck" you'd like.

These are the sorts of complicated nymphs that you should tie and fish only if you get a lot of enjoyment at the bench tying difficult flies. When you tie them by the half dozen or dozen of a size and color, the steps ease out, become far less difficult. The results are pretty, kind of cute, and they do catch trout. I'm not sure they catch any more trout than the less difficult Peeking Caddis, but there is a sense of satisfaction in tying on a fly that you've tied yourself, and that you think is pretty, even if it turns out that trout don't care.

FREE-LIVING AND NET-SPINNING CADDIS LARVAE

Free-living and net-spinning caddis larvae (Hydropsyche) *are most often some shade of olive, from drab to bright. Trout might see them in either a somewhat straight posture or curled up.*

The simplest approach to the green rock worms, and the closely related net-spinning caddis, which are most often green as well, but are sometimes tan, is with a twisted-yarn body finished off with a fur thorax. Add a beadhead to attract the attention of trout, and you have a fine rock worm imitation. You also have a Beadhead Serendipity, though on a bit larger hook than that used for the universal searching pattern (see page 123). It is reinforcement of the concept that the best searching-nymphs look a little like a lot of things, and in many cases almost exactly like something that is very abundant in nature.

Most brisk riffles, such as this one on the Deschutes River, are loaded with net-spinning caddis larvae, and trout are always on the lookout for them.

YARN CADDIS LARVA

A nymph similar to the Serendipity can be tied with a tightly twisted fur noodle (see page 53). The result will be a bit rougher, but trout haven't been discovered to notice the difference between rock worms tied with yarn and fur. Choose your material to suit yourself. If you collect rock worms in a particular shade of tan or green in your home waters, and have the right color fur but the wrong color yarn, tie with what you have unless you have other reasons to run to your local fly shop. Be sure to try your fur colors wet, however, before you conclude you've found the perfect match. On the experimental rock, dyed furs often change color when wet.

Z-lon, and many similar fibers, are not yarns, but can be used in a suitable thickness, and twisted so that when wound they form segmented bodies.

YARN CADDIS LARVA

Hook:	Curved scud, size 10–16
Bead:	Gold
Weight:	10–15 turns nonlead wire
Thread:	Brown 6/0 or 8/0
Abdomen:	Green or tan Antron yarn or Z-lon
Thorax:	Brown dubbing

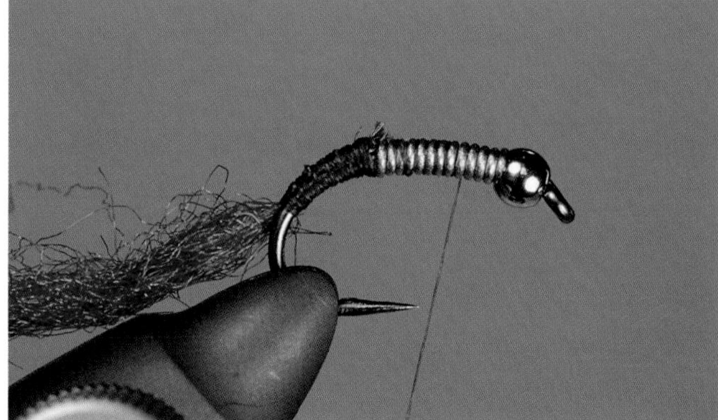

Step 1. Debarb the hook and slip a tapered bead to the eye, with the open end toward the rear. Wind ten to fifteen turns of nonlead weighting wire, and jam the front end into the back of the bead, or tight against it. Start

your thread behind the weighting wire, and use enough turns to form a slight tapered ramp to the back shoulder. Tie in your yarn behind the shoulder, and use enough turns of thread to level out the transition from the hook shank up onto the weighting wire.

Step 2. Twist the yarn into a tight skein, capture the end in your hackle pliers, and take it forward in tightly abutted turns to a point about one-fifth the shank length behind the bead. Be sure to leave plenty of room for the thorax fur. Retwist the yarn as you take turns forward, to keep it tight. Let it relax after the last turn, before tying it off, to keep the tie-in point from forming a lump.

Step 3. Fix a small amount of dubbing to the thread. Wind it forward in two to four turns to fill in the space between the abdomen and the back of the bead. Tuck a whip-finish in the space between the fur and the bead, and clip your thread. Tidy up the fur if you'd like, for the larva. If you leave it long, it can represent the wing cases of the pupal stage of the same insect. You will often find the precise same dressing listed as both a larva and a pupa, with the only difference being the tidiness or looseness of the fur thorax.

LACE CADDIS LARVA

You can capture the fleshiness of the natural caddis larva more closely with bodies wound of soft lace tubing. You might also coax trout into holding on to these imitations a bit longer before they expel them as bad goods. Though it's at least slightly speculative, it's not a bad guess that a trout detects the incorrect texture of a dubbed or hard body quite quickly. A nymph with a soft stretch lace body might not be ejected so instantly. When you're fishing deep, and must wait for information about a take to be transmitted up the leader and through the indicator to your eye, every hesitation helps.

Tubing comes in several thicknesses, suitable to small, medium, and large hooks, and in all colors of the natural insect spectrum. It is, however, semitransparent, and when stretched, it is thinner, less opaque. The color of whatever is under it will not necessarily dominate the color of the tubing, but it might keep the true color of the tubing from becoming the final color of the fly body. You must be careful, when tying with lace, to use a thread color, or to construct an underbody, that agrees with the color of the tubing.

You can also wrap an underbody of one color, and cover it with tubing of another, to create an undercolor and overcolor. By using a bright thread or floss color, and covering the hook, then wrapping clear tubing over it, you can achieve a transluscence that is present in some natural insects, though unfortunately, not often in caddis larvae.

I'll list the Lace Caddis Larva in the two most common colors of the naturals, green and tan. You can vary the brightness of your undercolor to achieve any shade of green, to imitate larvae you collect in your home waters. The nymph can also be tied without a bead, which will make it more exactly imitative. Other variations can be tied with a brass or tungsten bead for brightness or a quicker sink, or with a colored glass bead to reinforce or contrast with the color of the lace body.

Lace patterns can take many forms; the common material to all of them is the soft body. From left: olive standard, with green glass bead, red glass bead, and black tungsten bead; tan standard, and tan with gold bead.

LACE CADDIS LARVA

Hook: Curved scud, size 10–16
Weight: 10–20 turns nonlead wire
Thread: Green or brown 6/0, 3/0, or silk
Underbody: Working thread, or floss
Abdomen: Lace tubing, green, brown, or clear
Thorax: Tannish brown dubbing

If you choose thread for the underbody, it's wise to avoid fine 8/0 except on small nymphs. Instead, use 6/0 or even thicker 3/0, or silk thread.

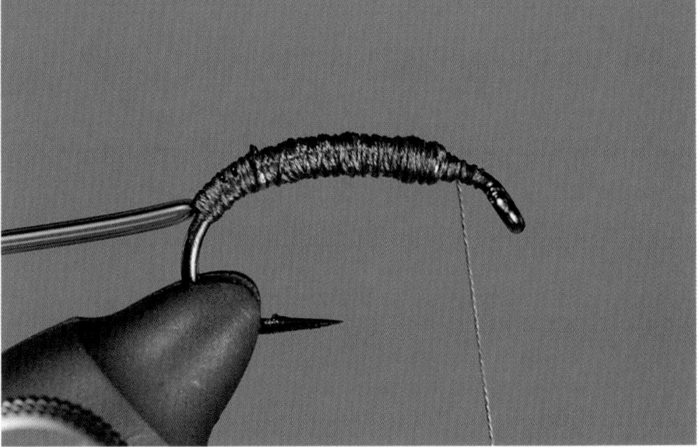

Step 1. Debarb the hook, fix it in the vise, and wind weighting wire over the center half to two-thirds of the shank. Start your thread in front of the wire, use enough turns to lock it in, and overwind past the wire and halfway around the bend of the hook. Return the thread to the back shoulder of the weighting wire. Tie in a few inches of tubing just behind the wire shoulder, with four or five tight turns of thread. Stretch the tubing slightly, and overwrap it tightly with thread halfway down the bend and back. Overwrap the weighting wire and hook shank with thread until it is covered, and you have a fairly even underbody, from the tubing tie-in point to the front shoulder of the weighting wire.

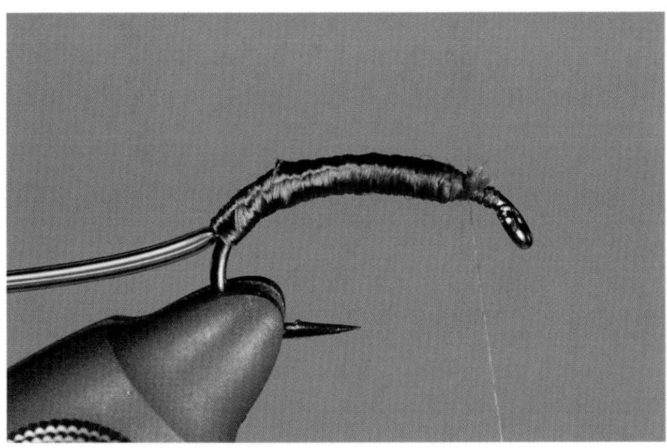

Alternate Step 1. Debarb the hook, fix it in the vise, layer the weighting wire, start the thread, and tie in the tubing as in Step 1 above. Tie in a few inches of floss the color you'd like for the underbody. Wrap it forward to the front shoulder of the weighting wire, tie it off there, and clip the excess. It should form an even underbody, and cover all of the weighting wire and hook shank.

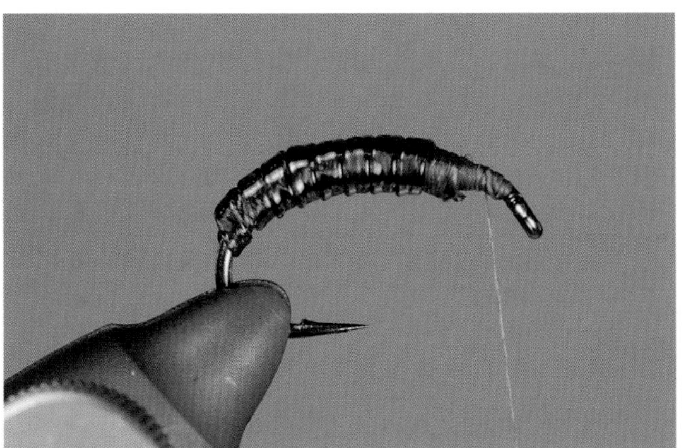

Step 2. Stretch the tubing a bit, and wind it forward in tightly adjacent wraps to a point two or three hook-eye lengths behind the eye. Continuing to stretch it, tie it off with four or five tight wraps of thread. Clip the excess, then secure the end of the tubing with several more turns of thread.

Step 3. Apply a small amount of dubbing to the thread. Wind it forward from the end of the abdomen to just behind the hook eye. Form a neat thread head, whip-finish, clip the thread, and cement the head.

Step 4. The natural free-living caddis larva is a compact beast, with few peripheral parts beyond its legs. The dark dubbed thorax of the imitation copies the darkened plates on the head and three thoracic segments. These are nonmoving, and small. The fly is more imitative if you leave the thorax tightly dubbed, but there are those among us who can't stand tidiness, and have to muss it up if we've achieved it. By picking out the dubbing with a dubbing hook, you can cause the fur to represent legs, and also to make the finished fly look a bit like a pupa, with its swept-back wing cases. It's your choice.

LACE MICROCADDIS LARVA

Before leaving lace tubing, Ed Engle has a nice chapter on microcaddis in his *Tying Small Flies,* and it includes a lace-bodied pattern that is not wound in the normal fashion. It's worth covering here because it's a simple way to imitate caddis larvae in size 16 down to 22. You need tubing of a size that will slip over the hook eye and a thin underbody of thread. That will usually be one thickness up from the size you would wind as a body on the same size hook.

It's interesting, but not necessarily important, to note that what all entomologists call microcaddis differs from what most angling literature refers to as microcaddis. In angling, the term *microcaddis* has been used to indicate any caddis larva, pupa, or adult size 18 and smaller. In taxonomic terms, microcaddis is the common name for the family Hydroptilidae, the members of which are so small that imitations would need to be tied on hooks size 28, 30, 32, and even smaller. When you camp next to a stream, leave the lantern on after dark, and forget to put the butter in the cooler, microcaddis adults are the tiny dark dots that make it look as if somebody got excited with the pepper shaker over the butter tub.

If you choose to ignore true microcaddis, and call the general run of tiny caddisflies by that term, you're far from making a mistake, except to a taxonomist. Several families of caddis are represented by tiny larvae. In all families of caddis, the larvae are tiny when they first leave the egg. Many case-building caddis leave construction for later instars, and spend their first few weeks or even months in a free-living form. A small lace larva dressing has a lot of counterparts in nature.

LACE MICROCADDIS LARVA ***Ed Engle***

Hook:	Straight-shank or curved scud, size 18–22
Thread:	Olive, tan, or desired undercolor, 3/0, 6/0, or silk
Body:	Olive, tan, or clear lace
Head:	Peacock herl

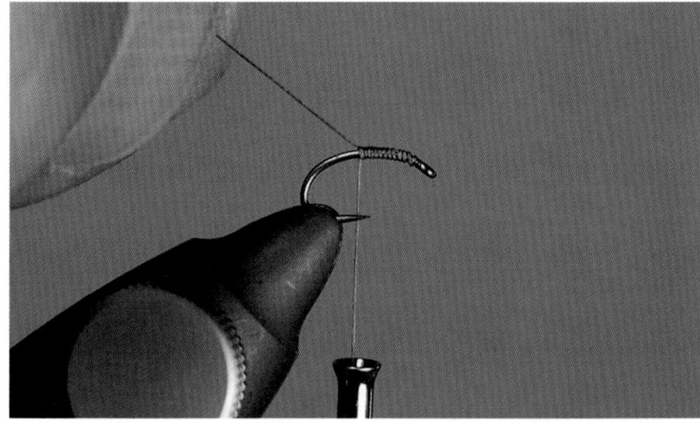

Step 1. Use a single layer of thread to make an underbody. This should cover the hook shank completely, leaving no gaps. One way to do this is to hold the tag end of your thread vertically over the hook shank, and let each turn of thread around the hook shank slide down this sloped tag. The tag forces the wrap of thread to seat itself against the one before it. When you get to the point on the hook where you want to tie in the tube body, clip the tag.

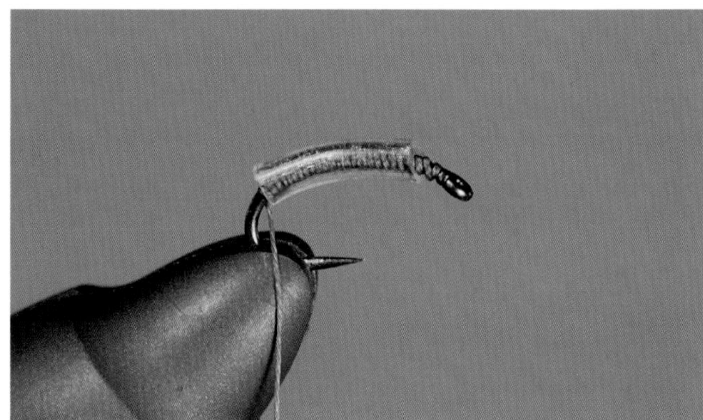

Step 2. Cut a section of tubing three-quarters the length of the shank, slip it over the hook eye, and stop at your thread.

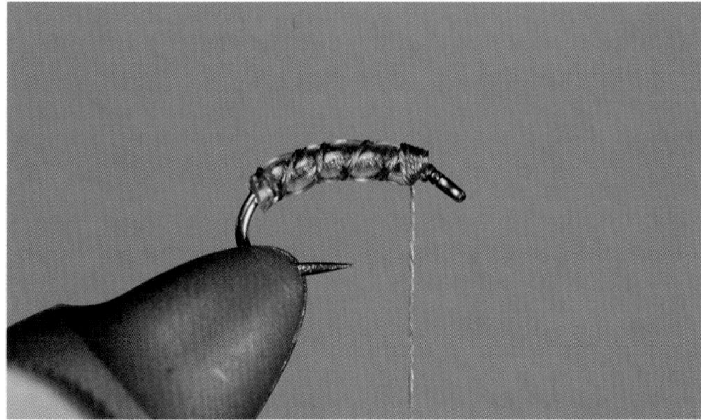

Step 3. Secure the back end of the tubing with a couple turns of thread. Spiral the thread forward to the end of the tubing, similar to a rib. Take a few extra turns there to secure it.

Step 4. Tie in a single peacock herl. Take two to three wraps of herl forward, leaving room to make a fly head that does not crowd the hook eye. Clip the excess herl, take minimal turns of thread to form a head, and whip-finish.

Microcaddis larva patterns, usually in olive, but restricted only by the thread and tubing colors on your tying bench, are excellent when fished as droppers off dry flies. They're also good in combination with other, larger nymphs, when rigged with more standard nymphing setups and fished along the bottom.

CADDIS PUPAE

In the pupal stage, all caddis have essentially the same shape. They vary widely in size, from a portly size 6 down to a small, but still somewhat bulbous, size 20. They range in color from very pale cream, almost white, to very dark green, almost black. It seems that to match all of them, you would need to tie and carry patterns in an extreme range of sizes, over a vast spectrum of colors. But a small academic exercise has helped me condense that down to a very narrow set of colors, each tied in a restricted set of sizes. I hope it will help you, as well.

It's difficult to take good photos of caddis pupae, at least for me. I don't like to take stomach pump samples from a trout I plan to release, though I do take throat pump samples on occasion. Pumping a trout caught during a caddis emergence is the one best way to capture caddis pupa samples. The second best way is to take several kick-net samples, tweezer through them searching for the cylindrical cocoons that encase the pupae. You won't find many, but if a hatch is in progress, you will find one once in a while.

To take a photo of a caddis still cocooned, it must be surgically removed from the tight silk windings in which it is has entombed itself. The surgery metaphor is not an accident: in my aquatic insect photo kit, I carry fine-pointed tweezers, hemostats, and scissors—almost everything from a medical kit except a scalpel, and I probably should have that. The silk cocoon is tough; the insect inside is extremely fragile. About half the time when trying to extract one, the patient is lost, and is no longer suitable for photos. The other half of the time, the subject squirms so much that it's almost impossible to get it to pose for a photo. As a result of all these problems, I have many bad photos of caddis pupae, but very few good ones.

For my little foray into academia, however, I looked through all the photos of pupae I had, good or bad, and noted their sizes and colors. It wound up being a sample of only about thirty, probably not statistically significant.

Green caddis pupa.

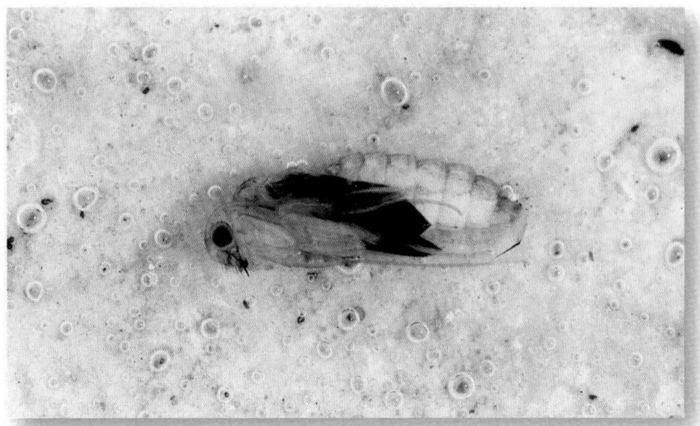

Tannish cream caddis pupa.

Golden brown caddis pupa.

However, I suspect it revealed good information about the ranges of sizes and colors of caddis pupae fed on by trout.

I had to crank some guesswork about color into my equations, which I confess makes them less valid. Caddis pupae removed from their cocoons can be in any stage of the transformation from larva to adult, and they'll be different colors at different points in the transition. The mature adult caddis is in the end contained within the exoskeleton of the pupa, which is called the *pharate adult*. The colors of the pupal body darken as it approaches maturity, and the colors of the wing cases and thorax darken a lot. So in many cases I was forced to estimate from an insect captured early in its transformation what it might look like later, in its trip up to the surface for emergence, which is when a trout would have a chance to eat it, and you and I would want to imitate it.

The result of looking at my photos and including my guesswork about eventual colors narrowed the need for caddis pupa imitations considerably. I found three colors almost exclusive in my photos: green, tannish cream, and golden brown bodies, all with dark brown wing cases. These body colors have been interpreted in various fly-fishing books as olive, dirty cream, and amber or ginger, terms with which I have no quarrel, since they result in about the same colors in the resulting imitations. The size range for each color, in my sample, broke down roughly to size 12 to 18 for green, size 12 to 20 for tannish cream, and size 8 to 14 for golden brown.

I am certain that extensive collecting over the broad geographic range of caddis, which is everywhere in the world that trout live, would turn up important caddis pupae outside these narrow color and size ranges. I am also certain that shade variations exist within all of the colors, and that trout might become so picky that they insist on a fly that is the precise right shade of the color. But I suspect a small fly box that averaged out the listed colors, in the correct sizes, would almost always contain a working imitation for almost any caddis pupa situation you might encounter on this continent.

BEADHEAD DUBBED CADDIS PUPA

The easiest way to match caddis pupae is simply to tie a dubbed-bodied larval imitation and leave the thoracic dubbing mix untrimmed. You could easily reduce it to the even simpler formula of always tying the fly the same way, and fishing it deep for caddis larvae, shallow for caddis pupae. Your fly boxes would be a lot lighter, and in truth you'd probably solve most of the subsurface caddis problems you get into on streams and rivers.

It's important to remember that some dyed furs lose their colors when wet, whereas most synthetics do not. A wide range of materials can be used for the following dubbed pupal patterns, but be sure, before you settle on a dubbing color and tie a big batch of flies with it, that the material retains the color you're after when you dunk it in water. Unless you've discovered some way to catch fish that I don't know about, your fly is going to get wet when you present it to trout.

BEADHEAD DUBBED CADDIS PUPA, GREEN

Hook: Curved scud, size 12–18
Bead: Gold
Weight: 8–15 turns of nonlead wire
Thread: Brown 6/0 or 8/0
Abdomen: Green dubbing
Thorax and wing cases: Brown dubbing

BEADHEAD DUBBED CADDIS PUPA, TANNISH CREAM

Hook: Curved scud, size 12–20
Bead: Gold
Weight: 8–15 turns of nonlead wire
Thread: Brown 6/0 or 8/0
Abdomen: Tannish cream dubbing
Thorax and wing cases: Brown dubbing

BEADHEAD DUBBED CADDIS PUPA, GOLDEN BROWN

Hook: Curved scud, size 8–14
Bead: Gold
Weight: 10–20 turns of nonlead wire
Thread: Brown 6/0 or 8/0
Abdomen: Golden brown dubbing
Thorax and wing cases: Brown dubbing

Step 1. Debarb the hook, slip a tapered bead over the shank, wrap nonlead weighting wire behind the bead, and jam the front of the wire into the back of the bead, or tightly against it. Start your thread behind the back shoulder of the wire, and form a slight ramp to the wire before taking the thread halfway down the bend of the hook. Twist a fair portion of dubbing fairly tightly to the thread. Dub a body forward over three-quarters of the shank. It should be about as fat at the back as it is at the front.

Step 2. Fix a smaller amount of brown dubbing loosely to the thread. You are going to tease it out; stray and wild fibers sticking out should not bother you. Wind this forward from the end of the abdomen to the back of the bead. Tuck a whip-finish tight in behind the bead, and clip your thread.

Step 3. Use your bodkin point or a dubbing roughing tool to tease out the thorax dubbing. Draw it down and back so that it represents both the legs and wing cases of the natural caddis pupa. If a lot of wild fibers protrude from the top, you can cut them off. If you leave them, they might represent the antennae of the natural, which this simple tie omits.

I often make the mistake of fishing this type of fly on the swing, in fairly fast water, as if it were a wet fly. But trout don't often make the mistake of taking it that way when I do. Natural caddis pupae do not have the strength to swim upstream against any but the weakest currents. If you're fishing very soft water, swinging the fly is workable, but a slow current doesn't give a swinging fly much animation. It's generally best to fish caddis pupa patterns along the bottom, rigged in whatever way it takes to get the fly there, drifting along freely, or to suspend them inches to a foot or so deep, beneath a strike indicator or a high-floating dry fly. In this way you imitate the pupa in one of its two staging areas: along the bottom, just after it has cut its way out of its cocoon but hasn't yet started its trip to the top, or near the surface, after it has completed its swim and is resting in preparation for that last aquatic adventure of its life, when it breaks through the surface film and frees itself as the aerial insect.

Z-WING CADDIS PUPA

Mike Mercer's Z-Wing Caddis Pupa is a more exact imitation, and a more exacting tie. The Z-lon wing captures some of the flash of the natural. Caddis pupae are buoyed to the surface, in many cases, by gases trapped between the exoskeleton of the pupa, loose and about to be cast off, and the inner skin of the adult caddis, about to be launched. These gases are highly reflective, and might be the trigger that key trout to strike. The Z-lon in Mercer's pattern might be the bright spot trout notice before committing to the imitation.

Z-WING CADDIS PUPA, GREEN *Mike Mercer*

Hook: Curved scud, size 12–18
Bead: Copper
Weight: None, or 6–10 turns nonlead wire
Thread: Olive 6/0 or 8/0
Rib: Chartreuse 3/0 Monocord or similar
Body carapace: Dark golden brown turkey tail feather section
Abdomen: Green fur and Antron dubbing mix
Wing cases: Dark dun Z-lon
Collar: Bright green Antron dubbing
Head: Peacock herl

Z-WING CADDIS PUPA, CREAM *Mike Mercer*

Hook: Curved scud, size 12–20
Bead: Copper
Weight: None, or 6–10 turns nonlead wire
Thread: Tan 6/0 or 8/0
Rib: Cream 3/0 Monocord or similar
Body carapace: Dark golden brown turkey tail feather section
Abdomen: Cream fur and Antron dubbing mix
Wing cases: Cream Z-lon
Head: Light gray ostrich herl

Z-WING CADDIS PUPA, AMBER *Mike Mercer*

Hook: Curved scud, size 8–18
Bead: Copper
Weight: None, or 6–10 turns nonlead wire
Thread: Tan 6/0 or 8/0
Rib: Copper wire
Body carapace: Light brown marabou
Abdomen: Golden brown fur and Antron dubbing mix
Wing cases: Ginger Z-lon
Antennae: Wood-duck flank fibers
Head: Tan marabou

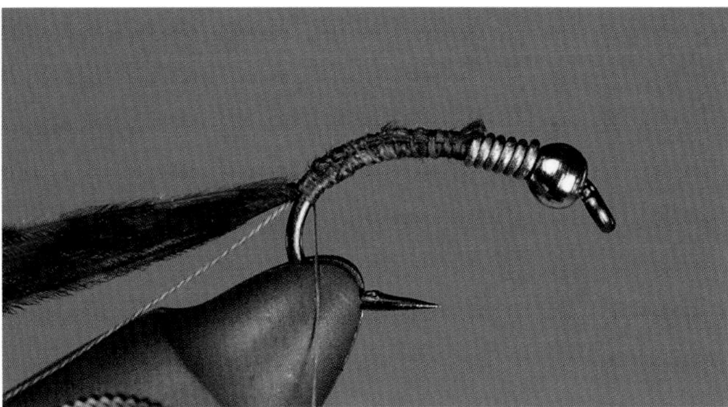

Step 1. Debarb the hook and slip a bead to the eye. Fix the hook in the vise, and wrap six to ten turns of nonlead wire around the shank. Press the weighting wire into the back of the bead, or tight to it. Start your thread behind the wire, build a slight ramp to the back shoulder, and take the thread halfway down the hook bend. Tie in a few inches of ribbing thread. Clip a section of turkey feather about half the width of the hook gap, and tie it in by the narrow end, with the dark side down, at the end of the thread wraps.

Step 2. Dub a stout and only slightly tapered abdomen forward over two-thirds to three-quarters of the hook shank.

Step 3. Draw the body carapace feather section forward to the front of the abdomen, tie it off there, and clip the excess. Wind the ribbing forward over the carapace in evenly spaced wraps, tie it off, and clip the excess.

Step 4. Select a substantial number of strands of Z-lon, fold them in half to create a V-shaped wedge or loop in the center of them, and tie this wedge or loop in at the front of the abdomen. As you overwrap the tie-in point, hold the extended fibers down and to each side of the abdomen, which will result in protruding wing cases. Clip the Z-lon so each wing case reaches almost to the end of the abdomen.

Step 5. If a collar is called for, dub just two or three turns of it, the same diameter as the front of the abdomen, over about half the space between the wing-case tie-in point and the back of the bead. Be sure to work this back against the front of the abdomen, so there is no gap.

Step 6. Tie in two to three peacock herl fibers. Gather them with the thread, and twist them into a rope. Take three to four turns forward between the end of the abdomen, or the front of the collar, and the back of the bead. Separate the thread from the herl, tie off the herl, and clip the excess. Seat a whip-finish between the herl and back of the bead, and clip the thread.

DEEP SPARKLE PUPA

Research for the late Gary LaFontaine's book *Caddisflies* took him underwater, in scuba gear, for the point of view of the trout. He concluded that sparkles of light reflected off bubbles of gas extruded from the body were the trigger that prompted trout to strike a natural caddis pupa. He sought that in his imitations, and found it in Sparkle Yarns, commonly sold under the brand name Antron. He incorporated these fibers in his pupal patterns in both a dubbed underbody and a sheathed overbody. He tied his caddis pupae in both deep and emergent versions. Though I use the emerger as often as the nymph, Gary's Deep Sparkle Pupa becomes the subject of a book on nymphs for streams and stillwaters.

He called for carrying the style in four primary colors and eleven secondary colors. That might be beneficial, but I don't have the tying discipline to accomplish it. I'll describe the Deep Sparkle Pupa here in the three basic colors my own research has revealed are those of the dominant naturals on the wide range of streams and rivers that I fish for trout. I recommend that you learn to tie the style, and extend your tying only when your own collecting reveals the need for one of the secondary colors.

DEEP SPARKLE PUPA BROWN AND BRIGHT GREEN *Gary LaFontaine*

Hook: Standard nymph, size 12–16
Weight: 10–15 turns nonlead wire
Thread: Brown 6/0 or 8/0
Overbody: Medium olive Sparkle Yarn
Underbody: Pale green fur and Antron mix
Legs and antennae: Brown partridge fibers
Head: Brown fur and Antron mix, or brown marabou or ostrich herl

DEEP SPARKLE PUPA CREAM *Gary LaFontaine*

Hook: Standard nymph, size 12–20
Weight: 10–15 turns nonlead wire
Thread: Tan 6/0 or 8/0
Overbody: Tan Sparkle Yarn
Underbody: Cream fur and Antron mix
Legs and antennae: Gray partridge fibers
Head: Tan fur and Antron mix, or tan marabou or ostrich herl

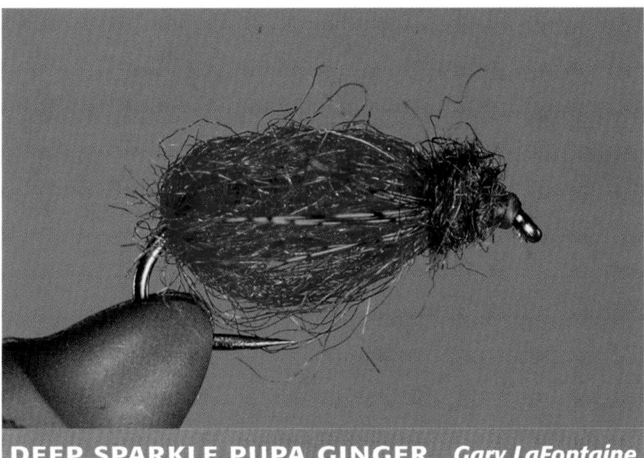

DEEP SPARKLE PUPA GINGER *Gary LaFontaine*

Hook: Standard nymph, size 8–18
Weight: 10–20 turns nonlead wire
Thread: Brown 6/0 or 8/0
Overbody: Amber Sparkle Yarn
Underbody: Ginger fur and Antron mix
Legs and antennae: Brown partridge fibers
Head: Brown fur and Antron mix, or brown marabou or ostrich herl

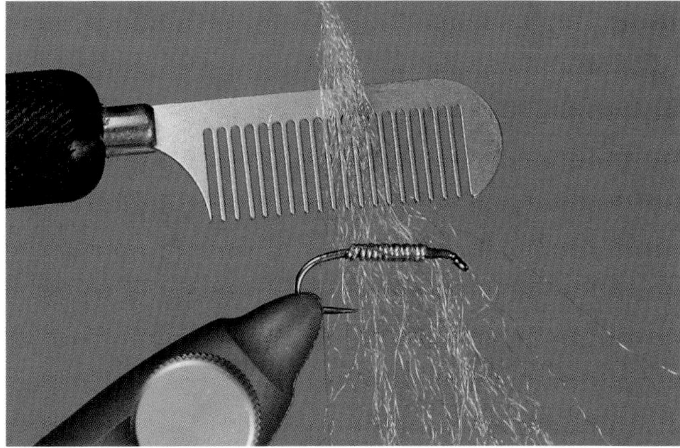

Step 1. Fix the hook in the vise and take ten to fifteen turns of weighting wire around the shank, positioned in the center. Start the thread and build slight ramps to the front and back shoulders of the wire. Take the thread to the bend of the hook. Clip a two- to three-inch skein of Sparkle Yarn. If your yarn has more than one strand, separate them and use just one. The overbody should be somewhat sparse. Use a fine-tooth comb to tease out the skein.

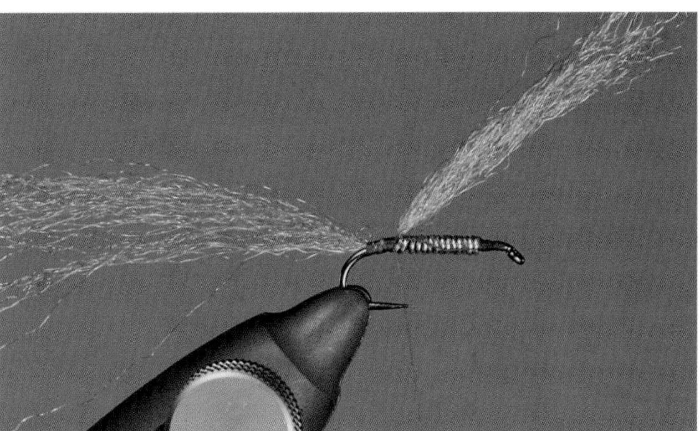

Step 2. Tie the center of the Sparkle Yarn skein in at the bend of the hook. Overwrap it to the back shoulder of the weighting wire. Leave half sticking out the back, the other half over the front.

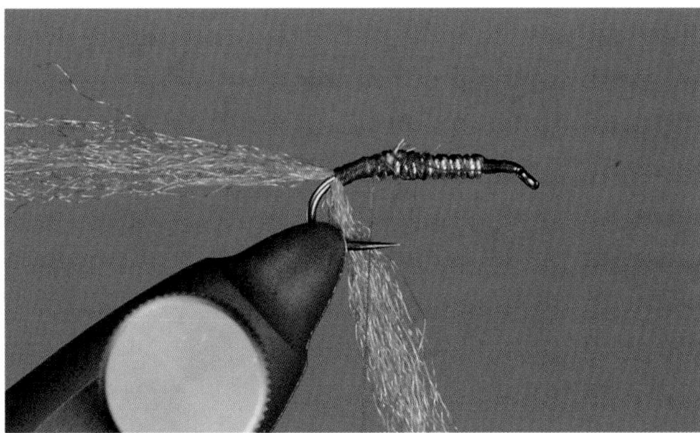

Step 3. Draw the front half of the skein back and down with your off hand, and overwrap it with thread so that it ends protruding from the underside of the hook.

Step 4. Use a loose and fibrous dubbing material, teasing it out if necessary, to make a fairly fat and untapered body over three-quarters of the hook shank. LaFontaine used a chopped Sparkle Yarn that he called Touch Dubbing. It is available commercially from the kind folks at the Book Mailer, highly recommended, and used here.

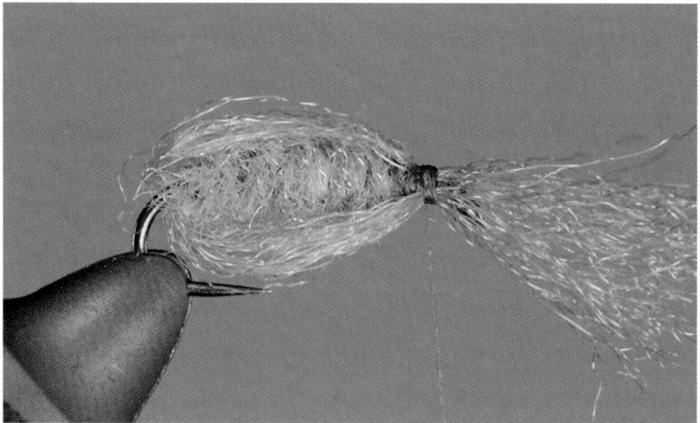

Step 5. Bring the upper skein of Sparkle Yarn over the top of the underbody, and tie it off with a couple loose turns of thread. Repeat with the lower skein, bringing it forward beneath the underbody, and tying it off loosely. Do not cinch it down, and don't clip the excess.

Step 6. Use your bodkin point to tease the overbody into a loose and sparse *bubble* around the underbody. It should be as evenly distributed as you can make it, and not tight against the underbody.

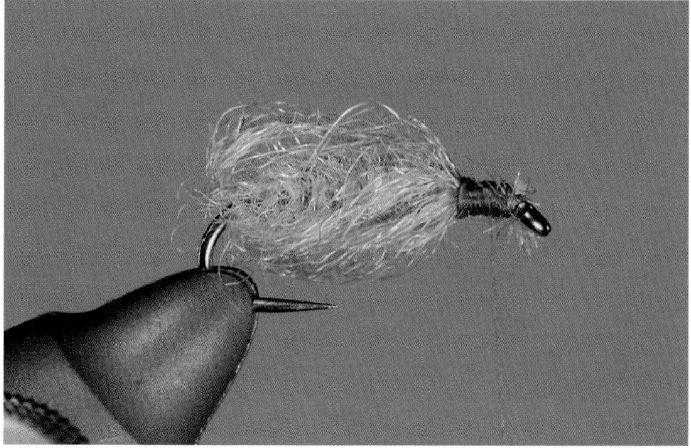

Step 7. Use several tight thread turns to lock the overbody into place. Clip the excess.

Step 8. Remove a few fibers from a partridge feather stem, measure them so they extend to the point of the hook, and tie them in on the near side, in front of the overbody. Repeat on the far side. Clip the excess butts.

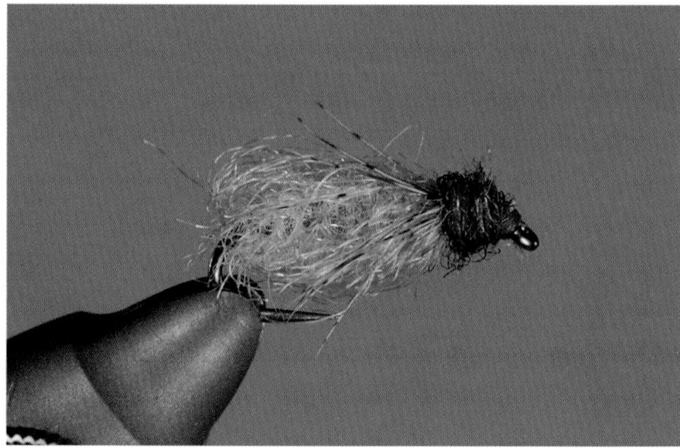

Step 9. Dub a small head, or tie in and wind two to three turns of ostrich or marabou herl. Tie it off, clip the excess, whip-finish, and clip the thread.

As their name implies, Deep Sparkle Pupa patterns are designed to be fished deep. The naturals often drift along the bottom after cutting their way out of the pupal chamber, then swim toward the top fairly rapidly, buoyed by those trapped gases, before staging once again just beneath the surface prior to breaking through for emergence. Your imitation can be fished at any of those levels, but it's best to recall that the naturals contest the currents only in the mid-depths. They drift freely along the bottom, and again toward the top. Your imitation should be rigged to tumble along the bottom, or to drift almost without drag just beneath the surface. A standard shot-and-indicator rig will suffice for fishing the bottom. A yarn indicator, or high-floating dry fly, will serve as support for the same dressing fished shallow.

I have had some luck fishing Deep Sparkle Pupa patterns on the swing, rigged with floating lines and long leaders, presented precisely as if they were wet flies, during fairly heavy hatches. But I've never done as well swinging them as I have fishing them on the drift, either top or bottom.

PULSATING CADDIS PUPA

It has recently become popular to incorporate glass beads into caddis pupa patterns to capture that essence of air bubbles the naturals display to trout. It's a fine idea, but it is often done in heroic ways that require starting the thread, stringing the beads on the hook, clipping the thread, restarting it at the bend behind the beads, and sometimes even clipping and restarting the thread between each couplet of beads. Other methods require the construction of separate bead bodies that are made up and then tied in to trail the hook. All of these methods are fine, in terms of imitation, but they're delaying tactics in terms of getting a few flies tied with which you can go out and imitate caddis pupae.

One simple method to get beads onto a hook, and get an effective result, is to string them on the shank, start the thread behind the hook eye, overwrap the beads to space them and lock them in place, then take turns of loose dubbing forward between them, and finally to tease the dubbing out. The result is similar to that achieved by Gary LaFontaine's Sparkle Pupa concept: an underbody surrounded by a halo of fibers. In this case the underbody is a line of reflective glass beads. If you use Sparkle Yarn, or a fur and Antron mix, your halo of outer fibers will be reflective as well.

The Pulsating Caddis Pupa was originated by Jim Pettis. Many more ways to apply beads to caddis patterns can be found in Joe J. Warren's book *Tying Glass Bead Flies.* For the purpose of this book, that condensed box of flies that match hatches wherever in the world you might find them, I've interpreted the Pettis concept into the three most common colors in which I've found the naturals.

PULSATING CADDIS PUPA, GREEN *Jim Pettis*

Hook: Curved scud, size 12–16
Underbody: Green glass beads
Thread: Brown 6/0 or 8/0
Overbody: Light brown fur and Antron dubbing mix
Legs and antennae: Brown partridge
Head: Dark brown fur and Antron dubbing mix

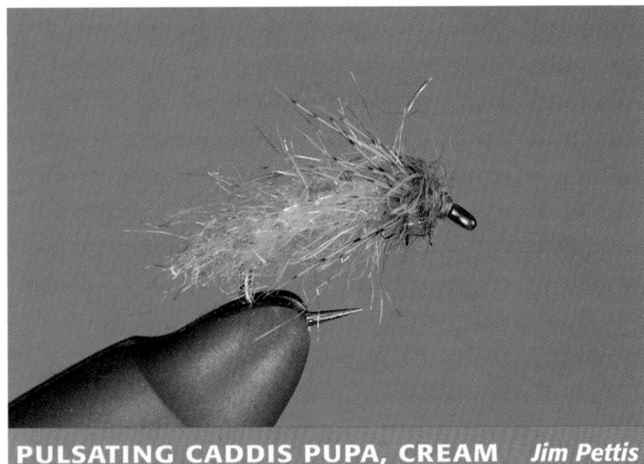

PULSATING CADDIS PUPA, CREAM *Jim Pettis*

Hook: Curved scud, size 12–20
Underbody: Clear glass beads
Thread: Tan 6/0 or 8/0
Overbody: Cream fur and Antron dubbing mix
Legs and antennae: Gray partridge fibers
Head: Tan fur and Antron dubbing mix

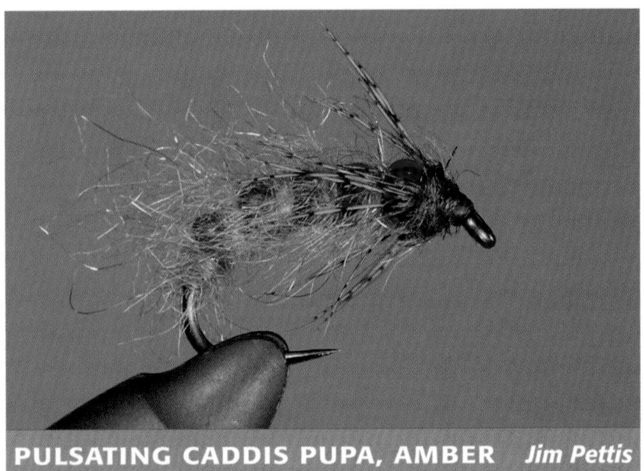

PULSATING CADDIS PUPA, AMBER *Jim Pettis*

Hook: Curved scud, size 8–18
Underbody: Red or amber glass beads
Thread: Brown 6/0 or 8/0
Overbody: Golden brown fur and Antron dubbing mix
Legs and antennae: Brown partridge fibers
Head: Brown fur and Antron dubbing mix

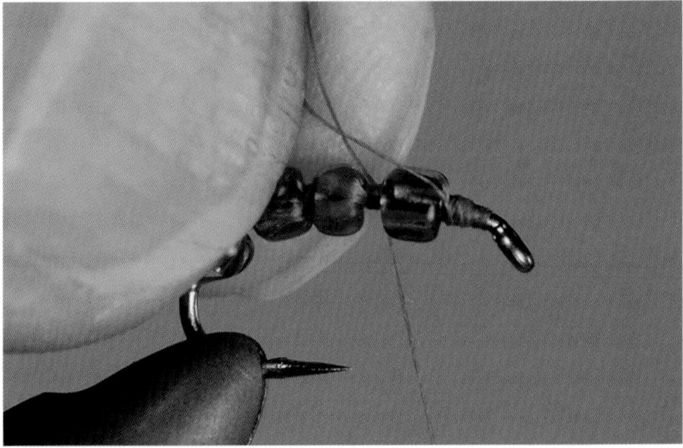

Step 1. String three to five beads on the hook, using a bead size consistent with the hook size, and a number of beads that will cover about half the hook shank. Start your thread behind the hook eye. Hold your first bead in place about one-quarter the shank length behind the eye, and leap the thread over it. To accomplish this thread leap, lock the bead where you want it by bracing it with the nail of your off-hand forefinger. Then take a pinch wrap (see page 45) by securing a thread loop between your off-hand thumb and forefinger, right behind the bead, and letting this loop wrap slide into place behind the bead. It sounds difficult, but becomes very quick and easy after a fly or two.

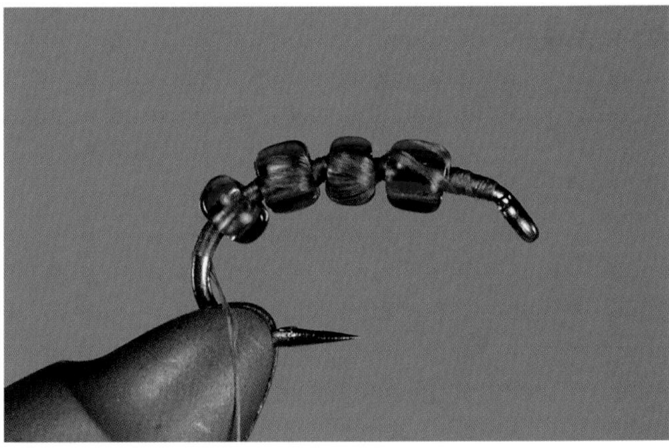

Step 2. Layer thread over a slight gap, hold the second bead in place, and repeat the thread leap to lock it in. Finish with the beads fairly evenly spaced, and the last bead well around the bend of the hook.

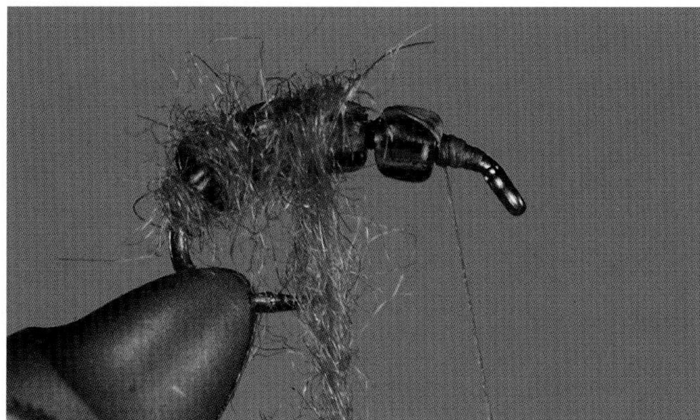

Step 3. Twist a skein of dubbing loosely to the thread, or use a thread loop for a loose and spiky dubbing. Take a turn or two of dubbing behind the last bead, then one or two turns between beads, working forward. Finish with a turn of dubbing in front of the last bead.

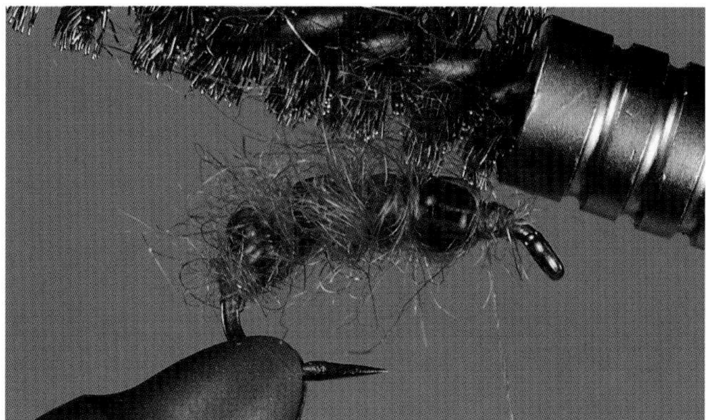

Step 4. Use your bodkin point or a dubbing brush to tease the fur and fibers out around the bead underbody. It should be sparse and very fibrous. If it becomes too unruly, clip it to shape with your scissors. But don't tidy it up to the point where no fibers are left to pulsate in the current. The beads, and their color, should show through this loose overbody.

Step 5. Clip eight to ten partridge fibers from the feather stem, and measure them so they reach the hook point or a bit farther. Caddis pupae have long legs and antennae. Tie them in on the far side of the hook, splaying them rather than gathering them into a tight leg bundle. Repeat on the near side. The result should look almost like a wound hackle. You could use a turn of partridge hackle if you have feathers small enough, but for the sizes in which most caddis pupae are tied, 12 and smaller, a partridge feather usually has fibers that are too long when wound.

Step 6. Fix a small amount of darker dubbing to the thread. Take two or three turns of dubbing forward to the hook eye. The dubbing should be positioned so that it causes the leg and antennae fibers to sweep back. Make a neat thread head, whip-finish, and clip the thread.

I'm in high favor of this particular concept for caddis pupae. It combines several things: the glint of the beads, the reflectance of the trilobal Sparkle Yarns, the roughness that somehow seems to creep into all of my flies, even when I try to keep it out. The most difficult part of tying the Pettis Pulsating Pupa is getting the beads onto the hook. I find that glass beads in bulk at hobby shops are less than consistent in size. I use tweezers, and perform the operation near but not over a wastebasket. If a bead is recalcitrant for any reason, and doesn't want to slip easily onto the hook, I drop it instantly and pick up another. My slightly superstitious belief is that a bead reluctant to go on the hook doesn't belong on the fly, and if it got there, might bring bad luck. Glass beads are cheap.

Bead your hooks in advance. If you're going to tie a half dozen or dozen Pulsating Pupa patterns of a particular size, which I recommend you do, then bead all of the hooks and set them aside before beginning to tie. Be careful when you pick up each beaded hook; you don't want them to slide off on their way to the vise.

These unweighted glass-bead patterns can be fished deep by rigging with indicator and split shot. They're also excellent for fishing shallow, suspended beneath a yarn indicator or dry fly. You might need to pinch a tiny shot six to eight inches up the tippet, just to get them through the surface film and down to where trout expect to see the naturals drifting along, waiting their time for the final break through the surface film.

FOX POOPAH

Originated by Redding, California, guide Tim Fox, the Fox Poopah is an excellent dressing when you decide it's necessary to get down to fairly exact imitation of caddis pupae. The wound underbody of silver tinsel or Krystal Flash gives it the sparkle of light that is beneficial to caddis pupa patterns. The overbody of Vernille, Velvet Chenille, or Ultra Chenille captures the precise shape of the pupal body. It's an excellent dressing during a hatch, when trout are selective to naturals.

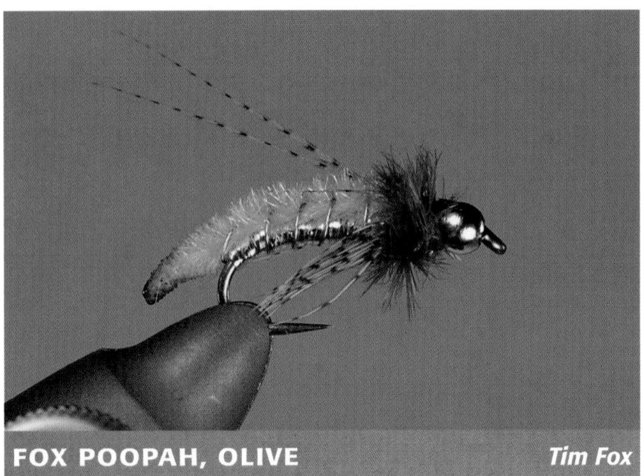

FOX POOPAH, OLIVE *Tim Fox*

Hook: Standard nymph, size 12–18
Bead: Gold
Weight: 10–15 turns fine nonlead wire, optional
Thread: Brown 6/0 or 8/0
Rib: Fine gold or copper wire
Underbody: Silver tinsel or pearl Krystal Flash
Body: Olive Vernille, Velvet Chenille, or Ultra Chenille
Legs: Partridge fibers
Antennae: Wood-duck flank fibers
Head: Brown ostrich herl

FOX POOPAH, TAN *Tim Fox*

Hook: Standard nymph, size 12–18
Bead: Gold
Weight: 10–15 turns fine nonlead wire, optional
Thread: Brown 6/0 or 8/0
Rib: Fine gold or copper wire
Underbody: Silver tinsel or pearl Krystal Flash
Body: Tan Vernille, Velvet Chenille, or Ultra Chenille
Legs: Partridge fibers
Antennae: Wood-duck flank fibers
Head: Brown ostrich herl

FOX POOPAH, BROWN *Tim Fox*

Hook: Standard nymph, size 12–18
Bead: Gold
Weight: 10–15 turns fine nonlead wire, optional
Thread: Brown 6/0 or 8/0
Rib: Fine gold or copper wire
Underbody: Silver tinsel or pearl Krystal Flash
Body: Brown Vernille, Velvet Chenille, or Ultra Chenille
Legs: Partridge fibers
Antennae: Wood-duck flank fibers
Head: Brown ostrich herl

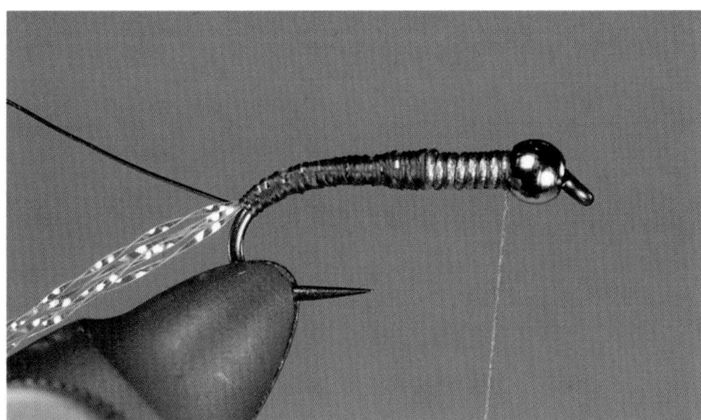

Step 1. Slip a bead on the hook, take ten to fifteen turns of nonlead weighting wire that are undersized for the hook on which you're tying. You'll want to use .025-inch wire on hooks in sizes 10 and 12, .015-inch on sizes 14 and 16, and omit the weight on smaller hooks. Start the thread behind the wire, and build a slight ramp to the back shoulder. Tie in a few inches of ribbing wire, along with the underbody tinsel, or three to five strands of Krystal Flash. Overwrap the body and rib materials well down on the bend of the hook. Take the thread to the back of the bead.

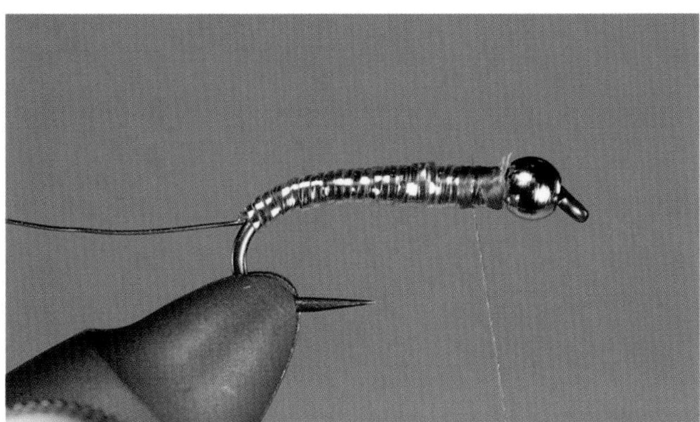

Step 2. Wind the underbody forward to the back of the bead. If you're using several strands of Krystal Flash, it will be necessary to twist them together, and retwist them with each wrap around the hook shank, or they will splay and not cover the weighting wire. You can twist them once and catch them with your hackle pliers, if you find this easier. Tie the underbody off behind the bead, clip the excess, and return your thread to a point about one-fifth to one-quarter the shank length behind the eye.

Step 3. Singe the tip of a short section of overbody chenille, forming a short tapered tip. Measure it so the end extends just beyond the bend of the hook, and tie it in at the end of the underbody.

Step 4. Hold the chenille overbody firmly in place directly on top of the hook shank, and overwrap it with four to six evenly spaced turns of the ribbing wire. Do not let the chenille migrate to the far side of the hook. If it does, use your fingers to boss it back into position on top of the shank.

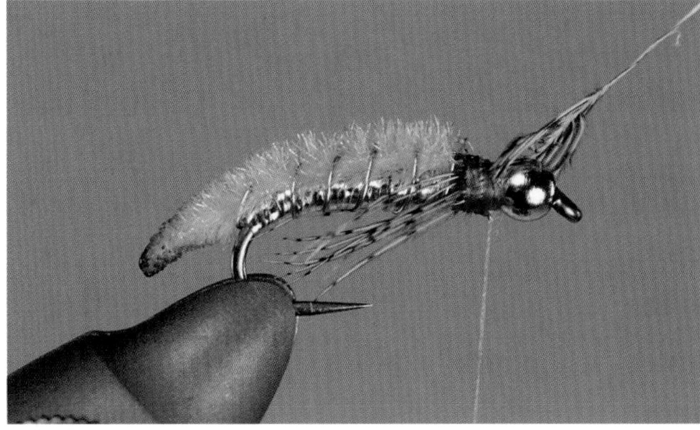

Step 5. Prepare a partridge feather by cleaning fuzz from the base, reversing the remaining fibers, clipping out the tip, and realigning the fibers into their original orientation. Hold this on top of the shank, at the end of the underbody, with an equal numbers of fibers splayed to each side. Do not scrimp on the partridge; the fibers rep-

resent both legs and wing cases on each side of the natural. Tie the feather in so that the fibers extend beyond the hook point. Adjust it for length after a couple loose turns of thread, then lock it down and clip the excess. On small hooks, it might be easier to remove the fibers from the feather and tie them directly in on each side.

Step 6. Even the tips of two wood-duck flank fibers, remove them from the feather, and measure them just beyond the end of the chenille overbody. Tie them in and clip the excess butts. Clip two ostrich herl fibers from the feather, and tie them in by the butts, behind the bead. You can wrap them as they are, but I prefer to twist them together to lessen the chances that they'll separate when you wind them, which creates a head with gaps.

Step 7. Take two to four herl wraps to fill the gap between the end of the body and the back of the bead. Tie off the herl, clip the excess, and tuck a whip-finish behind the bead. Clip the thread.

SUMMARY

My view that caddis pupae fall into three primary color schemes might be an oversimplification, but fly tiers, as opposed to trout, are prone to overcomplication. Complexity sells. I once showed a series of flies I'd designed—a rare happening, because I'm not a dedicated fly designer—to the buyer for one of the contract tier companies. "They're too simple," he told me. "They'll never sell."

I didn't have a problem with that. Half of the business of a commercial tying operation is to provide flies that catch trout. But that turns out to be the second half. The first half is to catch trout fishermen. If they fail to do that, then the flies will never get bought and tested against trout. It all makes sense, and is rooted in the knowledge that a fly fished with confidence will catch more trout than one fished without it. But I grew up fishing simple flies with confidence, and continue to make the same mistake.

I recommend you pick at least one free-living larva pattern, and tie it in green and tan in a narrow range of sizes, 12 to 16. That's probably all you'll ever need, but you can add others if you find them necessary in your own fishing, based on your own collecting. You will also be well served by at least one cased caddis dressing, most likely George Anderson's well-tested and highly approved Peeking Caddis, in just a couple of sizes and colors. These cased larval dressings could easily serve as searching nymphs; they are designed to be fished along the bottom, most often when a specific caddis larva is dominant in the food chain, but also when trout are not feeding selectively on that one insect.

Imitations of caddis pupae are much more important than those for larvae. When pupae are abundant and available, it will be during an emergence. Sometimes the hatch will be heavy, sometimes the pupae will come off in a constant trickle. Trout might see a lot of them, and feed selectively, or see an occasional pupa, and feed eagerly and opportunistically when they can get one. If trout are selective and you don't have a nymph that at least resembles the insect they are taking, you're not likely to catch very many fish. If trout are feeding opportunistically, you increase your chances greatly if your fly resembles the insect they're taking most often: the caddis pupa.

You should choose at least one of the listed pupa dressings, tie it in at least the three colors I've emphasized—green, cream, and golden brown—each in a narrow range of sizes, 12 to 16. If you need to expand your coverage, it's likely to be in the direction of tiny, unless you get onto water with a heavy hatch of fall caddis, in which case you'll want an amber pupa dressing in about size 8.

Caddis imitations should take up about the same amount of room in your selective-nymph box as the mayflies, though you'll find that searching nymphs, if chosen carefully, will often serve for both groups. I'll have to confess that my finest day fishing over caddis pupae is now long in the past, but was with a size 16 Gold-Ribbed Hare's Ear. That searching nymph was exactly the right size and color, and almost precisely the right shape, for a net-spinning caddis species that enjoyed an evening emergence on the Deschutes River. The first trout or two that took the Gold-Ribbed Hare's Ear teased its rough fur into an even better imitation. The longer I fished it, the more trout I caught on it, until what must have been a stout trout whacked it, broke my 4X tippet, and it was too dark to tie on another.

It's important to remember that caddis often emerge just before dark. It's wise to arm yourself with a tiny flashlight.

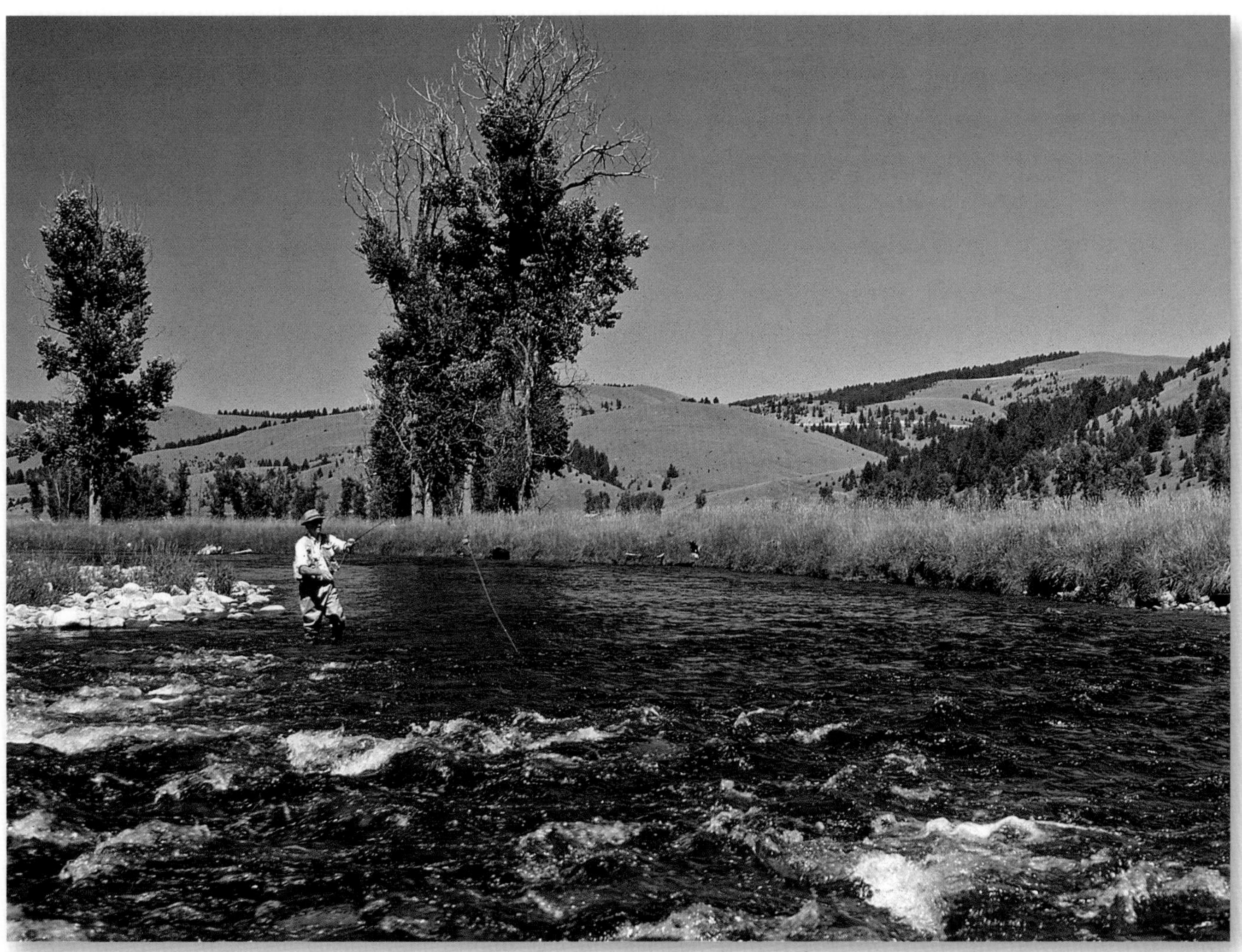

A minimal number of caddis nymph dressings, representing the most common larvae and pupae, will prepare you to solve a lot of moving water situations.

CHAPTER 21

Moving Water Midges

The term *midge* has been used historically, in angling literature, in reference to small flies, size 16 and under. In taxonomic terms, *midge* refers to a member of the order Chironomidae. In recent years, most angling literature has used the term in this literal sense, and I'll use it that way here: a midge is a chironomid, not a small imitation of a mayfly or caddisfly or any other fly.

Midges move up in importance, in angling terms, as current speed slows down. They're least important on small mountain and foothill streams, more important in the lower gradients of mature river systems, most important in spring creeks and tailwaters—and of course, on lakes and ponds. Since an angling life often follows a fairly similar progression, starting off on small, brisk waters, moving through medium-sized freestone streams and small rivers, and finally gravitating toward the types of spring creek and tailwater meccas where matching hatches becomes the goal, midges tend to become more critical as you gain experience. That has certainly been true in my own wanderings on fly-fishing waters.

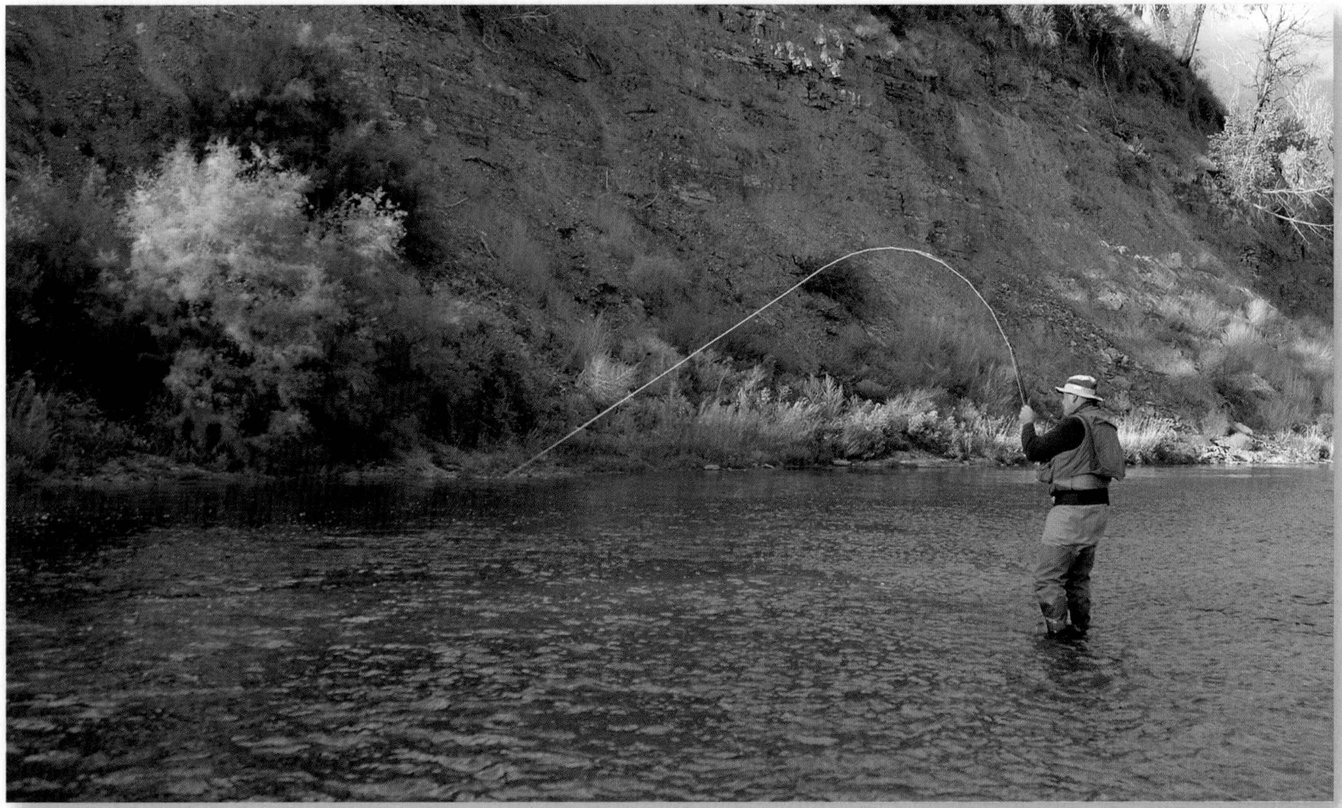

Most moving-water midge fishing will be on the fairly smooth water of spring creeks and tailwaters, such as the Bighorn River in Montana.

Midges in stillwaters seem to arrive in three size ranges. The first is tiny, imitated with size 20 to 24 nymphs. On ponds I fish most often, I call these the *small* hatch. The second is moderate, sizes 16 and 18. I fish these often, and call them the *big* hatch. The final size is very large; their imitations are sometimes tied on long-shank hooks in sizes 8 and 10. These are restricted to northern stillwaters; the farther north you go, the larger lake and pond midges tend to get. I don't have a name for these. But the subject of this chapter is midges in *moving* water.

Stream midges rarely exceed the size range of the smallest lake and pond midges. When you consider midges for moving water, think about spring creeks and tailwaters, and consider that a size 18 imitation will likely be outsized.

Most of my midging has been done on the Deschutes, Missouri, and Bighorn Rivers, all tailwaters. The Deschutes is boisterous, but I've found midges important only on its rare smooth runs and edge currents, never where it's rough. The other two rivers could almost be considered long flats, and midges are important from end to end, wherever trout are found, which in those two rivers is everywhere. You might find midges important on any creek, stream, or river that you fish. But you'll rarely find them important on any flows that are not at least somewhat smooth. The most important recent innovations in midge nymph patterns have been made on the San Juan River in New Mexico, the South Platte River in Colorado, and the Colorado River in Arizona—all tailwaters where midges are tiny and prolific.

About half the pattern styles that are tied for moving-water midges imitate the larval stage. The other half imitate pupae. Midge larvae are essentially wormlike tubes, little different at one end than the other, unless you're looking through a microscope, in which case you'll see a head at one end and fleshy prolegs at the other. Midge pupae are more tapered, have budding wing cases, thoracic segments, and heads that give them a hunchbacked appearance. When you're talking the average size of a moving-water midge, sizes 20 and 22, there is small distinction between a larva and a pupa. I'm going to move out on a limb and guess that a lot of successful patterns that are tied to match midge larvae are taken by trout as midge pupae. When trout feed high enough in the water column to be visible, and to send subsurface riseforms to the top, it's certain they're taking pupae, not larvae.

When trout feed selectively on midge pupae, it's also certain that you need to imitate what they're taking if you're going to fool very many of them. In my experience, I've found that trout feeding on midges are tuned to size first, slenderness second, and color an often remote third. I've had fair success over quite snotty Bighorn trout with a size 22 Pheasant Tail Nymph, a *Baetis* mayfly nymph imitation, when midges were on the menu and no mayflies were in sight. You can begin your midge fishing with tiny searching dressings, and extend it into imitations if you find it necessary on your own waters.

I often find midge imitations necessary on the moving waters that I fish, and carry a small number of tiny dressings to match midges. Most of them are extraordinarily simple.

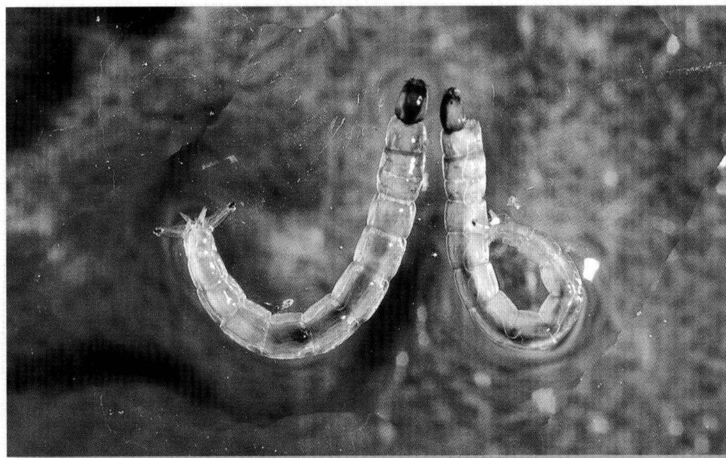

Many patterns tied to imitate moving-water midge larvae are taken by trout for midge pupae. In streams and rivers, larvae are available far less often than the later emergent stage of the insect.

When trout feed on midges selectively in moving waters, it's nearly always to pupae either just beneath the surface or in the film itself, preparing to break through for emergence.

WIRE MIDGE

The two most common colors of midge pupae, in moving water, seem to be black and a brown so dark it is almost black. I've also collected them in tan, green, and red. If I could carry only one color midge dressing, which in truth is pretty close to what I do carry, it would be black with a silver rib. My second would be red, not necessarily because I see red naturals second in abundance, but instead because I often use a red wire-bodied dressing as weight to deliver a less heavy but darker imitation to the few inches of depth that I desire. When trout are not fussy, I take a fair number of trout on the Red Wire Midge. When they're selective to a particular midge, trout usually ignore the red nymph and take the other almost exclusively. But I've found that the impenetrable rule of doubles applies: If I remove the nymph that is not taking any trout, I reduce my take, even if I replace the Red Wire Midge with a microshot that weighs about the same.

You'll want to tie and carry Wire Midges, which are technically midge larva imitations, not pupa patterns, in black, red, and green. You should acquire those wire colors in sizes small, brassie, and medium.

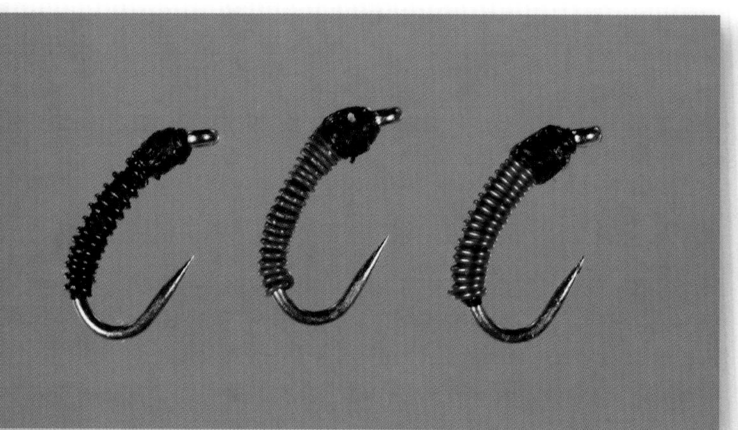

You'll find constant employment, in both streams and stillwaters, for Wire Midges in black, green, and red, sizes 18 to 22.

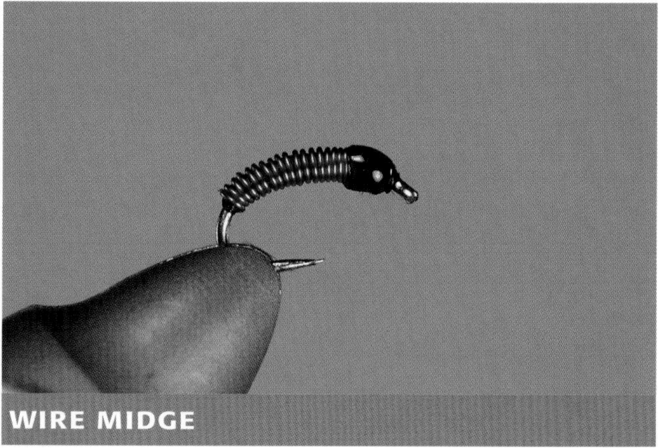

WIRE MIDGE

Hook:	Curved scud, size 18–22
Thread:	Black 8/0
Body:	Black, green, or red Ultra Wire

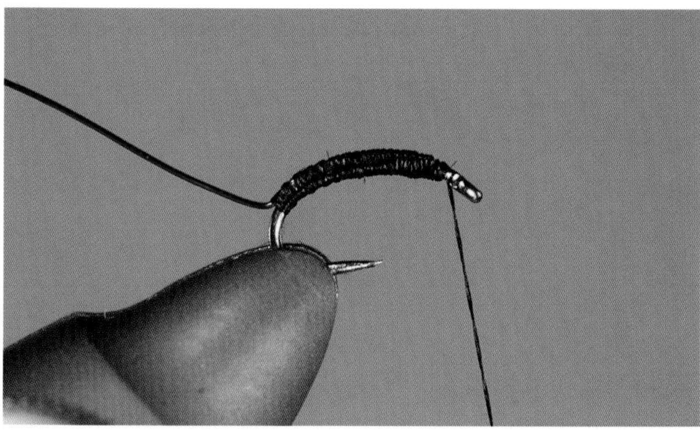

Step 1. Start the thread behind the eye of the hook. Clip three to four inches of wire in the appropriate diameter for the hook, and tie it in behind the eye. Layer thread over it well around the bend of the hook, and take a second layer of thread back to the hook eye.

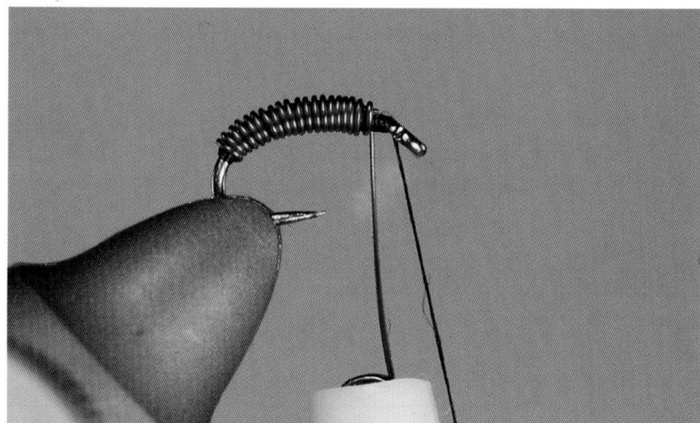

Step 2. Wind the wire in adjacent turns forward, stopping about one hook-eye length behind the eye. In small sizes, it helps to wind your wire with hackle pliers. Tie off the wire, clip the excess, and form a slight thread head that extends over the front one or two wire wraps. Whip-finish, clip the thread, and apply a drop of head cement.

THREAD MIDGE

In his fine book *Tying Small Flies,* Ed Engle credits the thread midge concept to Gary Willmuth, who has guided for many years on the San Juan River tailwater in New Mexico. On waters where trout feed constantly on an abundance of midge pupae, and where they see an excess of anglers and their imitations, they become highly selective, and your own imitations need to be quite close to the naturals. If you're able to acquire a trout for a sample, it's wise to carefully use a throat pump, see exactly what the trout have been taking. In most cases you'll find a mixture of many things, but the predominant insect will be midge pupae. Match the size and color with a thread midge, and you will increase your chances of holding more trout in your hands.

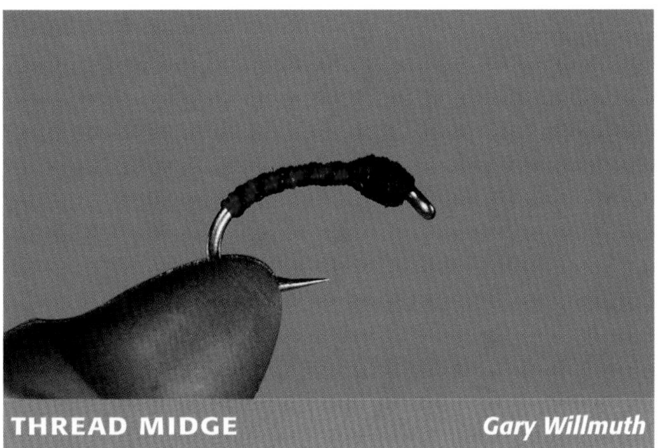

THREAD MIDGE *Gary Willmuth*

Hook:	Curved scud, size 18–24
Rib:	White, black, or brown 6/0 or 8/0 thread
Abdomen:	Black, red, green, or cream 8/0 thread
Thorax:	Black thread

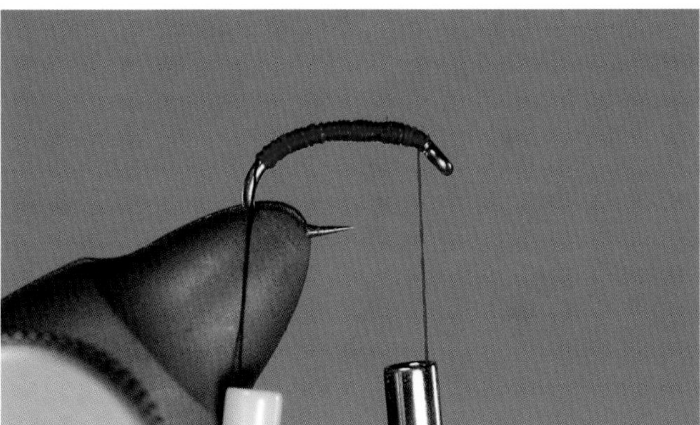

Step 1. It's easiest to tie this fly, which should always be easy to tie, when you use two colors of thread: one for the abdomen, one for both the rib and thorax, or head, of the fly. Begin with both colors spooled on bobbins. Start the abdomen color behind the head. Capture the rib and thorax color under it, and use the abdomen color to overwind the rib color halfway around the bend of the hook. Be sure your thread wraps are adjacent, to cover the hook shank. Leave the rib color dangling at the bend of the hook, and make another solid layer of the abdomen thread to the hook eye.

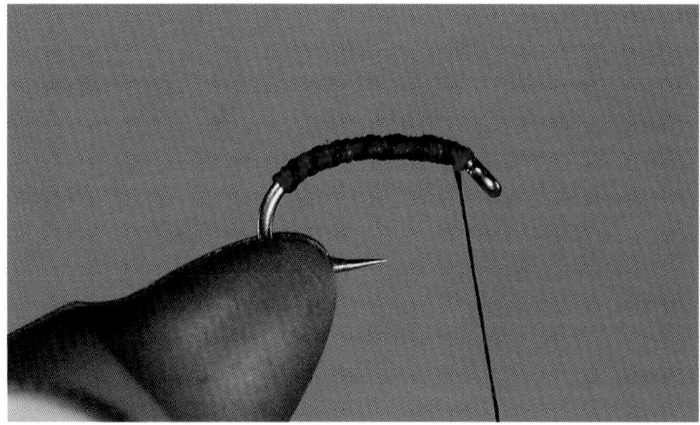

Step 2. Tie off the abdomen thread with a whip-finish or a couple of quick half hitches. Clip this thread and set the bobbin aside. Take up your ribbing and thorax bobbin, and wind it forward over the abdomen in four to six evenly spaced turns, forming the rib.

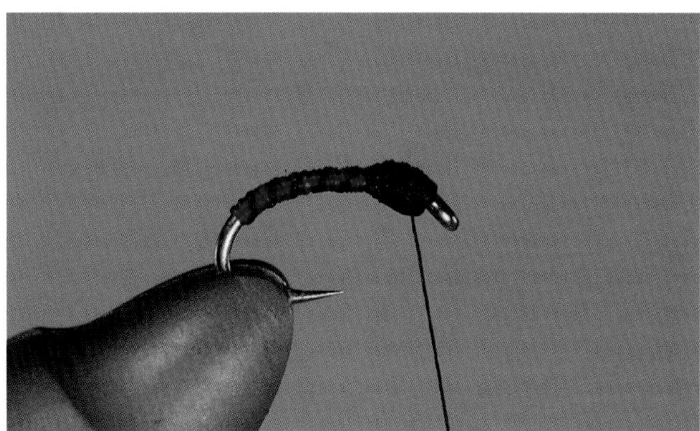

Step 3. Take enough turns of the ribbing and thorax thread to form a lumpy segment behind the hook eye. Whip-finish at the eye, and clip the thread.

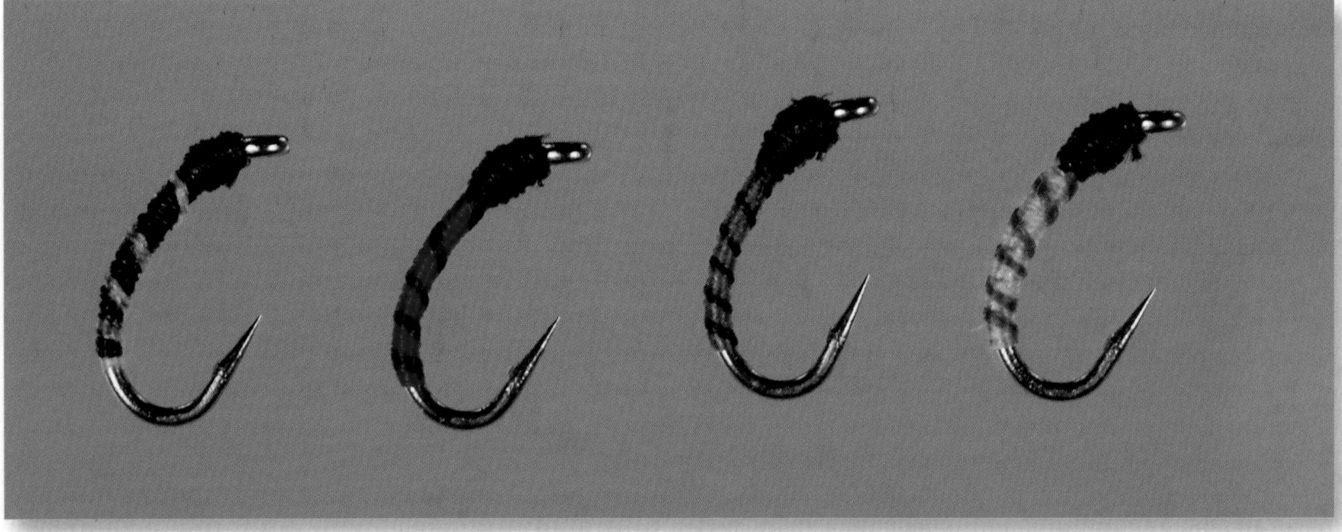

Thread Midges should be tied (left to right) in black, red, green, and tan.

The simple finished Thread Midge should have a very slender body, distinct ribbing, and an expanded thorax and head. It is often called a Thread Midge Larva, and it could easily be mistaken for a midge larva by a trout, but in all the samples I've taken from actively feeding trout, pupae dominate. They're tiny, almost always dark, have a substantial curve in the abdomen, and that gathering of furled legs and antennae and wing cases that enlarges the short thorax. The Thread Midge, tied on a curved scud hook with a slender body and slightly thicker thorax, looks more like a pupa than it does a larva. It is an excellent tie to use in a tiny size, trailed behind a Wire Midge a size or two larger.

I fish this tandem most often over fish that are working visibly and so near the surface that their takes sometimes break the film, usually with the dorsal fin or tail, but sometimes even with the top of the head. The water is always smooth, and the currents are normally a difficult set of contradictions. It's tough water on which to fish a dry fly, but those visible rises always tempt me into it. Even the best floating midge imitation usually harvests little but frustration.

It's always tempting to tie a two-foot 6X tippet to the hook bend of the midge dry, and drop a midge pupa off that. But the disadvantages are distinct: any dry fly small enough to match the emerging adults is too small to use as an indicator for a suspended pupa. You won't be able to see the dry fly well enough to mark a take to the nymph. The dry fly will take on water quickly and subside, either after an unseen take or two, or after you've caught a fish on the nymph.

It's better to rig to fish the Thread Midge, or a brace of midge nymphs, without the dry fly. If trout are high in the water, feeding just subsurface, that means nipping off the dry that's been failing, slipknotting a pea-sized yarn indicator two to three feet up the leader, tying a Wire Midge to the tippet, adding a foot or so of one size finer tippet, and then a Thread Midge.

Pea-sized yarn indicators in white and black, an inch or two apart on your leader, will help you fish midge pupa patterns in the low light of dusk, when the naturals often become active, and trout begin to feed selectively on them.

I use white yarn until dusk, then switch to black yarn, or add a second pea-sized indicator of black yarn a few inches from the white one, fishing them both. The last time I used this combination on the Bighorn River, I had no black yarn. Reflections of cottonwood trees on the far bank darkened the surface in places. In the spaces between cottonwood reflections, the surface reflected the sky, and was silvery. As light faded, the white yarn indicator I'd been using showed well on the dark surface, in the cottonwood reflections, but disappeared as soon as it drifted into the silvery reflection of the sky. So I cut my leader six inches from the white indicator, tied in a size 16 Black Snowshoe Caddis, tied the trailing tippet with

When you're casting midge pupa patterns rigged with yarn indicators against different backgrounds, such as those caused by the reflections of cottonwood trees opposite the swimming geese, it helps to have both light and dark indicators, so you can follow the drift of your nymphs no matter what surface they're on.

the two midge nymphs to the hook bend of the floating caddis, and went back to fishing.

When I cast this combination onto water with dark reflections, the white indicator was visible, and marked takes. I could not see the black dry fly. As soon as the setup drifted out of a cottonwood reflection, and into water that reflected the sky, the white indicator disappeared, but the black caddis suddenly showed up as a silhouette against the water. If it twitched or went under, I'd set the hook, and a trout would dance in the evening air. That happened a lot.

Almost every trout took the smaller and darker Thread Midge.

DISCO MIDGE

Often when midges are about to emerge, such as the one on the left, they exude gases between inner and outer exoskeletons, become shiny and almost white.

Originated by Colorado tier Bill Fitzsimmons, the Disco Midge uses a body of Krystal Flash to capture the colors of both the midge pupa and its natural reflectance. Like caddis pupae, many midge pupae trap gases between the inner adult and outer pupal cuticles. These can cause the insect to turn almost white in the instant before it emerges through the surface film. It is reasonable to assume that trout would key in on this brightness wherever it happens.

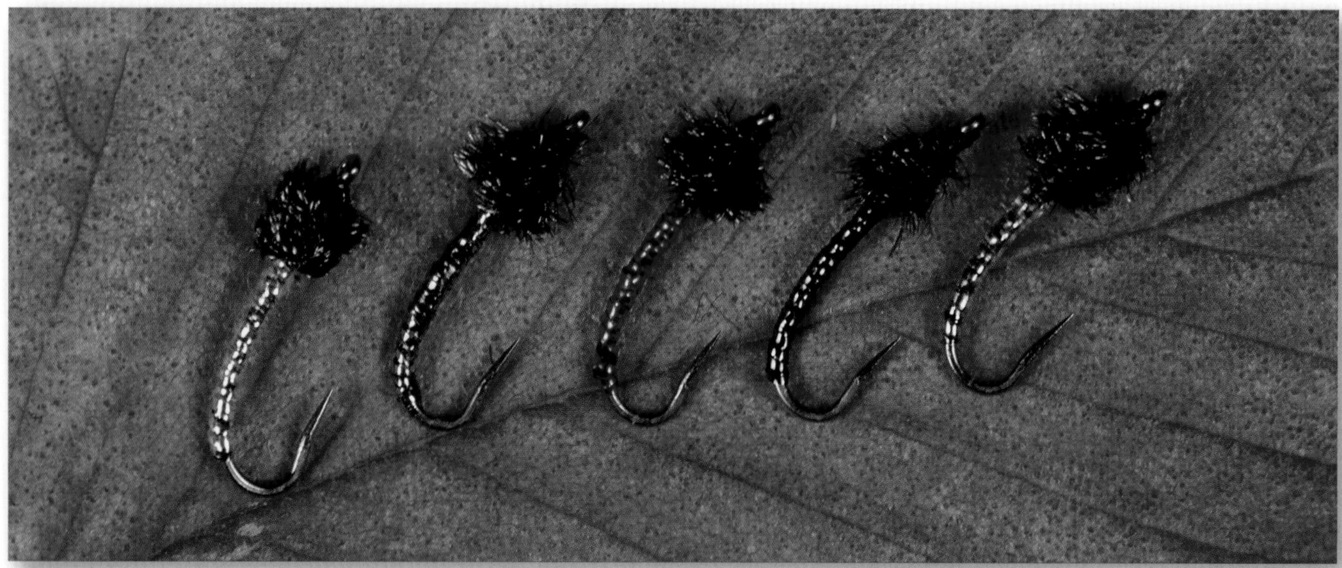

Some useful colors for the Disco Midge include pearl, peacock, red, dark blue, and light blue.

DISCO MIDGE *Bill Fitzsimmons*

Hook: 3XL curved-shank, size 18–22
Thread: Black 8/0
Body: Pearl, peacock, red, or blue Krystal Flash
Thorax/head: Peacock herl

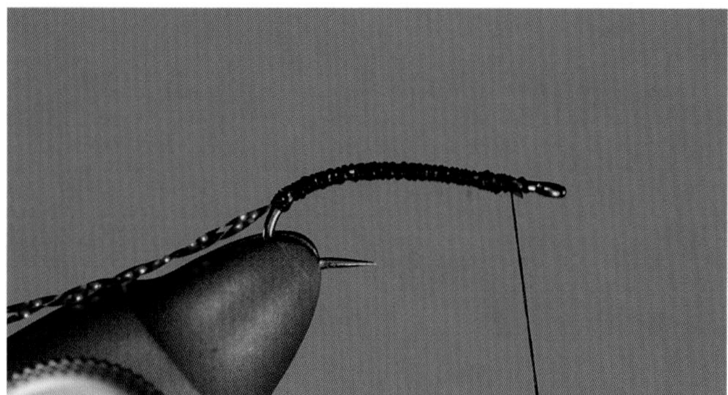

Step 1. Start your thread behind the eye of the hook. Tie in four strands of Krystal Flash, and bind them well down on the curved part of the hook shank. Bring your working thread back to the hook eye.

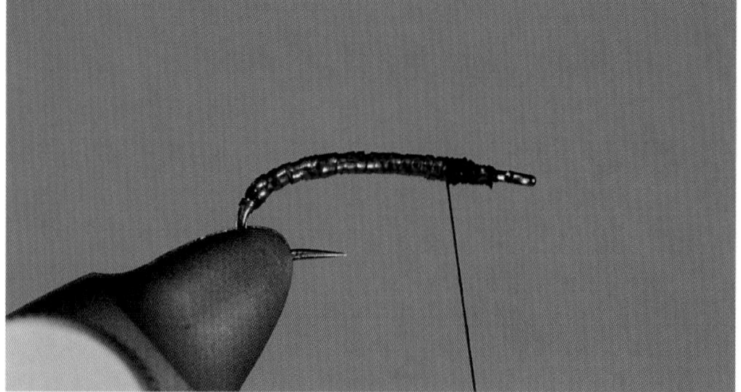

Step 2. Twist the Krystal Flash strands together, and wrap them forward in tightly adjacent wraps almost to the hook eye. Tie them off there and clip the excess. If you have trouble keeping the strands together, twist them and use your hackle pliers to hold them together while wrapping them. It will be necessary, whether you use fingers or hackle pliers, to twist the Krystal Flash strands frequently as you wind them forward.

Step 3. Tie in two peacock herls. Gather them together with your thread, twist them into a rope, and take two to four turns of herl forward to the hook eye. Let the herl separate from the thread, tie it off, and clip the excess. Form a neat thread head, whip-finish, and clip your thread.

ZEBRA MIDGE

The Zebra Midge was originated by a guide on the Lees Ferry stretch of the Colorado River, in Arizona. But the same fly shows up as a variation of Pat Dorsey's Black Beauty midge pattern, created for tailwaters such as the South Platte, in Colorado. Such simultaneous originations are common with good ideas. Since they are similar, and can therefore be considered a theme on which color and size variations can be worked, I'll list both the Black Beauty/Zebra Midge and Dorsey's Mercury Midge together. One is white, the other black. You can collect midge pupae on your own streams, and tie other colors to match them. It's not a secret that midges are more abundant on stillwaters than they are on most streams, and that these same dressings will work as well on lakes and ponds as they do on moving waters. There is no meaningful distinction between stream and stillwater midges, except that those in moving water will almost always be at the tiniest end of the size range.

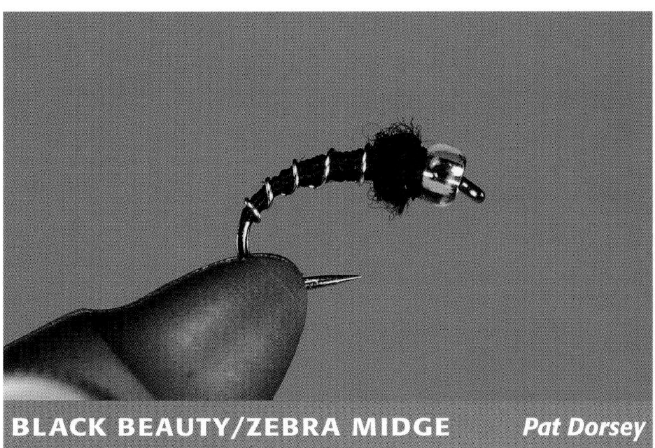

BLACK BEAUTY/ZEBRA MIDGE *Pat Dorsey*

Hook: Curved scud, size 18–24
Head: Hi-Lite silver glass bead
Thread: Black 70 Denier or 8/0
Rib: Fine silver wire
Body: Working thread
Thorax: Black dubbing

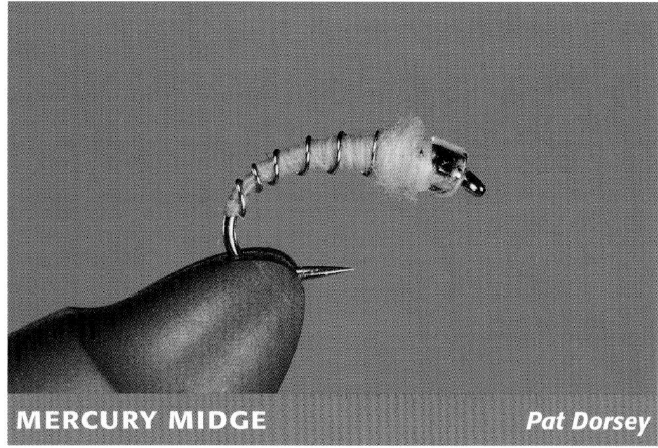

MERCURY MIDGE *Pat Dorsey*

Hook: Curved scud, size 18–24
Head: Hi-Lite silver glass bead
Thread: White 6/0 or 8/0
Rib: Fine copper wire
Thorax: Working thread, or cream dubbing

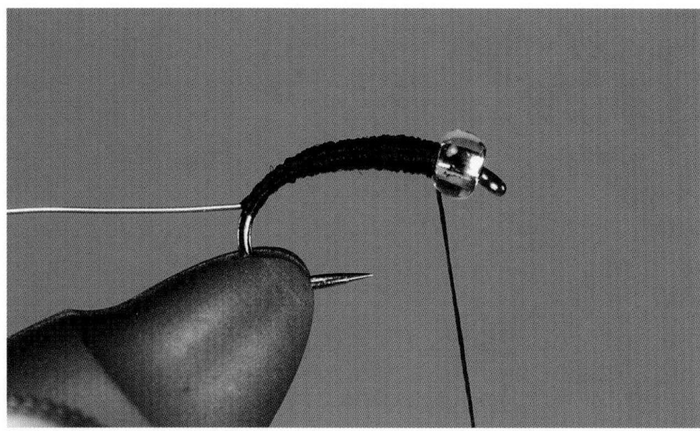

Step 1. Fix a glass bead on the hook, and place the hook in the vise. Start the thread behind the bead, tie in several inches of ribbing wire, and overwrap the wire well around the bend of the hook. Use several layers of working thread to form a body that is tapered from slender at the back to still slender but somewhat thicker behind the bead.

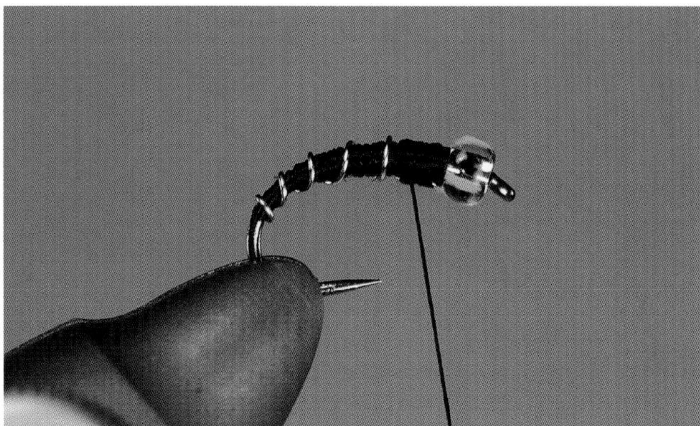

Step 2. Take four to six evenly spaced turns of ribbing wire, stopping about a bead width behind the beadhead. Tie it off there and clip the excess wire.

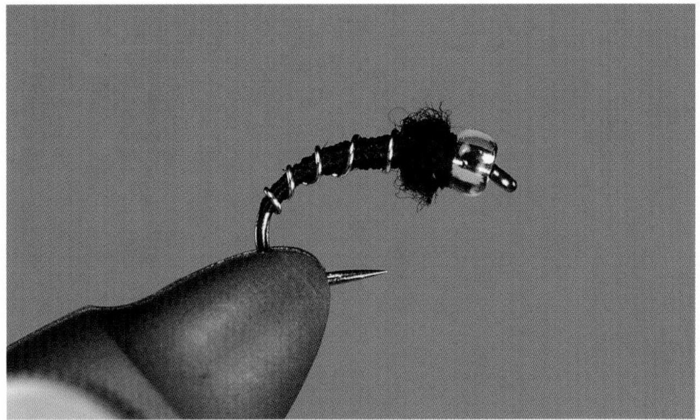

Step 3. Fix a small amount of dubbing on the thread, and take two to three turns forward to the back of the bead. The diameter of the thorax should be about the same as the diameter of the beadhead. Tuck a whip-finish between the back of the bead and the thorax dubbing. Clip the thread, and the simple fly is finished.

Like all tiny midge pupa patterns, the Black Beauty, or Zebra Midge, and the Mercury Midge are quick, easy ties. The hardest part is getting the bead onto the hook. Use tweezers, bead half a dozen to a dozen of a size at a time, then tie them quickly. The added bit of flash at the head makes this an excellent concept, and it's one you should carry in a couple of colors if you intend to spend any time on spring creeks or tailwaters.

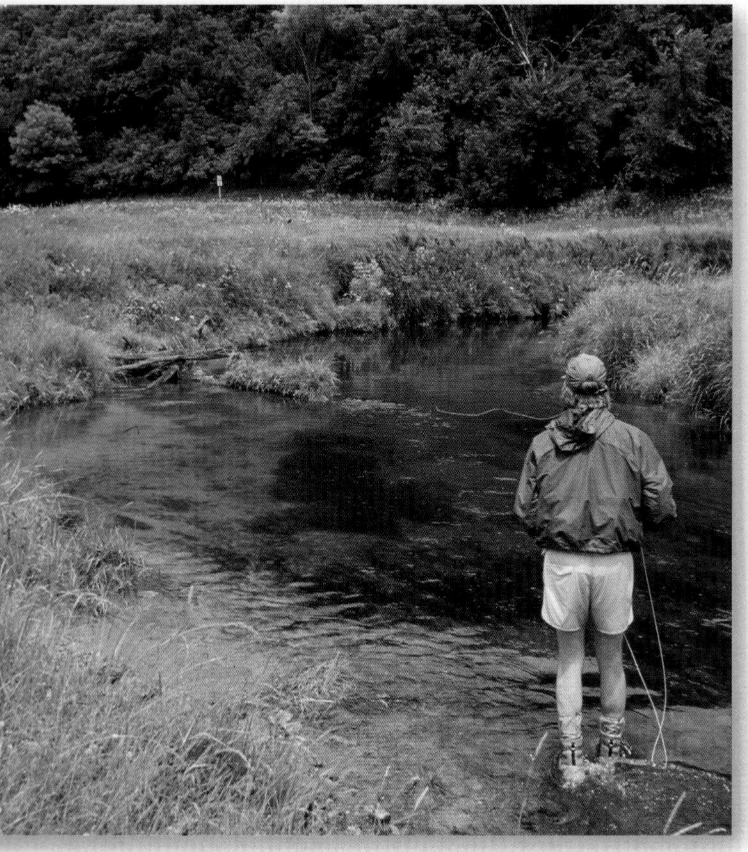

Whenever your travels take you to spring creeks or tailwaters, be aware of the need for a few patterns to match midge pupae.

SUMMARY

If you ever get into working trout on smooth water, and they defy all of your efforts with dry flies, yet you're unable to observe what they're taking, don't waste too much time before making the switch to a tiny indicator with a pair of midge pupa dressings dangled behind it. If trout are frustrating you during a small mayfly hatch, refusing your drys, you'll at least be able to observe duns, which is your clue to try small mayfly nymphs. When the subject is midges, the clues will often be almost invisible. You won't notice the adults on the surface unless you seine for them with a net. It's very difficult to tell when trout are feeding on midges, and even more difficult to separate surface from subsurface feeding.

Some problems in medicine are *diagnosed by elimination:* the disease is determined by the absence of indications that the symptoms might be caused by anything else. Midge pupa feeding is about like that: you realize that it's happening because you can see that trout are feeding, but you can't see anything that they might be taking. The absence of clues to any other kind of feeding is your main clue that it's time to try midges.

On waters where midges are dominant, tiny larva and pupa patterns tied for midges become fallback searching patterns. You'll rarely go wrong trailing a size 18 to 22 midge pupa pattern behind a larger nymph, rigged to fish near the bottom, on a spring creek or tailwater that has lots of midges and also gets hammered hard by anglers. You can rig with the standard shot and indicator, but that might be too coarse on smooth water with even currents and modest depths. Instead, use a hinged yarn indicator, and a single length of fine tippet about the depth of the water. Tie a Wire Midge to the tippet, dangle a smaller Thread Midge, Disco Midge, Zebra Midge, or Mercury Midge as a trailer, and pinch a microshot on the tippet halfway between them. You'll fish the bottom, but you'll also get news about takes delivered almost instantly to that fluffy indicator.

This is a short chapter, about a subject—midges—that is taxonomically much more complex than many others. But the flies tied for these tiny insects should be simple, and you should tie them as variations on very few themes. For moving waters, you need just a few colors, in a restricted number of very small sizes. In truth, if you get the size right, the shape near, and the color approximate, then your success will depend on your presentation more than your pattern.

CHAPTER 22

Craneflies

If you were to set up your kick-screen net in a shallow riffle with a bottom of very fine stones and pea gravel, and if you then used your brogues to dig deep into the substrate upstream from the net, essentially shoveling out whatever might lie buried a few inches deep beneath the streambed, you would almost certainly come up with a few cranefly larvae. You might find enough of these big, grublike insects to conclude that they are the dominant trout food in that bit of water. It's possible you'd be right. It's also possible that trout don't wear brogues.

Cranefly larvae look a little like truncated, fat earthworms. The prescription for fishing imitations of them is usually based on the reasoning that a lot of them get into the currents during high flows, and you should fish cranefly larva patterns when the water is rising or falling after a good rain. That's possible, but I don't enjoy fishing muddy water, which is when this formula predicts trout might be eager for cranefly larvae, and therefore susceptible to their imitations.

It's my guess that cranefly larvae get exposed to trout on occasion, most often when they take a wrong turn in the depths of their gravel beds and go up instead of down; they do burrow around blindly down there. It's also my guess that no sane trout would pass up a chance

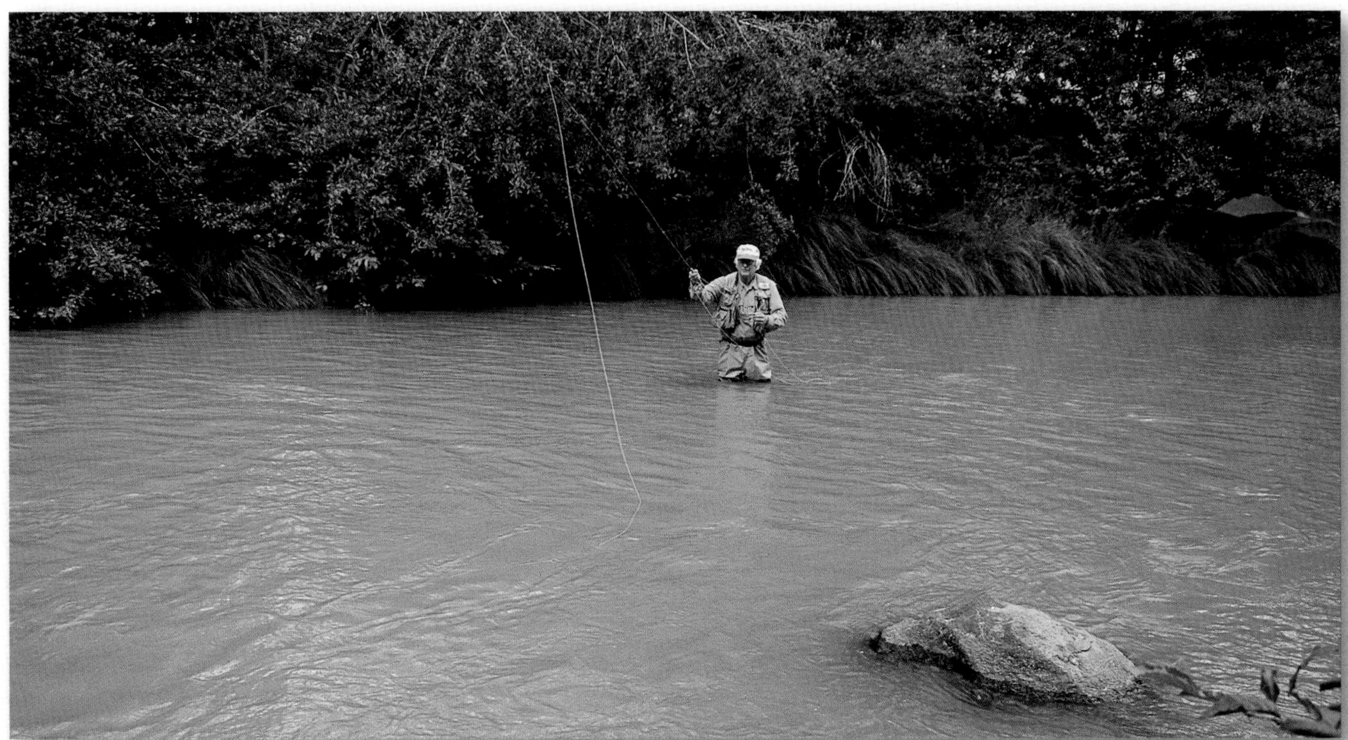

The general prescription is to fish cranefly larva imitations when the water is high and off-color. Though they work then, they are also excellent patterns to try in any water where you collect the naturals, no matter the color of the water.

to gather a fat cranefly larva exposed along the bottom. So I suspect you'll be very unlikely to ever find a trout feeding selectively on cranefly larvae, and selective feeding is my criteria for the necessity of an imitation.

Having said that, I'll confess that in waters harboring an abundance of these big, juicy insects, an imitation makes a great searching nymph. So I'll offer a couple of quick ones here. I do advise you, however, to consider that other insects, such as golden stonefly nymphs, live higher in the gravel, are even more likely to be knocked into the currents by high water, and are more likely models for imitation if their numbers approach those of craneflies.

Cranefly larvae are corpulent fellows, a fat mouthful for any trout. Many have a greenish aspect, which should be reflected in your imitations.

Some cranefly larvae have an almost shiny translucence, an aspect captured by using reflective materials in your imitations.

Most of the larvae I have collected have been either dark with a green aspect, or light with a tan or almost amber aspect. They have shiny, reflective skins, though reflectance requires light, and imitations of them will be taken along the bottom, where light is low, and if fished according to the usual prescription, in off-color water on dull and rainy days, when light is at best soft. My advice is to ignore the prescription, and to try these as the large lead nymph in a two-fly combination whenever your collecting reveals more than a few of the naturals in the gravel. My suspicion is that you'll catch most of your trout on whatever small nymph you choose as your trailer. But you'll also catch trout on imitations of cranefly larvae.

Members of this group pupate on shore, so there is no need to consider imitations of that stage of the insect.

CRANEFLY LARVA

Though the few pattern descriptions you find for cranefly larva imitations usually call for lots of weight on the shank, to get them down in high water, I recommend you keep your weight modest, giving you the option to fish them in shallow riffles, or wherever else you might find the naturals in less-than-deep water. You can always add split shot to the leader to get them to the bottom in heavy water, during or after a rain.

CRANEFLY LARVA, OLIVE

Hook:	3XL or 4XL, size 4–8
Weight:	15–25 turns of nonlead wire
Thread:	Black 6/0 or 8/0
Tail:	Gray fluff from base of hackle feather
Rib:	Olive stretch lace
Body:	Olive dubbing
Head:	Black dubbing

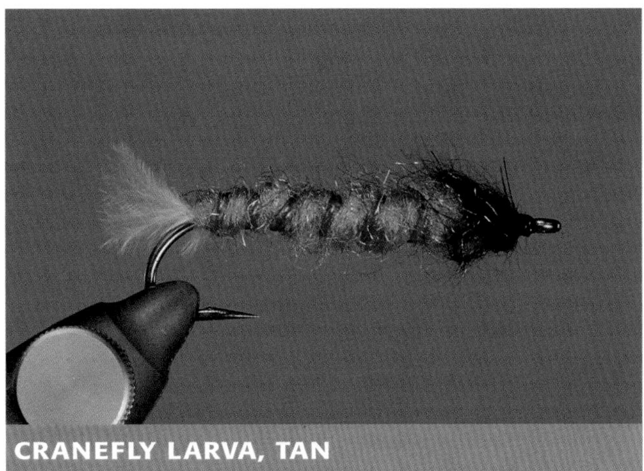

CRANEFLY LARVA, TAN

Hook:	3XL or 4XL, size 4–8
Weight:	15–25 turns of nonlead wire
Thread:	Black 6/0 or 8/0
Tail:	Gray fluff from base of hackle feather
Rib:	Amber stretch lace
Body:	Golden tan dubbing
Head:	Black dubbing

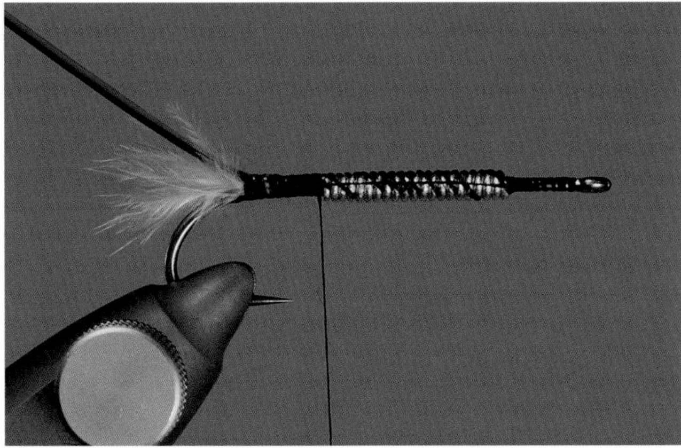

Step 1. Fix the hook in the vise and layer the shank with weighting wire. Start the thread behind the eye, and use enough turns to lock in the wire. Don't worry about building thread ramps at front and back shoulders. Strip a clump of fluff from the base of a saddle or hen hackle feather. Measure this about the length of one to one and a half hook gaps, and tie it in at the bend of the hook. Tie in several inches of tubing for the rib.

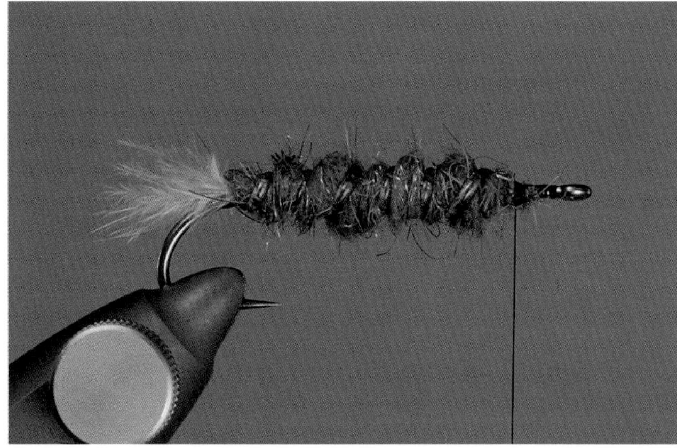

Step 2. Twist a fat amount of dubbing onto your thread, and wrap it forward to a point about one-sixth the shank length behind the hook eye. It should be portly, and have little taper. Take six to eight evenly spaced turns of ribbing over the dubbing. Tie it off and clip the excess.

Step 3. Dub a head the same diameter as the body, tapering down to the hook eye. Make a thread head, whip-finish, clip the thread, and apply head cement.

GLASS BEAD CRANEFLY LARVA

Glass beads are reflective, and also form a somewhat corpulent body, though the use of glass beads precludes weighting wire. You'll need to add split shot or putty weight to your leader if you want to get these imitations to the bottom. You could tie them with tungsten beads; that might be wise. Though the following dressings are not based on any exact pattern, the concepts for tying with glass beads are covered in Joe J. Warren's *Tying Glass Bead Flies.*

GLASS BEAD CRANEFLY LARVA, OLIVE

Hook:	3XL or 4XL, size 6–10
Beads:	Green
Thread:	Olive 6/0 or 8/0
Body:	Olive dubbing

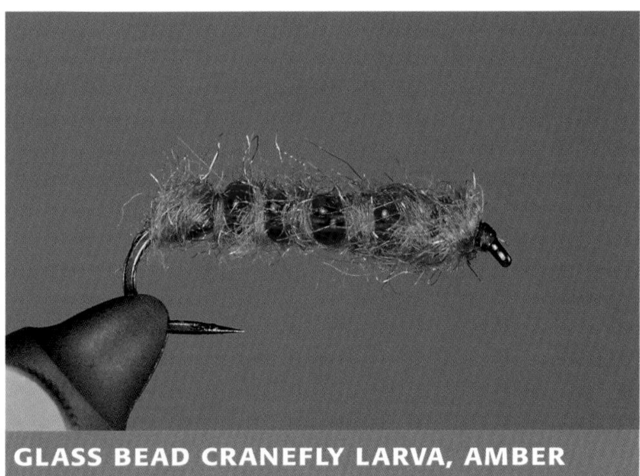

GLASS BEAD CRANEFLY LARVA, AMBER

Hook:	3XL or 4XL, size 6–10
Beads:	Red or amber
Thread:	Tan 6/0 or 8/0
Body:	Golden brown dubbing

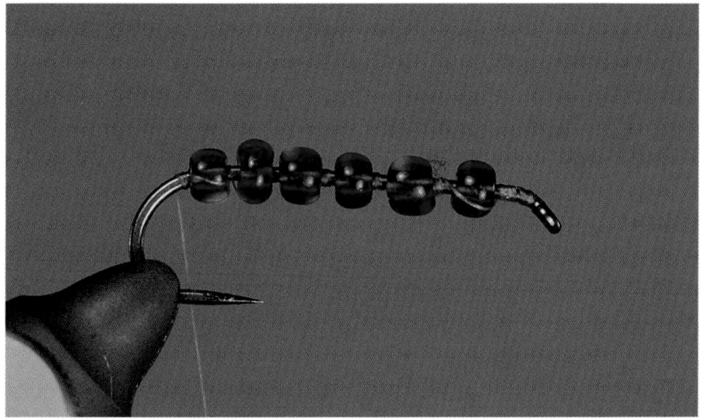

Step 1. Fix enough beads on the hook shank to cover about two-thirds of it; don't crowd the shank, or you'll not be able to wind dubbing between the beads. Start your thread behind the hook eye, and use pinch wraps between beads to lock them in place and take your thread to the bend of the hook. The beads should be fairly evenly spaced, though it's not critical that they be precise.

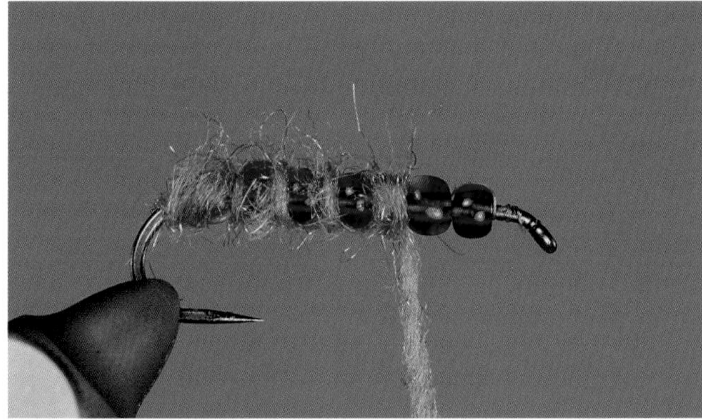

Step 2. Fix a long and fairly thin skein of dubbing to the thread. Take two or three turns behind the last bead, then wind it forward, taking one or two turns of dubbing to fill in the spaces between beads.

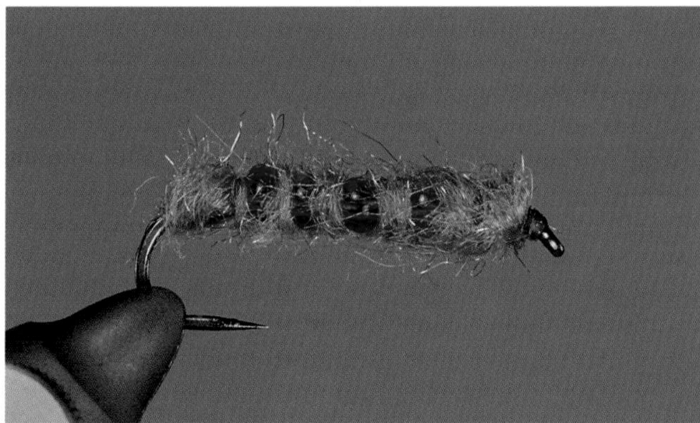

Step 3. Finish with two or three turns of dubbing between the front bead and the hook eye. Make a thread head, whip-finish, clip the thread, and apply head cement.

OLIVE CRANEFLY LARVA

A shellback of Thin Skin over the entire back of a cranefly larva pattern captures the shiny, reflective quality of the natural nymph. If there is any light down there where your nymph tumbles, the plastic stretch material will capture it and wink it to the trout. The following dressings are based on John Barr's Cranefly Larva, listed in his book *Barr Flies,* but the colors and materials have been slightly adjusted to agree with the cranefly naturals I collect most often. Cranefly larvae vary in color from stream to stream, one reason you should always collect in your own waters before tying more than a few imitations for any insect.

CRANEFLY LARVA, OLIVE ***John Barr***

Hook: 3XL curved shank, size 6–10
Weight: 15–25 turns nonlead wire
Thread: Olive 6/0 or 8/0
Tail: Gray fluff from pheasant, partridge, or hen feather
Rib: 3X monofilament
Shellback: Clear Thin Skin
Body: Olive dubbing

CRANEFLY LARVA, TAN ***John Barr***

Hook: 3XL curved shank, size 6–10
Weight: 15–25 turns nonlead wire
Thread: Tan 6/0 or 8/0
Tail: Gray fluff from pheasant, partridge, or hen feather
Rib: 3X monofilament
Shellback: Clear Thin Skin
Body: Golden brown dubbing

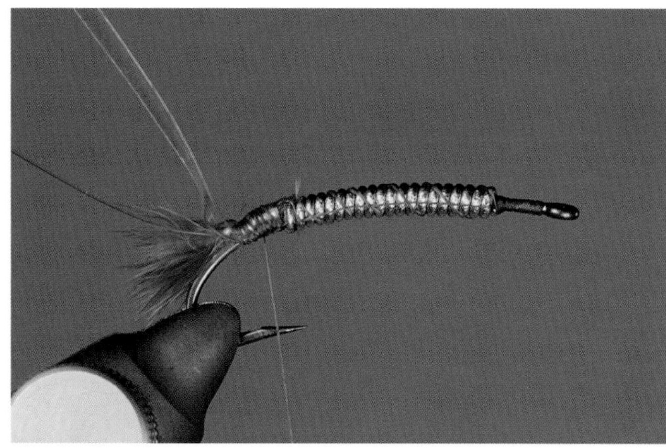

Step 1. Fix the hook in the vise, and layer the shank with fifteen to twenty-five turns of nonlead wire. Start the thread behind the eye, and overwrap the wire to a point straight above the hook barb. Don't worry about making thread ramps to the wire shoulders. Secure a bit of fluff from the base of a feather, measure it about the length of the hook gap, and tie it in. If it is too long, you can pinch it shorter. Tie in several inches of 3X ribbing. Cut a strip of Thin Skin one-half to two-thirds the hook gap width, and tie it in at the base of the tail.

Step 2. Use the direct-dubbing method to create a somewhat portly body. It should taper slightly at both ends, and should end about a hook-eye length behind the eye, leaving room to tie off the shellback and ribbing, and to place a head.

Step 3. Bring the shellback forward over the body, and tie it off behind the hook eye. Clip the excess.

Step 4. Bring the ribbing forward over the shellback in six to eight evenly spaced turns. Tie it off and clip the excess. Form a thread head, whip-finish, clip the thread, and apply head cement.

Step 5. If desired, use a dubbing roughing tool to tease out the body dubbing. Don't make it too rough; the natural has no significant appendages. But a few loose fibers create a halo effect, and add life to the fly.

SUMMARY

I collect many cranefly larvae in my sampling, wherever in the world fishing takes me. I have no doubt that trout eat cranefly larvae whenever they get a chance at them. Trout take imitations of cranefly larvae, quite often with eagerness. I suspect it's rare that trout eat cranefly larvae selectively. I'm never certain, when a trout takes my cranefly imitation, that the trout has mistaken the imitation for a cranefly larva. But these nymphs do take trout, and it will never hurt to have a few imitations in your nymph boxes. Tie them in olive and tan, in sizes 6, 8, and 10. If you fish them, you'll catch trout on them. If you run into a mysterious abundance of cranefly larvae, you'll be prepared for them.

CHAPTER 23

Sow Bugs and Scuds

Moving-water scud and sow bug patterns are most important in spring creeks, tailwaters, and the meadow reaches of freestone streams, all waters where aquatic vegetation has a chance to take root. You might find small populations of scuds, and more rarely sow bugs, in quiet edge waters, backwaters, and pools left stranded when high flows recede in spring on freestone streams. But you won't find good populations of trout in any of those marginal waters. Your use of patterns imitating these crustaceans will usually be restricted to gentle, weedy waters.

SOW BUGS

Aquatic sow bugs, also called cress bugs because of their heavy presence in watercress beds, can be abundant in spring creeks and tailwaters, especially where you find rooted vegetation or woody debris. They thrive in places where flows are controlled and spates are tamed, so that silt settles and plant beds are not washed out. This is sometimes, though not always, a good circumstance for aquatic insects such as mayflies, midges, and some caddisflies. It's very beneficial for sow bugs. As an example, if you hoist a few bottom stones from a tailwater such as the Bighorn River in Montana, you'll find that they're coated with plush beds of what is commonly called moss, but which is actually a combination of rooted plants and algae. It thrives in controlled flows, especially in drought years, when no high-water flush ever happens to clean those stones.

These close-cropped plant mats shelter several types of animal life in great numbers. Midge larvae are safe there. Aquatic annelids—worms—crawl around between rock surfaces and the plants that hug those surfaces. Aquatic sow bugs, which have little ability to swim, find safe haven there, and can be found in abundance. They thrive in similar numbers in Ozark tailwaters. They also live in stillwaters, perhaps in even greater abundance. But they spend most of their time in lakes and ponds deep in bottom ooze or hidden in leaf packs, where trout can't easily get at them. They have no emergence, so there is no point in their life cycle where they must risk trout predation, at least in waters without movement.

In moving water, they get knocked loose from their vegetative retreats often enough that you'll frequently find them in throat pump samples taken from trout that

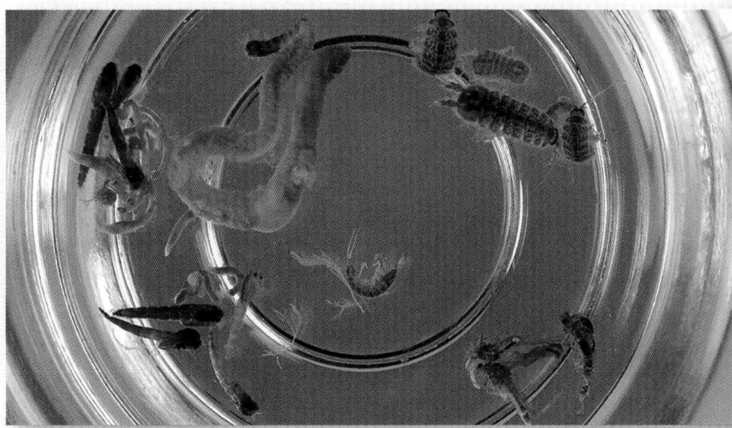

The trout from which this throat sample was extracted was feeding nonselectively, but it clearly knew what to do about an aquatic sow bug when it saw one. The largest sow bug, in the upper right-hand corner, is about a size 18.

are feeding opportunistically. This does not make them necessary as imitations. But it does mean that a pattern tied to approximate them will find favor with trout that are obviously not passing up a chance at a natural when it's available.

I happen to have a vial that's been getting in the way, rolling around on my desk as I've been writing, since last October, when Jim Schollmeyer and I last fished the Bighorn. It's a throat sample from a trout I caught on a size 22 midge pupa pattern dangled beneath a tiny, white yarn indicator. In the interests of science or curiosity—it's hard to parse those two out—I just poured the contents of the vial into a petri dish, and counted its specimens. They broke down this way: seven tiny midge larvae, eight midge pupae, three *Baetis* mayfly emergers, one aquatic worm that in terms of calories probably equals everything else put together, and six aquatic sow bugs. That trout had been feeding at relative random, though when I hooked it, it had turned to selective feeding high in the water column, and therefore was likely focused on midge pupae. But not much earlier in its day, judging by the lack of decomposition of those sow bugs, it had been feeding near the bottom.

It becomes obvious, both from hoisting Bighorn River rocks and from looking at that throat pump sample, that a two-nymph tandem of a worm dressing trailed by a sow bug pattern would be deadly on the Bighorn tailwater. That turns out to be true. It's what about half the guides on the river will have their clients fishing about half the time.

Whenever trout hold in or near weedbeds, but are clearly not feeding on the surface, they'll almost certainly be susceptible to small sow bug imitations fished at their level.

AQUATIC SOW BUG

Natural aquatic sow bugs are crustaceans. They don't swim. They have small heads, flat carapaced backs, seven pairs of legs that emanate from segments along their whole length, and stubby, forked tail-like structures at the back. Imitations for them are often complex, but it's my suspicion that a simple pattern is at least as effective. I can only speculate on that, because my own pattern for them is the abbreviated Aquatic Sow Bug, and I haven't tied or tried the more intricate patterns. Whenever I've found sow bugs in samples taken from trout, they've been mixed with other groceries, a sign that small searching patterns might be effective, and also that your imitations for sow bugs need only be approximations. Those that I've collected have all been the same color as their environment: light to dark gray.

The natural aquatic sow bug has a flat profile, is wider at the stern than the stem, has long antennae, short forked tail-like apparatuses, and seven pairs of legs. Most are gray.

AQUATIC SOW BUG

Hook: Curved scud, size 14–22
Thread: Black 6/0 or 8/0
Rib: Copper wire
Body: Muskrat fur

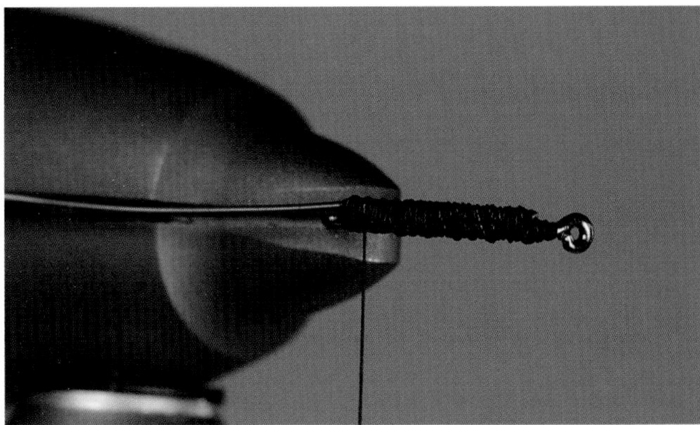

Step 1. Fix the hook in the vise, layer the shank with thread, and tie in the ribbing wire. If the wire is heavy, which will help the nymph sink, then lay it the length of the shank, along one side, and overwrap it with thread. This will slightly widen the finished fly, making it look a bit more like the broad-backed natural, something you'll appreciate, but the trout will not likely even notice.

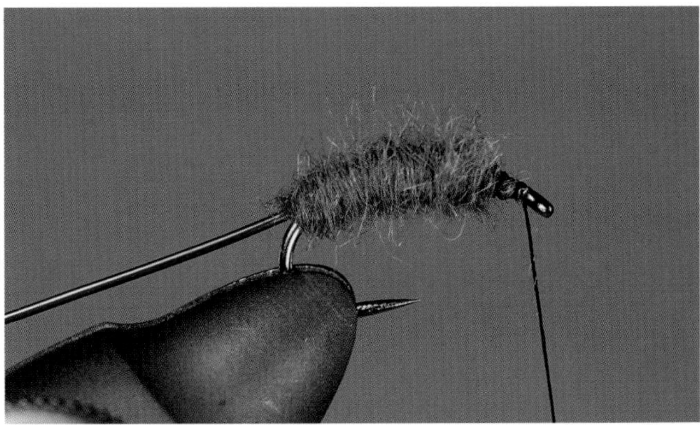

Step 2. Dub a fairly fat and untapered body from halfway down the bend of the hook to a point just behind the hook eye. I prefer muskrat belly fur for this tie; it is pale compared with back fur, and has fewer and shorter guard hairs, making it easier to work as dubbing.

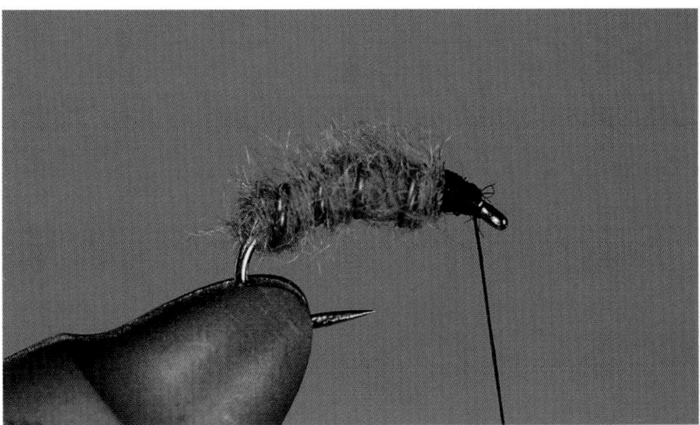

Step 3. Wind the rib forward in three to five evenly spaced turns. Tie it off, clip the excess, form a thread head, whip-finish and cement the head, and the simplest imitation you'll ever tie is finished.

SOW BUG

If you desire to get into exact imitation, of this or any other beast that trout make a living eating, then I implore you to take up collecting first, and base what you tie on what you see, and beyond that, what you know that trout are taking selectively, not just randomly. Whenever trout feed opportunistically, you can catch them on searching dressings that are within the size and color range of whatever they've been taking.

However, the wish to tie a complicated and imitative dressing is enough, without regard to the need for it, if intricate tying is your motivation. The following dressing incorporates many of the ideas that go into a more imitative Sow Bug dressing.

SOW BUG

Hook:	Standard nymph, size 16–22
Weight:	Outriggers of nonlead wire, or flattened wire
Thread:	Gray
Tails:	Gray goose or turkey biots
Rib:	3X monofilament
Shellback:	Clear Thin Skin
Body:	Gray fur and Antron mix
Legs:	Picked-out body dubbing

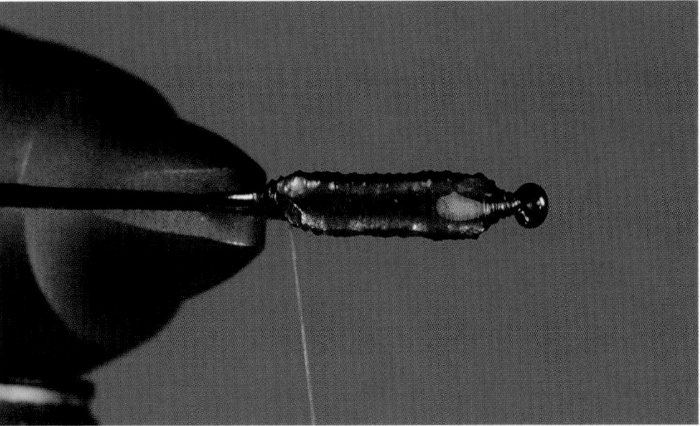

Step 1. Layer the shank of your hook with thread. From nonlead wire that is the diameter of the hook shank or a bit fatter, clip two sections about one-half to two-thirds the shank length. Lash one section to the far side of the

hook, the other to the near side, to form outriggers. It's difficult to cut these short enough to leave room for the head and tails. Start by lashing the wire to the top of the hook shank, from the front, with a few turns of thread. Then clip it to length at the back, and roll it to the far side of the hook before completing the lashing. Repeat on the near side. Cover with thread, and coat with head cement or Flexament.

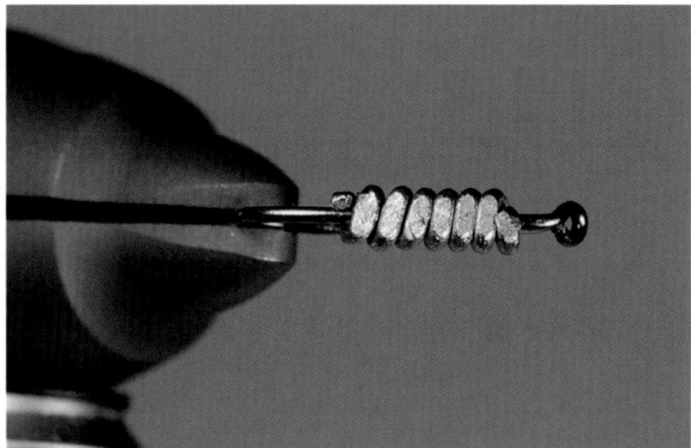

Alternate Step 1. Using nonlead wire the diameter of the hook shank or a bit fatter, take turns over about two-thirds the shank length. Leave room for the head and to tie in the tail. Use your debarbing pliers to flatten the wire. Cover the wire with thread, and coat it with head cement or Flexament.

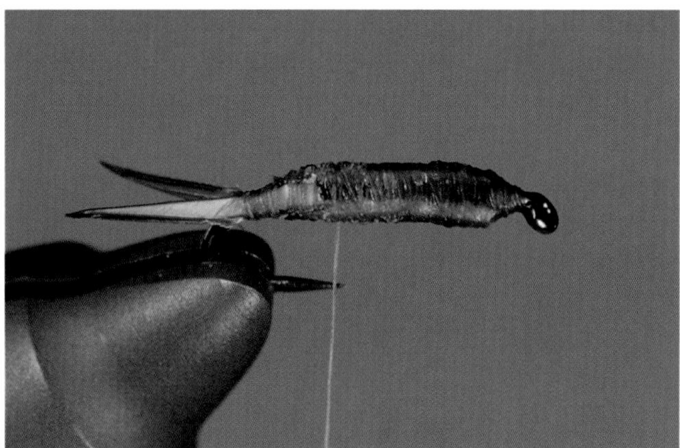

Step 2. Measure a biot half the length of the hook shank, and tie it in on the near side of the hook with two or three tight turns of thread, just enough to hold it in place. Be sure the curve of the biot is toward you. Measure a second biot the same length, and tie it in on the far side of the hook. Position the biots to form a forked tail, and secure them with several more turns of thread before cutting the excess and overwrapping the butts.

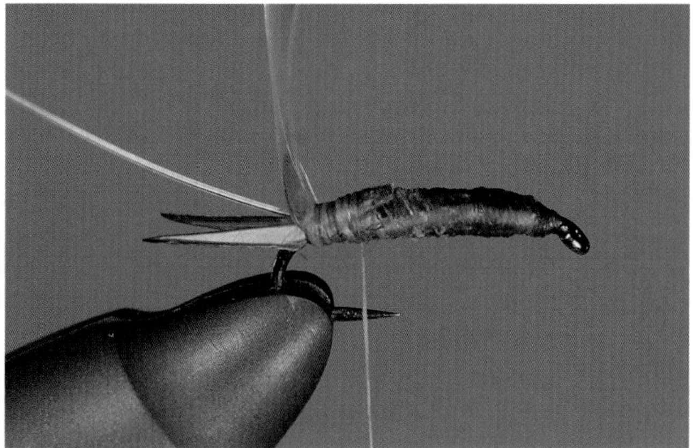

Step 3. Tie in a few inches of ribbing monofilament at the base of the tails. Cut a strip of Thin Skin about two-thirds the width of the hook gap. Tie it in at the base of the tails.

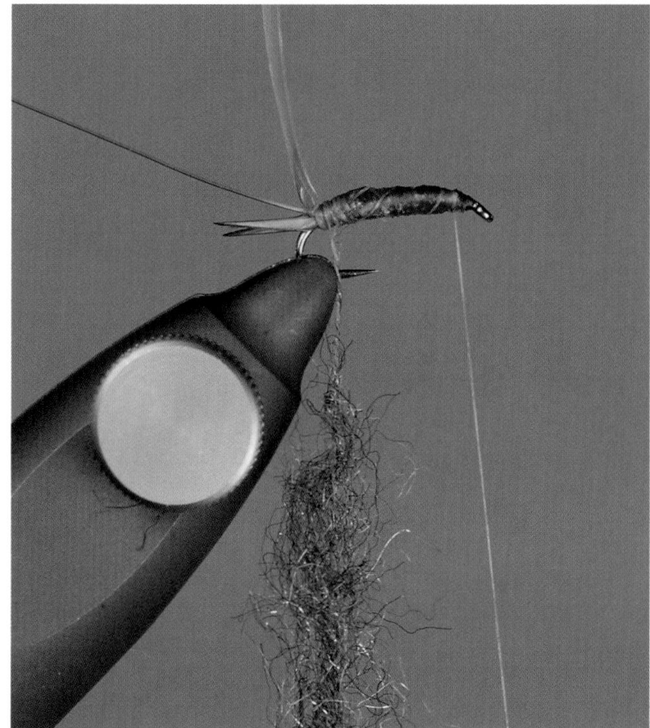

Step 4. Using a loose fur and Antron dubbing mix, tease it out into a short but wide skein, and touch it to well-waxed tying thread. Form a dubbing loop, twisting it just enough to capture the fibers. Do not twist it into a tight dubbing rope.

Step 5. Wind a body forward to a point far enough behind the hook eye to leave room to tie in the shellback and rib, and to form a head. The natural sow bug is wider at the back than the front, so your body either should have no taper, or should taper from wider at the back to narrower at the eye. At this point it should be an unruly affair.

Step 6. Pull the Thin Skin shellback over the body, and tie it off behind the head. Wind the monofilament ribbing over the shellback in four to five evenly spaced turns. Try to work the rib through the underside dubbing as much as possible, to keep from matting it down, though some matting is inevitable. Tie off the ribbing, and clip the excess shellback and ribbing.

Step 7. Form a thread head, whip-finish, clip the thread, and apply head cement. Use your bodkin point or a dubbing roughing tool to tease out the dubbing to the sides to widen the nymph, and down to represent the excessive number of legs owned by the natural aquatic sow bug.

Sow bugs are almost always found in relatively slow flows: spring creeks, tamed tailwaters, and the more peaceful edges or low-gradient stretches of freestone streams. They do not swim when knocked loose by currents. Imitations of them, or searching dressings fished for them in waters where the naturals are abundant, should be dead drifted in the bottom zone.

Because the water where aquatic sow bugs live is rarely fast, the best rig is usually the lightest that will get the nymph down where you want it. That is almost always a hinged indicator rig, with a yarn indicator, straight tippet of a single diameter and as long as the water is deep. Add a couple of nymphs, one a sow bug imitation, the other a scud or another sow bug, ten inches to a foot or so apart. If needed, pinch a microshot or two between the nymphs. Because the naturals vary from too small to imitate up to about size 16, it would never hurt to trail one in that size by another in size 20 or 22. It's my guess, based on a lot of fishing with such combinations, that you'll catch more trout on the smaller sow bug imitation than you will the larger one.

SCUDS

Scuds are more important in lakes and ponds than they are in moving water. But they are present and sometimes populous in slow stretches of many freestone streams. Like their relatives the aquatic sow bugs, they can be dominant in spring creeks and tamed tailwaters. The defining need for scuds is rooted vegetation. The more flows become stabilized in any stream or river, whether by spring sources or a dam, the more vegetation takes root, and the more scuds you'll find. They are crustaceans, do not leave the water for emergence, and have no moment in their life cycle when they're suddenly concentrated. They breed and are present in the full range of sizes, in all seasons of the year.

It has often been written that scuds become most important when aquatic insects are least important, which would mean fall and winter. To a certain extent that is true; if scuds are the only thing trout can find to eat, trout will focus on rooting them out of their weedbed sanctuaries and gunning them down in the currents. But trout feed on scuds whenever they get a chance, and they seem to get chances whenever they're holding on or near the bottom in relatively slow and weedy water. It is not unusual to catch a trout that has been feeding opportunistically, to sample what it has been eating, and to find at least one or two scuds, sometimes several, in the mix.

If you catch trout that have been feeding on more than the occasional scud, an imitation should be tied to the end of your tippet soon, at least in combination with a searching dressing or an imitation of something else, perhaps a sow bug.

Scuds have one peculiarity that needs to be pointed out, because it influences the imitations that have been tied to match them: when they're preserved, they turn orange or pink or an almost parchment white. Many tiers have collected them, placed them in vials filled with alcohol, taken them home, imitated them after they'd been pickled for some hours or even days. As a result, you see scud imitations in a variety of colors, some of them fluorescent. The astonishing thing is, they work. I doubt that they work as scud imitations, but trout take them, and you should tie some. But be sure to observe the colors of the naturals when you collect them, and match what you see when you're on the stream, not back at the vise, for most of your scud imitations.

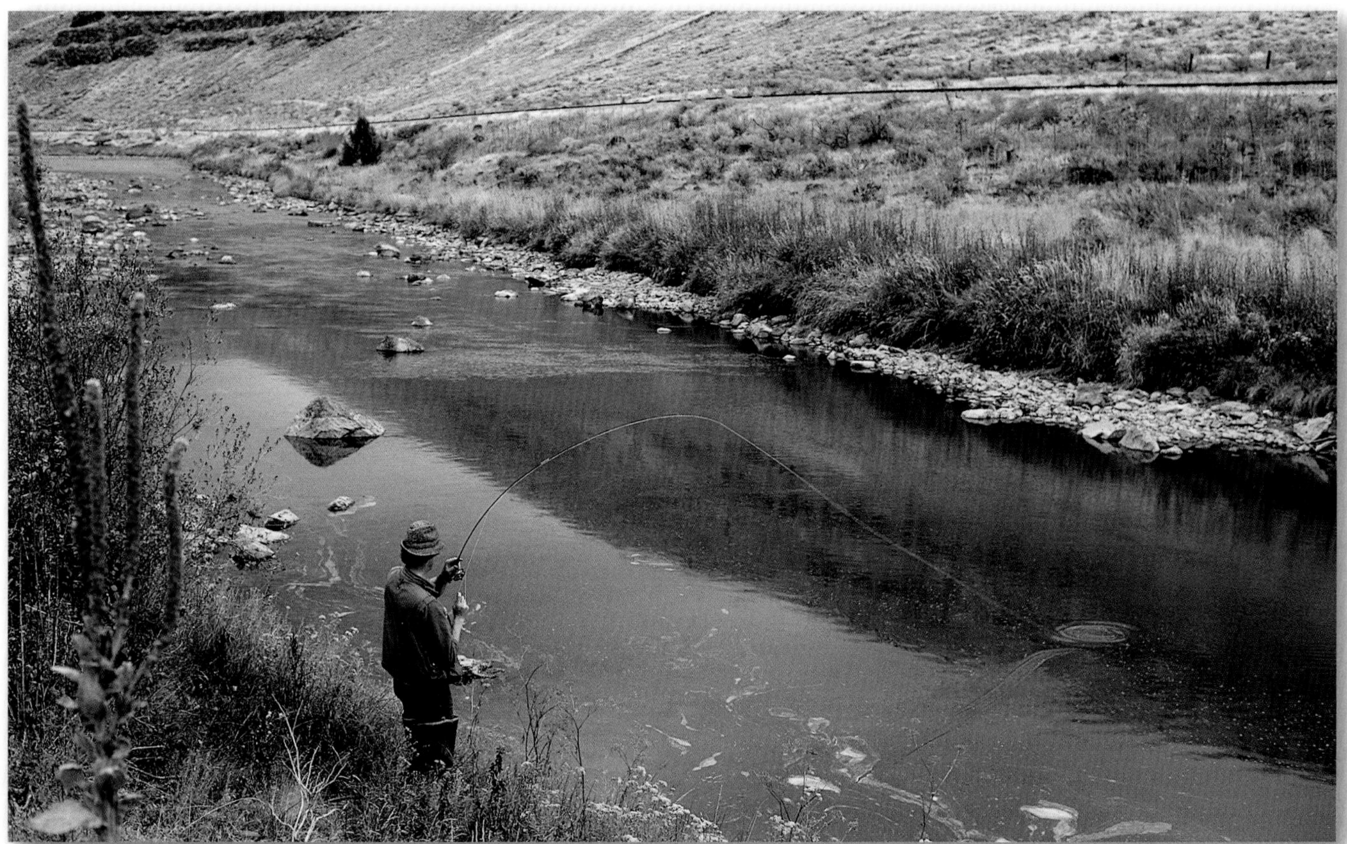

On many arid, and therefore alkaline, streams that have been turned into tailwaters, vegetation takes root in pools, and scuds can be the most important food source for trout, and therefore the most likely candidates for imitation, when flows are slow outside of irrigation season.

Scuds take on the color of the vegetation in which they live as camouflage, or they would live even shorter lives than they do.

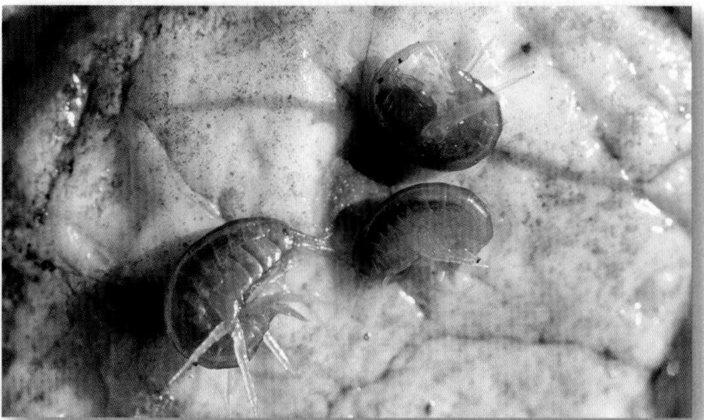

Though scuds are usually curled nearly into balls when you collect and observe them, they're straight when swimming, which is when we can assume trout see them most often.

To carry this admonition a bit further, don't imitate scuds removed from trout, either in autopsies of trout you've killed to eat, or from throat pump samples. Stomach acids do the same thing to scuds as preservatives: they change their colors. Take the time to scoop a handful of vegetation from the water, and inspect it for scuds. They'll be kicking around in there. They'll be wearing the colors you should match. Most often, they will be the exact color of the vegetation from which you collected them.

Scuds carry their eggs on their bellies. The eggs are bright. I've read scientific studies that show trout prefer, or at least take in exaggerated proportions, scuds with eggs attached. So it's not unwise to slip a bit of fluorescent dubbing into the center of the body for at least some of your scud dressings.

The addition of a bead makes a scud imitation less imitative, but often more effective. I add beads to most of mine. I hope that the wink of light from the bead attracts more trout to the fly. I've never fished a beaded scud against an unbeaded one, together on the same leader, but I suppose it's the sort of experiment that should be done. If it is done, then the two flies will have to be switched at given intervals, say half an hour, to eliminate the advantage of either the point or the dropper position. I suspect that the position of the nymph has more influence than the bead or lack of it, but I have an entire lack of evidence for my suspicion. I hope you will perform that experiment and let me know your results. Perhaps by the time you do, I'll have done it myself, and we can compare notes.

A final note about scuds, the result of keeping hundreds of them in an aquarium at one time: when they're collected in a net or held in your hand, scuds will curl almost into little balls; when swimming, they're stretched out straight. Since it can be assumed that when a trout takes a scud, the scud is likely to be swimming, imitations of scuds should be tied on straight-shank, not curved-shank, hooks. Hooks that have been called *curved scud hooks* all through the book, used for midge and caddis pupae, and for myriads of searching-nymphs, are not the best for scuds. Manufacturers call them scud hooks. I've followed their prescription. But I don't prescribe them for scuds.

OLIVE SCUD

In the smallest sizes for scuds, 18 and 20, I often use no more than the dubbed and ribbed Aquatic Sow Bug dressing listed above, but with an olive body in place of the muskrat belly fur. Most scuds taken by trout in moving water will be in or near weed beds, and therefore the color of the weeds, some shade of green. They'll be small. A very simple imitation will take trout for you, especially when fished in tandem with a larger nymph, which might be a searching dressing or a larger scud imitation.

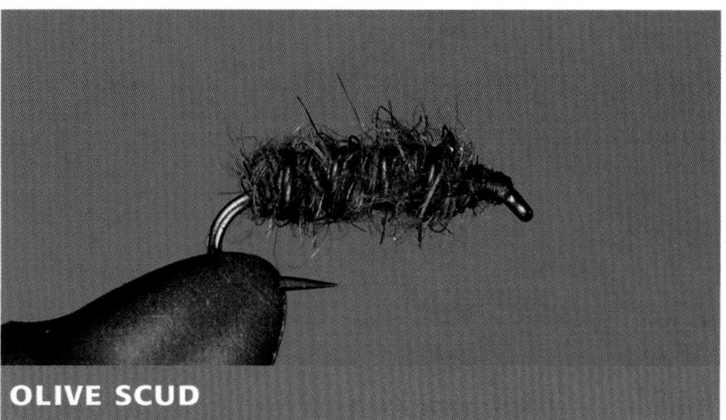

OLIVE SCUD

Hook: Standard nymph, size 18–20
Thread: Olive 8/0
Rib: Copper wire
Body: Olive dubbing

The steps in tying the Olive Scud should be self-evident. If not, they're the same as those listed for the Aquatic Sow Bug dressing given above. Rigging should be the same as well, usually with a hinged indicator, straight leader, and a microshot or two pinched to the leader between the larger and smaller nymphs in a two-nymph setup.

DUBBED SCUD

The Dubbed Scud is a basic pattern style listed in Jim Schollmeyer's book *Nymph Fly-Tying Techniques,* and is a slight abbreviation of other, more complicated, scud dressings. Most of the time, when trout take scuds in moving water, they do so opportunistically. They might take them in greater proportion than other foods around them, if scud populations are higher than other aquatic foods, and in that case it's good to show trout an imitation. But you do not need to show them an exact copy of the natural. I've never seen a stream or river situation in which one of the following Dubbed Scud dressings was not close enough to the naturals to take trout.

DUBBED SCUD, OLIVE

Hook: Standard nymph, size 12–16
Weight: 10–15 turns nonlead wire
Thread: Olive 6/0 or 8/0
Rib: Fine copper wire
Shellback: Olive Scud Back or clear plastic
Body: Olive fur and Antron dubbing mix

DUBBED SCUD, GRAY

Hook: Standard nymph, size 12–16
Weight: 10–15 turns nonlead wire
Thread: Gray 6/0 or 8/0
Rib: Fine copper wire
Shellback: Gray Scud Back or clear plastic
Body: Gray fur and Antron dubbing mix

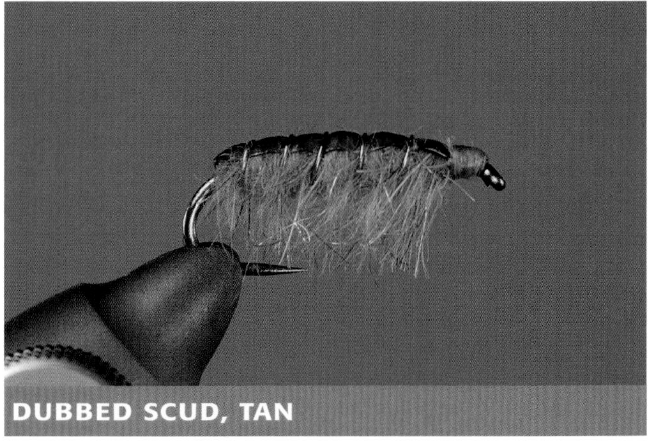

DUBBED SCUD, TAN

Hook: Standard nymph, size 12–16
Weight: 10–15 turns nonlead wire
Thread: Tan 6/0 or 8/0
Rib: Fine copper wire
Shellback: Tan Scud Back or clear plastic
Body: Tan fur and Antron dubbing mix

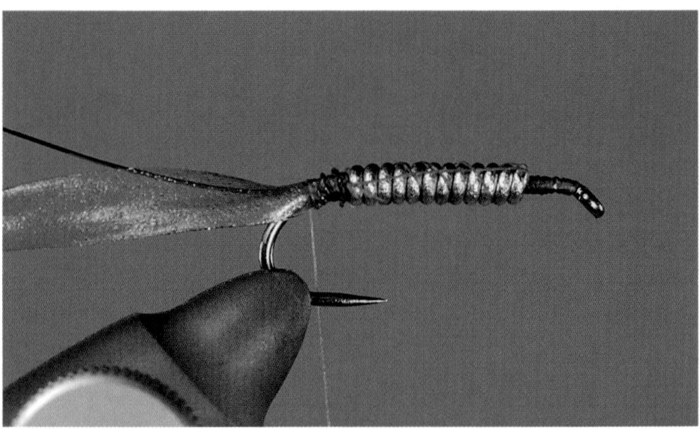

Step 1. Debarb the hook, fix it in the vise, and wrap ten to fifteen turns of nonlead wire around the shank. Start the thread, overwrap the weighting wire without worry about thread ramps front and back. Take the thread to the bend of the hook. Tie in a few inches of ribbing wire. Tie in a section of Scud Back, or cut a strip of Ziploc bag one-half to two-thirds the width of the hook gap. Tie it in at the hook bend.

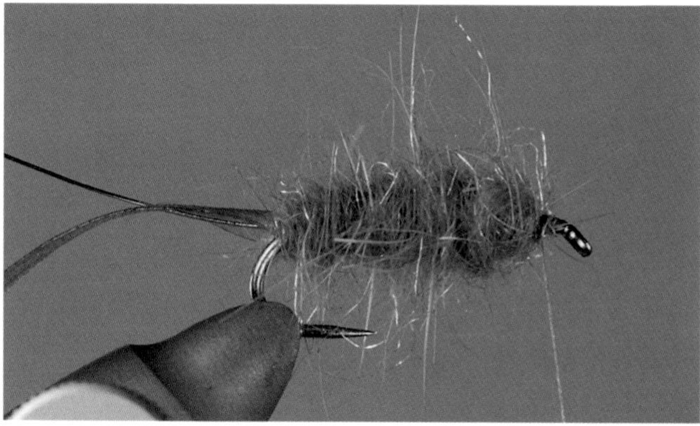

Step 2. Wind a fairly portly dubbed body forward, leaving room behind the hook eye to tie off the shellback, ribbing, and to form a head. This should be loosely dubbed, not tight. If you find it easier for the loose body required, use a dubbing rope, do not twist it tight, and wind it forward.

Step 3. Use your bodkin point or a dubbing roughing tool to tease out the body dubbing. Stroke the fibers downward, to represent those myriad legs of the natural.

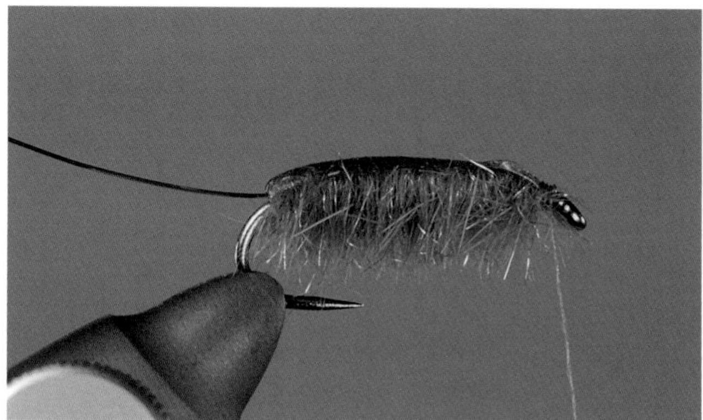

Step 4. Bring the shellback forward over the body, and tie it off behind the hook eye. Clip the excess shellback material. Slide your scissors in along the hook point, and clip the teased body fibers parallel to the body.

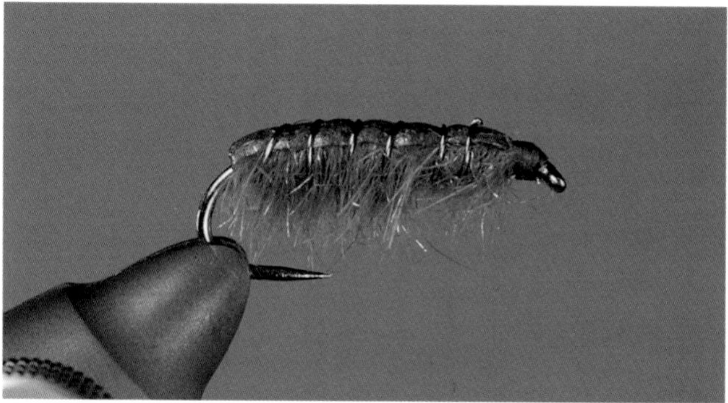

Step 5. Wind the ribbing forward in four to six evenly spaced turns. Work the wire back and forth through the fibers to keep from matting an excess of them down, though some will be captured under the wire. Tie off the wire, clip the excess, form a neat thread head, whip-finish, and cement the head.

Step 6. Use your bodkin or dubbing roughing tool again, if necessary, to tease out any fibers that have been caught under the ribbing wire.

These dubbed and clipped dressings are as close as you need to come to scuds, in stream and river environments. You'll usually use them in spring creeks and tailwaters, most often in and around beds of rooted vegetation. In these sorts of slow and often modestly shallow currents, fishing the standard shot-and-indicator rig might be a bit heavy-handed. It's often better to use a lighter yarn indicator, a hinged leader of one diameter rather than tapered, and a two-nymph rig.

It's standard among those with whom I fish to use a size 12 or 14 scud, usually olive, as the big fly, and to trail it with a size 18 or 20 beadhead searching nymph or Flashback Pheasant Tail. It's a killing combination in the types of waters where scuds thrive, because you'll also find blue-winged olive *(Baetis)* nymphs in the same waters, along with a wide variety of small midge larvae and pupae, sow bugs, and other organisms that arrive in such variety that trout are more selective to size and presentation than they are to shape and color.

If you would prefer to do this sort of fishing with a beadhead on your larger nymph, you can simply add one to the series of Dubbed Scuds.

BIGHORN SHRIMP

It's not unwise to step away from the colors of the naturals, and to tie a few scud dressings in bright colors. They work. I'll not be the one to tell you that they work because trout think they're scuds. But trout take them for something, and they're tied to look like scuds, so we would call them that, except that they're usually misnamed *shrimp,* to which scuds are related, and for which they're often mistaken.

The following dressings, used on the Bighorn River but useful on all sorts of waters as searching dressings, imitate scuds, not shrimp. It's useful to note that on some tailwaters, such as the Lee's Ferry stretch of the Colorado River downstream from Glen Canyon Dam, the water is raised and lowered at such dramatic speeds that scuds are often stranded on gravel beds. They die, turn white, orange, and even pink. When the water rises again, they are washed away, and trout feed on them, at times selectively. In that circumstance, the following dressings can be considered imitative.

BIGHORN SHRIMP, ORANGE

Hook: Curved scud, size 10–14
Weight: 10–20 turns nonlead wire
Thread: Fluorescent orange 6/0 or 8/0
Shellback: Clear Thin Skin over copper Krystal Flash
Rib: Copper wire
Abdomen: Yellow-orange Antron dubbing

BIGHORN SHRIMP, PINK

Hook: Curved scud, size 10–14
Weight: 10–20 turns nonlead wire
Thread: Fluorescent orange 6/0 or 8/0
Shellback: Clear Thin Skin over red Krystal Flash
Rib: Copper wire
Abdomen: Pink Antron dubbing

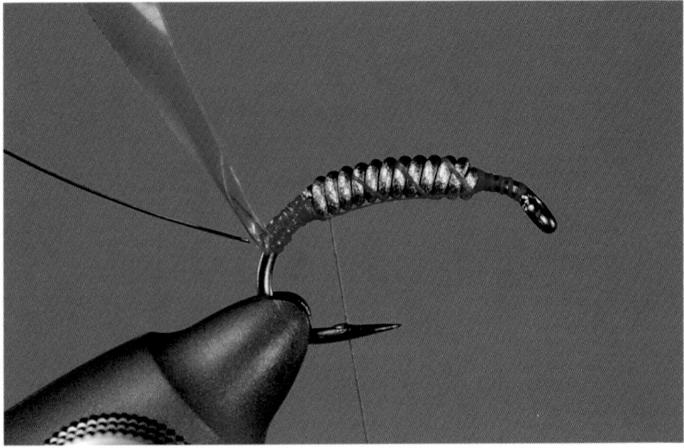

Step 1. Debarb the hook, fix it in the vise, and wrap ten to twenty turns of nonlead wire around the shank. Start the thread behind the hook eye, overwrap the lead, and take it halfway around the bend of the hook. Do not worry about building thread ramps to the weighting wire shoulders. Tie in a few inches of ribbing wire. Cut a strip of Thin Skin one-half to two-thirds the width of the hook gap, and tie it in.

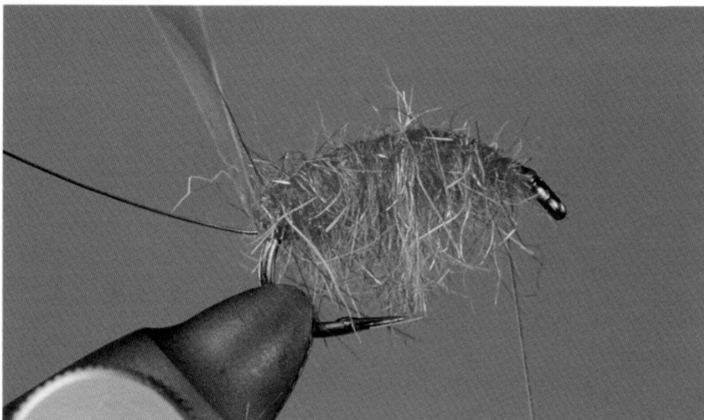

Step 2. Wrap a loose skein of dubbing forward from the bend of the hook to just behind the hook eye, leaving room to tie off the shellback and to form a head. Tease this dubbing downward with your bodkin point or a dubbing roughing tool. Hold it down and clip it about even with the hook point.

Step 3. Bring the shellback forward over the body, and tie it off behind the eye. Clip the excess. Bring the ribbing forward in four to six evenly spaced wraps over the shellback. Be sure to work the wire back and forth through the clipped dubbing, to mat down as little as possible. Tie off the ribbing, clip the excess, form a thread head, and whip-finish the fly.

Step 4. Use your bodkin point or dubbing roughing tool to tease out any fibers that have been matted down by the ribbing.

BEADHEAD SCUD

The addition of a bead makes a scud dressing less imitative, because no natural scud bears any appendage that could be mistaken for a bright head. But a bead might make a scud imitation more effective. You'll use scud patterns often, in moving water, as lead flies in searching situations, in weedy water where your collecting reveals that lots of the naturals kick around among the plant leaves and stems. A bead, in that case, adds that bit of brightness that might catch the attention of a trout feeding on or near the bottom, often in channels cut through the vegetation beds, and almost always opportunistically. The scud dressing in your two-fly tandem should be a fairly large size 12 to 16. The smaller point fly, on a ten- to twelve-inch tippet tied to the hook bend of the scud dressing, could be a size 16 to 20 searching nymph, midge larva or pupa, or small mayfly nymph imitation.

BEADHEAD SCUD, OLIVE

Hook:	Standard nymph, size 12–20
Bead:	Gold
Weight:	10–15 turns of nonlead wire
Thread:	Olive 6/0 or 8/0
Rib:	3X monofilament
Shellback:	Olive Scud Back or clear Thin Skin
Body:	Olive Scud Dub, or fur and Antron mix
Eggs:	Fluorescent red dubbing

BEADHEAD SCUD, GRAY

Hook:	Standard nymph, size 12–20
Bead:	Gold
Weight:	10–15 turns of nonlead wire
Thread:	Gray 6/0 or 8/0
Rib:	3X monofilament
Shellback:	Gray Scud Back or clear Thin Skin
Body:	Gray Scud Dub, or fur and Antron mix
Eggs:	Fluorescent red dubbing

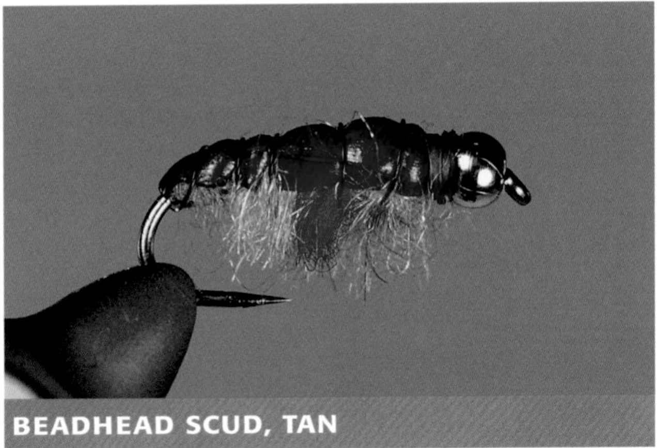

BEADHEAD SCUD, TAN

Hook:	Standard nymph, size 12–20
Bead:	Gold
Weight:	10–15 turns of nonlead wire
Thread:	Brown 6/0 or 8/0
Rib:	3X monofilament
Shellback:	Tan Scud Back or clear Thin Skin
Body:	Brown Scud Dub, or fur and Antron mix
Eggs:	Fluorescent red dubbing

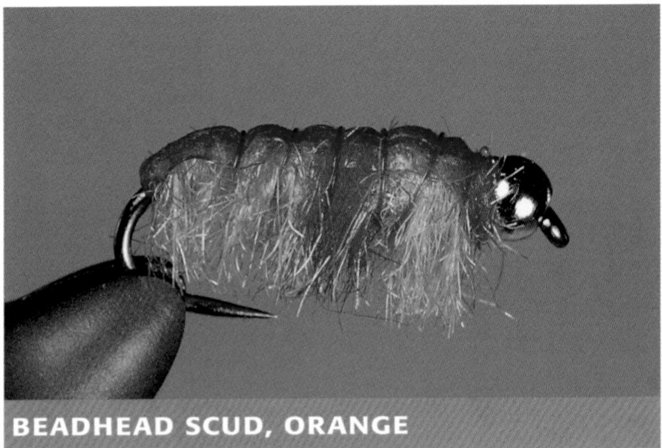

BEADHEAD SCUD, ORANGE

Hook:	Standard nymph, size 12–20
Bead:	Gold
Weight:	10–15 turns of nonlead wire
Thread:	Orange 6/0 or 8/0
Rib:	3X monofilament
Shellback:	Orange Scud Back or clear Thin Skin
Body:	Orange Scud Dub, or fur and Antron mix
Eggs:	Fluorescent red dubbing

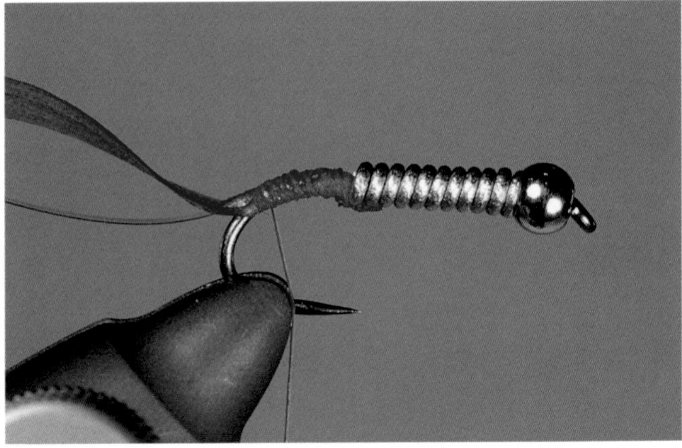

Step 1. Slip a taper-drilled bead onto the hook, and place the hook in the vise. Wrap ten to fifteen turns of nonlead weighting wire around the hook shank, and jam the front end of the wire into the back end of the bead. Start the thread behind the wire, and tie in a few inches of monofilament ribbing. Overwrap it a short way past the bend of the hook. Tie in a strip of Scud Back Thin Skin about two-thirds the width of the hook gap, and overwrap it to the back shoulder of the weighting wire.

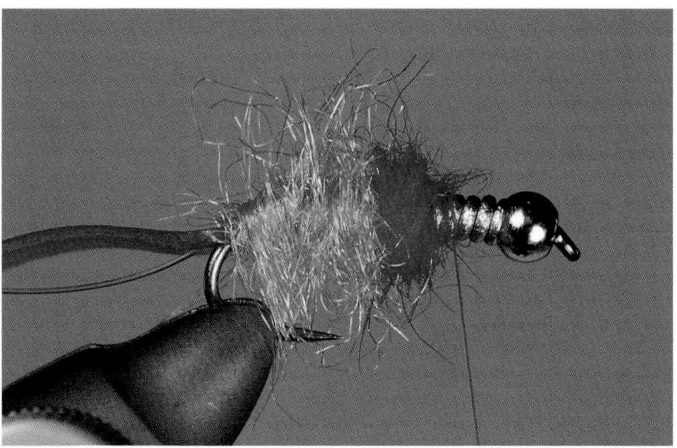

Step 2. Wax a few inches of thread, tease out a skein of dubbing, lay it against the waxed thread, and capture it in a thread loop. Twist it into a loose dubbing rope. Wrap this forward just short of the midpoint of the shank. Twist a small amount of bright red dubbing loosely onto the thread, and take a couple of turns in the center of the shank.

Step 3. Repeat Step 2, making a loose dubbing rope and winding it forward to the back of the bead. At this point the body should be a shaggy mess; don't do anything to correct that.

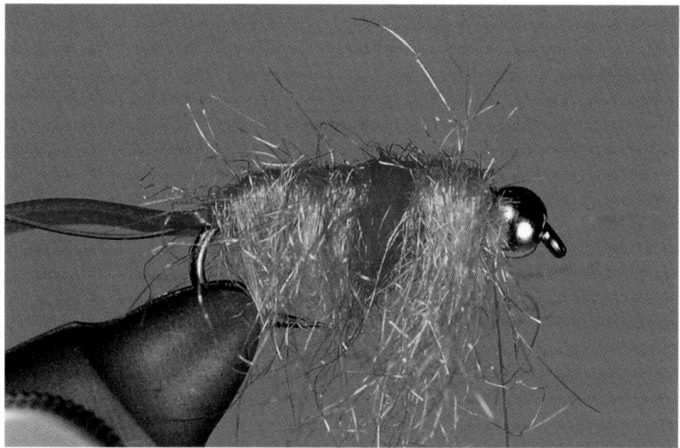

Step 4. Use your bodkin point or a dubbing brush to tease the fur out from both sides of the body, stroking it downward. Again, don't tidy it up just yet.

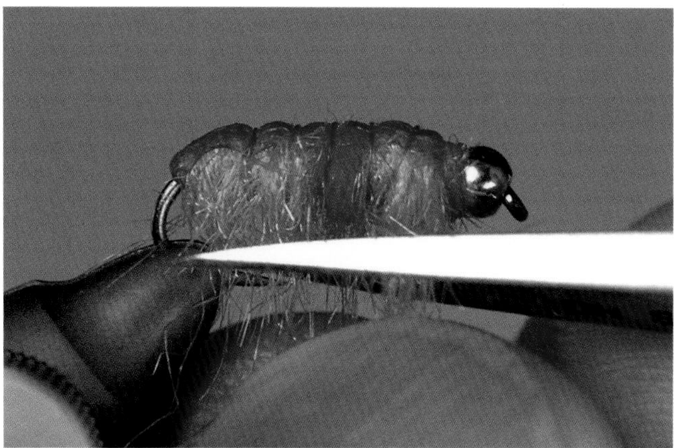

Step 5. Bring the shellback forward over the body, and tie it off behind the bead. Clip the excess. Wind the rib forward in four to six evenly spaced turns, being careful to mat down as little of the dubbing as possible. Tie it off and clip the excess. Whip-finish, clip the thread, and apply head cement. At this point you will probably find it necessary to tease some of the dubbing downward again. Holding the dubbing down with your off-hand thumb and forefinger, slide your scissors in at about the level of the hook point, and clip the dubbing.

SUMMARY

You do need sow bug and scud dressings for moving waters, but you don't need many. A single aquatic sow bug dressing, whether simple or complicated, should serve you. One of the dressing styles for scuds tied in olive, gray, and tan, each in a range of sizes from 14 to 18, should cover all the situations in which you want to fish over abundant naturals.

Rigging for sow bug dressings, and for small scuds, should usually be as the point fly, or trailer, in a two-fly setup. The larger and heavier lead fly will often be a San Juan Worm or a bigger scud dressing. You'll benefit from a light rig in such waters. A hinged leader, dropped off a fan of strike indicator yarn, with a tippet of a single diameter and about the depth of the water, will usually work better than the more coarse shot-and-indicator rig. Because spring-creek and tailwater currents are usually even in both depth and current speed, you almost always have a fairly long reach of water in which you can let your two-nymph rig reach the bottom. Such currents are ideal for the hinged-indicator method.

Place your cast well upstream of the lie you'd like to fish. Make an upstream roll cast the instant your line lands, to position the strike indicator upstream from the nymphs. Continue to mend line to give the indicator a free drift to your position. Turn and feed line into the drift as the indicator continues downstream past you. Watch for the tiniest twitch of that fluff of yarn; rarely do trout reveal themselves by tugging it under. When a natural sow bug or scud, or an imitation of either, drifts into their gun sights in spring-creek or tailwater currents, trout simply accept it in passing, and reject it at once when—not if—they detect it's a fraud. The indicator will hesitate or twitch more often than it will take a sudden dive. React quickly, but gently.

Sow bug and scud imitations will be most useful on spring creeks and tailwaters with tamed flows and aquatic vegetation.

CHAPTER 24

Hellgrammites and Fishfly Larvae

Hellgrammites and fishfly larvae are large and fierce predaceous insects that are common in eastern trout streams, less abundant throughout the West, and absent from the Great Basin region. They are so closely related, and so similar in size, form, and color, that a single imitation will fish for both. I have not encountered, read, or been told about selective feeding by trout on them. But they are present in many streams, and it is certain that a trout, given a chance at one, will not pass it up. The natural insects are often used for bait, if that is any indication about the worth of imitations.

Hellgrammite is the name for the larval stage of the adult dobsonfly, a big and bashful insect that is not often observed. In the larval stage, hellgrammites can be distinguished from fishflies by the presence of tufted gills along the sides of the abdominal segments. Fishfly larvae lack these, but have two long breathing tubes extending from the end of the abdomen. These give fishfly larvae access to atmospheric oxygen, and allow them to live in less-than-troutlike habitats. Both, however, are common in foothill and lowland trout waters, and are especially associated with smallmouth streams.

My own experience with the group is too thin to base any fishing notes upon. I have collected one hellgrammite in all of my kick-netting around the West, and have captured a single adult. Trout were not feeding selectively on them in either circumstance. I turned over just a few rocks in North Carolina's Davidson River, and collected enough larvae to see why one would want to carry an imitation of them on that water. I was being tutored on the water by Kevin Howell, owner of Davidson River Outfitters in Pisgah Forest, and coauthor with his father Don Howell of *Tying & Fishing Southern Appalachian Trout Flies*. We were fishing higher in the water column, with Bird's Nest nymphs suspended beneath small, white yarn indicators, and did very well without

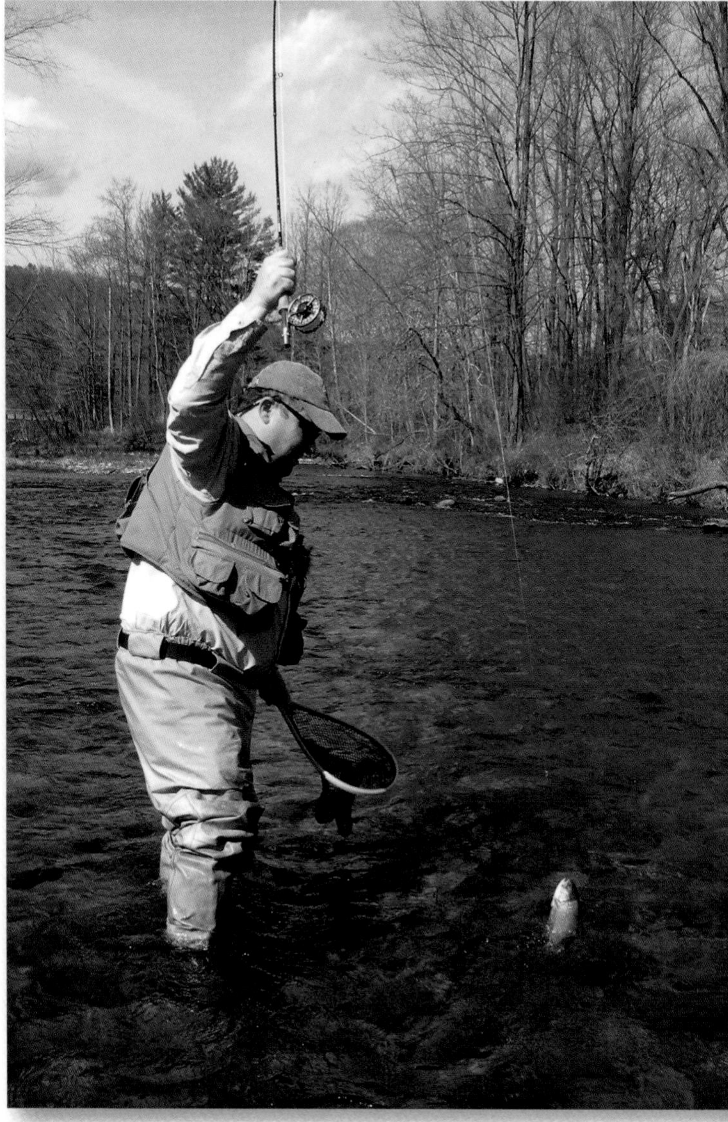

Kevin Howell on his home stretch of North Carolina's Davidson River, in water where turning over a few rocks will reveal quite a few large fishfly larvae.

Hellgrammites and fishfly larvae (shown here in two year classes) are large and approximately the color of the bottom on which they live. These were collected from the Davidson River in North Carolina, and photographed after being preserved in alcohol.

resorting to bottom bumping. But I collected the larvae, thinking they were hellgrammites.

Later, in the parking lot of Kevin's store, local biologist Jonathan Stepp looked at the insects and said if I got them home and under a microscope, I would find that they were fishfly larvae. He was right; they were fishflies. But a trout would never have noticed the absence of gill tufts and the presence of breathing tubes, and a hellgrammite imitation would have fished fine for them. A salmon-fly nymph imitation would likely work for both hellgrammites and fishfly larvae, if you were ever on a stream with the naturals present, and you lacked a nymph to match them.

BLACK WOOLLY WORM

It has long been considered that the Black Woolly Worm is an adequate imitation for hellgrammites and fishflies. Unless you get into an abundance of naturals, and see clear signs that trout are taking them, a Woolly Worm might be all you ever need for them. Certainly that old-fashioned fly will take trout, whether they mistake it for a hellgrammite, fishfly, or just something big and edible rolling along the bottom. Since my own information is so scant, and many good imitations for these insects are built around the Woolly Worm concept, I turned to Gary Soucie's book *Woolly Wisdom* for ideas. It is full of good ones.

BLACK WOOLLY WORM

Hook:	4XL, size 6–10
Weight:	15–25 turns of nonlead wire
Thread:	Black 3/0 or 6/0
Tail:	Red wool yarn
Body:	Black chenille
Hackle:	Grizzly, palmered

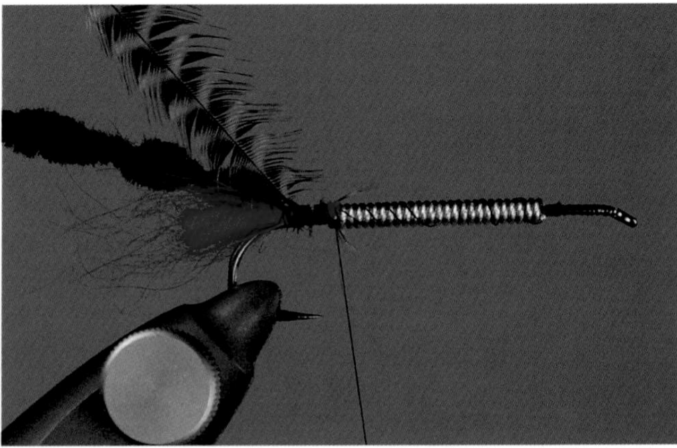

Step 1. Debarb the hook, fix it in the vise, and layer about three-fourths of the shank with weighting wire. Start the thread behind the hook eye, layer the shank, and overwrap the wire to the hook bend. Tie in a short tuft of wool yarn. Remove fibers from one-eighth inch of

chenille, and tie it in at the base of the tail. Select a long rooster neck or saddle hackle with fibers at the butt that are about two hook gaps long. Prepare it by stripping fuzz from the base and running your thumb and forefinger along it in opposition to the direction of the fibers, to splay them out. Leave enough room for one turn of chenille behind the hackle, and tie it in by its tip.

Step 2. Take one turn of body chenille behind the hackle, then wrap the rest forward to a point about one hook-eye length behind the eye. Tie off the chenille there and clip the excess.

Step 3. Wind the hackle forward over the body in five to eight evenly spaced turns. Tie off the stem, clip it, form a neat thread head, whip-finish, and cement the head.

The red wool tail might serve the same attractive purpose as a winking bead. It's hard to know what trout are thinking, but it's safe to say they're not thinking deeply. If you would like to alter your Woolly Worm to be more precisely imitative, omit the red tail.

HELLGRAMMITE

Also found in *Woolly Wisdom,* the Hellgrammite is a rough dressing targeted to this particular insect. It captures the size, shape, and color of it with a tangle of long black and brown hackles wound the length of the hook shank, then clipped to the shape of the natural. The result is ragged, but somewhat realistic, and it will certainly catch trout in the presence of hellgrammite or fishfly naturals.

HELLGRAMMITE

Hook:	4XL, size 4–8
Weight:	15–25 turns nonlead wire
Thread:	Black 3/0
Body:	Two black and two brown hackles, palmered and trimmed

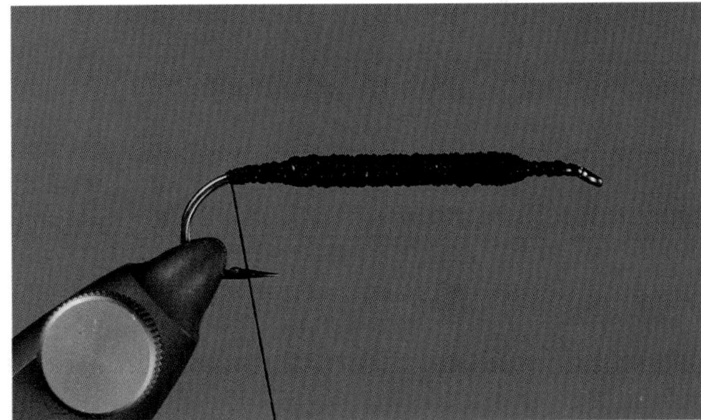

Step 1. Debarb the hook and fix it in the vise. Layer two-thirds to three-quarters of the shank with weighting wire about the diameter of the hook shank. Start the thread behind the eye, and use as many turns as necessary to build thread ramps to both wire shoulders and to cover the wire. You do not want to use 8/0 thread for this fly; it will take an unreasonable amount of thread to cover the weighting wire. Coat the thread with head cement or Flexament.

Step 2. Select two brown and two black feathers from a saddle patch, or from the unused end of a rooster cape. It does not matter how long the fibers might be. Stroke the fibers of each feather against the grain, to flare them out from the stem. Tie them in by their tips, at the bend of the hook.

Step 3. Wind one feather to the hook eye in evenly spaced turns. Tie it off. Wind a second feather of the opposite color through the first. Try to keep from matting more fibers down than you must, but it's necessary to mat lots of them down. You can tease them out with your bodkin point, if you want, after winding each hackle, but the result is going to be unruly any way you do it.

Step 4. Wind the last two hackle feathers one at a time. Tie off the stems, and clip the excess. Form a thread head, whip-finish, and apply head cement. Use your bodkin point again, or for the first time if you haven't earlier, to tease out fibers that have been covered by subsequent hackle wraps.

Step 5. Trim the hackles on the top and bottom of the fly, giving it a flat profile when viewed from the side.

Step 6. Trim the sides of the fly at a slant, from wide at the front to narrow at the back. The result both captures the flattened profile of the natural hellgrammite or fishfly, and also gives the appearance of the projections that come off each abdominal segment of the insect.

The Black Woolly Worm and Hellgrammite should both be fished with a dead-drift presentation, tumbling along the bottom. If their internal weight is sufficient, you can rig them directly under a hard indicator. A yarn indicator that would hold up such a heavy nymph would have to be large enough to frighten birds and fish. If boisterous water calls for it, you might need to add split shot or putty weight to the leader ten to twelve inches from the fly. The naturals tend to be most abundant in currents that have leveled out, lost a lot of their drive. You will normally find no need for added weight.

MURRAY'S HELLGRAMMITE

Harry Murray's famous Hellgrammite has many attributes of a streamer, and might be mistaken by trout for something other than the natural it imitates. That makes it more effective; the best searching dressings can always be fished for more than the single insect they were created to match. It's no secret that the following dressing can be tumbled along the bottom to imitate a hellgrammite or fishfly larva, or it can be given action like a streamer to imitate a leech or pollywog out for a swim across the currents. It can be fished in all of the ways that a Black Woolly Bugger might be, and it will meet with similar success.

MURRAY'S HELLGRAMMITE *Harry Murray*

Hook:	2XL or 3XL, size 4–10
Weight:	15–25 turns nonlead wire
Thread:	Black 3/0
Tail:	15–20 black ostrich herls
Hackle:	Dark blue dun, palmered over body
Body:	Black chenille
Pincers:	Black rubber legs

Step 1. Debarb the hook, fix it in the vise, wind weighting wire over two-thirds to three-quarters of the shank, and coat it with thread and either head cement or Flexament as you did for the above Hellgrammite dressing. Peel or cut a substantial number of ostrich herls from the stem. Do not scrimp, or the resulting fly will appear anemic when it gets wet. Clip the butts to even them, and tie them in at the bend of the hook. Use your fingers to pinch the fibers—do not cut them—to about two hook-shank lengths.

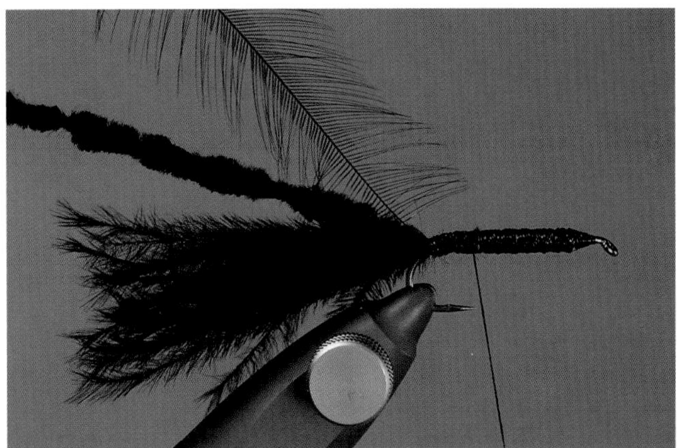

Step 2. Tie in a section of chenille at the base of the tail. Select a hackle feather with fibers about two hook gaps long. Stroke the fibers contrary to their natural direction, to stand them at an angle from the stem. Tie the hackle in by the tip, leaving room for a single turn of body chenille behind it.

Step 3. Take a turn of chenille behind the hackle, then wind the rest forward to a point one and a half to two hook-eye lengths behind the eye. Leave room for the rubber pincers. Tie the chenille off and clip the excess.

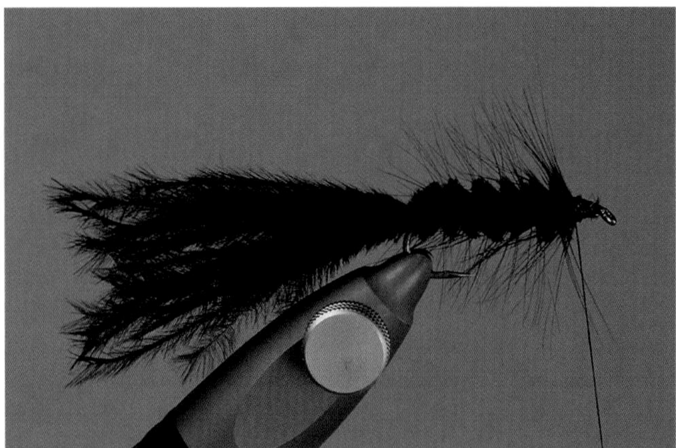

Step 4. Wind the hackle forward in five evenly spaced turns through the chenille body. Tie it off at the end of the body, and clip the excess stem. Again, don't crowd the head.

Step 5. Measure two rubber-leg sections about the length of the hook shank. Tie them in tight behind the hook eye. Clip any excess behind the head, and use enough thread turns over the rubber to form a neat thread head. Whip-finish behind the pincers, clip the thread, and apply head cement.

OLE HELLGY

The most realistic imitation I've seen for the hellgrammite and related fishfly larva is Kevin Howell's Ole Hellgy, tied for the North Carolina streams where I fished with him, and observed what I thought were hellgrammites but turned out to be fishfly larvae. Those insects had a dark brick red aspect to them, clearly because the rocks on which I found them were that same color. Kevin's dressing uses a mix of dubbing that captures that color. It's wise to bear in mind that the colors of all aquatic insects will reflect the substrates on which they live, and that you might need to vary your dubbing color to match hellgrammites and fishfly larvae on your own waters.

OLE HELLGY
originated and finished fly tied by Kevin Howell

Hook:	3XL curved nymph, size 2–8
Weight:	25 turns of nonlead wire
Thread:	Black 6/0
Underbody:	Black wool yarn
Tail:	Dark brown or black rabbit fur
Rib:	Red wire
Gills:	One olive-brown and one black emu feather
Abdomen:	Peacock herl
Shellback:	Turkey tail feather section
Thorax:	Big Nasty dubbing, Ole Hellgy color
Pincers:	Brown rubber legs

For the thorax, Kevin uses a proprietary Big Nasty dubbing mix, Ole Hellgy color, available from his Davidson River Outfitters (www.davidsonflyfishing.com). He describes it as a complicated mix of dark brown, black, dark olive, and a touch of red rabbit fur, blended in a two-thirds-one-third mix with groundhog hair with the guard hairs left in.

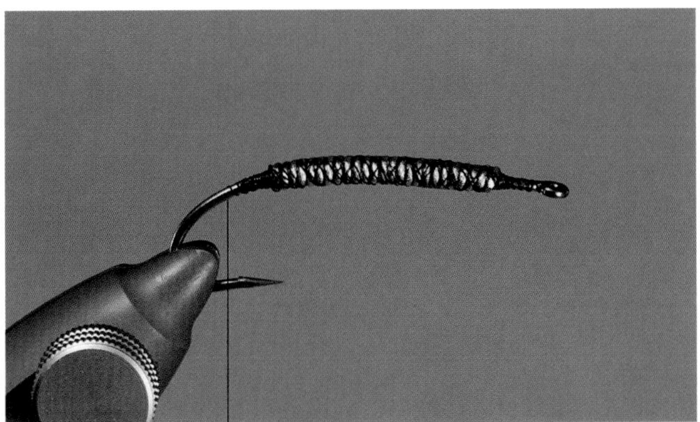

Step 1. Debarb the hook, fix it in the vise, and lay a thread base from the eye to a point directly above the barb. Weight the shank with twenty-five turns of nonlead wire. Layer thread over the wire, flatten the wire with pliers, then coat it with head cement or Flexament.

Step 2. Tie in a skein of wool yarn behind the weighting wire. Wrap the yarn over the wire to the front of the weighting wire, then one-third of the shank length back, to form an underbody for the fattened thorax. Tie off the yarn and clip the excess.

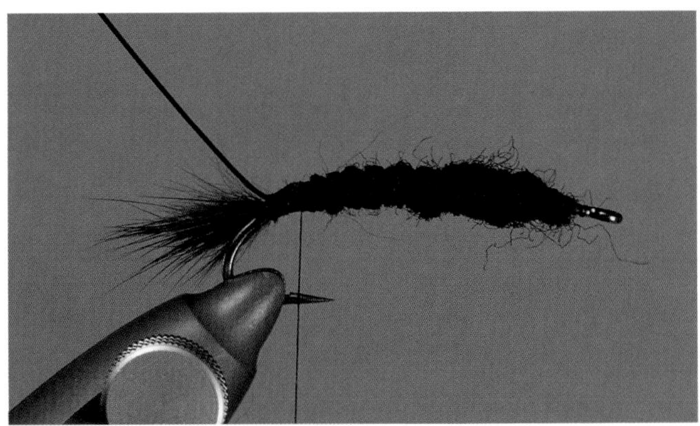

Step 3. Clip a substantial patch of dark brown or black rabbit fur from a Zonker strip. Measure it one-third to one-half the length of the shank, and tie it in at the end of the underlayment of thread. Clip the excess. Tie in the ribbing wire.

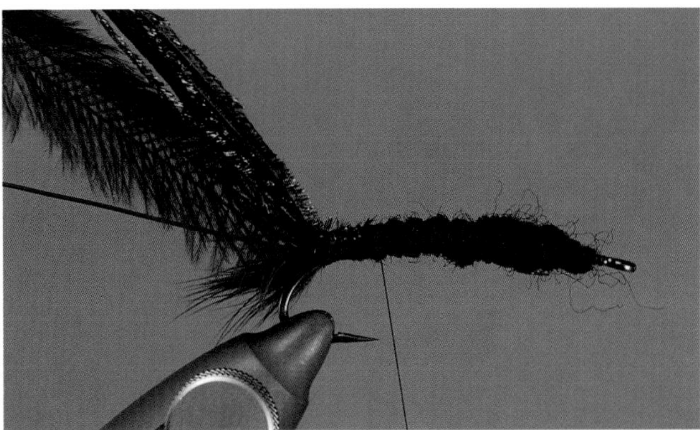

Step 4. Prepare one olive-brown and one black emu feather by stroking the fibers so they stand at ninety-degree angles to the feather stem. Find the point on each feather where the fibers begin to have some substantial fuzziness to them, tie them in at the base of the tails, by their tips, and clip the excess. Tie in six to eight peacock herls by their tips.

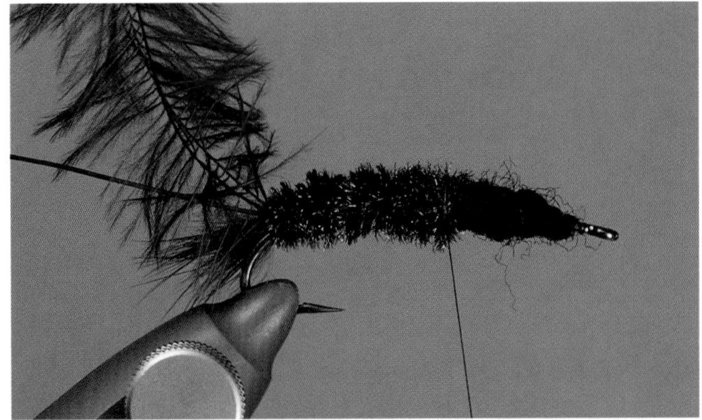

Step 5. Gather the peacock herls with the thread, or form a loop and make a herl rope. Wind this forward over the rear two-thirds of the shank. Tie it off and clip the excess.

Step 6. Palmer the two emu feathers the length of the abdomen, tie them off, and clip the excess. Counterwind the ribbing wire through the herl and emu to the end of the abdomen. Tie it off and clip or break the excess. Shear the top and bottom of the emu fibers flush with the peacock herl body.

Step 7. Cut a section of turkey tail feather about the width of the hook gap. Tie it in at the end of the abdomen with its shiny side up, so that when you pull it forward there will be no wasp-waist effect, and the dark side will be up.

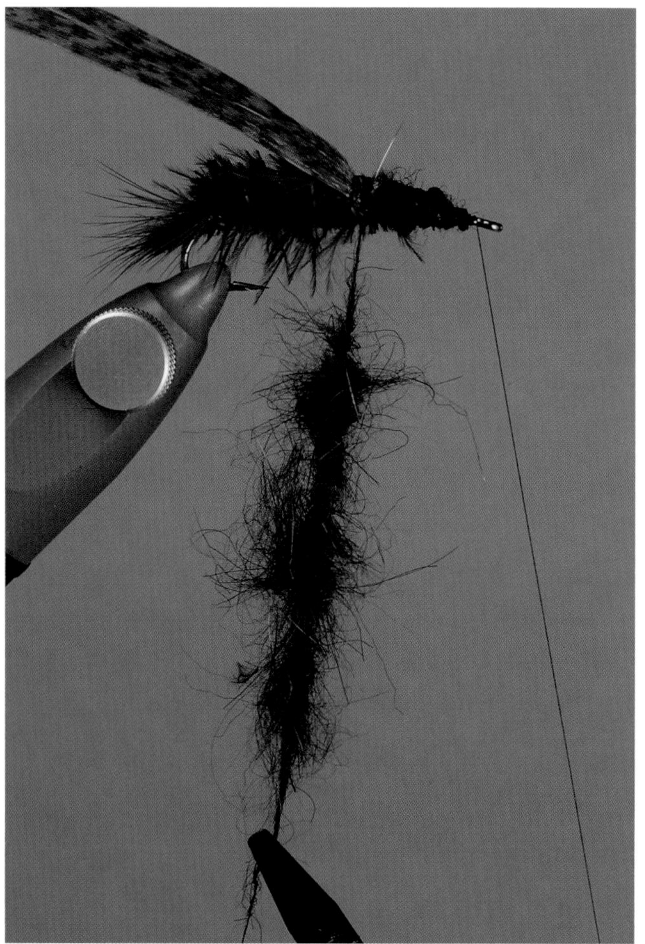

Step 8. Apply sticky dubbing wax to your tying thread. Create a wide and loose skein of dubbing mix, and tack it to the thread. Form a dubbing loop and twist it into a thick and fibrous dubbing rope (see page 50).

Step 9. Dub a substantial thorax, tapering to a point one or two hook-eye lengths behind the eye. Leave room to tie off the shellback and to tie in the pincers.

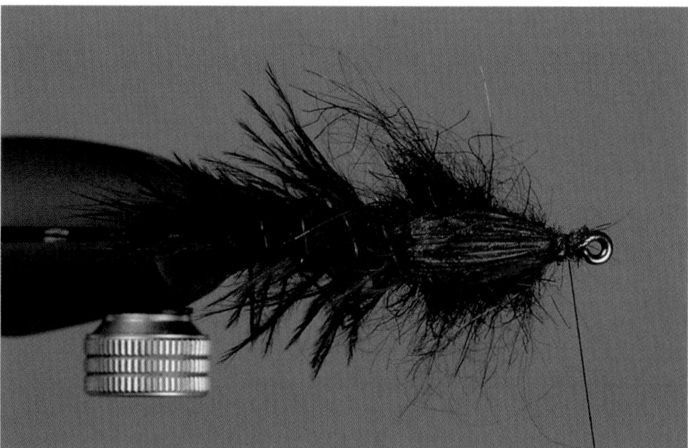

Step 10. Draw the shellback over the thorax, and tie it off with several tight turns of thread. Clip the excess.

Step 11. Fold a length of rubber legs so the two tips are even. Tie it in behind the hook eye. If necessary, clip the tag of rubber that forms behind the tie-in thread wraps. Form a head over the pincer tie-in point, whip-finish, clip the thread, and apply head cement.

Kevin's dressing is obviously intended to be fished on or very near the bottom, with a dead-drift presentation. In the brief time I fished with Kevin, I noticed he's a master at using his line tip as an indicator. His beautiful but relatively low-gradient home stretch of the Davidson River, near his shop in Pisgah Forest, lends itself to an upstream or cross-stream cast, carefully tended downstream drift, and keen watchfulness of any abnormal movement by the line tip or leader.

If you fish more boisterous water, or water that is even slightly off-color, you might be wise to suspend the heavy Ole Hellgy, or any other imitation of the large hellgrammites and fishfly larvae, beneath a fairly large indicator. The new balloons will probably become the ideal. But there is a reason Kevin uses his line tip, or a less intrusive indicator when he uses one: on brisk but even flows, in clear water two to three feet deep, a big, brash indicator floating overhead might as well have a horn to honk. It's going to frighten trout, unless they've never had a fly tossed at them.

SUMMARY

You won't find many situations in which you need an exact imitation of either a hellgrammite or fishfly larva. It's likely, however, that you'll catch lots of trout on a nymph that looks a lot like them, especially if the naturals are abundant in the water you're fishing. A kick-net sample in a riffle or bouldered run, or simply turning over a few bottom rocks, will reveal the presence or absence of the naturals to you. If any are present, trout will be aware of them, and will be happy to accept a nymph that looks like them. Either tumble it along the bottom, or give it a bit of teasing action, though that last retrieve works only with the Murray's Hellgrammite, and the fly, when fished with such movement, no longer represents the natural for which it is tied.

A large, weighted hellgrammite nymph makes an effective delivery system for a smaller nymph, which might in turn catch more fish for you than the larger imitation. It's surprising how often you will catch trout on a small fly trailed behind a large one, decide that you no longer need the large one, only to remove it and suddenly stop catching trout. The large nymph gets the attention of trout. If they choose to take the small one, that should not bother you.

Just as often, if natural hellgrammites or fishfly larvae are present, trout will accept the large imitation, and ignore the smaller nymph trailing behind it.

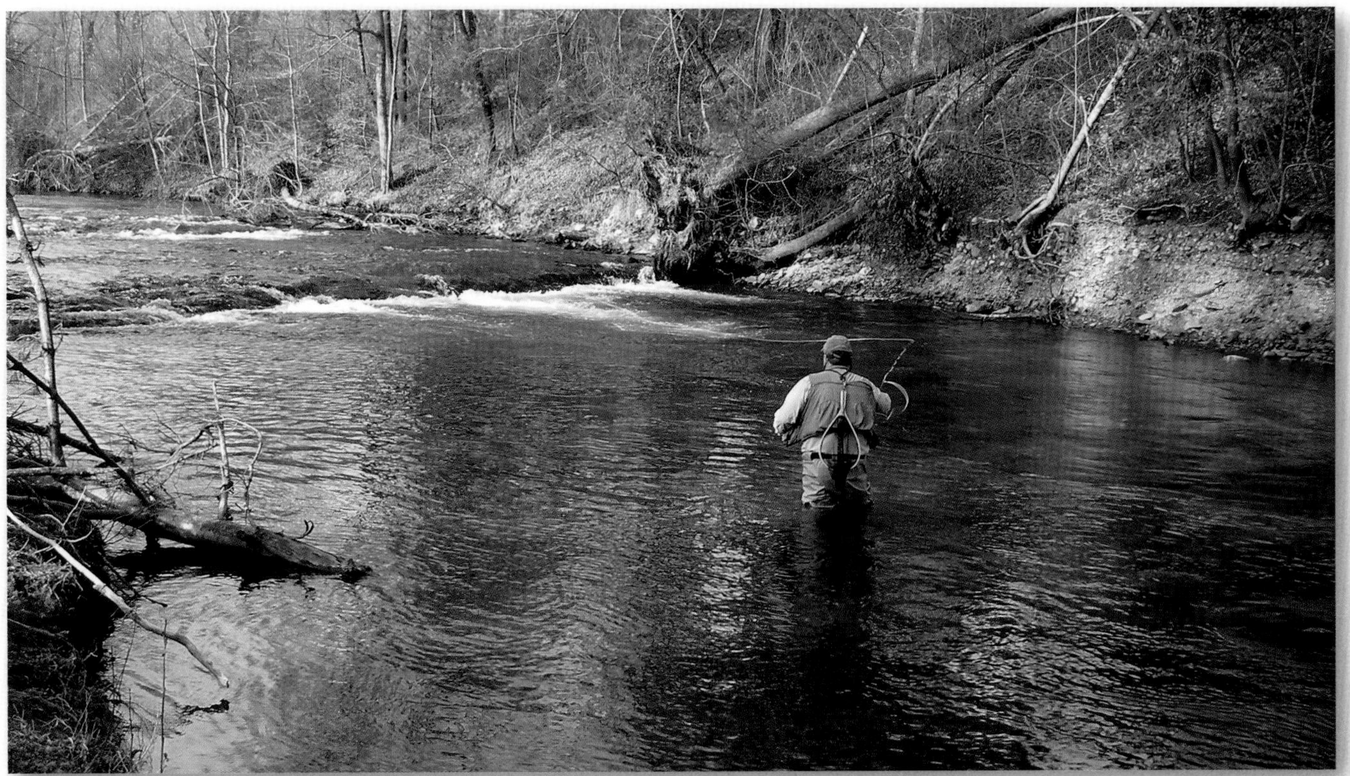

Kevin Howell on the Davidson River, where he designed his Ole Hellgy imitation for the common fishfly larva, which is almost precisely like the more famous hellgrammite.

CHAPTER 25

Aquatic Worms

I would prefer to place the San Juan Worm in the section on searching nymphs, because it's quite likely best when used as such. But it's an imitation of a specific trout food form, and therefore belongs here in its own chapter. It will be a short one. What can be said about worms, and about the simplest flies that can be tied to match them? A defect in my personality has kept me from fishing them. I suppose it's a continuation of the same philosophy that makes some folks dry-fly purists, other folks content to fish wet flies but never downstream, still others okay with nymphs but disdainful of strike indicators. I have in my past drawn my own line, without realizing it, at an imitation of a worm.

It's far from reasonable. I am fine with wet flies, upstream or down. I had a secret quarrel with strike indicators until, a long time in my past now, I slipped one on once when nobody was looking, and it turned a frustrating and fishless late-winter day on the Deschutes into a fine reason to be out in the cold fishing. We all have our own lines drawn. I have usually found that relaxing my line a bit has resulted in more fun, not less of it, so I have tied a dozen San Juan Worms and added them to my

Chuck Rizzuto, dean of guides on New Mexico's San Juan River tailwater and originator of the San Juan Worm, playing a trout on his home river.

searching-nymph box. They're a big bright spot in that box, but they haven't gotten wet yet. They catch my eye, and I'm certain that one day soon they'll begin to get dunked, and I'll have fun doing it . . . if I catch trout on them, which is almost certain.

Chuck Rizzuto, dean of the San Juan River and long a guide on the river, is the originator of what has become one of the most popular trout flies of all time. I have fished with Chuck on his home water, at a time when the Corps of Engineers was working on the dam. The water was somewhere between cloudy and muddy. I was not able to put much pressure on the trout. Chuck was so tuned to the movements of his indicator that he detected strikes I had no idea had happened. He and his San Juan Worm accounted for quite a few fish that day.

The original San Juan Worm, and still the most popular, is tied with bright red Vernille, Ultra Chenille, or Velvet Chenille, all brand names for a chenille that is wound on a stiff enough core to keep its shape in the water. Most of the natural aquatic worms I've collected are a very light brown, almost reddish, but far from bright red. I recommend tying the fly in what is called "worm brown," and also in the original red. I've seen it in nearly every color you can imagine, and I imagine they would all work. But I have no experience with these worm imitations, so I would be going too far out on a limb to give a list of preferred colors.

The original San Juan Worm was tied on a hook shank without weight. The thread color is the body color. Now that fine wires are available in all sorts of colors, it's easy to wind the body of Ultra Wire and have both the color you're after and a bit of weight to get the fly down. It's also possible to add a bead to the San Juan Worm, which might or might not make it more effective. Maybe I'll make it next season's experiment to not only fish San Juan Worms, but also figure out which style is most effective, in my experience.

Aquatic worms are common in the bottom silts of streams and rivers, thriving in the gravel of riffles and on rocks that have gathered moss, or a layer of aquatic vegetation.

Though most aquatic worms are the same color as earthworms, bordering on reddish brown, few are the bright colors in which imitations are usually tied for them. These bright red flies work, however, so it would be wise to carry the San Juan Worm in both natural and bright colors.

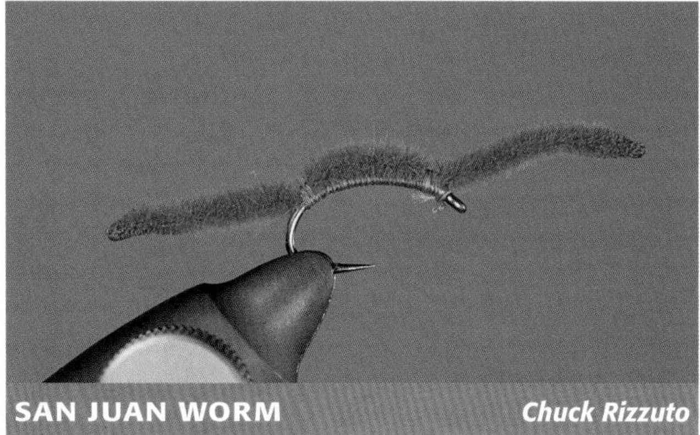

SAN JUAN WORM *Chuck Rizzuto*

Hook: Curved scud, size 10–18
Thread: Tan or red 6/0 or 8/0
Body: Worm brown or red Vernille, Ultra Chenille, or Velvet Chenille

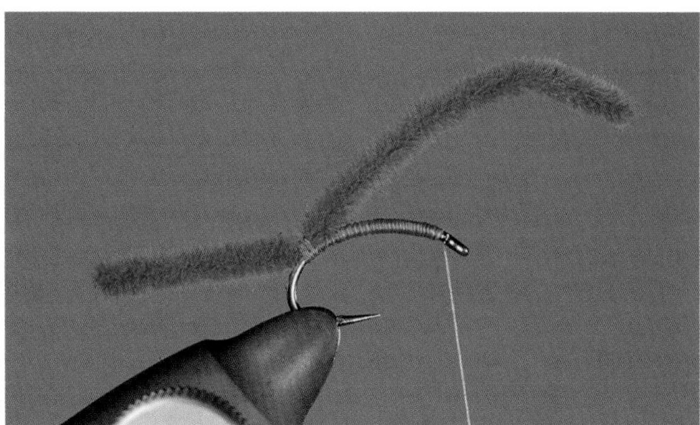

Step 1. Debarb the hook and fix it in the vise. Start the thread behind the eye, and layer it partway around the bend of the hook, covering all of the shank with tightly adjacent thread wraps. Cut a section of body material about three to four hook-shank lengths long. Hold it so

it is centered at approximately the midpoint of the shank, and tie it in with four to five tight thread turns at the end of the thread body. Return the thread to the hook eye, again with adjacent turns that cover the first layer. A single layer of thread will let the hook color dominate the thread color when the fly gets wet.

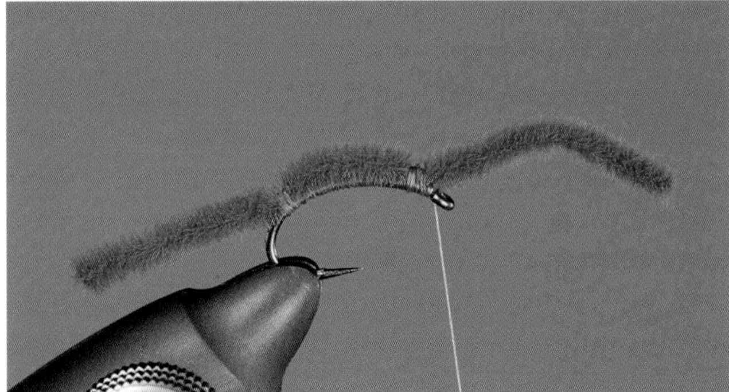

Step 2. Draw the body material over the top of the hook shank, and tie it in with four or five turns of thread. Hold the front section of body material up and out of the way. Make a thread head in front of it, whip-finish, clip the thread, and apply head cement.

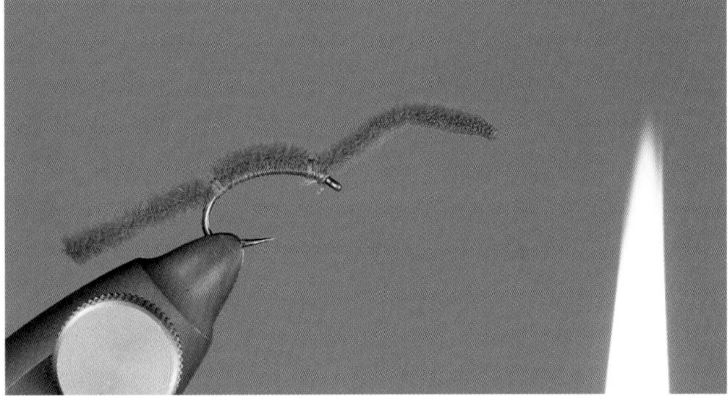

Step 3. Use a candle flame or cigarette lighter to singe both ends of the body. Move the flame to the end slowly; if you get it too hot, the chenille will abruptly melt too far back. It's a good reason to use an excessive length of body material until you've got the knack for shaping the ends without igniting them.

To tie a San Juan Worm with a wire body, choose a wire that is the same color as the chenille you will be using, and a diameter finer than the hook wire. It's questionable whether it's better to weight the shank, or to tie the fly without weight and pinch shot to the leader to get it to the bottom. It's certain that you want to fish the San Juan Worm on the bottom, no matter how you choose to get it there.

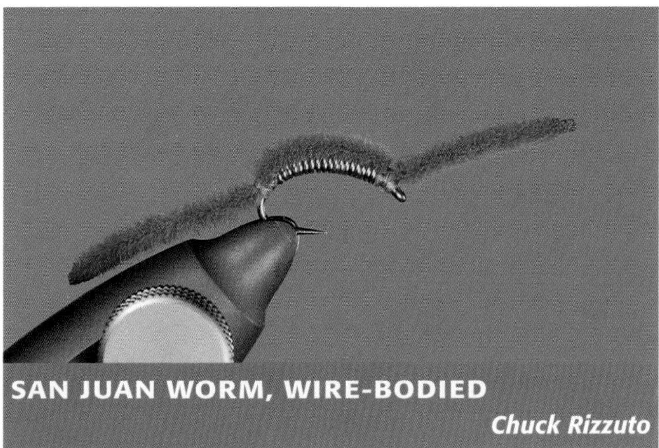

SAN JUAN WORM, WIRE-BODIED
Chuck Rizzuto

Hook: Curved scud, size 10–18
Underbody: Copper or red wire
Thread: Tan or red 6/0 or 8/0
Body: Worm brown or red Vernille, Ultra Chenille, or Velvet Chenille

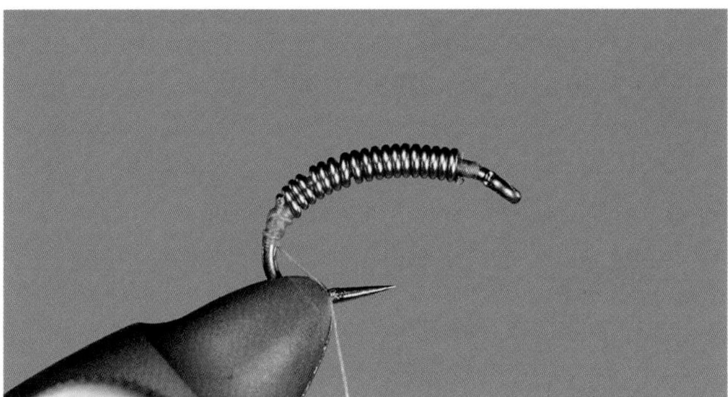

Step 1. Start the thread behind the eye, and layer the shank well around the bend of the hook. Start the wire at a point about straight above the point of the barb. You will have difficulty if you try to skimp on wire; it will be almost impossible to start the wire if you hold it by a short stub. Instead, give yourself one-half to three-quarters of an inch to hold with your off-hand thumb and forefinger, and place the first few turns precisely where you want them, against this steady anchor. Clip this excess later. Take tightly abutted turns of wire forward to a point about two hook-eye lengths behind the eye.

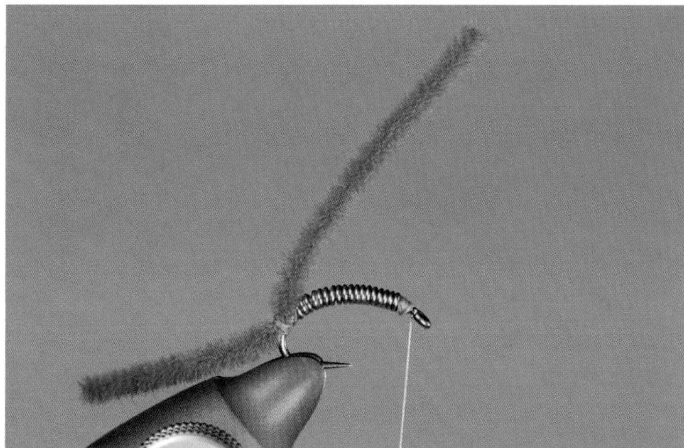

Step 2. Measure a section of chenille three to four times the hook-shank length, and center it on the shank. Tie it in with four to five tight turns of thread behind the wire underbody. Take your thread forward through the wire, wrapping between the wire turns.

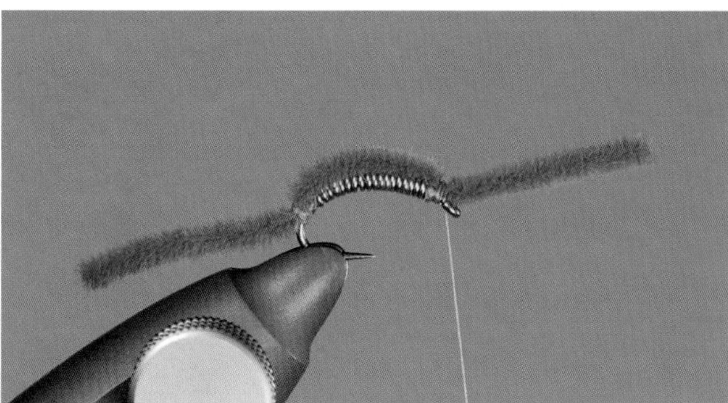

Step 3. Bring the chenille forward over the underbody, and tie it off with four to five turns of thread behind the hook eye. Hold up the front section, make a thread head, whip-finish, clip the thread, and apply head cement.

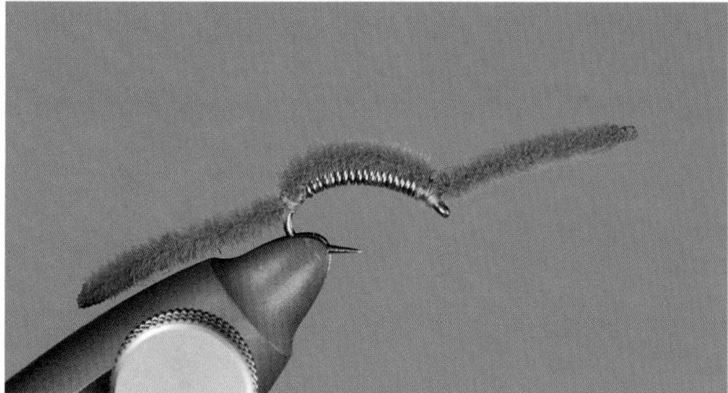

Step 4. Singe the ends of the worm with a candle flame or cigarette lighter.

It's easy to add a bead to a San Juan Worm, but it must be taper-drilled, and the diameter of the hole must allow passage of both the chenille and hook shank. Use a hook one size smaller than you would for the same length worm with a thread or wire body. If you have trouble getting the chenille through the bead, it might help to singe the end as the first step. It's best to simply use a bead big enough to accommodate the chenille easily, so you aren't forced to use tweezers or pliers to push and pull it through.

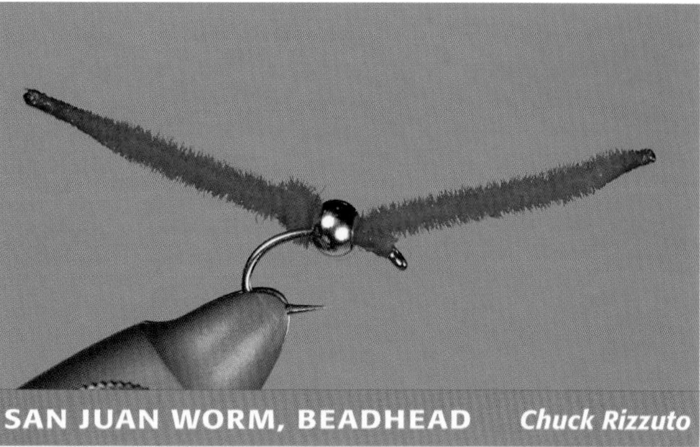

SAN JUAN WORM, BEADHEAD *Chuck Rizzuto*

Hook: Curved scud, size 10–18
Bead: Gold
Thread: Tan or red 6/0 or 8/0
Body: Worm brown or red Vernille, Ultra Chenille, or Velvet Chenille

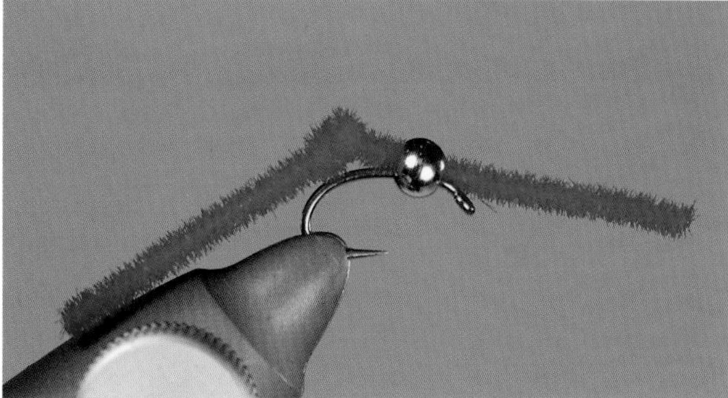

Step 1. Clip a section of chenille four to five times the length of the hook shank. Make an overhand knot in the center and draw it tight. Run one end of the chenille through a bead, entering from the open end of the taper. Run the hook point through the narrow end of the tapered hole, and thread the bead to the hook eye. Fix the hook in the vise.

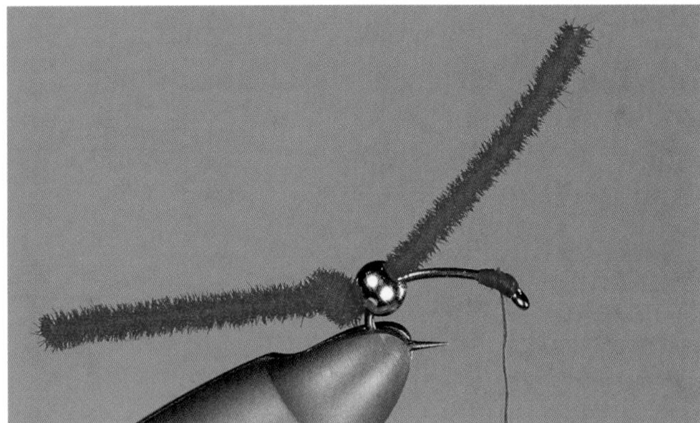

Step 2. Move the bead and chenille to the bend of the hook, out of the way. Start the thread behind the eye, and take enough turns to form a bump that will block the bead.

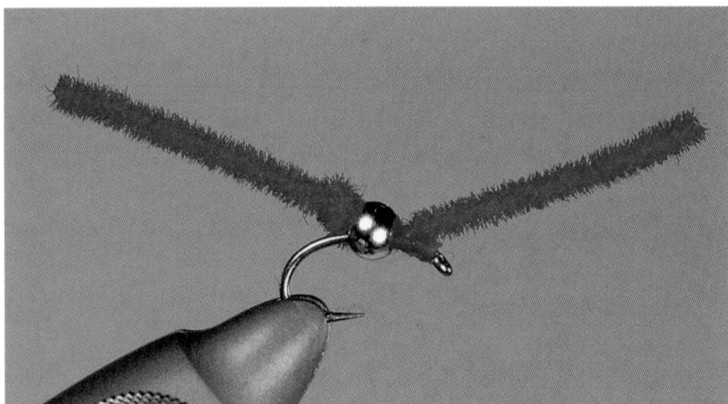

Step 3. Draw the chenille knot tight against the back of the bead. Move the bead forward until it is jammed against the thread bump. Take four to five thread turns over the chenille, just in front of the bead. The thread locks it in place from the front, and the knot from the rear. Move the thread in front of the chenille, whip-finish over the bump, clip the thread, and apply head cement.

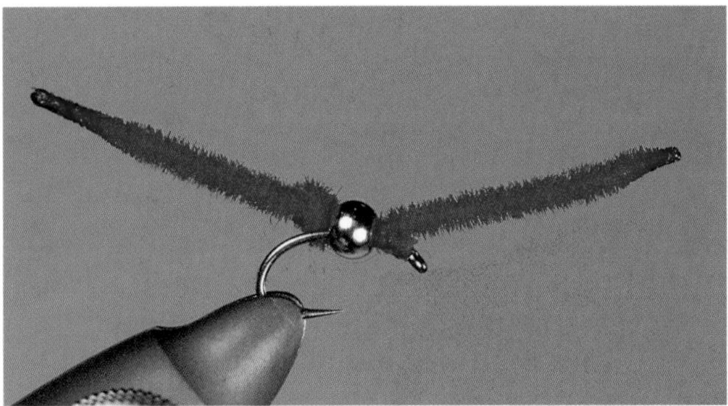

Step 4. Singe the ends of the chenille, being careful not to overheat it and burn up more than you want. Worms have tapered ends, so don't worry about a long taper if you have sufficient body length left to represent a real aquatic worm, unhappy and writhing at the idea of being knocked loose in the currents.

Aquatic worms like gravel and fine sediments. You will kick them up in nearly every riffle sample you take, in every stream you fish. I have collected them from Patagonian Chile north into British Columbia. They are most abundant where sediment is finest. Spring creeks and tailwaters allow the deposition of the smallest particles, so your use of the San Juan Worm imitation will be most common on the types of waters where Chuck Rizzuto originated the fly: the San Juan River tailwater in New Mexico.

SUMMARY

The San Juan Worm is one nymph everybody should have in the fly box, to add some color if for no other reason. Unless you're as foolish as I am, and let artificial reasons keep you from getting this excellent artificial wet, you'll catch lots of trout on it.

Most water where the worm is fished has subdued flows, either by spring sources or the taming of a dam. The best rig for these types of flows is the hinged indicator: a fan of yarn, a tippet of a single diameter and a bit longer than the water is deep, the San Juan Worm at the end of the tippet, and usually a small scud or sow bug dressing dropped off the worm on a ten- to twelve-inch tippet. A couple of microshot, or a pinch of putty weight, will almost always be needed to get the brace of flies to the bottom.

This is the most common setup used by guides on western tailwaters such as the Bighorn, Missouri, and San Juan Rivers. The client casts the rig slightly upstream from the boat; the guide strokes a proper cadence on the oars to give the combination of flies a long and drag-free drift. The indicator tilts, suddenly stops, or moves in some way contrary to the current. The guide bellows, "Set the hook!" and if you fail to do that too many times, you will be instructed to pay attention to your indicator.

Perhaps that is why I don't use the San Juan Worm as often as I should. When I'm afloat on a river, I tend to be more interested in the scenery than I am the career of my indicator.

CHAPTER 26

An Imitative-Nymph Box

Your imitative-nymph box should reflect your preferences. If you spend most of your time on small streams, fast mountain waters of all sizes, or foothill streams still steep enough that they rush right along, your searching-nymph box should be big, but your imitative box can be smaller. Trout don't get a chance to study what trots past them in such swift waters. They make quick decisions: take it or let it pass. If they failed to accept more than they rejected, examining most of what they see with their secondary senses of taste and texture, they would soon go out of business, which to a trout means fading away and expiring. Nymphs from your searching box will serve you in almost all fast-water situations.

If your focus is brisk water, but you'd like to add a few specific nymph imitations to your box, be sure to include the Flashback Pheasant Tail in sizes 18 to 22 for times when trout are taking tiny insects. You'll not always notice when it's happening; if you add a size 20 Pheasant Tail as a trailer behind whatever you normally fish on fast water, you'll be surprised how often it's the one interviewed by trout. They take it in water so fast you'd think they'd never notice it. If you fish fast waters in the West, then you'll want to add imitations of the large salmon-fly and golden stonefly nymphs, unless your searching box contains Charles Brooks's Montana Stone, which might be as good as you can get for the salmon-fly imitation. If you prowl eastern streams, substitute a hellgrammite dressing for the salmon-fly nymph.

Caddis are abundant in both fast and slow waters. If your focus is fast water, then your imitative box should contain larval dressings in a couple of colors, green and tan, and a narrow range of sizes, 12 to 16. Add pupal patterns in the three important colors, green, cream, and golden-brown, in the same small set of sizes: 12 to 16.

You won't find it necessary to add many imitative nymph patterns to your searching selection if you spend most of your fishing time on fast creeks, streams, and rivers. If your searching-nymph box is big enough, and has some empty rows for expansion, you might be able to add your imitative efforts to it, and cut what you carry to one box. That is always beneficial in the sort of wading that swift water requires: the less you carry, the more time you'll spend upright.

If you spend any portion of your allotted trout-fishing time on spring creeks and tailwaters, or if your mountain and foothill streams are pleasantly interrupted by long meadow-stream stretches, then the size of your imitative-nymph box should be right up there with that of your searching box. If you spend most of your time fishing spring creeks and tailwaters, then your imitative-nymph box should be outsized. You might even expand into a mayfly nymph box, caddisfly box, small stonefly box, add a midge box, and a combined scud, sow bug, and San Juan Worm box.

For gentle waters, start by selecting the more imitative options from the lists of pattern styles for each insect type. Spring creeks and tailwaters have more abundant niches for insects, but they are less varied. As a result, they have higher populations of a limited number of species. That translates into trout focused on a single nymph, larva, pupa, or crustacean a higher percentage of the time. In peaceful flows, trout are also allowed more time to examine what the currents deliver past them. They become selective. A searching nymph might still be close enough, in size, form, and color, to the natural they're taking. But you're far more likely to need an imitative dressing to catch trout on slow water than you are on fast water.

If you fish slow water often, your imitative-nymph box should contain imitations of small blue-winged olive mayfly nymphs *(Baetis)*, and also small crawlers such as the pale morning dun nymph *(Ephemerella inermis)*. I wouldn't want to visit a spring creek or tailwater without

Wire Midges in green, red, and black, sizes 18 to 22, and Thread Midges in the same set of colors and sizes, to imitate midge larvae and pupae. At least as important would be the white and black indicators necessary to fish these just beneath the surface, where selective trout tend to focus on them when the naturals are abundant.

You need to add sow bug and scud dressings to your imitative-nymph box for moving waters only if you fish waters with rooted aquatic plant beds. Such vegetation will be loaded with scuds, and in some cases sow bugs as well. Your patterns for them might be as simple as the dubbed and ribbed Aquatic Sow Bug and Olive Dubbed Scud, but you should have something to represent them. I don't encounter sow bugs often enough to carry anything beyond the simplest dressing for them. If you fish Ozark tailwaters, your nymph box would look different from mine.

Scuds are so prevalent in some plant-filled waters that your imitations should be based on what you scoop from the water. It's educational to hoist a fistful of what we call *weeds,* lay them out on a dry rock, see what scurries out. In almost every weed-choked stream where I've performed this maneuver, the dominant trout food has been a scud, ranging in size from 12 to 20, almost the exact color of the vegetation in which it lives.

Carry a few San Juan Worms even if you never intend to fish a tailwater, where they're most effective. They'll be a colorful presence in your imitative-fly box. They'll cheer you up a bit every time you open it. Sometime in your future, they will probably save a fishing day for you.

Your imitative-nymph box should not be entirely full when you start any season. Leave lots of expansion gaps. Some of these will be filled by favorite nymphs that you develop over time, as you fish your own waters, collect your own natural nymphs, larvae, pupae, and crustaceans, and tie, buy, or devise your own patterns to match them. Those killing nymphs naturally become favorites. You might be wise if your newfound favorites begin to outweigh the traditional nymphs normally prescribed for specific insects. You would fish these favorites with confidence, and that would ensure that you catch more trout on them.

You should also leave room in your imitative-fly box to insert flies that you buy from fly shops located near waters that you visit. It's never wise to take a trip to a specific stream or river, especially if it's famous and well attended, without stopping at the nearest fly shop and asking what's happening, and what's solving it. You'll buy at least a handful of flies, some of which you'll never use, but you'll end up with local knowledge, on which it's difficult to place sufficient value. One or two of those dressings might be the magic solution. You should always leave room in all of your fly boxes to add magic. Over a long period of time, you'll find that your boxes of all sorts tend to be heavily weighted toward flies that have supplied magic in some fishing situation, somewhere on this planet. Those will eventually become the flies you tie to your tippet most often, and they'll become the flies on which you catch most of your trout.

The final bit of room in your imitative-nymph box should be left for the experiments you tie out of your portable tying kit, if you carry one. I don't carry one on every trip. Sometimes the trip is too short, or the situation too inconvenient, for tying. But I like to have a kit handy for any trip that approaches a week in one place, and where I'll have a table on which to tie, even if it's only a campsite picnic table.

In my own fishing, I get the ultimate enjoyment from finding feeding trout, collecting what they're eating, constructing something that matches it, catching the trout on flies I've worked out myself, right there next to the water. This usually takes two or three days at minimum. Those flies are almost always based on designs originated by others. They almost always become my favorites. Perhaps this book will serve you, if in no other way, by giving you enough tying ideas around which to build your own set of nymphs, both searching and imitative.

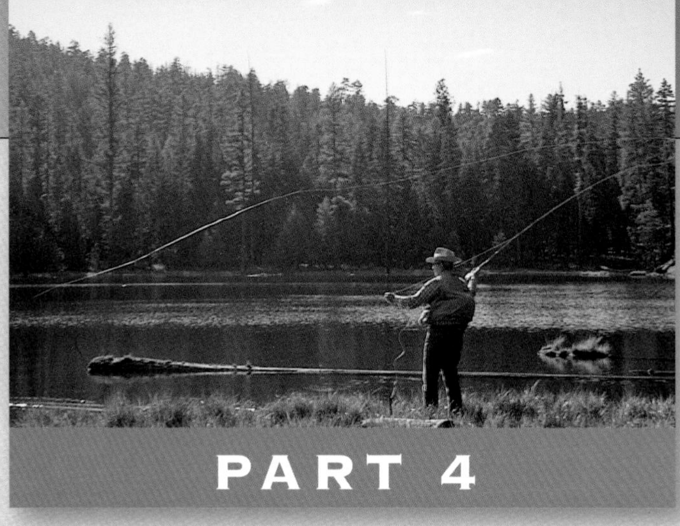

PART 4

Nymphs for Stillwaters

CHAPTER 27

How to Murder a Woolly Bugger

The Woolly Bugger is treated as a streamer in many books. In others it's considered a nymph. I listed it as a streamer in my own *Trout Flies.* It's tied on a long-shank streamer hook. It has a tail as long as or longer than the body. It's usually fished with a stripping retrieve, rarely with a creeping retrieve such as a hand-twist. All of those things define streamer, to me. But Randall Kaufmann's *Fly Patterns of Umpqua Feather Merchants,* which might be called the definitive source, lists the Woolly Bugger as a nymph. For the purpose of this book, which is about nymphs, and the present chapter, which is about how to murder this pattern, I'll reach for Randall's definition. But I still don't know if the final answer is in: is the Woolly Bugger a nymph or a streamer?

Stillwater leeches swim with snakelike undulations of their long bodies. The Woolly Bugger, with its active marabou tail, is one of the best imitations you can find for one.

Perhaps it's a streamer when it's fished like one, on a fast retrieve, and a nymph when it's fished as an imitation of an aquatic insect, crustacean, or leech, usually on a slow retrieve.

The Woolly Bugger is an excellent dressing for both streams and stillwaters. If you don't carry a few of them in olive and black, sizes 6 to 12, you're probably making some sort of mistake, though you might have good reasons for making it. I catch a lot of trout on it, often along the edges of rivers while floating, more often along the edges of lakes and ponds while casting from a float tube or pram, but just as often while slowly trolling the depths or casting from anchor, over suspended structure and plant beds in a stillwater of any size. I feel more as though I'm fishing a streamer than a nymph when I do all of the above. But I also often fish a Woolly Bugger as an imitation of a specific trout food form. When I do that, I feel as if I'm fishing a nymph as opposed to a streamer. That's how we'll treat it here.

The Woolly Bugger is generally considered an imitation of a leech. It's excellent for that, and can be considered a nymph when it's fished for that. With its undulating marabou tail, a Woolly Bugger retrieved at anything from a hand-twist to a trot can look like a leech sneaking along, or ambling along with its snakelike swimming motion. Leeches can swim fairly briskly. We can assume that they have senses to inform them when a hungry trout approaches. It's not unreasonable to suspect that when a leech knows a trout is on its tail, it might kick in its afterburners. A Woolly Bugger cast out, allowed to sink, and retrieved with modest to fast strips might look more like a leech than many more exact leech imitations. So you can consider the Woolly Bugger, fished just as you normally tie it, as an excellent nymph imitation for a stillwater leech.

WOOLLY BUGGER, OLIVE *Russell Blessing*

Hook:	3XL or 4XL, size 6-12
Weight:	15-25 turns nonlead wire
Thread:	Olive 3/0 or 6/0
Tail:	Olive marabou with green Krystal Flash
Body:	Olive chenille
Hackle:	Brown hen or grade-three rooster

WOOLLY BUGGER, BLACK *Russell Blessing*

Hook:	3XL or 4XL, size 6-12
Weight:	15-25 turns nonlead wire
Thread:	Black 3/0 or 6/0
Tail:	Black marabou with green Krystal Flash
Body:	Black chenille
Hackle:	Black hen or grade-three rooster

Step 1. Debarb the hook, fix it in the vise, and wrap about twenty turns of nonlead weighting wire. Start the thread behind the eye, and overwrap the weighting wire to the hook bend. Gather the end fibers of a marabou feather, measure them the length of the hook, and tie them in at the bend. For a fluffier Woolly Bugger, or to economize by tying three flies with one feather, gather the fibers from one side of the feather, cut or strip them from the feather, measure them the length of the hook, and tie them in. Measure three to four Krystal Flash strands just short of the end of the tail, and tie them in on either side of the tail.

Step 2. Tie in several inches of chenille at the base of the tail. Select a hen or poor-grade rooster hackle feather with fibers about twice the length of the hook gap. Prepare it by stroking the fibers from tip to butt, in opposition to their natural direction. Tie the feather in by the tip, with the convex side toward you, so that when wrapped they will sweep toward the back of the hook.

Step 3. Take a turn of body chenille behind the hackle, then wrap the body forward, and tie it off just behind the hook eye. Clip the excess chenille.

Step 4. Palmer the hackle forward in five to eight evenly spaced turns. Tie it off behind the hook eye, and clip the excess stem. Form a thread head, whip-finish, clip the thread, and cement the head.

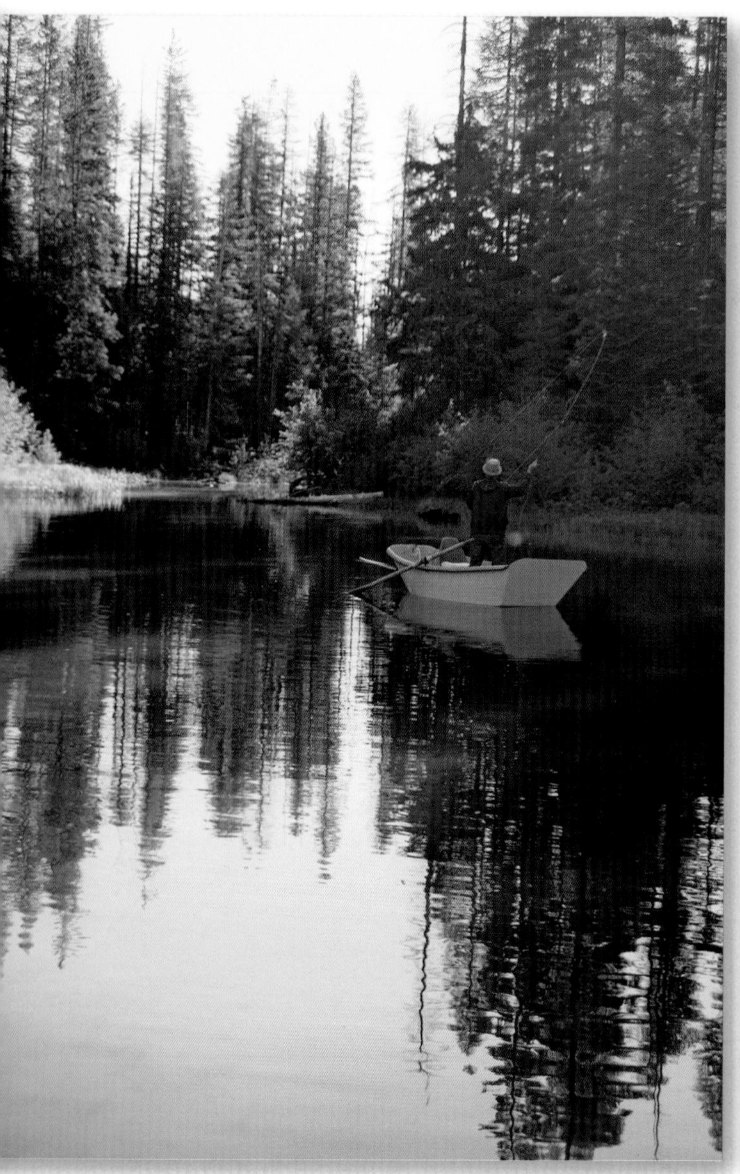

My father setting the hook to a trout feeding on cased caddis swimming awkwardly among the stalks of rooted plants.

The Woolly Bugger, in a literal pinch, can be made to fish for a lot of other stillwater food forms, in addition to the leech for which it might have been intended. I don't recommend you neglect tying imitative nymphs for all those others, but it won't hurt to know that if you're out of anything that resembles certain insects and crustaceans, and run into trout feeding selectively on them, you can often shape a Woolly Bugger to resemble them enough to fool at least a few fish. Sometimes you'll be able to fool a lot of trout on a modified Woolly Bugger.

My dad and I fished a small, clear lake in Oregon's Cascade Range once. It had forests of stalked plants trailing from eight- to ten-foot depths almost to the surface. They were somewhat scattered, enough that the long, trailing leaves of one plant did not quite brush the tips of those around it. We were able to find casting lanes between those plants, down the lengths of which we were able to cast, and through the modest depths of which we were able to retrieve our flies.

Our flies weren't working. Dad was using wets; I was using an Olive Woolly Bugger but fishing it as a streamer, with all sorts of retrieves, trying to show it to trout in a variety of ways. After we spent quite a fruitless while casting and retrieving, a trout made a mistake about Dad's wet fly. I think he stopped his retrieve in disgust to ponder the poor quality of our fishing, while his fly was still in the water, and a trout came along and whacked it. However it happened, we had a stomach autopsy. My late father always felt that trout dinners were a natural part of trout fishing, and the first fish of what had been lining up to be a fishless day didn't enjoy much chance.

I slit its belly and squeezed the contents into a white pickle jar lid, added water, stirred the stew of what the trout had been eating. An approximate dozen vegetation-cased caddis larvae, taken case and all by the trout, separated themselves out. Two or three were still alive, their

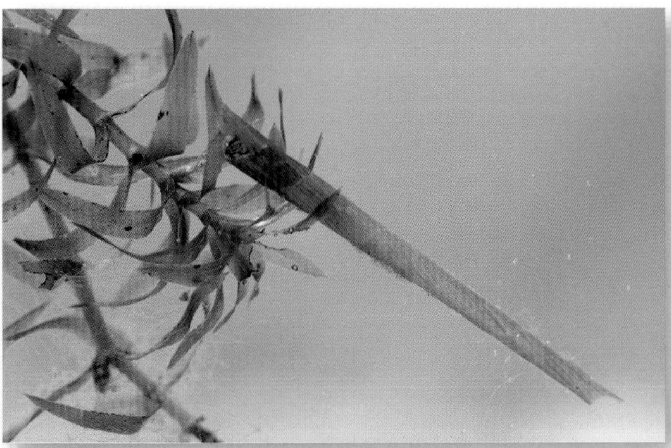

Some cased caddis are able to swim feebly (Leptoceridae)*; trout dislodge them from their pastures in the vegetation, feed on them as they try to return to safety.*

An Olive Woolly Bugger shorn of all its appendages can be a close enough imitation to a cased caddis to fool trout.

long, feeble legs clawing for purchase on their less lucky relations, who were already dead. I tweezered the living ones out and released them over the side of the boat. I watched as they swam slowly and awkwardly away, using their forelegs in feeble breast strokes. You can learn a lot about how to retrieve an imitation by watching the way a natural moves in the water.

My fly boxes of that time contained no imitations of those cased caddis. They were about size 10, very slender, olive like the plants among which they'd been living, and out of which they had constructed their cases. They were long-horned sedge larvae (Leptoceridae), a common cased caddis that has the rare ability to swim, though not with much agility. I speculated that the trout were seeing them moving from leaf to leaf, or plant to plant. Trout might have been cruising, brushing the vegetation, turning to eat anything that got dislodged. However it might be happening, it was clear from the single sample that cased caddis larvae were the main thing on the trout menu at the moment.

I had a portable fly-tying kit on shore, but didn't want to stop fishing long enough to row in, tie up some imitations, row back out. By the time Dad and I would get back to casting, the menu might have changed. I sat and thought awhile, then looked at the Olive Woolly Bugger I already had tied to my tippet. Its body, shorn of all its peripheral parts, would be about the size, shape, and color of those cased caddis. I went at it instantly, with fingernails and nippers.

A long cast, a twenty-second countdown, and a few feet of hand-twist retrieve later, I provided Dad the rest of his dinner. I murdered another Olive Woolly Bugger for him, and he set into the pleasant work of catching my dinner, scolding me while he did because I caught more trout and released them. But somebody had to do it; we couldn't have eaten all the trout that we caught on those butchered flies the rest of that day.

Scuds are often prolific in lakes and ponds, especially those with heavy vegetation beds. They are crustaceans, not insects, and have an entirely aquatic life cycle. They are in the water all year round, in a full range of sizes. You can often do well by imitating the largest of them, even in the absence of evidence that trout are feeding on them. They range from too small to imitate up to about size 12. Their imitations are often tied on curved-shank *scud* hooks, but as I explained in the chapter on scuds, when they swim they're straight. I've often been caught on a lake or pond without any specific scud dressings, and have always been able to salvage at least some of the day by performing some brutalities on a size 12 Olive Woolly Bugger.

The natural scud has no tail, a tightly carapaced back, and seven sets of walking legs and several sets of addi-

Scuds are among the most prolific trout foods in stillwaters. Recall that when swimming, they're straight as sticks.

Your smallest Olive Woolly Bugger, when trimmed of all but its underhackles, and with those trimmed short, can look a lot like a scud if you lack a closer imitation.

A size 10 or 12 Olive Woolly Bugger with its tails thinned, and all but a few wisps of hackle left at each side to represent legs, can be a very effective damselfly nymph imitation.

tional appendages on the abdominal segments, according to J. Reese Voshell Jr. in his excellent aquatic reference, *A Guide to Common Freshwater Invertebrates of North America.* If you lack something that looks even a little like that, you can cut the tails off the smallest Olive Woolly Bugger in your box, which in mine is usually a size 12. Then tug as many hackle fibers as possible to the downside of the fly, and trim them about even with the point of the hook. Cut off the remaining hackles on the sides and back of the fly, and you have a reasonable imitation of a large olive scud. It is no surprise when a trout mistakes it for the real thing.

Damselfly nymphs live in the same stillwater vegetation beds inhabited by scuds and leptocerid caddis larvae. They make most of their living creeping along stalks and leaves, ambushing smaller life forms, including scuds and cased caddis. When damselfly nymphs are ready for emergence, they swim toward shore in ones and twos, or sometimes in bunches, in a migration that can cause selective feeding, and might require accurate imitations. But it's fairly rare to catch a stillwater trout, examine its stomach contents with a throat pump or via my dad's more thorough method, and not find at least two or three damselfly nymphs among the other, and often dominant, things the trout has been eating. Those same trout will almost always be susceptible to something that looks at least a little like a damselfly nymph.

Damselfly nymphs are long and slender, and swim with snakelike side-to-side undulations of the body. Most are slow swimmers, but some, such as this Calopterygidae, are capable of short bursts at high speed.

I'm never caught on a stillwater without a few damselfly imitations these days, but it happened often in my early days, because I didn't fish lakes and ponds as often then as I do now, and hadn't constructed a fly box specific to stillwaters. When you begin tying flies into a stillwater-nymph box, the first thing in it should be olive damsel nymphs. If you haven't gotten around to that vital step yet, you can still have some success when trout are selective to damsels, and a lot of success when trout are not eating them exclusively, but are open to the idea of taking one whenever it's available. You can use a trimmed size 10 or 12 Olive Woolly Bugger to make trout think a damselfly nymph is creeping by, looking like groceries.

Start the conversion by thinning out about half the marabou from the tails, lengthwise. Don't shorten it; instead, reduce its thickness. Then cut or pinch all of the hackle off the back two-thirds to three-quarters of the body. Finally, pinch or clip all hackle fibers from the top and bottom of the forward portion of the fly. What you have left should be a sparse tail, long slender body, and a few wisps of hackle off the port and starboard bow that look like legs. Fish it slow, with a hand-twist retrieve or very short and slow strips, and any trout that sees it should approve. It has worked for me almost as often as an exact imitation.

Stillwater trout feed often on dragonfly nymphs, but rarely with selectivity, out of lack of opportunity. The naturals are large at maturity, and contain more nutrients than almost anything a trout can capture short of a minnow or mouse. They can be abundant in lakes and ponds, but they're fairly near the top of the food chain, and the law of predation deems that they be fewer in number than their prey or they'd have to eat each other. I've told the story before of placing about 150 scuds in an aquarium, along with three dragonfly nymphs. I got busy writing a book and forgot to check the operation as often as I should. I noticed that the number of scuds diminished fast, but I forgot to look into the aquarium for a couple of weeks. When I finally did, I had to search for a long time to find anything alive. I pulled a stick out of the water, looked at its underside, and found a single portly dragonfly nymph clinging to it. I didn't let my finger get near it.

I did take it back to the water where I'd found it, and released it.

Trout are a step higher on the food chain, and they don't play catch-and-release with dragonfly nymphs. You'll often find one or two in a sampled stomach, but mature specimens are too large to extract with a throat pump, so you'll have to apply my dad's sampling technique to find out if a trout has been eating dragonfly nymphs. If they're present in the stillwater you're fishing, which they are in almost every lake and pond on every continent, you can assume trout see them at least on occasion. If a trout gets a chance at one, it won't be passed up.

If your supply of nymphs tied specifically for dragonfly larvae is as thin as mine often is, it's nice to know that you can convert a size 6 or 8 Woolly Bugger into a workable imitation in a hurry by truncating its tails. Use your fingers to get a good grip on the marabou in about the middle, and rip the back end off. The remains of the fly will be about the size, shape, and color of a natural dragonfly nymph, certainly close enough for trout to mistake it for one.

I've caught so many trout on a Woolly Bugger, modified merely by shortening its tail, that I don't worry as much as I should about tying specific dragonfly nymph imitations. I don't recommend that you follow me on this, but if you lack tying time, and find yourself on a stillwater where trout are eating dragonfly nymphs, your situation won't be hopeless if you have an Olive Woolly Bugger to murder.

Portly dragonfly nymphs are among the biggest bites that stillwater trout ever get to enjoy. It's rare that they feed selectively on them, but also rare that they'll pass up a chance at one.

A size 6 or 8 Olive Woolly Bugger with its tail shortened is not far from being the best dragonfly nymph imitation you can tie.

CHAPTER 28

Stillwater Mayflies

Stillwater mayflies are dominated all across the continent by the genus *Callibaetis,* a scientific name in such continual use by anglers that it has become the common name of the insect. In the adult stages, these are the speckle-wing duns and speckle-wing quill spinners. As nymphs they're swimmers, closely related to the moving-water *Baetis* covered in chapter 18, of which they could be said to be the stillwater version. But they tend to average much larger, size 12 to 16 as opposed to size 18 to 20.

Speckle-wing hatches can be terrific on lakes and ponds, and at times in spring creeks and meadow streams, in water where rooted plants thrive and the currents are very slow. When duns are on the water, trout might seem selective to them. On cool and wet days they might be on the water from several seconds to a minute or more, before they take wing. Trout approve; you'll have no trouble noticing that duns go down in swirls, and it's very likely that you'll be able to catch a pleasing number of trout on floating imitations such as size 12 to 16 Olive Comparaduns or Quigley Cripples.

The trout that provided this throat pump sample appeared to be feeding on stillwater Callibaetis *duns, but instead was taking nymphs, along with a few spinners and a couple of stray longhorn sedge pupae.*

In my youth I fished many mountain lakes with hatches of *Callibaetis.* I nearly always camped, and the evening meal was often provided by the day's fishing. I did not kill trout without opening them up to see what they'd been eating. It didn't take long to realize that even during the heaviest *Callibaetis* hatches, when trout were visibly feeding on floating duns, nymphs were represented in stomach samples by a ratio of about ten to one over duns. On days when trout would take drys, I continued to fish them, and still do. But I learned that I could do better by fishing a nymph on days when the hatch was sparse, or whenever I wanted to get greedy, catch even more trout than the satisfying number that were willing to take the dry. Greed for fish happens a lot when you're young.

The best formula for *Callibaetis* might be to suspend a nymph dressing on a couple feet of 5X or 6X tippet, tied to the hook bend of the dry fly you're using to imitate the dun of the same insect. Then you'll get the satisfaction of seeing an occasional surface take. But you'll also discover that the sudden disappearance of the dry is just as exciting, and means precisely the same thing: a trout out there and dancing with your fly in its mouth. It will just happen a lot more often if you offer trout the choice of both the dry and the nymph.

Callibaetis have two to three broods per year. The first hatch happens in early spring, whatever time that occurs in your latitude and at your altitude. In most places it begins in April or May and continues for two to three weeks. That brood lays its eggs, those eggs hatch, the nymphs eat and grow and become a second generation, usually in midsummer, which might be anywhere from late May to early August. The second brood lays its eggs, those hatch, and the nymphs become a third generation in the same season, usually in early to late fall, September or October.

Each succeeding generation has a shorter time to consume groceries and attain size, so each is smaller than the one before it. If the mature nymph in the spring brood is a size 12, then the summer brood will be size 14, and the fall brood size 16. If the spring brood is size 14, then the summer brood will be size 16, and the fall brood size 18. At that point, you can use the same flies for the stillwater *Callibaetis* that work on moving-water *Baetis* nymphs.

Distribution of the speckle-wings is a bit weighted to the West, but a count of species in a printout from Mayfly Central lists eight from the West and six from the East. They are important stillwater mayflies across North America, in the United States and Canada.

Populations of other stillwater swimmer mayflies might be nearly as dense as *Callibaetis.* Some, such as the gray drakes *(Siphlonurus),* are larger. But they have the habit of crawling out on protruding vegetation for emergence, rather than hatching out in open water. In some cases, this might happen in water where reed stems probe sufficient depths that trout enjoy access to the nymphs. It might be beneficial to imitate gray drake nymphs in that case. As they do in moving water, these larger nymphs usually migrate into water so shallow, scant inches, that trout are reluctant to follow and feed on them.

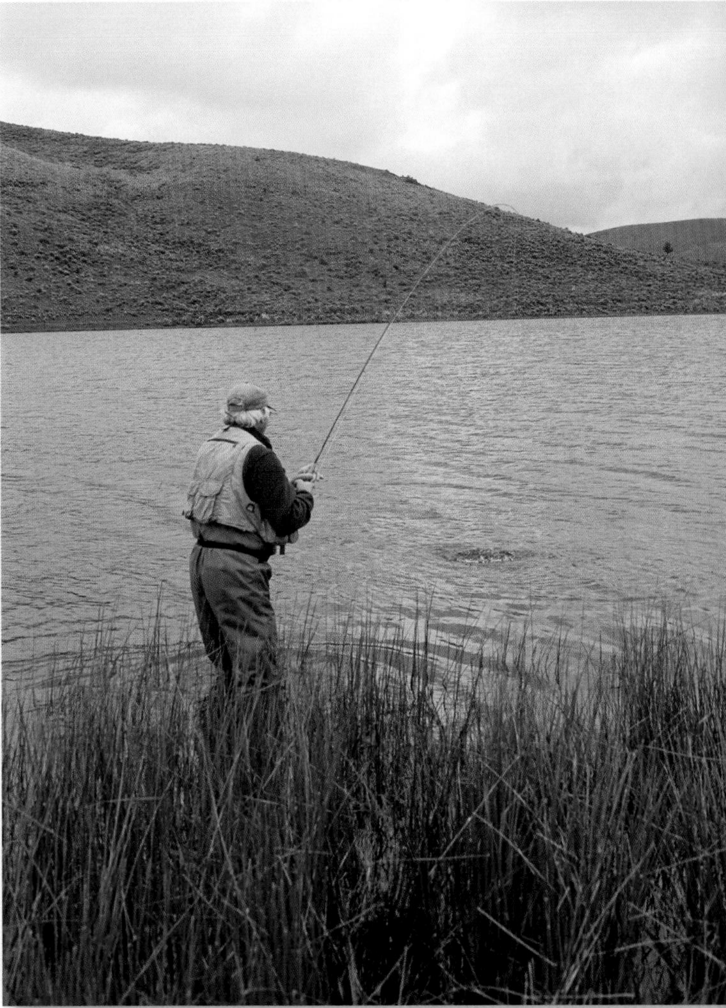

Callibaetis *mayflies have three broods in an average season, so the nymphs are available to trout from spring through fall. Emergences can be best on cloudy days.*

The stillwater Callibaetis *nymphs are closely related to the moving-water blue-winged olives* (Baetis). *They range from size 12 to 18. In their smallest sizes, you can use the same Pheasant Tail Nymphs you use for blue-winged olives in rivers and streams.*

Callibaetis emerge out in open water, where trout can get at them. The few that I've observed in nature, in the process of leaving the bottom, swimming to the top, and breaking through the surface for emergence, have accomplished it all in a rush. The swim is unbroken. I've read that they can be indecisive: start for the top, retreat to the bottom, repeat the process several times before finally dashing all the way to the surface and emerging. This might happen, I've just not seen it. I've also not done any skin diving. The few *Callibaetis* nymphs that I've watched emerge leave the vegetation as near the surface as they can get, swim with a fast and unbroken motion to the top, and break through the surface film without hesitation.

Most *Callibaetis* nymphs have enough mass to penetrate the film in a lake or pond without the necessity of beating their heads against it, as a small midge often must. It's possible that the tiniest autumn *Callibaetis* stage at the surface, before breaking through. I've not noticed it. I have raised them in aquariums. Even the large ones have some trouble breaking the surface. But the tension in a small aquarium is magnified many times over that in any stillwater.

FLASHBACK PHEASANT TAIL

All stillwater nymphs adapt to the color of the vegetation in which they live. If they did not, few would survive to pass on their contrarian genetics to subsequent generations. Most *Callibaetis* nymphs are shades of green to olive-tan or olive-brown. It's not difficult to find material colors listed as *Callibaetis,* typically a grayish olive. I have found this close enough to the naturals in all the waters I've fished. But my favorite nymph dressing, the one I use most when I'm on a stillwater and *Callibaetis* are hatching or I suspect they're about to, is the Flashback Pheasant Tail in size 12 to 16 (see page 112). You can do a lot better in terms of imitation. But it's a nymph you should have with you, for searching fishing and in smaller sizes as a *Baetis* imitation. Try it first; you might find it's all you ever need.

Once, when rearing *Callibaetis* in my aquarium, I was able to observe the nymphs as they emerged into duns. Just before the final transformation, the nymphs turned a shiny color that was almost bronze. I assume it was due to gases extruded between the inner adult exoskeleton and the outer nymph cuticle, to separate them, though that is speculation. The brassie color of the nymph just before emergence is not speculation, though it might not always happen out in nature. If it does, it would explain the success of the Flashback Pheasant Tail during *Callibaetis* emergences.

FLASHBACK PHEASANT TAIL

Hook:	Standard nymph, size 12-16
Thread:	Brown
Tail:	Pheasant tail fibers
Rib:	Fine copper wire
Body:	Pheasant tail fibers
Wing case:	Pearl Flashabou or Krystal Flash
Thorax:	Peacock herl
Legs:	Pheasant tail fibers

TURKEY QUILL *CALLIBAETIS*

I fish a pond in the treeless, windswept wheatlands of central Oregon. It has what might be considered an excessive population of *Callibaetis* mayfly nymphs in its shallow vegetation beds. The pond is spring-fed; there is no inlet or outlet, and therefore no spawning water for trout. It is planted with a few triploid rainbows each year, and these quickly grow fat. It's not a natural situation, but it is the perfect laboratory in which to get educated about the relationship between *Callibaetis* and trout.

One May morning the pond and the air around it were both cold, but in the way of that semidesert country, the sun promised warmth later in the day. I knew speckle-wing duns would be on the water starting about an hour before noon, lasting for enough hours to keep me happy. But I was eager to start catching a few trout earlier, and that meant fishing a nymph until the duns began to show.

I waded knee-deep into a cove that was only three to four feet deep and floored with a solid bed of plants. I rigged with a microshot ahead of a *Callibaetis* nymph, because I wanted to be ready with a floating line, not an intermediate or Sink-Tip, when the hatch started later. I began casting, giving the nymph a few seconds to sink, then retrieving it with a hand-twist. The line twitched a couple of times, and tugged back against my hand once, before I finally got the hook set and was able to play and land a nice trout, about two pounds.

As I released that first trout and prepared for the next cast, I noticed a bulge in the foot-deep shallows behind me. I turned and flicked the fly back there. It landed with a slight smack about five feet from where I thought the trout might be. I didn't give it any time to sink. Instead, I retrieved it like a streamer. After about ten feet of retrieve, I'd decided the cast was wasted, when suddenly a V-wake built up about five feet from the fly, and arrowed in a swift curve right onto it. I felt a terrific thud, but was for some unusual reason able to quell my urge to rear back and set the hook with force. That would have been a disaster.

The trout weighed about four pounds. The nymph was Phil Rowley's Turkey Quill *Callibaetis,* tied from his book *Fly Patterns for Stillwaters.* Phil is involved with Brian Chan in Stillwater Solutions, a product line of materials designed and dyed specifically for lake and pond food forms, and marketed by SuperFly in Edmonton, Alberta. To tie Phil's fly as he describes it, you need the materials he designed specifically for it. But you can catch at least a few trout if you stick to the idea but substitute some minor materials, as long as you keep the colors near to those of the naturals you collect in your own waters.

TURKEY QUILL *CALLIBAETIS* ***Phil Rowley***

Hook: Standard nymph, size 12-16
Thread: Tan or olive 6/0 or 8/0
Tail: Microfleck turkey flat fibers, tan
Rib: Single strand of Pearl Krystal Flash
Counter rib: Fine gold wire
Legs: Microfleck turkey flat fibers, tan
Body: Mottled turkey tail
Wing case: Mottled turkey tail

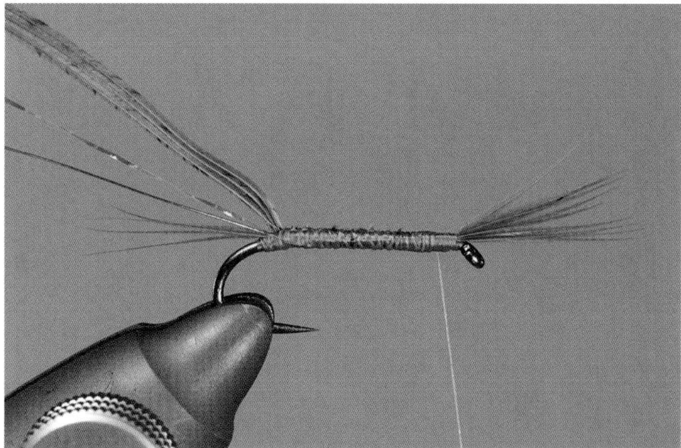

Step 1. Start the thread behind the eye, and layer it to the bend. Twist the thread clockwise to tighten it, and make a slight thread bump there. Measure three to five turkey flat fibers one-half to two-thirds the shank length and tie them in, splaying them against the thread bump. Tie in a few inches of Krystal Flash and gold wire ribbing. Take the thread to the eye. Measure six to ten turkey flat fibers one-half to two-thirds the shank length, and tie them in with the tips over the eye. Clip a narrow section of mottled turkey, three to six fibers, and tie them in by the tips, overwrapping them with thread to the base of the tail and back to the eye.

My wife playing a trout on a pond, in the kind of shallows where trout go out of their way to chase down natural Callibaetis *nymphs, and the Turkey Quill* Callibaetis.

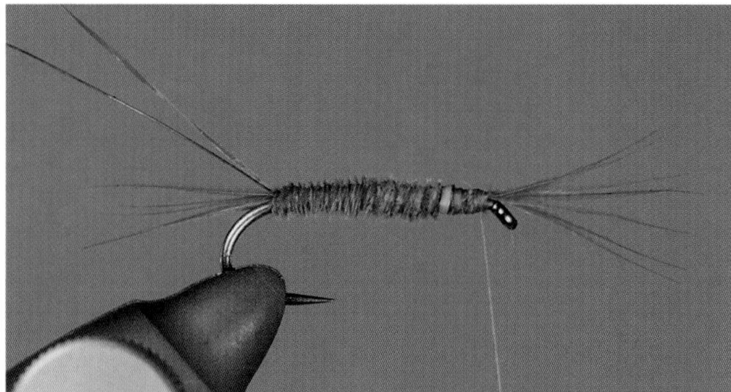

Step 2. Wrap the mottled turkey tail section forward as herl, from the base of the tail to about a hook-eye length behind the eye. Space the turns more tightly at the front than the back, to build up a slightly thicker thorax than abdomen. Tie it off and clip the excess.

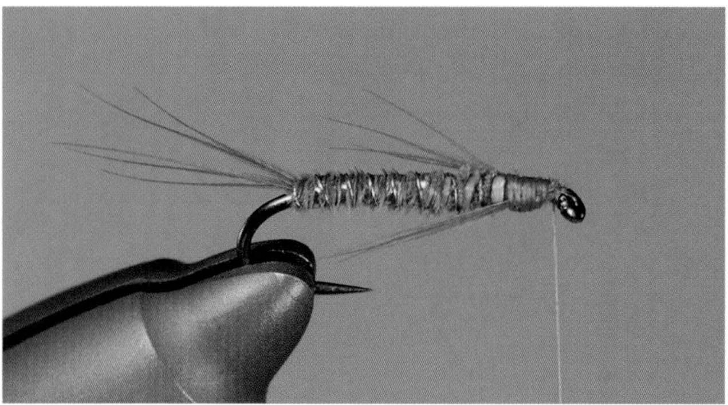

Step 3. Wind the Krystal Flash rib forward in six to eight evenly spaced turns, in the same direction as the herl, to the end of the body. Tie it off and clip the excess. Counterwind the gold wire rib over the body and Krystal Flash ribbing. Tie it off and clip or break off the excess. Separate the legs equally, draw them back alongside the body, and secure them with a few turns of thread.

Step 4. From a mottled turkey feather that has been lightly coated with Flexament or sprayed with artist's fixative, clip a section about half the hook gap wide. Tie this in with the shiny side down, the tip to the back, over the head of the fly. Use just two to three tight turns of thread to secure it.

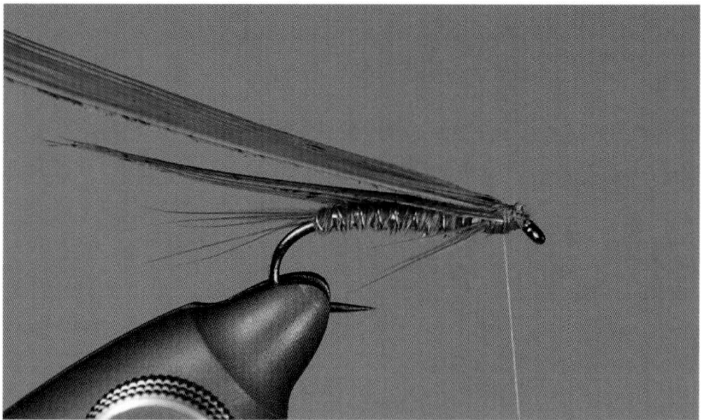

Step 5. Draw the forward section of wing case over the back, and take several more turns of thread to secure it.

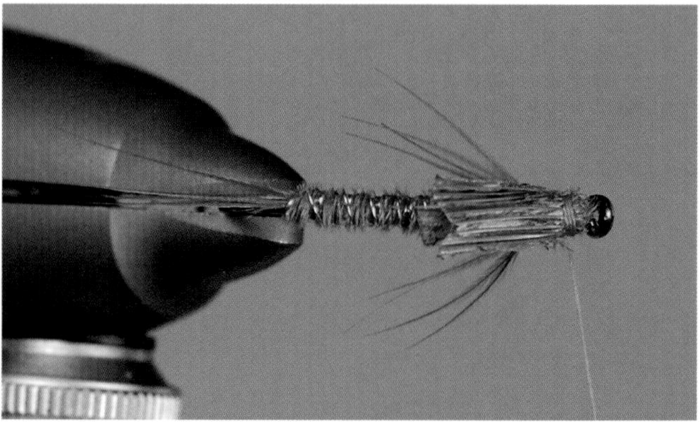

Step 6. Gather the two wing cases, under and over, together in the fingers of your off hand, folding them above the body. Clip them with your scissors at a slant, so the resulting cut leaves a natural notch in the wing cases. Use enough thread turns to form a neat head, whip-finish, clip the thread, and apply head cement.

Phil Rowley recommends tying his Turkey Quill *Callibaetis* nymph in olive and tan. I tie it in a single color, using materials from Stillwater Solutions and labeled *Callibaetis.* It has always served me very well. I use this as my imitative dressing when naturals are very abundant and I suspect trout might be a bit snotty. Though I always fish it at the level of any plant beds, retrieving it slowly just above them no matter their depth, I prefer to cast it in the shallows, over trout that are exposing themselves at least occasionally. I like the fly best when it draws those murderous V-wakes to it.

GILLED NYMPH

Shane Stalcup's Gilled Nymph, from his *Mayflies Top to Bottom,* is a pattern concept best applied to the largest *Callibaetis,* sizes 14 and 16, on long-shank hooks. When tied in smaller sizes, it's a bit more complex than might be necessary, and the ostrich herl used to tie it might be outsized for the hook on which you're tying it. In those large sizes, it is an excellent imitation.

If you choose to tie a nymph as precise as Shane's, it's wise to collect naturals first, and be sure to get the colors exactly right. Since *Callibaetis* nymph colors will vary with substrate colors from place to place, you'll need to do your own research. Always remember that the species of an insect, in the nymphal stage, does not determine its color. It will take on the coloration of the vegetation on which it lives, and that will differ not only from pond to pond and lake to lake, but also from place to place within the body of water, and from time to time as the colors of the vegetation change with the seasons.

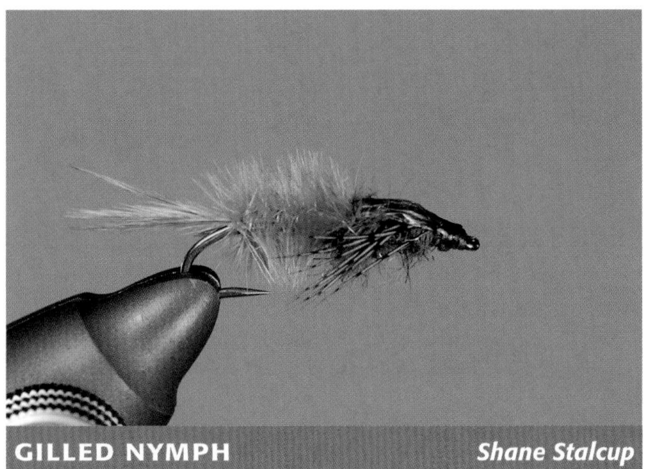

GILLED NYMPH ***Shane Stalcup***

Hook:	2XL or 3XL curved shank, size 12-16
Thread:	Olive 6/0 or 8/0
Tail:	Olive ostrich tips
Rib:	Fine copper wire
Body:	Olive ostrich herl
Wing case:	Dun or olive Medallion sheeting
Thorax:	Olive dubbing
Legs:	Gray or brown partridge

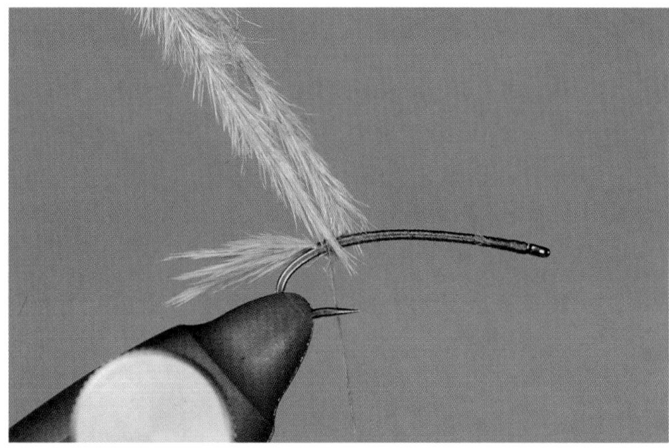

Step 1. Debarb the hook, fix it in the vise, and layer thread from the eye to a point straight above the point of the flattened hook barb. Though Shane does not call for weighting this fly, you might experiment with underweighting it: using nonlead weighting wire in either just a few turns, or the normal number of turns but with wire one size finer than standard for the hook. Measure three ostrich herl tips one-half to two-thirds the length of the shank, and tie them in. Do not clip the herls; the rest forms the body of the nymph.

Step 2. Tie in a few inches of ribbing wire. Grasp the butts of the herls together, and twist them into a rope. Wind this forward to a point one-fifth to one-quarter the length of the shank behind the eye. Tie it off and clip the excess stems.

Step 3. Wind the ribbing forward through the herl. Work it back and forth as you go, to mat down no more ostrich fibers than necessary. Tie the ribbing off at the end of the body, and clip or break the excess. Cut a section of sheeting a little less than the hook-gap width, and tie it in at the end of the body. Be sure to overwrap it with thread back far enough to avoid a wasp-waist effect.

Step 4. Dub a thorax that tapers from wide at the back, narrowing to end one or two hook-eye lengths behind the eye. Prepare a partridge feather for legs by removing all but a few fibers on each side, stroking these fibers back, cutting out the tip, then stroking the remaining fibers back into their original alignment.

Step 5. Hold the leg feather in position over the top of the thorax, and tie the butt in with a couple of pinch wraps. Before securing it, tug it into position on top of the thorax, so the legs reach just short of the hook point. Tie it off with several more tight wraps of thread, and clip the excess butt.

Step 6. Bring the wing case forward over the thorax and legs. Tie it off behind the hook eye, and clip the excess. Use enough thread turns to form a neat head. Whip-finish the head, clip the thread, and apply head cement.

This excellent imitation depends on the fibrous ostrich herl to imitate the gills of the natural nymph. It will work well with a hand-twist retrieve, but can also be fished with short strips, and even long pulls, somewhat streamerlike, to represent the *Callibaetis* nymph on its brisk swim to the surface for emergence.

SUMMARY

I recommend you carry the Flashback Pheasant Tail in sizes 12 through 22, for many reasons that don't involve *Callibaetis* nymphs. If you get stranded on a lake or pond during activity that points to the success of an imitation, try the Pheasant Tail if you don't have anything closer. In my experience, it will work well enough to keep you happy, and in many cases will work better than a more imitative dressing.

If you fish stillwaters as often as I do, especially in spring, when streams and rivers are typically unfishable with snowmelt or runoff from heavy rains, and also a time when *Callibaetis* nymphs are at their largest and in their most active stage, then you'll likely want to experiment with closer copies. Be sure to collect specimens from the waters you're fishing before tying a bunch of imitations for them. You might discover that your size and shape are perfect, but your color is far off from the naturals. In the case of the stillwater *Callibaetis,* that can be critical.

Once you've settled on a dressing, and a color that suits what you've collected, then tie it in a range of sizes from 12 to 16. It's likely those few flies are all you will ever need for *Callibaetis* nymphs . . . until you visit another body of water, where they might be a different color.

You will also encounter big Hex *(Hexagenia limbata)* mayfly nymphs in scattered lakes. They live only where the bottom consistency is correct for their burrows: firm enough to tunnel in without being so soft it collapses, the same requirement they have in moving water. Not all states and provinces have lakes with suitable bottoms. Not all waters with suitable bottoms have Hex populations. Their distribution is spotty. They emerge at dusk or after dark. In my home state, Oregon, it is not legal to fish for trout beyond an hour after sunset, which is about when the Hex hatch might become important.

I speak more from theory than concrete experience when I say that the same nymphs you tie for the Hex in streams and rivers will work as well on lakes and ponds.

I collect gray drake nymphs *(Siphlonurus)* quite often in Cascade Range lakes. I'm sure trout eat them. But as they near emergence, and in theory would become more important, they migrate into thin shallows. All of the lakes in which I've found them have resident osprey. I've never found trout daring enough to follow the migration of gray drake nymphs into the shallows. They wouldn't survive long if they did.

In stillwaters where I've found the greatest abundance of these naturals, I've done fairly well with my All-Fur Swimmer (see page 103) in a beadhead version, size 10 or 12, fished near but not in the shallows. I like to relate it to the presence of the big swimmer nymphs. But I've never been able to collect concrete evidence that trout take the nymph as an imitation of the gray drake natural, which would be indicated by gray drake nymphs in throat or stomach samples of trout taken on the All-Fur Swimmer.

Perhaps trout move onto the shallows as light fades, and osprey nap. Since I'm not willing to break Oregon's law and fish at night, I can only speculate. On your waters, where night fishing is legal, an imitation of a gray drake nymph fished after dark might work wonders. So might a Woolly Bugger or almost anything else that looks like something nutritious on the prowl at night and good to eat, to a trout.

You'll encounter the scattered Hexagenia limbata *hatch on lakes and ponds across the land. If you do, it will be late in the evening or after dark, and you'll need something to at least come close to them, because of their large size.*

If you encounter a Hex hatch on a stillwater, you'll be able to fish it with the same flies you tie for moving waters: Clark's Hex Emerger (left), Jorgensen's Hexagenia *Nymph (center), and Andy Burk's* Hexagenia *(right).*

CHAPTER 29

Stillwater Midges

Midges can be divided by size into three categories: *small,* from size 20 to 24; *big,* from size 14 to 18; and *very large,* from size 8 to 14, on long-shank hooks. These last are often called "bombers" in the region where they are most common, the famous Kamloops Lakes area of British Columbia, Canada. But such very large chironomids are found all across the northern tier of the continent, from New England and the higher midwestern and Great Plains states to Washington and Oregon, as well as all of the Canadian provinces, where they are most important and best known.

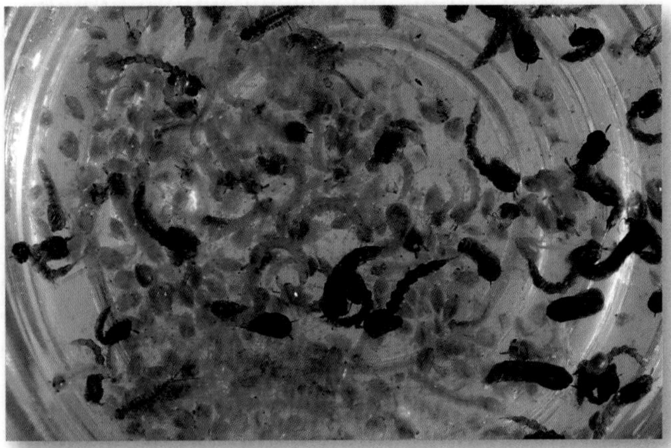

An occasional midge pupa, even if it's only size 16 or so, shows up like a large black silhouette in the water to a trout when it's surrounded by a vast seething mass of zooplankton forms.

I have noticed over a long period of minor study, both by peering into clear stillwaters and by analyzing the occasional throat or stomach sample, that *big* and *very large* midge pupae often stand out from their surroundings. The stillwater food chain usually consists of a thriving and pulsating mass of very tiny and almost invisible forms, mostly zooplankton and phantom midges. Trout feed on this. But an occasional midge pupa will be suspended, midwater, in that mass of tiny bites. It will usually be dark, and might show to trout only as a silhouette. Even if it's just a size 14 or 16, it will loom large among the abundance of tiny organisms all around it.

I have seen cruising trout spot such a suspended bit of groceries from ten feet, turn abruptly toward it, and dash to take it, as if some sort of race were on. Clearly to a trout, there is: it's a race to get to that helpless bit of nutrients before another cruising trout spots it.

In my experience, a suspended midge pupa imitation, or more often a pair of them, cast out and simply let to drift beneath an indicator, will catch an outsized number of stillwater trout. I suspect it's that separation factor: trout are used to seeing an occasional pupa suspended and helpless among a myriad of smaller organisms, and they have no reason to pass up such a serendipitous bite.

When spring turnover hits a lake, especially a northern one with large midges, it can loft bloodworm larvae into the water column, and trout will feed selectively on them. Shown here are natural bloodworms and some of Brian Chan's imitations of them.

If you see signs of midge activity, and trout cruising and seeming to feed on them, but fail to catch trout on surface imitations, don't wait long to switch to a sunk pattern suspended a foot or so beneath a yarn indicator.

Stillwater midge larvae live on and even in the bottom, if it's soft, or in vegetation, making small tubes on the surface of leaves, stems, or the bottom itself, or digging into the bottom ooze. They'll drift in stillwater wind currents at times, but usually in small numbers and an inconsistency of sizes and colors. However, when a lake turns over in spring, they can be swept up into mild lake currents and become suspended in sufficient numbers to cause selectivity. I've seen this happen on Lake Tunkwa in British Columbia, while fishing with Brian Chan. Unfortunately, Tunkwa is part of a two-dam chain on a river system, and one lake was being drained into the other at that moment. As a consequence, the water was stirred by more than turnover, and it was too cloudy with silt to take advantage of the suspended midge larvae. It's too bad; they were bright red bloodworms, big enough to be imitated with size 8 or 10 3XL nymphs.

Midges pupate in those same larval tubes or in the bottom ooze. I've also seen them in the flocculant ooze, the slimy pond snot that has a consistency and color about like half-hardened lime Jell-O. Midge larvae live in this; they construct a transparent cocoon and pupate inside. I suspect when you catch a trout that has a lot of vegetable matter mixed in with a diet of plankton and midge larvae and pupae, they might be nosing into this ooze and picking the midges out of their cocoons like berries. But I don't know of any way to fish a fly among such slurry, so the best thing I've found is to fish a suspended pupa in the nearest clear water. This works very well.

Most midge pupae emerge from larval chambers on the bottom, or in vegetation rooted to the bottom. Studies have shown that they often stage about eighteen inches above the bottom, apparently waiting for some trigger that tells them conditions are perfect up top for their emergence. Then they release, sometimes in great numbers, and move through the water column toward the surface. The distance might be anywhere from a foot to thirty feet or even more. The movement is accomplished by a combination of an undulating swimming motion and gases trapped between the outer pupal and inner adult exoskeletons. It can be a gradual buoying toward the top, or a fairly brisk dash, though a slower ascent is more common.

Pupae often stage once again just a foot or so beneath the surface. If trout see many suspended so near the top, you will see the fish cruising and feeding. Sometimes you'll see a fish break the surface, but almost always with the dorsal fin or tail. It's an indication of feeding on pupae inches deep, not on adults on the surface itself. If you fail to make this distinction, and fish a dry fly while trout feed on submerged pupae, midges can drive you crazy.

Make this small rule for yourself: If you fish a floating imitation for midges over trout that appear to be rising, and don't catch anything in about half an hour or so, make a quick switch to a small yarn indicator and a pupa pattern, about the size and color of the adults you see on the surface, and suspend it just a foot or so deep. It won't solve the problem every time, but you'll be surprised how often that indicator begins to disappear, and how satisfying it is to see that happen.

Small size 20 to 24 and *big* size 14 to 18 midge pupae can be imitated with the same patterns listed in chapter 21 for moving-water midges. I am partial to wire midges in sizes 16 and 18, red, green, and black, because they catch a lot of trout for me, but also because they are heavy enough to assure that any pattern fished in tandem with them will get escorted through the surface film and tugged to the depth I'd like them to attain, which is determined by the length of a single-diameter tippet. I also like the Mercury Midge and Black Beauty or Zebra Midge, with their bright beads, in sizes 18 and 20. To go smaller than that, I turn to simple Thread Midges, again in red, green, and black (see page 239).

The only stillwater departure from flies tied for moving-water midges is in the *very large* types across the northern lattitude of trout ranges. Some of these have full-year, or even two-year, life cycles. They have all that time to eat and grow; their imitations can sometimes be tied on size 8 and 10 hooks with 3XL shanks. When such bombers are staged, either near the bottom or just under the surface, trout will not accept anything that does not look at least a little like them. When only a few are around, trout will not be selective to them, but they will never neglect to take one when their constant cruising exposes one.

I have a favorite lake that has heavy hatches of both *small* and *big* midge larvae, ranging in size from 22 up to about 14. Once in a while as I wade the shoreline, I'll see the cast shuck of a size 10 midge pupa. Once in a rare while, I'll do a throat sample on a trout, and it will contain one or at most two of these big pupae, along with that typical myriad of smaller food forms. They are black, or so dark brown that they appear to be black. It is clear that trout see these monsters very sporadically. It is also clear that they take one whenever given a chance. A simple size 10 or 12 black midge pupa pattern, in any style, works very well on that lake, though in a typical day fishing it, I would not see even one of the naturals.

The best fly patterns, and also fishing information, related to these large midges comes out of the Kamloops, British Columbia area, famous for the Kamloops lakes and the portly Kamloops rainbow trout. I have had the luck to fish with Brian Chan and Phil Rowley, though not often enough. They are at the center of study and development of patterns for those very large midges. Two excellent resources for patterns and tactics are Phillip's book *Fly Patterns for Stillwaters* and Brian and Skip Morris's *Morris & Chan on Fly Fishing Trout Lakes.*

KAMLOOPS BLOODWORM

Big bloodworm larvae find themselves stranded on wind or turnover currents annually, almost always in spring. They are blind, and are not able to discern which direction would take them back to their preferred ooze on the bottom, where they can burrow out of danger from trout. Their swimming is aimless; they accomplish what little forward movement they make by whipping their bodies back and forth. When exhausted they simply ride the slight currents, letting fate deliver them to the ooze or to the trout. Brian Chan's Kamloops Bloodworm is an excellent dressing to suspend above the bottom if you spot even a single bloodworm adrift in the water. Trout will likely be seeing more of them than you do, and always know what to do about them.

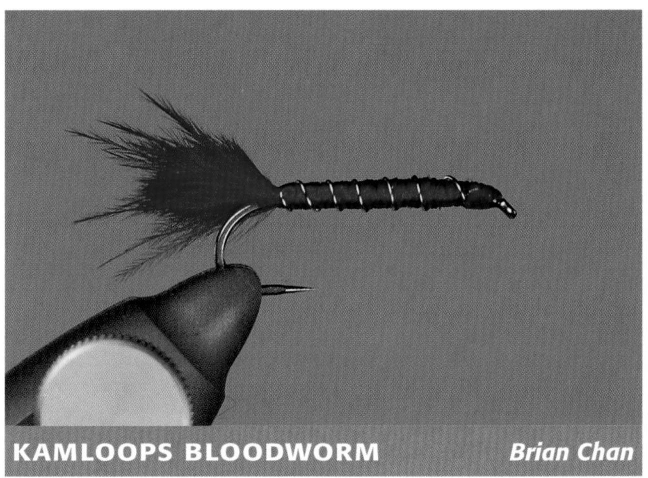

KAMLOOPS BLOODWORM ***Brian Chan***

Hook:	3XL, size 10-14
Thread:	Red 6/0 or 8/0
Tail:	Tuft of red marabou
Rib:	Fine copper wire
Body:	Red floss

The original calls for a body of Super Floss, available from SuperFly, which is thicker than standard rayon or silk floss. If you use thinner floss, overwrap the tail butts and ribbing the length of the shank, and use two layers of floss, to give a bit of bulk to the body.

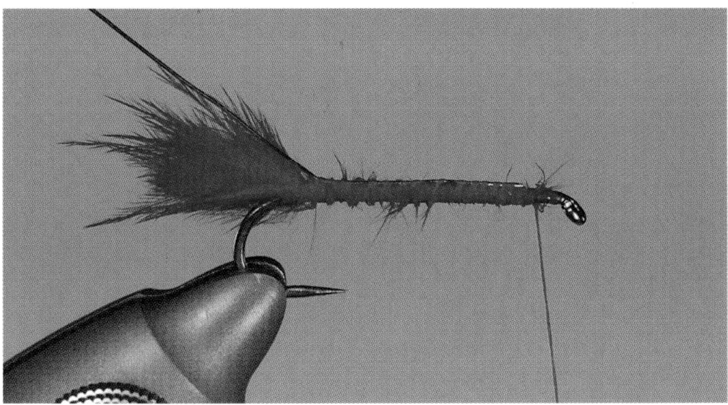

Step 1. Fix the hook in the vise, and layer the shank with thread. Clip or peel a bunch of marabou from the feather, and measure it about one-half the shank length. The red marabou fluff from the base of a red-dyed saddle hackle feather is excellent for this fly. Tie in the marabou and overwrap the butts to the hook eye. Tie in the ribbing wire at that point, and overwrap it to the base of the tail and back to the hook eye.

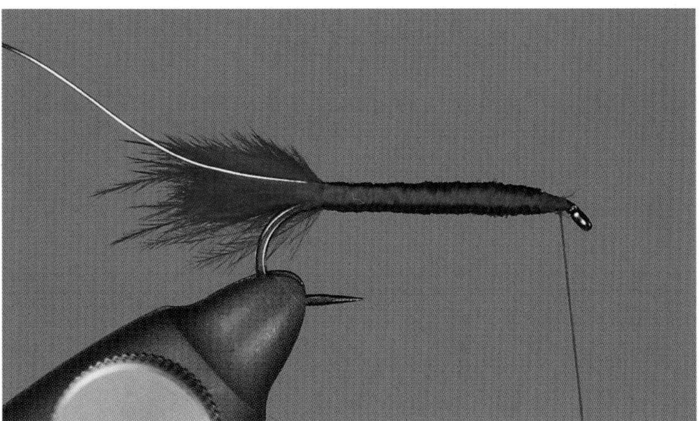

Step 2. Tie in several inches of floss. Wrap a single layer to the base of the tails, and another back to the tie-in point. Tie it off and clip the excess. If you are using heavier Super Floss, tie it in at the base of the tail and take a single layer forward.

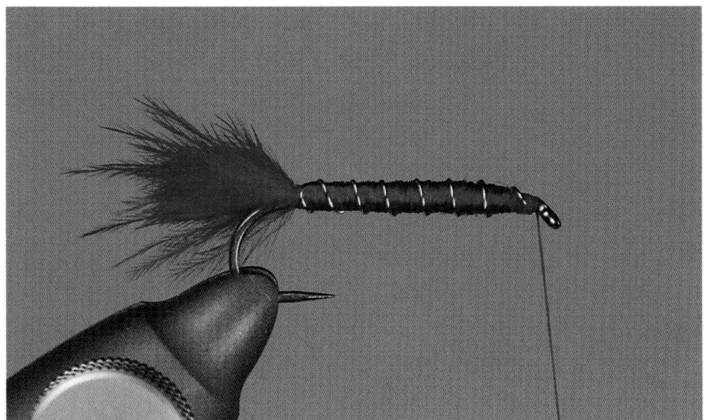

Step 3. Counterwind the ribbing wire forward over the floss body in six to eight evenly spaced wraps. Tie it off behind the hook eye, and clip the excess. Form a thread head, whip-finish, clip the thread, and apply head cement.

It will not take a very large part of a single evening to tie enough Kamloops Bloodworms to last a season. You won't use them often, though you also might find yourself fishing them in searching situations on lakes and ponds, when you see no evidence of bloodworms in the water, but don't know what might work better. It's surprising how often a bright red dressing, fished in tandem with a black pupa pattern, will intercept cruising trout. It's also no secret that the San Juan Worm you tied for aquatic worms in rivers and streams (see page 275) will be suitable for bloodworms if you have no exact imitations. Trout have trouble telling a wormlike midge larva from a worm, and cannot separate their imitations any better.

Trout take far more midge pupae than larvae in lakes. Most of the patterns you tie for midges should be for pupae (Chironomidae).

Most of your midge patterns should be tied to imitate pupae, not larvae. I suspect that most larval patterns are taken by trout as pupae. In my experience, when trout feed on midge larvae, they do so opportunistically, taking them along with so many other things that the larvae are outweighed by the etceteras. But trout feeding on pupae often see them in great numbers, when the naturals are staged, or they see them as standouts in a pelagic field crowded with microscopic bites, in which case they are not necessarily selective to them, but are awfully glad to get them. Usually when trout feed on pupae suspended in a stew of tiny organisms, the few midge pupae in a throat or stomach sample will outweigh, if not outnumber, the other items.

CHAN'S CHIRONOMID

Brian Chan's Chironomid can be tied over the full range of natural sizes, from about size 18 up to size 10 or 12. But it's a bit difficult to tie on small hooks, and is most effective in the larger sizes of the northern bombers, sizes 10 to 14. The original is tied on a straight-shank hook, but all midge pupa patterns can be tied as well on curved scud hooks. Because these are functionally 2X short, and most very large pupae are tied on long-shank hooks, you will need to tie on larger sizes if you use the shorter curved styles. I prefer midge pupae on the rounded hooks.

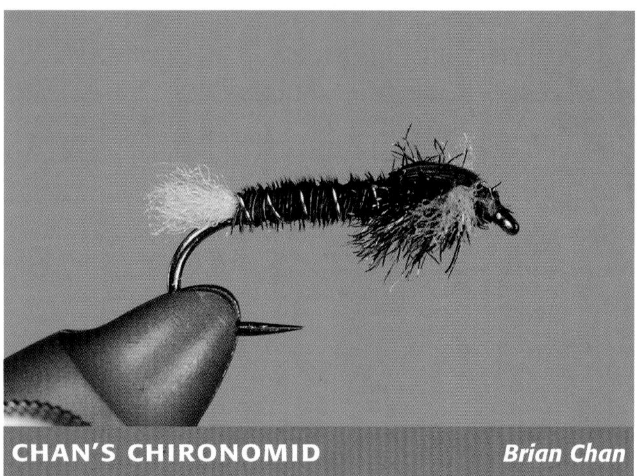

CHAN'S CHIRONOMID *Brian Chan*

Hook:	Standard nymph, size 10-14
Thread:	Brown 6/0 or 8/0
Tail:	White polypro yarn
Rib:	Copper wire
Abdomen:	Pheasant tail fibers
Wing case:	Pheasant tail fibers
Thorax:	Peacock herl
Gills:	White Antron or polypro fibers

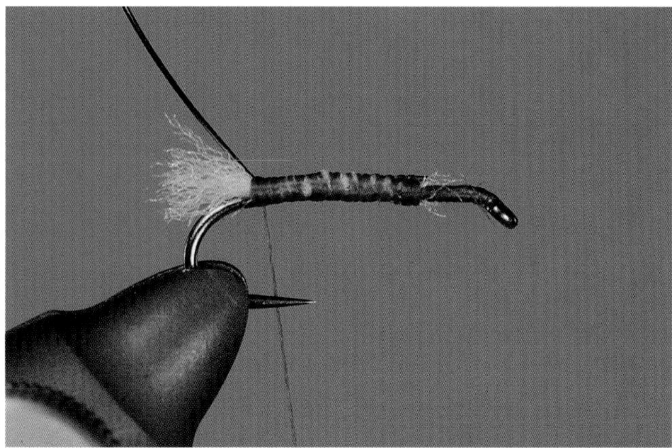

Step 1. Fix the hook in the vise, start the thread behind the eye, and layer the shank to the hook bend. Tie in a very short tuft of polypro yarn; it should reach from the tie-in point to the outside curve of the hook bend, or just a bit farther. Overwrap the polypro forward the length of the shank. Tie in a few inches of ribbing wire, overwrapping it the length of the shank to the base of the tail tuft, to maintain an even underbody.

Step 2. Tie in three to four pheasant center tail fibers by their tips, and wind them forward, stopping one-quarter to one-third the length of the shank behind the eye. Tie them off and clip the excess. Counterwind the ribbing wire over the pheasant herl in four to six evenly spaced turns, to lock it in against the teeth of hungry trout. Tie the wire off and clip the excess.

Step 3. Tie five to ten pheasant tail fibers in by the butt end, at the end of the abdomen. Tie two to three peacock herls in at the same place, but by their tips. Select a strand of white polypro yarn about the same length and thickness as the tail tuft. Tie this in across the hook shank about two hook-eye lengths behind the eye, using a few figure eights of thread. Do not trim the ends to length at this point; it's easier to wind the thorax herl with the gill tufts long rather than short.

Step 4. Wrap a couple turns of peacock herl behind the polypro gill tufts, and another turn in front. Tie it off and clip the excess. Gather the pheasant tail wing-case fibers together; it helps make a tight wing case if you give them a bit of twist before pulling them over the thorax. Draw them forward, and tie them off behind the hook eye.

Step 5. Clip the excess wing-case butts. Make a neat thread head, whip-finish, clip the thread, and apply head cement. Clip the polypro gill tufts the width of the peacock herl thorax.

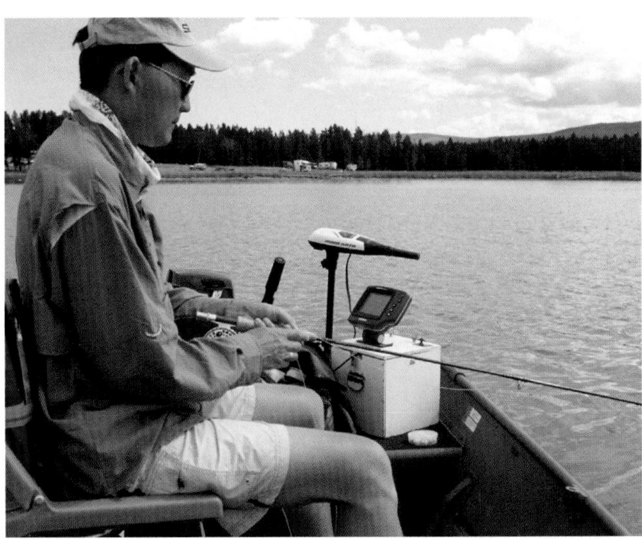

Kamloops biologist and midge specialist Brian Chan fishing from his boat, set up with a depth finder at his side.

CHAN'S FROSTBITE CHIRONOMID PUPA

Many large midge pupae, in the moments before emergence, take on the same brassie coloration as the *Callibaetis* mayfly nymphs hatching in my aquarium. Trout can key on them in this vulnerable moment, and you will do well with a fly pattern that matches the reflective body rather than the color of the pupa before it pumps gases between its inner and outer cuticles. Brian Chan's Frostbite Chironomid is designed to capture that reflectance and color.

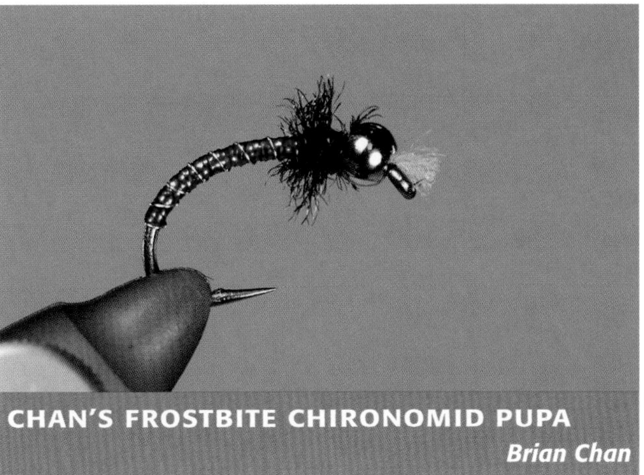

CHAN'S FROSTBITE CHIRONOMID PUPA
Brian Chan

Hook:	Curved scud, size 6–16
Bead:	Copper
Thread:	Black 6/0 or 8/0
Gills:	Tuft of white polypro yarn
Rib:	Silver wire
Abdomen:	Red, black, or brown Frostbite or Krystal Flash
Thorax:	Peacock herl

For the abdomen, the original calls for two strands of Frostbite of the appropriate color unraveled from a woven strand. If you lack Frostbite, available from SuperFly, try the Krystal Flash.

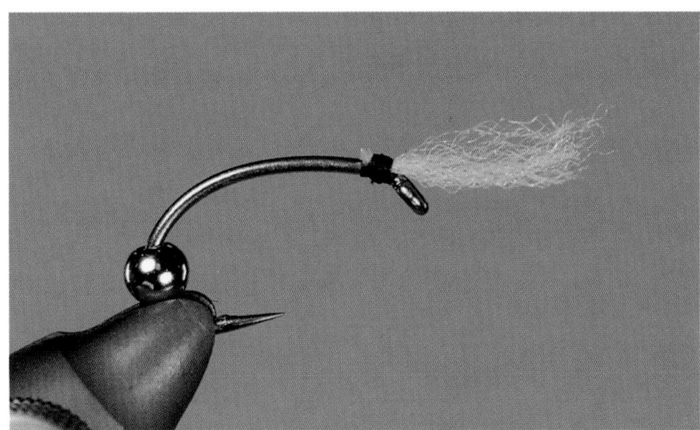

Step 1. Debarb the hook, slip a bead over the bend with the narrow end of its taper toward the hook eye. Fix the hook in the vise, and place the bead back out of the way, down on the bend of the hook. Start your thread with

just a few turns behind the hook eye. Separate a small amount of polypro yarn from the main skein, and clip it short. Tie it in with minimal turns of thread, with the end protruding over the eye. Apply a whip-finish and clip the thread.

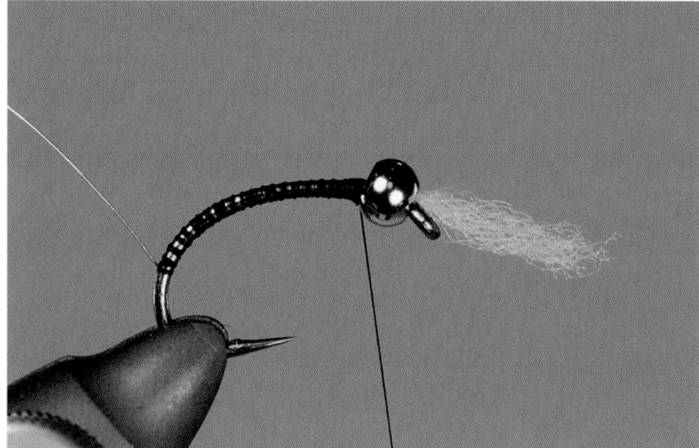

Step 2. Advance the bead to the polypro gill tuft, and push it over the tie-in point as far as you can against the hook eye. Restart the thread behind the bead. Tie in the ribbing wire, and overwrap it well around the bend of the hook. Return the thread to the back of the bead.

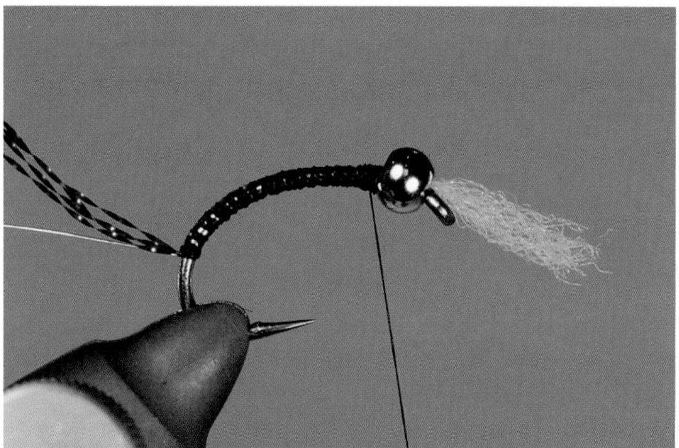

Step 3. Tie in three to six strands of Frostbite or Krystal Flash. Overwrap it to the ribbing wire and back, ending with your thread at the back of the bead.

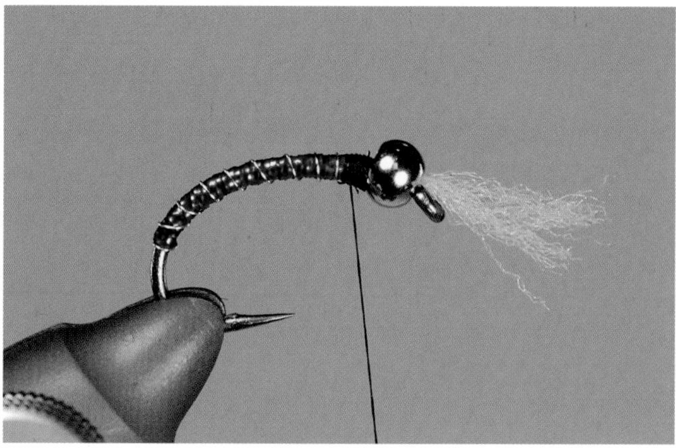

Step 4. Wrap the Frostbite or Krystal Flash body forward to the back of the bead, tie it off, and clip the excess. Counterwind the ribbing over the body in six to ten evenly spaced turns. Tie it off and clip or break the excess.

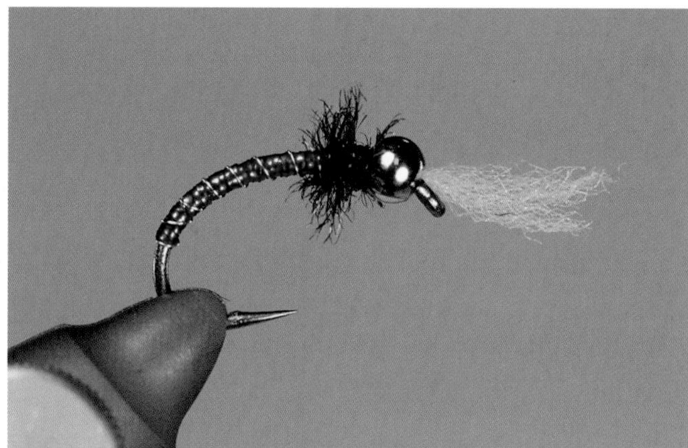

Step 5. Tie in two or three peacock herl fibers behind the bead. Wind them forward in two or three turns behind the bead. Tie off and clip the excess herl. Whip-finish between the herl and the back of the bead. Clip your thread.

Step 6. Clip the polypro gill tuft to the length of the hook eye, or a bit longer.

CHROMIE

I'm not sure if Phil Rowley's Chromie is a color variation of Brian's Frostbite Chironomid, or if the Frostbite is a variation of the Chromie. But they're both tied with the same set of steps listed above. I've seen enough midge pupae, in aquariums, with a whitish sheen in the moments before emergence to value a dressing with a shiny body.

CHROMIE *Phil Rowley*

Hook:	Curved scud, size 8-14
Thread:	Black 6/0 or 8/0
Bead:	Black
Gills:	Tuft of white polypro yarn
Rib:	Red Flashabou, Krystal Flash, or wire
Body:	Silver Flashabou or Krystal Flash
Thorax:	Peacock herl

SUMMARY

Most large midge pupae I've encountered on lakes and ponds have been black, or so dark brown they were nearly black. I think what Henry Ford said about Model A Fords can be modified for midges: You can fish any color pupa pattern you want, but be sure the other one in the tandem is black.

Don't let this chapter's emphasis on flies for the very large midges of the northern regions mislead you into thinking that midges in stillwaters are mostly large, and only those are important. I suspect that those in the midrange of hook sizes, say 14 to 18, are taken most by trout, and are most important in most places. Imitations for them are the same as those used for moving water, and I urge you to refer to chapter 21 as the basis for most midges that you tie for stillwaters.

The very smallest midges, sizes 20 to 24, are more important in the southern tier of trout stillwaters. The largest bombers, sizes 8 and 10, tied on long-shank hooks, are an aberration unless you fish in the North. It is not an accident that most of our chironomid writing and fishing advances arise in a region where midges are largest. That makes the biggest of them most important there.

Those advances in fishing techniques apply to midges of all sizes, and in all waters. I catch far more trout on midge pupae suspended beneath strike indicators now than I ever caught before using floating lines and long leaders, or any type of sinking line. Midge pupae should usually be fished in one of the two zones at which the naturals tend to suspend: just off the bottom or just beneath the surface. When trout are active, and even an occasional fish can be seen cruising, taking something on or near the surface, then one or two midge pupa patterns dropped on a foot or two of tippet from a yarn indicator will put your nymphs at just the right depth. I often fish a single size 16 black midge pupa pattern on just ten inches of tippet, and catch lots of trout doing it.

If you see no signs of trout feeding or cruising, then suspect they might be interested in a midge pupa suspended just above the bottom. Brian Chan keeps a depth sounder in his boat, and uses it to find fish and to scope out the depth and structure of the bottom as well. While in the boat with him on one of his favorite British Columbia lakes, I asked, "How do you figure out the right depth to fish a midge pupa near the bottom if you don't have a depth finder?"

Brian hooked his hemostat to the bend of his fly, dropped it overboard, watched for the obvious sudden slack in the line when it hit bottom. He brought it back up, said, "You tie on an untapered leader a few feet longer than that depth. Tie a barrel knot in the leader eighteen inches short of that mark. Then put a sliding indicator on the leader, so it stops when it hits the knot. Tie on one or two midge pupa patterns at the end of the tippet, and pinch some putty weight or a microshot between them. Casting is no fun, but when you've got your rig out there, and have given it time to sink, your pair of nymphs will be suspended eighteen inches off the bottom, right where trout cruise and look for midge pupae."

It worked. The water we fished was more than twenty feet deep.

CHAPTER 30

Damselflies

Damselfly nymphs are predaceous. Their primary weapon is a long, hinged lower jaw with what seem like fangs at its end. The nymph creeps around in the submerged vegetation, stalking, or lies without movement along stems and leaves, lurking. When an innocent midge larva, mayfly nymph, or scud gets into range, that lower labium shoots out, grabs the prey, drags it to the damselfly's mouth, where the victim is slowly consumed. To get a feel for how it would work if we had the same apparatus, ball up one fist and press it to the bottom of your jaw. Now frown at your son, daughter, dog, or cat. When they drift over to see what trickery you're up to, shoot that hand out and grab them. Don't consume them.

Damsel nymphs are long, very slender, have three leaflike tail gills at the end of the abdomen, and wide heads with beady eyes, sometimes red or green, more often black, out on the sides. Their aspect is a long, even taper, from wide at the front to narrow at the back, then those trailing gills. When they swim, which is rare except during migration for emergence, they tuck their long legs along the sides of the body. They depend on camouflage for the success of their hunt, and are the color of whatever vegetation they live among. Usually that is some shade of olive, but in some waters the olive tips toward tan or brown. They range in size from immature specimens less than half an inch long to fully grown nymphs nearly two inches long, big enough to be imitated on long-shank size 4 and 6 hooks. Most of the mature damsel nymphs that trout eat, in my own collecting, are in the 3XL size 10 to 12 range.

Damsel nymphs have two phases of availability to trout. The first is almost continuous, as they grow from eggs sown in summer, hatched in late summer or fall.

Damselfly nymphs (Coenagrionidae) are long and slender, with three willow-leaf gills at the end of the abdomen, and wide heads with eyes at the sides. Their general aspect is a very slender taper from wide at the front to narrow at the after end.

It's fairly rare to catch a stillwater trout that hasn't included at least a few damselfly nymphs in its diet. That is why an olive damsel imitation is an almost constant producer on lakes and ponds, and should always be considered as a fallback fly, when you have no idea that something else might work better.

Damselfly nymphs live in vegetation wherever they find it in a lake or pond, but they must make their way toward shore, or protruding vegetation, for emergence. They seem to prefer reed and cattail stalks. During their migration, they'll move toward the edges in numbers that can turn trout selective.

They are thus available in their early stages of growth from fall through winter and into early and even late spring. They start out as little wisps, perhaps a quarter inch long when trout begin to take them along with the pelagic stew of zooplankters and midges. By the time they reach half an inch long, they begin to stand out in stomach samples, so that you might imagine a trout making a concerted effort to turn and take one, or even begin to nose into the vegetation, flush them out, gun them down.

By late spring they have reached full size, averaging around an inch long, and trout are clearly glad to take them whenever they get a chance. By then trout must be making their own chances often, driving through vegetation beds, feeding on whatever they've managed to disturb, which will often be scuds, but just as often damselfly nymphs that are in the vegetation hunting for scuds.

I confess to enjoying meals of trout wherever a lake or pond has no inlet or outlet stream for natural spawning, and holds only planted trout. I don't recommend that you kill trout, but if you do, then always examine what they've been eating. That always provides the best evidence about what sort of fly you should tie to your tippet. I rarely catch a stillwater trout in any season, except late summer and early fall, that fails to contain at least one or two damselfly nymphs. Since some damselflies have two-year life cycles, it's not uncommon to catch trout with a mix of sizes, and at all seasons. That makes damselfly nymph imitations constant producers in stillwaters. If you ever arrive at any lake or pond, stand at its edge, and wonder what fly you should try, start with an olive damsel in size 12 or 14 unless you get the sense that something else might work better.

The second phase of availability occurs when the nymphs have reached full size, are told by the seasonal light cycle that their time for emergence has arrived, and must make it to shore from wherever they've been living, so the adults can escape the nymphal shucks. The nymphs crawl out of the water to emerge. They'll hoist themselves out on any emergent vegetation: a lily pad, a protruding limb from a fallen log, the floating tops of submerged weed beds. But their most common emergence site is the edge of a forest of reeds or cattail stalks.

When damsels sense that their time is right, they leave their offshore plant beds and begin the long, slow swim toward shore. They generally live in plants rooted to the bottom, therefore at some depth. As they move out of it, they usually move higher into the water column, and become more and more exposed to trout predation. This happens in spring, but spring can happen in different months depending on elevation and latitude. It will be April in the southern tier of states, May in most of the middle tier, and June or even early July in the northern states and Canadian provinces. At some point in the stillwater season, trout will usually see enough migrating damselfly nymphs to become selective to them. When that happens, you need to have an imitation for them.

Two aspects of a natural damselfly nymph are obvious to us, and are presumably triggers to trout. The first is those dominant eyes. The second is their undulating swimming motion. They swim with a sinuous side-to-side wobble that can be brisk when they're fresh, but looks as though it's played in slow motion when they are on the move over long distances, during their migration, when they quite likely get tuckered out. They often pause to rest during their long swim, at which time their legs splay out, one guesses to act as parachutes and impede their descent.

I've read that when a trout gets after a damsel nymph, the nymph's defense is to dive toward the bottom. I can't confirm this, but have no reason to deny it. I don't know how to imitate it, and in truth I don't usually know it when a trout is suddenly on the tail of my fly. I do know that I get a large proportion of takes when my nymph is on the sit, and I consider it beneficial to incorporate periods of no retrieve at all in whatever retrieve I am using with a damselfly nymph. Usually that is a slow hand-twist.

Because so many takes come on a slow retrieve, or on no retrieve at all, it is useful to incorporate materials that impart movement to the fly even when it's making little or no forward progress. Marabou, with its soft texture and wavery response to water, is incorporated into most successful damsel imitations.

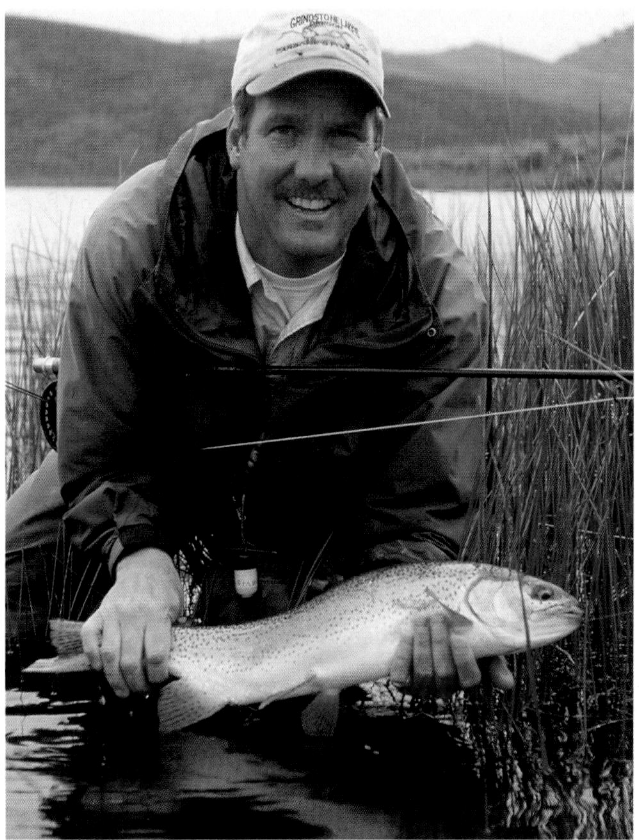

Pat Windsor, a guide on the Grindstone Lakes in central Oregon, shows the hefty results of fishing a damsel imitation along lake reed edges.

BABY DAMSEL

One of the most valuable damsel nymph dressings was designed by Brian Chan, the British Columbia stillwater expert, to imitate the immature naturals found in almost every trout sample throughout the seasons. It has become a go-to pattern for me, for use in all seasons except the period of the actual migration, when a larger dressing is more appropriate.

BABY DAMSEL *Brian Chan*

Hook: Curved scud, size 14-18
Bead: Gold
Weight: 4 to 6 turns nonlead wire, optional
Thread: Olive 8/0
Tail: Olive marabou
Rib: Fine gold wire
Body: Olive marabou

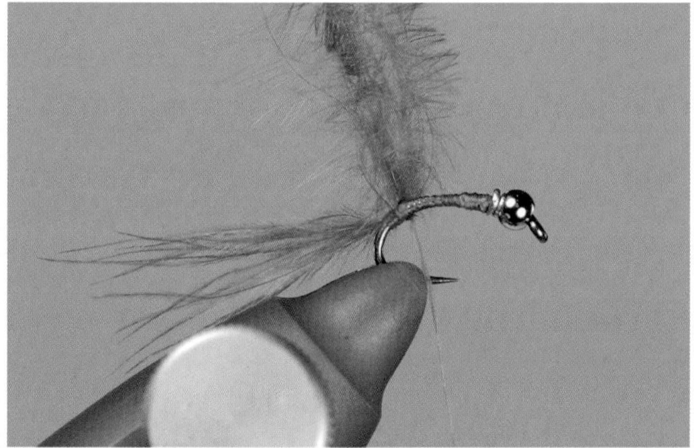

Step 1. Place a bead on the hook, and fix the hook in the vise. Wrap a few turns of nonlead wire behind the bead, and jam them into the back end of it. Keep the weight scant; if you use more than a tiny amount, the fly will sink too fast when you fish it in and around shallow weed beds. Start the thread behind the weighting wire, and layer it partway around the bend of the hook. Measure the tips of a few marabou strands two to three times the hook length. Tie these in with three to four tight turns of thread.

Step 2. Hold the butts of the tail fibers out of the way, and tie in the ribbing wire. Overwrap it with thread to the back shoulder of the weighting wire, or to the back of the bead if you omit the wire.

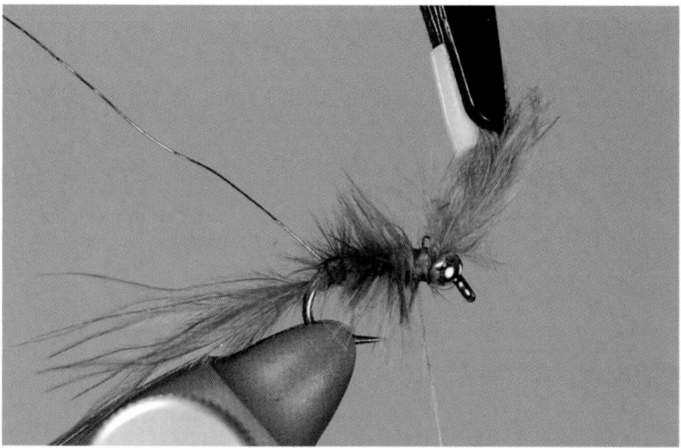

Step 3. Capture the marabou tail butts in your fingertips, or attach hackle pliers to them. Twist them into a rope, and wind them forward to the back of the bead. Tie them off there and clip the excess.

Step 4. Counterwind the ribbing through the marabou herl body in three to six evenly spaced turns, working it back and forth as you go forward to avoid matting down any more fibers than necessary. Tie it off and clip or break off the excess. Whip-finish behind the bead, and clip the thread.

I catch an outsized number of trout on Brian's small damselfly nymph imitation, in part because it's a quick tie, and I don't mind tying a few in a hurry on a camp table alongside a lake, and in second part because it's a great fly to fish in combination with a midge pupa dressing when you don't know precisely what is happening on a stillwater, but would prefer catching a few trout to taking a hike or a nap. I rarely fish the Baby Damsel, either by itself or in combination with any other fly, with anything but a hand-twist retrieve.

Most imitations for larger, more mature damsel nymphs incorporate eyes, because they are such a prominent feature of the natural that they might be the trigger that prompts trout to strike. We might not always know what these triggers are, but if you suspect one, it never hurts your chances if your nymph captures it. You can buy preformed monofilament eyes in black, red, and green, large, medium, and small. I recommend that you do. If you'd like to form your own, however, it's not difficult, and you can build up a good supply in a hurry.

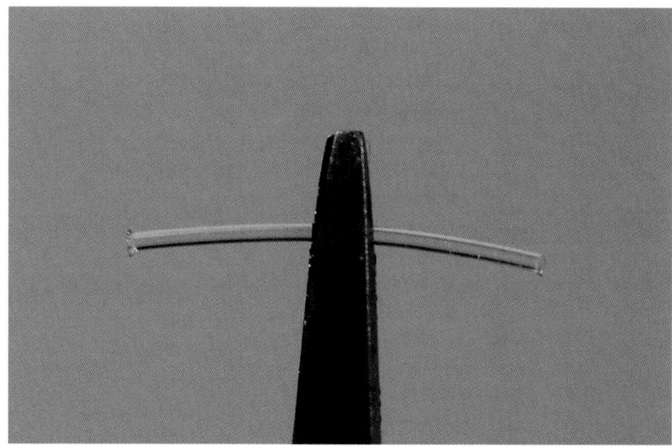

To create your own monofilament eyes for damselfly nymphs, start with about a half-inch section of 40- to 50-pound-test mono. Center it in your debarbing pliers, near the narrow tip. The width of the pliers at this point will determine the width of the finished eyes.

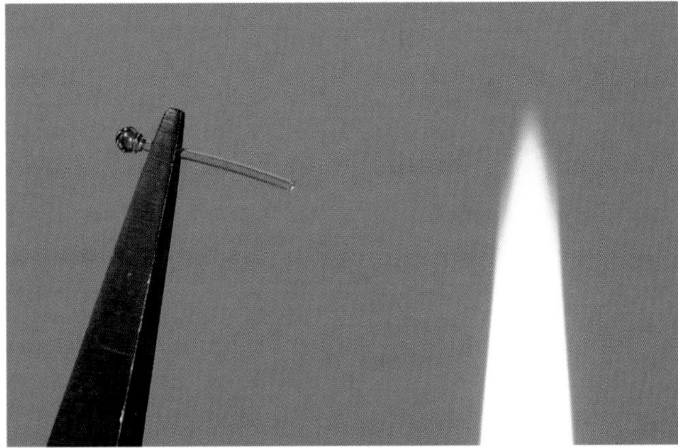

Slowly bring the mono near the flame, until it begins melting and balling up toward the pliers. When it reaches the pliers, remove it from the heat and blow on it to cool it. Turn the pliers and burn the other side.

The finished eyes will be the width of the pliers. You can adjust the size of the eyes by using heavier mono or a longer section. You can adjust the width by placing the mono closer to the pliers tip or farther down the taper.

The basic formula is to hold a half-inch section of 40- to 50-pound-test monofilament in the tip of your debarbing pliers, and melt each side into a ball with a cigarette lighter or candle flame. You can buy mono with a greenish or reddish cast, though it's difficult to find black. You can create larger or smaller eyes by using a longer or shorter piece of mono. You can make wider or narrower eyes by placing the mono closer to or farther from the tapered tip of your pliers.

The one warning I'll extend is to be careful with your burn rate. If you get the mono too hot, it will ball up abruptly, and often drop away from the pliers and onto your lap. You'll end up with holes in your pant legs. If you're wearing shorts, you might tip over your tying bench. Hold the mono near enough to the flame to get it softened and rolling into a ball toward the pliers, then move it slowly closer as the stub shortens into an eye. If it ignites, which it will often, just blow it out.

MARABOU DAMSEL, OLIVE

Though many damselfly imitations have been tied to capture every complexity of the naturals, I've seen no evidence that trout are mystified by all the additions. I recommend you start by tying the simplest fly possible that has mono eyes and a marabou tail. The Marabou Damsel is tied in many variations, but the quickest tie might be the most suitable.

MARABOU DAMSEL, OLIVE

Hook:	Curved nymph, 3XL, size 8-14
Weight:	8-12 turns nonlead wire
Thread:	Olive 6/0 or 8/0
Eyes:	Preformed mono eyes
Tail:	Olive marabou
Rib:	Copper wire
Body:	Olive marabou
Wing case:	Olive marabou
Thorax:	Olive dubbing

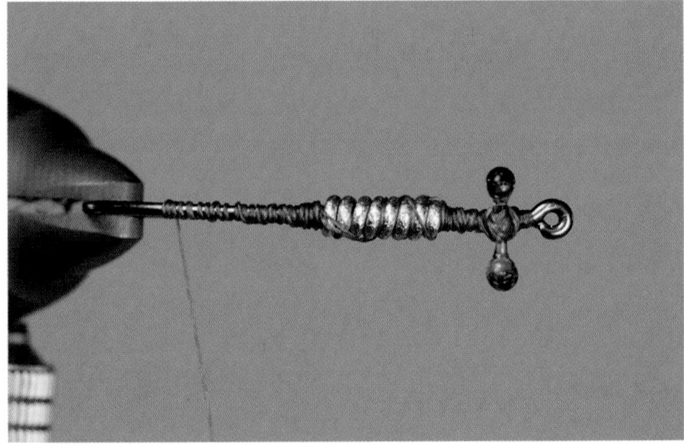

Step 1. Fix the hook in the vise, and position a few turns of nonlead weighting wire on the front half of the shank. This is an attempt to capture the natural's habit of diving when seen by a trout; when you stop retrieving, it goes down slightly by the bow. Place the mono eyes one to two hook-eye lengths behind the eye. Tie them in with several figure eights of thread and a few more turns that

go under the far eye, up and around the shank in front of the eyes, under the near eye, and up and around the shank behind the eyes. Build slight thread ramps to the front and back shoulders of the weighting wire, and take your thread to the bend of the hook.

Step 2. Gather the tip fibers of a marabou feather, or peel the fibers from one side of a feather. Measure them the length of the hook, and tie them in at the bend of the hook.

Step 3. Hold the butts of the tail marabou up and out of the way with your off hand. Tie the ribbing wire in at the base of the tail, and overwrap it to the back shoulder of the weighting wire. Continue forward with the thread, leaving it at the front shoulder of the wire.

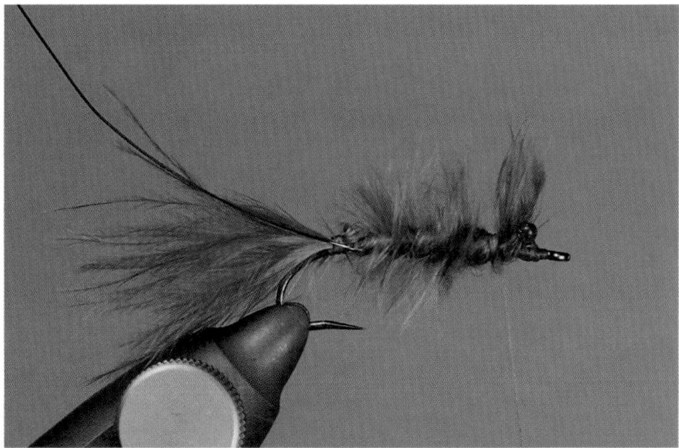

Step 4. Wind the tail marabou butts forward as herl, ending at the front shoulder of the weighting wire. Tie it off there. Do not trim the remainder. If your fibers are too short to leave any remainders, you might have to tie in a bit of marabou for the wing cases in the next step.

Step 5. Counterwind the ribbing forward to the end of the body in five to seven evenly spaced turns. Tie it off and clip or break off the excess. Fold the remaining marabou butts back over the body, and take several turns of thread to hold them in place. They should extend to the midpoint of the body, no farther, and should be sparse rather than thick. Damselfly nymphs have unobtrusive wing pads that do not turn black when the nymphs reach maturity, as do those of mayflies and stoneflies. If the butts are too long, which will be normal, use your fingers to pinch them to the length and thickness desired. Resist the urge to use your scissors; you don't want to cut clean lines here.

Step 6. Twist a long and fairly thin amount of dubbing to the thread. Take two or three turns to fill in the gap between the end of the body and the eyes. Make one figure eight set of turns between the eyes. Take a final turn of dubbing in front of the eyes. Use enough thread turns to form a neat thread head, whip-finish, clip the thread, and apply head cement.

In its most common variations, either the Marabou Damsel has a turkey feather section wing-case, or marabou herl is wound forward between the eyes, in place of the dubbing. I prefer to tie it the way it's listed and shown, but the trout haven't expressed any preference for this particular tie over any other version of it. The key is to keep the colors consistent between the marabou herl and the dubbing; I usually use what is called Caddis Green dubbing, but that might not agree with the shade of marabou you have on your bench. Try to match them. If you use the same marabou for the thorax as you do for the abdomen and wing case, that problem is automatically solved for you.

No matter the materials you use to tie this fly, be sure to keep it sparse. The naturals are wispy, and your imitations should reflect that.

D. T. DAMSEL

Nearly every angler who has ever fished a damselfly migration has rushed home and created an imitation in his own image, named it for himself. You can find dozens of them; I haven't found one that fails to work. That is why I tend to look first for simplicity, and second for those triggers, in any dressing I tie for my own nymph boxes. One of the most interesting dressings, which I haven't tried but have tied and intend to fish next season, uses rabbit fur rather than marabou to capture the undulating swimming movement of the natural nymph.

D. T. DAMSEL *Dan Allen and Tim Tollett*

Hook: 2XL, size 10-14
Weight (optional): 8-12 turns nonlead wire
Thread: Olive 6/0 or 8/0
Eyes: Black mono
Tail: Olive rabbit fur
Rib: Pearl Flashabou
Abdomen: Olive rabbit fur dubbing
Thorax: Dark olive fur dubbing

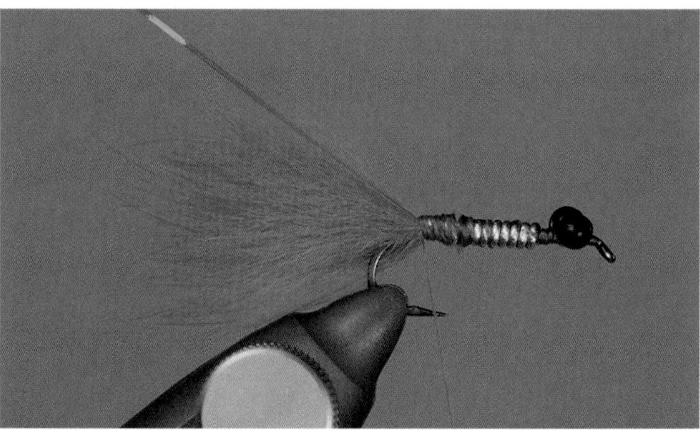

Step 1. Fix the hook in the vise, wind a few turns of lead, start the thread, and affix a set of eyes with figure eights of thread, as you did in the above Marabou Damsel. Secure the weighting wire close behind the eyes, and build slight thread ramps to both shoulders. Clip a substantial section of rabbit fur from the hide. A good

source is olive rabbit strip cut for strip leeches. The tail on this fly, like that on most damsel imitations, represents the body as much as those leaflike tails. Measure the tail the length of the shank, tie it in, and overwrap the butts to the back shoulder of the weighting wire before trimming. Tie in a single strand of pearl Flashabou.

Step 2. Use a dubbing fur with no guard hairs, or remove the guard hairs from the underfur if you clip your dubbing from the hide. Dub a fairly slender abdomen forward just past the midpoint of the hook. Bring your ribbing forward in four to six evenly spaced turns, and tie it off at the end of the abdomen.

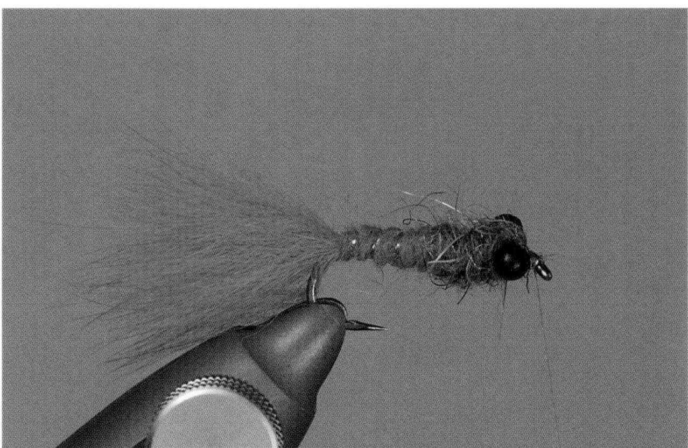

Step 3. In dubbing cut from the hide, leave the guard hairs in, or use a rough dubbing mix that is a little darker than the fur used for the tail and abdomen. I prefer a fur and Antron mix, for the tiny bit of sparkle, and also for the fibers that stick out and might represent legs of the natural. Make a fairly long dubbing skein, twist it to your thread, and wind two or three turns behind the eyes, a figure eight between them, and finish with a turn in front. Make a neat head, whip-finish, clip the thread, and cement the head.

The D. T. Damsel was designed by Tim Tollett and Dan Allen, of Frontier Anglers Fly Shop in Dillon, Montana. It can be tied with marabou for the tail. If you omit the weight, or underweight it, using nonlead wire finer than the diameter of the hook shank, the body will be more slender. If you plan to fish it only in the shallows, with a slow hand-twist retrieve, the unweighted version will be better. I prefer to use just a few turns of nonlead wire on all of my damselfly nymph patterns to get them to the depth I want. But that is usually just one to three feet; if I want them deeper, I accomplish it with a sinking line, not with weight on the fly or leader.

AFTERSHAFT DAMSEL

If you desire to tie a more complex, and also more imitative, dressing for the stillwater damselfly nymph, then Phil Rowley's Aftershaft Damsel, from his book *Fly Patterns for Stillwaters,* should please you. It offers a couple of tying ideas that you should know about. You'll need ring-necked pheasant rooster back feathers dyed olive. Aftershafts are the long, maraboulike feathers attached to the undersides of the bird's back feathers. You can buy a dyed skin. You can find the aftershaft feathers dyed and packaged. Or you can buy a natural skin, pluck the aftershaft feathers, and mark them with a green permanent pen. I find it remarkably easy to buy the dyed feathers prepackaged.

AFTERSHAFT DAMSEL *Phil Rowley*

Hook: Curved nymph, 3XL, size 8-12
Weight (optional): 5-10 turns nonlead wire
Thread: Olive 6/0 or 8/0
Eyes: Olive Vernille, Ultra Chenille, or Velvet Chenille, knotted
Tail: Tips of olive marabou feather
Rib: Copper wire or pearl Krystal Flash
Body: Butts of tail fibers
Wing case: Olive raffia
Thorax: Olive ring-necked pheasant aftershaft

Step 1. Debarb the hook, fix it in the vise, and take five to ten turns of nonlead wire in the thorax region of the shank. Start the thread behind the eye, and layer the front quarter of the shank. Cut a two-inch section of chenille, and tie two abutted overhand knots in it. Lay this across the shank, two eye lengths behind the eye, and lash it down with a few figure eights of thread. Draw the tag of the off-side eye behind the eye, and lash it to the shank. Repeat with the near eye. Trim the excess.

Step 2. Layer the shank with thread, and the weighting wire as well, if you've added it. Align the tips of a marabou feather, measure them the length of the entire hook, not just the shank, and tie them in at a point straight above the hook barb point. Hold the butts out of the way, and tie in the ribbing. Overwind it to the back shoulder of your weighting wire, or to a point about the diameter of the chenille eyes behind those eyes.

Step 3. Grasp the tail butts and twist them to form a herl rope. If they are long, use your fingers to wind them forward. If they are short, attach your hackle pliers and wind the body with the pliers. Stop at that point about the diameter of the chenille eyes behind the eyes. Tie off the marabou and clip the excess. Counterwind the ribbing through the marabou herl body, working it back and forth if necessary to avoid matting down fibers.

Step 4. Select a section of raffia about one-half to two-thirds of the hook gap in width. If it's not dyed olive, mark one side with a waterproof pen. Tie it in at the end of the abdomen with the olive side down. Select an aftershaft feather, and prepare it for tying by removing the long fibers from the tip. Pinch them off with your fingers.

Step 5. Form a thread loop a bit longer than the aftershaft feather. Wax one thread of the loop with very sticky dubbing wax, or use your bodkin to apply head cement to one thread. Tack the aftershaft feather to this thread, with the tip toward the hook, the butt at the far end of the loop.

Step 6. Close the loop on the aftershaft feather, being sure to catch it in the center, so the thread aligns with the stem. You might find it easier to use a dubbing loop spinner tool for this operation. Twist the end of the loop, twirling the aftershaft feather into a herl rope. This is the same process used for a dubbing rope (see page 50). It is similar to the method used to make a peacock herl rope, but the aftershaft is not tied to the hook shank before the loop is created.

Step 7. Wind the marabou herl rope in two or three turns forward to the nymph eyes. If you have enough, cross turns between the eyes and take a final turn in front of them. But these are optional; the main purpose of the long aftershaft fibers is to represent the legs of the natural. Do not trim them short. Tie off and clip the excess loop. Return the thread behind the eyes.

Step 8. Draw the raffia forward over the thorax, and use a few thread turns to secure it there. Take your thread forward to a point just behind the hook eye. Bring the remaining raffia forward between the chenille eyes and tie it off. Cut the excess. Make a thread head, whip-finish, clip the thread, and apply head cement.

This is the most imitative dressing you will need for damselfly nymphs. When it's wet, all of its parts will be active, even when you're not retrieving it. Phil ties the fly in tan as well as the listed olive. He also recommends mixing a couple of colors, olive and tan or olive and brown, for the marabou tail and body. This gives the finished fly a mottled appearance, common among the larger naturals.

As always, I recommend you collect the naturals in your own lakes and ponds, and match the colors you find dominant. You won't go wrong tying and carrying a basic supply in olive; damsels rely on camouflage both to capture prey and to avoid becoming prey. They're usually found living on vegetation some shade of green, and can almost always be matched with materials in the color that has come to be called olive.

SUMMARY

In chapter 27, I mentioned a way to prune an Olive Woolly Bugger into an acceptable damselfly nymph imitation. It works surprisingly well, but I don't like to rely on it. If nothing else, it does not provide the satisfaction of having tied a specific dressing to match a particular insect, which, at least to me, is a major part of what fly fishing is all about. I consider it necessary to carry Brian Chan's Baby Damsel. I also like to have one more imitative pattern in my box. It is almost always the Olive Marabou Damsel in size 12, tied on its 3XL hook.

That is a small supply of flies for such a major insect. The damselfly nymph is one of the most important stillwater food forms for trout, and therefore one of the few critical imitations to carry in your stillwater-fly box. If the migration is on, and you lack something that imitates the insect, or that you can crop into a rough imitation, it's likely that you're going to enjoy some time sitting on a lakeside log watching trout feed with big bulges just beneath the surface, and with not much you can do to stop them.

When damsels are on the move, I prefer to rig with a clear intermediate line. It gets the nymph down a foot to three feet. The clear line, sunk just below the surface, seems to disturb trout less than a floating line. I use it most of the time on stillwaters when I'm not fishing dry flies on the surface or probing the depths when trout are down. If you fish stillwaters much, or intend to, and don't own a clear intermediate line, you might find that it improves your fishing more than this or that precise imitation.

If plant beds are deep, say ten to twenty feet, and I want to get my damsel nymph down to them, then I rig with the appropriate sink-rate line out of a shooting-taper system that I always carry. Usually it will be either the Type IV fast-sinker or Type VI head, which I call the *depth charge.* If you don't own some sort of depth-charge line, one that plummets, then it is the second acquisition I recommend, right after the clear intermediate.

When you switch to a sinking line, don't use a long leader. That just lets the nymph ride high above the line tip, and defeats the purpose of using the right sink-rate line. Keep the leader around six to at most eight feet, and attach the fly with a Duncan loop knot, to give it freedom of motion. Retrieve with a hand-twist, most of the time, but intersperse this creeping retrieve with short strips and pauses. Trout might prefer the nymph on any one of the movements: slow, fast, or stopped. If you discover they want only one, then use just that one. By trying all three on each retrieve, you begin to sort out what the trout like best.

I remember a story told by the late Ron Brown, the well-known Montana guide introduced to me at the annual Badger Flyfishers Trout Unlimited banquet in Madison by the great Wisconsin guide Jim Rhomberg. Ron and his clients were sitting in a boat on a famous lake, fishing damselfly nymphs, catching trout with such regularity that it distressed those in other boats around them. Some were watching their retrieves with binoculars, trying to figure out what they were doing different. Ron instructed his clients to make quick twitches with their line hands, making it look as if they were using a short, quick, and constant strip.

"Just move the line on every tenth twitch," he told them. "Before long I could see anglers all over the lake doing this frantic twitching retrieve, and not one of them ever caught a fish doing it." You can imagine that nymph at rest down in the depths, taking a little hop every once in a while, then resting again. Trout must have liked it. I liked the story, but I wasn't watching from one of those other boats.

Insert an occasional burst of speed into your retrieve. For the most part, creep your damsel nymph along, or let it simply idle. You won't always feel the takes to your damselfly nymph. If your line makes a subtle movement away from you, or begins a sneaking lateral move, raise the rod to set the hook. You certainly won't detect all of the takes that you get. But you will catch a lot more trout than you would by stripping a damselfly imitation like a streamer.

CHAPTER 31

Dragonflies

Dragonfly nymphs belong to the same order of aquatic insects as damselflies, Odonata, and have the same hinged lower jaw for hunting, though it's more massive and more effective. They lie in ambush or prowl in plant beds and along the bottom. When one moves into range of prey, or prey moves into range of it, that jaw shoots out almost with the speed of a rattlesnake striking. The average victim will be a scud, mayfly or damselfly nymph, midge or caddis larva. It might also be a smaller dragonfly nymph, a pollywog, or a small fish. A dragonfly nymph will kill and eat anything that does not kill and eat it.

Dragonfly nymphs can be broken down into two types, one very important to anglers, the other much less so. Most important are the *climbers,* which do their hunting or ambushing somewhat actively, either along the surface of the bottom or higher in plant beds. They're often available to trout. Less important are the *silters,* sometimes called *sprawlers.* These hunker on the bottom, work their way into the debris, have fine hairs all over their bodies that help hold the debris on top of them. They camouflage themselves with detritus. They rarely venture up into the vegetation. Trout don't get much chance at them except when they pull up stakes and migrate toward shore, once in their two- to three-year lives, for emergence.

Almost all of our focus in this chapter will be on the climbers, because they're more often available to trout, and more useful as models for imitation. Climbers have wide heads, with prominent eyes to each side. The thorax is often pinched in. The abdomen is long and fairly fat. The result is a slight hourglass shape. The legs are long, brittle, and I can tell you from personal experience, crunchy when you fry dragonfly nymphs with onions and eat them. Possible triggers to consumption—by trout, not by you or me—might be those big eyes, the prominent legs, the large size of the insect, and its hourglass shape.

Climber dragonfly nymphs (Aeschnidae) are large and hourglass-shaped, and have big, dominant eyes and stubs for tails. Because they clamber about in vegetation, trout get chances at them far more often than they do at silters.

Silter dragonfly nymphs (Libellulidae) commonly camouflage themselves with silt and debris, and are not likely to be abundant in the trout diet except during their migration for emergence.

Mature dragonfly nymphs can attain lengths of three inches, though one and a half to two inches is more common. A 3XL or 4XL size 6 hook is about average, and the most popular size for these big insects. They have a three- or even four-year life cycle. It's wise to remember that although the mature nymphs are big, they are available to trout only in the last weeks of winter through spring and early summer. Then they emerge, and the smaller first-, second-, and sometimes third-year classes are left to appeal to trout. That means trout will always see dragonfly nymphs, but they will see the largest of them only early in the year. It's always a good idea to carry patterns in smaller sizes: 8, 10, and even 12.

Dragonfly nymphs migrate toward reed and cattail edges for emergence. Smart trout cruise there to intercept them. Smart anglers cast dragonfly nymph imitations, or shortened Woolly Buggers, to intercept the trout.

When ready for emergence, dragonfly nymphs must make it to shore, or to protruding vegetation. Like damselflies, they seem to prefer reed and cattail edges, and will migrate toward these if the pond or lake owns any. They will also crawl out on lily pads, floating vegetation beds, limbs or logs, or the shoreline. They are most available to trout during this migration, and fly patterns fished to match them will be most effective when the naturals are on the move toward shore. The closest I've seen to a trout selective to them was a rainbow with three in its stomach, each the same size and color. That trout was clearly onto them, though it wasn't getting many of them. My scant observations do not preclude more frequent selectivity to the nymphs; they're too large to extract with a throat pump, so the only way to know a trout has fed on them is to kill the trout and examine its stomach.

Dragonfly emergence occurs at dusk or after dark on sunny days, to avoid bird and frog predation. You will observe a rare dragonfly cryptic in the vegetation, making the slow transition from nymph to adult on a reed or cattail stalk, in late afternoon on a cloudy day. Most often you'll see lots of cast shucks in the shallows, and adults in the air, but you'll rarely get to observe that transformation unless you amble out at night with a flashlight.

The migration begins in late April and May in waters across the southern and low-altitude parts of the middle range of trout distribution, and it will be a rare stillwater that holds trout but fails to hold dragonflies. Most emergences take place in late May and June in the moderate altitudes and latitudes, where most trout fishing is done. In the northern tier of states and provinces, and in waters at higher altitudes, migration and emergence can be delayed into July and even August. You will want to fish size 6 imitations until you see lots of adults out and buzzing about on your own waters. After that you'll catch more trout on nymphs in smaller sizes.

Colors of climber dragonfly nymphs tend toward dark olive and olive-brown. You should either collect naturals from your own waters, or at least observe the submerged vegetation over and around which you'll be fishing. The naturals will take on the coloration of their habitat, and your flies should do the same thing. As with damsels, arm yourself with at least a few in olive, but be prepared to tie variations in brown or even tan.

Dragonfly nymphs do not migrate high in the water column as the related damsels do. Instead, they make their movements toward shore either on the bottom or not far above it. As a consequence, you'll want to fish imitations deep, but you will probably want to avoid getting constantly hung up on limbs and logs. It's a good plan to have at least one dragonfly nymph style that floats. Don't fish it as a dry fly. Instead, rig it with a Duncan loop knot to a short leader, say four to at most six feet long, and use an appropriate sink-rate line to get it to the bottom. Let your line drape across the bottom; the floating dragonfly nymph will ride above it a foot or two, and keep you out of trouble with debris down there in the depths. It will also ride up where trout are more likely to notice it.

The naturals have internal gill chambers in their abdomens. Oxygen-rich water is taken in through the anal orifice, washed over the gills, and expelled through the same aperture. If you watch one at rest, it will appear to be breathing, which in fact it is. This same mechanism serves to propel the insect in an emergency. Water is drawn in the back end, the abdomen is clamped down, the water is driven out with force, and the result is jet propulsion on a three- to five-inch scale. The insect folds its legs along its sides, and jets along in those short bursts. It can't go far that way, but it can go surprisingly fast. One could assume that when a trout is in pursuit, a dragonfly nymph has its jets kicked in, and is moving as fast as it can. The best retrieve is a series of short strips followed by a pause. This imitates the resting phase of the natural, but also allows your nymph, if it's a floater, to reposition itself above snags on the bottom.

I'll confess that the imitation I use most often for dragonfly nymphs is by murdering a size 6 or 8 Olive Woolly Bugger, truncating it by pinching off the back part of the tails, as described in chapter 27. I'm more attuned to the imitation of damselfly nymphs and midge pupae on stillwaters, but I'm also aware that trout focus on dragonfly nymphs at times, and rarely pass a chance at one. Nymphs tied to match them can be necessary when the migration is on. They can also be useful as lead flies in a two-fly tandem, usually trailed by a scud or midge pupa dressing, any time you would like to explore for trout by fishing over the tops or along the sides of submerged vegetation.

BEAVERPELT

The Beaverpelt could be considered a variation on the Carey Special, a simple dressing long used as a dragonfly nymph imitation, tied with an olive chenille body and olive pheasant rump feather hackle. The hackle is long, and opens and closes around the chenille body when the fly is retrieved, much as the legs of a natural dragonfly nymph close alongside its body when it jets forward. The original Beaverpelt was tied with dubbed beaver fur, including the guard hairs, in place of the chenille body of the Carey Special, and had the same pheasant rump hackle. I use it in a form that is a bit modified from the original, using olive-dyed beaver fur, tying in and winding the hackle, then finishing with a turn or two of the same fur at the head. You could add eyes, and it would be even more realistic. The Beaverpelt has been modified almost endlessly. But it might be best left as a quick tie, the kind you can construct by the half dozen or dozen on a camp table next to the lake. It will get you back onto the water, and into the business of catching trout that are feeding on dragonfly nymphs, in a hurry.

BEAVERPELT *Don Earnest*

Hook:	3XL curved nymph, size 4-10
Weight:	10-20 turns nonlead wire, optional
Thread:	Olive 6/0 or 8/0
Body:	Olive-dyed beaver fur or similar
Hackle:	Pheasant rump
Head:	Olive-dyed beaver fur or similar

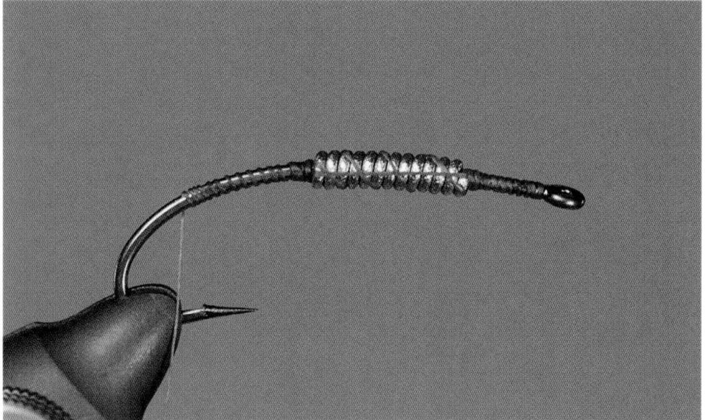

Step 1. Debarb the hook, fix it in the vise, and weight it if desired, which I recommend. Start the thread behind the hook eye, and layer it to the bend, locking in the weighting wire if you've weighted the fly.

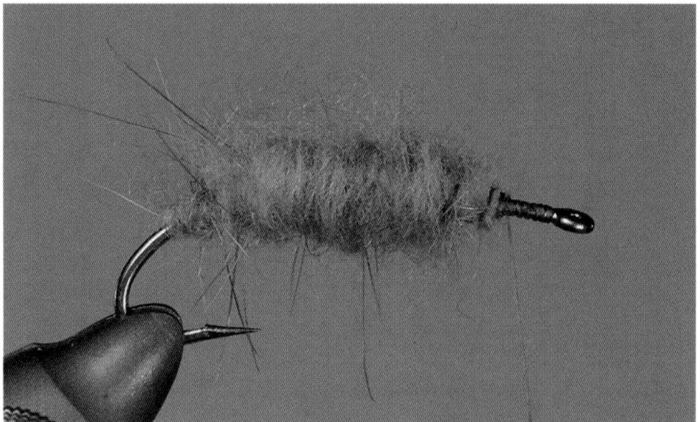

Step 2. Use the direct-dubbing method or a dubbing loop to create a fairly portly body. Resist the urge to tidy it up, if it's spiky; the water will take care of that for you, when you fish the fly. The body should end about one-fifth the shank length behind the eye.

Step 3. Tie in a pheasant rump feather at the end of the body, by the stem, and wind two to three turns of it, which should exhaust the feather. Tie it off and clip the excess tip. Hold it in a swept-back position with your off hand, and take thread wraps up onto the windings until the hackle remains in position.

Step 4. Fix a small amount of the same dubbing to the thread, and take two or three turns of it tapered down to the hook eye. Be sure to wrap it back onto the hackle, covering the thread wraps that hold the hackle in its swept-back position. Make a neat thread head, whip-finish, clip the thread, and apply head cement.

The general prescription is to tie the Beaverpelt or Carey Special without weight, and to fish them with a sinking line. I prefer enough weight on the shank to deliver the fly through the surface film and down a foot or so. That makes it effective where plant beds are shallow, which is fairly common in warm coves and along the fronts of reed edges, where I often fish dragonfly nymph imitations. If you don't weight the fly at least a little, then you will be forced to use a sinking line to fish it. If you use a few turns of weighting wire, you'll be able to fish it with a floating line, which is often best for the situation, and also leaves you in position for a quick switch to a dry fly if a hatch starts.

It won't be a hatch of dragonflies. I've seen trout take a very occasional dragonfly adult out of the air, but I've never seen them remotely selective to them, with the exception of a remote lake in the Chilean Andes. Those trout had never seen an angler. We were able to catch them on bass poppers.

HENRY'S DRAGON NYMPH

You need a dragon nymph imitaion that sinks, and another that floats. It helps if the one that sinks rides with its hook point up, because the naturals travel the bottom corridor, and you're going to want to get your fly down to where trout expect to see it. A fly tied with barbell eyes lashed to the top of the hook shank flips and rides eyes-down, point-up. One of the best was designed by lake specialist Henry Hoffman, of super grizzly hackle fame. The original is tied with his proprietary Chickabou, or hen back patch, dyed olive.

HENRY'S DRAGON NYMPH ***Henry Hoffman***

Hook:	2XL or 3XL, 1X or 2X heavy, size 6–10
Thread:	Olive 6/0 or 8/0
Eyes:	Lead barbell eyes
Tail:	Olive Chickabou
Rib:	Copper wire
Body:	Six to twelve olive Chickabou feathers
Wing case:	Turkey tail feather section
Legs:	Chickabou tips
Thorax:	Olive dubbing

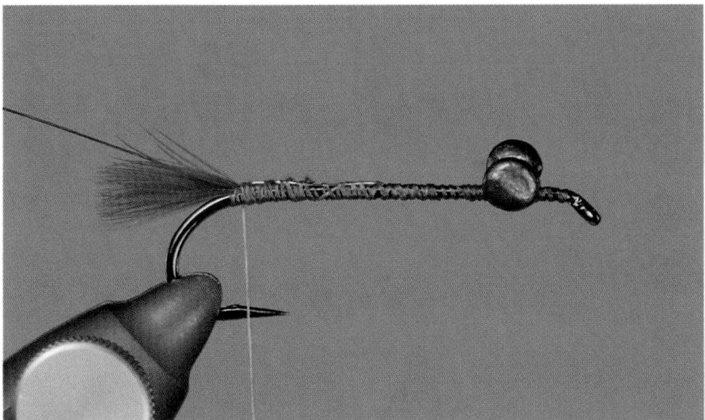

Step 1. Debarb the hook, fix it in the vise, start the thread behind the eye, and layer the front quarter of the shank. Use several figure eights of thread, and circular turns under the eyes and over the hook shank, to secure the barbell eyes about two hook-eye lengths behind the eye. Layer thread to the bend of the hook. Align the tips of a Chickabou feather, measure them about one-third the shank length, and tie them in. Clip the excess feather. Tie in three to four inches of ribbing wire.

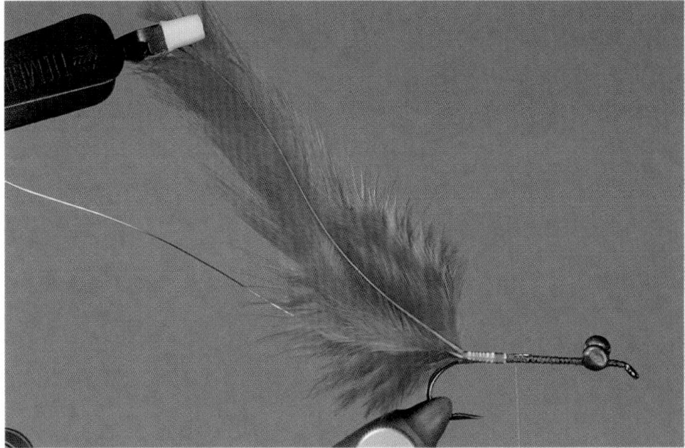

Step 2. Select two Chickabou feathers that are equal in length. Strip the fuzz from the butt ends of the stem where they are thickest. Meld them with concave sides together, and tie them in by the butts at the base of the tail. Bring the ends together and capture them in your hackle pliers.

Step 3. Wind the Chickabou feathers forward together, stroking them back after each turn to keep them compact. Two feathers should cover one-quarter to one-third of the shank.

Step 4. Tie in a second pair of Chickabou feathers the same as you did the first set in Step 2.

Step 5. Wind the second pair of feathers forward, again stroking them back after each turn, to abut each turn tightly against the one before it. Tie in and wind a third, and perhaps fourth, set of feathers in the same way, stopping about a barbell-eye width behind the fly eyes.

Step 6. Trim the forest of hackle to a tapered shape, about the width of the barbell eyes in the front, narrow at the back, tight along the top and bottom. Refrain from cutting off the tail. Counterwind the rib through the trimmed hackle, working it back and forth as you go to seat it into the hackle without matting it down.

Step 7. Remove the hook from the vise, invert it, and reinsert it upside down, just as the finished fly will ride in the water. Dub a thorax that tapers from the width of the abdomen down to nothing just behind the eyes. Measure a substantial bundle of Chickabou fibers so they will reach the hook point, and tie them in on the far side of the hook. Repeat on the near side. Trim the leg butts.

Step 8. Add a small amount of dubbing to cover the leg butts, and to form a taper as a base for the wing case. Using a turkey feather that has been pretreated with Flexament, clip a section about the width of the hook gap. Fold it and cut a corner at one end to notch it. Hold it in place just behind the eyes, measure it about one-third the body length, and tie it in behind the eyes. Trim the butts.

Step 9. Add sufficient dubbing to cover the wing-case butts. Take two to four figure eights of dubbing between the eyes, and a turn or two in front of the eyes, tapering down to the hook eye. Form a thread head, whip-finish, clip the thread, and apply head cement.

The finished Henry's Dragon Nymph is designed by Henry Hoffman to ride with its hook point up, helping avoid snags when it's fished on the bottom, where it belongs.

Henry's Dragon is a patient tie, and you need to be adept with scissors. You wouldn't want me to give you your next haircut. But practice helps, and the truth is, you don't need to give it a professional styling before it will catch trout. It's a very realistic tie, but also one that incorporates quite a bit of practicality: that upside-down ride ensures that you won't lose as many of them as would a standard tie on the same hook.

PREDATOR

A floating dragonfly nymph might be the best performer, and is certainly your best defense against predation by snags. Some flies use foam underbodies for flotation. Skip Morris's Predator makes it a lot easier by using foam as an overbody.

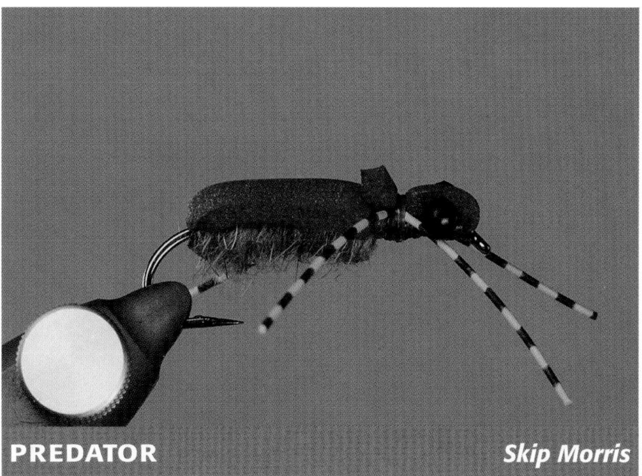

PREDATOR *Skip Morris*

Hook: 2XL or 3XL, size 6-12
Thread: Brown 3/0
Overbody: Brown 1⁄16-inch-thick foam
Underbody: Olive dubbing
Eyes: Black monofilament eyes
Legs: Brown or speckled rubber legs

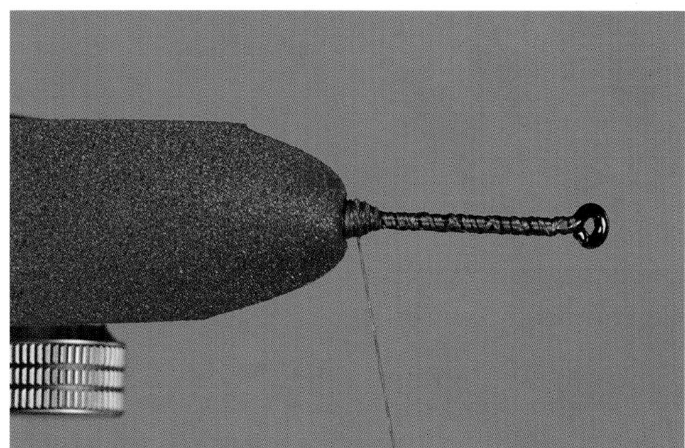

Step 1. Debarb the hook, fix it in the vise, and take two or three layers of thread over the shank, to form a firm underlayer. Cut a one-and-a-half- to two-and-a-half-inch strip of foam, depending on the size hook you're using, about one and a half times the width of the hook gap. Taper one end slightly with a couple of corner cuts. Fold this tapered end around the hook shank at about the midpoint. Hold it tightly and lash it to the shank with several firm turns of thread.

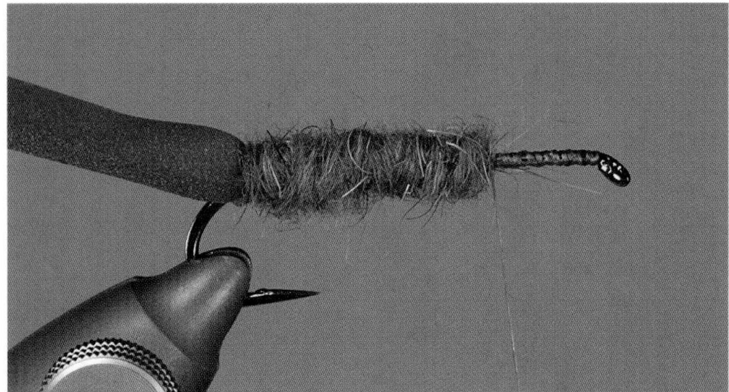

Step 2. Continue lashing the foam overbody to the bend of the hook. Dub a substantial body forward over the foam tie-down wraps, covering two-thirds of the hook shank.

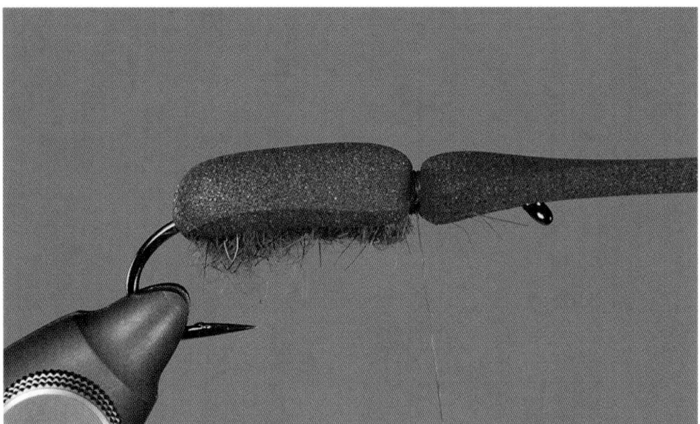

Step 3. Bring the foam overbody forward, fold it around the hook shank at the end of the underbody, hold it firmly, and take ten to fifteen tight turns of thread over it to secure it in place. Be sure that your first turns are as tight as the last, or the loose early turns will go slack when you bear down on the later ones. Use 3/0 thread; if you use 8/0, it will cut the foam.

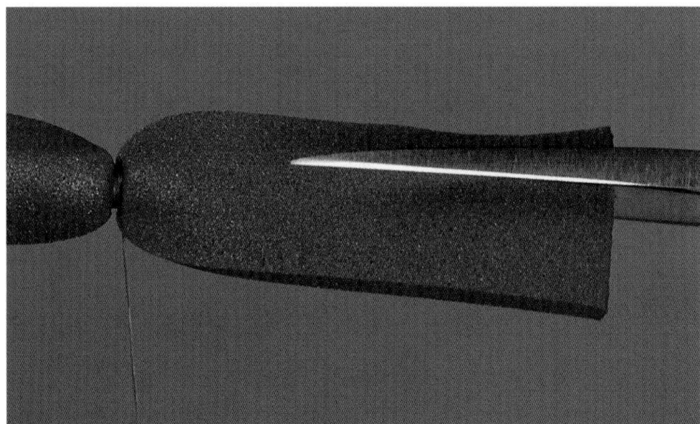

Step 4. Cut the remaining foam strip in front of the tie-down point to one-half its original width. If you aren't tying on a rotary vise, it might be helpful to remove the fly from the vise to do this. Be careful not to cut into the carapace that you've already formed over the rear two-thirds of the hook.

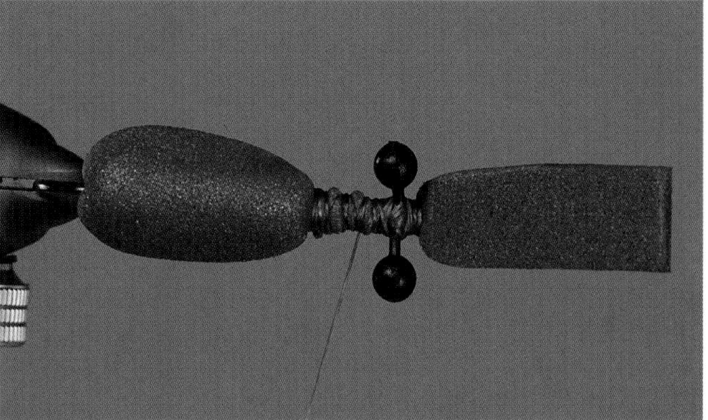

Step 5. Lash the foam overbody tightly to the shank from the end of the abdomen forward to the hook eye. Lash a set of monofilament eyes to the top of the shank just behind the hook eye.

Step 6. Draw the foam back between the eyes. Tie it off with ten to fifteen tight turns of thread halfway between the eyes and the end of the abdomen. Clip the excess foam so that it extends to the top of the abdomen or just a little more, to serve as a wing case.

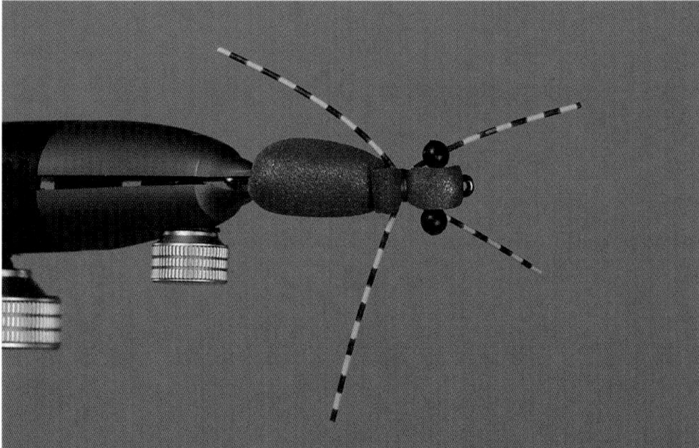

Step 7. Tie in a section of rubber leg on each side of the body. Take one or two whip-finishes over the leg tie-in point. Clip the thread, and apply head cement. Draw the back legs together just beyond the end of the hook, and clip them there. Draw the front legs together, and clip them at about the hook-shank length.

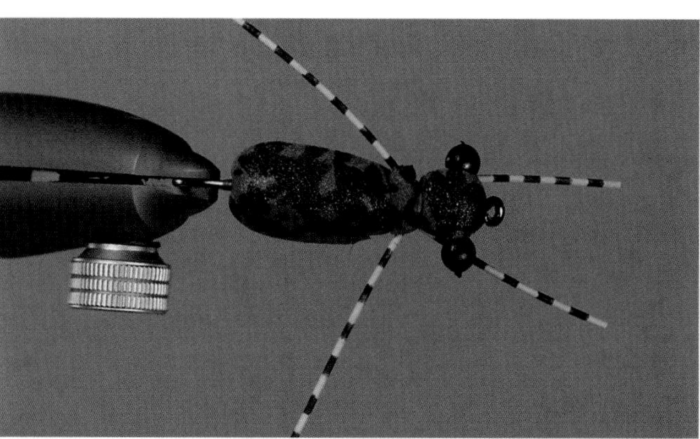

You can use waterproof marking pens to make your finished Predator resemble any dragon in the lake.

If the dominant dragonfly nymphs in your lakes and ponds are shades of green, which will not be unusual, then it's not difficult to take a permanent marker pen to the brown Predator. The result might be a mottled olive-brown, which is the most common dragonfly nymph color of all.

DRAGGIN

A final way to float a dragonfly nymph imitation uses a foam underbody, rather than the bold overbody employed by Skip in his Predator, to float the fly above vegetation and snags, up where trout can see it, and where you're less likely to lose it. Phil Rowley calls for a core of round foam on his Draggin, but you could substitute any closed-cell foam, as long as you don't lash it down so tightly that you collapse all of its flotation chambers.

DRAGGIN ***Phil Rowley***

Hook: 4XL, size 4-8
Thread: Olive 3/0 or 6/0
Underbody: Black round or sheet foam
Body: Olive Krystal Chenille and Antron dubbing, spun together
Wing case: Brown Swiss straw, raffia, or Medallion sheeting
Thorax: Olive-dyed deer hair, spun and clipped
Legs: Mottled silicone or rubber legs
Head: Olive Antron dubbing
Eyes: Black foam or monofilament eyes

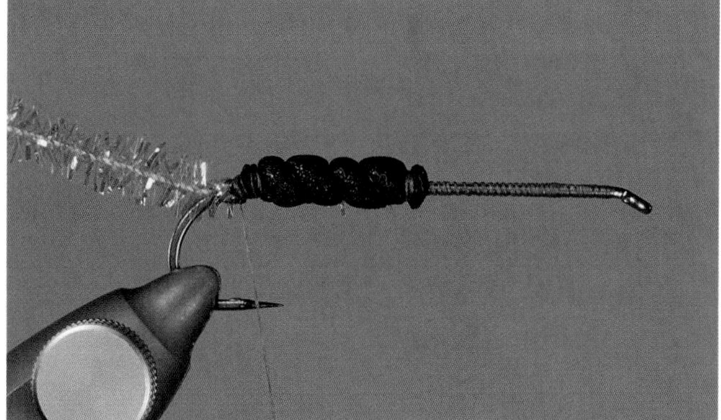

Step 1. Debarb the hook, fix it in the vise, and layer it with thread from the eye to the bend. Tie in a two- to three-inch strand of Krystal Chenille, and overwrap the butts to the midpoint of the shank. If you're using round foam, clip a piece half the shank length long. If you're using sheet foam, cut a strip about the width of the hook gap, and cut a section half the hook gap long. Lay the round foam on top of the shank, or fold the sheet foam around the shank. Tie it down firmly at the midpoint of the hook, and overwrap it, loosely enough not to cause collapse, to the hook bend. Tie the back end down firmly.

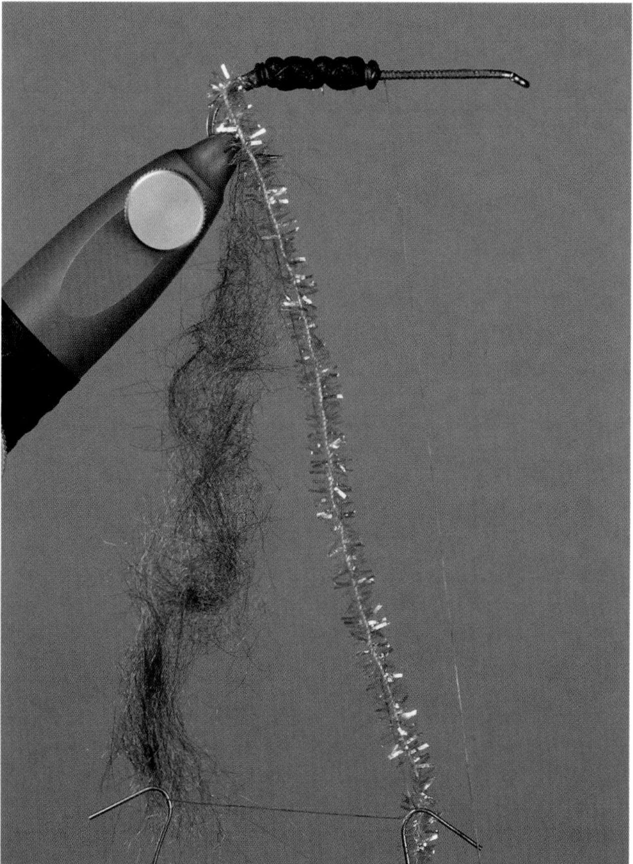

Step 2. Wax three to four inches of thread with a sticky wax. Form a long dubbing loop, catching the thread over the forefinger of your off hand, or in the arms of a dubbing loop tool, returning the bobbin to the vise to take

several securing turns of thread. Work dubbing into a long, loose skein, and place it against the waxed side of the loop, so it sticks. Bring the Krystal Chenille down and align it with the other thread of the loop.

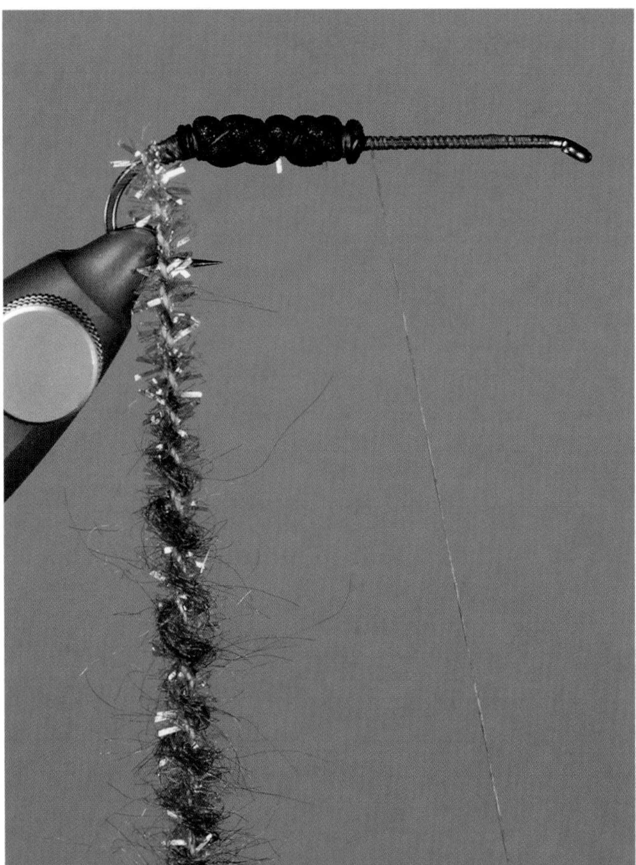

Step 3. Collapse the two strands of the dubbing loop together, and spin the end to form a spiky dubbing rope with lots of reflectance in it.

Step 4. Wrap a very portly abdomen forward to a point just past the midpoint of the shank. It should be shaped about like a football, tapered at both ends, with lots of flashy strands protruding.

Step 5. Cut a strand of wing-case material about the width of the hook gap. Tie it in just in front of the abdomen, overwrapping it partway up onto the front of the abdomen. Do not worry about the wasp-waist effect; in the case of the hourglass-shaped dragonfly nymph, that's what you're after.

Step 6. Clip a clump of deer hair from the hide. It should be a little smaller in diameter than a lead pencil. Clean fuzz from the butts and clip the tips so the remaining hair is about an inch long. Hold this on top of the hook shank, just in front of the abdomen, and take two loose turns of thread around it. Let go of the hair as you draw the thread tight. If it does not spin and flare all the way around the shank, use your fingers to distribute it. Take several more flaring wraps of thread forward. Hold the hair back, and tie in a pair of rubber legs on each side of the shank, just in front of the spun hair.

Step 7. Prepare a second clump of deer hair by removing fuzz from the butts and clipping the tips. Hold this over the shank in front of the first clump and the legs. Use the same fingers that hold the clump to hold the rubber legs back out of the way. Take a couple loose turns of thread around the hair, and release it to spin around the shank while you draw the thread tight. Take several more flaring turns of thread forward. Use the thumb and fingernail of your tying hand to compact the hair.

Step 8. Trim the spun hair flat on the top and bottom, about the width of the abdomen on the sides. Hold the rubber legs out of the way as you make each cut. Be sure you have enough bare shank left to complete the eyes and dubbed thorax.

Step 9. Bring the wing-case material forward, and tie it off in front of the spun hair. Do not trim the excess; fold it back and take a few turns over it to hold it back out of the way. Cut a section of round foam about the width of the abdomen. If you don't have round foam, cut a narrow strip of sheet foam the same length and round its corners. Hold it on top of the shank halfway between the wing-case tie-down point and the hook eye. Tie it in with several figure eights of thread, forming big eyes.

Step 10. Using the direct-dubbing method, fill in the space between the spun hair and the eyes with dubbing. Take one or two figure eights of dubbing between the eyes, and finish with a turn of dubbing behind the hook eyes. Bring the wing-case material forward, and tie it off behind the hook eye. Do not trim the excess. Return the thread to the wing-case tie-off point behind the eyes.

Step 11. Draw the wing-case material back between the eyes, and tie it off firmly there. Do not cut the excess. Use one or two five-turn whip-finishes to tie off the fly. You don't want such a complex mechanism to unspool because of a bad finishing knot. Clip your thread, and apply head cement over the whip-finishes.

Step 12. Clip the remaining wing-case material to about one-quarter the length of the fly. Draw the back legs together, and clip them just a bit longer than the end of the body. Clip the front legs to about hook-shank length.

Large insects always lend themselves to exact imitation. They are fun to tie on winter evenings. They look very good lined up in a stillwater-fly box. They certainly catch trout, and the buoyancy of this one defends it, at least to an extent, from loss to snags. The Draggin is not a nymph you want to fish among a tangle of submerged logs and limbs, or out in more open water on a light tippet. But it is quite effective over and among submerged plant beds, when fished with a sinking line and short leader to get it down very near the bottom.

A person who is usually short of tying time could wonder what would happen if a monastically simple Beaverpelt were tied with an underbody of a little foam rather than a little weighting wire. An endless number of experiments are still to be made in the world of stillwater fly fishing. I'll assign that one to you.

SUMMARY

I've already mentioned that you need one dragonfly nymph in a weighted version, the other with a foam underbody for flotation. It won't be even mildly surprising that the weighted nymph is designed to be fished in relatively shallow water, with a floating or clear intermediate line, while the floating nymph is designed to be fished on a sinking line that plummets it to the bottom.

Retrieves for both weighted and floating dragonfly nymphs should combine a creeping hand-twist, some sharp but short strips to imitate their jet propulsion, and some time on each cast spent at rest. Trout will usually prefer one of the three speeds; if you employ them all on every cast, you'll soon figure out which trout like best. Once you've solved this, fish with the retrieve that is most effective, or continue to intersperse them in case the one that is working suddenly fails, and trout begin to prefer the one that they earlier disdained.

For the nymphs shown, I've stuck as close to the originators' prescriptions as possible within the limits of the materials on my tying bench. But the colors of the naturals vary with colors of the substrate on which they live. They're chameleons; if the bottom or plant color changes over the seasons, they'll change colors with it. Always collect in your own waters, and match your tying efforts to what you find where you're going to be fishing.

CHAPTER 32

Stillwater Caddisflies

Always remember that selectivity predicts the need for imitation. If trout feed on something with fair regularity, but very rarely with selectively, those trout will almost certainly take an imitation for it, but they will also take an imitation of something else that is available in the same sort of constant but low-grade numbers. The same trout will almost certainly be susceptible to a wide range of searching patterns.

Stillwater patterns of instant renown often originate in just these sorts of situations. The trout are hungry, perhaps just after ice-out. They're seeing an occasional insect of a certain kind, and smacking into it when they do, probably along with half a dozen other kinds. The inventor of the Wonder Nymph stumbles onto a sample of the insect, often with a throat pump just after the trout has taken a couple of the prototype naturals, and they're still squirming in the sample.

Our miracle worker paddles furiously to shore, concocts an imitation of the insect on the camp table, though a dozen better ones might already exist. He rushes back and applies the new nymph against the trout. It works wonders, and gets its name honestly. But almost any old Nondescript might have worked as well. Never deny yourself this pleasure, however. It's the basis for most effective personal favorites, and also for many fine flies that become famous old dependables.

Only selectivity demands imitation. When trout see an abundance of just one insect, surface or sunk, they begin to focus on it. In time—a short time; we're talking about the daily duration of a hatch here, a matter of one to four hours—trout fail to recognize anything else as food. A searching nymph, or the best imitation of the wrong insect, will not be seen as something the trout desire to eat at that moment, because it doesn't resemble what they've keyed out as their only food source at that moment.

Caddis larvae are an example. Stillwater trout feed on them often, taking them case and all, since their cases are made of vegetation. The nutritious insect can easily be digested; the remains of the case can just as easily be passed. But selectivity to cased caddis is rare, because they rarely congregate. When trout take them, they will almost always take something else that crawls, swims, or trots past. This is not to imply that imitations of cased caddis lack all importance. It's just to inform you that their importance as models for fly patterns does not equal their abundance in lakes and ponds.

Think of this difference, if no other: stillwater *Callibaetis* mayfly nymphs become active at emergence, swim to the surface, break through and emerge as duns. All of this takes place in relatively restricted areas over plant beds or shoals, in a time period defined by the hatch. When it happens, trout see a lot of *Callibaetis* nymphs at one time, in one area. They become selective to them. Caddis larvae, on the opposite hand, go to the ground, sealing their cases to vegetation or the bottom, wherein pupation takes place. As larvae, they become an absence in the weeks just before an emergence, rather than a concentrated presence. You don't often need to imitate them. I pointed out one of the exceptions in chapter 27, on murdering the Woolly Bugger.

You will always be wise, when considering the weight given any imitation type in your fly box, to calculate out the availability and abundance of the natural, and the ways in which it causes selective feeding by trout.

Caddis larvae in moving water can be free-living or cased. All caddis in lakes are cased. They might be broken into swimming and crawling, but it wouldn't mean much, since even those that are capable of swimming from plant to plant spend most of their time crawling on vegetation or the bottom. When my dad and I encountered trout feeding selectively on swimming cased caddis

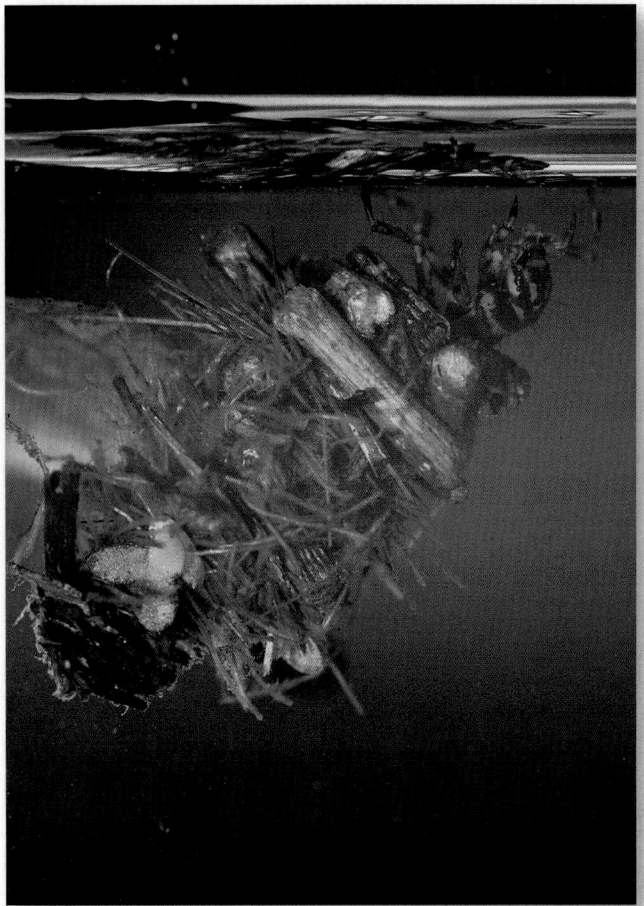

On rare occasions when cased caddis larvae float in the surface film, trout become selective to them, and you'll need an imitation to fool those trout.

(Leptoceridae) in a mountain lake, and I solved that case by shearing a brushy Olive Woolly Bugger of all its appendages, it might have been solved just as well with an Olive Gold-Ribbed Hare's Ear or Herl Nymph, two nymphs that you should be able to find in your searching-fly box, if you put that box in your boat bag and carry your boat bag on lakes and ponds.

Gary LaFontaine, in his *Caddisflies,* reported that certain large cased caddis in lakes float to the surface and congregate just after ice-out. Ron Cordes and Randall Kaufmann report the same thing in *Lake Fishing with a Fly.* I have frequently seen cased caddis adrift at the surface in spring and early summer, usually associated with reed edges but not necessarily with ice-out. Whenever I've seen this, trout have been busy responding to it, though I'm not sure they were selective. But I do know that an imitation proved useful, and I do recommend that you carry at least half a dozen of one cased caddis pattern designed to float.

I also know that anything that resembles a cased caddis larva will work wonders in most stillwaters, when fished as a searching nymph.

OLIVE WOOLLY WORM

Perhaps the original Wonder Nymph was the Woolly Worm. I don't know many folks who fish it anymore, but if you think about the abundance of stillwater food forms that are olive, in keeping with the most common plant color, and around size 10 to 14, then you'll know that trout can mistake it for more than just a cased caddis larva. An Olive Woolly Worm cast long over shallow plants on a floating line, clear intermediate, or wet-tip, and allowed to sink for a count of ten to fifteen seconds before being crept back toward you with a hand-twist retrieve, will not very often leave you feeling like an anachronism. It will keep you busy catching trout.

WOOLLY WORM, OLIVE

Hook: 2XL or 3XL, size 8-14
Weight: 10-20 turns undersized nonlead wire
Thread: Olive 6/0 or 8/0
Hackle: Grizzly hen or grade-three rooster
Body: Olive chenille

Step 1. Debarb the hook, fix it in the vise, and weight the shank. Start the thread behind the eye, and overwrap the shank and weighting wire to the bend. Tie in the body chenille there. Select a hackle feather with fibers about one and a half to two hook gaps long. Hold the tip and

run a thumb and forefinger the length of the feather to flare the fibers. Tie it in by the tip. Some people prefer the concave side toward the shank, so the hackle will be swept back when wound. Others prefer the convex side toward the shank, so the hackle will lean forward when wound. I like the look of the latter, but think it is best for moving water, where I no longer use Woolly Worms. In stillwaters, I think the swept-back hackle looks more natural.

Step 2. Wind the body to the hook eye, and tie it off. Attach your hackle pliers to the hackle butt, and wind it forward in as many evenly spaced turns as the length of your feather allows. Finish with a turn or two at the end of the body. Tie it off, clip the excess stem, whip-finish, clip the thread, and apply head cement.

To me, the Olive Woolly Bugger is specific for stillwaters. I prefer it sparsely hackled, with soft hen rather than stiffer rooster. I know that it looks cocky when tied with a red tag for a tail, and with many turns of tightly spaced hackle that tip forward rather than back. Properly tied, it's supposed to look almost like a bottle brush. But in all of my collecting in stillwaters, I've found lots of insects with six legs and rough vegetation cases, but I've never collected one that remotely resembled a bottle brush.

The Woolly Worm would look more like a cased caddis if you clipped its hackle short. That is often done, and the result is magically transformed into a pattern called the Cased Caddis, which might make you feel better about fishing it. If that is true, whack at it. You won't hurt it, and it probably will fish better because you have more confidence fishing something called a Cased Caddis than you would an out-of-date Woolly Worm.

GUNNY SACK

The concept of trimming a Woolly Worm might have been perfected in the ancient Gunny Sack. I doubt it was created specifically to imitate cased caddis larvae, but it does as good a job of that now as it did when horse and chicken feed were purchased in burlap bags. The original calls for dyed brown grizzly hackle palmered the length of a burlap body, then trimmed. You could easily substitute one brown and one grizzly hackle, and chenille for the body. Because I have no burlap on hand, I'll show it tied with what I do have. If you'd like to try the original, you'll find burlap at your fly shop or craft store, or it can be ordered for you.

GUNNY SACK

Hook:	3XL, size 6-14
Weight:	10-20 turns of undersized nonlead wire
Thread:	Brown 6/0 or 8/0
Tail:	Brown and grizzly hackle fibers
Body:	Burlap or brown chenille or dubbing
Hackle:	Grizzly and brown, trimmed

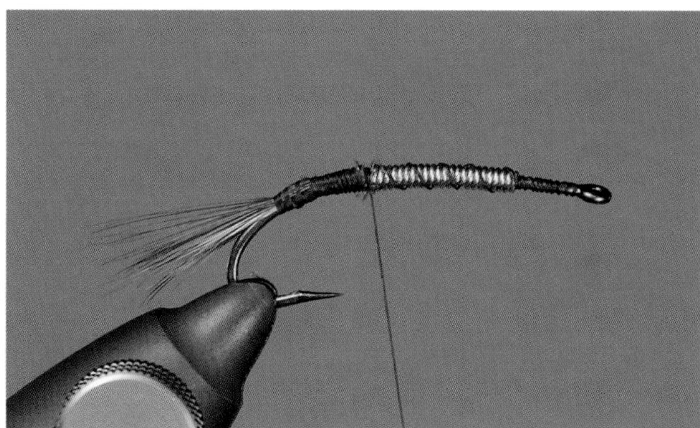

Step 1. Fix the hook in the vise, wind weighting wire, start thread, and coat the shank and wire to the bend. Measure a substantial amount of grizzly hackle half the shank length, and tie it in at the bend. Repeat with the same amount of brown hackle. The tail should be stubby and stout.

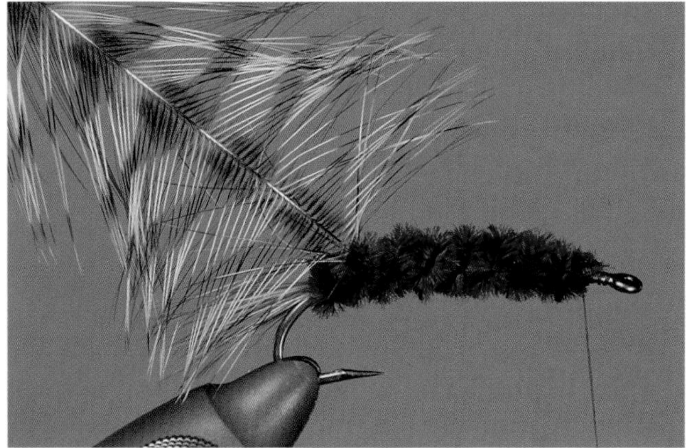

Step 2. Tie in several inches of burlap or chenille. If you're using dubbing, tie in the hackle first, then use the direct-dubbing method to twist a fairly thick amount of dubbing to your thread. Select one low-grade grizzly and similar brown hackle feather, and prepare them by holding the tips and flaring the fibers from the stem. Don't worry about the length of the individual fibers. Make sure they are overlong hackle feathers. This is a good fly on which to use those long and soft cape feathers that often get wasted. Tie them in together, by their tips, in front of the body material. Take one turn of body behind the hackles, then wind or dub the body forward to a point just behind the hook eye.

Step 3. Grasp the two hackle butts together in your fingers if they are long enough, or in hackle pliers if they are shorter. Wind them forward, keeping them together, in distinctly spaced turns to the hook eye. Finish off with a couple of turns behind the hook eye. Tie off the stems and clip the excess. Whip-finish and clip the thread. Apply head cement.

Step 4. Trim the hackle about the width of the hook gap in front, tapering down to about half that at the back. Be careful not to cut off the tail, though in truth trout haven't reported any interest in whether this appendage is present or absent. If you'd like to make tying the nymph easier, omit it.

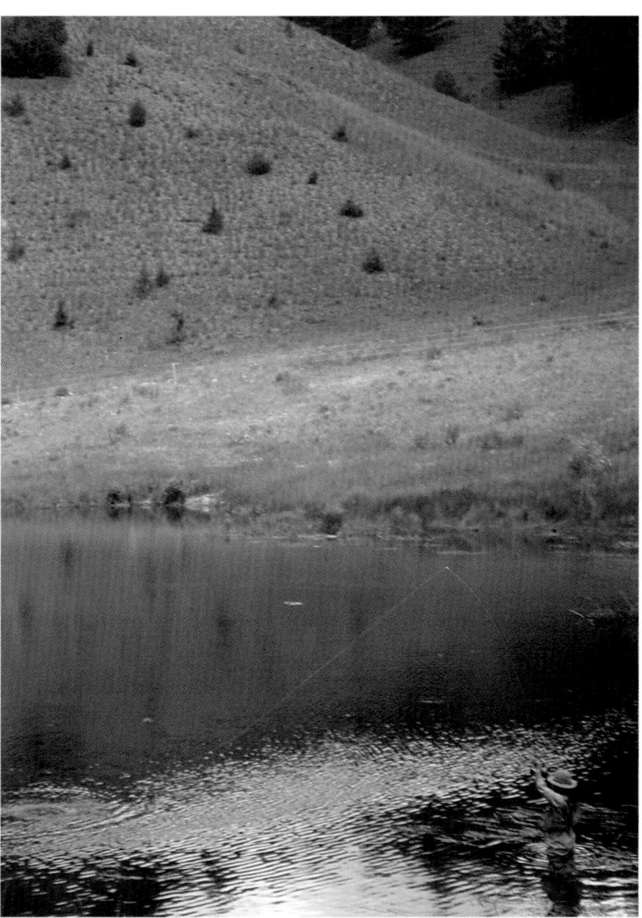

Cased caddis larvae work the vegetated edges of stillwaters of all sizes, and trout of all sizes work the caddis, taking them case and all.

HUSMASK

The old Woolly Worm and what is essentially its trimmed version, the Gunny Sack, are the ideas behind many more modern flies that imitate cased caddis larvae. One of the most interesting is the Husmask, which in Swedish means cased caddis, from Gary Soucie's book *Woolly Wisdom*. You can match the naturals you collect in your stillwaters simply by varying the colors of the hackles you use.

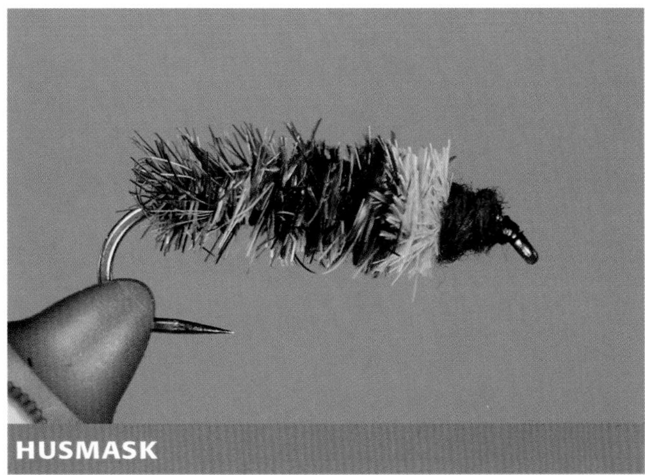

HUSMASK

Hook: 3XL, size 10-12
Weight: 10-20 turns nonlead wire
Thread: Brown 6/0 or 8/0
Body: Working thread
Body hackle: Brown, grizzly, and green, palmered and clipped
Thorax hackle: Ginger, pale olive, or white, palmered and clipped
Head: Brown dubbing

Though weight is listed in the dressing, consider replacing it with a strip of closed-cell foam lashed to the shank, which will cause the fly to float in the surface. When the cased caddis naturals this fly imitates are taken opportunistically by trout, which will be most common, they will be clambering among vegetation stems and leaves, or will be slowly sinking because they've lost their grip, must get to the bottom and climb back up. When they're taken selectively, which will be most rare, they'll be floating, awash in the surface. Searching nymphs will likely take trout when they're feeding on submerged cased caddis. When trout feed on them drifting at the surface, you need a floating imitation or you're sunk.

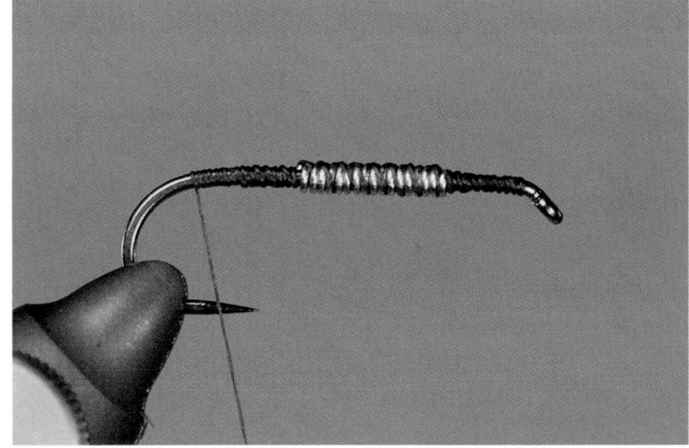

Step 1. Fix the hook in the vise. Weight the shank with ten to twenty turns of nonlead wire. Standard procedure calls for wire the diameter of the hook shank. I prefer to underweight most lake nymphs, so they penetrate the film and sink slowly when fished on a floating or intermediate line. To get deep, I go to a sinking line. So I use weighting wire that is one size undersized, which in nonlead means .015 inch, because nonlead is available only in that diameter and .025 inch. Start the thread, and layer the shank and weighting wire to the hook bend.

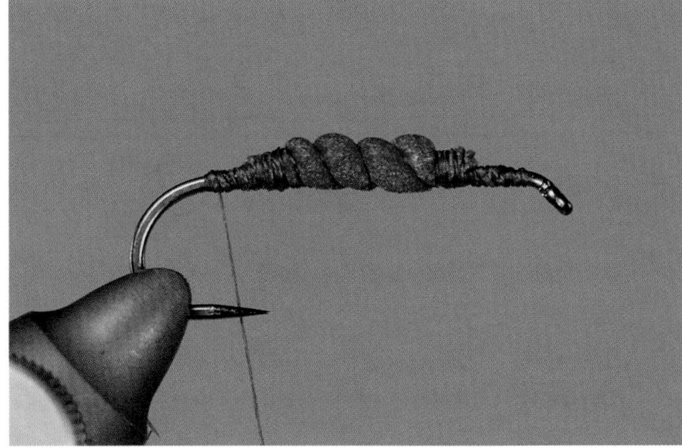

Alternate Step 1. Fix the hook in the vise. Start the thread and make two to four loose layers over the shank, forth and back, to make a secure base for the foam. Cut a strip of foam about half the length of the hook shank long and half the hook gap wide. Fold the foam around the shank, tie it in tightly at the front, then take a few widely spaced thread loops over it to the back. Lash the back tightly.

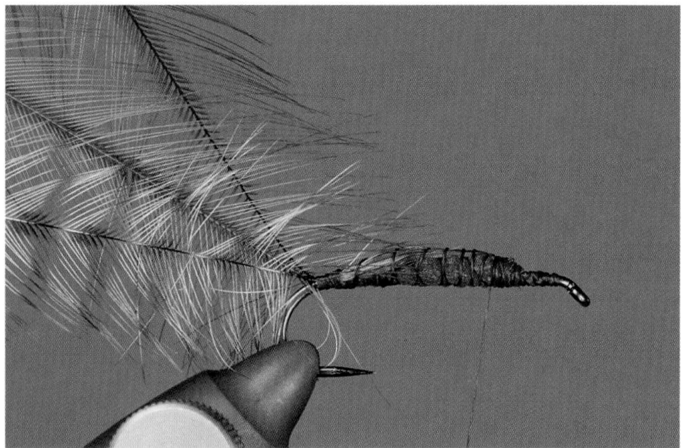

Step 2. Select long neck or saddle hackle feathers in green, brown, and grizzly, or a combination that reflects the colors of the cased caddis you collect in your own stillwater trout fishing. Prepare each hackle by holding the tip and stroking the fibers in opposition to their normal flow, to flare them. Tie each in at the bend of the hook, by the tip. Overwrap the tips to a point about one-third the shank length behind the eye.

Step 3. Wind each hackle forward separately, in as many turns as you can get, and tie each off. Do not cut the stems until the last hackle is wrapped and its stem secured. Overwrap the stems with thread almost to the eye, and clip the excess.

Step 4. Prepare a light-colored hackle by holding the tip and stroking the fibers opposite to their normal direction. Tie it in by the tip, and wind it forward half the distance to the hook eye. These hackle wraps should be tightly spaced; they can be wrapped over top of each other without hurting anything. Tie the hackle off and clip the excess.

Step 5. Trim the hackle with little taper from front to back. The result should be somewhat round, and about the diameter of the hook gap.

Step 6. Twist a small amount of dubbing to the thread, and form a tapered head from the front of the trimmed hackle down to just behind the hook eye. This represents

the head of the insect protruding from the case, and should be small. Use enough thread turns to make a neat thread head. Whip-finish, clip the thread, and apply head cement.

This fly, when tied with a foam underbody, belongs in a book about dry flies, not nymphs. But it represents the larval stage of the caddis, not the adult, stranded in the surface film. If you ever see trout working reed or cattail edges, or above shallow submerged weed beds, and the takes are big and bold but it's difficult to see what the trout might be taking, suspect either damselfly nymphs or floating cased caddis. If it's not time for the damselfly migration, try fishing this dressing on the patient sit, with an occasional twitch to represent the struggles of the natural. Takes to the fly will be precisely like those to a dry fly.

These few dressings lay the groundwork for all the cased caddis larval imitations you might ever need. The idea is to represent the vegetation case with the body of the fly, and the protruding head with the dubbed or thread head of the fly. If you do not run into situations in your fishing where trout seem selective to cased caddis, then I recommend you tie no more than a half dozen or so, as preventative medicine, to carry constantly in your stillwater-fly box. If you do encounter trout feeding on them, then you will want to collect the naturals and match them in size, shape, and color. Unless you fish lakes a lot, it's unlikely you'll ever notice trout being selective to cased caddis.

Stillwater caddis pupae are shaped the same as those from rivers and streams. If the size and color are right, you can fish the same imitations for them that you use on moving water.

Caddis pupae are more important. Each species of stillwater caddis retreats to its pupal chamber at roughly the same time of year, and emerges from it in a one- to three-week period, usually within a two- to three-hour window each day. When such an emergence happens, trout often focus on the pupae as they rise to the surface, and you need to fish a nymph that is at least an approximation to catch any trout.

Some caddis emerge in daylight, but in my experience, most begin coming to the surface just before dark, and many finish emerging after daylight has gone. You can fish mayfly hatches and damselfly migrations at midday. If you're going to enjoy the best caddis activity, you'll need to be on the water at dawn and dusk. In midsummer, such long hours might force you to nap at midday, when you're not likely to be missing much.

Caddis pupae have fringed swimmer paddles on their hind set of legs. Many stillwater forms use these to stroke toward shore, sometimes swimming just beneath the surface.

All caddis pupae have effective swimmer paddles on their hind pairs of legs. These are powerful, and propel the insect efficiently. When a caddis pupa cuts free of its chamber and heads for the top, it swims briskly. Some of the larger ones make it in one long dash, from as far as fifteen to twenty feet down. They're boosted by gases trapped under the pupal cuticle. I've seen trout respond to the sight of a pupa by arrowing out of a cruising pod and making a swift turning take in the mid-depths. In clear water, trout can spot a caddis pupa from distances that are greater than those fifteen- to twenty-foot depths.

For smaller stillwater species, sizes 12 to 18, the standard moving-water caddis patterns that you tied in chapter 20 will serve as well on lakes and ponds as they do in rivers and streams. It's a rough rule that if you see quite a few caddis adults begin to appear on the surface, usually at evening, and you see trout working them, but you can't solve the situation with a floating fly, you should try a pupal dressing in the approximate size and color of the adult. It's common for the adult to be a different color than the pupa, but you have to start somewhere until you procure a sample of the natural pupa, and the adult color is a good place to start. When fished on the same floating line and dry-fly leader, the pupa, retrieved slowly, should at least get you a foolish fish, from which you might be able to extract a throat pump sample to get a look at the true colors of the pupa.

Larger caddis pupae, sizes 6, 8, and 10, can call for more exact imitation, though if you lack them, you might also be surprised to discover that a searching dressing such as a Gold-Ribbed Hare's Ear, or a dragonfly nymph imitation such as the Beaverpelt, might take at least some trout. One of those dressings might solve the problem to your own satisfaction. But all of those *mights* might lead you to the conclusion that a specific dressing for larger stillwater caddis pupae is a good investment of your tying time. I agree.

STILLWATER CADDIS PUPA

Most of the work on large caddis comes out of the same region as that on large midges: the Kamloops Lakes area of British Columbia. It's the center of distribution for the traveling sedge *(Banksiola)* that gets trout excited in late spring and early summer. The traveling sedge emerges during daylight. The large adult motors erratically toward shore rather than taking to the air. This behavior is likely a defense against heavy bird predation. The inland lakes in which it developed either had no native trout, or had trout numbers that were very restricted by a lack of spawning tributaries. In the presence of normal trout populations, traveling for an adult caddis would be maladaptive behavior. This might be the reason why the traveling sedge hatch is the most important hatch in many northern-tier lakes in the years after they've first been stocked with trout, but then that importance slowly gives way to midges, damselflies, leeches, and scuds after a few years of violent fishing over the caddis. Traveling sedge numbers begin to dwindle in the presence of large numbers of trout.

Wherever you find them, however, they still lead to explosive fishing. Never neglect dry flies during the traveling sedge hatch. It's the rare occasion when you can successfully fish them retrieved like streamers. A pupa dressing, cast out and allowed to sink deep, then brought toward the top, in what has been called the *sink and draw,* can also incite brutal strikes.

STILLWATER CADDIS PUPA *Brian Chan*

Hook:	2XL or 3XL, size 8-12
Weight:	15-25 turns nonlead wire
Thread:	Brown 6/0 or 8/0
Rib:	Lime green floss or yarn
Abdomen:	Mix of bronze, green, and gold sparkle dubbing
Wing case:	Pheasant tail fibers
Thorax:	Mix of bronze, green, and gold sparkle dubbing
Legs:	Tips of wing-case fibers
Throat:	Peacock Angel Hair or Ice Dub
Head:	Peacock herl

Step 1. Debarb the hook, fix it in the vise, and weight it substantially. Start the thread and overwrap the shank and weighting wire to the hook bend. Tie in the ribbing. Mix the dubbing colors by blending them in the palm of your hand, if you're tying just a few flies. Use a coffee grinder to make a larger amount of the blend if you're tying by the dozen. Dub a fairly portly body to a point just past the middle of the hook shank. Wind the ribbing forward in four to six evenly spaced turns. Tie it off and clip the excess.

Step 2. Tie in a small amount of Angel Hair or Ice Dub, on the underside of the hook, at the end of the abdomen. Use a pinch wrap (see page 45) for the initial thread turn, then secure the throat and clip the butts. Draw the tips of the fibers out past the end of the hook, and clip the excess there.

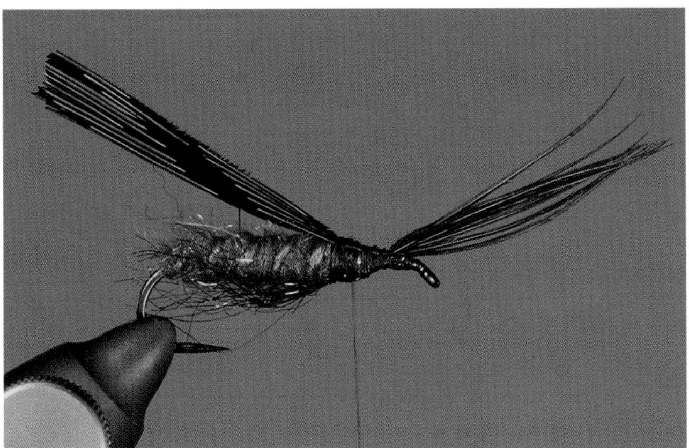

Step 3. Even the tips of twelve to eighteen pheasant tail fibers by holding them at a ninety-degree angle to the stem. Clip or strip them from the stem. Measure them the length of the hook, and tie them in one to two hook-eye lengths behind the eye. Overwrap them to the end of the abdomen. The tips will serve as legs, the butts as the wing case.

Step 4. Dub a thorax forward from the end of the abdomen about halfway to the hook eye. Be sure to make the first wraps back over the wing-case tie-down point, to avoid any wasp-waisting. Split the leg fibers in half. Hold the near half of the fibers back, and position them with a single turn of thread. Hold the far half back on the opposite side of the thorax, and secure them with a few turns of thread.

Step 5. Draw the wing-case fibers forward over the thorax, tie them off securely, and clip the butts.

The traveling sedge is most famous on British Columbia lakes, and most abundant where it evolved in the absence of predation by trout.

Step 6. Tie in a couple of peacock herls by their tips. Catch them along with the thread, and twist them into a herl rope. Wind them forward two or three turns to the hook eye. Separate the herls from the thread, and secure them with several turns of thread. Clip the excess herl. Make a neat thread head, whip-finish, and apply head cement.

Biologist and writer Brian Chan lives in Kamloops, British Columbia. His Stillwater Caddis Pupa is designed for the traveling sedge, the caddis that is so famous in that area. It's likely that the same pattern will take trout wherever you find them feeding on the larger types of caddis pupae.

HOLLYWOOD CADDIS

Gordon Honey is a longtime guide in the same Kamloops region. Gord's criteria for a good fly are first that it catch trout, and second that it be a quick tie. His Hollywood Caddis got its name from the bright materials with which it is tied. It imitates the same traveling sedge pupa as Brian Chan's Stillwater Caddis Pupa, and like Brian's, it's a good model for any lake and pond caddis pupa you collect in your waters and need to imitate.

HOLLYWOOD CADDIS *Gordon Honey*

Hook: Curved scud, size 6-12
Bead: Copper or gold
Weight: 10-15 turns nonlead wire, optional
Thread: Olive 6/0 or 8/0
Rib: Yellow floss
Abdomen: Dark olive fur and Antron dubbing mix
Thorax: Pheasant Tail Angel Hair

Step 1. Debarb the hook, slip a bead to the eye, and fix it in the vise. If you want to add weight, take ten to fifteen turns, and jam them into the back end of the bead. Start the thread, and overwrap the weighting wire to secure it. Tie in a few inches of ribbing floss, and overwrap it well down around the hook bend. Dub a fairly thick body forward to a point about a bead width behind the bead. Wind the ribbing forward in four to six evenly spaced turns, tie it off, and clip the excess.

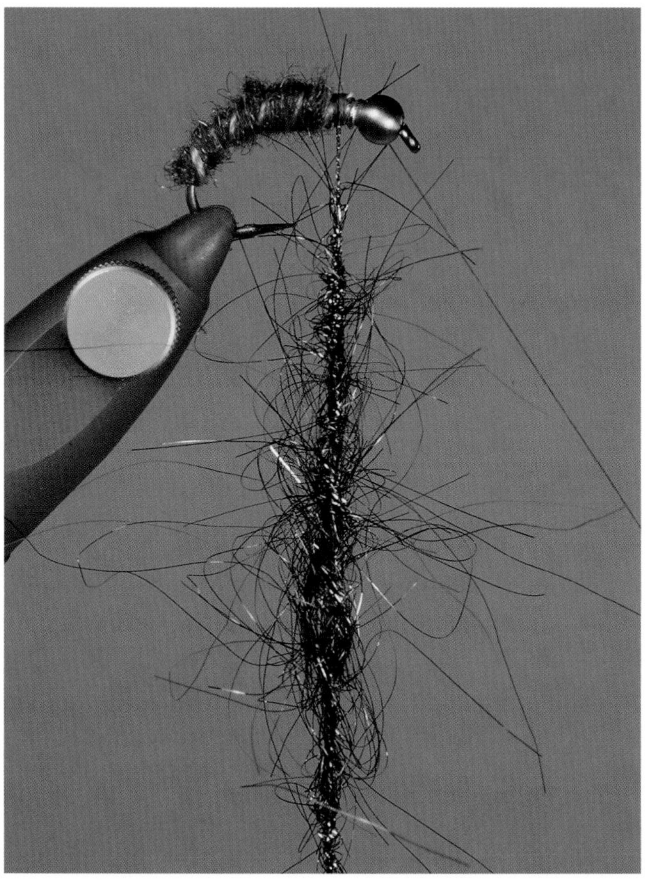

Step 2. Gather a small skein of Angel Hair in the palm of your hand, and rough it up into a ball. Tack it to your waxed thread, and catch it in a dubbing loop. Spin the loop loosely; do not tighten it into a rope. This will be the most unruly dubbing loop you have ever created.

Step 3. Wind the dubbing loop from the end of the abdomen to the back of the bead in three to four turns. Tie it off with a few turns of thread, and clip the excess dubbing loop.

Step 4. Use your off-hand thumb and fingers to stroke the Angel Hair back, and place a whip-finish tight behind the bead. Clip your thread.

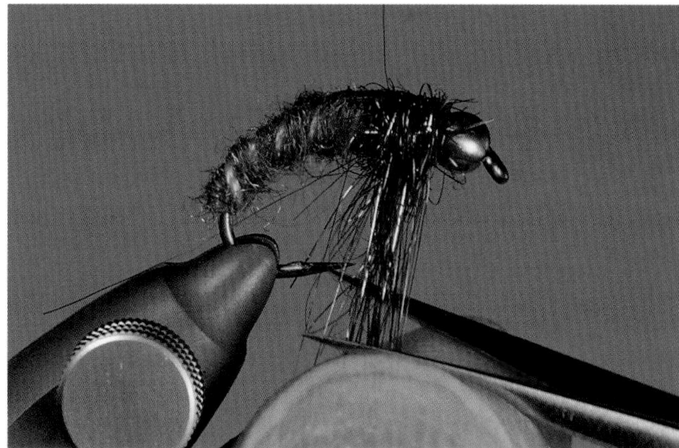

Step 5. Stroke the Angel Hair to the underside of the hook. Hold it in the thumb and forefinger of your off hand, and clip it at a length that will let it reach to the end of the body. Stroke the fibers back and down, to give the appearance of legs and wing cases.

Gordon Honey does not call for weighting this fly, preferring instead to let his line choice determine the depth at which he fishes it. When tied on a heavy-wire hook, it will penetrate the film and sink a foot to several feet if given enough countdown time, even when fished on a floating or intermediate sinking line. Phil Rowley, in *Fly Patterns for Stillwaters,* expresses his preference for this fly, and for wind-drifting it on a floating line. The drift of the float tube, pontoon boat, or pram causes a curve in the line. When that curve magically begins to straighten, Phil suggests you set the hook.

ANTRON CADDIS PUPA

A concept that will work well for the larger caddis, but can also be applied to smaller caddis that you find in lakes, is the Antron Caddis Pupa, listed in Jim Schollmeyer's book *Nymph Fly-Tying Techniques.* It uses lace tubing overwrapped with Antron to capture the segmentation of the natural, and the sheen of the air bubble that many caddis use to boost them on their rise to the surface. The given colors can be varied to match any caddis pupa you might encounter on your own stillwaters.

ANTRON CADDIS PUPA *Jim Schollmeyer*

Hook:	Curved scud or standard nymph, 2X heavy, size 8-16
Bead:	Gold or brass
Weight:	8-12 turns nonlead wire
Thread:	Brown 6/0 or 8/0
Overbody:	Tan or cream Antron dubbing
Underbody:	Olive rubber lace or ribbing material
Thorax:	Brown fur and Antron dubbing mix
Wing cases:	Brown or black Antron yarn
Legs:	Natural CDC
Head:	Brown fur and Antron dubbing mix

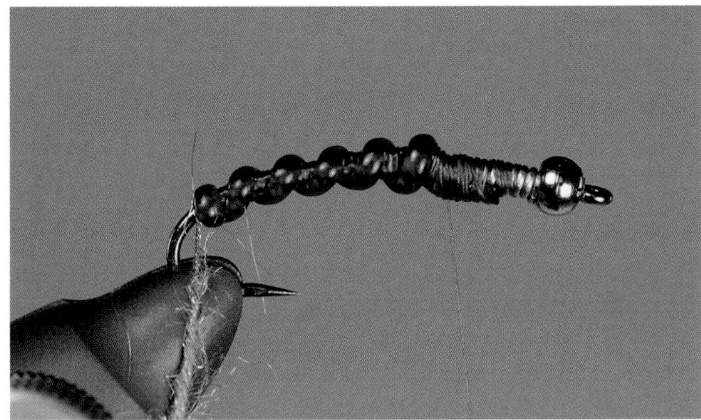

Step 1. Slip a bead onto the hook, and fix the hook in the vise. Weight it with a few turns of nonlead wire jammed into the back of the bead, or braced against it. Start the thread behind the weighting wire, make a thread ramp onto the shoulder of the wire, and overwrap the shank onto the bend. Make a thin dubbing loop of light-colored Antron dubbing, and leave it dangling out of the way. Tie in the rubber lace or rib, and wind it in spaced wraps to a point about one-third the shank length behind the bead. Tie it off and clip the excess.

Step 2. Wind the Antron dubbing loop forward in the gaps between the lace. Tie it off, clip the excess, and use a dubbing brush to tease it out. It should form a sort of halo effect around the underbody.

Step 3. Dub a thorax forward to fill in half the gap between the end of the abdomen and the back of the

bead. Clip an inch or two of Antron yarn, separate the strands, and tease one strand out with a hair comb. Lay this across the shank in front of the thorax. Tie it in with a few turns of thread. Draw the ends back along each side of the hook, and use several more turns of thread to hold them swept back and down. Clip them so they reach to the hook point, or just short of it on a long-shank hook.

Step 4. Align the tips of a CDC feather, hold it on the underside of the hook, and measure the tips to the hook point or just beyond it. Tie the feather in and clip the excess.

Step 5. Use dubbing to fill in the space between the wing case and leg tie-in point and the back of the bead. Tuck a whip-finish behind the bead, and clip the thread.

SUMMARY

I recommend you tie and carry at least half a dozen each of a sinking and a floating cased caddis larva dressing, in a narrow range of sizes, from 8 to 12. Those will arm you to fish a sunk pattern in and among vegetation beds, and a dry pattern on those rare occasions when trout feed on cased caddis captured in the surface film.

Keep your tying for stillwater caddis pupae to a minimum until you encounter a situation in which trout request them. Nymphs out of your stream and river boxes will fish for the smaller ones you might find important.

If you have a trip planned to the northern tier of states and provinces, then you should tie at least a few of the dressings designed specifically for the larger traveling sedge and rush sedge pupae. A large Gold-Ribbed Hare's Ear might fool some fish when large caddis are on the move, but you'd be dependent on the presence of foolish fish. You would be much smarter to tie a dozen each of Brian Chan's Stillwater Caddis Pupa or Gord Honey's Hollywood Caddis, in sizes 8 and 10.

If your trip will be prolonged, and timed for the late-spring and early-summer emergence window, you might get separated from that short supply in a day or two. Trout in the northern lakes, where they feed on traveling sedge pupae and a variety of other stillwater riches, are sometimes big, always strong, and react with violence when stung in the jaw. Tie some extra.

CHAPTER 33

Water Boatmen and Back Swimmers

Water boatmen and back swimmers are aquatic Hemiptera, related to terrestrial stinkbugs. They have beetlelike carapaced forewings held over their bodies, with flying hind wings tucked under them. When they want to take off, they swim to the surface, lift the forewings, loft the hind wings, and whir away. Flight is a means for dispersal, not mating as in mayflies. If the lake or pond in which they live dries up, they abandon it and fly away to look for better habitat. Though most boatmen and back swimmers remain in water their entire lives, a portion of every population suffers wanderlust, and takes to the air even when the old body of water remains suitable. This is nature's way of ensuring the colonization of new lakes and ponds.

Dispersal flights happen in spring and fall. These insects are less important, in angling terms, when they take off, more important when they land. It's a rare sight, but it's been reported that they land like raindrops or hail.

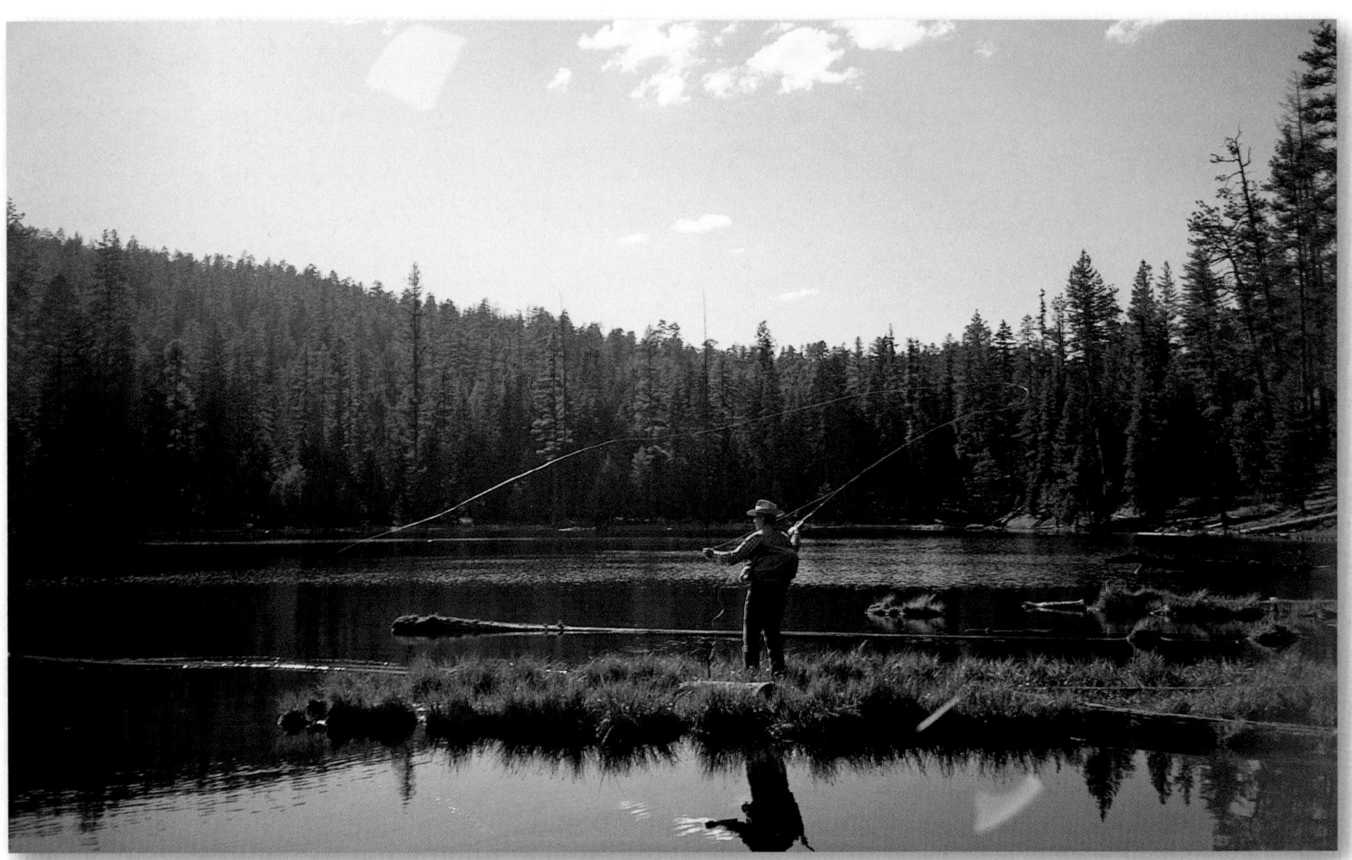

Water boatmen and back swimmers depend on atmospheric oxygen, and are most abundant in shallow lakes and ponds with extensive shallows and vegetation beds.

I've seen an occasional water boatman descending to the water near me, but I've never witnessed a hailstorm of them, the kind of activity that would get trout boiling after them. I have, however, seen lots of trout feeding on water boatmen with enough focus that their bellies were packed with them and contained little else.

Both of these insects breathe atmospheric oxygen, which they get by swimming to the surface, tucking a bubble of air along the body and under the forewings, and swimming back to their homes in the aquatic vegetation. Oxygen is transported out of these bubbles and into their tracheal systems. As the insect uses up the oxygen in the bubble, the balance with nitrogen is upset, and more oxygen diffuses out of the water and replenishes the supply in the bubble, enabling a water boatman or back swimmer to remain underwater for several minutes.

The water boatman has a dark, mottled back and a lighter underside. Each set of legs is used for a different purpose: the front for winnowing food, middle for gripping vegetation, and hind for swimming.

WATER BOATMEN

Water boatmen are most abundant in lakes and ponds, but they also can be found in vegetation beds in moving water if the currents are almost nil. The key is rooted vegetation. Wherever plants take root in still or very slow water that is shallow enough for the naturals to make their dash to the surface for air, you'll find water boatmen. I have fished over them in the almost still pools of tailwaters that have had their flows shut down after the irrigation season. If you encounter such a situation, they could be considered moving-water insects. It's rare. You'll almost always fish over them in lakes and ponds with extensive vegetated shallows.

Trout cruise these shallows, watching for water boatmen risking that trip to the top. If you see trout cruising in singles, pairs, or pods, and they make occasional swift turns and rushes to take something subsurface, they're probably feeding on boatmen. Sometimes you'll see the trout nosing in and out of the weeds, with frequent darts to feed. They're usually flushing out water boatmen and gunning them down, though they might also be feeding on dislodged scuds and damselfly nymphs. At such times they'll eat whatever looks alive, but a high percentage of the time they're seeing water boatmen, more than anything else, stroking away, trying to escape the trout.

All insects have three sets of legs. Each pair of the water boatman's legs are specialized. The front legs are scooplike, held close to the mouth, and used to winnow through the thin layer of diatomaceous growth on aquatic plant leaves and stems. Boatmen feed primarily on vegetable matter, but will not reject a midge larva or small scud if their front legs scoop one in. Their middle legs are adapted to clinging to the vegetation, holding them in position against the buoyancy of the captured bubble. Their hind legs are long and fringed with hairs, oarlike, and give the bugs their name: water boatmen. They stroke along very efficiently, most often either up to get a bubble of air or down to return to their hides in the vegetation.

Water boatmen and back swimmers take a bubble of air under the water with them, and extract oxygen from it. The reflectance of the bright bubble might be the trigger to strikes by trout.

Three aspects of a water boatman are distinct, and might be triggers to trout predation. The first is their dark carapaced forewings, covering the entire back of the insect. The second is the bubble of air, brightly visible along the insect's underside. The third is those long hind legs. Any imitation you tie for water boatmen should capture at least one or two of these features. When the naturals are largest, in late fall through winter and into early spring, your flies should be tied on size 12 and 14 standard nymph hooks, and should reflect each of the three important aspects of the water boatman.

MIDGE NYMPH, OLIVE

Hook: Curved scud, size 14-24
Weight: 5-6 turns nonlead wire
Thread: Olive 8/0 or 10/0
Rib: Copper wire
Body: Olive dubbing

Water boatmen are present in their greatest numbers, but smallest sizes, in late spring through the summer. That is when trout are most likely to cruise the shallows and along undercut banks, feeding on all that abundance. The smallest imitations for them can be as simple as a ball of olive dubbing on a size 18 or 20 hook. I have had some success on trout selective to tiny water boatmen by fishing an olive Midge Nymph (page 75). It is cast in the path of a cruising trout, and simply allowed to settle in front the fish. It can also be twitched along within the trout's vision, to attract attention, if the trout seems not to have noticed the small nymph.

A high percentage of your fishing with water boatman patterns will be done to visible, cruising trout, in water two to at most four feet deep. Your main problem will be to keep the fly at a depth where trout will notice it. It's not easy to strike a balance between enough weight to penetrate the surface film and not so much that the fly plummets to the shallow bottom. The olive Midge Nymph has enough weight in its ribbing wire to get it sinking, but not so much that it will sink to the bottom quickly.

STILLWATER BOATMAN

Gary Anderson, a noted stillwater angler from Wenatchee, Washington, has instructed me a few times on his home waters in the seeps lake region of that area. Gary has lots of solutions to stillwater trout, and one of his solutions for water boatmen is to tie a very small and simple imitation, then suspend it on a couple feet of fine tippet beneath a tiny strike indicator, while he waits for a cruising trout to move into view. If the trout's path will take it near the nymph, he merely lets it sit. If necessary, Gary will move the fly just enough to catch the trout's attention. The key is sufficient weight on the fly to make it sink slowly, and the right length tippet to suspend the nymph at the level trout are cruising.

STILLWATER BOATMAN *Gary Anderson*

Hook: Standard nymph, size 16-20
Weight: 4-6 turns nonlead wire
Thread: Olive 8/0
Legs: Black rubber legs
Body: Peacock herl

Step 1. Fix the hook in the vise, and take just four to six turns of nonlead weighting wire. Start the thread behind the eye, and secure the weighting wire. Lay an inch or more of fine rubber-leg material across the wire at the midpoint of the hook, and lash it down with figure eights of thread. Layer thread to the hook bend. Tie in two or three peacock herls by their tips.

Noted Washington angler Gary Anderson on the shallow lake where he developed many of his water boatman patterns and techniques.

Step 2. Capture the herl in a thread loop, or twist it together with the thread, to make a herl body secure against the teeth of trout. Wind it forward over the legs and to the hook eye. Clip the excess herl, make a thread head, whip-finish, and apply head cement.

Step 3. Bring the legs together above the body, and clip them about the length of the hook shank. Be careful not to stretch them when you do this, or they'll spring back short.

This simple nymph is designed to be suspended in the path of cruising trout. It can also be cast to cruisers, on a floating or clear intermediate line, and retrieved in front of them. You'll have to calculate your casting angle to place the fly far enough in front of a moving trout that it sinks to the right level, and so the arrival of your line and leader don't alarm the trout. When trout are in shallows, exposed to overhead predation, they will be spooky. That's the major reason you want to suspend your fly at the right depth, and animate it when a trout approaches it. What a trout sees is a bit of detritus that suddenly springs to life. That appearance of life might be the most important trigger any nymph can own.

It's also effective to fish such shallows with a sinking line and floating nymph. The cast can be made, and the line allowed to settle to the bottom, while the fly suspends once again, but above the line instead of beneath an indicator. When a trout moves into sight, the nymph can be animated, and the result is the same. Gary Anderson also recommends fishing a floating water boatman on a floating line, with a microshot pinched to the tippet a foot or two from the nymph. The same dressing could be tied with an underbody of foam instead of weighting wire, and your fly would suspend from the bottom and not the top. When brought to life, it would then dive, rather than climb toward the surface, as a weighted fly would when suspended under an indicator.

There is no evidence that trout are particular about which direction a water boatman takes, up or down, but your fishing situation might make it easier to suspend a floating nymph above the bottom rather than a weighted nymph from the surface. Your fly boxes should prepare you for both types of presentations if you fish many shallow, weedy stillwaters, the kind that can be loaded with boatmen.

WATER FLOATMAN

Phil Rowley's Water Floatman is designed to solve the same problem, but over a more mature stage of the insect, therefore with a larger nymph. A foam shellback floats the fly. A Krystal Chenille body gives it the brightness of a bubble of air. Phil calls for Super Floss for the legs, but I have substituted rubber legs.

WATER FLOATMAN ***Phil Rowley***

Hook: Standard dry fly, size 10–14
Thread: Black 6/0 or 8/0
Shellback: Black sheet foam
Body: Olive Krystal Chenille
Legs: Brown Super Floss or rubber legs

Step 1. Fix the hook in the vise, start the thread behind the eye, and layer the shank to the hook bend. Cut a thin sheet of foam into a strip about two-thirds of the hook gap wide. Tie this in at the bend of the hook. Tie the Krystal Chenille body material in at the base of the shellback. Take the thread to the midpoint of the hook, and tie in a length of leg material with figure eights, across the shank.

Step 2. Wrap the Krystal Chenille forward, around the legs, and tie it off behind the hook eye. Clip the excess.

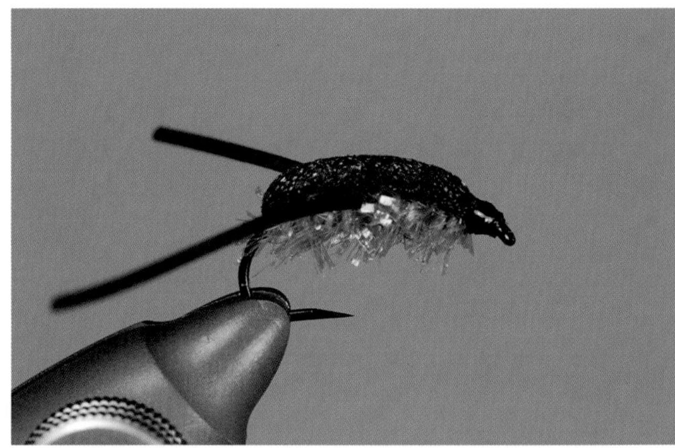

Step 3. Bring the shellback forward over the body, and secure it behind the hook eye. Clip the excess. Make a neat thread head, whip-finish, clip the thread, and apply head cement.

Step 4. Draw the legs out to a point just beyond the end of the hook bend, hold them together, and clip them to that length. Be careful not to stretch them; they'll recoil and be short.

BOATMAN

The reflective Krystal Chenille in Phil's dressing imitates the bubble taken under the water by the natural water boatman. Jim Schollmeyer's Boatman dressing accomplishes the same thing, but uses white Antron dubbing rather than Mylar trapped in chenille. It also has mono eyes, which it might be wise to incorporate into any of the water boatman and back swimmer dressings.

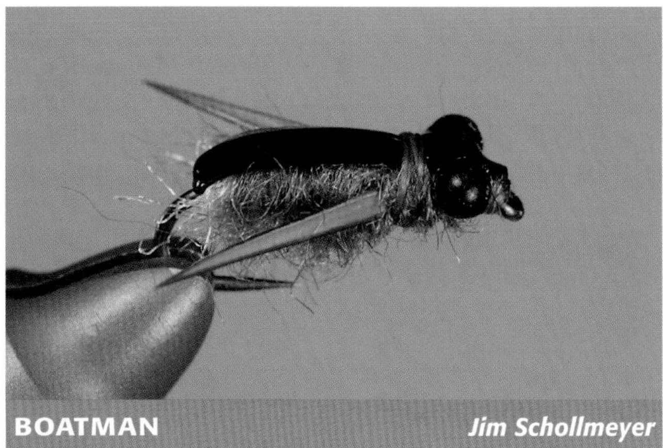

BOATMAN *Jim Schollmeyer*

Hook:	Standard nymph, size 14-16
Weight:	10-15 turns nonlead wire
Thread:	Olive 6/0 or 8/0
Eyes:	Amber or black mono eyes
Shellback:	Black Thin Skin or similar
Air bubble:	White or clear Antron dubbing
Abdomen:	Olive Antron dubbing
Legs:	Olive goose biots
Thorax:	Olive Antron dubbing

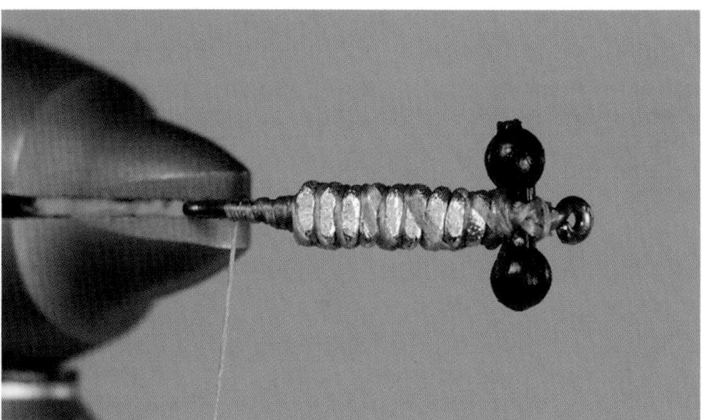

Step 1. Fix the hook in the vise, weight it with a few turns of nonlead wire, and start the thread behind the eye. Layer the shank, securing the weighting wire, and return the thread to a point about one or two hook-eye lengths behind the eye. Burn a set of mono eyes (see page 307) or select a premade set of eyes with a width a bit narrower than the hook gap. Tie them in with figure eights. Jim recommends flattening the weighting wire wraps slightly with flatnose pliers.

Step 2. Cut a strip of Thin Skin about two-thirds the width of the hook gap. Tie it in at the bend of the hook. Twist a small amount of white or clear Antron dubbing to the thread, and take a single turn of it at the tie-in point for the shellback. Tease it out slightly to trail the hook. This represents the natural's bubble of air.

Step 3. Use a dubbing loop to create a fairly loose and fibrous dubbing body forward to a point about one eyeball width behind the eyes. Measure a goose biot to the end of the hook, and tie it in on the near side. Repeat on the far side, and clip the butts.

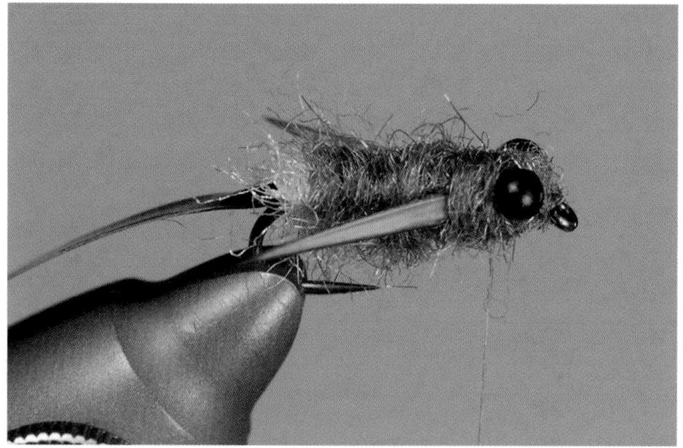

Step 4. Fill in behind the eyes with dubbing. Take a turn of dubbing between the eyes, one in front of them, and another back between them. End with the thread behind the eyes.

Step 5. Bring the shellback forward. Tie it off with several turns of thread behind the eyes. Take the thread in front of the eyes, with one long turn on the underside of the thorax. Tie the shellback off behind the hook eye. Form a thread head, whip-finish, clip the thread, and apply head cement.

BACK SWIMMERS

Back swimmers are very similar to water boatmen in shape, but they average a little larger, and their behavior is remarkably different. They are predaceous, and because of that bright bubble and their showy colors, they don't do well at stalking. Most of the time, they hang in the surface film, butts-up, taking in atmospheric oxygen while they watch for prey with big, black eyes. If something moves within range, they use their long, fringed, oarlike hind legs to stroke down and capture it. They often hunt pelagically, hanging in the surface far from shore, feeding on phantom midges that rise and fall in the water column in daily rhythms, in turn feeding on phyto- and zooplankton.

Back swimmers are similar in shape to water boatmen, but they're very different in attitude. Their brightness is a rarity among aquatic insects, and they act as if they're more often hunters than hunted.

Back swimmers act as if they consider themselves to be at the top of the aquatic food chain. With the exception of trout, they might be. I have seen them swimming briskly and boldly through clear lake water, acting as if they fear nothing. Their coloration adds to that perception: some are almost black on the back and silver on the underside, but most I've collected and photographed are gleaming white, almost silver. Ernest Schwiebert, in his book *Nymphs,* calls them "pale moon-winged back swimmers," a name as beautiful as the insect itself. But they bite. Actually they pierce an insect, tadpole, or small fish with a sharp proboscis, and inject enzymes designed to break down tissue, yours if you hold one carelessly in your hand.

I've collected many back swimmers, but I've rarely found one in a trout stomach sample, though water boatmen show up there, often in numbers that reflect selective feeding. Back swimmer brightness might be a warning to trout about that stinging bite. It's possible that they fear nothing because trout fear to eat them. That is speculation. But their position so high up the food chain, by the law of predation, means their numbers will never approach those of water boatmen. That is not speculation.

If you ever find need for an imitation of a back swimmer, I suspect that either a white-winged Coachman Wet or a Prince Nymph, with its white biots on the back, will be all you need. The key is the retrieve. The naturals stroke along at about the speed that a feeding trout cruises, which is fast for an aquatic insect. I have no doubt that a trout could chase one down. I also have no doubt that a Coachman or Prince, fished with the standard stripping wet-fly retrieve, looks a lot like a pale moon-winged back swimmer out on the prowl.

The coachman wet fly (left) or Beadhead Prince Nymph (right) might be all you ever need to match the bold pale moon-winged back swimmers.

SUMMARY

You should arm yourself with at least one floating water boatman dressing, and one that is weighted enough to penetrate the surface film and sink a few inches. It seems counterintuitive, as it did with dragonfly nymphs, that the sinking nymph is best fished on a floating or intermediate line, whereas the floating nymph is best fished on a sinking line. The line tip dredges the bottom, while the floating water boatman follows along behind, suspended a few inches to a foot or two above the bottom, or above plants if you're fishing over dense vegetation. That will be the most common scenario in which you fish water boatman imitations: shallow water, dense vegetation, and cruising, feeding trout. Be sure to use a short leader, to keep the imitation down where you want it, when you fish a floating nymph on a sinking line.

Often trout set up a pattern, nosing along for twenty to fifty feet or more just about a foot from the bank, feeding on whatever they find. Then they turn around and repeat the same patrol in the opposite direction. If you are able to discern the pattern of such a trout, and place in its path either a sunk water boatman beneath an indicator, or a similar dressing floating above a sinking line, then animate the fly when the trout returns into view, you will be surprised at the number of smart stillwater trout that suddenly become foolish.

CHAPTER 34

Stillwater Scuds

Scuds are more important in stillwaters than they are in streams and rivers. You'll find them only in the slowest stretches of moving water, most often in spring creeks or tailwaters, where plants have a chance to take root, where winter and spring spates do not scour the plants out, and take the scuds with them.

Lakes and ponds never suffer scouring spate flows. Plants take root wherever the substrate is suitable and the water is shallow and clear enough for sunlight to strike the bottom. Plants are absent only in water that drops off into abrupt depths all around a shoreline that is too rocky for plants to take root along the edges, or over bottoms such as sand or nonhospitable types of silts, where plants don't do well. Not only are such stillwaters barren of scuds, but they attract few other aquatic life forms, and have sparse populations of trout.

You find plant growth, and therefore scuds, in extensive shallows and over shoals. In waters that are opaque, usually darkened by tannin, sunlight does not penetrate more than eight to ten feet, and that will be the depth at

You will always find scuds in or very near vegetation. If you anchor over plant beds such as these, count a scud dressing down to the tops of the vegetation, and retrieve it slowly, you are almost certain to entertain some trout.

which plant growth ends. In lakes with normal clarity, sunlight will reach the bottom at fifteen to twenty-five feet, and you'll find rooted vegetation, usually loaded with scuds, down to those depths. In alpine lakes, which are often almost as clear as the mountain air around them, sunlight might strike to the bottom at thirty to thirty-five feet. If it does, you'll usually find at least a thin scattering of plants, and therefore scuds. The same high lakes will almost always have coves or shoal areas that are shallower and vegetated, where you find fishing scud imitations easier, and also more profitable.

None of this eliminates the probability of finding trout deeper than the limits of sunlight. When you find them in those darkened depths, however, they won't be feeding on scuds. When you approach any stillwater, always look for its vegetation first, then calculate your rigging for the depth you'll have to reach in order to place your nymph, or pair of nymphs, either along the edges of the plant beds, or right over the top of them.

Trout patrol the edges of vegetation beds, setting up patterns of movement, just as they do along the banks of lakes and ponds, where you'll also find scuds. Trout cruise over the tops of thick vegetation, watching for whatever moves, darting in to take it. Trout nose through sparse plant beds, dislodging whatever lives there, turning swiftly to take anything that tries to escape, such as a cased caddis larva, damselfly or dragonfly nymph, or water boatman. In stillwaters with heavy populations of scuds, trout are more likely to flush them than they are anything else, almost always in colors that provide camouflage among that same vegetation.

It's rarely a mistake to include an olive scud dressing, in size 12 to 16, as either the lead fly or trail fly in any pair of nymphs that you use to explore a stillwater, when you have no idea what trout might be taking. The more vegetation you find in any lake or pond, the more likely scuds will be important to trout, and therefore to you, in that bit of water.

It's always helpful to inform yourself about the abundance or absence of particular food forms as soon as you begin fishing any new stillwater. You can do a bit of collecting, using the same kick net you use in moving water, though awkwardly. Or you can lash a kitchen strainer to a dowel or discarded broomstick, as described in chapter 4, and probe the vegetation with that. Scoop up some plants in your net, the strainer, or your fist if you lack anything else. Toss them into your dishwashing pan, or anything else with a light-colored bottom. See what swims out. Imitate whatever is most plentiful. In stillwaters where plants are abundant, about half the time the most prolific food form will be scuds.

If you're afloat, and have an anchor, you can do some minor collecting by locating a plant bed, dropping your anchor into it, dragging it for some distance to collect plants, hoisting it quickly. Most aquatics will drop out before the anchor reaches the surface. But enough will remain to give you an idea about what might be down there for trout to eat. In my own experience using this collecting method, the dominant foods have almost always been damselfly nymphs and scuds. That might only indicate that swifter and less cryptic beasts, such as dragonfly nymphs and water boatmen, abandon ship when it surprisingly sets sail—their habitat has never done that before! But the presence of a few of any trout food form in a plant sample lofted off the bottom and pulled up through several feet of water is an indication that there were probably a lot more individuals in that same group present when the sample left the bottom. If I see a few of something, I always suspect that trout are seeing a lot of the same thing, and that's what I imitate.

The best way to collect scuds in stillwaters is to dredge up some vegetation, let them squirm out. They will almost always be the same color as the plant growth in which you find them.

Again, about half the time, scuds will be the dominant trout food. If I can't get a sample, for lack of an anchor or any other reason, I assume the presence of scuds unless there is an absence of vegetation.

Scuds are crustaceans, with hardened and carapaced backs, and what seems to be a blur of legs and swimmer appendages emanating from the underside of the thorax and abdomen. They breed all year round, and are constantly available in a range of sizes from tiny 20s up to large 12s. They are curled whenever you capture them and hold them in your hand. When they swim in and around vegetation beds, which it's easy to assume is the most likely time for trout to see and eat them, they'll be swimming like sticks, with all those leglike swimmers awhir, seemingly directionless.

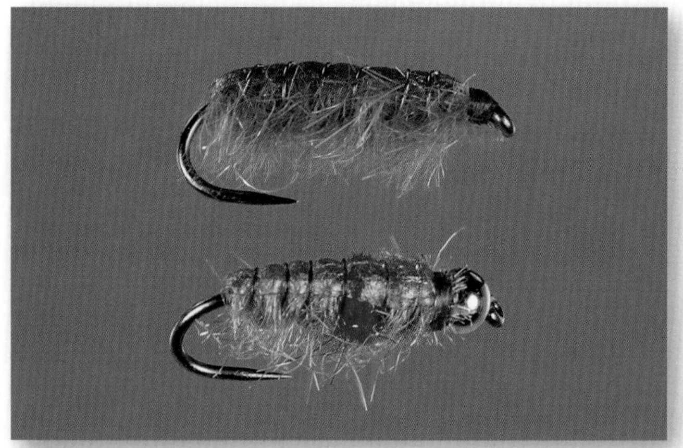

Your selection of stillwater scud imitations should be based on those you've tied for rivers and streams, such as the Dubbed Scud (top) and Beadhead Scud (bottom). The same narrow set of colors and sizes will work, and you might as well carry your stream-fly box that contains them.

Nymphs for stillwater scuds can be almost precisely those that you tie for scuds in moving water (see chapter 23). The basics should be a small supply built around the Dubbed Scud and Beadhead Scud, both styles tied in olive, gray, and tan, sizes 12 to 16. They should amount to at least a couple of rows in your stillwater-fly box, more if you fish stillwaters often and get separated from nymphs with fair regularity. You might simply carry your stream box when you fish a stillwater. If I'm in a boat, I'm rarely without my entire collection of fly boxes, which are all stored in a single waterproof boat bag, so that I can grab it and go on any trip without forgetting the boxes that I need when I get wherever I'm going. If I'm in a float tube or pontoon boat, then my capacity will be limited, and I would rather have a separate set of scud dressings added to my stillwater-fly box.

If you weight your stream scud dressings lightly, depending as I do on weight attached to the leader to get them deep, then you'll want to tie a fresh set of nymphs for lakes, anyway. Your scuds for lakes and ponds will always be reaching for vegetation growth, which will always be somewhat deep and will often be very deep, so your nymphs tied to imitate them on stillwaters should be more heavily weighted than those for moving water.

Though your basic set of flies should arise from the same set of styles listed in chapter 23, there are a few different ideas that you should consider applying to stillwater scud imitations. I'll list them here, and refer you to that earlier chapter for most of your scud dressings, with the admonition to tie them with a few extra wraps of weighting wire. Note that if an originator has called for a curved scud hook for a pattern, I have followed that prescription. But you should feel free to tie any listed scud pattern on a standard nymph hook with a straight shank.

GLASS BEAD SCUD

The following glass bead dressing, from Phil Rowley's book *Fly Patterns for Stillwaters,* is a simple tie. Many bead-bodied dressings call for knotting the thread between beads, clipping it, starting it again between the next set of beads. The result might be beautiful, but the tying is certain to be tedious. If fly tying itself is your hobby, and trout fishing is a distant adjunct to it, then it's easy to find more complex bead patterns for scuds. My tying time is usually constricted, because I'd rather go fishing, so I'm always in favor of the simplest way to get a fly together, so long as it works. Phil's pattern is about the fastest way to incorporate beads into a killing scud dressing. You don't need to restart your thread between each pair of beads.

GLASS BEAD SCUD *Phil Rowley*

Hook:	Curved scud or standard nymph, size 10-16
Beads:	Olive glass
Thread:	Olive 6/0 or 8/0
Body:	Olive Antron dubbing, or fur and Antron mix

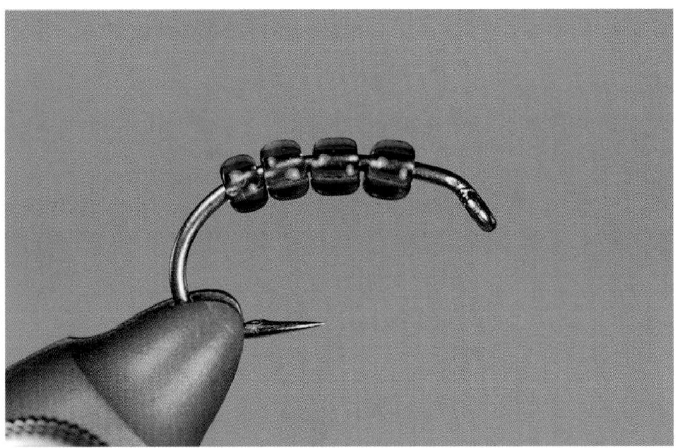

Step 1. Place enough beads on the hook to cover a bit more than half the shank length. When spaced with dubbing turns, they will cover it completely. If you use too many beads, you will not have room for dubbing between them. If you use too few, the fly will be out of aesthetic balance, though interviews with trout have indicated that they're not concerned with pretty, though that doesn't mean that you should neglect it.

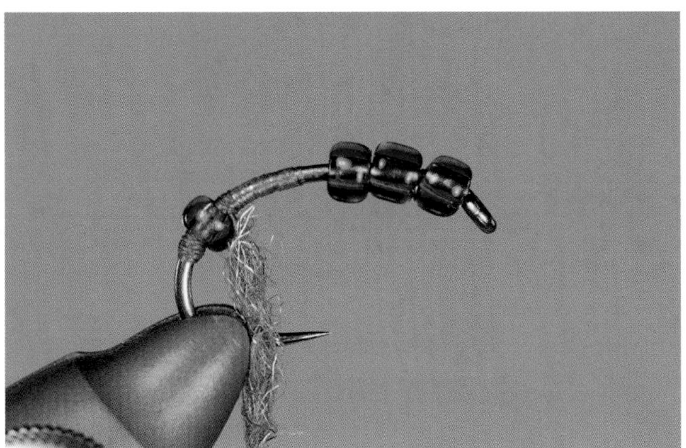

Step 2. Slide the beads forward against the hook eye, and start the thread behind them. Layer the shank around the bend of a curved hook, or to the beginning of the bend of a straight-shank hook. Build a thread bump big enough to block passage of a bead. Slide the rear bead against the bump, and take your thread over the bead. Use a few turns of thread to lock it in place. Use the direct-dubbing method or a dubbing loop to create a realtively thin dubbing skein.

Step 3. Wrap the dubbing forward in the spaces between beads. Use one to at most three turns of dubbing in each gap, then push the next bead back against the dubbing, take the dubbing over it, and fill the following gap with dubbing. The dubbing should be about the thickness of the beads. Stop the dubbing in the last gap, and take the thread forward over the last bead to the hook eye.

Step 4. Form a thread head that locks in the front bead. Whip-finish, clip the thread, and apply head cement. Use your bodkin or a dubbing roughing tool to tease the dubbing to the underside of the hook. It should extend to about the level of the hook barb.

This glass bead fly is necessarily unweighted. Depend on the sink rate of your line to deliver it down to the vegetation you want to fish. You can also use it as a trailer behind a heavily weighted dragonfly nymph. But it fishes most naturally when trailed behind something less obtrusive, or used as the lead fly in front of a smaller midge pupa pattern.

FAST-SINKING SCUD

In his book *Active Nymphing,* Rich Osthoff lists his Fast-Sinking Scud as his favorite fly for rousting big brook trout and goldens from high alpine lakes. Though it's likely that in its bright orange version, the nymph is taken by trout more as a serendipitous mouthful of protein than it is as an imitation of scuds they've been feeding on in recent moments, it is an effective pattern, well worth having in your stillwater-fly boxes.

The orange Fast-Sinking Scud is designed to be cast well in front of spotted cruising trout, but it will be just as effective when fished in searching fashion, over water into which you're not able to see so well, but you suspect contains trout on the prowl. The fly should be fished with a combination of slow strips, fast strips, a hand-twist, and plenty of rest stops in which it simply sits and sinks. If you find a part of the retrieve that trout like best, then forget the others and focus on that.

Osthoff ties the same fly in an olive variation. It is much more realistic, in terms of the naturals, and is the one you would want to tie on when you're fishing around vegetation, rather than casting over cruising, and therefore hungry, trout. The Olive Fast-Sinking Scud is an excellent imitation of the most common naturals, and will do well as the basis for a few size and color variations that will match any scuds you might find in stillwaters, anywhere. In its larger sizes, it imitates the upper range of naturals, but that's often wise; scuds in the full range of sizes are always out there, swimming blindly through aquatic vegetation, getting fed upon by trout. The Olive Fast-Sinking Scud follows excellent stillwater logic: the average bite that a trout eats in a lake or pond is olive, size 12 to 16, and moving at a slow crawl.

FAST-SINKING SCUD, ORANGE *Rich Osthoff*

Hook: Standard nymph, size 6-16
Weight: 10-15 turns nonlead wire
Thread: Orange 6/0 or 8/0
Tail: Rooster pheasant breast fibers
Shellback: Clear Scud Back or Thin Skin
Back stripe: Strip of silver Mylar tinsel
Underbody: Yarn
Rib: 3X to 5X monofilament
Body: Orange fur and Antron mix

If you fish alpine lakes, or any others where you have a chance to spot cruising trout, you can plot your casts to place a Fast-Sinking Scud in the path of trout, at the right depth to catch their attention when they arrive.

FAST-SINKING SCUD, OLIVE *Rich Osthoff*

Hook: Standard nymph, size 12-16
Weight: 10-15 turns nonlead wire
Thread: Olive 6/0 or 8/0
Tail: Hen pheasant breast fibers
Shellback: Clear Scud Back or Thin Skin
Back stripe: Strip of silver Mylar tinsel
Underbody: Yarn
Rib: 3X to 5X monofilament
Body: Olive fur and Antron mix

The fly in the photo was tied by Rich Osthoff and has been fished by me, so it's not pristine, but is blooded.

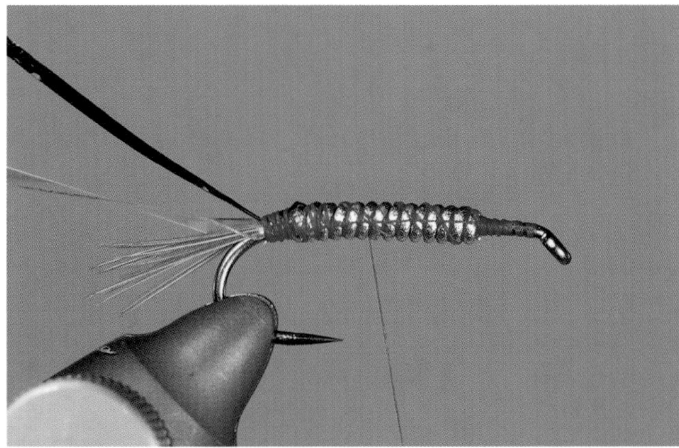

Step 1. Fix the hook in the vise, and weight it over the back two-thirds of the shank. Start the thread, and overwrap the weighting wire to secure it. Measure eight to twelve rooster pheasant breast feather fibers two-thirds the length of the shank, and tie them in at the bend. Cut a strip of shellback material about half the hook-gap width, and tie it in at the base of the tail. Tie in a single strip of Mylar, with the silver side down, so that when brought forward, the silver side is up.

Step 2. Use any color yarn for the underbody, as it won't show through. Tie it in over the weighting wire, and wrap an underbody that is slightly fatter at the tail end, tapered down toward the hook eye. Accomplish this by twisting the yarn tightly to fatten it toward the back, and letting it relax and spread out as you approach the eye. Tie it off and clip the excess. Tie in several inches of ribbing monofilament far enough forward of the end of the underbody that you can take a turn of body dubbing behind it.

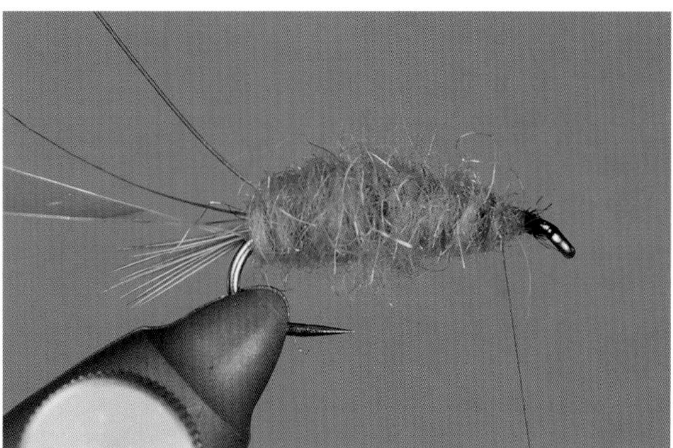

Step 3. Fix dubbing to the thread, and wind a body forward that follows the taper of the underbody, from fat at the back to slender at the front. Taper it down to the hook eye, leaving room to tie off the racing stripe and shellback.

Step 4. Bring the Mylar strip forward over the center of the nymph back, and tie it off behind the eye. Draw the shellback over the body, and tie it off securely. Clip the excess Mylar and shellback.

Step 5. Wind the ribbing mono forward over the body and shellback in five to six evenly spaced turns. Tie it off securely and clip the excess. Make a neat, tapered thread head, whip-finish, and clip the thread. Osthoff, a commerical tier in Wisconsin, has noted deterioration of the plastic shellback if head cement is applied, and omits it.

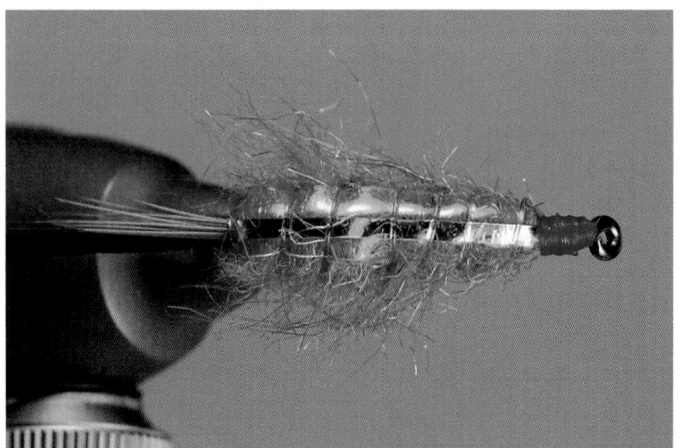

Step 6. Use a dubbing roughing tool to brush the underside of the body out to both sides.

SUMMARY

Most of the flies that you tie for scuds in stillwaters should be similar to those that you tie for streams, with the addition of a bit more weight. If you already tie the Orange Bighorn Shrimp (see page 260), then you'll also already be armed to fish the scud as an attractor. If not, try Rich Osthoff's ideas and his Fast-Sinking Scuds. When sight-fishing, it's usually best to use a floating line and fairly long leader, ten to twelve feet, or a clear intermediate line and moderately long leader, eight to ten feet. Place the fly well in front of a cruising trout: ten feet is minimum, twenty to thirty feet might be necessary to keep from spooking the fish. Let the fly sink. If the trout turns toward it, continue to let it sink. If the fish makes a dart, or suddenly stops where you think the nymph sits at rest, assume the trout has taken the nymph and set the hook.

If the trout seems to be passing without noticing the nymph, give it a few twitches, then let it sit some more. If a trout follows, pause, give the fish a chance to catch up and inhale the nymph. When it stops or turns, set the hook.

When using scud imitations in their more common application, for exploring submerged plant beds, shoals, and shallow coves, choose your line sink rate for the depth you need to achieve to reach the vegetation. If it's shallow, use a floating or intermediate line and long leader. If the water is deeper than four to five feet, go to a wet-tip or full-sink line. The deeper the water, the faster your line should sink, and the longer you'll have to count to get it down. If the water is deeper than fifteen to twenty feet, you'll be best served by what I call a "depth charge" line, which is usually the fastest-sinking shooting taper I can find for the rod I'm casting.

No matter how you get a scud imitation to the depth you desire, you'll want to keep it in the strike zone as long as possible on each cast. If you strip it in fast, it not only will move like no natural scud ever did, but also will lift up in the water column, almost always out of range of trout feeding along, above, and among plant beds. A hand-twist retrieve, moving the nymph little more than enough to keep in contact with it so you can detect takes, is usually best. It moves the nymph slowly, like an aimless natural scud, and also keeps your fly in the strike zone much longer than a faster retrieve would.

CHAPTER 35

Leeches

Stillwater leeches often come to bad ends because of trout. Not all of those ends are precisely predictable. I fished my favorite windswept lake one day last spring, during a morning midge hatch. A few trout already bulged in the shallows, plucking midge pupae hanging from the rafters, when I arrived just after dawn. Mist came off the water. Yellow-headed blackbirds quarreled in the cattails. A flock of mallards squawked off in alarm when I wadered up and waded into the shallows where those scattered trout fed.

The rises were too scattered to hit with any consistency, so I rigged as I almost always do on a stillwater when I want to pass the time until trout commit themselves fully to a hatch: I tied on a size 12 Beadhead Black Woolly Bugger, in a foreshortened form that I've found deadly for me. Because I knew I would be switching to midge patterns before long, and would want to fish them in or just under the surface, I used a floating line and ten-foot 3X leader. I began casting, giving the fly a few seconds to sink, retrieving it with a slow hand-twist. It's a formula that has taken countless stillwater trout for me, and it didn't fail for long that morning.

The first trout was a rainbow, about three pounds. It jumped several times and fought with strength, but was docile enough when brought to hand that I decided to cradle it upside down, and extract a throat pump sample. It was no surprise that it contained quite a few midge pupae, but I was surprised to find three fat leeches, each about two inches long. They had been taken long enough ago to be dead, but not so long ago that they had begun decomposing. I released the trout, feeling guilty that I'd deprived it of its morning groceries.

I squeezed the bulb to dispense the leeches and midges into a film canister, tucked it in a vest pocket, and continued fishing the Black Woolly Bugger until the midge hatch took over. By the time that ended, around ten o'clock, I'd already caught a satisfying number of trout for the day. I let down the tailgate of the rig, set up my photo gear, and poured the contents of the film canister into a small, flat dish. After taking a few photos of the leeches mixed in with the midges, I left them in the dish on the tailgate, switched waders for hiking boots, and took off across the broad, rolling wheat country for a

The author releasing the pond trout that provided a throat pump sample with three dead leeches in it.

The three leeches in the photo were taken by a trout around dawn, were extracted and photographed at midmorning, and by noon had been pilfered by a blackbird, in which it's assumed they ended their misadventure.

long walk. I saw some deer, jumped a rooster pheasant, watched a small hawk sit on the uplifted blower arm of an abandoned wheat combine, scouting the nearby sage flat for the flicker of movement that might give away one of the cottontail rabbits that called the combine home.

When I got back to the rig an hour later, the leeches were gone from the dish in which I'd left them. It took a long time to puzzle out their disappearance. They were dead, so they hadn't crawled away. While I sat and thought, one of those blackbirds landed in a nearby cattail, tried to start an argument with me, and I knew instantly who had done it.

Those unlucky leeches had started their day undulating along the bottom of the lake, probably as happy as leeches get. They were eaten by a trout, which abruptly ended any happiness. Then I extracted them from the trout and posed them for photos. They ended their day in the belly of a blackbird . . . unless that bird got attacked by the hawk also hanging around the lake.

Leeches are sightless. They move blindly over the bottom, in and out of vegetation beds, and sometimes swim pelagically out in open water, which probably gets them into the sort of adventures outlined above. I've seen them cruising long distances on broad, soft lake bottoms, leaving trails etched into the silt behind them, kicking up puffs of it as they move along. I've also seen small leeches, an inch long or less, hanging from the surface film, looking a bit like large midge pupae. I've never seen evidence of a trout feeding exclusively on leeches, but I have found two or three leeches in enough stillwater samples to know that trout take them very often, quite likely almost daily.

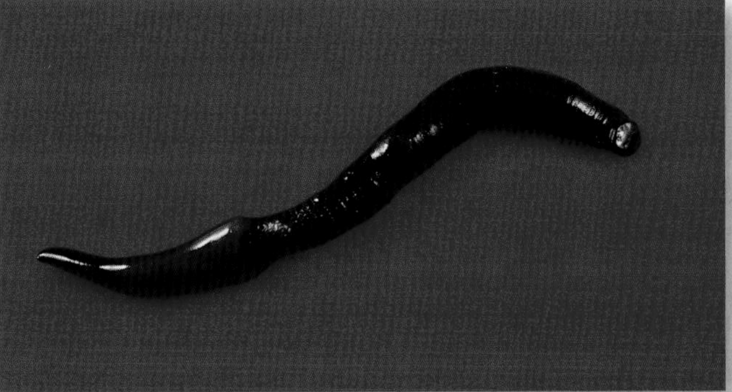

Leeches look much like earthworms, when they're stretched out at rest. When swimming, however, they undulate a lot like miniature snakes, though the motion is up and down rather than side to side.

My favorite variation of the Black Beadhead Woolly Bugger (top) is the undersized, underweighted, and foreshortened version on the bottom.

Most of the leeches I see swimming in lakes and ponds are large, two to three inches long, and fat enough to provide a lot of nutrition to a trout. But almost all of the leeches I've found in trout stomach contents have been small, an inch to an inch and a half long, and slender. I don't know if that reflects the law of abundance—there are usually greater numbers of the smaller life stages of any organism around—or if trout become leery about eating big leeches. I just know that it's very common to find small leeches eaten by trout, rare to find big ones. Many folks fish size 4 and 6 leech imitations, but the most knowledgeable stillwater anglers I know use sizes 10 and 12.

We think of leeches as bloodsuckers, and some are, but most of them feed most of the time on detrital ooze, along the bottom. Rick Hafele and I recently paddled a canoe up the shallow arm of a big lake in British Columbia, following the trickle of an inlet stream up to a short portage into a smaller lake. The arm was just a few inches

Black, Olive, and Brown Beadhead Woolly Buggers are standards for leeches in lakes and ponds.

deep, too shallow for trout, and heavily vegetated. We saw dozens, and soon hundreds, of big, black leeches as we paddled along. Rick speculated that they found a rich stew of digestable algae and other vegetable matter in the bottom ooze. When we disturbed the water with our paddles, the leeches would turn and undulate in a hurry toward us. They might have been feeding on salad, but they might also have been glad at the arrival of an occasional moose.

Many leeches are black, or a green so dark it's almost black. Some are dark brown or rust. These are often called blood leeches. It's not uncommon to see tan leeches with black speckles in the Canadian lakes I've fished. They could be considered pretty if they weren't leeches. I've never imitated them. I've also seen small leeches in olive to bright green, though not often. Whatever pattern you settle on for leeches, it would be wise to tie a few in each of three primary colors: black, brown, and olive. In some styles, add blood red. That will cover all of the likely possibilities.

Woolly Buggers are standard for leeches, with good reason: they have the elongated shape of a natural leech. When retrieved, or allowed to simply sink, their long marabou tails undulate. I suspect that the swimming motion of a leech is the trigger to a take more often than the shape of the fly. The pattern in the following three colors will cover most of your need for leech imitations, and will work for a lot of other trout food forms as well. (For tying steps, see page 283.)

BEADHEAD WOOLLY BUGGER, BLACK

Russell Blessing

Hook:	3XL, size 6-14
Bead:	Gold
Weight:	10-20 turns nonlead wire
Thread:	Black 6/0 or 8/0
Tail:	Black marabou with 6-8 Pearl Krystal Flash fibers
Body:	Black chenille
Hackle:	Black hen or grade-three rooster

BEADHEAD WOOLLY BUGGER, OLIVE

Russell Blessing

Hook:	3XL, size 6-14
Bead:	Gold
Weight:	10-20 turns nonlead wire
Thread:	Olive 6/0 or 8/0
Tail:	Olive marabou with 6-8 Pearl Krystal Flash fibers
Body:	Olive chenille
Hackle:	Brown hen or grade-three rooster

BEADHEAD WOOLLY BUGGER, BROWN

Russell Blessing

Hook:	3XL, size 6-14
Bead:	Gold
Weight:	10-20 turns nonlead wire
Thread:	Brown 6/0 or 8/0
Tail:	Brown marabou with 6-8 Pearl Krystal Flash fibers
Body:	Brown chenille
Hackle:	Brown hen or grade-three rooster

BEADHEAD MOHAIR LEECH

Mohair is an old but still very popular material for leech patterns. The Mohair Leech was originally tied with yarn unraveled from worn-out sweaters, but you can now buy the yarn carded or spooled. I recommend you purchase black, red, brown, and olive. If you don't have mohair handy, you can quickly construct something very similar by using any long-fibered natural or synthetic dubbing material, trapped in a loose dubbing loop, and teased out after it is wound (see page 50).

The Mohair Leech is a simple tie, and you should keep it that way, so you can get a few tied in the size and color you need, and get back onto the water quickly. I have found it most useful in the original brown, tied slender on size 12 hooks. The concept came out of the Kamloops region, from commercial tier Jack Shaw. A few of the lakes I've fished in that area are almost black with tannin; in those waters, a black pattern will show a more visible profile to trout. If you're fishing less opaque waters, and collect olive leeches, then that should be your color of choice. Red is called for often to represent *blood leeches,* a color I have yet to collect, perhaps because when one gets on me, I'm not patient enough to wait for it to take on that coloration. But red carries its color into dark waters, and it catches trout, so it's worth tying along with the others.

BEADHEAD MOHAIR LEECH *Jack Shaw*

Hook: 3XL, size 6-12
Bead: Gold
Weight: 10-20 turns nonlead wire
Thread: Black, brown, olive, or red 3/0 or 6/0
Body: Black, brown, olive, or red mohair

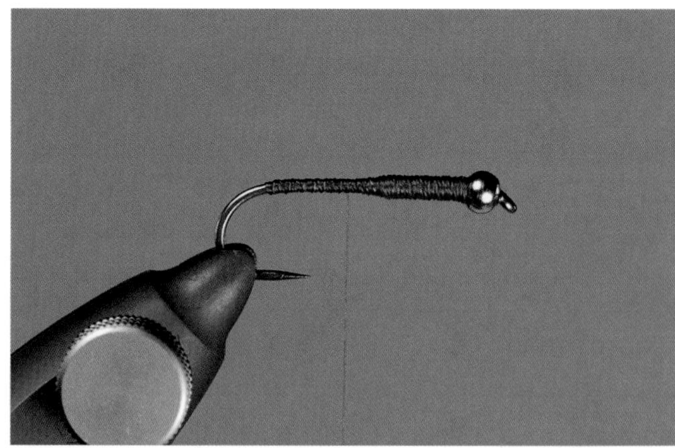

Step 1. Slip a bead onto the hook, and fix the hook in the vise. Wind weighting wire and press it forward into the open back end of the bead, or tight against it if it won't fit inside. Start the thread behind the wire, and secure the wire with a thread ramp up onto the shoulder. Overwrap the weighting wire with thread, and layer the hook twice, back and forth, to create an undercolor for the mohair body.

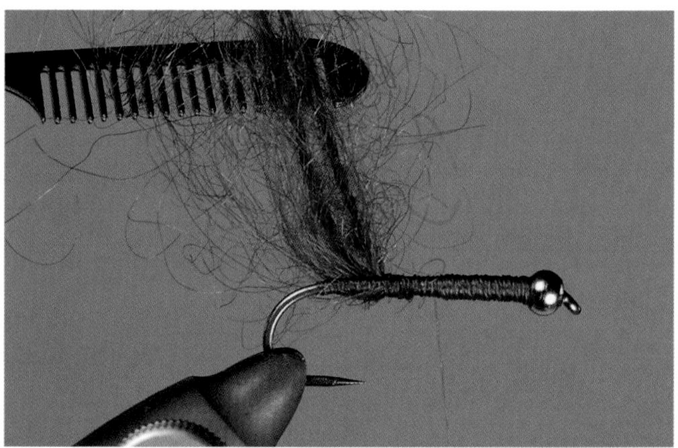

Step 2. Take your thread to the approximate midpoint of the hook shank. Double the mohair yarn around the thread, slide it down to the top of the hook shank, and use several turns of thread to secure it. If the mohair has insufficient fuzzy loose fibers, hold the two strands together, and use a comb to rough out the fibers slightly. With mohair designed for tying, this will not usually be necessary.

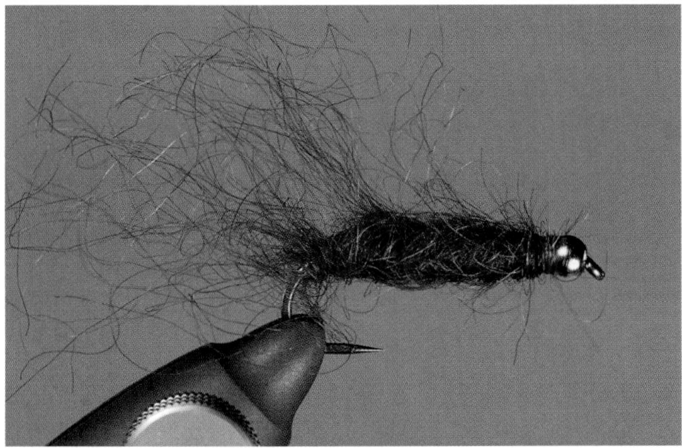

Step 3. Wind the mohair forward to the back of the bead. Use your off hand to stroke the mohair back after each turn of the yarn. Tie it off behind the bead, tuck a tight whip-finish or two at the end of the body, and clip the thread.

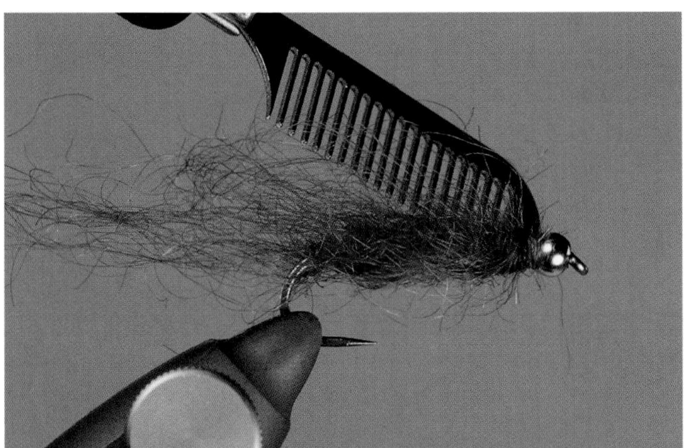

Step 4. Use your comb or a dubbing roughing tool to tease the mohair back along the hook shank. The fibers that trail should be about a hook shank long. If necessary, trim any long and stray fibers, but don't tidy it up too much; when it is in the water, it will slim down and undulate like a natural leech.

GLENN'S LEECH

Glenn Gerbrandt's leech dressing, mentioned in Phil Rowley's *Fly Patterns for Stillwaters,* has a rabbit strip body. It's an excellent design, and very simple. It has the advantage of stacking its weight to the front, so that when the fly is at rest, it will swim downward, a very natural thing for a trout to see a leech doing when the fish comes upon one and decides to eat it.

You can use any color rabbit strip you can find, or dye, but the original calls for brown. I've found black and olive just as useful. Barred strips will give the fly some mottling, and add life, though the naturals are either speckled or solid. You should collect in your own waters, and consider variations that suit your own leeches. The most common will be black, olive, and brown.

GLENN'S LEECH *Glenn Gerbrandt*

Hook: Curved scud, size 8-12
Weight: 10-15 turns nonlead wire
Thread: Black, brown, or olive 6/0 or 8/0
Tail: Black, brown, or olive rabbit strip
Rib: Gold or copper wire
Body: Black, brown, or olive marabou

Step 1. Debarb the hook, fix it in the vise, and place the weighting wraps toward the front half of the hook. Start the thread, and layer the shank, securing the weighting wire wraps. Cut a section of rabbit strip about one-half inch long, and tie it in behind the weighting wire, with the hairs positioned to trail the hook.

Step 2. Tie in the ribbing wire. Gather the tips of a good number of marabou fibers, align them, and peel or cut the fibers from the marabou feather stem. Tie them in by their tips, at the base of the tail. It might help to tame the fibers by wetting them.

Step 3. Wind the marabou forward as herl. Tie it off behind the hook eye, and clip the excess. Counterwind the ribbing wire forward through the herl, to secure it against the teeth of trout. Tie it off, clip or break off the excess. Form a thread head, whip-finish, clip the thread, and apply head cement.

BRISTLE LEECH

The late Gary LaFontaine's Bristle Leech might be considered a wild idea, but some of the best flies begin as just that: ideas that spring out of observation, and when applied to a hook, so nontraditional that they look wild. But this one reflects that bit of dust that leeches kick up as they swim along silty bottoms.

Gary was always looking into water, watching the behavior of trout and the things they eat. He noticed that big trout cruising in lakes could be attracted to a sudden puff of silt, and would attack whatever caused it. So he designed a leech dressing that he could cast out, let settle to the bottom, then tug to life when a spotted fish moved into sight of it. The result is his Bristle Leech. If you fish stillwaters that have silt bottoms relatively free of snags, and with the kind of water clarity that lets you spot feeding fish, then try this dressing. It works in a narrow set of circumstances. It might be taken for a crayfish as often as for a leech. But the trout you take with it might be the biggest of your season.

The original Bristle Leech called for a gray rabbit strip body and gray marabou. I tie it in black, and it works for me in that color. I haven't had enough opportunities to try the black against the original gray, because I get into too few situations where the concept can be put through trials. If you spend lots of time on stillwaters that are suited to this fly and method, it is your job to run it through color, size, and behavior experiments. I just pull it out occasionally, where conditions are suitable, and catch a trout with it.

BRISTLE LEECH *Gary LaFontaine*

Hook:	4XL, size 4-10, bent to keel shape
Weight:	15-25 turns nonlead wire
Thread:	Black 3/0 or 60
Bristles:	30- to 50-pound-test monofilament
Body:	Black rabbit strip, wound
Wing:	Two black marabou feathers

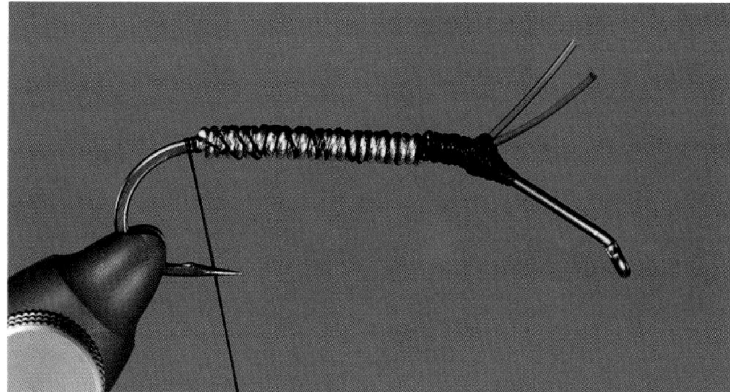

Step 1. Debarb the hook, and use your pliers to bend about one-third of the hook so that the eye is almost level with the plane of the hook point. Wrap the keel part of the shank with nonlead wire. Start your thread in front of the wire. Fold a two-inch section of hard mono in half, and tie it in at the bend in the hook. Cut the tips a bit short of the hook eye.

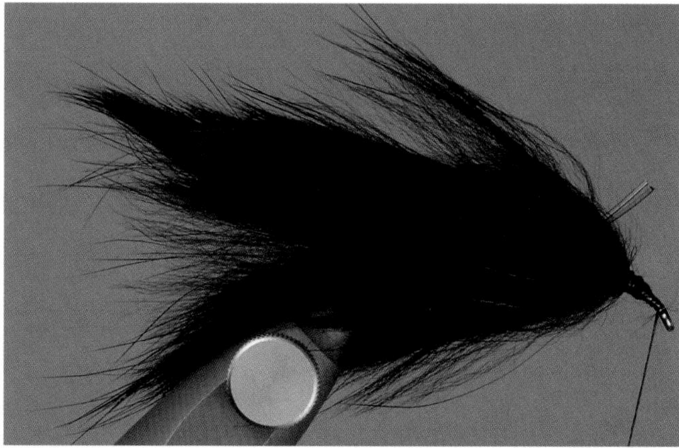

Step 2. Tie a rabbit strip in at the hook bend, and wind it forward to a point about halfway between the bristles and the hook eye. Stroke the fur back as you make each turn, to avoid wrapping the fur down. Tie off the strip and cut the excess.

Step 3. Choose two full marabou feathers, hold them together so their tips are aligned, stroke the fibers to gather all of the tips, and measure the feathers so the tips are about a hook-shank length beyond the bend of the hook. Tie them in at the end of the body, and clip the excess. Use enough thread turns to secure them and to form a stout thread head. Whip-finish once or twice, clip the thread, and apply head cement.

You could accomplish almost the same thing by tying the fly with barbell eyes rather than the bristles. But it might not kick up the same puff of bottom duff. And it wouldn't be Gary's fly if you tied it without using his methods. But Gary would likely agree that if you observe what's going on in the world of trout and trout foods, then his bristles are just one tying trick to consider in your attempt to make a nymph solve a trout fishing situation. If they don't work, it's time to come up with your own trick. The more you know about tying nymphs, the more tricks you'll be able to apply against trout.

SUMMARY

Your stillwater-fly boxes should contain Black and Olive Woolly Buggers at a minimum. If they do, they might hold the solution to all of the leech situations you ever encounter. It's likely you'll want specific leech dressings if you spend more than a few days a season on lakes and ponds. My inclination is toward nymphs on the simple side of the scale, in the smallest size range. I think that retrieve is more important than pattern. The critical factor is a fly line of the right sink rate to get the leech imitation close to the bottom in whatever depth water you're fishing.

The cast should be fairly long, to extend the time the nymph remains at fishing depth, and simply to cover more water and therefore increase the chances a trout will notice the nymph. I've caught as many trout on the drop, using leech patterns, as I have on the retrieve. Always watch the point where your leader or line enters the water. If it starts sinking faster, stops sinking, moves to one side or the other, or if the V-wake the sinking line causes as it sinks changes in any way, set the hook. If no trout is there, drop the rod to let the fly settle again. Then begin retrieving with a hand-twist or very slow strip.

Trout take leeches by opening their mouths and flaring their gills, creating a suction that inhales them. Quite often you'll feel a tap. That was a trout attempting to draw your fly into its mouth against the tension of your line. Drop the rod; the trout will often circle and make a second attempt. After a measured beat or two—remember the British dictum to say, "God save the queen"?—set the hook again. You'll be surprised how often a trout is suddenly out there and on.

CHAPTER 36

A Stillwater-Nymph Box

If you spend few days fishing lakes and ponds in a typical season, you can usually catch trout out of the same nymph boxes you carry on moving water. Most of the patterns you'll tie to your tippet will be out of the searching-nymph box: fur Midge Nymphs; Fox Squirrels; A. P. Beavers and A. P. Olives; herl nymphs like the Flashback Pheasant Tail, Herl Nymph, and Beadhead Prince; such wire-bodied nymphs as the Brassie and Copper John. Many flies plucked out of your stream searching-nymph box will work as searching nymphs on stillwaters.

A few nymphs out of your moving-water imitative-nymph box might even work, in an emergency, as imitative patterns on stillwaters. Once I got into a hatch of large traveling sedges, on my return from fishing the salmon-fly migration on the Deschutes River, and caught some trout with an imitation of that big, black, and ugly nymph. I'd cast it out, let it plummet to the bottom and rest there until a trout came into view, then swim it toward the surface, just as the big caddis pupae around it were doing. The trout made a few mistakes about it, but I'd likely have done better with a more realistic pattern.

If you spend more than a few days on stillwaters in any average trout-fishing season, you need a separate stillwater-nymph box for a couple of reasons. First, aquatic insects in lakes and ponds are a bit like those in spring creeks and tailwaters: they live in a restricted set of niches, and there's a tendency toward a greater abundance of a narrower set of species than you find in the varied habitats of freestone streams. Trout see more individuals of a specific food form and tend to be selective more often in stillwaters than in brisk waters.

Second, while a few food forms in lakes and ponds overlap those found in streams, such as some mayfly nymphs, caddis pupae, and most scuds, many more of the most important insects are not similar at all. Midges in streams and stillwaters are alike at the tiny end, but you find very few large midge larvae or pupae in moving water, although they're abundant and trout often feed on them selectively in stillwaters. Damselfly nymphs, dragonfly nymphs, water boatmen, and leeches all acquire major importance in lakes and ponds, but rarely cause selective feeding in streams. You do not need imitations of any of them in your moving-water nymph boxes. You will reach for imitations of each of them in a stillwater season.

The table of contents of your stillwater-nymph box should begin with a few Black and a few Olive Woolly Buggers in sizes 6 to 12, most to fish as they are, a few to shape into rough imitations of an important insect or crustacean for which you lack a pattern. I tie my truncated Woolly Buggers as small as size 14, on long-shank hooks.

Your stillwater-nymph box should contain imitations of the ubiquitous *Callibaetis* mayflies, even if it's just the Flashback Pheasant Tail Nymph in sizes larger than you would use on streams. The largest size PT I find useful on moving water is size 16. That is the smallest I would use on lakes and ponds. Sizes 12 and 14 are more imitative of the speckle-wing nymphs at maturity, which is when trout most often focus on them.

You need a range of midge pupa patterns from size 10 to 20, in black, red, and olive. If your fishing tends to take you to the northern tier of states and provinces, then you might not need to extend the size range, but you do need to be sure they're tied on 3XL hooks.

I would feel unarmed on a lake at any time of year without a few Baby Damsels, just because I rarely catch a stillwater trout, even if it appears to be feeding selectively on something else, that has not taken at least two or three small damselfly nymphs recently. I have often extracted them with a throat pump, found them still living, set up miniature aquariums, and taken their photos. In spring and early summer, a stillwater-nymph box that lacks an

Col. Tony Robnett with the sort of bend in his rod that can be expected if you apply the correct stillwater nymph to the prevailing situation.

imitation for mature damselfly nymphs is certain to let you down on many days. Trout will be feeding with bold swirls, just subsurface, and you will fish for them in frustration if you don't have something long, slender, and olive to show them.

A stillwater-nymph box should have at least a few dragonfly nymphs that are weighted, to fish near the bottom in the shallows, on floating or intermediate lines, and also a few dragon nymphs that float, to plumb the deeper depths over vegetated bottoms, shoals, and drop-offs, trailing above lines that plummet.

Most lake and pond caddis larvae and pupae can be imitated with nymphs out of your moving-water searching box. If you fish where large traveling sedges motor around on stillwaters, however, you need a specific imitation of a size 8 or 10 caddis pupa in your box. And I have gotten into situations often enough where cased larvae get pinned in the surface film to want an unruly imitation of them at hand. It's like the damselfly migration: trout will be taking at or near the surface with big swirls, and you need something that at least roughly resembles what they're taking, or you're going to be a mere spectator to all that activity that looks so easy to solve. It is, with the right nymph.

You need a water boatman that sinks, to suspend in shallow water at the end of a floating line, or intermediate, or beneath an indicator. Cast it out, wait for cruisers to move into view, animate the sunk fly in front of them. You also need a floating water boatman, for the opposite reason: to suspend off the bottom, still in the shallows, above a sinking line or microshot heavy enough to tug it down. Again, let it sit until a trout moves into view, then bring it to life right in front of the fish.

Most of your scud patterns for lakes and ponds can be based on the same styles you would use in rivers and streams, but they should almost always be more heavily weighted, and therefore should be tied separately for your stillwater-nymph box. I would not feel unarmed if all I carried were a row of olive scuds in the simplest Dubbed Scud style, sizes 12 to 16. I'd tie others if my collecting in a particular stillwater indicated a need for them.

Any stillwater-nymph box should have substantial room for leech imitations. A few of them might be large, but you'll find trout susceptible to smaller sizes, 10s and 12s, far more often than they are to the more common 6s and 8s. Most of mine carry beadheads. Though that makes them less imitative, they do seem to catch more trout, and that is the most important way to measure the success of a pattern.

You can do all of your stillwater searching and imitative fishing out of the same nymph box, if it reflects the full range of stillwater food forms. I do recommend that you leave a fair amount of vacant space in yours. You'll fill those expansion gaps with favorites that you find catch trout for you. You'll also fill them with experiments: flies that you tie based on what you collect in your own stillwaters. You might even find that your own flies outfish the standards, and the experiments of others, over the years.

The perfect stillwater-nymph box would arise out of your own collecting and tying. Flies that you invent yourself do not always catch more trout, but they do provide an elevated sense of accomplishment with every trout that you bring to your hand.

Conclusion

I was on the Bighorn River, fishing over a midge hatch with Jim Schollmeyer, not doing as well as Jim, and not very happy about my lack of success. A few trout were coming to the few standard midge nymphs that I had with me, which was not the full complement of them that I should have tied before the trip. My supply of tiny pupae, in sizes 20 to 24, was scant.

Tracy Peterson, who guides on the Yellowstone River most of the time but also on the Bighorn on occasion, joined us for dinner, and had to listen to a long lament about my lack of luck over the midges. He described the standard pattern for the hatch on that river: the one nymph I needed to solve all of my problems. Let's call it the Killer Midge. Tracy enumerated its list of materials, carefully described how it was tied.

Jim and I are both early risers. The next morning, after breakfast, and an hour or two before the nearest fly shop opened, I rifled through my portable tying kit to see what I had that approached the Killer. I could only approximate what I'd heard Tracy describe, but decided it was better to come close than to fish through a second day with the same flies that had failed the first day. So I tied a half dozen rough attempts at what I thought might fit the Killer's description, and pinned them into my nymph box.

Trout were eager for these flies. I spent the day happy, until the last of them departed; six size 22 nymphs don't last long when you're fishing them on 6X tippet over Bighorn River browns and rainbows. Jim and I got off the river after dark, as usual, far too late to visit the fly shop and procure some real Killer Midges. So I tied a dozen of the same approximation after the next breakfast, then lobbied for a late launch, after the shop opened. When I held a half dozen purchased samples of the real Killer Midge in my hand, they were perfectly tied, and very pretty. Mine were almost comically unlike them.

I fished the Killer over the same hatch that day. It didn't move a trout. I nipped it off and tied my mistake back to the tippet. Trout showed their approval once more.

Neither of those nymphs made it into this book. The Killer didn't work for me, though it had for hundreds of others, and failed to find a place in my own fly boxes, so I can't recommend it to you. My misinterpretation of the Killer remains untested beyond that one trip, has never been fished by anybody else but me, and hasn't even earned a name. If it ever becomes successfully tested, it's still too ugly to bring out in the open.

It's best when patterns are pretty and catch trout as well. John Barr's Copper John might be the best example: it's well dressed and shapely, but more important, when applied to water, it catches lots of trout. It's also fine if a pattern is ugly and catches trout. But such patterns are likely to please only their creators. They rarely enjoy the sort of contagion that lets them infect one fly box and then the next, until they find their way into common usage.

Your searching-nymph box should be based around those few flies that have been contagious, that have spread from box to box until they're in use almost everywhere. There is always a reason behind such success: they catch trout for lots of folks, in a wide variety of trout-fishing situations.

Your imitative-nymph boxes, for both streams and stillwaters, should be based on proven patterns, some of them ugly but most of them not. There's a reason that they too have become standards: they catch lots of trout for lots of folks, but in narrower sets of selective situations.

All of your nymph boxes should have expansion gaps, plenty of room left over to fill with flies that arise out of your own fishing, whether you create them yourself or buy them locally, to meet the specific needs of a hatch that is happening where you happen to be fishing. Those nymphs in which you have confidence, because they've consistently caught trout for you, become the most important patterns to tie and carry.

I hope that all of yours are not ugly like most of mine.

Bibliography

Barr, John. *Barr Flies.* Mechanicsburg, PA: Stackpole Books, 2007.

Best, A. K. *Production Fly Tying.* Boulder, CO: Pruett Publishing, 1989.

———. *A. K.'s Fly Box.* New York: Lyons & Burford, 1996.

———. *Advanced Fly Tying.* Guilford, CT: Lyons Press, 2001.

———. *Fly Fishing with A. K.* Mechanicsburg, PA: Stackpole Books, 2005.

Borger, Gary. *Nymphing.* Harrisburg, PA: Stackpole Books, 1979.

Brooks, Charles E. *The Trout and the Stream.* New York: Crown Publishers, 1974.

———. *Nymph Fishing for Larger Trout.* New York: Crown Publishers, 1976.

Cordes, Ron, and Randall Kaufmann. *Lake Fishing with a Fly.* Portland, OR: Frank Amato Publications, 1984.

Engle, Ed. *Tying Small Flies.* Mechanicsburg, PA: Stackpole Books, 2004.

———. *Fishing Small Flies.* Mechanicsburg, PA: Stackpole Books, 2005.

Hafele, Rick. *Nymph-Fishing Rivers and Streams.* Mechanicsburg, PA: Stackpole Books, 2006.

———. *Favorite Fly Patterns and How to Fish Them.* Gresham, OR: Apolosis, 2006.

Hafele, Rick, and Dave Hughes. *Western Hatches.* Portland, OR: Frank Amato Publications, 1981.

Hafele, Rick, and Scott Roederer. *Aquatic Insects and Their Imitations.* Boulder, CO: Johnson Books, 1987.

Harvey, Geroge W. *Techniques of Trout Fishing and Fly Tying.* New York: Nick Lyons Books, 1990.

Hellekson, Terry. *Popular Fly Patterns.* Salt Lake City, UT: Peregrine Smith, 1977.

Howell, Don, and Kevin Howell. *Tying and Fishing Southern Appalachian Trout Flies.* Pisgah Forest, NC: Davidson River Outfitters, 1999.

Hughes, Dave. *Nymph Fishing.* Portland, OR: Frank Amato Publications, 1995.

———. *Wet Flies.* Mechanicsburg, PA: Stackpole Books, 1995.

———. *Trout Flies.* Mechanicsburg, PA: Stackpole Books, 1999.

———. *Essential Trout Flies.* Mechanicsburg, PA: Stackpole Books, 2000.

Jorgensen, Poul. *Modern Fly Dressings for the Practical Angler.* New York: Winchester Press, 1976.

Judy, John. *Slack Line Strategies for Fly Fishing.* Mechanicsburg, PA: Stackpole Books, 1994.

Juracek, John, and Craig Mathews. *Fishing Yellowstone Hatches.* West Yellowstone, MT: Blue Ribbon Flies, 1992.

Kaufmann, Randall. *Fly Patterns of Umpqua Feather Merchants.* Glide, OR: Umpqua Feather Merchants, 1998.

Koch, Ed. *Fishing the Midge.* Rockville Center, NY: Freshet Press, 1972.

LaFontaine, Gary. *Caddisflies.* New York: Nick Lyons Books, 1981.

———. *Trout Flies, Proven Patterns.* Helena, MT: Greycliff Publishing, 1993.

Lawrie, W. H. *All-Fur Flies and How to Dress Them.* London: A. S. Barnes, 1967.

Leeson, Ted, and Jim Schollmeyer. *The Fly Tier's Benchside Reference.* Portland, OR: Frank Amato Publications, 1998.

———. *The Benchside Introduction to Fly Tying.* Portland, OR: Frank Amato Publications, 2006.

Machiavelli, Niccolo. *The Prince* and *The Art of War.* New York: Barnes & Noble Collector's Library, 2004.

Martin, Darrel: *Fly Tying Methods.* New York: Nick Lyons Books, 1987.

———. *Micropatterns.* New York: Lyons & Burford, 1994.

Mathews, Craig, and John Juracek. *Fly Patterns of Yellowstone.* West Yellowstone, MT: Blue Ribbon Flies, 1987.

McCafferty, W. Patrick. *Aquatic Entomology.* Boston: Jones and Bartlett Publishers, 1983.

McGee, Allen. *Tying and Fishing Soft-Hackled Nymphs.* Portland, OR: Frank Amato Publications, 2007.

Mercer, Mike. *Creative Fly Tying.* Mill Creek, WA: Wild River Press, 2005.

Merritt, R. W., K. W. Cummins, and M. B. Berg. *An Introduction to the Aquatic Insects of North America,* 4th ed. Dubuque, IA: Kendall/Hunt, 2008.

Morris, Skip, and Brian Chan. *Morris and Chan on Fly Fishing Trout Lakes.* Portland, OR: Frank Amato Publications, 1999.

Osthoff, Rich. *Active Nymphing.* Mechanicsburg, PA: Stackpole Books, 2006.

Richards, Carl, and Bob Braendle. *Caddis Super Hatches.* Portland, OR: Frank Amato Publications, 1997.

Richards, Carl, Doug Swisher, and Fred Arbona, Jr. *Stoneflies.* New York: Nick Lyons Books, 1980.

Rizuto, Chuck, and Roy Stoddard. *Flyfishing the San Juan.* Farmington, NM: Three Rivers Publishing, 1988.

Rosborough, E. H. "Polly." *Tying and Fishing the Fuzzy Nymphs.* Harrisburg, PA: Stackpole Books, 1978.

Rowley, Philip. *Fly Patterns for Stillwaters.* Portland, OR: Frank Amato Publications, 2000.

Sawyer, Frank. *Nymphs and the Trout.* London: Stanley Paul & Co., 1958.

Schollmeyer, Jim. *Hatch Guide for the Lower Deschutes River.* Portland, OR: Frank Amato Publications, 1994.

———. *Hatch Guide for Lakes.* Portland, OR: Frank Amato Publications, 1995.

———. *Hatch Guide for Western Streams.* Portland, OR: Frank Amato Publications, 1997.

———. *Nymph Fly-Tying Techniques.* Portland, OR: Frank Amato Publications, 2001.

Schollmeyer, Jim, and Ted Leeson. *Trout Flies of the West.* Portland, OR: Frank Amato Publications, 1998.

———. *Trout Flies of the East.* West Yellowstone, MT: Portland, OR: Frank Amato Publications, 1999.

———. *Tying Emergers.* Portland, OR: Frank Amato Publications, 2004.

Schullery, Paul. *American Fly Fishing.* New York: Nick Lyons Books, 1987.

Schwiebert, Ernest. *Nymphs.* New York: Winchester Press, 1973.

———. *Trout.* New York: E. P. Dutton, 1978.

Shenk, Ed. *Fly Rod Trouting.* Harrisburg, PA: Stackpole Books, 1989.

Solomon, Larry, and Eric Leiser. *The Caddis and the Angler.* Harrisburg, PA: Stackpole Books, 1977.

Soucie, Gary. *Woolly Wisdom.* Portland, OR: Frank Amato Publications, 2005.

Stalcup, Shane. *Mayflies Top to Bottom.* Portland, OR: Frank Amato Publications, 2002.

Voshell, J. Reese, Jr. *Guide to Common Freshwater Invertebrates of North America.* Blacksburg, VA: McDonald & Woodward Publishing, 2002.

Warren, Joe J. *Tying Glass Bead Flies.* Portland, OR: Frank Amato Publications, 1997.

Whitlock, Dave. *Dave Whitlock's Guide to Aquatic Trout Foods.* New York: Nick Lyons Books, 1982.

Index

Fly patterns with detailed tying instructions are listed in bold.

Active Nymphing (Osthoff), 352
Advanced Fly Tying (Best), 159
Aftershaft Damsel
materials for, 311
tying steps, 312–313
A. K.'s Fly Box (Best), 196, 206
Allen, Don, 310, 311
All-Fur Flies and How to Dress Them (Lawrie), 76
All-Fur Nymph, 76–77
Black, materials for, 78
Cream, materials for, 78
Gray, materials for, 77
Hare's Ear, materials for, 78
Olive, materials for, 77
tying steps, 78–80
All-fur nymphs
instructions and materials, 77–80
overview of, 76–77
All-Fur Swimmer, 105, 106, 169, 192, 295
materials for, 103
tying steps, 103–104
All-Fur Wet, 76–77
Anderson, Gary, 342, 343
Anderson, George, 211, 234
Antron Caddis Pupa
materials for, 338
tying steps, 338–339
A. P. Beaver, 91, 150, 169, 362
materials for, 93
A. P. Black, 8, 32, 50, 8, 95, 99, 106, 150, 169, 192–193, 196
materials for, 4, 91
tying steps, 92–93
A. P. Hare's Ear, 91
materials for, 94
A. P. Herl, 91, 95
materials for, 94
A. P. Muskrat, 91, 150, 169
materials for, 94
A. P. Olive, 91, 362
materials for, 94
Aquatic Entomology (McCafferty), 185
Aquatic Sow Bug, 6, 257, 280
materials for, 5, 252
tying steps, 253
Arbona, Fred, Jr., 199
Astorga, Juan-Ramon, 141–142
Avon River, 107

Baby Damsel, 314, 362
materials for, 306
tying steps, 306–307
Back swimmers, 340–341, 346–347
Badger Flyfishers, 314
Barker, Mims, 196
Barr, John, 130, 132–136, 201, 249, 364
Barr Flies (Barr), 130, 133, 136, 201, 249
B/C Hopper, 135
Beadhead Biot Little Brown Stonefly Nymph
materials for, 201
tying steps, 201–203
Beadhead Biot Little Yellow Stonefly Nymph, materials for, 203
Beadhead Biot Stonefly Nymph, 201
Beadhead Black Beauty, materials for, 13
Beadhead Dubbed Caddis Pupa
Golden Brown, materials for, 223
Green, materials for, 222
Tannish Cream, materials for, 223
tying steps, 223–224
Beadhead Fox Squirrel Nymph, 66, 130, 177
Beadhead Green Rock Worm Nymph, 64, 66
Beadhead Hare's Ear, 8, 90–91, 192, 207
materials for, 90
tying steps, 90
Beadhead Mohair Leech
materials for, 358
tying steps, 358–359
Beadhead Pine Squirrel Nymph, 103, 106
materials for, 84
tying steps, 84–85
Beadhead PMD Nymph
materials for, 178
tying steps, 178–179
Beadheads, weighting with, 48
Beadhead Scud, 350
Gray, materials for, 262
Olive, materials for, 261
Orange, materials for, 262
Tan, materials for, 262
tying steps, 262–263
Beadhead Serendipity, 122, 216
materials for, 123
tying steps, 123–124
Beadhead Squirrel Nymph, xi, 4
materials for, x
Beadhead Woolly Bugger
Brown, materials for, 357
Olive, materials for, 357
Beadhead Woolly Bugger, Black, 355
materials for, 357
Bead-Nabber, 25
Beads
selecting, 30–31
storage for, 26–27
using, 66–69
Beaverpelt, 334
materials for, 317
tying steps, 318
Best, A. K., 159, 196, 206
Big Hole River, vii–viii, 13, 97
Bighorn River, 4, 6, 30, 153–154, 237, 240–241, 252, 260, 278, 364
Bighorn Shrimp
Pink, materials for, 260
tying steps, 260–261
Bighorn Shrimp, Orange, 354
materials for, 260
Biot, 33
Biot Nymph, 161–162, 168
materials for, 162
tying steps, 162–164
Bird, Cal, 95, 199
Bird's Nest, 105, 265–266
Brown, materials for, 95
Olive, materials for, 97
Olive-Brown, materials for, 97
tying steps, 96–97

Bird's Stone
materials for, 199
tying steps, 199–200
Black Beauty, 12, 298
Beadhead, materials for, 13
materials for, 13, 243
tying steps, 243–244
Black Beauty Emerger, materials for, 13
Black Snowshoe Caddis, 240–241
Black Ugly Nymph, 206
Black Woolly Worm, 144, 204, 268
materials for, 266
tying steps, 266–267
Blessing Russell, 144, 283, 357
Blue Ribbon Flies, 121
Blue-Winged Olive Nymph (standard body), 164, 167, 168
materials for, 165
tying steps, 165–166
Blue-Winged Olive Nymph (stretch body)
materials for, 167
tying steps, 167–168
Boatman
materials for, 345
tying steps, 345–346
Bobbins, 24
Bodkin, 25
Box Canyon Stone, 196
Braendle, Bob, 213
Brassie, 31, 125–126, 128, 211, 362
materials for, 69, 126
tying steps, 126–127
Bristle Leech
materials for, 360
tying, 361
Brooks, Charles, 33, 97–99, 102, 196, 204, 279
Brown, Ron, 314
Burk, Andy, 189, 192

Caddies/ holders for tools, 26
Caddisflies (LaFontaine), 62, 226, 328
Caddisflies, for moving water
instructions and materials, 211–234
overview of, 208–210, 234–235
Caddisflies, for stillwaters
instructions and materials, 328–339
overview of, 327–328, 339
Caddis Green, 310
Caddis Super Hatches (Richards and Braendle), 213
Carey Special, 317, 318
Cased Caddis, 329
Cement/glue, 26
Chan, Brian, 290, 297, 298, 300, 301, 303, 306, 307, 314, 334, 336, 339
Chandler, Ken, 69, 125, 126
Chan's Chironomid
materials for, 300
tying steps, 300–301
Chan's Frostbite Chironomid Pupa, 303
materials for, 301
tying steps, 301–302
Chenille, 34
Chromie, materials for, 303
Chung, Rim, 157, 159
Clark, Lee, 187
Clark's Hex Emerger
materials for, 187
tying steps, 187–188
Coachman Wet, 346–347
Coffee grinder, 27
Colorado River, 237, 243, 260
Columbia River, 185
Copper John, 4, 26, 31, 33, 61, 66, 130–140, 142, 170, 173, 201, 207, 211, 362, 364
Chartreuse, materials for, 134
Green, materials for, 134
materials for, 130
Red, materials for, 134
tying steps, 131–133
Zebra, materials for, 134
Cordes, Ron, 328
Craneflies
instructions and materials, 246–250
overview of, 245–246, 250
Cranefly Larva
Olive, materials for, 246
Tan, materials for, 247
tying steps, 247
Cranefly Larva (Barr's)
Olive, materials for, 249
Tan, materials for, 249
tying steps, 249–250
Craven, Charlie, 135
Creative Fly Tying (Mercer), 170, 173, 179
Czech Nymph, 29, 148
materials for, 145
tying steps, 146–147

Damselflies
instructions and materials, 306–313
overview of, 304–306, 314
Daring Dark, 7–8
version 1, materials for, 7
version 2, materials for, 7
Daring Light, 7, 8
Daring Olive, 7
Davenport, Tug, 69, 125, 126
Davidson, Andy, 105, 185
Davidson, Marie, 105
Davidson River, 265–266, 273
Davidson River Outfitters, 265, 266, 270, 273
Deep Sparkle Pupa
Brown and Bright Green, materials for, 226
Cream, materials for, 227
Ginger, materials for, 227
tying steps, 227–228
Delaware River, 30
Deschutes River, viii–x, 10–13, 85–87, 91, 97, 98, 179, 196, 204, 206, 235, 237, 274, 362
rock experiment, 62–65
Disco Midge, 241, 244
materials for, 242
tying steps, 242
Dorsey, Pat, 12, 13, 243
Draggin
materials for, 323
tying steps, 323–326
Dragonflies
instructions and materials, 317–326
overview of, 315–317, 326
D. T. Damsel
materials for, 310
tying steps, 310–311
Dubbed Scud, 280, 350, 363
Gray, materials for, 258
Tan, materials for, 258
tying steps, 258–259
Dubbed Scud, Olive, 280
materials for, 258
Dubbing
direct method, 49–50
loop method, 50–53
material for, 33–34
twister for, 25–26
wax for, 26

Engle, Ed, 12, 126, 157, 220, 239

Fall River, 192
Fast-Sinking Scud, 354
Orange, materials for, 352
Fast-Sinking Scud, Olive, 352
materials for, 353
tying steps, 353–354
Favorite Fly Patterns and How to Fish Them (Hafele), 66
Field & Stream, viii, 85
Fishfly larvae. *See* Hellgrammites and fishfly larvae
Fishing the Midge (Koch), 74
Fitzsimmons, Bill, 241
Flash
selecting, 31–32
using, 66–69
Flashback Gold-Ribbed Hare's Ear, 90
Flashback Hare's Ear, 178
Flashback Pheasant Tail, 4, 32, 66, 119, 154, 156, 168, 192, 259, 279, 295, 362
materials for, 58, 112, 290
Fly box. *See* Nymph box
Fly Fisherman, 85
Flyfishing & Tying Journal, 80, 187
Fly Patterns for Stillwaters (Rowley), 290, 298, 311, 338, 350, 359
Fly Patterns of Umpqua Feather Merchants (Kaufmann), 282
Fly Rod & Reel, 85
Fly-Tying Methods (Martin), 107

Fox, Tim, 232
Fox Poopah
Brown, materials for, 232
Olive, materials for, 232
Tan, materials for, 232
tying steps, 233–234
Fox Squirrel Nymph, 34–35, 54, 64, 91, 192, 193, 201, 207, 362
Frontier Anglers Fly Shop, 311
Fur(s)
hackle, tying a, 54–56
noodle, tying a, 53
selecting, 34–35
Fur nymphs
all-, 76–80
instructions and materials, 73–106
midge nymphs, 73–76
overview of, 72–73, 106

General Stonefly Nymph, 203–204
materials for 204
tying steps, 204–206
Gerbrandt, Glen, 359
Giant Salmon Fly Nymph
materials for, 197
tying steps, 197–198
Gilled Nymph, 173–176
materials for, 174, 293
tying steps, 174–175, 293–294
Girdle Bug, Black, 144
materials for, 142
tying steps, 142–143
Girdle Bug, Brown, 142, 144
Glass Bead Cranefly Larva
Amber, materials for, 248
Olive, materials for, 248
tying steps, 248
Glass Bead Scud
materials for, 350
tying steps, 351
Glenn's Leech
materials for, 359
tying steps, 360
Glue/cement, 26
Gold Bead Biot Epoxy Golden Stone Nymph, 201
Golden Stonefly Nymph, 204
materials for, 197
Gold-Ribbed Hare's Ear, 21, 35, 85–87, 91, 152, 176, 185, 196, 201, 211, 235, 334, 339
Flashback, 90
materials for, 87
Olive, 328
tying steps, 88–89
Graham, Larry, 138–140
Gray Nymph, materials for, viii
Green Damsel, 16
materials for, 15
Green Paradrake, 3
Guide to Common Freshwater Invertebrates of North America, A (Voshell), 286
Guinea, material from speckled, 33
Gunny Sack, 331
materials for, 329
tying steps, 329–330

Hackle, fur, 54–56
Hafele, Rick, 2–4, 8, 64, 66, 67, 113, 115, 159–160, 168–169, 178, 179, 200, 356–357
Half-hitch
technique, 43
tool, 25
Halford, Frederick, 76
Hare's Ear, 15, 91, 177
Harrop, René, 183
Hellgrammite, 269
materials for, 267
tying steps, 267–268
Hellgrammites and fishfly larvae
instructions and materials, 266–273
overview of, 265–266, 273
Henry's Dragon Nymph
materials for, 319
tying steps, 319–321
Henry's Fork, of the Snake River, 13, 91, 154, 155, 179, 181
Herl
counterwound, tying, 58–59
rope, tying, 59–61
selecting, 32
Herl Nymph, 115, 152, 211, 328, 362
materials for, 113
tying steps, 113–114
Herl nymphs
instructions and materials, 108–119
overview of, 107–108, 119
***Hexagenia* (Burk's)**, 192
materials for, 189
tying steps, 190–191
***Hexagenia* Nymph (Jorgensen's)**
materials for, 188
tying steps, 188–189
Hoffman, Henry, 319
Holders/caddies for tools, 26
Hollywood Caddis, 339
materials for, 336
tying steps, 337–338
Honey, Gordon, 336, 338, 339
Hooks
curved scud, 29
long-shank curved nymph, 29
long-shank nymph, 29
overview of, 28–29
standard dry-fly, 29
standard nymph, 29
standard wet-fly, 29
storage for, 26–27
Howell, Don, 265
Howell, Kevin, 265–266, 270, 273
Hughes, Bill, 284, 285, 287, 327–328
Husmask, 333
materials for, 331
tying steps, 331–332
Imitative nymphs for moving water
caddisflies, 208–235
craneflies, 245–250
hellgrammites and fishfly larvae, 265–273
mayflies, 152–193
midges, 236–244
nymph box for, 279–280
overview of, 10–14
scuds, 251, 256–264
sow bugs, 251–255, 264
stoneflies, 194–207
worms, aquatic, 274–278
Improved Sofa Pillow, 204

Jorgensen, Poul, 182, 188

Kamloops Bloodworm
materials for, 298
tying steps, 299
Kamloops Lakes, 296, 298, 334
Kaufmann, Randall, 282, 328
"Killer Midge," 364
Klinkhamer Special, 29
Koch, Ed, 74
Krystal Flash *Baetis* Nymph, 159
materials for, 160
tying steps, 160–161
Krystal Flash bodies, tying, 58

Lace Caddis Larva, 217
materials for, 218
tying steps, 218–219
Lace Microcaddis Larva
materials for, 220
tying steps, 220–221
Lacing, 31
LaFontaine, Gary, 34, 62, 68, 226–229, 328, 360, 361
Lake Fishing with a Fly (Cordes and Kaufmann), 328
Lawrie, W. H., 76
Leaded Stone, 204
Leeches
instructions and materials, 357–361
overview of, 355–357, 361
Legs, rubber/silicone, 32
Lightning Bug, 21, 31, 66
materials for, 138
tying steps, 138–140
Little Brown Stonefly Nymph, materials for, 196
Little Yellow Stonefly Nymph, materials for, 197
Lynch, Gene, 69, 125, 126

Madison River, 13, 91, 97, 120
Marabou Damsel, Olive, 314
materials for, 308
tying, 308–310
Marabou Nymph, 173–174
Marigold, Ross, 120–121
Marryatt, George, 76
Martin, Darrel, 107

Materials, selecting
beads, 30–31
biot, 33
chenille, 34
dubbing, 33–34
flash, 31–32
furs, 34–35
guinea, speckled, 33
herl, 32
lacing, 31
legs, rubber/silicone, 32
overview of, 30
partridge, 33
ribbing, 31
tinsel, 31
wires, 31
wood-duck, 33
yarns, 34
Ziploc bags, 35
Matthews, Craig, 121, 123
Mayflies, for moving water
instructions and materials, 156–192
overview of, 152–156, 192–193
Mayflies, for stillwaters
instructions and materials, 290–294
overview of, 288–289, 295
Mayflies Top to Bottom (Stalcup), 161, 173, 293
Mayfly Clinger Nymph, 185
materials for, 182
tying steps, 182–184
McCafferty, W. Patrick, 185
McCleod River, 169
Mercer, Mike, 170, 173, 179–181, 224, 225
Mercury Midge, 298
materials for, 243
tying steps, 243–244
Merwin, John, 85
Meyer, Deke, 144
Midge, defined, 236
Midge Nymph, 74–75, 362
Black, materials for, 75
Cream, materials for, 75
Gray, materials for, 75
Olive, materials for, 75
Tan, materials for, 75
tying steps, 76
Midge Nymph, Olive, materials for, 75, 342
Midges
instructions and materials, 75–76
overview of, 73–75
Midges, for moving water
instructions and materials, 238–244
overview of, 236–237, 244
Midges, for stillwaters
instructions and materials, 298–303
overview of, 296–298, 303
Midge with No Name, materials for, 11
Missouri River, 30, 237, 278
Mitchell, Neal, 137–138
Modern Fly Dressings for the Practical Angler (Jorgensen), 182, 188
Montana Stone, 33, 67, 97–99, 106, 109, 128, 196, 204, 279
materials for, 99
tying steps, 99–102
Morris, Skip, 298, 321
Morris & Chan on Fly Fishing Trout Lakes (Morris and Chan), 298
Moving water, nymphs for. *See* Imitative nymphs for moving water; Searching nymphs for moving water
Murphy, Rick, 128
Murphy's Two-Wire Brassie, 130
materials for, 128
tying steps, 128–129
Murray, Harry, 269
Murray's Hellgrammite, 273
materials for, 269
tying steps, 269–270
Muskrat Nymph, viii–x, 8
materials for, ix

Nat Greene Flyfishers, 137
Noodle, fur, 53
Nymph box
for imitative nymphs for moving water, 279–280
for searching nymphs for moving water, 149–150
for stillwaters, 362–363
time to replace, 4–6
Nymph-Fishing Rivers and Streams (Hafele), 2, 178, 200
Nymph Fly-Tying Techniques (Schollmeyer), 4, 204, 258, 338
Nymphs (Schwiebert), 182, 346
Nymphs and the Trout (Sawyer), 107

Ole Hellgy, 273
materials for, 270
tying steps, 271–272
Olive Beadhead
materials for, 105
tying steps, 105–106
Olive Comparadun, 288
Olive Nymph
materials for, 166
tying steps, 166–167
Olive Scud, materials for, 257
Osthoff, Rich, 352–354

Parachute Adams, 11
Partridge material, 33
Patterson, Jack, 137–138
Peacock Herl Nymph, 3–4, 8, 113
materials for, 3
Peacock Herl Nymph, Beadhead
materials for, 115
tying steps, 115–116
Peeking Caddis, 211–212, 215, 234
Cream, materials for, 212
Olive, materials for, 212
tying steps, 212–213
Peeping Caddis
materials for, 213
tying steps, 214–215
Peterson, Tracy, 364
Pettis, Jim, 229, 230
Pheasant Tail (Sawyer's), 107–108, 111, 112, 156
materials for, 108
tying steps, 108–109
Pheasant Tail (Troth's), 112, 156
materials for, 110
tying steps, 110–111
Pheasant Tail Beadhead, materials for, 113
Pheasant Tail Flashback Squirrel, materials for, 112
Pheasant Tail Nymph, 11, 58, 111–113, 119, 153–154, 156, 161, 164, 178, 201, 207, 237, 279
Pinch wrap, 45–46
Pine Squirrel Nymph, 83
Pit River, 169
Pliers
hackle, 23–24
needlenose, 23
PMD Trigger Nymph
materials for, 179
tying steps, 179–181
Poxyback Swimmer, 175–176
materials for, 170
tying steps, 171–173
Predator, 323
materials for, 321
tying steps, 321–322
Prince Nymph, 116, 119, 346–347
Prince Nymph, Abbreviated
materials for, 118
tying steps, 118–119
Prince Nymph, Beadhead, 362
materials for, 117
tying steps, 117–118
Pulsating Caddis Pupa
Amber, materials for, 230
Cream, materials for, 230
Green, materials for, 229
tying steps, 230–231
Puyans, André, 4, 8, 91, 93–95

Quigley Cripple, 288

Rabbit Leech, 35
Red Fox Squirrel Nymph, 103, 106, 149, 152
materials for, 81
tying steps, 81–83
Rhomberg, Jim, 314
Ribbing, 31
Richards, Carl, 199, 213
Rio Huemules, 141–142
Rio Rivadevia, x–xi
Rizzuto, Chuck, 275–278
Roaring Fork River, 125
Roberts, John, x

Robnett, Tony, 11
Rosborough, Polly, viii, ix, 8, 15, 16, 19, 20, 33, 53, 54, 185
Rowley, Phil, 290–292, 298, 303, 311, 313, 323, 338, 344, 345, 350, 359
Royal Wulff, vii, 137
RS Quill, materials for, 159
RS-2 (Rim's Semblance, version 2), 157, 161, 168
  materials for, 158
  tying steps, 158–159
Rubber Leg Copper John, 142
  materials for, 135
  tying steps, 135–136
Rubber-legged nymphs, 141–144
  instructions and materials, 142–144
  overview of, 141–142, 144
Rusty Spinner, 169

Sacramento River, 169
Saito, Megaku, 19–20
Saito-San Special, materials for, 19
San Juan River, 237, 239, 275, 278
San Juan Worm, 34, 264, 274–275, 278, 280, 299
  materials for, 275
  tying steps, 275–276
  Ultra Chenille, 275
  Velvet Chenille, 275
  Vernille, 275
San Juan Worm, Beadhead
  materials for, 277
  tying steps, 277–278
San Juan Worm, Wire-Bodied
  materials for, 276
  tying steps, 276–277
Sawyer, Frank, 107–109, 111, 112, 156
Schollmeyer, Jim, viii, x, 4, 6, 66, 153, 204, 252, 258, 338, 345, 364
Scuds, for moving water
  instructions and materials, 256–263
  overview of, 251, 264
Scuds, for stillwaters
  instructions and materials, 350–354
  overview of, 348–350, 354
Schwiebert, Ernest, 182, 346
Searching nymphs, defined, 8
Searching nymphs for moving water
  Czech nymphs, 145–148
  fur nymphs, 72–106
  herl nymphs, 107–119
  nymph box for, 149–150
  overview of, 7–9
  rubber-legged nymphs, 141–144
  twisted-strand nymphs, 120–124
  wire- and tinsel-bodied nymphs, 125–140
Serendipity, 57, 124, 216
  materials, for, 121
  tying steps, 121–122
Shank
  weighting the, 47–48
  wrap technique, 46–47
Shaw, Jack, 358
Shenk, Ed, 74–75
Shenk's Special, 74–75
Skues, G. E. M., 76
Snake River
  Henry's Fork, 13, 91, 154, 155, 179, 181
  South Fork, 97
Soucie, Gary, 266, 331
South Platte River, 125, 128, 157, 237
Sow Bug
  materials for, 253
  tying steps, 253–255
Sow bugs
  instructions and materials, 252–255
  overview of, 251–252, 264
Sparkle Pupa, 34
Sports Afield, viii
Squirrel Leech, 35
Stalcup, Shane, 161–164, 173–174, 293
Stepp, Jonathan, 266
Stillwater Boatman
  materials for, 342
  tying steps, 342–343
Stillwater Caddis Pupa, 339
  materials for, 334
  tying steps, 334–336
Stillwaters, nymphs for
  back swimmers, 340–341, 346–347
  caddisflies, 327–339
  damselflies, 304–314
  dragonflies, 315–326
  leeches, 355–361
  mayflies, 288–295
  midges, 296–303
  nymph box for, 362–363
  overview of, 15–18
  scuds, 348–354
  water boatmen, 340–347
  Woolly Buggers as, 282–287
Stillwater Solutions, 290, 292
Stoneflies
  instructions and materials, 196–207
  overview of, 194–196, 207
Stoneflies (Richards, Swisher, and Arbona), 199
SuperFly, 290, 298, 301
Swisher, Doug, 199

Thread(s)
  base layer, 42
  breaking and rescuing, 42–43
  selecting, 29–30
  starting the, 42
Threader, 24
Thread Midge, 240–241, 244, 280, 298
  materials for, 239
  tying steps, 239
Tinsel
  holders for, 27
  selecting, 31
Tinsel-bodied nymphs. *See* Wire- and tinsel-bodied nymphs
Tollett, Tim, 310, 311
Tools, tying bench
  Bead-Nabber, 25
  bead storage, 26–27
  bobbins, 24
  bodkin, 25
  cement/glue, 26
  coffee grinder, 27
  dubbing twister, 25–26
  dubbing wax, 26
  half-hitch tool, 25
  holders/caddies for tools, 26
  hook storage, 26–27
  pliers, 23–24
  threader, 24
  tinsel/wire holders, 27
  tweezers, 25
  vise, 21–23
  whip-finisher, 24
Troth, Al, 110, 112, 156
Trout and the Stream, The (Brooks), 98
Trout Flies (Hughes), 282
Trout Unlimited, 137, 314
Tunkwa, Lake, 297
Turkey Quill *Callibaetis*, 290
  materials for, 291
  tying steps, 291–292
Tweezers, 25
Twisted-strand nymphs
  instructions and materials, 121–124
  overview of, 120–121, 124
Twister, dubbing, 25–26
Tying & Fishing Southern Appalachian Trout Flies (Howell and Howell), 265
Tying and Fishing the Fuzzy Nymphs (Rosborough), viii, 19, 53, 185
Tying bench
  overview of, 19–21
  tools for, 21–27
Tying Glass Bead Flies (Warren), 229, 248
Tying kit, portable
  checklist for, 40
  overview of, 38–39
Tying Small Flies (Engle), 12, 126, 157, 220, 239
Tying techniques
  direct dubbing, 49–50
  dubbing-loop method, 50–53
  fur hackle, 54–56
  fur noodle, 53
  half-hitch, 43
  herl, counterwound, 58–59
  herl rope, 59–61
  hook in the vise, mounting the, 41–42
  Krystal Flash bodies, 58
  order of, 61
  overview of, 41
  pinch wrap, 45–46
  shank wrap, 46–47
  thread, breaking and rescuing, 42–43
  thread, starting the, 42
  thread layer, base, 42

weighting with beadheads, 48
weighting the shank, 47–48
whip-finish, 43–45
yarn body, twisted, 57

Umpqua Feather Merchants, 144

Vise, 21–23
Voshell, J. Reese, Jr., 286

Warren, Joe J., 229, 248
Water boatmen
instructions and materials, 342–346
overview of, 340–342, 347
Water Floatman
materials for, 344
tying steps, 344
Wax, dubbing, 26
Weighting
beadheads, 48
shank, 47–48
Western Hatches (Hughes and Hafele), 2, 168
Whip-finish
technique for, 43–45
tool for, 24
Whitlock, Dave, 34–35, 54, 80–81, 83, 103, 106, 149, 193, 201
Williamson River, 19, 168–169, 185
Willmuth, Gary, 239
Wire
holders for, 27
selecting, 31
Wire- and tinsel-bodied nymphs
instructions and materials, 125–140
overview of, 125, 140
Wire Midge, 240–241, 244, 280
materials for, 238
Red, 238
tying steps, 238
Wire Midge Larva, materials for, 37
Wood-duck material, 33
Woolly Bugger, 29, 34, 144, 187, 269, 282, 287, 295, 357
Brown, 186
Tan, 186, 193
tying steps, 283–284
Woolly Bugger, Black, 193, 269, 361, 362
materials for, 283
Woolly Bugger, Olive, 193, 284–287, 314, 317, 328, 329, 361, 362
materials for, 283
Woolly Wisdom (Soucie), 266, 267, 331
Woolly Worm, 34, 266, 328, 329, 331
See also Black Woolly Worm
Woolly Worm, Olive
materials for, 328
tying steps, 328–329
Worms, aquatic
instructions and materials, 275–278
overview of, 274–275, 278

Yakima River, 138
Yarn body, twisted, 57
Yarn Caddis Larva
materials for, 216
tying steps, 216–217
Yarns, 34
Yellowstone Angler Fly Shop, 211
Yellowstone River, 97, 206, 364

Zebra Midge, 298
materials for, 243
tying steps, 243–244
Ziploc bags, 35
Zug Bug, 73–74
Z-Wing Caddis Puppa
Amber, materials for, 225
Cream, materials for, 225
Green, materials for, 224
tying steps, 225–226